WORLD CHRISTIANITY
POLITICS, THEOLOGY, DIALOGUES

edited by

ANTHONY O'MAHONY
and
MICHAEL KIRWAN

'Christianity is not a village affair.'
Francis, Cardinal Arinze

MELISENDE
LONDON

In memory of
Judson Trapnell
(1958-2003)

World Christianity:
politics, theology, dialogues
edited by
Anthony O'Mahony and Michael Kirwan

First published 2004
by Melisende
an imprint of
Fox Communications and Publications
39 Chelmsford Road
London E18 2PW
Tel: 020 8498 9768
Fax: 020 8504 2558
e-mail: melisende@btinternet.com
www.melisende.com

ISBN 1 901764 38 9

Edited by Leonard Harrow
Printed at the Cromwell Press, Trowbridge, England

CONTENTS

CONTRIBUTORS

Francis, Cardinal Arinze, born in Nigeria, Archbishop of Onitscha from 1967 to 1985. From 1985-2002 he was President of the Pontifical Council for Interreligious Dialogue, Rome. His most recent studies include—*Meeting Other Believers*, Leominster, Gracewing, 1997; 'The Role of the Catholic University in the Promotion of Interreligious Dialogue', *Louvain Studies*, Vol. 23 (1998); 'Public Morality in a Global Society: Catholics and Muslims in Dialogue', *Theology Digest*, Vol. 49 (2002).

Bishop Kenneth Cragg has served as both scholar and bishop in the lands of the Middle East and also held academic posts in the UK, Lebanon, Nigeria and the USA. He is the author of many studies in contemporary relations between the Semitic faiths. He is an Honorary Fellow of Jesus College, Oxford, and Hon. DD. of the University of Leeds and former Bye-Fellow of Gonville and Caius College, Cambridge. His most recent books include—*Islam Among the Spires: an Oxford reverie* (1999), *Muhammad in the Qur'an: The Task and the Text*, (2000), *Am I Not Your Lord? Human Meaning in Divine Question*, (2002) all published by Melisende, London. A recent *Festschrift* was published in his honour—*A Faithful Presence, essays for Kenneth Cragg*, edited by David Thomas with Claire Amos, London, Melisende, 2003.

Michael Kirwan, SJ, Heythrop College, University of London, lectures in Systematic and Pastoral Theology. His principle interest is in Political and Liberation Theologies, with special attention to the theme of religion and violence in the modern world. His publications include: 'The Struggles of Perpetua: Vision, Narrative and the Meaning of Martyrdom' in H B Browne and G Griffith-Dickson (eds), *Passion For Critique: Essays in Honour of F J Laishley*, Ecumenical Publishing House, Prague, 1997; 'Millenial Appetites and the Refusal of Somatocracy' in S E Porter, M A Hayes and D Tombs (eds), *Faith in the Millenium*, Sheffield Academic

Press, 2001, pp. 348-359; 'The Limits of Interpretation: the Gadamer-Habermas Conversation' in P Pokorny and J Rosovec (eds), *Philosophical Hermenutics and Biblical Exegesis*, Mohr Siebeck, Tubingen 2002, pp. 68-83; articles on culture and religion in *The Month, passim. Discovering Girard*, DLT London, forthcoming 2004.

Anthony O'Mahony, Heythrop College, University of London, Director of Research and Lecturer in Theology at the Centre for Christianity and Interreligious Dialogue and with a specialist interest in contemporary Christianity and Christian-Muslim relations. His publications include *Palestinian Christians: Religion, Politics and Society in the Holy Land* (1999); *Christians and Muslims in the Commonwealth*, (2001); *The Christians communities in Jerusalem and the Holy Land: Studies in History, Religion and Politics*, (2003); *Eastern Christianity: Studies in Modern History, Religion and Politics* (2003); *Patriarchs, Prophets and Mystics: Christian Politics and Theology in the Middle East* (2004); *Catholics and Shi'a in Dialogue: Studies in Theology and Spirituality* (2004).

Catherine Cowley, a sister of the Assumption and a lecturer in Theology at Heythrop College, University of London. She has a specialist interest in business ethics and is a member of the Institute for Religion and Public Life.

Anna Abram, Heythrop College, University of London—a specialist in Christian Ethics, also with an interest in Christian-Jewish relations in modern Europe. She has published in *Collectanea Theologica, Studia Telogiczine*, and *The Month* (London). She was born in Poland.

Inger-Marie Okkenhaug, Department of History, University of Bergen, Norway. She has published numerous studies on women and the modern Christian missionary movement including—*The Quality of Heroic Living, of High Endeavour and Adventure: Anglican Women and Education in Palestine, 1888-1948*, E J Brill, Leiden, 2002 and 'Education, Culture and Civilization: Anglican Missionary Women in Palestine' in *The Christians communities in Jerusalem and the Holy Land: Studies in History, Religion and Politics*, edited by A O'Mahony, University of Wales Press, 2003.

Ian Linden, CMG, formerly Director of the Catholic Institute for International Relations, currently professor at the School of Oriental and African Studies, involved in interfaith dialogue with Shi'ite Muslims in Iran and is currently authoring a book on globalization and ethics. He has also published widely on religion and politics in modern Africa: *The Catholic Church and the Struggle for Zimbabwe*, London, Longman, 1979; (with Peter Clark) *Islam in Modern Nigeria: A Study of a Muslim community in a Post-Independence State, 1960-1983* (Grunewald-Kaiser Verlag, 1985); and *Church and Revolution in Rwanda*, Manchester University Press, 1977.

Peter Gallagher, SJ, a Jesuit who teaches the history of philosophy at Heythrop College, University of London. He studied theology in France where he became acquainted with the work of Michel de Certeau; he wrote his doctoral thesis at Kings College, London on Gnosticism. He has published a recent study 'Seeking the European Self: Three "other selves" of Michel de Certeau', *The Way: Contemporary Christian Spirituality* Vol.41 (2001) and has made several contributions to *The Month* (London).

Alister McGrath is Professor of Historical Theology, University of Oxford and Principal of Wycliffe Hall, Oxford. Among his many books are *Christian Theology: An Introduction*; *The Christian Theology Reader*; *An Introduction to Christianity: Historical Theology*; *Reformation Thought*; and his most recent study is *The Future of Christianity*, Basil Blackwell, Oxford, 2002.

David Tombs, a Lecturer at the Institute of Ecumenical Studies, Trinity College (Belfast and Dublin). He did his postgraduate studies and research at Heythrop College, University of London. His publications include 'The Legacy of Ignacio Ellacuría for Liberation Theology in a "Post-Marxist" Age', *Journal of Hispanic/Latino Theology*, Vol. 8 (2000) and a recent monograph *Latin American Liberation Theology*, Leiden, 2003.

John Watson is an Anglican priest and a leading expert on Oriental Christianity in the Middle East with particular reference to the Coptic Christians of Egypt. He has authored numerous works including *Among the Copts*, Sussex Academic Press, 2000; 'Abba Kyrillios: Patriarch and Solitary', *The Coptic Church Review*, 1996; 'The Transfigured Cross. A study of Father Bishop Kamel (1931-1979)', *The Coptic Church Review*, 2000.

Peter Riddell, London Bible College Graduate School, Brunel University. He is a leading specialist in the study of contemporary Islam, Christian–Muslim relations and religion in South-East Asia. His most recent publications include—*Islam and the Malay-Indonesian World: Transmission and Responses*, C Hurst and Co, London, 2001; Co-edited with Tony Street, *Islam: Essays on Scripture, Thought and Society—A Festschrift in Honour of Anthony H Johns*, Leiden, E J Brill, 1997; 'The Diverse Voices of Political Islam in Post-Suharto Indonesia', *Islam and Christian-Muslim Relations*, Vol. 13 (2002); 'Muslims and Christians in Malaysia, Singapore and Brunei', in *Christians and Muslims in the Commonwealth*, (2001); and 'Arab Migrants and Islamisation in the Malay World during the Colonial Period' *Indonesia and the Malay World*, Vol. 29 (2001).

Judson Trapnell was a graduate of the Catholic University of America where his doctoral research was on the English Benedictine monk Bede Griffiths' theory of religious symbol and practice of dialogue. He published widely on Christian theological encounter with other faiths—*Bede Griffiths: A Life in Dialogue*, Albany, New York: State University of New York Press, 2001; 'Suffering and Compassion: A Jewish-Buddhist-Christian Dialogue', *Horizons*, Vol. 27, (2000); 'Indian Sources on the Possibility of a Pluralist View of Religions', *Journal of Ecumenical Studies*, Vol. 35 (1998); 'Bede Griffiths as Culture Bearer: An Exploration of the Relationship between Spiritual Transformation and Cultural Change', *American Benedictine Review*, Vol. 47 (1996). Judson Trapnell died in 2003.

Stanislaw Grodz, SVD, a Polish Catholic priest who has done postgraduate study and research into the historical and contemporary encounter between Christianity and Islam at the Centre for Islam and Christian–Muslim Relations, Selly Oak College, University of Birmingham and on contemporary African Christian Theology at the Catholic University of Lublin, Poland. He has recently published a study 'Towards Universal Reconciliation: the early development of Amadou Hampâte Bâ's ecumenical ideas', *Islam and Christian-Muslim Relations*, Vol. 13 (2002).

Basil Cousins is doing postgraduate study and research into the historical and contemporary encounter between Russia and Islam at the Centre for Christianity and Interreligious Dialogue at Heythrop College,

University of London. He has recently published a study 'The Russian Orthodox Church, Tatar Christians and Islam' in *Eastern Christianity: Studies in Modern History, Religion and Politics*, London, 2003.

David M Neuhaus, SJ, is an Israeli Jesuit who teaches in the Seminary of the Latin Patriarchate of Jerusalem and at Bethlehem University. He is a research fellow at the Shalom Hartman Institute, Jerusalem. He completed a PhD at Hebrew University, Jerusalem in Political Science and degrees in theology and Scripture in Paris and Rome. His publications include *Justice and the Intifada: Palestinians and Israelis speak out* (edited with Kathy Bergen and Ghassan Rubeiz), Friendship Press, New York, 1991, *Kritische Solidarität: Einige Überlegungen zur Rolle privilegierter Christinnen und Christen im Kampf der Enteigneten*, Aphorisma Kulturverein, Trier, 1995, 'L'idéologie judéo-chrétienne et le dialogue juif-chrétien', *Recherches de Science Religieuse* (1997), 'A la rencontre de Paul; Connaître Paul aujourd'hui: changement de paradigme', *Recherches de Science Religieuse* (2002), as well as articles in reviews such as *Al-Liqa'* (Arabic), *Pastoral Psychology* and *Mishkan*.

Rocco Viviano, SX, an Italian Catholic priest who recently completed postgraduate studies on the theology of interreligious dialogue and research into contemporary Christian-Muslims relations in the Philippines at the Centre for Christianity and Interreligious Dialogue at Heythrop College, University of London.

INTRODUCTION

The first planning meetings for the conference on World Christianity took place two months before the horrific attacks on the Twin Towers in 2001. The conference itself, at Cumberland Lodge, Windsor Great Park, unfolded in March 2002, in a post-11 September world. The papers given at the conference now appear in print, just as the second Gulf War, which must surely be read as a more or less direct reprisal for the September atrocities, has concluded: with a military victory for the coalition forces, but also with a bitterly controverted political legacy. To expect of the papers collected here an authoritative synthesis of these seismic, still unresolved, upheavals, would clearly be inappropriate, and they are not presented as such. Of course these events are the background against which the papers were written. Nevertheless, their overall thrust is less towards geopolitics than towards a sympathetic, but not uncritical, appreciation of the diversity and vitality of Christianity around the world.

The overall theological stress is on the incarnation, as Cardinal Arinze sets out when he cites Jn 3: 16: 'God so loved the world that he gave his only Son, so that everyone who believes in him may not perish but may have eternal life.' This quotation is the most potent response to critics like Hannah Arendt, who see in Christianity only a denial of, a flight from, the world and its demands. It affirms that Christianity, despite its aberrations, is called to an *amor mundi*, a readiness to care for the world and to take responsibility for it. As the papers show, the Christian *amor mundi* has taken striking and surprising forms: whether as a proto-emancipatory movement for women's education in nineteenth-century Africa (Inger-Marie Okkenhaug) or as the irruption of the poor among the crucified peoples of Latin America (David Tombs); as a critical commentary on apocalypse (John Watson) or on globalisation (Catherine Cowley, Alister McGrath).

Is such an optimistic survey misplaced, given the 'sheer dark face of religious performance' (Kenneth Cragg) of the world religions in history? Here, more than anywhere, a different—for some a more anxious, jarring—note is sounded, in the wake of the September atrocities. During the week after the bombings a popular UK radio station commemorated the harrowing events by playing John Lennon's *Imagine* every hour: 'Nothing to kill or die for/And no religion, too'. The only hope for humanity, we were being told, lies in a utopian effacement of all distinguishing and divisive characteristics based on nation, class or creed; the inability of many people to conceive that such 'globalising' indifferentiation might actually be the motor of 'fundamentalist' terrorism rather than a solution to it, remains like an ideological Gordian knot, which so far neither a hawkish American 'unilateralism' nor a weakened and divided European 'multilateralism' has successfully managed to untie.

For good or ill, religion is part of the world picture, and a renewed understanding of the symbiosis of the terms 'world' and 'Christianity' is confirmed by recent literature exploring the analogous and overlapping dichotomy of 'religion' and 'global order'. Globalisation is the phenomenon which has attracted most attention, especially among Western academics:

> But where is religion in all this? Certainly it is often ignored (globalisation is seen overwhelmingly as an economic and technological matter). Yet religion too, has recently emerged into political and social consciousness internationally, if only or mainly as a result of the resurgence of a militant Islam and in particular its challenge to modern (Western) values and power. However, the notion of a religious resurgence or renewal goes wider than this and what it involves invites exploration, specifically as to its place and part in the global order of post-Communism and globalisation, including the associated question marks raised against the modern world as such, now almost exclusively seen in terms of market capitalism and liberal democracy.[1]

There is a positive, 'globally Christian' response to be made: the resources of the Church's social teaching and of virtue ethics are proffered here as ways of exploring and responding to this new global context; there is also a renewed reflection upon Christianity's self-understanding

---

[1] John Esposito and Michael Watson, 'Introduction' to their edited collection, *Religion and Global Order*, University of Wales Press, Cardiff, 2000, 1-2.

as the guardian of the public sphere. But the overall spirit and thrust of many of these essays is to set out the internal and external plurality of Christianity, and see what challenges and opportunities emerge.

Internally, the regional studies show a shift in Christianity's centre of gravity, from the West to the East and South (and a consequent re-evaluation of the West's 'questionable heritage'). Essays here on Africa, Asia, and the Middle East testify to this shift. Overlapping in many ways with this regional awakening, Christianity has once again to face its own credal diversity (ecumenical relations, the attraction of 'fundamentalism') and theological plurality (the irruption of liberation theologies). Paradoxically, as Kirwan suggests, one outcome of the success of the local theologies of the South is that we now seem to be lacking a strong and authentic European theological 'voice'.

Externally, Christianity has always existed in a religiously plural world, as Anthony O'Mahony points out, and one of the central tasks for current theology is to develop strategies for entering the meaning system of other religions and traditions. It is perhaps not surprising that many of the contributions here explore Christianity's relationship with Islam, and the need to engage in an honest and informed dialogue and engagement. The challenge and risk of dialogue takes different forms in Nigeria and Malaysia than it does in Egypt, though in all cases a mutual respect of the respective claims to distinctiveness needs to be a feature of theological discourse. Once again the doctrine of the Incarnation is key: as O'Mahony insists, the paradox of the 'word made flesh' cannot be downplayed, even in the name of a theocentrism which may seem to offer a more irenical way forward for Christians and Moslems.

Such observations regarding Christianity's inter-religious tasks will surely hold good for the more general condition of plurality within which Christianity finds itself, though there is no sustained attempt here to make such connections. Collectively, as has already been declared, these contributions cannot pretend to offer anything like a synthesis of the diversity they explore; they are better conceived as snapshots of Christianity, taken at a moment of acute and painful intensification of the global encounter and possibly an axial age of historical significance. For this reason there is no conclusion or summary, since this would be to impose a false uniformity, the more so since the contributors seek to avoid all sense of 'triumphalism' and religious colonialism. It is a Jewish critic, George Steiner, who understands this best when he writes of being gripped, as a child, by 'the intuition of the particular, of diversities so numerous that no labour of classification and enumeration could exhaust them.'

> At that hour, in the days following, the totalities of personal experience, of human contacts, of landscape around me became a mosaic, each fragment at once luminous and resistant in its 'quiddity'—the Scholastic term for integral presence revived by Gerard Manly Hopkins. There could be, I knew, no finality to the raindrops, to the number and variousness of the stars, to the books to be read, to the languages to be learned.[2]

The insight is at once intellectual, aesthetic and intensely moral; it shapes the religious humanism of all Steiner's writing. What it challenges and refutes is the 'disappearance of religion', either as a fact or as a *desideratum*. Is it possible that Christianity in a 'post-Lennon' context might recognize itself in this ecstatic commitment, both as celebrant of 'the holiness of the minute particular', and as a champion and guardian of religious 'otherness' in the world? An affirmative answer to this question is implicitly or explicitly offered by the scholars who have contributed here, not least by Kenneth Cragg who appropriately refers us to Dag Hammarskjöld's question: how does one carry responsibility for God, for faith, and not just in responsibility to God? Nor is it just the contributors who show themselves ready to rise to this challenge: the conference as a whole was particularly memorable as a vivacious experience of ecumenical exchange and discovery, of risks taken and acknowledged. It is perhaps a small ray of hope, given the dark anxiety of the past two years, but a very real one.

Religion continues to play a large part in forging and preserving political frontiers, inspiring the sense of historic community, and refreshing the sense of self-differentiation from the other on which historical identities depend. The persistence of religious warfare says a lot about the power of religion in a supposedly 'secular' world. It may be power to do harm rather than good; it may reflect the imperfect understanding of their religions by adherents who seem incapable of absorbing lessons of charity,

---

[2] George Steiner, *Errata; an Examined Life*, Yale University Press, New Haven, 1998, 3-4.

peacemaking, resignation or social co-operation, but it does show the strength of religious affliction as a source of identity.

'To be rooted', Simone Weil, once remarked, 'is perhaps the most important and least recognized need of the human soul.' That is to feel oneself at home in the world; to have a sense of place. However, Christian witness has been characterised as 'Walking in the Pilgrim City'.

> Therefore Jesus also suffered outside the city gate in order to sanctify the people by his own blood. Let us then go to him outside the camp and bear the abuse he endured. For here we have no lasting city, but we are looking for the city that is to come (Hebrews, 13: 1 2-14).

Blessed and cursed by a peculiar 'hopelessness,' Christians claim fellowship with Christ who suffered outside the city gate, and are called to follow him into that wilderness beyond the camp, that region other than the earthly *civitas*, from which we might discern another city. This other city shows the structures of this world, which seem so solid and so real, to be afflicted with an ephemeral quality, a kind of unreality, so as to make them a source of anxiety rather than a resting place for our restless hearts (Luke 12: 12-34). The definition of pilgrimage is given as 'a journey—usually of considerable duration—to some sacred place as an act of religious devotion. 'In this definition the salient elements of the contemporary concept of pilgrimage are contact with the sacred and displacement. And so we exist in a state of perpetual pilgrimage to our true *patria*, following 'Jesus the pioneer and perfecter of our faith, who for the sake of the joy that was set before him endured the cross, disregarding its shame, and has taken his seat at the right hand of the throne of God' (Hebrews 12.2).

Dwelling 'outside the camp' need not entail a removal to a place apart. Christianity was from its earliest days a predominantly urban phenomenon, enacting its peculiarly homeless form of existence within the institutional confines of the late ancient city. Though there have been within Christianity from its earliest times monastic intuitions which would locate themselves in a withdrawing to uninhabited places, for the vast majority of Christians in the first four centuries physical withdrawal from the city was not an option, nor was it held up as an ideal. At the same time, the Gospel call to homelessness is not a purely internalised indifference to this life, nor an invisible kind of pious detachment. When Paul speaks of those 'who walk not according to the flesh but according to the spirit' (Romans 8:4), he is not contrasting a spiritualised Gospel, which asks only for faith, to the carnal law which demands specific, visible actions. The Gospel, no less than the Law, requires actions, gestures and rituals—collection for the poor in Jerusalem, baptism, faithful participation in the Eucharist. What are called for are actual, concrete social practices by which the community of the Church is manifested as 'a chosen race, a royal priesthood, a holy nation, God's own people'. That which marks out the Church as a distinctive community of people a 'nation' must be visible so it may 'proclaim the mighty acts of him who called you out of darkness into his marvellous light' (1 Peter 2:9).[3]

The concern for an understanding of the 'other'—seeing the relationship of the one to the many, struggling with the questions of identity and difference, unity and diversity—has been a serious preoccupation of post-modern philosophy. In a somewhat different though not unrelated arena, contemporary Christian theologians have been increasingly aware of the necessity to formulate a theology, or set of theologies, that takes serious account of the 'otherness' as it is reflected in the existence of a great variety of forms of human religiousness. The French Dominican theologian, Claude Geffré, suggests that there is a risk involved in the work of theology. Since theology is a hermeneutical task 'from beginning to end', it involves 'the risk of distortion and error', but unless theology is willing to take that risk by presenting a creative interpretation of Christianity, it runs the no less serious risk of 'simply handing on a dead past'. Thus Christian theology draws upon: *ressourcement*—reaffirmation of Christian identity by appeal to its ancient sources; and *aggiornamento*—renewal through the modernisation of Christian thought and institutions.

Without having the pretension of installing a new world order, Christianity holds a prophetic and counter-cultural power against the risks of, not only dehumanisation, but also fragmentation between persons and ethnic and religious communities. As a religion of incarnation, Christianity not only announces to every human being the gratuitous salvation of God, but it works in healing cultures and all creation. The

---

[3] Frederick Christian Bauerschmidt, Walking in the City, *New Blackfriars: special edition— Michel de Certeau, SJ*, Vol. 77 (1996), 504-518.

Church announces Jesus Christ as an event of universal salvation for all humanity, including those who belong to other religious traditions. But the witness of the Gospel must learn not to confuse the universality of the mystery of Christ with that of a Christianity understood as a historical religion inseparable from its Western form, and to maintain a distance between the Church as means of salvation and the Kingdom of God that doesn't cease to go beyond its frontiers, which at present can present themselves as borders.

However, Christianity faces other challenges which often seek to de-root spirituality from commitment, religious identity and compassion for the world and God's creation. One challenge is the growth in extreme revulsion from the world and the desire to destroy it. Just as we can expect more and more religions of worldly compromise—more syncretic abominations, more prosperity-cults, more theocracies—so we can expect more of the opposite: movements of withdrawal from the world, of self-isolation in introspective ghettos and, ultimately, more fanatics resolved to precipitate Armageddon. In atomised, rootless societies with little respect for authority and rampantly non-judgemental values, religious movements could get replaced altogether by individual 'personal faith'. Most 'personal' religions, however, are not really religious at all; to call them so is to mask self-indulgence. The 'religion' of divinised humanity is usually narcissism masquerading as generosity of soul. Worship on one's own, without the discipline of sharing, is lightly ritualised arrogance.[4]

Religious behaviour differs from secular behaviour not because it involves belief but because it is linked with committed attitudes to transcendence. The sense of transcendence distinguishes the sacred from the profane. But we should not expect religions to be unaware of the world. The sense of transcendence is an addition to a worldly perspective, not a substitute for it. When religions become absorbed with the world, they cease to be religions. When they ignore it, they cease to be effective. Yet matter and spirit, for most people, for most of the time, have been mutually charged, thoroughly interpenetrated or inseparably fused. States and faiths have always corrupted each other. The pretence of religion has been politically exploited, to justify wars and terrorism, to impose social ethics, to bolster elites or legitimate revolutions, to sanctify authority or

---

[4] See the reflections by Felipe Fernández-Armesto, *Religion*, London, Phoenix 1997, Collection—Predictions, 45-47.

subvert it. These observations find an echo in the thought of the Irish-American writer and political scientist David Walsh:

> Even the discovery of God does not lift us out of this world. For as long as he wills it we must remain in this life to work out as best we can the meaning and direction we must follow within it. The light of transcendent illumination is a piercing beam from beyond, but it does not illuminate the surrounding area. The mystery of the whole remains. The difficulty of articulating the consequences of revelation for the modern secular world is evident in the confusion concerning the relationship between religion and politics.[5]

'Always be ready to make a defence to anyone who asks for a reason for the hope that is in you, and make it with modesty and respect' [1Peter 3: 15-16]. Since the middle ages, this biblical text has been considered to state the fundamental charge given to the theologian. One could say that four fundamental features of theology thus appear: it is an articulation of the ground of one's hope; it arises as a response to questions about the way Christians live their lives; the norm for that hope and practice is Jesus Christ; and reasons may be given for that hopeful practice, whether those addressed are fellow Christians or others. Taking the text of First Peter as a fundamental challenge, theology may be conceived thus as a mediation of the Christian gospel within a cultural context. Addressing two not entirely distinct audiences, those who have already accepted the gospel and those who have not, theology faces two tasks, one primarily *ecclesial* and the other primarily cultural. How these tasks are conceived and interrelated is a basic question for the conception of theology. For most of the Christian tradition both dimensions and roles of theology have been visible.

Today the Christian tradition has a global presence unsurpassed in its history. It is by far the largest religious faith in the world today and is likely to remain so. It has recently experienced large growth in Africa and Asia, and in the latter continent it is set for further expansion. The freeing of Eastern Europe and Russia from the secular tyranny of

---

[5] David Walsh, *Guarded by Mystery. Meaning in a Postmodern Age*, Catholic University of America Press, Washington, DC, 1999, 98-99.

Communism has given new life to Eastern Churches and society. However, the Christian tradition continues to express itself in multiplicities; despite the decline in 'denominationalism' and the ecumenical movement, the blocks remain—Catholic, Eastern Orthodox, and Protestant. Unity in diversity is the foundational principle which gives the Christian tradition its uniqueness and strength—division weakens it. However, Christianity exists as unity and diversity and that defines the nature of particularity and universality in such a way that it offers the world a sustaining beatific vision. In the Catholic tradition, however, there is a subtle interplay between the particular and the universal in the concept of catholicity. As Henri de Lubac pointed out, there is a sense in which, for the Church fathers, catholicity meant a gathering together rather than a spreading out, a cohesion around a centre which unites the disparate elements in their diversity.[6] That is the Eucharist; in which the universal Christ is mediated in particular form. Each eucharistic community is not a mere part of a whole, as if Christ could be divided into parts, but a microcosm, a mini cosmos in which the cosmic Christ is wholly present. One becomes more united to the universal the closer one is attached to the particular community gathered around one particular altar. For this reason Paul can refer to the local assembly in Rome as *hole he ecclesia*, the whole Church (Romans 16: 23).

A word of thanks in particular must go to the Principal of Cumberland Lodge, Dr Alistair Niven, and the dedicated work that Dr Jutta Huesmann put into the preparation of the conference and her continuing commitment to the publication of this book.

We would wish to acknowledge the generous support of the British Province of the Society of Jesus who have made this publication possible.

Finally, during the preparation of this volume, we learnt of the sad death of Judson Trapnell. We would like to dedicate this work to the memory of this fine scholar.

Anthony O'Mahony
Michael Kirwan
October 2003

---

[6]   Henri de Lubac, *The Motherhood of the Church*, Ignatius Press, San Francisco, 1982, 174.

CHRISTIANITY AND THE REALITIES OF LIFE TODAY

Francis, Cardinal Arinze

The religion which Jesus Christ founded was meant by him for every people, time, place and culture. Like her divine Founder, Christianity has never been, and never will be, without challenges. It is therefore encouraging and stimulating that this particular St Catharine's Conference has chosen as its theme 'World Christianity: a contemporary encounter between religion, politics and culture'.

I appreciate the honour of being asked to propose some reflections to you at the opening of this conference. I shall focus on 'Christianity in the Realities of Life Today.' After a brief word on Christ founding a world Christianity and on this religion progressively articulating her self identity, I shall move on to consider more directly how Christianity meets other religions and the many cultures in the world and how it tries to respond to the questions that people ask today on social and political matters. We shall conclude by asking Christianity how it wants to be seen today and tomorrow.

Christianity a world religion

When Jesus Christ became man and came into this world, he was well aware of having been sent on a mission by his Eternal Father. And his mission was to the whole of humanity. God loved the world so much that 'he gave his only Son, so that everyone who believes in him may not perish but may have eternal life' (Jn 3: 16). Christ came to save all humanity, 'to gather together into one the scattered children of God' (Jn 11: 52).

Jesus consciously founded the Church as the budding forth of the Kingdom of God that he came to inaugurate. He gathered disciples. He taught them. He performed miracles in their presence. Nearest to him were the twelve specially chosen Apostles. Then there was an outer circle of 72 disciples. Women who followed him are also mentioned.

Jesus sent his Apostles, and through them the whole Church, to the whole world to bring his Good News of salvation. They are to be his witnesses 'not only in Jerusalem but throughout Judaea and Samaria, and indeed to earth's remotest end' (Acts1: 8). 'As the Father sent me', he said them, 'so am I sending you' (Jn 20: 21). And he gave them a divine guarantee of assistance: 'And look, I am with you always; yes to the end of time' (Mt 28: 20).

Christ therefore intended to found a world religious community, not a club for a few elite members, not a sect, not a tribal region, not even a national association, and much less a racial body. The Church began indeed like the small mustard seed. But her divine Founder meant her to grow into a big tree in whose branches the birds of the air would take shelter (cf Lk 13: 20-21; Vatican II: *Lumen Gentium*,5).

From the small flock of apostles and disciples the Church manifested to the world on Pentecost day when people from many countries heard the Apostles under the inspiration of the Holy Spirit speaking their various languages (cf Acts 2: 4). Three thousand converts were made on that day (cf Acts 2: 41). Numbers grew. Missions began. The faith reached Samaria, Antioch, Corinth, Athens, Cyprus, Rome, Alexandria and Persia. Some evangelisers went to Asia. Europe became more and more at home in the Church. When the first Europeans reached the Americas the missionaries followed. In more recent centuries Africa south of the Sahara received the faith, as also did Oceania. There is no doubt that Christianity is a world religion.

Christianity articulating her self identity

As the Church grew, she had gradually to articulate her self identity. She manifested her faith in the Lord Jesus Christ through prayer, through transmitting the teaching of the Apostles and through community life. Her relationship with Judaism was only slowly appreciated and expressed. It was a delicate development in which even the top and best leaders like Peter and Paul could have different views or approaches (cf. Acts 11: 1-18; 15: 1-2; 23-29: Gal 2: 11-21).

Purified by fire of Roman empire persecution, the early Church led by heroic martyrs gave unmistakable witness to Christ. Taking the best from Greek philosophy, the Church began to articulate her Credo in the formulae hammered out by the Councils of Nicea, Constantinople, Ephesus, Chalcedon and others. Roman law and culture also influenced the early formulations of Church law.

As the centuries rolled by, a certain measure of institutionalisation was unavoidable. The Church, however, always saw it as her *raison d'être* to preach the Gospel of Jesus Christ. And undisputable witnesses of Christ such as martyrs, virgins, hermits, mendicant consecrated people and monastics were always there as a challenge to the spirit of the world and as a healthy dimension of Church life along with hierarchical and institutional charisms.

While the doctrine of the faith does not change, our understanding of it and of its implications can and should grow. Thus the Church has come to realise the evil of slavery and usury, has deepened her appreciation of the human right to religious freedom, and has modified her attitude towards other religions and towards democracy and science. As St Vincent of Lerins wrote, there is to be development of doctrine in the Church, but not the introduction of new doctrines nor a change of doctrine. Progress in understanding of the faith is to be 'along its own line of development, that is, with the same doctrine, the same meaning and the same import' (*The First Instruction*, cap. 23: PL50, 667–668).

Along the centuries, Christianity has had to face persecution, internal divisions, heresies, schisms, encroachments by political authorities on the religious sphere, and, more recently, agnosticism, liberalism, secularism, materialism, communism and atheism. Because of the very fact of the missionary effort of the Church, Christianity has had to ask herself what her stand is with reference to religions and cultures, which she meets in the wider world. All this has helped Christianity to articulate better her self-identity. One of the best of recent statements on how the Church sees herself is the Dogmatic Constitution, *Lumen Gentium*, of the Second Vatican Council (1962–1965). There the Church is presented as 'a kind of sacrament or sign of intimate union with God, and of the unity of all mankind' (*Lumen Gentium*, 1).

World Christianity meeting other religions

A world religion such as Christianity cannot avoid meeting other religions. This is not a new phenomenon. The early Church met with Greek polytheism, Roman religions, emperor worship, Egyptian cults and various forms of Oriental ways of worship. Emerging as it did from Judaism, early Christianity had, as has already been said, to examine its relationship with the Jewish faith too.

As Christianity spread, it had some contact with Hinduism and Buddhism. It was Islam, however, that presented a major challenge. At first considered as a type of Christian heresy, it had to be accepted as a separate religion. In Europe, although Christianity gained dominance, Jewish communities remained and there were places and periods which saw interaction among Christians, Jews and Muslims.

In our times religious plurality has asserted itself as a major dimension of modern life. Hinduism and Buddhism as earlier religions, Islam coming seven centuries after Christ, traditional or tribal religions, Sikhism and Zoroastrianism are religions which are very much alive today. The relative ease of modern travel and the increasing desire of people to go to other lands, have resulted in Christians living and working with people of other religious convictions as never before in the past two thousand years.

While not introducing any new doctrine into the deposit of faith which she received from the Apostles, Christianity has made progress in her attitude towards other religions. By looking deeper into the Gospel, the sacred tradition of the Church and the teachings and lives of the Saints, the Church is asking herself what the Holy Spirit is saying to her today regarding other religions (cf. Apoc. 2: 29). For the Catholic Church, the Second Vatican Council made history by being the first General Council to issue a major document on her relations with other religions. In the declaration, *Nostra Aetate*, the council states the openness of the Church to all that is true, good, noble or holy in other religions and exhorts Catholics to co-operate with their followers to promote the spiritual and moral good of humanity (cf. *Nostra Aetate*, 2). The council says that God's plan of salvation includes not only Christians but also Jews, Muslims, Hindus, other believers and all people of good will, under certain conditions (cf. *Lumen Gentium*, 16), although only in the Church will people find in their completeness and abundance all the means to salvation. A theological assessment of the other religions and their role in salvation is still developing among theologians.

The positive and co-operative attitude of Christianity toward other religions can be illustrated by three recent events: the Jewish-

Christian-Muslim colloquium organised by the Ecumenical Patriarch Bartholomew I in Brussels last December, the dialogues promoted by the Archbishop of Canterbury, Dr George Carey, in January 2002 between Christians and Muslims at Lambeth Palace, among Jews, Christians and Muslims in Alexandria, and the World Day of Prayer for the major religions of the world called by Pope John Paul II in Assisi also in January 2002.

The number of other initiatives of Christians meeting people of other religions is indeed high. Other speakers may provide further details. What is undisputed is that Christians today do have a positive attitude to and a will to co-operate with, people of other religious convictions.

One Christianity in many cultures

One other reality in which the world of Christianity has to live is the plurality of cultures. Christianity began in West Asia, generally called the Middle East today. But soon the centre of this religion moved to Europe. Most missionaries along the centuries have come from Europe. This fact carries with it the danger of identifying Christianity with European culture. Even as early as 1659 the Vatican Congregation for the Evangelisation of Peoples advised and warned the European missionaries being sent to Asia to respect the cultures of Asian peoples and to promote evangelisation not europeanisation. The famous Instructions read:

> Put no obstacles in their way, and for no reason whatever should you persuade these people to change their rites, customs, and ways of life, unless these are obviously opposed to religion and good morals. For what is more absurd than to bring France or Spain or Italy or any other part of Europe into China? It is not these that you should bring but the faith which does not spurn or reject any people's rites and customs, unless they are depraved, but on the contrary tries to keep them ...
>
> ... Admire and praise what deserves to be respected.
>
> (*Collectanea SCPF* 1, n. 135, p.42)

If only missionaries had heeded this advice, as Fathers Matteo

Ricci and Roberto de Nobili did, the image of Christianity in Asia today (especially in India and China) might have been different.

With the 'discovery' of America and the spread of the Gospel of Jesus Christ in Africa south of the Sahara and in Oceania in the past 500 years, the challenge of inculturation becomes more pronounced in the Church. Christians cannot avoid asking themselves the following questions: The faith is the same worldwide. Christianity has the same articles of faith, the same worship and the same code of conduct everywhere. But how does this universal Christianity become local? How does the Gospel of Jesus Christ become incarnated in the cultures of the Japanese, the Thai, the Indians, the Ghanaians and the Indios of Latin America?

How can the tree that is Christianity grow in these and similar cultures as on its own native ground and produce local fruit which can at once be recognised as Christian and at the same time as authentically local? How can the Church live, work and be seen as indigenous and not as a visitor with passport and visa? What local gifts has the Church in these cultures produced and offered for sharing and exchange to the universal Church?

Ecumenism focuses on prayer and other initiatives to promote the reunion of Christians. Along the corridors of history, the various Christian Churches, rites or communions have developed an impressive variety of patrimonies, rites, theologies and traditions. A re-united Christianity will have to seek ways to treasure all this variety and maintain diversity in unity. Christianity, ever ancient and ever new, has within herself the capacity to meet all cultures, to exalt, adopt, and adapt all it can, and to challenge what deserves to be changed.

Christianity meeting social and political needs of humanity today

Christianity does not remain inside the church building. It does not dwell in the sacristy. Much less is it fossilised in the Vatican Museum.

Christianity is alive. It is dynamic. It is a contributor to modern society. It has something to contribute to people's every day life. It is not a matter of Sunday morning Mass only.

What has Christianity to say to people today in their human relations, human love, marriage, family relationships, work, trade and commerce, politics and government, science and culture, fine arts and ecology?

How is the Gospel to be translated into the realities of daily life? How does the modern person live this faith, the person of telephone, telefax and email, the diplomat in Brussels, Geneva and the UNO in New York, the business person in Wall Street, Hong Kong and Tokyo, the professor in the literature or fine arts department, the politician, the media practician and the economist at the World Economic Forum, or the activist at Porto Alegre, Durban or Bangkok?

Moreover, people cannot refrain from asking themselves where the competence of Christianity comes in and where it should necessarily stop. In view of the ethical and religious dimensions which political, social or scientific decisions can have, it is easy to see that Christianity does have a say in many questions that on the surface seem to be merely political, social or scientific. This also shows the difficulty of unanimity and the possibility of differing stands.

The Catholic Church has articulated in a very coherent way her teaching on many areas of social and political life. Expected soon is a book on the social teaching of the Church to be published by the Pontifical Council for Justice and Peace. Pope John Paul II has travelled around the world, making 95 apostolic journeys, sharing this nourishment. There is no doubt that for us Christians our religion, celebrated in liturgical worship, enlightens and directs every sector of our lives and unites them in one vital synthesis, so that a good Christian is necessarily a good citizen (cf. *Gaudium et Spes*, 43).

Christianity and examination of conscience

To conclude, and as a contribution to our discussion, let us pose some questions to the Christians of today.

If Jesus Christ came back to earth today, what would he be likely to think of the Church he founded? Would he see her as a mother of the nations, as a bridge-builder between the individual and God and between individuals, peoples and cultures? Would he see the Church as a welcome companion to people in their life journey, as a good Samaritan at the side of those left half-dead by economic pressures and racial prejudices? Would he see the Church as indeed an able manager of educational and medical institutions, but also and above all as a convincing personal witness pointing to himself as the source of her faith and commitment? What would Christ say of the efforts of the Church today to give people hope and a sense of direction in life?

Is the proclamation of Jesus Christ seen as a priority so that people have a chance to believe in him? 'How can they believe in him if they have never heard of him? And how will they hear of him unless there is a preacher for them?' (Rm 10: 14).

Does institutionalisation of Christianity scare people away from the Church? What can be done to preserve both the minimum of necessary institution and the maximum of required spiritual charism? What messages do modern Saints like John Bosco, Theresa of Lisieux, Blessed John XXIII, Blessed Cyprian Michael Tansi and the Servant of God, Mother Teresa of Calcutta, convey to our times?

The answers to questions such as these will help Christians today to assess how world Christianity is encountering religion, politics, and culture today, how the face of Christianity is likely to be today and tomorrow, and how Christianity can be more and more present in the realities of life in our times. May God give us the grace not to fail in making our personal and group contribution.

RESPONSIBLE TO FAITH:
RESPONSIBLE FOR FAITH
Kenneth Cragg

I

It will be well for our Conference on 'World Christianity and Contemporary encounter' in the sundry realms of 'Religion, Politics and Culture' if we take up at the outset the ground of belief and the nature of a faith's authority. Nowhere were the stakes more sharply summarised than by Dag Hammarskjöld in his private diary of Christian devotion. He said, as it were, to himself: 'you fancy you can be responsible *to* God: can you carry the responsibility *for* God?'[1] In his role as Secretary-General of the United Nations an organisation which allowed no mention of 'God' in its Charter, he was acutely aware of the place of his deeply Christian devotion in the arduous quest for world peace and in diplomacy inside the conflicts of nations.

'To' and 'for'—prepositions are always tediously important in all languages. 'Responsible to God and faith'—that is orthodoxy, the sense of an obligation to be loyal to what is perceived, and received, as the due claim of a faith's authority. This usually entails a deference to the acknowledged custodians of doctrine, ritual and practice, be they *'ulama'* in Al-Azhar, Cardinals in Rome, presbyters in Geneva or their counterparts everywhere as the *magisteria* of 'the things most surely believed among us.'

The quality both of the mind and heart in such custodianships is a large dimension of the contemporary transactions of the inter-faith. Clearly the due role of scholars, preachers, lawyers, witnesses reaches back into the temper of the faith itself, its originating formulation and its range of self-critique. On what grounds does a faith claim to be true? There belongs our believing 'responsibility *to* faith,' in discerning loyalty and honest discipleship. But if we are to be adequate with these they take us into 'responsibility *for* faith'—seeing that, otherwise, our fidelity would

---

[1] Dag Hammarskjöld, *Markings*, trans. L S Sjoberg and W H Auden, NewYork, 1964, xvi.

decline into a mere 'faith in faith.' If authority has to be somehow 'intrinsic' to faith, it cannot well be so in the presence of sleeping conscience or a lazy mind.

Dag Hammarskjöld had an intriguing solution to setting religion at the heart of the United Nations in so far as architecture could supply it. (How to do so doctrinally was vastly more difficult.) He designed a 'Quiet Room,' with no identifiable symbols that would be familiar to explicit world religions. It had white walls and was lit only by a shaft of light from an aperture in the roof. The light fell on a block of Swedish iron-ore in the centre, a product from his native land. Unwritten was a message from the Book of Deuteronomy: 'choose you this day whom you will serve.' Out of iron we build bridges that connect: out of steel we contrive the surgeon's scalpel that heals: or we fashion guns and bombs and tanks and weapons of destruction. 'I set before you good and evil'— the same iron. 'Choose you ...'

It was an architectural response both to the religions and the secular godlessness of those 'United Nations.' It was a paradigm of inter-faith dialogue wrung from a personal Christian discipleship by the very pressure of a world role of peace with diversity. Our task here is with how we inter-relate our Christian conviction—commitment to that same diversity, that same confrontation of cultures, that same arena of statehoods presiding over disparate accounts of all things transcendent or denying that these exist.

II

However vexing the diversity between religions (if we let it be such, beyond complacency and sloth), there is at least one common factor, namely forfeiture of the transcendent or what might be called a recession in the sense of God and of the will to worship. Such recession of religious belief is more widespread and expressive in the West but is present everywhere, seeing that the factors inducing 'secularisation' respect no religious frontiers. Even the most instinctively self-protective of faiths, those bastioned in retentive habits of mind, are beset by modernity and its challenge to religious belief and practice.

It will be well to examine the factors which have induced this discounting of the transcendent, this forfeiture of wonder and moral obligations, in which the West is most conspicuous but which defy the seclusions that would escape them. Honest realism requires that we begin with them in our 'responsible *to* and *for* situations' concerning faith and worship.

One obviously contributing factor is the sheer sophistication of technology. We have grown accustomed to assuming that all 'problems' have a technique—solution. Many of the old impulses to prayer and piety seem to be absorbed into reliance on human skills and mechanical competence. If we pray, will it not be rather that these agencies will not miscarry than as it were an unmediated dependence on divine action? That sort of eliding of divine relevance will only be corrected if we dwell in a daily gratitude for which all human competences in our well-being and survival exist inside the divine entrustment of the world into the purview of human operation.

The partial dimension of human ability to manipulate and inventively harness the natural order has to be kept always within the inclusive endowment of a creature-hood truly made managerial, by intelligence, in an intelligible world. There is essentially no reason why a world always marvellous to shepherds should be less to astronauts or genetic engineers. Only the cognisance, or the will for it, will be wanting. Manifestly, there is no dis-inventing, backing out of human technology. The only sane answer is to acknowledge and revere the liability it imposes. That duly appreciated, prayer—for sanity, consecration and honesty—becomes all the more indispensable. Are not those very virtues at the heart of the scientific enterprise?[2] Provided we resist the intoxication to

---

[2] Religious faiths must beware of reproaching sciences and scientists for lack of religious feeling. Their entire enterprise readily constrains to a sense of wonder and surprise as well as being an education into that honesty which is the core of moral obligation. Thus, for example, Richard Dawkins in the oddly entitled *Unweaving the Rainbow: Science, Delusion and the Appetite for Wonder,* Oxford, 1998, xi. After affirming his sense of scientific 'wonder' he goes on: 'I believe that an orderly universe, one indifferent to human pre-occupations, in which everything has an explanation even if we still have a long way to go to find it, is a more beautiful, more wonderful place that a universe tricked out with capricious *ad hoc* magic.' The latter were never religious. Moreover, are not the sciences precisely our ' pre-occupations' in what—by its very legibility to mind—is not 'indifferent' to them but deeply amenable to their ministries of enquiry and 'explanation'. Moreover, Dawkins here has entirely ignored how laboratories reach out into markets and techniques into trade—the industrial, the commercial, the economic, the social, the moral, the spiritual, the political integrally engaging with each other. All intellectual wonder becomes myopic if it does not 'wonder' around all the liabilities science engenders.

which proud techniques are liable, whereby we say: 'We are the masters' or 'We are on our own,'[3] Christian faith need have no fear of forfeiting its theology in the world of technology.

Even so, laboratories are very confining places where attention is more and more—and necessarily—focused on less and less, as the price of successful research. Thus its sundry foci which yield 'discoveries' require to be returned to the totality of the global scene to which they belong and from which they were withdrawn.

Another noteworthy factor in the spread of secularisation and loss of divine perspective comes from an increasing distrust in the capacity of language. Jacques Derrida, Michel Foucault and others tell us that language resembles a game. It is a convention for communication that can never carry 'the really real' but will always condition it by its 'manner of speaking.' Our logocentrism means we are in a sort of Kantian impasse whereby the instrument (not now of knowing but of telling) in being such frustrates the end it serves. This—it is held—supremely the case when language ventures into metaphysics or metahistory.

What is at stake here deserves longer reckoning than context allows, but at least those who deny language 'meaning' still use it for the case they make. A certain common sense may be legitimate in being sceptical about their scepticism. Islam is the most assertively logocentric of all faiths with its doctrine of 'the eternal Qur'an'. Integrity with it has to mean a careful relation to whatever challenges believing confidence concerning it—as is the case for all contemporary religion.[4]

Another factor making for modern distrust of religious belief—systems is the suspicion that they are inherited from cultural accidents of birth. When this suspicion is registered a sense of their sheer optionality emerges. Is the sense that 'mine' is 'authentic' an accident of birth? If so, what does their continuing co-existence mean for the exclusive authority of any? The claim of each and all seems severally self-intrinsic, with no feasible court of appeal that might finally decide on their disparities. Do not peace and harmony, therefore, demand that they are optional in every sense, possessed of an authority that is only inward and private? If,

---

[3] See Iris Murdoch, *The Sovereignty of Good,* London, 1970, 79: 'We are simply here.'

[4] The point of 'logocentric' in respect of the Qur'an, and of its being in deep contrast to Christian Christology (and the resulting new Testament concept of being 'scriptures') was examined in my *The Education of Christian Faith*, Brighton, 2000. See also *Muhammad in the Qur'an*, London, 2001.

however, faiths are left in these terms will they not cease to be categorical? 'Being categorical' was why the believer was 'responsible to' them: it would seem to make him now also 'responsible for them'.

There is a claim for Christian faith that it is 'public truth.'[5] This surely can only mean that it is deserves and claims to be offered to, and shared by, all humanity. It is committed to a world-wide relevance. It can never be privatised as if it belonged only to an 'elect,' a single culture or a destined race. Its New Testament, by existing at all as a text of 'gospels' and 'letters,' witnesses to its world wideness as meant for, and living in, dispersion, with neither sacred land, nor sacred language. Given inter-religious co-existence, it keeps a vital sense of mission and a willed accessibility.

Its 'public truth' quality—in this vital sense—cannot, however, mean that it 'goes' like some Highway Code that all drivers must obey, or like arithmetic that must disallow any wayward 'two plus two equals five.' These 'public truths' have their sanctions none may safely, or sanely, ignore. The sanctions of Christian faith are not of that order. If 'its truth makes us free', only in freedom, not coercion, may it do so.

We come, finally, to a fourth factor lying behind the growth of irreligion, namely the dark and sinister face of religious history, the performance of religions. Not only do we have 11 September in mind. That was only a dramatic symbol of how perverse bigotry and zealotry can be. Examples litter history like 'Legion' in the Gospel. Did not James Joyce wryly observe: 'We have had too much of God in Ireland'? or Nietzsche gibe: 'If you would breathe the pure air keep away from churches.' The record in history of religious faiths has been such as to provoke many to cry: 'A plague on all your houses!! Whether out of anxious perplexity or in angry revolt. Emotions this way in the West have been sadly intensified since the drama of 11 September 2001. It was well to urge that this event was *not* Islam and many Western leaders hastened to do so. Yet the perpetrators all had Muslim names. Some left behind them well—thumbed copies of the Qur'an from which they had drawn their deadly logic. Indeed, it was not Islam—not the Islam of Muhammad pre-Hijrah in a Meccan defencelessness at that point

---

5   See e.g. Lesslie Newbigin, Lamin Sanneh and Jenny Taylor, *Faith and Power: Chritianity and Islam in 'Secular' Britain*, London, 1989 and Newbigin, *The Gospel in a Pluralist Society*, Grand Rapids, 1989.

unquestioned,[6] nor of the likes of Jalal al-Din Rumi nor of Abu-l-Kalam Azzad and a multitude of others in their genuine *Islam*. As with so many of the atrocities of Christian history or of contemporary Zionism, we can only ambiguously say of these that there were *not* Christianity, nor were they Judaism.

For some then these days, there is the need to repudiate all religion as only and ever demonic, a licensed insanity due to be allowed no more license. Humans are better shaping their own morality without reference to God or Allah or to 'Benameeker'.[7] This must mean for Muslims an end to the traditional *Dar al Islam/Dar al-Harb* division of the world, between the politico/religious regime of Islam and a world fit to be power-subdued to it. Equally we must ask whether the President of the United States does not have a *Dar al-Harb* concept of his own, in respect of states he dubs as 'an axis of evil', due for righteous invasion? There is something terrifying in a 'war against terror' that identifies a *Dar al-Harb* elsewhere in a unilateral conclusion around what makes it so.

Ought religion to be inherently combative to the point of armed conflict in its name? What then of its integrity? The issue presses—Islam this way or not Islam this way? Is there not something idolatrous, something blasphemous, in that Quranic phase about being *hizb-Allah*? Is Allah a 'Partisan'? When 'His throne encompasses the heavens and the earth.' *Hizb* is a political term and, taken at face value, must mean some 'annexation' of the divine, of which we would have to say, with the Qur'an: 'Exalted be He above all that ye associate.' If the Irish 'have had enough of God in Ireland,' have we all had enough of Gods in global society?'

---

[6] See the discussion of the transition from a religion as 'message' minus political power in Mecca to one empowered state-wise in Medina in Zakaria Bashier, *Hirjah, Story and Significance*, Leicester, 1983. He notes that 'there were no hypocrites in Mecca, 'there was no need for them,' (p. 71). They only emerged when, in Medina, the victory of Islam was clear. 'Musing on why there was no fighting even in self-defence during the Meccan years, he asks: 'Perhaps it was that Islam needed a period of time in which to establish itself peacefully and on the merit of its own intrinsic spiritual and moral strength' (p. 104). The question would seem to follow: why not always on such grounds?

[7] The name Friday gives his 'supreme deity' in Daniel Defoe's *Robinson Crusoe*.

III

If these four are salient factors in the trend to an agnostic or even an atheist 'secularity' in the stress of contemporary society in its global reach, what follows for responsibility concerning faith? They certainly argue a genuine repentance, an honest sense of guilt and a quest for gentleness in mood and mind. These must also mean a greater openness to interior perplexity from self-interrogation and a self-awareness that seeks true sincerity—that *ikhlas* which the Qur'an so often stresses as crucial to *Din*. How far then does *Dawlah* corrupt or discount or exclude it, from factors politics can never exclude and will often incite? How evident it becomes that we, believers, are 'responsible *for* faith in ever presuming to be responsible *to* it'.

At once a paradox looms. How are we to decide what by its entire *raison d'être* must decide us? A faith has surely to be authoritative, even adamant, about its writ and truth. Do we not stand under them as subjects of their warrant? Indeed. But this quality in religious conviction and commitment cannot well be arbitrary, a tyranny—real or potential—to which the believer brings no security, has no role of critical consent. Both our crucial prepositions ' to and for' have to be there in the equation, if either is to hold.

Allegiance is less than worthy if it is not dynamic and perceptive, if its confidence is passive, traditional, slothful or routine. Only so can it also have that quality which rightly cries, in the ancient words: 'I can so do no other. So help me, God.' To be religious, it has been said, is not simply to hold a view but to do so as one who must. 'The distinctive religious act is an unconditional surrender.'[8] Orthodox Jews, loyal Muslims would agree. The late Pakistani scholar, Fazlur Rahman wrote: 'A mental state of responsibility from which an agent's actions proceed must always recognise that the criterion of judgement about them lies outside them.'[9] 'He/she' are 'under authority'. Yet somehow receiving it so has to be within the liability of the submission that obeys it.

Accordingly, we have now to ask—in prelude to our whole Conference theme—how sundry faiths relate their truth—convictions to

---

[8] Baron Von Hugel, *The Mystical Element in Religion*, London, 1908, Vol. 1, 72, see also 46.

[9] Fazlur Rahman, *Major Themes of the Qur'an*, Minneapolis, 1980, 29. He is expounding the concept of *taqwa*, or 'God-fearingness,' the essence of which is that one knows oneself commanded. Fazlur Rahman was in spiritual exile from Pakistan in the cause of scholarly freedom and became an important influence from his chair in Chicago.

the mutual presence of disparate systems of rite, doctrine, culture and ethics? Living so far, as we now do, globally, only accentuates these issues of tolerance and dialogue and witness. There are no more local privacies in which we can contrive to be immune from one another. If 'World'— as in our Conference title—is adjective to the noun 'Christianity' then all that the world contains has to be 'grist to its mill,' and not only to its mill but to its mind. Its witness has to engage with all it meets and not cringe from the awkward questions that world—inclusion presents.

It is just this sense of unprecedented exposure, whether to paradox or perplexity that sends some believers back to 'final' re-assurers, like an infallible church or a sacrosanct book, wherein they 'let lie or let rest' all for which they can be no longer otherwise responsible. Thus, for example, John Henry Newman abhorred all 'liberalism' as the blight on all confidence, the bane of all certainty. God must have ensured a sound repository for His truth in the Church of Rome, this mercifully delivering soul and mind from the need of 'private judgements'—that terrifying duty of having somehow oneself to underwrite the truth on which one rested. 'Certitude is to know that one knows' and that boon Mother Church bestows. But is not such entire trust in her no less as act of 'private judgement' for which one presumably had considered grounds? Had one then merely shifted the theme of such 'judgement' from a Gospel to an institution, from 'one in *whom* one could believe' to '*what* one could rely on.' The most absolute reliance was, anyway, being made by an option so—and there—to make it.

A comparable shift of the centre of gravity of one's faith has often been made in respect of the Bible, or the Qur'an, as havens of shelter from doubt, one had no occasion to interrogate as to how and why they could still fulfil that office. Or; more fittingly, one might reason rather like old John Bunyan when he assured himself that other faiths, like Islam, were 'only a think-so' by which trusting souls were wrongly re-assured. When that very thought 'tempted him' (his phrase) to wonder whether his own belief in Saviour Jesus was likewise only 'his think-so,' his anxiety betook him to 'beloved Paul.' Paul had believed what John Bunyan believed and 'beloved Paul' was no deceiver. Poor ignorant John could trust what the great Paul had trusted. Thus we all find proxies for our own misgivings, the better to be rid of them. Yet all of these return us to ourselves when we ponder why we did so. A true *consensus fidelium* is not of an exonerating kind, though truly fellowship corroborates faith.

Or there is a way of resolving responsibility *to* and *for* by starting and ending with one's own premise. A writer in *Fundamentalism and the Word of God* sets his issues thus: 'The fact is that here we are faced in principle with a choice between historic evangelicalism and modern subjectivism: between a Christianity that is consistent with itself as one that is not: in effect between one that is wholly God–given and one that is partly man–made.'[10] The 'God–given,' 'man–made' distinction has often been invoked while the criteria, in either case, are either dogmatic or assumed. 'Christianity consistent with itself' deserves and demands to be more privately identified. We see that even certitudes become argumentative about themselves. We may yearn for indubitable oracles but confessing them will always be a decision for which we were liable.

It would seem to follow that decisive faith must always be corrigible, revisable, dynamic in its canon of fidelity. Has 'development' not often figured in the very narrative of dogma? Newman believed and taught that there were truths somehow latent inside an original core or deposit (itself a standing problem for decision) awaiting the wisdom which would one day recognise their latency and bring them into circulation. Some Muslims have argued for the prescience of the Qur'an. Jewry allows the oral law to 'develop' the written Torah of Sinai.

Thus living faith cannot rightly be a sort of 'fideism', a mere 'faith in faith'. Yet, by strange paradox, faith in faith creatively, dynamically, seriously, is what it can only be. That intrinsic quality is caught in the very ambiguity of the English word, denoting both the content of belief and the act of faithful trust that is fidelity. It remains, then, to try to see this Christian vocation to faith/fidelity in encounter with the religious diversity which, in the contemporary world, is its sharpest challenge. 'Politics and Culture' must belong to other papers. 'Religion' here must be the bearing of Christian faith/fidelity on today's Islam.

For alike in Asia and Africa and via the dispersion of—now— some quarter of all the world's Muslims outside any *Dar al-Islam* in the old traditional sense of a *religio/regio*, Islam is where, in a primary kind of way, the relevance of Christianity obtains in distinctively urgent terms. Those terms, in the light of all the foregoing, have to do supremely with that 'making gentle' of religious claim, and awe-tied its temper, as the only authentic credential in being 'on behalf of God' in His human

---

[10] J I Packer, *Fundamentalism and the Word of God,* London, 1959.

world. Thanks to the Incarnation and the Passion of Jesus, understood as the clue to Messianic meaning and so, in turn, the very credentials of the divine nature, such 'gentleness' has been definitive for Christian theology ever since the New Testament, however grossly betrayed in the course of Christian centuries.

What is the potential for its being comprehended in its essential terms so that it might be imprinted into Islamic reading of Allah? The question must be answered from inside Quranic trends towards it, not as something externally commended as by alien auspices. The dynamic 'becoming' of any and every faith, in the direction the contemporary world most direly needs, had to emerge from inside its own resources of tradition and imagination. What, then, are the Muslim potentials for a 'gentle' compassionately patient Islam such as an anxious world most surely needs to have it be? How, if at all, can the Christian mind and spirit serve the hope?

There must be no spiritual imperialism, yet sometimes the outsider may see more clearly what the hopeful factors are as evident in another faiths wrestling with its own counsels in response to common riddles or demands.

It might be said that the current religious crisis is made the more exacting by historic features of Islam self-assurance as housing 'final prophethood' and constituting 'the very religion of Allah.' That impression of a strongly assertive religion has been deepened in recent months, inducing in some quarters a tragic 'Islamaphobia' which only 'darkens counsel by words without knowledge.'

That must be foresworn. One way may be to take the course of Islamic thought back into Mecca where—as we have earlier seen—Islam was only and ever a message, innocent of the power dimension, proudly and impressively so in its patient 'suffering for truth's sake.'[11] There, at Mecca, was—and forever remains—the essential Islam. The Hijrah which sought a power—regime and impressively achieved it in Medina is

---

[11] This dimension in Muhammad's mission features very clearly in the Qur'an. For example, Surah18.6: 'Is it that you are distressing your soul over the way they are.' The sharp enmity to him of the Meccan Quraish was a major factor in the Hijrah—the sense that they were incorrigible in their animosity. He knew from previous messengers' experience that there were hazards to face in the prophetic vocation (Surah 51.51-52). In this respect Muhammad was on very Biblical ground. See discussion in my *Muhammad in the Qur'an: The Task and the Text*, London, 2001.

doubtless rooted in the Qur'an and integral to Muslim self-possession. Yet it is always proper to recall and to insist that Hijrah was on behalf of the Meccan word. It was never a forsaking of the defining city to which, indeed the prophet returned via the Medina story. Power there was never an end in itself, still less a venture into barren brigandage. Its purposiveness pays tribute to its source in the pivotal religious message concerning the unity of Allah, the folly cum evil of idolatry, and the reality of human obligation to humankind.

There can be no doubt about the priority of the Meccan in all things Islamic—the eye-line of *Salat* as the *qiblah* of *taqwa*; the careful orientation of every mosque, the unique destination of *Hajj* in pilgrim journey; the birthplace of the Prophet; the source of the Islamic calendar; the seed-bed of Mohammed's vocation and the very navel—piety has it—of the earth.

The argument must therefore be that the 'what' of Meccan meaning governs the 'how' of Medinan regime, and that the latter, right in the 7th century setting of Arabia, is no longer right in a 21st century global scene. In its there—and—then, Arab tribes desperately needed the bond which monotheism gave then under a unified heaven abrogating tribal feuding.[12] Our world now is desperately needing a sense of 'one world' where religions no longer criminally divide us by sanctioning nation—states with exclusive mandates to impose their versions on us all.

That Islam was meant 'for all seasons'[13] is the proud claim of its finality. That finality must mean that it registers what a changed 'season' now demands and satisfy it by discerning application of a current (not an antiquated) relevance. It is a logic clearly sustained by the familiar principle of *asbab al-nuzul* as the right clue to exegesis.[14] If 7th century immediacies during Mohammed's *Sirah,* or life-course as prophet, determined how *ad hoc* passages were to be understood, then what of the immediacies of a new century? What the Qur'an meant then needs

---

[12] In so far as patron deities sponsored tribal interests, plural worships were the bane of social cohesion. To 'unify' heaven gave hope of unifying human bonds. A clear case can be made for Mohammad's power quest in *that* context. The modern situation differs altogether in that religions have sanctioned division and must learn to belong with the global sanction of civil society among nations.

[13] Echoing the title of Shabbir Akhtar's study of Islam—*A Faith for All Seasons*, London, 1990.

[14] I.e. 'occasions of the sending down.' These have long been the stock-in-trade of exegetes. Report concerning them was a major factor in the development of Tradition.

articulating into what it must mean now, since it is in no way fit to be consigned to a museum where relics only survive as being such.

It is clear, furthermore, that the onus for this responsively responsible exegesis rests, by Sunni tradition, squarely on the community via its *Ijma'*, or 'consensus' as creative reading of the Qur'an and *Shari'ah* via the 'enterprise' of *Ijtihad,* pioneering loyal renewal. This grace of wise initiative has to be steadily 'laicised' so that the right to engage in it is open to all and not circumscribed or hindered by a monopoly in it of crippling pundits thinking only under turbans of mental lethargy, or fear. That the principle of 'development' is there and available is not in doubt. For it fulfils the dictum of the prophet that his 'people would never converge on an error.' Safety lies in communal mind when duly ascertained, so that the old Tradition translates into 'Islam is (will be) what Muslims say it is.'[15]

This whole situation is taken from the realm of aspiration—or some would say, even in this Conference, a dream of the wishful mind—and moves into evident practical significance by the fact, already noted of widespread Muslim Diaspora into the West. This quarter of the world's Muslim population are 'back in Mecca' in that they no longer enjoy a *Dar al–Islam* situation as Medina contrived and bequeathed it. They cannot create more Pakistans.[16] But they are certainly *Dar al-Islam* in their liberty to pray, to build mosques, to go on *Hajj,* to pay alms and celebrate their *mawlids,* keep their Ramadan and do ablutions at the call of the muezzin. What, then, lacks of their Islam?

Moreover, in most of this dispersed existence they are free to participate in the life of politics, to exercise democratic suffrage and bring their faith and ethics to bear on civil life. The absence of Medinan style caliphate need not be deplored as exiling them from a political legitimacy. For no faith can think to dissociate itself from power issues, indispensable as these are in the due sanity and discipline of human society. The current error would be to require that such power dimensions should be the exclusive and oppressive monopoly of the one faith, reducing all other faithful to wan inferiority, living on a demeaning sufferance.

---

15 A favourite dictum of the Canadian Islamicist, Wilfred Cantwell Smith, giving extreme form to the themes of *Ijma'* and *Ijtihad.* It has an obvious circularity in that only by reference to 'Islam' are right 'Muslims' known as qualified to tell.

16 There being no more majority areas where partitioning could happen, though extremists might want to visualise them.

This theme of 'civil society'—often described as 'the secular state'—need not imply a total 'secularisation' that consigned all religion to a sorry limbo. On the contrary, 'secular' in the limited sense intends no rejection of belief but only a 'level situation' for all faiths, consistently with a 'law and order' whose definitions they all share but which none arrogate to themselves alone. Such a concept makes in practice for a better health of faith at heart. In fact a historically hegemonic religion may well stay so, for obvious reasons,[17] while faithfully conceding the mutual presence of 'minority' ones. Then the hard art of being a minority as well as the taxing art of being a majority will alike be the better learned.

That this is the *de facto* situation for significant numbers of Muslims here and now gives ground for hope that defining and fulfilling a congruent Islamicity will develop by its stimulus and challenge. Of course, the very logic of the situation will evoke counsels-and passions-of resistance, of bigotry and defensiveness. Fear is often a dark counsellor. Much will obviously turn on the quality of Christian relation. Hence new measures of being responsible *with* faith as well as *to* and *for* it. It will, perforce, be harder for Islam to revise its Medinan Muhammad in a return with him to Mecca than it was for Christianity to repudiate the 'Christendom' of its 4th century Constantine. The Prophet was always more integral in that, via the Hijrah, he was effectively his own Constantine.

Yet there are already precedents to indicate that the Mecca accent can again prevail.[18]

---

[17] Migrants into a country do not deprive it if its historical character and legacies. Culture, language, ethos and tradition have a staying power which has, in turn, to be the very fabric of any 'hospitality'. A right tenure of 'minority status' will need to discern and implement an accommodating relation that can, hopefully, be reciprocal. The temper of religious 'presence' has much to do with that hope. It is a new dimension of 'responsibility for ...'

[18] At the time of the Indian uprising of 1857 many Muslims were 'in low despair,' assuming that with Empress Victoria on their 'throne' they were not *Dar al-Islam*. Sayid Ahmad Khan assured them that—with all the 'religious' tests in place—their Islamic condition was complete. He founded what became Aligarh University to enable a better self-possession of their minds by education and a reasoned emulation of 'those governing British.' Similarly, in 1925, after the termination, by the Turks, of the ancient caliphate, the Egyptian scholar, 'Ali 'Abd al-Raziq, wrote a famous treatise to prove that the caliphate had never been indispensable to a right Islam. *Islam wa Usul al-Hukm*, 'Islam and the sources of rule', Cairo, 1925. His thesis was disputed bitterly but never refuted.

Opting for Pakistan may have seemed to many the *sine qua non* of authentic survival for Indian Islam. Yet its creation inevitably left millions of Indian Muslims to a condition in which that allegedly vital factor could never belong. If the reality of Pakistan would hope to vindicate the one logic the dis-empowered Islam of partitioned India would have to demonstrate the contrary, the two logics disputing the other's validity. At least it must be clear that the power issue was and is an open question.

IV

The final consideration, however, in any 'making gentle' of religious faith and moral mandate must lie in the concept it has of divine nature. Theology is the ultimate clue both for hope and despair. For, in the ultimate reckoning, worshippers will be characterised by whom they worship, inasmuch as worship has custody of the ideal being–in–the–self. Something of the image the external world has of Islam relates closely to the perceived theology by which Islam is popularly measured. It is often that of supreme and absolute sovereignty, even at times arbitrary in an almightiness answerable only to an inscrutable will–an almightiness where there can be no 'ought,' no necessary obligation, no accountability. No 'making gentle' of the faithful should then be looked for in His mortal minions.

It is manifest that this popular notion of Islamic theism is all awry. Whatever may have been the fortunes of determinism, such a theism is quite un-Quranic. It contravenes the whole theme of a creation entrusted into human creaturehood and that creaturehood honoured and guided in its deputy quality by the sustained ministry of prophethoods sent to remind, encourage and educate those high trustees. Such is the clear theme of Surah 2.30 and the 'setting of a sub-lord, the human, over the created order,' making humankind 'colonists' in the earth (11.61). That our 'subsidiarity' is a genuine 'lordship' cannot be in doubt.

Such high dignity, corroborated by both halves of the *shadadah*, represents—to use Christian terminology—a certain *kenosis on* the part of God in that, through our given liability, there is about that which God wills a clear element that lets it turn on us, the will of God being then done only as and where we will it shall be done. This is our *islam*. [19] An

---

[19] Making the urgent distinction marked by the absence or presence of the capital 'I'— seeing that Arabic lacks that device. Islam would then be the structure finalised only in

Allah who has human 'deputies' and prophetic 'agencies' in measure entrusts His purposes by having us consciously share their goals and serve their ends by our willing (i.e. *muslim*) means.[20]

To miss this Quranic truth of our human stature would be to repudiate alike creation and the Prophet, the one being a fiction or a fate, the other being an irrelevance. As has been aptly said 'Puppets need no prophets.' It is Islamic to realise that the things of God are—in measure—responsibly the things of humankind to appreciate and to fulfil. Creation is heaven's magnanimity in self-expending compassion and intention. We humans have to know, and take, ourselves as a divine enterprise at serious earthly risk—the risk of a 'most Moved Mover' who is neither tyrant nor absentee, whose throne encompasses all that is.

This mystery of life and being as 'over to you, you humans' is captured in the question of Surah 7. 172, addressed to all humanity continuously through their generations: 'Am I not your Lord?' It is a negative question and, like all such, expects the answer Yes! But waits for it. 'Yes' is the binding answer it has humanly received. We are 'bound over' to the acknowledgement of Allah as Lord.[21] This is the Lord who has also said: 'Upon you are your own souls.'[22] This 'Disposer supreme' is the more greatly great in having willed for us a stake in that sovereignty, rejoicing to make room for our frail humanity within His majesty Self-sufficing, He who is *Allah al-samad* (112. 4).

A religion that knew it so would need to reproduce that gentleness and arrive—as many Sufis congenially did—at 'One who had enjoined upon himself mercy' (Surah 6. 54) in a divine Self-inscription His mortals must surely emulate in their own religious tribute of submission. It was well said of Christians that they could not well be aggressive with the meaning of the Cross nor serve the wounded hands with a clenched fist. May it not also be true that the authority Islam wields should conform to the generosity of the Allah it serves?

Muhammad and the Pillars of *Din*: islam the 'surrender' to God long earlier exemplified by e.g. Abraham, Salih and Ayyub and all *muslims* antecedent to its Meccan/Medinan completion. (There is the same distinction around the 'm' and the 'M').

[20] On the role of divine agency—always within omnipotence duly understood—see *The Weight in the Word*, Brighton, 2000, and also *op. cit.*, note 11 above, chapters 7 and 8.

[21] See my *Am I not Your Lord? Human Meaning in Divine Question*, London, 2002.

[22] Surah 5. 105: 'You are in charge of your own souls,' i.e. divine sovereignty does not override personal liability for selfhood. Hence the frequent refrain: 'It was their own selves they wronged,' in comment on wilful waywardness.

We are returned, in conclusion, to how far our responsibility to our faith is a searching liability *for* it—for its being duly present in contemporary terms, for its awed exercise of the vocation its truth would have it perceive. In Christian terms that liable sense of things might well tell itself in the final words of an impressive series of Broadcast Talks in the nineteen-forties. They were given by a celebrated historian, Herbert Butterfield. He said:

> Remember a principle which gives us both a firm rock and leaves us the maximum elasticity for our minds: The principle: Hold to Christ, and for the rest be totally uncommitted. [23]

I remember how it seemed to me at the time a truly heartening advice—to respond entirely to the Christ who, in the Christ-event which, is the Gospel, gives us the inclusive referent to God—loved, known and adored through Him. On more mature reflection, one realises that one cannot escape being committed to much else, in clinging only to Christ. Witness Robert Browning's poem *Christmas Eve*, where the poet, traversing from the vulgar chapel, to stupendous Rome, to the lecture hall at Groningen, learns that he can only have Jesus in the company he keeps. [24] Faiths are always responsible for what their faithful have made of them. For these identify each other—which, as in an aphorism, is the paradox for which they are responsible. Being a 'world-Islam' or a 'world-Christianity' only makes us the more liable for magnanimity.

---

[23] Herbert Butterfield, *Christianity and History*, London, 1949, 146.

[24] Robert Browning, *Poetical Works*, Oxford, 1905, 396–409. Despairing about what he found uncouth in the tawdry Chapel with its poor preaching and its feeble music, he visualises an aerial journey to High Mass in St Peter's and thence to the German academy where the scholar doubts that any of the Gospel 'ever happened.' Browning finally returns where he had begun, determined 'to bear with all that Christ will bear with.'

CURRENT THEOLOGICAL THEMES IN WORLD CHRISTIANITY
Michael Kirwan SJ

Introduction

In this article I attempt to delineate within our present geopolitical situation a confrontation between political theology and political myth, and to see within this situation an imperative to 'reconceive' Europe theologically.

The conference which gave birth to it in autumn 2001 originally set out to consider some of the 'challenges which face world Christianity': a globalised economy; Christian ethics in a diverse world community; the encounter between Christianity and other faiths; the homogenisation of culture. Nowhere in the planning was there a foreseeing of the post-11 September scenario: we did not then imagine, nor could we imagine, the United States leading a crusade entitled 'Operation Infinite Justice', drawing nations together against an 'axis of evil'. It is as if the world had survived with relief the transition to a new millennium, only for the forces of a fearsome apocalypse to be unleashed one year later. The tentative programme for the conference looked different: centred on urgent themes, for sure, but even so this was a conversation that has been cut across, leaving us with the simple questions: what are we to talk about now, and how are we to talk about it? Do we concede that there is a new agenda—'all changed, changed utterly'—or do we try and pick up where we left off, before we were so rudely and violently interrupted?

This image of a 'rudely interrupted conversation' is intended to echo the philosophical programme of Critical Theory, or the 'Frankfurt School', which was and is a multi-disciplinary exploration of modernity as an 'unfinished project'. From its beginnings in the early part of the last century, Critical Theory has sought to hold fast to the goals and values of Enlightenment and universal rationality, despite the terrible catastrophes—totalitarianism, technological domination—brought about by the perversion of these ideals. In its most contemporary version, Jürgen Habermas has tried over many years to continue this project in terms of a Theory of Communicative Action, in which he views rationality as oriented towards an 'ideal speech situation'.

One month after the World Trade Centre atrocity, Habermas gave a speech accepting a peace prize in Germany, in which one can almost detect a sense of frustration at his train of thought being interrupted, as it were. He had prepared himself to talk about the challenge of genetic technology, but in the wake of the September atrocities he now finds he has to revisit an old theme: secularization:

> Despite its religious imagery, fundamentalism is, as we know, an exclusively modern phenomenon. What struck us immediately about the Islamic perpetrators was the imbalance between their ends and their means. This reflects an imbalance that has emerged in the perpetrators' home countries between culture and society in the wake of an accelerated and radical modernization.
>
> What under more fortunate conditions might have been considered a process of creative destruction offers these countries no prospect that can adequately compensate for the suffering caused by the collapse of traditional ways ... Even in Europe, where centuries have been spent trying to work out a sensible accommodation with the Janus head of modernity, 'secularization' is still accompanied by highly ambivalent feelings, as evident in the controversy over biotechnology. There are obdurate orthodoxies in the West as well as in the Middle and Far(ther) East, and among Christians and Jews as well as Muslims. Those who wish to avoid a 'clash of civilisations' must therefore keep in mind the still-unresolved dialectic in our own western process of secularization.[1]

The idea of a 'clash of civilisations' has become notorious through Huntington's 1997 book, *The Clash of Civilisations and the Remaking of World Order*, though as we shall see later, the phrase has resonances other than those of Islamic-western tensions. My citing of Habermas here is appropriate, because most of what is understood by 'political theology',

---

[1] From: 'Faith and Knowledge—an Opening'. Speech by Jürgen Habermas, October 2001.

at least from a European Catholic perspective, has been elaborated through conversations with critical theorists, including Habermas. For over thirty years, theologians such as Edward Schillebeecx and Johann Baptist Metz have sought to engage with Critical Theory, taking advantage of its insights, but also challenging and attempting to correct its negative view of religion, and in particular to stress the emancipatory potential of the Christian faith.[2] To borrow a useful typology from Charles Davis:[3] there are three intellectual options open to us, each defined in terms of the stance it takes towards modernity, and each having its own theological variant:

—neo-conservatism (which he describes in Habermas' terms as the ambiguous relation to modernity typified by 'frightened liberals')
—postmodernism, whose theological variants include the work of Mark C Taylor, as well as John Milbank and *Radical Orthodoxy*
—and the view of modernity as an unfinished project, put forward by Critical Theory and political theologians.

I will assume as correct the diagnosis of neo-orthodoxy as an understandable but ultimately inconsistent intellectual stance, and will not attempt to delineate it further. So our choice of an appropriate theological stance lies between the remaining two options. The most striking recent attempt to delineate a postmodern theology is that of 'Radical Orthodoxy', associated with John Milbank and other Cambridge theologians, which proposes a robust view of ecclesiology as the only 'true' politics. Christians are called to forsake their false humility, and to come out fighting against the distortions of a bankrupt modernity which persistently denies its own disguised theological suppositions:

For several centuries now, secularism has been defining and constructing the world. It is a world in which the theological order is either discredited or turned into a harmless leisure-time activity of private commitment. And yet in its early

2 For overviews of the relation between Critical Theory and Political Theology, see Arens (1997), and Peukert (1992).
3 Charles Davis, 1995, *Religion and the Making of Society*.

manifestations secular modernity exhibited anxiety concerning its lack of ultimate ground—the scepticism of Descartes, the cynicism of Hobbes, the circularities of Spinoza, all testify to this. And today the logic of secularism is imploding. Speaking with a microphoned and digitally simulated voice, it proclaims—uneasily, or else increasingly unashamedly—its own lack of values and lack of meaning. In its cyberspaces and theme-parks it promotes a materialism which is soulless, aggressive, nonchalant and nihilistic.[4]

Hence Radical Orthodoxy's attempt to 'reclaim the world' by resituating its concerns and activities, including politics, within a theological framework. In *Theology and Social Theory* Milbank attempts a 'sceptical demolition of modern, secular social theory, from a perspective with which it is at variance ... Christianity'. He calls on modern theology to reject its *pathos*, the false humility which sees theology being 'positioned' by secular reason rather than the other way round.

The idea that Enlightenment secularity is finally to get its theological come-uppance is a headily attractive one, but it needs to be recognised that this is not the only possible reading of Europe's religious history. Paul Valadier has challenged the tendency of the Pope and others to dismiss Europe's as a 'culture of death';[5] this is dangerous talk, he says, because it conjures up the image of a dying animal, waiting to be put out of its misery, rather than a sick patient who needs to be nursed back to health. Europe's ills—depression, barbarism, materialism—should be regarded as evidence of a malaise *in* society rather than *of* it; if we replace the metaphor of imminent death with that of sickness, a very different theological strategy suggests itself. Above all, Valadier is challenging Europe's 'Promethean myth', the reading of its history since the Enlightenment as nothing but the long, progressive attempt to emancipate itself from the Christian message and its God—an overcoming of theocentrism by anthropocentrism. The one true God is replaced by false gods: progress, the technological taming of nature, emancipation from religion—a Promethean will which issues in two forms of totalitarianism, consumer society and communism.

---

[4] *Radical Orthodoxy*,1. See also William T Cavanaugh, 'A Fire Strong Enough to Consume the House', 1995, for a re-reading of the European 'wars of religion'.

[5] Paul Valadier, 'Europa und seine Götter', 1996, 15-29.

Valadier counters this argument when he asserts that the Promethean delusion is only one particular moment of European history, though a very important one. It reaches its climax in 19th century history of philosophy, and more resembles a childhood illness rather than the purest expression of reason. Thinkers like Hobbes and Machiavelli are rather seeking to limit (evil) humanity—on this account, it is Christianity which is too optimistic! What more accurately characterises Europe is its chronic and pervasive weakness of will and the modesty of its projects, rather than unbridled arrogance.

This, I would suggest, has even greater force in the present climate. Radical Orthodoxy's confidently muscular discourse on the shortcomings of liberalism and the rhetorical superiority of the Christian meta-narrative now comes across as supremely tactless: not, as it were, what we really want to be whispering into the ear of the ailing patient. Certainly, our disappointment is profound. The decade preceding September 2001 was one of flickering possibilities: of a new post Cold-War world order; of new democratic openings in Latin America, South Africa and elsewhere; of humanitarian interventionism; of international responsibility for justice against the instigators of state-sponsored violence; of fresh perspectives on human rights and debt relief. Many of these developments have not lived up to their promise, few have been entirely without shadow, but in any case it is this conversation, more a tentative stammering, which has been cut across and all but silenced by the brutal and simplistic rhetoric of two fundamentalisms.[6]

Political myth or political theology?

To understand the international mobilization of the last nine months, we will find ourselves turning to old, well-trodden territory. I refer to an earlier strand of political theology which for the purposes of this discussion will be better described as 'political mythology'. Carl Schmitt's

---

[6] See Barber's analysis of a struggle between 'Jihad' and 'McWorld' (1995). The 'return of religion' which was a subject of discussion even before 11 September is too vast a theme to be considered here: see the special issue of *Millennium* (Journal of International Studies), 2000, on 'Religion and International Relations', as well as Esposito and Wilson (eds), *Religion and Global Order*, 2000. The relationship between religion and violence is likewise a perennial theme: see Juergensmeyer's *Terror in the Mind of God*—updated just before the September bombings!

curious Catholic restorationist programme of the 1920s is described by Matthew Lamb as 'a completely immanent project with no trace of the transcendence of Christian faith',[7] one which led Schmitt to pledge his allegiance to National Socialism. The unpalatable features of his political theory—his assertions that politics can only be based on a strongly dominative sovereign who is capable of deciding between conflictive interest groups, and that knowledge is power to control and impose extrinsic order upon natural and historical realities which are inherently combative in nature—are not news. They continue a long tradition of political anthropology taking in Augustine, Luther and Hobbes, which centres on a conception of politics as *katéchon*: *Katécho* means 'to hold back, hold fast, to bind, restrain'. Many myths (and even Scripture—see 2 Thessalonians 2: 1-12) speak of a power or person, a *katéchon*, which keeps chaos in check; a conception which in Thomas Hobbes' *Leviathan* (1651) is introduced at the very outset of modern political thought.

While the *katéchon* is a mythical–religious concept, one can certainly question the extent to which it is a Christian one. Its fundamental paradox concerns the *katéchon* as a means of preventing chaos which is itself violent; the force of anarchy ('Leviathan'), is itself a source of order. This is the Augustinian understanding of the 'pax Romana', the strictly qualified and limited peace which comes from imperial domination. The more modern tradition of Political Theology associated with Johann Baptist Metz and Jürgen Moltmann[8] consciously seeks to distance itself from this gloomy and reactionary distortion of Christianity.

This is understandable, but it should also be evident that much of Schmitt's analysis merits close attention, not least the *Freund-Feind* distinction, 'friend or foe', which is reproduced in President Bush's insistence that we are either for his crusade against terrorism or we are on the side of the terrorists, with no possibility of a neutral stance. Schmitt states in his *Concept of the Political*, 'The specific political distinction, from which political actions and motivations derive, is the distinction between Friend and Enemy'. For Palaver (1998) the *Freund-Feind* distinction is a necessary

---

[7] Matthew Lamb, 'Political Theology' in *The New Dictionary of Theology*, ed. J Komonchak *et al*, Gill and Macmillan, Dublin, 1990, 774.

[8] For an exposition 'Leviathan theology' and of alternatives to it, see Jürgen Moltmann, 'Covenant or Leviathan? Political Theology for Modern Times', *Scottish Journal of Theology* 47 (1994). J B Metz also addresses this tension in *Faith in History and Society*, 149-158. See also Wolfgang Palaver, 'Hobbes and the Katéchon: The Secularization of Sacrificial Christianity'.

diagnostic instrument, applicable to historical examples as well as the contemporary situation. It appeared to Schmitt himself to be clearly applicable to the Cold War; since the end of communism, this global bipolar Friend-Enemy structure has even proliferated rather than disappeared, so that we have a world full of local conflicts, a 'hot peace' (Palaver, 1998: 11). Schmitt's development of this doctrine is an uncomfortable argument for the primordial status of strife in human affairs, one which does not allow for the possibility of neutrality or pacifism (the famous fragment of Heraclitus is cited here: 'Strife is the Father of all').

Schmitt finds scriptural backing for this view in Genesis 3.15: 'I set an enmity between you and the woman ...'; God similarly wills division between human beings in the story of the Tower of Babel. As a result of the Fall, God has established hostility between human beings; anyone who attempts to deny or alleviate this enmity stands on the side of Satan against God. Such a temptation of Antichrist is manifested, for Schmitt, in the universalist drive to establish a World State, as well as in pacifist or non-aligned movements. By contrast, one's enemy is 'God-given', providential, and therefore a part of the world order—a critique which may be compared with the dystopic visions of *1984* and *Brave New World*, where modernity's violence is concealed under a peaceful facade.

Despite these biblical allusions, Schmitt's emphasis is more mythological than theological, as Palaver demonstrates. Schmitt stands in an extremely ambiguous relation to Catholic tradition and to biblical revelation, whereas in the work of the French–American cultural theorist René Girard there is a convergence with some of Schmitt's basic analyses, though this time in the service of the Gospel message rather than of the immanentist project dismissed by Lamb. Girard is known for his description of how a society, galvanised by its fear of chaos and loss of identity, will seek for a 'scapegoat', whose destruction will restore peace. What Girard also points out is how conflict escalates through the mutual and sterile fascination of rivals, becoming identical doubles the more they try to differentiate themselves from 'the other'.

For Girard, 'myth' means the tale that a society tells about itself in order to deny its violent origins, and to hide from itself the continued operation of this violence.[9] Once this story has been exposed for the

---

[9] Gillian Rose's chapter on Girard and Thomas Mann is eloquently titled 'Myth out of the Hands of the Fascists'. See *The Broken Middle*, Blackwell, Oxford, 1992, 115-152.

sham of half-truths that it is—to echo Habermas, a 'process of creative destruction', except that for Girard and Milbank it is the corrosive power of the Christian gospel that does this—then societies have to take responsibility for their conflict and aggression, and find more lastingly constructive ways of dealing with them. Even the most sophisticated political and justice systems are never entirely free of this mythical and violent past, and to present themselves as such (i.e. when a nation sees itself as providentially guided or 'sacred'), is idolatry. A political theology arising from this appoach will consist in a relentless and rigorous desacralisation of any given political order, what R A Markus describes with reference to Augustine as a 'refusal to bless the State'.[10] What is less obvious is what are the concrete and positive political options that may come from such a theology; as I suggest later, what may be at stake here is the debate within liberation and political theology about the necessity of an 'eschatological reserve' which prevents us from fully embracing any single political system, however benign.

Europe's theological 'other'

Implicit in what has been said so far, then, is a tension between 'political mythology' and 'political theology'; I shall return in the final section of this article to a consideration of why such a contrast might be helpful, but will do so by way of a detour. The challenge is to articulate a fresh European theological perspective; one way of sharpening this challenge is to consider for a moment what has happened to the most distinctive of Europe's theological conversation partners, Latin American theology of liberation. I hope the detour will be illuminating on a number of levels, but specifically I am suggesting a parallel between the political backdrop against which liberation theology exercised such a powerful imaginative hold, and the move towards European integration. For all its specifically *theological* novelty, the impact of the theology of liberation is inconceivable without a shared pan-Latin American political vision, inspired by first Cuba and then Nicaragua, of a broadly socialist and even revolutionary character. It is the interplay between this specific supra-national

---

[10] R A Marcus 1989, 'Refusing to Bless the State'.

perspective, and the gospel read from the perspective of the poor, which gives liberation theology its distinctive flavour.[11]

Rather than survey the vast literature concerning the nature and extent of liberation theology's alleged demise, I will confine myself here to three specific proposals:

> —Latin American liberation theology is experiencing a transition or tension between socio-economic and cultural analyses;[12]
> —Liberation theology faces a new agenda in post-dictatorship countries, with a new concern for transitional issues of truth, justice, memory, reconciliation, forgiveness, and a 'deepening' of democracy;
> —Latin American theology in general should be ready to reflect upon its own poetic and literary 'mytho-logos', instead of conventional social analysis.

George de Schrijver argues that a paradigm shift has occurred in liberation theology. He sees in much of its contemporary literature a tension between socio-economic and cultural analyses, and, controversially, a 'retreat' from the former into the comparative tranquillity of cultural debate. The reasons alleged for liberation theology's decline as a theory about socio-economic reality are well-known: it has not responded adequately to the fall of communism; it needs to revise its judgement on market economies, which can no longer seriously be regarded as intrinsically evil; the dependency theory upon which it relied has lost credibility since the 1980s. This demise of dependency theory entails the necessity of a revision of its verdict on the market economy; the challenge for the Third World, and for liberation theology, is to build up the kind of space in civil society that can regulate the excesses of capitalism, i.e. the social democratic model (Germany) as a 'blueprint' for other nations. 'It

---

[11] The most important expression of this would be the meetings of the Latin American Episcopal Conference in Medellin (1968) and Puebla (1979) which helped to orientate the church during these decades. The inability of Europe to develop a comparable united episcopal/ecclesial voice since the Second Vatican Council may be noted here as a theme for further investigation.

[12] G de Schrijver, 'Paradigm Shift in Third-World Theologies of Liberation: From Socio-Economic Analysis to Cultural Analysis?', in George de Schrijver (ed), 1998, *Liberation Theologies on Shifting Ground*, 3–83.

is imperative for liberation theology to espouse a social-democratic version of its initial enterprise; only then will it be able to keep pace with modern theory-formation in the social sciences, and to gain relevance for the political action of Christians in the context of complex modern societies.' Such a shift implies a change in method and a new agenda for action, since, under postmodern conditions:

> [w]hat is mainly striking is not only the fragmented panorama of the fields of action but also the determination to uncouple those fields from any unifying centre that might command the march for revolutionary change. This dispersal sharply contrasts with the Marxist revolutionary consciousness, whose force is based on the exploited people's collective will 'to overthrow the seemingly unchangeable state of affairs'. This collective will is essential in the formation of a unified class consciousness, yet it is obviously this core element which, in the new approach, has been relegated to the background. (de Schrijver: 31)

A second factor in the evolution of liberation theology is the unfinished business of the transition from dictatorship to democracy, above all where this includes urgent discussion about human rights and reconciliation, which now constitutes the biggest single political challenge for many Latin American countries. A 'theological' analysis is required here in two respects: firstly, the distinctive history of the Latin American continent since its 'discovery' is one of sacralised violence—the Conquest itself being very explicitly and necessarily a military-ecclesial enterprise; and secondly, the contemporary challenge in countries such as Argentina, Chile and El Salvador, which suffered under military dictatorship is in part a religious one, since the painful transition to democracy involves a complex negotiation of the competing demands of religiously loaded values such as truth, memory, reconciliation, forgiveness, justice. The Church is usually one of the main actors in these processes, and of course the majority of South America's population is at least culturally Roman Catholic. Failure then, to incorporate a theological analysis would be a severe impoverishment of our understanding of these processes.[13] For all

---

[13] For a continent-wide survey of this theme, see Jeffrey Klaiber, SJ, *The Church, Dictatorships and Democracy in Latin America*, 1998.

of these countries, the transition to stable democracy and 'normalisation' is fraught by the dilemma spoken of by Ricardo Lagos (before his election as Chile's President): how to explain:

> [t]he drama of a country that has seen emerge from its own entrails those who murder, torture, cut throats, and even burn other human beings, and who brazenly walk the streets at our side, without our understanding where these people came from, or how it was possible that our society give origin to this, to these thousands who seem to be normal beings.

To mention just some of the literature which picks up, explicitly or implicitly, on the religious aspects of this dilemma: Graziano's study of 'Divine Violence' traces the ritual and religious symbolic dimensions of torture under military dictatorship in Argentina; similarly, William Cavanaugh's study of ecclesial resistance to the Pinochet dictatorship posits the Church's eucharistic discipline as a counterpoise to the 'anti-liturgy' of torture.[14] In post-dictatorship contexts, Tomás Moulian describes the public reception of the Rettig Report in Chile as 'a great symbolic act by which the State assumed responsibility, and at the same time a euphemistic civic liturgy, a spectacular act of evasion', while Alexander Wilde draws our attention to 'irruptions of memory' during the Chilean transition.[15] He writes out of a concern with how democracy, once achieved and consolidated, can be 'deepened', citing a key text which addresses the healing but dangerously amnesiac traditions of Chile's collective memory, evocatively entitled 'the soft ashes of forgetfulness'.[16] Wilde also attempts a comparison with literature on Vichy France, and on the 'divided memory' of the two Germanies dealing with the legacy of Nazism. In all of these texts, whether they seek to articulate and understand the horrors of state terrorism, or to map out the way forward to healing and reconciliation, the resort to religious conceptuality is unavoidable—for depicting evasion and occlusion, as well as resources for resistance and meaning.

---

[14] Frank Graziano, *Divine Violence*, 1992; William Cavanaugh, *Torture and Eucharist*, 1998.
[15] Tomás Moulian, *Chile Actual: Anatomia de un Mito*; Alexander Wilde, 1999, 'Irruptions of Memory: Expressive Politics in Chile's Transition to Democracy'.
[16] Elizabeth Lira and Brian Loveman, 1999, *Las suaves cenizas del olvido*.

For a third perspective, I refer briefly to Juan Noemi's suggestive observations concerning the conditions for a truly inculturated Latin American theology.[17] Noemi argues that a principal reason for the inadequacy of liberation theology has been the epistemological narrowness of its sociological and philosophical foundations: 'The theological problem rests in the fact that philosophy is not a luxury for the theologian, but a necessity which determines the seriousness and the very possibility of her task, and Latin America has not been reflected upon philosophically' (47). This does not simply concern the 'problem' of Marxism, but refers to the poverty, up to now, of all scientific attempts to 'think Latin America', especially when we compare this poverty with the richness of the continent's literature:

> This is well-known in Latin America and can be recognised by anyone who reads any of our poets or novelists. I am thinking of Neruda, García Marquez, Rulfo and Jorge Amado. In them and in others we are presented with a rich logos which we cannot deny simply because it still lacks a corresponding philosophical tradition, so that it remains a 'mytho-logos'. Certainly a careful reading of *One Hundred Years of Solitude* offers a more profound and complete understanding of Latin America than the most sophisticated socio-economic analysis elaborated in the framework of dependency theory. But the transition from a mytho-logos to a philosophical logos (to what the Greeks called theo-logos, distinguishing it from the content of the poetry in their myths) has scarcely begun. Theology is weakened by this situation. The theologian lacks the philosopher who can unravel and articulate the mytho-logos of the poet. (Noemi: 29)

These three challenges to liberation theology—the 'paradigm shift' from socio-economic to cultural analysis, which must be embraced if liberation theology is to retain effectiveness; the move from prophetic denunciation of injustice to the less clear-cut tasks of healing, reconciliation and of 'deepening' democracy in post-dictatorship societies; the invitation to draw on literary rather than sociological imagination

---

[17] J Noemi, 'Rasgos, Imperativos y Desafio' in Noemi and Castillo, 1998, *Teología Latinoamericana*.

for 'thinking Latin America'—these together imply a fundamental repositioning and refocusing of this distinctive theological style.

Conclusion: 'It is time to proselytise European success'[18]

I am suggesting that European theology is being called to a similar repositioning. We may posit a kind of *communicatio idiomata* here, a recognition of the shared challenges and shared resources for European and Latin American theology and of the mutual applicability of their insights. Noemi argues against the alleged provincialism of liberation theology, whenever it has tried to set itself up over and against the 'occidental European cultural space': such an opposition is a denial of Latin America's ethno-cultural diversity. He quotes Octavio Paz, 'We are and we are not Europeans':

> The richness of the Latin American will not be confined to a provincial folklorism. Indigenism is not an alternative to Herodianism. We should assume without complexes and in all its dynamic complexity our 'mestiza' reality. We are 'mestizos', and we are and we are not Europeans, we are and we are not indigenous. (Noemi: 57)

If Latin Americans are, and are not Europeans, can the same be said of Europeans themeslves? This paradox is addressed specifically by Timothy Garton-Ash when he asks: *Will Europe never be Europe because it is becoming Europe?*

Garton-Ash explains this paradoxical question by indicating four meanings of the term 'Europe': 'Will the current European Union of fifteen states (Europe, sense 1) never attain the long-dreamed-of final condition of coherent political unity (Europe, sense 2) because it is now committed to including most other states on the geographical continent of Europe (sense 3) ... because it is reverting to the bad old ways of competing nation-states in pre-1945 Europe' (sense 4).' The Nice negotiations concerning increased membership and voting rights were

---

[18] Will Hutton, *The World We're In*, 2002, 358.

indeed chaotic and undignified; nonetheless the summit was a symbolic and psychological breakthrough to bringing the formerly communist countries of the 'other Europe' into the European Union: finally, for the EU, the penny has dropped about what 1989 was all about.

Garton-Ash goes on to envisage a putative European 'orchestra' of between forty and forty-two states, which, including Russia, would double the current EU population of 375 million.

Fantastical as this may seem, what has already been achieved is already fantastical enough: 'Now, for the first time ever in European history, most states on the European continent are freely committed to designing, by consent, a non-hegemonic order for most of Europe.' What then becomes apparent is the gulf between this extraordinary momentum towards unity and the immense fragility and even sickness of the mechanisms and institutions which are supposed to sustain it. Paradoxically, Europe is in danger because it fails to excite the imagination:

> While quite a few Europeans will display the European flag on their vehicle registration plates, there is precious little else of inspiring symbolism, mystique, or what Walter Bagehot, in writing about the British constitution, called simply 'magic.' For most Europeans, Europe is boring. This *grand ennui* is a real danger to the whole project, and a limit to what it can become. ... the combination of mind-curdling institutional complexity and the missing trans-European public sphere make public drama or mystique most unlikely to emerge around European institutions for the foreseeable future. Europe may just have to get by without it.

Nor, as some hope and others fear, will Europe become a superpower to rival the United States. It does not have, nor will have for some time, the capacity to focus political will, backed by economic might and military force, for the concentrated projection of power outside its borders. But this shouldn't worry us, says Garton-Ash, any more than the mermaid of the fairy tale who wanted to be a girl: '... she doesn't need to be so unhappy. She just has to know who she is.' On this view, Europe is most satisfactorily regarded as 'a process rather than a structure, a method rather than a piece of architecture ... Europe will, indeed, never be Europe, because it is becoming Europe. But this does not mean that it must return to being Europe again.'[19]

This dates from before 11 September, however; since then, William Hutton's plea for a more robust recasting of European identity may be more pertinent. In his own version of the 'clash of civilisations' he castigates British vacillation about European integration: *The World We're In* is 'a book for the idea of Europe', with the quest for European unity crucial in providing a 'countervailing force to the US around which a more enlightened and liberal global order can be formed'; a counterweight, therefore, not so much to the US itself as to the social and economic conservatism which has now eclipsed its liberal tradition. Globalisation may be inevitable, but what can and should be resisted is a globalised version of this dominant American ideology. For sure, the renaissance of American liberalism will need to be fought on American territory:

> However, Europe can help in two ways. It can be explicit about the importance of those liberal values itself; and it can demonstrate that they work effectively as a platform upon which to construct a just economic and social order. The old world, in short, needs to be come an exemplar of what is possible for the new world—and, around the rebirth of a hard but tolerant liberalism, it needs to offer the rest of the world in general, and the Islamic world in particular, a settlement based on interdependence, reciprocity of obligation and the recognition that there is a global interest. It is the moment when Europe must come of age. (Hutton: 18)

Paradoxically, it is Europe which offers the possibility of a genuinely postmodern respect for plurality, while 'America' is locked into modernity's self-identity and brutish will to power. America has become the world's sole superpower (or 'hyperpower', if you will), while relinquishing the responsibility that goes with this status; Europe, says Hutton, must take up the mantle.

---

[19] For further discussion of the challenge posed to European democracy and its institutions by the logistics of expansion and unification, see Larry Siedentop's *Democracy in Europe*, 2001.

Although he recognises the importance of religious factors that have contributed to the shaping of the two 'civilisations'—evangelical fundamentalism in the United States, social Catholicism in Europe— Hutton's strident call-to-arms cries out for and deserves a sustained theological analysis. America's presumption of its providential role in world affairs, and of the overriding primacy of its interests, together with the dualism of its *Freund/Feind* distinction, do not receive an explicit religious label from Hutton, but these categories are familiar to political theology. Moltmann's describes two models, 'Leviathan' and 'Covenant', according to their underlying anthropologies (respectively, negative and positive). It is ironic that he appeals to America as an example of the positive, covenantal idea of the State, taken by Puritans into the New World along with the notion of America as a covenanted nation; this:

> presupposes a positive anthropology in order to legitimate a critical theology of power as well as democratic institutions for the control of power. 'All men are created free and equal and endowed by their Creator with inalienable rights', as the American Declaration of Independence explains. The political doctrine of the demons, according to which (uncontrolled) power as such is evil (Jakob Burckhardt), is usually cited here. (Moltmann: 25)

By the same token, Enlightenment Europe for Moltmann represents the Leviathan model of the State, whose negative anthropology legitimates a positive theology of power, authority and sovereignty. Human beings are evil and chaotic, and therefore need a strong State to protect them from others and from themselves. A reversal, in other words, of Hutton's positive appraisal of Europe over against the prevailing American hegemony.

I have sought to explore some of the theological implications of the current challenge to Europe's self-understanding, a challenge robustly articulated in its economic and political aspects by Will Hutton's analysis. There are a number of theological tools to hand:

The tradition of post-war European Political Theology which seeks to 'keep faith' with modernity and with the ideals of Reason and Enlightenment, I suggest, remains an appropriate project for Christianity. It stands as heir to and in tension with the older attempt at 'Political

Theology' (better understood as a kind of political myth), whose restorationist objective need not invalidate the applicability of some of its concepts. I also advert to the transformed context of Liberation Theology as a resource for the renewal of European theology: ways forward include an emphasis on cultural as well as socio-economic analysis, attention to the theological issues around reconciliation, inclusion and the 'deepening of democracy';[20] the development (by way of its own literary and cultural resources) of a genuinely European *theo-logos* out of its 'mytho-logos'. It is precisely because Europe's 'grand narrative' is exhausted and incredible, because its gods have failed, that it is freed to act and judge wisely, to challenge and to 'refuse blessing'.[21]

To put this another way, there is a need, like Habermas, to revisit the 'process of creative destruction' under its various names— secularisation, demythologisation—and to acknowledge it as still under way. We too are asked to be 'mestizos', to envisage a political order which can function liberatively and assertively, but without myths and without messianism. A refusal to bless Leviathan means refusing not just the more blatant blasphemies of absolutism, but also the logic of the Freund-Feind distinction itself.

In the light of this, there is perhaps one more question to be asked anew, one which features at the heart of political theology's self-definition: the debate about the 'eschatological reserve'. In the light of Auschwitz, Metz insists on the wrongness of any wholehearted Christian approval for any political project or system, no matter how humane or progressive. There must always be an 'eschatological reserve' which prevents us from idolising any messianic regime. For the Uruguayan liberationist Juan Luis Segundo, on the other hand, this is too reticent: surely, if we are faced with a comparatively benevolent and democratic government (as opposed, for example to a violent dictatorship), Christians should be allowed to name and celebrate this as a partial instantiation of

---

[20] A theme which seems to be extremely apposite given the concerns that there are interconnections between anxieties about immigration, the rise of the Far Right in a number of European countries, and a widespread disillusion with democratic processes and institutions.

[21] Cavanaugh gives the example of the incident in which a German foreign minister berates General Pinochet for his human rights record. Pinochet is taken aback, and asks how a German, of all people, can have the temerity to speak out so directly. The minister turns the question around: it is precisely *because* of what happened to his people in the Nazi era that he knows the danger of keeping silent.

God's kingdom, and to work accordingly on its behalf. An 'eschatological reserve' will only serve to paralyse the praxis of liberation.

The difference between the two theologians on this issue is not easily resolved, yet clearly requires attention if an effective theological version of Hutton's majestic call-to-arms is to be taken up. As Garton-Ash's article makes clear, the European project is a curious mixture of dynamism and *grand ennui*; it remains a limited project because it simply does not exert the fascination and symbolic power which one associates with national or regional identities. It is possible, of course, that the project could ultimately fail through lack of interest, but my argument in this article is that this low-key, pragmatic embrace of a 'demythologised' Europe is to be seen as precisely a theological strength, and needs to be trumpeted as such. Apart from anything else, this is to recognise the necessary risk involved in all talk of Europe returning to her 'Christian roots'. This is where my fairly crude distinction between political 'mythology' and political 'theology' must be put to work: there are too many demons and too many idols in Europe, still, for us to be able to dispense entirely with the bleaker insights of Schmitt; and yet a political theology for our times will refuse to be bound by them, and by their alleged inevitability, so that generous conversations of the past can resume, and new ones begin.[22]

References

Arens, E, 1997, 'Interruptions: Critical Theory and Political Theology between Modernity and Postmodernity', in Batstone *et al.* (eds.), 222-242.

Barber, B, 1995, *Jihad Versus McWorld*. Times Books, NY.

Batstone, D, Mendieta, E *et al.* (eds.), 1997, *Liberation Theology and the Americas*. Routledge, NY and London.

Browning, D S and Fiorenza, F (eds.), 1992, *Habermas, Modernity and Public Theology*. Crossroad, NY.

Cavanaugh, W T, 1995, ' "A Fire Strong Enough to Consume the House": The Wars of Religion and the Rise of the State', *Modern Theology* 11.4 (1995), 397-420.

—1998, *Torture and Eucharist: Theology, Politics and the Body of Christ*. Blackwell, Oxford.

—1999, 'The World in a Wafer: A Geography of the Eucharist as Resistance

---

[22] My thanks to Wolfgang Palaver for conversations which have assisted me in the writing of this article.

to Globalization', *Modern Theology* 15.2 (1999), 181-198.

Comblin, J, 1998, *Called for Freedom: The Changing Context of Liberation Theology.* Orbis, Maryknoll, NY.

Davis, C, 1995, *Religion and the Making of Society*, Cambridge University Press.

Esposito, J, and Wilson, M (eds.), 2000, *Religion and Global Order*, University of Wales Press.

Garton-Ash, T, 'The European Orchestra', *New York Review of Books*, 17 May, 2001.

Girard, R, 1997, [1972], *Violence and the Sacred.* Johns Hopkins UP.

—2000, *I see Satan Fall like Lightning.* Crossroad, NY.

Graziano, F, 1992, *Divine Violence: spectacle, psychosexuality & radical Christianity in the Argentine 'dirty war'.* Westview Press, Oxford.

Habermas, J, 2001, 'Faith and Knowledge—an Opening'. Speech by Jürgen Habermas accepting the Peace Prize of the German Publishers and Booksellers Association, Frankfurt, 14 Oct 2001.

de la Huerta, M Garcia, 1999, *Reflexiones Americanas: Ensayos de Intra-Historia.* LOM Santiago, Chile.

Hutton, W, 2002, *The World We're In*, Little, Brown, London.

Juergensmeyer, M, 2000, *Terror in the Mind of God: The Global Rise of Religious Violence.* University of California Press.

Klaiber J, SJ, *The Church, Dictatorships and Democracy in Latin America.* Orbis, Maryknoll, 1998.

Lira, E, and Loveman, B, 1999, *Las suaves cenizas del olvido.* LOM Edicíon, Santiago.

Malamud-Goti, J, 1996, *Game Without End: State Terror and the Politics of Justice.* University of Oklahoma Press.

Marcus R A, 1989, 'Refusing to Bless the State', *New Blackfriars* 70: 1989, 372-79.

Milbank, J, 1990, *Theology and Social Theory: beyond secular reason.* Blackwell, Oxford.

—et al., 1999, *Radical Orthodoxy*, London.

Millennium (Journal of International Studies), 2000, vol. 29/3; Special Issue: 'Religion and International Relations'. London School of Economics.

Moltmann, J, 1994, 'Covenant or Leviathan? Political Theology for Modern Times', *Scottish Journal of Theology* 47 (1994), 19-41.

Moulian, Tomás, 1997, *Chile Actual: Anatomía de un mito*, LOM-ARCIS, Santiago, Chile.

Noemi J C and Castillo FL, 1998, *Teología Latinoamericana.* Centro Ecuménico Diego de Medellin, Santiago, Chile.

Palaver, Wolfgang, 1995, 'Hobbes and the Katéchon: The Secularization of Sacrificial Christianity', *Contagion* 2 (Spring 1995).

—1998, *Die mythischen Quelen des Politischen: Carl Schmitt's Freund-Feind Theorie.* Beiträge zur Friedensethik 27, Kohlhammer, Stuttgart.

—[forthcoming] 'Die antike Polis im Lichte biblischer Gewaltanschauung. Die mimetishe Theorie René Girards zum Problem des politischen' in Gestrich, Christof (ed.), *Die Aktualität der Antike: das ethische Gedächtnis des Abendlandes*, Wichern-Verlag, 65-80.

Peukert, H, 1992, 'Enlightenment and Theology as Unfinished Projects' in Browning and Fiorenza (eds.).

de Schriver, G, 1998, *Liberation Theology on Shifting Ground*, Leuven University Press.

Siedentop, L, 2001, *Democracy in Europe*. Columbia University Press.

Sobrino, J, 1999, *La fe en Jesucristo: Ensayo desde las víctimas*. Editorial Trotta, Madrid.

Valadier, P, 1996, 'Europa und seine Götter: Eine kritische Gegenwartsanalyse', *ET: European Catholic Theological Association*, May 1996, 15-29.

Wilde, A, 1999, 'Irruptions of Memory: Expressive Politics in Chile's Transition to Democracy', *Journal of Latin American Studies* vol. 31/2, May 1999, 473-500.

Williams, J, 1996, *The Girard Reader*. Crossroad, NY.

CHRISTIANITY, INTERRELIGIOUS DIALOGUE AND MUSLIM-CHRISTIAN RELATIONS

Anthony O'Mahony

'I have been on my guard
not to condemn the unfamiliar.
For it is easy to miss.
At the turn of a civilization'[1]

'The observation that Christianity is the sustaining differentiation
at the heart of the modern world is a hard saying.'[2]

Crossing frontiers

Never before has history known so many frontiers as in our contemporary world, and at no period has there been such a frequent violation of frontiers as happens today. It would seem that the establishment and removal of frontiers is the order of the day. This contradictory process is a window into the plight of humanity in these times: a dialectical tension between demarcation of particular identities and crossing over to the other shore. If the consolidation of frontiers is characterized as ethnicity, tribalism, nationalism, and a certain type of religious fundamentalism; the crossing of them is known as a global awareness, the mixing of cultures, trans-nationalism and the expression of world religiosity.[3]

---

[1] From the poem *The Sleeping Lord*, by David Jones (1895-1974), Anglo-Welsh Christian poet and artist.

[2] David Walsh, *The Third Millennium: Reflections on Faith and Reason*, Georgetown University Press, Washington DC, 1999, 151.

[3] Felix Wilfred, 'The Art of Negotiating the Frontiers', *Concilium: Frontier violations: the beginnings of new identities*, no. 2 (1999), vii-xiii. Several Muslim-Christian frontiers have been outlined in Asia and Africa and the Mediterranean by M Marion, 'Les sept frontières chrétiennes devant l'Islam', *Esprit*, Vol.116, no.10 (1986), 39-59 and Anthony O'Mahony, 'Islam in Europe', *The Way: Contemporary Christian Spirituality*, Vol. 41, no. 2 (2001), 122-135.

We are struck by the ambiguity of the phenomenon of frontier crossing. Crossing over could mean a march of aggression that infringes upon the freedom and autonomy of the realm invaded. It could be overt and violent, as when a power intrudes into the territory—physical, cultural, spiritual—of the other; or it could be covert and subtle, nevertheless destructive, as in the transnationalization of capital and homogenisation of cultures. A sense of ambiguity marks the affirmation and negation of frontiers.[4]

However, the violation of frontiers is also often a matter of creativity. This aspect can offer great hope for the emergence of refreshing new identities and encounters and the envisioning of alternatives. To be able to cross over, one has to locate oneself at the margins or at the edges of the present identity. To position oneself at the frontier is to adopt a very advantageous standpoint inasmuch as one can assess one's identity in a very creative and critical way. There is a great epistemological potential in being positioned on the outer edge, where the view of things is bound to be quite different from the centre where one may not understand what it means to come *face-à-face* with another spiritual identity or religious territory.

It is important to note that the crossing of frontiers and the birth of the new are a sheer necessity for a new historical period or particular context. The reality or the search for authentic renewal from within tradition outgrows the bounds and frames in which it was set up and forces the crossing of frontiers and the breaking of the frame. A re-mapping of the territory and a re-drawing of the frontiers follow it—tradition is an ever-emerging source of theological creativity; rooted identity; and wise compassion.

'Always be ready to make a defence to anyone who asks for a reason for the hope that is in you, and make it with modesty and respect' [1 Peter 3: 15-16]. Since the middle ages, this biblical text has been considered to state the fundamental charge given to the theologian. One could say that four fundamental features of theology thus appear: it is an

---

[4] Claude Geffré, 'Chrsitianity and Culture', *International Review of Mission*, Vol. 84 (1995), 17-32; Cl. Geffré, 'Mission Issues in the Contemporary Context of Multifaith situations', *International Review of Mission*, Vol. 86 (1997) 407-409. See also Geffré's theological 'autobiography' which sets out these tasks for Christian theology, *Claude Geffré entretiens avec Gwendoline Jarczyk—Profession Théologien. Quelle pensée chrétienne pour le XXIe siècle?*, Albin Michel, Paris, 1999.

articulation of the ground of one's hope; it arises as a response to questions about the way Christians live their lives; the norm for that hope and practice in Jesus Christ; and reasons may be given for that hopeful practice, whether those addressed are fellow Christians or others. Taking the text of First Peter as a fundamental challenge, theology may be conceived thus as a mediation of the Christian gospel within a cultural context. Addressing two not entirely distinct audiences, those who have already accepted the gospel and those who have not, theology faces two tasks, one primarily ecclesial and the other primarily cultural. How these tasks are conceived and interrelated is a basic question for the conception of theology. For most of the Catholic tradition both dimensions and roles of theology have been visible.[5]

However, crossing, of course, is not simply an external event. It is also a spiritual experience. This 'journey as an enriching spiritual endeavour' has been taken up by the American Catholic theologian, David Burrell, who writes:

> We are, invited, in our time, on a voyage of discovery stripped of colonizing pretensions: an invitation to explore the other on the way to discovering ourselves. The world into which we have been thrust asks nothing less of us; those of us intent on discovering our individual vocations cannot proceed except as partners in such a variegated community. And as that journey enters the domain of faith, our community must needs assume interfaith dimensions. What once were boundaries have become frontiers, which beckon to be broached, as we seek to understand where we stand by expanding or minds and hearts to embrace the other. Put in this fashion, our inner journey can neither be syncretic nor procrustean: assimilating or appropriating. What is rather called for is mutuality of understanding and of appreciation, a critical perception which is already incipiently self-critical. Rather than reach for commonality, we are invited to expand our horizons in the face of diversity. The goal is not

---

[5]   Joseph A Komonchak, 'Defending Our Hope: On the Fundamental Tasks of Theology', (eds.) Leo J O'Donovan and T Howland Sanks, *Faithful Witness: Foundations of Theology for Today's Church*, Geoffrey Chapman, London, 1989, 14-26.

an expanded scheme, but an enriched inquirer: discovery
of one's own faith in encountering the faith of another.[6]

Felix Wilfred has observed several distinct moments in the early
history of Christianity when identity recorded itself a shift in its self-
understanding. Thus Christianity has re-drawn its own frontiers several
times. This has always been a critical act at crucial times. The first crisis
is connected with the times when the disciples of Jesus stood on the
crossroads of forging their identity either as a 'sect' within Judaism, with
strict Jewish membership and following its customs and traditions, or
opening up the way of Jesus beyond ethnic frontiers. What was achieved
after many struggles was in fact a frontier-moving act. The widening of
the circumference of the group led to the re-inventing of its identity. If
the first re-drawing of frontiers was thus a matter of *ethnos*—overcoming
the tendency of a reduction of Christianity within ethnical bounds—the
second frontier-moving act had to do with the *chronos*: against the
apocalyptic background of the imminent expectation of the Risen Christ,
Christian discipleship was viewed as something for a brief period. A
realization of the delayed *parousia* pushed the temporal frontiers of
Christianity with very significant consequences. It paved the way not
only for the consolidation of ecclesial structures providing for an
indeterminate period, but also for shaping the Christian identity anew.

Today we are witnessing a further shift or moment in Christian
history which witnesses to profound deepening or self-understanding in
relation to other religious traditions. This not only engages the Christian
tradition in a reassessment of its own Trinitarian unity, at present a
'fractured oneness' or how it understands itself from within, but also how
others bear witness to the Christian tradition from without.

This is of particular importance in the relationship between
Christianity and Islam, as here in this encounter the Muslim tradition
grasps within itself a particular understanding and interpretation of
Judaism and Christianity.[7] It is thus linked into the Jewish-Christian
other, and it is on a certain level held hostage by this relationship. Christian

---

[6] David Burrell writes in the preface to Roger Arnaldez, *Three Messengers for One God*, University of Notre Dame Press, 1994, VII.

[7] David Marshall, 'Christianity in the Qur'an', (ed.) Lloyd Ridgeon, *Islamic Interpretations of Christianity*, Curzon, Richmond, 2001, 3-29.

theologians are now becoming aware of a Christian identity within Islam, and what that says to the Christian tradition.[8]

Christianity was born into a religiously plural world and has remained in one ever since. At different times in its history it has been especially sensitive to this context. The mandate to go preach the gospel to the corners of the earth as well as its own socio-economic political position has resulted in a complex range of relations and response to other religions. In the modern period, and especially in the West, it stands unsure of its own distinct nature and deeply aware of its implication in various imperialist exploits. Although, I think this to be an unfair judgment on the historical record, and thus the Christian tradition of the West is only taking up half its responsibility. However Christians in the modern world cannot ignore the existence of other religions. Global communications, extensive travel, migration, colonialism, and international trade are all factors that have brought the religions closer to each other in both destructive and creative ways.

A brief look at some statistics may help; although reliability is a problem, no less than their interpretation, they do help configure our imagination. Gavin D'Costa has set out the case in comparing, for instance, the difference between 1491 and 1991. In 1491 roughly 19 percent of the world's population was Christian and while 2 percent of the non-Christian world was in contact with Christianity, 79 percent remained entirely or partially ignorant of its existence. Some 93 percent of all Christians were Europeans. Compare these figures with 1991, when 33 percent of the global population was Christian, with 44 percent of the non-Christian world being aware of Christianity, while only 23 percent had no contact with Christians or the gospel. The ethnic basis of Christianity has now radically shifted so that the largest Christian community is now to be found in Latin America, only then followed by Europe, with Africa third (and growing much faster then Europe), followed by North America and then South and East Asia.

To get a sense of the broader picture, it will be helpful to briefly survey the figures again for 1991 regarding the numerical strengths of world religions. After Christians (roughly 1.3/4 billion), Muslims are the largest religious group (962 million), followed by Hindus (721 million), with Buddhists then forming less than half the number of Hindus (327 million). New religions, notoriously difficult to classify and tribal religions

---

[8]   Kenneth Cragg, 'Islam and Other Faiths', *Studia Missionalia*, Vol. 42, 1993, 257-270.

constitute roughly 218 million; and finally, and in Western consciousness far more prominent, Sikhs with nearly 19 million and Jews with nearly 18 million.[9]

Christians cannot ignore the existence of other religions. Furthermore, with the awareness of their existence a host of theological, philosophical, methodological and practical questions are raised. Should for example, Buddhist mediation be used in Christian prayer and practice? How should religious education be taught? What kind of social and political cooperation or opposition is appropriate with people of other faiths? There are also fundamental theological issues at stake. If salvation is possible outside Christ/Christianity, is the uniqueness of Christ and the universal mission of the church called into question? Or if salvation is not possible outside Christ/Christianity, is it credible that a loving God would consign the majority of humankind to perdition, often through no fault of their own? Can Christians learn from other faiths? Can they be enriched rather than diluted or polluted from this encounter? Clearly, other religious traditions in varying degrees have also undergone their own self-

---

[9] Description and statistics are based on Gavin D'Costa, ' Theology of Religions', (ed.) David Ford, *The Modern Theologians*, Basil Blackwell, Oxford, 1997, 626-644. D'Costa has had a distinct and important contribution to a Christian theological response to other faiths—see *Theology and Religious Pluralism Trinity*, Basil Blackwell, Oxford, 1986; *The Trinity and the Meeting of Religions*, Edinburgh, T & T Clark, 2000; *Sexing the Trinity*, SCM Press, London, 2000. D'Costa has been concerned with the practices of other faiths, and although he continues to use the word 'religion' he is more than aware that the concept has a genealogy. Modernity constructed a discourse on religions, then turned to the study of religions and, more recently, the comparison of religions. D'Costa's work challenges this construction and seeks to further dialogue between world faiths in a way that accepts and works with some of the categories forged by modernity; see 'Postmodernity and Religious Plurality: Is a Common Global Ethic Possible or Desirable?', (ed.) Graham Ward, *The Blackwell Companion to Postmodern Theology*, Basil Blackwell, Oxford, 2001, 131-143. D'Costa continues to appeal to tradition based reasoning. At the centre of his challenge to these universalist methods which continue to work with an uncritical understanding of the term 'religion', is his appeal to the specific differences between faiths. D'Costa is keen to demonstrate that a religion is not simply a set of ideas, but a complex living practice in which beliefs are continually formed and transformed in a dialogue with its traditions, its institutions, and its cultural contexts. We can understand the distinctiveness of D'Costa's approach if we examine the debate that took place between 1987 and 1990 on Christianity and pluralism. In 1987 the liberal thinkers John Hick and Paul Knitter published a collection of essays entitled *The Myth of Christian Uniqueness*. D'Costa responded with *Christian Uniqueness Reconsidered: The Myth of a Pluralistic Theology of Religions*, Orbis, Maryknoll, New York, 1990, which posited Christology and Trinitarian theology as the two distinctive differences of the Christian faith.

questioning in the light of religious multiplicity, but that is another question.[10]

---

[10] The development of a Christian theology for the religious Other is an important area of exploration. For some time now the debate in the Christian theology of religions has centred on the question of the possibility of salvation for non-Christians. The answers to this question have often been placed in a threefold typology: exclusivism, inclusivism or pluralism. Exclusivists generally maintain that salvation is conditional on an explicit confession of faith in Jesus Christ, hence non-Christians are lost. Pluralists, on the other hand, maintain that salvation can be found in different religions in various ways, and that Christianity is one among many paths to the divine reality. Inclusivists agree that non-Christians may be saved, and if they are it may be through rather than despite their religion. Inclusivists differ from pluralists in believing that Christ is the constitutive cause of all salvation, therefore the salvation of a non-Christian. The work of the American Dominican theologian J A DiNoia claims to do two significant things. First, to go beyond the three approaches and suggest a fresh way of dealing with the question. Second, in doing so, to create a new agenda for Christian theology of religions. DiNoia, a Thomist with Barthian leanings, closely follows George Lindbeck's cultural–linguistic model of religion, arguing that the specific way of life, determined by the actual doctrines held, uniquely shapes and moulds the religious practitioner. The goal and means of the religious way are intrinsically related and cannot be separated. He then persuasively argues that the difficulty with pluralist and inclusivists is that they impose a soteriocentricism upon other religions where may be none. In contrast, DiNoia maintains one cannot say anything about the meaning of another religion apart from specific and proper attention to the ways in which its doctrines regulate its practice and stipulate the goal to be achieved by that way of life. In Christianity, eternal friendship with the blessed Trinity can be said to be the goal (salvation), which is carefully orchestrated, in minute detail, through the liturgical life of the community. To claim that other religions attain the same salvific goal is therefore problematic. DiNoia's argument creates a space for other religions to really disclose what they are about in their doctrines and practices, without *a priori* categorization. Hence the necessity of dialogue as the proper location for the disclosure of the 'Other'. Dialogue thereby becomes central to a theology of religions. Only in this process can we ask the question as to whether and how these ways of life relate to Christianity. DiNoia allows for the possibility that doctrinal truth and good actions can be found in other religions, without compromising the centrality of the incarnation as constitutive of salvation. But DiNoia is reticent on whether this goodness and truth can be said to be in principle the means of salvation for the non-Christian. He does not want to say 'yes', for this would tend to negate the view that doctrines constitute a way of life towards a particular goal which is not otherwise attainable. Nor does he want to say 'no', for this may limit the way in which God actually does work. What he prefers to say, when confronted by the question of non-Christian salvation, is that non-Christians will have a chance to attain salvation after death in a purgatorial state. Since DiNoia accepts that purgatory does not provide an opportunity for the reversal of life-shaping decisions taken prior to death, he allows that other religions may therefore have a providential, 'rather than specifically salvific', role (p.90). A religion may determine an individual's decision to 'acknowledge Christ' (p. 107) in the purgatorial state. Hence other religions may, at their best, be a kind of *preparatio evangelica*. DiNoia breaks fresh ground here in utilizing purgatory in this manner. For Reformation and Orthodox theologians who may have difficulties with the concept of

A global theological encounter

The theologian John Renard, once told a story to convey a warning. Once upon a time an itinerant grammarian came to a body of water and enlisted the services of a boatman to ferry him across. As they made their way, the grammarian asked the boatman, 'Do you know the science of grammar?' The humble boatman thought for a moment and admitted somewhat dejectedly that he did not. Not much later, a growing storm began to imperil the small vessel. Said the boatman to the grammarian, 'Do you know the science of swimming?'[11] Thus we are reminded that at beginning of the new millennium too much of our theological activity remains shockingly introverted. Instead of allowing an inherent energy to launch us into the larger reality of global religiosity, we insist on protecting our theology from the threat of contamination. If we continue to resist serious engagement with other theological traditions, our theology may prove as useful as grammar in a typhoon. One of the most important tasks of theology today is to develop strategies for determining how to enter into the meaning system of another tradition, not merely as a temporary member of that tradition, but in such a way as to see how they bear upon one another.[12]

---

purgatory he suggests they 'could content themselves with a less specified notion of prospective salvation or with an alternative account of what it might entail' (p. 191). DiNoia's solution allows for the universality of the offer of salvation and the specificity of its constitutive cause: Jesus Christ. DiNoia belives that in this approach he avoids an untenable exclusivism and has surpassed both pluralism and inclusivism. DiNoia finally argues that the stage is now set for Christianity to both criticize and defend itself in dialogue with others, rather then defending *a priori* views of salvific availability. See DiNoia's main work—*The Diversity of Religions: A Christian Perspective*, Catholic University of America Press, Washington, 1992; and further his various papers on the theme of theology and the religious other: 'Philosophical Theology in the Perspective of Religious Diversity', *Theological Studies*, Vol. 49, 1988, 401-416; 'Pluralist Theology of Religions: Pluralistic or Non-Pluralistic?', (ed.) Gavin D'Costa, *Christian Uniqueness Reconsidered*, Orbis Books, Maryknoll, New York, 1990,119-134; 'The Doctrine of a Religious Community about Other Religions', *Religious Studies*, Vol. 19, 1982-83, 293-307; 'Implicit Faith, General Revelation and the State of Non-Christians', *The Thomist*, Vol. 47, 1983,209-241; 'Varieties of Religious Aims: Beyond Exclusiveness and Pluralism', (ed.) Bruce Marshall, *Theology and Dialogue*, University of Notre Dame Press, Notre Dame, Indiana, 1991,247-272.

[11] John Renard, 'Islam and Christian Theologians', *The Catholic Theological Society of America: Proceedings*, Vol. 48 (1993), 41-54, 41.

[12] Emilio Platti, of the Dominican Institute for Oriental Studies in Cairo, has two interesting accounts of how this might be done in relation to the Muslim-Christian encounter: 'Risques respectifs du souci de fidelite dans l'Islam et dans le christianisme', *Christianisme,*

The concern for an understanding of the 'other'—seeing the relationship of the one to the many, struggling with the questions of identity and difference, unity and diversity—has been a serious preoccupation of post-modern philosophy. In a somewhat different though not unrelated arena, contemporary Christian theologians have been increasingly aware of the necessity to formulate a theology, or set of theologies, that takes serious account of the 'otherness' as it is reflected in the existence of a great variety of forms of human religiousness. The French Dominican theologian, Claude Geffré, suggests that there is a risk involved in the work of theology. Since theology is a hermeneutical task 'from beginning to end', it involves 'the risk of distortion and error', but unless theology is willing to take that risk by presenting a creative interpretation of Christianity, it runs the no less serious risk of 'simply handing on a dead past'. Thus Christian theology draws upon an axis: *ressourcement*—reaffirmation of Christian identity by appeal to its ancient sources; and *aggiornamento*—renewal through the modernization of Christian thought and institutions.

These observations find an echo in the thought of the Irish-American writer and political scientist David Walsh:

> Even the discovery of God does not lift us out of this world. For as long as he wills it we must remain in this life to work out as best we can the meaning and direction we must follow within it. The light of transcendent illumination is a piercing beam from beyond, but it does not illuminate the surrounding area. The mystery of the whole remains. The difficulty of articulating the consequences of revelation for the modern secular world is evident in the confusion concerning the relationship between religion and politics.[13]

One might add the relationship between the particular and the universal.

As we have now embarked on the third millennium, the major challenges for the mission of the Christian churches is not only atheism

---

Judaisme et Islam: Fidelité et ouverture (sous la direction de Joseph Dore), Editions du Cerf, Paris, 1999, 223-242, and 'Islam et Occident: Choc de theologies?', *Melanges Institut Dominicain d'études orientales du Caire*, Vol. 24 (2000), 347-379.

[13] David Walsh, *Guarded by Mystery. Meaning in a Postmodern Age*, Catholic University of America Press, Washington, DC, 1999, 98-99.

and religious indifference, but what amounts to a religious explosion and the proliferation of beliefs of all kinds. As we survey the religious supermarket, it is important to make the necessary distinctions between 'sects' in the strict sense of the term, the New Age, with its nebulous esoteric and mystical currents, and the increased vitality of the great non-Christian religions. The religious 'come-back' is a typical symptom of our post-modern age. It coincides with the death of the ideologies, and is a reaction to the failure of modernity to keep its promises in the face of secularization and the anxiety caused by meaninglessness. It is part of the great movement of the *re-enchantment* of the world, of humanity, and even of God. With regard to the urgency for mission, the most formidable challenge for the Christian faith is the historical experience of a plurality of religious faiths.

One observer has recently commented:

> The Western culture of modernity and the institutions of international society embedded in it are being challenged by the global resurgence of religion and cultural pluralism in international relations. As a result of this large-scale religious change international society is becoming a genuinely multicultural international society for the first time. A new approach to international order is required which overcomes the 'Westphalian presumption' in international relations. This is the notion that religious and cultural pluralism can be accommodated in international society, but must be privatized, marginalized, or even overcome—by an ethic of cosmopolitanism—if there is to be international order.[14]

A vital component of our contemporary situation is the growth of a certain awareness among the world's religious communities of the Other. The engagement between the religions has been characterized by two points of orientation; one of fear and one of hope, both elements

---

[14] Scott M Thomas, 'Taking Religious and Cultural Pluralism Seriously: The Global Resurgence of Religion and the Transformation of International Society', *Millennium: Journal of International Relations*, Vol. 29, no. 3, 2000, 815-841, 815. See also by the same author, 'Religious resurgence, postmodernism and world politics', (ed.) John L Esposito and Michael Watson, *Religion and Global Order*, University of Wales Press, Cardiff, 2000, 38-65.

poised between, on the one hand, conflict, and on the other, a deepening realization of the necessity and possibility of dialogue. The re-discovery of the 'virtue of compassion' might be one of the principal themes in this encounter. Anthony H Johns, the Australian Christian Islamicist has noted 'How can one re-discover what has never yet been fully realized ... such a compassion, in its fullness, is at best, something only dreamt of; or like the lost chord, is heard but once, and then vanishes into silence. Yet the memory of its haunting beauty has such power that it compels all who have ever heard it, to search to recover it, without ceasing'. One might say that the history of ecumenism and inter-religious dialogue will be the history of growth and development of this awareness and of actions inspired by it, and of changes brought about in this direct in relation to this creative virtue of engagement. However, this does not allow for some sought of neutral position *vis-à-vis* ones own religious identity and the Other. Those who adopt a theoretical, privileged position outside any specific faith community, and elaborate a general structure of religious 'truth' that can provide a space for every religious tradition, but which no body believes in, will not satisfy.[15]

Thus any dialogue requires respect of the dialogue partners and interest in their beliefs—especially if these beliefs are culturally and religiously different from our own. At the same time we must retain our own cultural and religious identity. Lack of commitment under the pretext of openness leads to no real dialogue, or to sham agreements. We cannot put our faith in parentheses to connect with another's faith.[16]

---

[15] Georges Cottier, 'Jésus, l'Eglise, le salut des non-chrétiens et la place des religions', *Studia Missionalia*, Vol. 50, 2001, 159-177; Charles Morerod, 'La relation entre les religions selon John Hick', *Nova et Vetera*, Vol. 75, 2000, 35-62; Geneviève Comeau, 'La christologie à la rencontre de la thélogie des religions', *Études*, no. 3931, 2000, 57-69; Terence W Tilley, 'Christianity and the World Religions—A Recent Vatican Document', *Theological Studies*, Vol. 60, 1999, 318-337.

[16] Cl. Geffré, 'La portée theologique du dialogue islamo-chrétien', *Islamochristiana*, Vol. 18 (1992), 1-23; 'La théologie des religions non-chrétiennes vingt ans après Vatican II', *Islamochristiana*, Vol. 11 (1985), 115-133; 'Théologie chrétienne et dialogue interreligieux', *Revue de l'Institut catholique de Paris*, Vol. 38, 1991, 63-82; 'Un salut au pluriel', *Lumière et vieno.* 250, 2001, 21-38; 'Les déplacements de la vérité dans la théologie contemporaine', (eds.) Gillian R Evans and Michel Gourgues, *Communion et reunion—Mélanges Jean-Marie Roger Tillard*, Leuven University Press, 1995, 309-321; 'Le pluralisme religieux et l'indifférentisme, ou le vrai défi de la théologie chrétienne', *Revue théologique de Louvain*, Vol. 31, 2000, 3-32; 'La vérité du christianisme à l'âge du pluralisme religieux', *Angelicum*, Vol. 74, 1997, 171-192.

This is particularly true with regard to Christian-Muslim encounters, when what is at issue is not only the identity of each tradition, but the future character of an engagement which encompasses approximately a half of humanity.[17] Christian-Muslim relations in all their multi-faceted complexity, religious in the strict sense, cultural, societal, economical, political, are fundamentally an encounter of believers called to give, through life and word, a witness. In these two living traditions is the giving of a witness in and of faith. Members of these two traditions know themselves to be called in faith to witness faith. The meeting of these two distinct overall witnesses, Christian and Muslim, is lived in countless concrete practical ways and adaptations and, hence, produces an endless number of encounters, both by individuals and by groups.[18]

Christian Troll has imaginatively reminded us that the Franco-Algerian Jesuit, Henri Sanson,[19] suggested that we should reflect on our Christian vocation towards Muslims 'in the mirror of Islam', that is, taking into account at every step the missionary vocation which our Muslim partners, in faith, know themselves to be charged with. We shall then reflect on our mission to Islam in the light of that of Islam, i.e. the Muslims' consciousness to be called by God, individually and collectively, to witness the Truth, to proclaim it, to establish the true religion and to invite all and everyone to membership in the *umma muslima*. This encounter with Islam as a missionary religion will lead us to greater precision in the grasp of the distinctive features of our Christian missionary vocation and message and of appropriate ways to respond to them today. For Islam is more than a social and political, a religious and humanitarian phenomenon, it is more a challenge to the growth of the Church. It is ultimately a theological issue as the heart of the *missio Dei*.[20]

---

[17] Thomas Michel, 'Christian-Muslim dialogue in a changing world', *Theology Digest*, Vol. 39, no. (1992), 303-320.

[18] Jacques Waardenburg, 'Critical Issues in Muslim-Christian Relations: theoretical, practical, dialogical, scholarly', *Islam and Christian Muslim Relations*, Vol. 8, no. 1 (1997), 9-26 and Thomas Michel, 'Social and religious factors affecting Muslim-Christian relations', *Islam and Christian Muslim Relations*, Vol. 8, no. 1 (1997), 53-66.

[19] Henri Sanson, *Dialogue interieur avec l'Islam*, Centurion, Paris, 1990.

[20] Christian W Troll, 'Witness Meets Witness: The Church's Mission in the Context of the Worldwide Encounter of Christian and Muslim Believers Today', *Encounter*, Vol. 4, no.1 (1998), 15-34.

There is a context to this engagement. The Muslim and Christian worlds have known violent confrontations. Muslim conquests which brought parts of the Christian world under Muslim domination; the Crusades still vividly remembered today; the expansion of the Turkish Ottoman Empire with its threat to Christian centres; the Armenian massacres and genocide; European colonialism of the 19th–early 20th centuries; the rise of Christian missions; the continuing difficult situations in which Christians find themselves in dominant Muslim societies, such as Sudan, Iran, Indonesia, Pakistan; the violent drama and massacre of the 'innocents' of 11 September 2001 in New York. It would be petty to try to figure out who is more guilty in these conflicts. History should make us all a little more humble.

The weight of this history may be why few approach Islam without strong feelings one way or the other. [21] Sound spiritual teaching reminds us that something must be clarified and freed within us in regard to Islam, for the Spirit of Jesus is the Spirit of peace and clarity. To quote a sage: 'We cannot change the past, but we do have a responsibility of how it is remembered.'

Sailing beyond the horizon

Christian theology of religions is an area within systematic theology that has lately undergone considerable development. The area has taken

---

[21] Since the events of 11 September 2001 there have been an increasing number of reflections on Christian-Muslim encounters, see Stanley L Jaki, 'Myopia about Islam, with an eye on Chesterbelloc', *The Chesterton Review*, Vol. 28, 2002, 485–502; Stratford Caldecott, 'The Mystery of Islam: Further Reflections', *loc. cit.*, Vol. 28, 2002, 521–530; Roch Kereszty, 'The Word of God: A Catholic Perspective in Dialogue with Judaism and Islam', *Communio*, Vol. 28, 2001, 568–580; David Novak, 'Pluralism and Interreligious Dialogue. Reply to Roch Kereszty', *loc. cit.*; Mahmoud M.Ayoub, 'The Word of God in Islam: Some Personal Reflections', *loc. cit.*; Roch Kereszty, 'Brothers in a Strange Land: A Response to the Responses', *Communio*, Vol. 29, 2002, 172–184; R. Kereszty, 'Toward a Christian Theology of Inter-religious Dialogue', *Communio*, Vol. 29, 2002, 579–97; Wilfried Dettling, 'Encounter and the Risk of Change: Religious Experience and Christian-Muslim Dialogue', *The Way Supplement*, no. 104, 2002, 67–74; Thomas Hughson, 'September 11 and Christian Spirituality in the United States', *The Way*, Vol. 42, 2003, 85–97; Peter Riddell, 'Christian-Muslim dialogue: a challenge for the new millennium', *St Mark's Review*, no. 184, 2001, 3–13; P Riddell, 'Islamic Perspectives on Globalisation', *loc. cit.*, no. 192, 2003, 10–17; Anthony O'Mahony, 'Reflections on the Encounter between Christianity and Islam', *The Merton Journal*, Vol. 9, 2002, 4–16; A O'Mahony, 'Islam face-à-face Christianity', *The Way Supplement*, no. 104, 2002, 75–85.

on greater definition in recent years as Christian communities throughout the world come to grips with a heightened awareness of other religious traditions, and with a growing desire on the part of Christians to pursue interreligious dialogue and other forms of positive engagement with Jews, Muslims, Hindus, Buddhists, and others. Theologians practicing this sub-speciality address such questions as these: Are any of the teachings of other religious traditions true? How should judgments about this issue proceed? Do other religions point their adherents in the right direction? Can Jews, Muslims, Hindus, and Buddhists be saved? Can they be saved by following the teachings of their religions? How should Christians relate to Jews, Muslims, Hindus, and Buddhists, and others? Should they attempt to persuade non-Christians to become Christians? Should they engage in dialogue with the adherents of other religions? What purposes does such interreligious dialogue serve?[22] Drawing upon a long and substantial tradition of inquiry about these issues within Christian doctrine and theology, the agenda of the theology of religions has taken on an increasingly systematic shape as more and more theologians within the Christian churches turn their attention to these questions.[23]

As has been observed by the Jesuit theologian and scholar of Islam, Patrick Ryan writing on the Christian encounter with other religious traditions suggests there is an important sense in which the Christian tradition has to become more *catholic*, in the root sense of the word: embracing the whole of human experience.[24] Any form of Christianity in the future will face two major challenges, each of which has theological and philosophical implications. The first of these challenges is polycentrism of intellect and the second one could sum up under the heading of the unity of humankind.

---

[22] J A DiNoia takes a interesting reading of reformed theologian Karl Barth in (ed.) John Webster, 'Religion and the religions', *The Cambridge Companion to Karl Barth*, Cambridge University Press, 2000, 243-257.

[23] Michael Barnes, SJ, *Theology and the Dialogue of Religions*, Cambridge University Press, Cambridge, 2002; and James L Fredericks, *Faith among Faiths: Christian Theology and Non-Christian Religions*, Mahwah, Paulist Press, New York, 1999.

[24] Patrick J Ryan, 'Sailing Beyond the Horizon: Challenges for the Third Millennium', *America*, 23 May 1998, 14-28. See also his 'Is Dialogue Possible with Muslims?', *America*, 31 December, 1994, 13-17; 'The Monotheism of the Excluded: Towards an Understanding of Islam', *The Month*, n.s., Vol. 16, no. 8 (1983), 264-267, and 'Creative Misunderstanding and the Possibility of Jewish-Christian-Muslim Trialogue', *The Month*, n.s., Vol. 31, no. 7 (1998), 267-274. See also Thomas F O'Meara, 'Tarzan, Las Casas, and Rahner: Aquinas's theology of wider grace', *Theology Digest*, Vol. 45, 1998, 319-327.

Augustine in the first millennium of the Christian era and Aquinas in the second lead the honourable procession of Christian intellectuals of those two millennia who retrieved the thought of Plato and Aristotle, the fountainheads of philosophical speculation in the millennium before Christ. These two doctors of the church transformed Greek thought in terms of their own respective grasps not only on that philosophy but also on the cumulative Judeo-Christian traditions of faith and hope and love.

As we start the third millennium, it might be suggested that those who would follow Augustine and Aquinas[25] over the next thousand years would have a task somewhat similar to that of their intellectual ancestors. But they will have to retrieve from many more non-Christian intellectual and faith traditions of the past century's new ways of thinking about the experience of Christian revelation. They will also have to do philosophy and theology and work out an ethics that borrow categories from broader perspectives. One most notably dimension is the inter-faith encounter. One could be tempted to say that the future of theology depends upon a more intensive 'inter-penetration' of systematic theology

---

[25] However, as J A DiNoia has reminded us Aquinas also has something to contribute to Christian theology's encounter with the alternative systems of belief and practice embodied in the world's major religious traditions. Thus, Aquinas' theology of the triune God and to introduce a concrete illustration, philosophical argument would be needed in conversation between Buddhists and Christians. Segments of the Buddhist community seem to be non-theistic in their doctrines, and their canonical and commentatorial literatures possess highly subtle explanations for the prevalence of theistic beliefs in other religious traditions. Presumably, in conversations with Buddhists, Christians would need to invoke patterns of argument analogous to those sketched by Aquinas in the Prima Pars of the *Summa* (and elsewhere). A readiness to advance such arguments would be a way of taking Buddhist objections to theistic beliefs seriously. Given the empirical bent of Buddhist patterns of reflection and argument, there would be considerable scope here for empirically based discussions such as those elaborated in the Five Ways and similar arguments. Patterns of argument appealing to objective states of affairs would have an important role in religiously pluralistic environment of some current theology. Only these kinds of arguments presuppose a field broad enough to sustain interreligious conversations. The issue can be joined in a common logical field, so to speak, where rival particularistic claims to universality would be taken seriously and debated. The readiness to advance arguments would make it possible for a true meeting of minds, though not necessarily agreement, to occur. It seems clear that, in order to rise to the occasion, logically speaking, appeals to history, narratives, texts, personal experiences, and the like would need to be combined with philosophical arguments having features of objective states of affairs as their context. Aquinas's incorporation of such arguments in his theology provides a model for Christian engagement in interreligious conversation. 'Thomism After Thomism: Aquinas and the Future of Theology', (eds.) Deal W Hudson and Dennis Wm Moran, *The Future of Thomism*, Notre Dame, Indiana, University of Notre Dame Press, 1992, 231-245.

and the history of religions. Some do not hesitate to speak of a new planetary ecumenism. We must agree with them inasmuch as the dialogue between religions coincides with the keener awareness of the unity of the human family and a more acute sense of the common responsibility of religions for the future of humankind and its environment.

But it would be absurd to think that the new 'dialogue' makes Christian ecumenism in the primary sense obsolete or secondary. The ecumenical dialogue within the Christian community which began to take shape in the early decades of the 20th century and which started to mature after the Second World War has shattered a certain type of absolutism and has generally promoted the dialogue of the Church, first with the other two monotheistic religions and then with the great Eastern religions.

The theology of religions has become an important chapter in Christian theology. But once again we find ourselves stammering because it takes time to shed our old habits and to understand that frank and open dialogue does not necessarily lead to false 'ecumenism', that is, to religious indifferentism.

A widespread consensus exists today among theologians that any exclusive model for understanding Christianity must be abandoned, whether it is that of ecclesiocentric absolutism or for whom Christianity is the only source of grace. However, on the other hand, it is not enough to adopt an inclusive religious model—Christ fulfils everything that is good, true, and holy in other religions—to believe that we have thereby demystified the absolute character of Christianity as an historical religion. Indeed, a fundamental tension remains between the demands of equality and reciprocity inherent in true dialogue and the legitimate claim of Christianity to be the religion of the absolute and definitive manifestation of God in Jesus Christ. If Jesus himself is only one mediator among others and not God's decisive manifestation for all men and women, then we can seriously question whether we have not already discarded the faith inherited from the apostles.[26]

For religions as well as cultures, globalization presents a double reef or dialectic: it can lead not only to destructive syncretism but also to

---

[26] My own reflections here owe much to the thought of Claude Geffré, 'Pour un christianisme mondial', *Recherches de Sciences religieuses*, 1998, 53–75, who observes, 'La croix est le symbole d'une universalité qui est toujours liée au sacrifice d'une particulariité pour renaître en figure d'universalité concrète, en figure de Christ', p. 64.

fundamentalist reactions.[27] It should be able, nevertheless, to favour an interreligious engagement on a planetary scale, without falling into the myth of world religion. Each religion, faithful to its proper identity, can witness to the universal search of the Ultimate or Last Reality, which no religious system can exhaust.

In other words, it is not at all certain that we yet possess an adequate theological response, which takes seriously the implications of interreligious dialogue without sacrificing Christian identity. In any event, it is not sufficient to go from Christocentrism to theocentrism as the adepts of a pluralistic theology of religions suggest. Every responsible Christian theology must maintain the normative character of Christology. Rather than adopting some general theocentrism, we must start at the very centre of the Christian message, that is, God's manifestation in the historical particularity of Jesus of Nazareth, and find there the justification for the dialectical nature of Christianity.

At one level it seems difficult to see how we can leave completely behind a certain inclusivism, that is, a theology of the *fulfilment* (to use a term present in Catholic theology since the Second Vatican Council) in Jesus Christ of all seeds of truth, goodness, and holiness contained in the religious experience of humankind. However it might be possible to reinterpret this notion of fulfilment in a non-possessive and non-totalising sense. Rather then renounce the confession of Jesus Christ, according to Claude Geffré 'Christians must renounce all claims to absolute truth precisely because they confess Jesus Christ as absolute, that is, as eschatological fullness that will never be revealed in history'. Can we ever cease to ponder the paradox of Christianity as a non-absolute religion, which nonetheless attests to the final revelation? Might we not say that we need to remain equally removed from the hybris of dialectical theology on the one hand and neo-liberalism, with its readiness to relinquish the Christological norm for the sake of facilitating interreligious dialogue on the other.

By virtue of the very demands of interreligious dialogue, we are ready to accept the historical particularity of Christianity. It would be an unwarranted pretension to claim that historical Christianity has been and will be able to encompass all the riches contained in the religious

---

[27] Cl. Geffré, 'La rencontre du christianisisme et des cultures', *Revue d'Ethique et de theologie morale. Le Supplement*, no. 192 (1995), 69-91.

history of humankind, still less in history itself. But we must not confuse the particular character of Christianity as an historical religion with the particular character of Christ as mediator of the Absolute in history. The link between God's presence and the contingent event 'Jesus as the Christ' will always remain in the eyes of the other religions as the scandal of the Christian claim. By confessing Jesus of Nazareth to be the Christ, the Church claims for Christianity a unique and unrivalled excellence.

In an effort to facilitate dialogue with other religions, certain theologians are tempted today to downplay this extravagant 'allegation' made by Christianity. In the encounter between Christianity and Islam this downplaying of the Christian difference is problematic as the Islamic tradition makes a direct connection between its own existence and the Christian claim to Christ as the God the incarnate one. They say, for instance, that to speak of Jesus' divinity is a 'manner of speech', that the incarnation is a 'metaphor' expressing his incomparable openness to God.[28] Or else they attempt to loosen the indissoluble link between the Christ of faith and the Jesus of history. The human Jesus would be only one historical manifestation, among others, of a transcendent and pre-existing Christ. In such a case, one may well wonder whether the uniqueness of Christianity is not jeopardized in the sense that Jesus would only become one of the several historical realizations of the Absolute.

Thus, in order to firmly establish the dialogical character of Christianity, it is preferable, to return to the very centre of Christian faith, that is, to the mystery of the incarnation itself in its most realistic and non-mythical meaning. The paradoxical character of Christianity originates in the paradox of the 'Logos made flesh'. There is, in the last analysis, only *one* genuine paradox in the Christian message—the appearance of that which conquers existence under the conditions of existence. Incarnation, redemption, justification, etc. ... are implied in this paradoxical event. In theology, paradox is not contrary to the demands of logical reason. Paradox does not result from logical contradiction, but

---

[28] Eric O Springsted in an interesting article on Christian encounters with other faiths, has suggested that the Incarnation may not in fact hinder dialogue but actually encourage it. Reflecting on the position of Simone Weil, he suggests that this central Christian doctrine may encourage dialogue if taken seriously as a value commitment constitutive of a way of life, and not just a position. In order to do so, he takes the example of Weil to show how she used the doctrine in practice and to show the theory of 'rootedness' she developed to explain that practice—'Conditions of Dialogue: John Hick and Simone Weil', *Journal of Religion*, 1992, 19-36.

from the fact that an event transcends all human expectations and possibilities. Thus for Christianity, to quote Paul Tillich, 'The Logos doctrine as the doctrine of identity of the absolutely concrete with the absolutely universal is not one theological doctrine among others; it is the only possible foundation of a Christian theology which claims to be *the* theology'. And again quoting Tillich, 'The paradox of the Christian message is that in *one* personal life, essential manhood has appeared under the conditions of existence without being conquered by them.'[29]

The Christological paradox is the foundation of the paradoxical condition of Christianity as a religion. Can we say that Christianity is based upon an original absence? And we must add that it is precisely this consciousness of a lack which is the condition of a relation to the other, the stranger, the difference. It is for this reason that dialogue with other religious experiences is written into the original vocation of Christianity. For each Christian, each community, and for Christianity as a whole, the goal is to be a sign of what is lacking.

Without having the pretension of installing a New World order, Christianity holds a prophetic and counter-cultural power against the risks of, not only dehumanization, but also fragmentation between persons and ethnic and religious communities. As a religion of incarnation, Christianity not only announces to every human being the gratuitous salvation of God, but it works in healing cultures and all creation. The Church announces Jesus Christ as an event of universal salvation for all humanity, including those who belong to other religious traditions. But the witness of the Gospel must learn not to confuse the universality of the mystery of Christ with that of a Christianity understood as a historical religion inseparable from its western form, and to maintain a distance between the Church as means of salvation and the Kingdom of God that doesn't cease to go beyond its frontiers, which at present can manifest themselves as borders.

Christian theological encounters with Islam

The Iraqi Jesuit, Paul Nwyia (1925-1980) grew up in the northern, Kurdish part of Iraq, in a mixed Christian-Muslim village. Reflecting

---

[29] Cl. Geffré, 'Paul Tillich et l'avenir de l'oecuménisme inter-religieux', *Revue des sciences philosophiques et théologiques*, Vol. 77, 1993, 3-22.

on his childhood, he remembered his first contacts with Muslims:

Searching far back in my memory, I rediscovered my first impression of my contacts with Muslims. Those contacts were frequent, for many Muslim religious leaders used to visit my family. But despite the real friendship on which these relations were based, I had a strong feeling that, in the eyes of these Muslim friends, we were and remained *strangers*: people who because of their religion were fundamentally different. What awakened this feeling in me was the superior attitude which these friends adopted, an attitude that only their religion could justify. They regarded themselves as followers of the true religion and manifested this conviction with such self-satisfaction and such contempt for others that they were the living image of those whom the Gospel describes as men with pharisaical traits. Many of them were very brave and their attitude towards us was often only unconsciously superior, but we always remained strangers in relation to them. This fact did not bother them; on the contrary, it made them feel that they were all the more faithful to their religion.[30]

Even as a child, Nwyia was sensitive to the tensions between Christianity and Islam. Not only is Islam different from Christianity; it sees itself as positively abrogating Christianity. Muhammad is the 'seal of prophets'; the revelation accorded to him supersedes all that came before.

Islam and the Scriptures of Judaism and Christianity

Christianity nevertheless has an important, if negative, role in Muslim self-understanding. Muslim writers have always been quick to claim that Islam's abrogation of Christianity mirrors the Christian abrogation of Judaism. A Christian might respond that this is unfair, since Christianity understands itself not as abolishing Judaism but fulfilling it. The Christian tradition continues to acknowledge Judaism as a source of its identity; it

---

[30] Paul Nwyia, 'Pour mieux connaître l'Islam', *Lumen vitae*, 30 (1975), 159-171.

at least claims to be constantly revisiting Judaism, and it continues to use—in its own fashion—the Hebrew Scriptures. Islam, by contrast, sees itself as the restoration of what Judaism and Christianity would have been, had they not become corrupted, especially with regard to their Scriptures.[31]

Within the long history of polemics between Muslims and Christians, the most persistent Christian response to the assertion of abrogation has been a straightforward rejection of how Muslims understand Christianity. Christian apologists have repeatedly insisted that the Qur'anic and post-Qur'anic comprehension of Christian doctrine is seriously flawed. The conflict centres on three issues: the reality of Jesus' crucifixion and death; the doctrine of the incarnation; and the Christian understanding of God as Trinity. The Qur'anic accounts of all three of these, as well as subsequent interpretations and elaborations, stand in sharp contrast with mainstream Christian self-understanding. Conversely, both Jews and Christians questioned Muhammad's prophetic status. This led Muslims to develop traditions of argument in vindication of Muhammad as prophet, and Christians in turn responded by articulating their own version of the 'signs of prophecy'.[32]

Muslims assert the superiority of the Qur'an by identifying it with the divine word (*Kalima*). This word is a divine attribute subsisting in God but distinct from God's essence. God is therefore the unique, total and exclusive cause of Scripture, and the Qur'an must be considered to be *uncreated*. Consequently the Prophet is simply the spokesman who hands on 'the supernatural dictation'[33] he receives from God.

However, qualifications must be made. Though Islam claims that Judaism and Christianity are superseded as independent traditions, it

---

[31] Frederick Mathewson Denny, 'Corruption', in *Encyclopedia of the Qur'an,* edited by Jane Dammen McAuliffe, Brill, Leiden, 2001, 439-440. On the Qur'an as Scripture and the qur'anic view of religion, see the work of Guy Monnot, for example: 'Le corpus coranique', in (ed.) Michel Tardieu, *La formation des canons scripturarires,* Editions du Cerf, Paris, 1993, 61-73; and 'L'ideé de religion et son evolution dans le Coran', in (ed.) Ugo Bianchi, *The Notion of Religion in Comparative Research,* 'L'Erma' di Brettschneider, Rome, 1994, 97-102.

[32] Jane Dammen McAuliffe, 'The Abrogation of Judaism and Christianity in Islam: A Christian Perspective', *Concilium,* 1994/3, 116-123, 117-118; Sarah Strouwsma, 'The Signs of Prophecy: the Emergence and Early Development of a Theme in Arabic Theological Literature', *Harvard Theological Review,* 78 (1985), 101-114, esp. 114.

[33] This phrase comes from the work of the eminent French Islamicist and mystic, Louis Massignon (1883-1962).

nevertheless sees the revelations accorded to Moses, the *Tawrat*, and Jesus, the *Injil*, as something like proto-Qur'ans: compilations of God's direct verbal revelation to Moses and Jesus. Consequently, it matters greatly how reliably or unreliably these traditions have been transmitted. And Muslims claim that the Jewish and Christian Scriptures are, in their present form, both textually and semantically corrupt. What Jews and Christians now recognize as their scriptures does not coincide with the Qur'an, God's full and final revelation. Since God's word does not change, this lack of consonance must result from more or less intentional alteration or corruption of the text. When Muslim theologians and apologists speak of Jewish and Christian corruption, therefore, they rarely use it to justify a wholesale rejection of either the Hebrew Bible or the Christian gospel.[34] Rather, they balance assertions about corruption with an insistence that both Testaments prefigure the advent of Muhammad and the success of his mission.

Islam: God's only revelation

Christian accounts of Islam vary, but they nevertheless generally draw attention to how Islam is expressive of a kind of natural law, given with the creation. Louis Massignon, for example, writes as follows:

> The goal of Qur'anic revelation is not to expose or justify supernatural gifts so as to be ignorant of them, but, in recalling them to the name of God, to bring back to intelligent beings the temporal and eternal sanctions—natural religion—primitive law, the simple worship that God has prescribed for all time—that Adam, Abraham and the prophets have always practised in the same way.[35]

---

[34] David Thomas, 'The Bible in Early Muslim Anti-Christian Polemic', *Islam and Christian-Muslim Relations*, 7 (1996), 29-38; Jane Dammen McAuliffe, 'The Qur'anic Context of Muslim Biblical Scholarship', *Islam and Christian-Muslim Relations*, 7 (1996), 141-158.

[35] Louis Massignon, *Examen du 'Présent de l'Homme Lettré' par Abdallah ibn Torjoman*, Pontifical Institute of Arabic and Islamic Studies of Rome, Rome, 1992 (following the French translation published in *Revue de l'Histoire des Religions*, 1886, Vol. XII), with a preface by Daniel Massignon, introduction by Père Henri Cazelles and observations by Père Albert (M J) Lagrange. *Collection 'Studi arabo-islamici del PISAI'*, No. 5, Rome, PISAI, 1992.

Jacques Jomier, another great Catholic Islamicist, complements this account:

> Islam is a natural religion in which the religious instinct which is present in the heart of each person is protected by a way of life, with obligations and religious observations imposed in the name of One who is, for the Muslim, the Qur'an revelation. It is a patriarchal religion, spiritually pre-dating the biblical promise made by God to Abraham, but which conserves the episodes of the life of the Patriarch involving his struggle against his fathers' idols and his voluntary submission to God, even his sacrifice of his own son. Islam re-presents Abraham (Father of the Prophets) as its great ancestor.[36]

For Muslims, Islam is not simply God's final revelation but also God's first.[37] Both cosmically and individually, human beings are born in submission (*islam*) to God. An important Qur'anic passage vividly depicts the primordial covenant which God forged with the creation:

> 'When your Lord brought forth their own behalf, saying, 'Am I not your Lord?' they said, 'Most certainly; we have testified'.

The verse closes with God's explanation that he had forged this covenant with humankind lest 'you say on the Day of Resurrection that "of this we were unaware."' (7:172) Thus other religious identities are seen as conflicting with a fundamental state of *islam*, a primordial Muslim identity.

A saying ascribed to Muhammad runs as follows: 'Every child is born a Muslim, but his father makes him a Jew, Christian or Magian/Zoroastrian'. Like all humans, therefore, Moses and Jesus were Muslim. Further, as prophets, they were privileged with a special divine covenant:

---

[36] Jacques Jomier, 'Le Coran et la Liturgie dans l'Islam', *La Maison-Dieu*, 190 (1992), 121–127, here 121.

[37] Guy Monnot, 'Ce que l'Islam n'est pas', *Communio* (French edition), 16 (1991), 28–41.

When We took their covenant from the prophets, from you
[Muhammad] and from Noah, Abraham, Moses and Jesus,
son of Mary, We took from them a binding covenant. (33:7)

God sent these prophets and others to particular peoples so that
they might remind their listeners of the primordial covenant, and summon
them to *islam* (submission). While Judaism and Christianity tend to think
of prophets as inspired, classic Islamic thought has functioned with what
might be termed a 'doctrine of dictation', with the human agent being
far more transparent. Prophets receive and transmit God's very words;
Muslims revere Jesus, Moses, and their prophetic predecessors as faithful
conduits of God's invariant message to humanity. Though Muslims
minimally recognise the importance of historical context, the Islamic
notion of prophet-as-divine-mouthpiece is essentially atemporal. God's
words, and God's will can never change: the message conveyed by Abraham
or Moses or Jesus or Muhammad has an inherent and inviolable continuity.
Muslims believe that these earlier messages as originally proclaimed were
perfectly consonant with the Qur'an. It was in order to account for the
evident inconsistency between these texts in the forms now available
that Muslim apologists and theologians developed a doctrine of scriptural
corruption. And this doctrine supports a wider vision of Islam abrogating
both Judaism and Christianity.

Doctrinal differences

The historic break caused by Islam did not influence in the slightest the
internal development of Christianity. One can study that development
today as a completely autonomous whole, as though Islam did not exist.
Christianity is wholly intelligible, to the extent to which it is intelligible
at all, without any reference to Islam. By contrast, Islam is not so
intelligible unless reference is made to Christianity.

Historically and theologically, however, Christianity inevitably
challenges and disturbs Islam; and Islam inevitably challenges and disturbs
Christianity. Neither religion can ignore the other, happy in its own
conviction and simplicity.

A Christian is disturbed and challenged by the Islamic refutation
of Christianity: that the Holy Trinity is *shirk* (polytheistic blasphemy);

that the crucifixion was only an apparition; that the stories about Christ and his mother in the Qur'an are the authentic ones, rather than those in the four Gospels. Similarly, a Muslim must be disturbed by what Christianity at least implies about Islam: that Christianity has not in fact been abrogated by Islam; that God became flesh in Jesus of Nazareth without ceasing to be God; that this same Jesus actually died and rose from the dead on the third day; that the Church, as a distinct historic body, makes absolute claims about itself. And this mutuality of disturbance is not confined to the order of theory: it expresses itself in the growth of distinct historic communities, with conflicting norms, laws and mores.

The central question is whether the Word of God is literally a word, or rather a living person. On this issue, Christianity and Islam frankly diverge, and all the other differences relate to this one. Whatever affinities between Christianity and Islam there may be, arising from their common links with Abraham, this question about the nature of revelation remains. Any dialogue which avoids it remains sentimental and superficial. The Qur'an has the highest respect for Christ and his mother, and speaks of him as a Word of God; nevertheless, the authoritative Muslim doctrine is that *the* Word of God is the Qur'an itself.

Building bridges

Paul Nwyia may have sensed the conflict between Islam and Christianity even as a child. But he was also aware, even then, that a Christian could not rest content with this situation. The passage quoted at the beginning continues as follows:

> One could easily have been tempted to react like them, to regard them as 'strangers' to transform the difference into indifference, or to meet their contempt with even deeper scorn. But this is precisely what my faith forbade me to do. To react thus would have meant doing away with the difference and, by that very fact, disowning my Christian identity. Hence I came to ask myself: 'How can I turn these strangers into the *neighbours* of which the Gospel speaks? How can I resist the temptation to react as they do, so that my way of seeing them may be different from the way

they look upon me?' I understood that to achieve this I would have to discover, beyond the image they projected of themselves, certain things in them or in their religion which could help me regard them as neighbours whom one must love.

This quest for understanding and for the love of neighbour led Nwyia to study and reflect on Islam throughout his life until his tragic death in 1980. Trained in France by Louis Massignon, Nywia became a widely renowned and celebrated scholar in the field of Islamic mysticism. His contributions included an edition of letters on spiritual direction by Ibn 'Abbad of Ronda, who was chiefly responsible for putting forward an understanding of Sufism as a spirituality available to all who put their trust in God. He also wrote on Islamic mysticism and Christianity, with special reference to the *Spiritual Exercises* of Ignatius of Loyola; and on the monastic character of early Muslim spiritual life.[38]

Nwyia reflected on the different ways in which Islam characterized the religious other, and what these revealed about Muslim self-understanding. For Nwyia, Islam's relations with other faiths are shaped by the tension between two antagonistic principles: mutabilities and immutability, between the diverse, changing forms in which religious commitment is lived on the one hand, and the unchangingness of Allah on the other. This tension has been operative since Islam began; it reflects the complex attitude of Muhammad towards the religious other: polytheists, Jews and Christians. Islam is faced with a crucial dilemma of how to find 'the synthesis between historical and spiritual truth'.[39]

Within the Qur'an, there are also discussions of how Muslims should relate towards Christianity. These vary in tone from unequivocal rejection to ambivalent co-existence. We find both warnings to Muslims not to make friends with Christians, as well as more positive calls for

---

[38] See Nwyia's second edition of Ibn 'Abbad de Ronda, *Lettres de direction spirituelle (ar-Rasa'il as-sugrä)*, Dar el-Machreq, Beirut, 1974, and also the following from among his numerous academic studies: 'Ibn 'Abbad de Ronda et Jean de la Croix: à propos d'une hypothèse d'Asin Palacios', *Al-Andalus*, 22 (1957), 113–130; *Ibn-'Abbad de Ronda (1332-1390): un mystique prédicateur à la Qarawiyin de Fès*, Catholic Press, Beirut, 1961; *Exégèse coranique et langage mystique: nouvel essai sur le lexique technique des mystiques musulmans*, Dar el-Machreq, Beirut, 1970.

[39] Paul Nwyia, 'Mutabilités et immutabilité en Islam', *Recherches de sciences religieuses*, 63 (1975), 197-213.

interreligious understanding. A dictum in the Qur'an placed on Muhammad's lips, 'to you your religion and to me mine' (109:6), can be interpreted in both these ways. It might suggest a gentle tolerance, honouring the diversities of culture and experience. Alternatively, it could be taken as expressing an exasperated weariness with how the differences in belief and ritual can never be resolved.[40]

Christianity's encounter with Judaism following the *Shoah* raises questions touching very deeply on the core identity of the Christian. Similar questions arise from its encounter with Islam, particularly as regards mission. The Jesuit Islamicists, Henri Sanson and Christian Troll, have suggested that Christians should reflect on their missionary vocation towards Muslims 'in the mirror of Islam'. This means that we should take into account at every step the fact that our Muslim partners are convinced in faith that they have a missionary vocation towards us, that they too are called, individually and collectively, to witness to the Truth. Only in this light can we discern with any sensitivity what a Christian missionary vocation towards Islam might amount to, and how might appropriately be lived out.[41]

Challenges to Islam

There are also tensions within Islam that may serve as a stimulus for Moslems to move beyond the impasse I have been sketching out. The German scholar, Josef van Ess, has documented three forms that sceptical challenges have taken in Islamic tradition. The first of these is theoretical and philosophical: it draws on the sceptical tradition in Hellenism. The second arises from doctrinal tensions and difficulties internal to Islam. The third is generated by practical and political concerns.[42] Scepticism, says van Ess, 'is something like the salt in the soup'; it makes theology interesting. Dogmatic speculation, of the kind put forward by Islam's

---

[40] Kenneth Cragg:, 'Islam and Other Faiths', *Studia missionalia*, 42 (1993), 257-270, here 257.
[41] Henri Sanson: *Dialogue intérieur avec l'Islam*, Centurion, Paris, 1990; Christian W Troll, 'Witness Meets Witness: The Church's Mission in the Context of the Worldwide Encounter of Christian and Muslim Believers Today', *Vidyajyoti Journal of Theological Reflection*, 62/3 (March 1998), 152-171, reprinted in *Encounters*, 4/1 (March 1998), 15-34.
[42] Josef van Ess, 'Scepticism in Islamic Religious Thought', in (ed.) Charles Malik, *God and Man in Contemporary Islamic Thought*, American University of Beirut, Beirut, 1972, 83-98.

great systematic thinker, al-Ghazzali, is 'like a game of chess' that becomes interesting only when there is an opponent, 'when the devil is playing on the other side'.

Van Ess speculates that Islam might have improved had the sceptical tradition continued into more recent times. He brings out the positive contribution made by scepticism to Islam. Islamic scepticism arose within the 'pluralistic outlook of a multiform society'. Islam was being challenged by the close proximity of other faith-systems, and was only one among many vigorous traditions: Christianity, Judaism, Zoroastrianism, Manichaeism, various forms of religious Hellenism. Scepticism was a stimulus to Islam's health and progress: 'Islam as well as Christianity ought to be glad about a time full of spiritual plurality, a time like ours'.

Contemporary pluralism is challenging Islam almost to breaking point. When it was more or less alone or apart, it did not need to ask fundamental questions about itself: it could take itself for granted. Where it was the dominant cultural and religious force, it could dismiss minority traditions out of hand. Today such attitudes are impossible. Today, Islam finds itself neither alone nor apart nor dominant. Moreover, like Christianity, it must also face the profound questions raised by modern intellectual discoveries, technological changes, and socio-economic globalisation.

However, one factor that makes it difficult for Muslims to face these questions, and for non-Muslims to understand the world of Islam, is that there is nothing like the Church in Islam. There is no worldwide organization with a strong sense of its own historical continuity, speaking and teaching authoritatively about itself. For all its fragmentariness, there is a Christian Church; there is no such organized, unitary, historical tradition in the world of Islam. 'Christianity' means something more than the physical or cultural space occupied by Christians; it means primarily the Kingdom of Christ, manifest in his Body, the Church. The word 'Islam' can only mean the world of Muslims.

In this context, van Ess's observation about the positive role of scepticism may need to be qualified. Scepticism can act as 'the salt in the soup' only if the soup is there to be tasted, out of a definite, secure vessel. When 'the salt of doubt' is sprinkled over the Christian world, when 'the devil' tantalizes and undermines or even checkmates Christian thought, the Church can sooner or later address the issue in an ecumenical council, a forum where the matter is considered and then somehow settled by an authoritative pronouncement. There is no such possibility in Islam.

If a Muslim thinker or theologian or even a whole Islamic state seeks to move Islam forward by asking fundamental questions, the question arises whether the result is still authentically Muslim. Because there is no central teaching authority in Islam, there is no possible answer to this question. There is, therefore, a permanent ambiguity about the nature of Islam. Nevertheless, Islam still needs to ask itself fundamental questions regarding its nature and origins. It cannot let these questions be asked only by people outside Islam; it needs to answer these questions for itself. Can it still be seriously and responsibly maintained that the Hebrew Scriptures have been falsified by the Jews and the Christians, and moreover that the original Gospel is lost, corrupted by the Christians? Islam is at a point when scepticism may be a creative force. Scepticism may help Muslims realise that the Jewish and Christian Scriptures—Scriptures which existed as we have then today long before Islam arose—are authentic. This may help Islam set about reconciling, in all truth and humility, the Qur'an with the Bible.[43]

The Muslim claim that Islam constitutes 'the essence of truth and religion' implies a sharp judgment on other religions. It is saying, for instance, that Christianity's true essence is found in Islam. But if that is so, then normal Christians ought to find themselves wholly at home in Islam. This is manifestly not the case. Perhaps Islam needs to ask itself some sceptical questions and move forward.

Agenda for the future

Several decades ago, the Lebanese Christian thinker Charles Malik, a former President of the General Assembly of the United Nations who helped draft the Universal Declaration of Human Rights, set out an

---

[43] For further explorations of this theme, see Ronald L Nettler, 'Mohamed Talbi, "For Dialogue Between All Religions"', in (eds.) Ronald L Nettler and Suha Taji-Farouki, *Muslim-Jewish Encounters Intellectual Traditions and Modern Politics*, Harwood Academic, Amsterdam, 1998, 171-199; and Ronald L Nettler, 'A Post-Colonial Encounter of Traditions: Muhammad Sa'id Al-Ashmawi on Islam and Judaism', in (ed.) Ronald L Nettler, *Medieval and Modern Perspectives on Muslim-Jewish Relations*, Harwood Academic, Luxembourg, 1995, 174-185.

agenda for ongoing Christian-Muslim encounter. The list of tasks that he gives is still worth reading.

One set of tasks centres round the sacred texts: how and why the Bible and the Qur'an were each formed; the intentions of the Bible and the intention of the Qur'an; the difference in their contents; why Muslims never read the Bible, whereas Christianity has fully incorporated the Old Testament into its theology and liturgy; how revelation is understood both in the foundational texts of the two religions and in subsequent tradition. Then there is the issue, already mentioned, about the word of God: in Christianity the Word is a person, while in Islam it is literally a word. A further set of issues centres on Muhammad's limited knowledge of Christianity. Must Muhammad's objectively deficient understanding be permanently binding on Islam, or can this knowledge be supplemented and corrected today by a fuller awareness of what Christianity is? It is worth noting, too, that the temporal and spiritual orders tend to be separated in Christian thought, whereas Islam makes no such separation.[44]

Malik's list, here quoted only selectively, brings home how wide the differences are between Christianity and Islam: a Christian committed to dialogue can only think of Jacque Maritain's dictum, *distinguer pour unir*. Moreover, these questions touch on the very identity of Islam, since Islam's self-understanding essentially refers to how it abrogates or supersedes Christianity. Even though, then, Islam may traditionally have set itself in confrontation with Christianity, it must face questions about its own identity that it cannot settle without involving authoritative representatives of Christianity. Perhaps, therefore, Islam's own internal tensions may lead it, eventually, to move forward. If so, the work of pioneers such as Paul Nwyia will not have been in vain.

---

[44] Charles Malik, *God and Man in Contemporary Islamic Thought*, 98-99.

CHRISTIAN ETHICS AND THE GLOBAL ECONOMY

Catherine Cowley

Christianity has been concerned with economic issues from its very origins because it takes the view that the world and all its activities are interconnected. It seeks to provide an overarching world view within which meaning is to be found. In our age it has found itself confronted with an alternative world view, one which believes that it too provides a system of meaning, a way of fully accounting for what it is to be human and how and why human persons act. That system is economics[1] and its current expression in free market ideology, most easily seen in what is referred to as the global economy.

Before discussing some aspects of the interaction between these two world views, I want to question a fundamental aspect of the term 'the global economy'. Let me be clear about what I am not saying. Although there is no one universally accepted meaning to the term globalisation (like the term 'justice' we tend to think we all mean the same thing by the same word, but we do not) there are common strands in the definitions. Thus I do not question the use of globalisation to describe the many ways in which space and time have been compressed by technology, information flows, trade and power so that distant actions have local effects. Neither do I deny that, particularly in financial markets, the process of integration is extensive and accelerating. Share prices, exchange rates and interest rates are converging due to their intimate interrelationships.

Financial markets do indeed exert tremendous influence on economic conditions. One consequence of the 24-hour operation of these markets is that every major event is immediately converted into asset prices, currency exchange rates and in-flows or out-flows of capital.

---

[1] For the interpretation of modern economic analysis as a secular religion, see Robert H Nelson, *Reaching for Heaven on Earth: The Theological Meaning of Economics*, Rowman & Littlefield, Savage, MD, 1991. This contrasts with Keynes view who reportedly said that economics should be 'a modest occupation similar to dentistry'.

Governments constantly watch the financial markets to gauge their response to political action, thus effectively leading to a reduced margin of action for governments.[2]

But note that I have been using the term 'globalisation'. To jump from there and call the economy 'global' is something of a misnomer. It is, in my view, a fallacy that we already live in a globalised economy.[3] The description 'global economy' presumes that we have completed the still unfolding phenomenon of globalisation. It presents a globalised situation as an already accomplished fact. To the contrary, I would argue that we are living in process, on a journey with some sort of destination for which we have no map, a destination which at the moment is not shared by all.

A substantial portion of humankind continues to subsist outside the circle of what purports to be the global economy. Many countries benefit; many do not. Measured either in terms of trade or direct investment, integration has been highly uneven. A few developing countries have managed to increase their trade a lot. They are the same countries that have attracted the lion's share of foreign direct investment. A recent study by the World Bank[4] showed that 24 countries, home to some 3 billion people, have seen growing economies and declining poverty rates.

However, another 2 billion people live in countries that have become less rather than more globalised. In these countries—including Pakistan, much of sub-Saharan Africa and parts of the former Soviet Union—trade has diminished in relation to national income, economic growth has been stagnant and poverty has risen. In short globalisation is not, and never has been, global. Much of the world, home to one third of its people, has simply failed to participate.

What this patchy integration suggests is that we need to avoid replicating (but from the opposite side of the argument) the mantra of globalisation that one size fits all. The world is just more complicated

---

[2] See, for example, Jonathon Perraton, *et al.*, 'The Globalisation of Economic Activity', *New Political Economy*, Vol. 2, No. 2 (1997) 257-277; Stephen Gill, 'European Governance and New Constitutionalism: Economic and Monetary Union and Alternatives to Disciplinary Neoliberalism in Europe', *New Political Economy*, Vol. 3, No. 1 (1998), 5-26.

[3] This view is held by, for example, George Soros in *The Crisis of Global Capitalism*, Little, Brown and Co., London, 1998.

[4] World Bank, *Globalisation, Growth and Poverty*, Washington, DC, 2001.

than that. There are very diverse problems which call for a wide range of solutions

A further reason for resisting the description of the economy as a global one is that it is, in many ways, a disempowering one. There is a deterministic rhetoric at work here which implicitly says 'Why are you bothering? It's already happened. You're too late.' It can lead to a hopeless resignation that brings down all effort. I challenge the ideology of globalisation which sees geographical locations as powerless in an era of global economic forces. I do, however, appreciate the enormity of forces shaping the world—not least how global, capital-based organisations select their locations at their convenience, playing localised social and political actors off against each other.[5]

But corporations have less power than myth says. For example, when discussing the size of transnational corporations as economic entities, we frequently hear that the 51 largest corporations have bigger sales than the GDP of nation states. However, this is a misuse of statistics. We are comparing oranges and fish. What GDP is measuring is 'value added' which is more similar to profits than to total sales. If we were to compare GDP and profits, not one corporation makes it into the top 100.

However, such myths are useful deflecting mechanisms for politicians who can blame others for their own failures or inaction. Perhaps globalisation is itself something of a myth that has been used to help reshape society in the interest of increasing the profitability of transnational corporations? Certainly the World Trade Organisation could be viewed as a strategy to overcome domestic resistance to transnationals' interests.

Another de-energising feature comes from the other side of the debate. Most Christians, however sensitive and conscientious, are probably tired of being harangued on the need for international economic justice, because they do believe it to be an imperative, but are unhappily aware that it will not come about very rapidly. Christian ethics, if it is to be true to itself, is not just about, or first and foremost about, working out what the evil is that we are to avoid—a list of 'Thou shalt nots'. Rather, it is about the good to be done. It is about how excellence is to come about, it is about how human flourishing is to be defined and worked towards. It is, therefore, *not* about an over-easy denunciation which, having denounced, considers the job done. Neither can it go beyond its

---

[5] For a discussion of the importance of location see Andrew Davey, *Urban Christianity and Global Order*, SPCK, London, 2001.

competence (for example, by providing over-detailed economic plans.) We need to remember Aristotle's salutary warning that we must not expect more precision from ethics than it can provide. It is for this reason that Catholic social teaching repeatedly points out that in the economic sphere it may offer guidelines towards solutions, but not the concrete solutions themselves.[6]

So what is within the competence of Christian ethics? What can it add to the vast literature generated by, for example, business ethics? The first thing to note is that the economy is not confined to business activity. Many other organisations and social institutions contribute to economic activity. There is, however, also a significant lacuna in business ethics. De George identified the need for business ethics to be multi-levelled.[7] By this he was referring to the level of choices and characters of *persons*, the policies and cultures of *organisations* and the arrangements and ideologies of entire social *systems*. Mainstream business ethics, whilst including in its view the first level, largely focuses on the managerial stratum of the second level. Very little is analysed at the third level.[8] It has remained resolutely micro-focussed, with good conduct within existing structures being seen as its remit. Even in discussion on 'social responsibility'—where it might be thought that almost by definition a wider horizon would have to come into view—the issues have been conceived in micro- and unilateralist forms. This results in central issues of business roles, power and resources being bypassed.[9] Christian ethics, on the other hand, particularly from within the Catholic tradition, encourages systemic analysis as well as the evaluation of individual acts.

But how it might do that in relation to economic activity is not, for many people, very obvious. I noted a little earlier that many are unhappily aware that international economic justice will not come about very rapidly. Many people of good will are also unhappily aware that they cannot see how Christian ethics is to be taken seriously in the

6 For example, John Paul II *Centesimus Annus*, Vatican Polyglot Press, Vatican City, 1991, n. 43.
7 Richard T De George, 'The Status of Business Ethics: Past and Future', *Journal of Business Ethics*, Vol 6 (1987), 206-11.
8 So, for example, although Boatright has a chapter entitled 'Ethics in Financial Markets', he deals only with the first and second levels, even though the financial sector seems one of the most obvious choices for third-level analysis. John R Boatright, *Ethics in Finance*, Blackwell, Oxford, 1999, 133-168.
9 This is not to suggest that a micro-focus has no value. Clearly it does. But business ethics needs more than just one level of analysis.

business world. It seems that we have two models, two visions of the world—that of free market ideology with its assumptions of neo-classical economics and the Christian world view. These two models seem to be talking about very different things, with the result that they just talk past each other. Those engaged in business will often perceive Christian ethics as being of only marginal relevance.

The very frames of reference seem to come from different planets. Those discussing business will be taking as some of their basic assumptions such features as utility theory, portfolio theory, arbitrage pricing, market efficiency, option pricing theory, the maximisation of shareholder value and the capital asset pricing model. Christian ethics will be referring to such assumptions as human flourishing, justice, the nature of the human person, the demands of community, solidarity and the rest.

Often when models differ widely the advocates of one model use it to define the other as inadequate. This is rarely fruitful. Each side can end up demonizing the other, and one is left tilting at windmills. If there is to be a true dialogue each 'voice' in the conversation needs to be heard. Common ground must be searched for, ground which perhaps is unnoticed because very different terms are being used to describe the same reality.

So how can we go about evaluation if we are using such different models? How do we know what to do with the guidelines offered by Christian ethics? If we want to decide whether a pen is a good pen, we have to know what pens are for, what the purpose of a pen is. If you think a pen is for eating soup, with you will probably conclude that most pens on the market are woefully inadequate. If you think they are for writing with, you will come to a different conclusion. So too with the economy. If we want to know if this is a good economy, we have to know what the purpose of the economy is. It is with such fundamental questions that we have to begin. If we cannot agree on the underlying purpose of the economy, we will not come to agreement on other issues such as the role of the business firm, or its relationship to the wider society.[10]

---

[10] Taking this approach enables us legitimately to side-step the stand-off about the prevailing orthodoxy which says that economics should not concern itself with ethics. This attitude was expressed forcefully and influentially by Lionel Robbins. Repudiating Hawtrey's claim that economics cannot be dissociated from ethics, he wrote 'Unfortunately it does not seem logically possible to associate the two studies in any form but mere juxtaposition. Economics deals with ascertainable facts, ethics with valuations and obligations. The two

Definition of the purpose of the economy

When considering the purpose of the economy as a whole, it is not sufficient to assert what the essential goal of business is—whether that goal be profit-maximization[11] or the provision of goods and services.[12] This goal will be important but it should neither dominate the discussion of the whole economy, nor should it be assumed that this goal can stand in isolation. There is what might be termed a 'for-the-sake-of' relationship. It is, therefore, also necessary to ask further what are the goods, and the ultimate good, for the sake of which the purposes of business might be pursued? How does it contribute to the purpose of the economy? By rejecting a micro-focus it becomes possible to reflect on the relationships between economic activity and the wider society. The moral justification of the market can only lie in the nature of its object, that is, the purpose of the economy. In the end one is asking: What is the ultimate good of human life?

A succinct summary of that purpose would go something like this:

> to provide all the goods which the resources of nature and industry can procure for all members of society. These goods ought to be plentiful enough to satisfy all those needs which

---

fields of enquiry are not on the same plane of discourse.' *An Essay of the Nature and Significance of Economic Science*, 3rd ed., Macmillan, London, 1984, 148. Obviously not all economists agree—Amartya Sen is an outstanding example of one who argues to the contrary in all his publications. See, for example, *On Ethics and Economics*, Blackwell, Oxford, 1987.

11 The most well-known justification for this is probably Milton Friedman,'The Social Responsibility of Business is to Increase Its Profits' (1970), reprinted in George D Chryssides and John H Kaler (eds.), *An Introduction to Business Ethics*, Chapman and Hall, London, 1993, 249-254. For a more recent example, Patrick Primeaux, and John A Stieber, *Profit Maximization: The Ethical Mandate of Business*, Austin & Winfield, London, 1995. For a standard financial management approach, see Arthur J Keown, *et al.*, *Basic Financial Management*, 7th ed., Prentice-Hall, Englewood Cliffs, New Jersey, 1996. For a succinct summary of the arguments exposing the fallacy that profit-maximisation will *necessarily* provide the basic motivational power of economic behaviour, see Kenneth J Arrow, 'Why Profits are Challenged' in *New Challenges to the Role of Profit*, Benjamin M Friedman (ed.), Lexington Books, Lexington, MA, 1978, 49-61. But old myths never die. For a recent refutation see Will Hutton, *The World We're In*, Little, Brown, London, 2002.

12 A well-argued case based on this is presented in Norman E Bowie and Ronald F Duska, *Business Ethics*, 2nd ed., Prentice-Hall, Englewood Cliffs, New Jersey, 1990.

are requirements for people to be able to realise their full and equal personhood, and raise society's members to a reasonable level of comfort.

It is worth noting here that reasonable people may reasonably disagree over what constitutes 'reasonable'. By definition it will be a moveable feast.[13] But also by definition it places in question whether some people in some places have more than is reasonable. It puts firmly on the agenda the question of de-development.

What we do have, with this definition, is a clear assertion that the economy has a purely *instrumental* function, it is a means to an end. It is not an end in itself. This can be seen clearly in *Gaudium et Spes* n. 64 [one of the most important documents issued by the Second Vatican Council]

The ultimate and basic purpose of economic production does not consist in the increase of goods produced, nor in profit nor in prestige; it is directed to the service of man, that is of man in his totality, taking into account his material needs and the requirements of his intellectual, moral, spiritual and religious life. Economic activity is to be carried out according to its own methods and laws, within the limits of the moral order, so that God's design for mankind may be fulfilled.[14]

It may seem strange to suggest that the economy should be meeting the moral, spiritual and religious dimensions of the human person. But economic activity is an important place of moral self-realisation. It is here that important virtues are developed. Catholic social teaching suggests that it is precisely through business activity that we grow in such characteristics as

---

[13] Adam Smith noted that the ability of a person to appear in public without shame, for example, requires that people have the accepted clothing and accessories for that particular society. In other words, some expressions of needs will be legitimately socially determined. Adam Smith, *An Inquiry into the Nature and Causes of the Wealth of Nations*, R H Campbell and A S Skinner (eds.), Clarendon Press, Oxford, 1976.

[14] Second Vatican Council, *Gaudium et spes* (1965), translated in Flannery Austin (ed.), *Vatican Council II: The Conciliar and Post Conciliar Documents*, Vol. 1, revised ed., Costello Publishing, New York, 1984.

... diligence, industriousness, prudence in undertaking reasonable risks, reliability and fidelity in interpersonal relationships, as well as courage in carrying out decisions which are difficult and painful but necessary, both for the overall working of a business and in meeting possible setbacks.[15]

Although I shall not be pursuing this particular point any further, it is important to bear it in mind as part of the purpose of the economy.

The skill of producing wide-spread wealth is a relatively new one in human history. For most of our history—and still today, in many parts of the world—existence was not about wealth creation. It was subsistence at basic or, at best, moderately comfortable levels. It is really only within the last 200 years or so that the idea that the purpose of the economy includes wealth creation has emerged, together with increasing skill at doing it. This skill has the potential to create a more humane life, which advances the kingdom of God. The Church recognises this, but also insists that wealth production should always be carried out in the context of the end of life on this earth, which is the formation of virtuous persons.

But Christian ethics for economic life are relatively undeveloped beyond the levels of generalities. And it is precisely here, with the issue of wealth creation, that Christian Ethics hits a problem. We have a well-developed ethics of distribution. We have rightly pointed to and criticised the market economy for growing inequality in the distribution of income[16] and creating poverty, or at least allowing it to grow. There is a vast and highly differentiated literature detailing these injustices, much of it from a global perspective. However, we do not have an equivalent ethics of production. Yet you cannot distribute what you have not produced. We should not presume that wealth creation somehow can be automatically taken for granted.

If we are to evaluate the market coherently within a Christian framework we need more than a well-developed theology dealing with

---

[15] *Centesimus Annus*, n. 32.
[16] The gap in per capita income (GNP) between the countries with the richest fifth of the world's people and those with the poorest fifth widened from 30 to 1 in 1960 to 74 to 1 in 1995. United Nations Development Programme, *Human Development Report 1999*, Oxford University Press, New York, 1999, 104–105.

poverty and injustice, the common good and materialism.[17] We also need to see more clearly what are the appropriate moral means or conditions for the creation of goods, services and wealth. We have, again rightly, rejected a 'trickle-down' *economic theory* of wealth creation and its associated sentiment that 'a rising tide lifts all boats'. But we have not, as yet, produced a *theology* of wealth creation—which seems strange when, as I said earlier, Christian ethics is above all about exploring the good that is to be done. To undertake such theology would require on the one hand, continuing to challenge economic prescriptions which assume as self-evident somewhat naive notions about the meaning of human life, such as more is always better. It would also require, on the other hand, taking seriously the practical criterion, namely, how do things really work in economics and what sort of changes would produce the effects we are looking for?

Without in any way assuming that the following is exhaustive, it seems to me that such a theology of production and wealth creation would need to include such themes as:

—Wealth creation that does not accumulate solely in the hands of the few.

—Wealth creation in an environmentally sustainable way so as to avoid an economics of exhaustion, expressly addressing issues of overproduction and overcapacity.

—Work as one expression of human creativity as a reflection of our nature in the image of God and a participation in God's creativity. How is this creativity to become a possibility for all workers, not just a favoured elite?

—As we are made in the image of Trinitarian God we have a need for community. It is an essential, not contingent, aspect of our humanity. Linked with this is the reality of our interdependence. How are economic systems to support community and reinforce the commitment to the common good?

—We have a God-given capacity to make choices for good and evil. How does economic activity reflect our human rationality and foster a mature responsibility for our actions on a global and local scale?

---

[17] For a rigorous discussion of many aspects of these issues, see Douglas A Hicks, *Inequality and Christian Ethics*, Cambridge University Press, Cambridge, 2000.

—Power relationships in decision-making processes.
—How is economic activity to be carried out so that an economics of exhaustion does not apply to those carrying out that activity?
—The duty to stand alongside the poor and disadvantaged and the need to ensure that they are empowered to develop their potential.
—How does our economic activity enable us to meet the obligation to serve implied in the injunction to love our neighbour?

So here we are, with at least the outline of what the purpose of the economy is. Modern economic life, however, like much of the rest of modern life, is based on what has turned out to be an extremely useful 'heresy'—that of autonomy. Because Christianity is rooted in the Judaic tradition, we share a very important point arising from what we can see in the Hebrew scriptures. Unlike some other world religions, Judaism has never held that an escape from the economic realities of life is the ideal for a religious person. Rather the religious relationship with God comes in the midst of the living of daily life, and economic dimensions of that life are as religiously significant as any other. The Christian tradition, with its strong emphasis on the active presence of God in the world, has always insisted that the whole of life is to be lived in conformity to God's will, and that therefore all aspects of our existence should be ordered to serve the end of virtuous and pious living. But modern economic relations recognise no such higher purpose. They derive in fact from a deliberate declaration of independence from the influence of such 'external considerations'.

The church statements that reflect on, and offer guidance to, the economy are attempts to restore the religious vision. The goal of the teaching is growth with equity (the purpose outlined at the very beginning) and the perennial target of condemnation is materialism—again recall that the definition spoke of 'reasonable' needs. Church teaching has never condemned capitalism as intrinsically evil, although some theologians have. Instead it has aimed its guidance at the reform of institutions, structures and personal life involved with the free-market economy i.e. the Church has wanted to journey with society and resource it as it makes decisions.

The global dimension

The fusion of Christian ethics and economics will take us into new
territory when we approach globalisation. We have to understand it in
cultural as well as political and economic terms. Globality is about human
meaning as well as social process; we have to explore human values and
identities as well as social institutions. This due not least to what Schumpeter
referred to as 'creative destruction'.[18] He was referring to the way
entrepreneurial innovation demolishes organisations and entire workplaces
and creates new ones. Such a view, as one might expect, is routinely
cited approvingly within the ideology of the free market. What is glossed
over is that Schumpeter was also clear that such creative destruction
would eventually destroy tradition and with it the cultural supports and
values without which the market cannot operate. A key service that
Christian ethics can perform here is to bring together the new possibilities
presented by globalisation, and values we want to uphold, such as
participation and justice, to see how our new possibilities can continue
to carry these values. By insisting that economic growth and technological
progress are not our supreme values and that the purpose of the economy
is an instrumental one, it leaves open the space to acknowledge that
politics, for example, is about much more inclusive goods.

It would be a mistake to accept the simplistic analysis that rejects
the global solely for the local—our world is just not like that. Nor is our
faith. On a technological level, we might assume that advances in
communications, and the compression of time and space are inevitable.
But on issues relating to economic developments, we must find a way to
pose the questions: who does this kind of globalisation benefit? What
kind of globalisation would benefit more people and how do we set
about achieving it? It is misleading to couch the debate in terms of polar
extremes, although that is often how it is presented. It is not the case that
the only alternative to the present form of globalisation is an end to all
economic progress. Globalisation is not a juggernaut to be stopped at all
costs; if the positive possibilities within it are to be realised, then we must
see it as a process that can, and must, be transformed, adapted, resisted
and guided.

---

[18] Joseph A Schumpeter, *A History of Economic Analysis*, George Allen & Unwin, London,
1955.

Despite all the talk about 'the iron laws of the market' etc., the globalising economy is not like the law of gravity. It is a human construct and like all human constructs it is changeable—perhaps not easily, but Christian ethics rejects the determinism which lies behind so many of the statements about the economy.

But there is another important difference between the economy and, say, the law of gravity. Although at quantum level, the observer is believed to change the phenomenon being observed, for all practical purposes gravity goes on its way irrespective of what we think about it. It was the same after the apple fell on Newton as it was before. The theory does not change the phenomenon to which it relates. Whether I know about or believe in gravity makes no difference to my fate if I jump off a cliff. Economics, like all social sciences, differs from the physical sciences precisely on this point. What is believed about a phenomenon makes a difference, even if the belief is not valid. This is because we base our decisions on our expectations about the future; but the future we are trying to anticipate is itself dependent on the decisions we are taking today which are shaped by our beliefs.

Ideas have behavioural consequences. If we believe things to be the case about the economy we will act in ways which reflect that. Hence the importance of what I was saying at the beginning about our beliefs about whether or not the economy is really global. Hence also the importance of what 'vision' we have of the world, of the human person, of what makes for human flourishing. This vision will govern what we come to accept as 'inevitable'.

Christian ethics keeps alive an alternative vision of what the world could be like. The Christian imagination is informed by the vision that we are made in the image and likeness of God. It enables us to imagine other arrangements, other states of affairs. We cannot work for what we cannot imagine. But our vision for the future must take account of the *truth* of what presently *is*. Only thus will we be able to identify the transformative possibilities hidden in the present.

Therefore perhaps at the moment one of the challenges for Christian ethics is to point to some truths which we have been ignoring. There are a couple in particular which I want to touch on. The first is that globalisation and urbanisation are inextricably linked by complex patterns of economic, political, social and cultural factors. The globalising economy is organised in and through cities, as node points in vast interconnecting networks and systems. The globalising economy is above all an urban phenomenon. By 2010 more than half the world will live in urban settlements. Britain is one of the most urbanised countries in the world. The 'desert' is now the city which requires our sustaining acts of contemplation, which helps to explain the growth of urban monasticism.

Yet we largely ignore this urbanisation—for example, consider the growth of a variety of spiritualities which seem rooted in a (romanticised) rural past and are couched in rural imagery. Why is it that we are so disinclined to acknowledge the urbanisation we see around us? Why are we so reluctant to understand ourselves as part of an urban society? Failure to take full cognisance of our urban reality means that we are left in a de-contextualised void. Yet the world is now an urban place and it is there that the globalising economy lives and moves and has its being, and the resources and concerns of the Church needs to acknowledge this. There is no other locus so touched by this economy. If we are to engage with the economy and shape our urban futures, we have a responsibility to develop models of urban theological practice which enable us to do this.

A second point is that as consumers we want prices to fall. As employees we want wages to rise. These two things, over time, are incompatible. For example, as buyers of pensions and insurance we want the best returns possible. As depositors with building societies and banks we want the highest possible rates of interest. As consumers of mortgages, bank loans and other forms of credit, we want to pay the lowest possible interest rates. This relies on the companies producing these goods and services (and the financial institutions which lend to them) creating shareholder value. In order to create this shareholder value management must cut costs through downsizing, out-sourcing, moving production to the places with the lowest labour costs and so on. Furthermore, we demand new products, or the same products at lower prices, or fresh food out of season,[19] and if we do not get them we switch to another company who will meet our demands. We cannot palm off all responsibility for economic decisions onto corporate executives. We, as consumers, are also responsible for the changes in the composition of the workforce and for the skills of some people being declared redundant. Many of our goods today are

---

[19] Even so, the subsidies paid by rich countries to their own agricultural sectors equals $350 billion a year, roughly 7 times the amount they spend on development aid.

cheap because they are produced in the global sweatshop. Our conflicting desires as consumers and as producers ensure that the symbiosis between poverty, globalisation and western consumerism continues.

As ethicists, we have been—rightly—concerned to highlight where the economy hits the poor, the marginalised, the oppressed, whether they be groups or whole nations. We have been extremely good at noticing the inequalities of distribution—whether that be in terms of income, investment, access to finance, trading rules and so on. We have been less adept at suggesting how the purpose of the economy can be nurtured by an ethics of production and wealth creation. We have, in the main, been slow to see and respond to the extraordinary linkage between globalisation and urbanisation.

We need to see how economic activity, in and of itself, can become more truly the vehicle for the moral self-realisation that is a necessary and integral part of a moral economy.

VIRTUE ETHICS AS
A TOOL FOR TACKLING GLOBAL
ECONOMIC ISSUES

Anna Abram

Introduction

Virtue ethics in recent years became one of the most exciting enterprises within ethics, including Christian ethics. The growing attraction of this enterprise is due to growing dissatisfaction with some central features of modern ethical theories. Preoccupation with the morality of particular, often controversial, actions and insufficiency of moral principles and rules for guiding moral life and solving moral dilemmas prompted writers such as Elizabeth Anscombe, Alasdair MacIntyre, Philippa Foot, Martha Nussbaum, James Keenan, Joseph Kotva, Jean Porter, Michael Slote, William Spohn and Robert Louden[1] to return to the concept of virtue that was central to the theories of Plato, Aristotle and Aquinas. This does not mean that virtue ethicists are disinterested in actions, principles and rules—they see them as important, but not as all there is to moral life. Instead, virtue ethicists look at the moral life as

---

[1] See Anscombe, 'Modern Moral Philosophy', in *The Collected Philosophical Papers of G E M Anscombe, Ethics, Religion and Politics*, Vol. III, Basil Blackwell, Oxford, 1981, 26–42, which appeared for the first time in *Philosophy* 33 (1958). It is widely regarded as having inaugurated the present revival of ethical interest in virtue; MacIntyre, *After Virtue: A Study in Moral Theory*, University of Notre Dame Press, Notre Dame, In, 1994(2); Foot, *Virtues and Vices and Other Essays in Moral Philosophy*, Basil Blackwell, Oxford, 1978; Nussbaum, *The Fragility of Goodness: Luck and Ethics in Greek Tragedy*, Cambridge University, New York, 1986; Keenan, 'Proposing Cardinal Virtues', *Theological Studies*, 56 (1995), 709–729; Kotva, 'An Appeal for a Christian Virtue Ethics', *Thought* 67 (1992), 158–180; Porter, *The Recovery of Virtue: The Relevance of Aquinas for Christian Ethics*, SPCK, London, 1994; Slote, 'Agent-Based Virtue Ethics', in R Crisp and M Slote (eds), *Virtue Ethics*, (Oxford Readings in Philosophy), Oxford University Press, Oxford, 1997; Spohn, 'Current Theology: Notes on Moral Theology: 1991: The Return of Virtue Ethics', *Theological Studies* 53 (1992), 60–75; R B Louden, 'Virtue Ethics and Anti-Theory', *Philosophia* 20 (1990), 94. For a good overview of virtue ethics, see D Statman (ed.), *Virtue Ethics: A Critical Reader*, Edinburgh University Press, Edinburgh, 1997, and L H Yearly, 'Recent Work on Virtue', *Religious Studies Review* 16 (1990), 1–9.

a whole with particular emphasis on *virtues*[2] as qualities that make up a well developed human character.

'Virtue ethics' is best defined as an approach[3] to ethics that centres on the self as a moral agent. It is an agent-orientated (as opposed to act- and or duty-orientated) ethics. It argues that by forming a good disposition of mind (that is virtue) we are able to act and live rightly—we act out of who we are. It is essential to recognize that although there exists a certain diversity in virtue ethics, there is a general agreement on the basic ideas. It is these basic ideas that I would like to present in this chapter. I have grouped them into four points: the idea of practice, the concept of the moral agent, the meaning of the moral good—the telos, and the universality of virtue language. I shall argue against an accusation of virtue ethics as being too theoretical and not practical enough and claim that virtue ethics is applicable to different spheres of human life. I will substantiate this claim by introducing virtue ethics to the sphere of global economy. The main point I would like to put forward here is this: 'global Christianity' is faced, amongst many, with a range of global economical issues; these issues can be addressed with the help of virtue ethics. I do not aspire to argue that virtue ethics can solve all the global economical problems. By disclosing a glimpse of what I called in the beginning as 'an exciting enterprise' I propose to use virtue ethics as a tool for addressing problems related to economic activities. The first operation of this tool will be the investigation of the idea of 'practice' in virtue ethics.

The idea of practice

Virtue ethics stresses the importance of practice, a participation of an individual in an activity that is undertaken alongside other individuals. Such participation is not simply mechanical motion, but it is purposeful and chosen doing. It involves *'the judgment of intellect'*.

---

[2] Virtue refers to human disposition that involves the judgment of intellect, leads to right action and directs towards the attainment of the moral good.

[3] I do not see virtue ethics as a separate part of ethics, but as an approach within ethics. In other words, ethics (in general) is not complete without this approach; it would be like medicine that ignores the whole area of the body's metabolism. My position is influenced by Jean Porter, who, following Aquinas, sees ethics as a unified concept in which virtue and its product, action, as well as moral good and community, mutually fit together. See *Moral Action and Christian Ethics*, (New Studies in Christian Ethics), Cambridge University Press, Cambridge, 1995.

The 'judgment of intellect' means two things: correct knowledge of the moral good—this means the ability to see what is the best kind of life for human beings to live. The second thing is the application of this knowledge to particular instances. Aristotle uses the term *phronesis*, translated as practical reason or prudence, to designate these two elements. When we have *phronesis* we are able to work out what actions we should perform in order to promote the moral good. This is what is referred to as 'virtuous practices'.

Alastair MacIntyre—mentioned in the introduction as one of the most influential writers on virtue—refers to very ordinary examples of practices such as football, chess, farming, the enquiries of science, the work of historians, architecture, painting and music. He stresses that it is the game of football or architecture and not just throwing a ball with skill or bricklaying that are examples of practices. For instance, planting turnips is not a practice but farming is. The concept of practice is central to an adequate understanding of the virtues. This concept, I believe, is crucial for relating virtue ethics to the sphere of business activity. It is not transporting people on coaches from one country to another that makes a virtuous practice but the well-functioning tourist industry is.

When we apply this understanding to global economics, let us say a multi-national company which is setting up a business in one of the countries of Eastern/Central Europe, correct knowledge of the moral good would mean the ability to understand and articulate what promotes the well-being of the people of the country concerned and the well-being of the company and choosing concrete actions that would contribute to the well-being of both. This involves working out what needs to be done in particular situations of a daily life.

Practice is never just a set of technical skills, even when directed towards some unified purpose (for example, having a well planted field of turnips or a well-organized multi-national company) even if the exercise of those skills can on occasion be valued or enjoyed for their own sake. What is distinctive in a practice is the way in which technical skills transform and enrich the goods and ends to which they are directed. Practices never have a goal fixed for all time; they are transmuted by the history of the activity.[4]

---

[4] See MacIntyre, *After Virtue*, 190 and 194.

Practices are not just in the here and now. They have a relationship with our predecessors in this practice. Here lie the historical and communal aspects of practice. Here practice begins to acquire a global extension. However, although practices are part of the life of the community, they must not be confused with institutions: 'chess, physics, medicine and economics are practices; chess clubs, laboratories, universities, hospitals and business companies are institutions.'[5] Practices and institutions are connected but they are not the same. Institutions are structured in terms of status and power, and they distribute money and status as rewards.[6] The ideals and the creativity of the practice are always vulnerable to the acquisitiveness and competitiveness of the institution. Here the role of virtues is clear: without them practices could not resist the corrupting power of institutions and the virtues could not be achieved.

It is noteworthy that MacIntyre clearly contrasts internal goods with external goods. The latter are only contingently related to practices and could in principle be obtained independently of them. Here he has in mind goods like prestige, status and money.[7] Internal goods (like friendship, care and concern for individual and community, fairness in judging others and oneself) are achieved only through participation in virtuous practices.[8] MacIntyre provides an implicit account of what makes a set of social and political arrangements justifiable. He says that these arrangements are justifiable only if they facilitate the leading of a good life. In order to facilitate the leading of a good life, social and political arrangements must sustain the practices which supply goods that would otherwise be unavailable. In other words, social and political arrangements are justifiable only if they foster virtue. Virtues can be adequately understood only by reference to a shared conception of the good. MacIntyre thinks that modernity has neglected virtues. Using the term 'modernity' he refers mainly to the modern economic order, which, in his view, has marginalized practices and is dominated by the pursuit of external goods. The practices which remain are under constant threat of corruption by acquisitiveness: the pursuit of external goods often comes into conflict with the realization of the goods internal to practices, and

---

[5] MacIntyre, *After Virtue*, 194.
[6] See MacIntyre, *After Virtue*, 194.
[7] See MacIntyre, *After Virtue*, 193.
[8] See MacIntyre, *After Virtue*, 204.

the corruption of a practice occurs when its participants pursue external goods at the expense of its internal goods.[9]

MacIntyre sharpens the distinction between external and internal goods when he says that 'external goods are always some individual's property and possession.'[10] Moreover, explains MacIntyre, they are such that the more someone has of them, the less there is for other people. This is sometimes the case with power, fame and money. External goods seem to be objects of competition in which there must be losers as well as winners. Although internal goods are the outcome of competition to excel (to reach excellence), they are achieved for the good of others (the whole community who participate in the practice). Virtues enable us to achieve goods which are internal to practices. In other words, internal goods can be achieved through participation in practices.

The participation in virtuous practices enables one to become skilful and to develop dispositions that will become a part of one's character. Virtues are not simply techniques but skills that suit us for life or become habitual—but not in the sense of mechanical operations. 'Habit' in this sense involves creative thinking and decision-making (practical reason) but, at the same time, expresses the inclination or orientation of a person's behaviour. Once virtue becomes part of character and settles into it (i.e., becomes a habit), it can communicate itself through skilful performances. Virtue facilitates moral growth. Virtue ethics proposes that being virtuous (which is expressed in right living) means having a basic set of virtues that enable a person to live well and act rightly. Being virtuous is not just having a particular disposition to act rightly in one sphere, such as being generous, for example. What it means, as many writers on virtue have recognized, is to have a fundamental set of related virtues, often referred to as 'cardinal virtues'.

Cardinal virtues are qualities which can be acquired by human effort of participation in practices that promote the moral good, are directed to, and in some degree constitutive of human happiness. The tradition of the cardinal virtues stems from Plato.[11] For him, the central

---

[9] See MacIntyre, *After Virtue*, 205 and 225.
[10] See MacIntyre, *After Virtue*, 190.
[11] See Plato's *Republic*, Book Four and *Gorgias*, T Irwin, (trans.) Clarendon Press, Oxford, 1979.

virtues were temperance, courage, prudence and justice. Aristotle adopted Plato's approach to the cardinal virtues. However, he expanded his list to include twelve virtues: bravery (or courage), temperance, generosity, magnificence, magnanimity, a virtue concerned with small honour (or proper ambition), mildness (or patience), truthfulness, wittiness, friendliness, modesty and proper indignation.[12] Aquinas, who adopted Plato's list and Aristotle's approach, is most associated with the idea of 'cardinal virtues' as he offers an extensive and rather persuasive account of these virtues.[13]

Aquinas articulates his set of cardinal virtues against an anthropology which classifies human faculties in terms of practical reason, will, and passions (irascible/concupiscible). He explains that prudence orders our practical reason; justice orders the will; temperance and fortitude perfect the passions, which are divided into the concupiscible or desiring power and the irascible or struggling power.[14]

Although Aquinas's account of traditional virtues seems coherent, it calls for further consideration. Jean Porter and James Keenan (modern followers of Aquinas) have undertaken such a task and have proposed two different approaches to the traditional list. Porter maintains Aquinas's classification, but translates it into more modern language. By contrast, Keenan, while still maintaining the idea of a fundamental set of related virtues, recasts 'fundamental' in terms of an anthropology of relationship (general, specific, self), and comes up with a list of cardinal virtues that are different from Aquinas's.[15]

Porter argues that the virtues of passions, that is, temperance and fortitude, can be identified with self-control and self-restraint

---

[12] See *Nicomachean Ethics*, T Irwin (trans.) Hackett Publishing Company, Indianapolis, 1985, 1107b–1108b (abbreviated as NE). Plato and Aristotle differed in their theories, especially about which virtues were essential. Nevertheless, they both maintained that the virtues were unified; that is, if a person were rightly formed by all the virtues in the right manner, there could be no possibility of a conflict between virtues. See, Plato, *Gorgias*, 477c; Aristotle, NE 1115a10–1138b10.

[13] See Porter, *Moral Action and Christian Ethics*, 194.

[14] See *Summa Theologiae: Latin Text and English Translation, Introduction, Notes, Appendices and Glossaries*, New Blackfriars, London, New York, 1963, 1a2ae 6.1, 2–3. (abbreviated as *ST*).

[15] Note that I do not claim that the traditional list does not consider human relationality. For example, justice, by nature expresses relational concern for the other. However, the relational concern in the traditional list is not as properly stressed and articulated as in the contemporary list.

(temperance) and courage, perseverance and patience (fortitude). With regard to justice[16] (the virtue of the will), Porter says that, first of all, this virtue requires that a person have some knowledge of what justice means. If the will orients one to his or her individual good, which on occasion may not be directed to a common good, then justice orients one to a common good. It is an other-regarding virtue. Porter suggests that justice can be understood in terms of conscientiousness, fairness and integrity. Conscientiousness can be described as 'a settled tendency to attend to, and to respect, the norms, the claims, and expectations that are incumbent on the individual as a member of a particular community or association, or as an adherent to a religious or moral framework of beliefs.'[17] Conscientiousness is necessary for obtaining the goods which are internal to practices. Rules and norms seem to play an instrumental role in the pursuit of goods. However, they cannot be treated the other way around, that is, the pursuit of goods cannot be seen as instrumental in formulating rules and norms. Otherwise, the meaning of justice can be lost. Fairness and integrity, in Porter's view, are 'two forms of an impersonal love for the good'.[18] In her understanding, these two forms seem to be conditional for love of oneself. Integrity means consistent willingness to construe one's own good in the context of some greater good, which one values more than one's own personal satisfactions. This willingness is grounded in one's own participation in the wider good, which bestows meaning and purpose on one's life.

The three cardinal virtues considered so far are closely linked to the fourth virtue, that is, prudence. The understanding and practice of fortitude, temperance and justice include an account of rationality. This means that the exercise of virtues involves prudence. (The same is true the other way around: the exercise of prudence involves the three other cardinal virtues). Prudence, as Porter points out, applies general principles to particular actions. 'Its central actions are to inquire with respect to what is to be done in a given situation, to form a judgment based on that

---

[16] Bernard Williams notes that justice is about ordering all our interior dispositions so that the claim of equality originates from within (see B Williams, 'Justice as a Virtue', in A O Rorty (ed.), *Essays on Aristotle's Ethics*, 1-40).

[17] Porter, *Moral Action and Christian Ethics*, 188. This understanding can be easily distorted. However, if understood correctly, it is a healthy capacity for the realization of individual and human good. Here the role of practical reason is very important.

[18] Porter, *Moral Action and Christian Ethics*, 193-194.

inquiry, and to command the action or actions so determined.'[19] For Aquinas, the components of prudence are: memory, reason, intellect, teachableness, cleverness, foresight, circumspection and caution. It is possible to say that prudence is a really complex capacity and it is not easily acquired. Therefore, it has to be acquired over time.

Keenan's understanding of cardinal virtues is based on relational ways of being. He understands human relationality in three ways: generally, specifically and uniquely. Each of these relational ways of being demands a cardinal virtue. As relational beings in general, we are called to justice. As relational beings specifically, we are called to fidelity. As relational beings uniquely, we are called to self-care. It should be noted that in Keenan's, unlike Aquinas's structure, cardinal virtues are not connected, and indeed they can be in conflict. Thus we are not called to be faithful and self-caring in order to be just, nor are we called to be self-caring and just in order to be faithful. None is auxiliary to each other. Each cardinal virtue is a distinctive virtue. The fourth cardinal virtue is prudence, which determines what constitutes the just, faithful, and self-caring way of life for an individual.[20] Keenan does not offer a detailed treatment of these virtues, however, his overall approach seems very plausible, especially for right living in a contemporary context.

Although there are similarities and dissimilarities in the two approaches to cardinal virtues, the relationship between them can be described as complementary. Thus, if we combine the two sets of virtues, an integrated person would have all six virtues: prudence, justice, temperance, fortitude, self-care and fidelity—these are the essential virtues for right living.[21]

If we translate the above approach to cardinal virtues to the sphere of economic life it becomes clear that a businessman/woman in order to be called 'morally mature' would need more than, for example, courage in taking risky decisions concerning future investment. He or she will need self-restraint in resisting the temptation of making

---

[19] Porter, *Moral Action and Christian Ethics*, 151.

[20] See, Keenan, 'Proposing Cardinal Virtues', *Theological Studies* 56 (1995), 709-729.

[21] Overall, virtuous behaviour consists of more than cardinal virtues. Other virtues are certainly important, but the cardinal virtues perfect the basic dimensions of being human that are needed for integrated virtuous behaviour. Here, because of the scope of this chapter I have considered only the basic virtues. Other virtues are derivatives of cardinal virtues.

disproportionate financial profits and will need to take into account demands of different relationships so that there is a right balance between self-care, fidelity and justice. A businessman/woman who possesses prudence, justice, temperance, courage, fidelity and self-care would act in a way that promotes the moral good and achieves internal goods (like friendship, solidarity, honesty, fairness, etc). Moral integrity of a business organization depends on the integrity of individual members of such an organization, their willingness to construe their own good and the good of their business company in the context of some greater good. It also depends on their participation as well as facilitation of virtuous practices. This applies not only to business directors but to all who are engaged in business life. A good businessman and woman would strive to know *what* is necessary for right living, *why* it is necessary and *how* in daily reality he or she can fulfil the demands of right living. Actions of such a person will be considered as human actions and not just actions performed by a human being. They will be intentional actions of a moral agent.

The concept of the moral agent

As we have just seen, virtue ethics accentuates the necessity of developing a deeper understanding of the activity and having reasons for an engagement in this activity. It works with the understanding of a person as moral agent. To view a person as moral agent means to accept that people are more than what happens to them. A moral agent is one who not only possesses the capacity to act, but one who has a capacity to choose which actions to perform, because he or she has moral understanding. Human beings are not simply formed by the interaction of psychological and environmental forces. They are not products of business activity but they are designers of such an activity. In other words, a person as moral agent can shape his or her future and can influence business practices. A moral agent has a capacity for intentional action. If this action becomes habitual, skilful, promotes the *telos* of the moral life and enables one to live rightly then this action becomes virtuous. It is embedded in the self. It characterizes (inwardly and outwardly) the self. The same is true the other way around. If, initiated in the self, action habitually does not promote right living and prevents one from attaining the moral good, this action becomes vicious. Hence, the self initiates actions, thus potentially, virtues and vices. Here lies the strong sense of our moral agency. This does not mean that we have unlimited possibilities. A person as moral agent, in choosing which actions to perform, takes into account his or her limited possibilities. He or she understands that society and culture are influential in what we become, but they do not determine us.

The overall idea of moral agency helps us to understand that, despite the limits of the world in which one lives, one is still able to shape responsibly the image of the person one ought to become. To be a moral agent is to accept responsibility[22] for one's personal history in which one has already become the person one's actions have formed. Having accepted the present, we become capable of governing what we ought to become. In order to govern our own and our society's future we need to have a concept of the moral good in the context of which we would be able to choose actions that would promote this good.

The idea of the moral good

Virtue ethics stresses the importance of the idea of the *telos*. The term itself, as translated from Greek, means an end, a goal or an aim. The idea of the *telos* comes from the Aristotelian concept of *eudaimonia*, often translated as the 'moral good', 'natural happiness' or 'the best kind of life for a human being to live'.[23] According to Aristotle, *eudaimonia* is the complete end, the only one that does not promote any other end. Aquinas adopts an Aristotelian approach to the moral good as the ultimate end of human life but also adds some precision to its understanding.[24]

---

[22] The self, through intentional actions, is responsible for forming its own character traits by repetition of these actions. Although the idea of responsibility is not developed by virtue ethics, it is closely connected with the idea of self as moral agent. By using the term 'responsibility' I suggest that the character one has is not just the outcome of environmental forces (although such forces are influential in the acquiring of character—we always have some sort of character) but is formed through reasoned choices and intentional actions. Thus, the self is aware of the limits of choices one can make and the environmental forces which are around, and, in spite of the limits, the responsible self is still able to make reasoned decisions.

[23] See Terence Irwin's explanation of *eudaimonia* which he identifies with 'living well' or 'doing well'. (*NE*, Glossary, 407-408). According to Aristotle, virtues are necessary for *eudaimonia*. (See, *NE* 1094b8, 1095b32).

[24] Note that Aquinas uses the Latin word *finis*. However, contemporary writers on virtue

Aquinas' account of the naturally good life for the human person sees the well-being of the individual and the community as mutually interdependent. He recognizes that no individual is able to live, much less lead a humanly good life, apart from the sustaining structures of the community. To put it simply, I cannot be happy in an eudaimonian sense if the rest of my society is unhappy. In the context of global economy moral good would mean empowering everyone and not just a few. My own well-being in a deep sense lies in the well-being of others. The moral good is a generic concept in the context of which the individual good should be defined. We can reach the moral good through realization of our individual goods which are, or should be, approximations of the moral good.

This understanding of the moral good is similar to what is usually meant by the 'common good'. The Christian tradition in general and the Roman Catholic approach in particular have emphasized the importance of the common good. Human beings are not just isolated individuals but are social beings called to live together in civic, political and global community. In this sense the moral good is an objective concept. However, since it is also a concept, in the context of which an individual good needs to be worked out, there is some sort of individualization of the moral good. Thus, the moral good is both objective and individualized.

In what sense is the moral good objective? It is in the sense that, as the ultimate end of human action, it should be desirable and worthy of choice. It is desired because of what it is. This statement sounds normative, and, indeed, the moral good is a normative concept. It could be said that this concept is based on the principle of worthy living. However, the normativity of the moral good has to be qualified further, in the sense that, although the moral good is connected to action, it cannot be simply reduced to it. The moral good to which action is directed is a state of being. Thus, the moral good is a dynamic concept in the same way as the human person is a dynamic being. Therefore, it can be best described as the way of living that consists in certain activities. These activities, as we noted in MacIntyre's account of virtue, are practices that promote internal goods such as knowledge, health, friendship and beauty, and to achieve

---

use the Greek term *telos*. They mean the same thing. The reason for using *telos* and not *finis* lies in the fact that virtue-centred ethics is seen as teleological ethics and *finis* is often used in deontological approaches. To avoid confusion, following contemporary writers on virtue, I use the word *telos* although other words like *finis* or *eudaimonia* can also be employed.

these goods we need virtues. Thus, virtues are necessary for the realization of the moral good. They enable us to achieve the moral good through right living, that is, through continuous (habitual) participation in what MacIntyre calls virtuous practices.

The idea of practices stresses the importance of daily activities in the attempt to achieve the moral good. Therefore, the moral good should not be understood as an end in the sense of something that can be achieved in a distant future. It is something that can be achieved here and now if enough effort is put into it. Moral good is the best kind of life for a human being to live that is worthwhile throughout—now and in the future. It is not just an unreachable ideal. Here lies the objective and ultimate sense of the *telos*. Virtue ethics helps us to see the meaning of the moral good that goes beyond one's own household and takes one to the idea of a global household. Here virtue ethics serves us a tool in addressing dangers and limitations as well as blessings of global economy. The phrase 'global economy' belongs to a universal language. It is the same language that virtue ethics speaks.

Universality of virtue language

Virtue ethics speaks a universal language. By this I mean, that every culture at every moment of history would have a list of basic virtues that constitute right behaviour. This list does not really change—what does change is the content of each virtue. For example, if we take patience (if patience is a virtue) we could say that patience has a different meaning in New York than in San Salvador. However, both New Yorkers and San Salvadorians would know whether their fellow citizens are patient or not. And it is here where different cultures and religions can find a common ethical ground. From this perspective global economy, not free of dangers, failures and limitation, can, however, become a growth-furthering enterprise. From this standpoint, global economical ethics does not have to be simply a set of impositions and constraints, obstacles to business behaviour but rather the motivating force of a successful life well-lived. In Christian terms, this is one of the ways of living out the commandment of love. Virtue ethics doesn't offer us a blueprint how to solve tensions within economic activity. However, it offers us a perspective from which business life can be viewed both critically and essentially.

Conclusion

If we relate virtue ethics more closely to the economic life we can say that although business life has its specific goals, goods and distinctive practices and people in business have their own particular concerns, loyalties, roles and responsibilities, there is no 'business world' apart from the people who work in the business, and the integrity of those people—their virtues and visions of the moral good—determines the integrity of the organisation and vice-versa. If the organization facilitates virtuous practices there is a good ground for developing virtues in the individual. This is the point where global economy—the product of human cooperation—and virtue ethics, with its stress on a person who makes choices that produce right behaviour and lead to a good human co-operation and the building of a good community, have common grounds for further explorations. This is a continuous challenge for Christian Ethics.

WOMEN IN CHRISTIAN MISSION: PROTESTANT ENCOUNTERS FROM THE 19TH AND 20TH CENTURIES

Inger-Marie Okkenhaug

In 1904 a Muganda Chief described the lack of a Christian boarding school for girls as 'the Muganda's broken arm', since boy's education was already established. As a response, the Ladies' Conference of the Church Missionary Society recommended that such a school should be built at Gayaza (today a 30-minute drive from Kampala). The school opened in 1905 and the first headmistress, Miss Alfreda Allen wrote, 'My conviction is that we ought to give these people, who are so eager and enthusiastic to learn, the best we can.'[1] By then Bishop Tucker had opened the school hall with the following message to the audience that included the Katikiro and many chiefs: 'There must be noble women in order to have noble men.' The first aim of Gayaza was to train Christian wives and mothers and to bridge the intellectual gap between husbands and wives. And when the time came for His Highness the Kabaka to marry, *it was to Gayaza that His Highness looked for a bride.*[2]

These glimpses from the history of the Church Missionary Society's High School for girls at Gayaza, Uganda, illustrate some of the many faceted phenomena of women and Christian mission. For one, the local population often welcomed the facilities the mission offered, including and not seldom especially, education for girls. Secondly the missionaries themselves gave priority to work among women, Thirdly this work among women had to be performed by women, and could be liberating and empowering for both Western women going out as missionaries and for the women being exposed to mission education. Finally, but not the least important: the impact of the missionary enterprise is even today considerable on girls and women in Sub-Saharan Africa, the Middle East and Asia. Gayaza is still considered one of the better

---

[1] *Gayaza High School, The first ninety years, 1905-1995*, eds. Joan Cox, Brenda Richards, Sheelagh Warren.

[2] *Ibid.*, 1-3. On Anglican mission and women in Uganda, see Elizabeth Dimock, *Women and the Church Missionary Society in Uganda, 1895-1939: Gender in an Imperial Setting*, Unpublished Ph.D., La Trobe University, Melbourne, 1995.

educational institutions for girls in Uganda. It is a boarding school and caters for the better off, and a Ugandan headmistress and teachers now run it. At Makerere University most of the female staff had attended either Gayaza or the Roman Catholic equivalent. The origins of this Christian mission, which can be characterised as the first global women's movement, originated in early 19th century Europe and the USA. Both Protestant and Catholic organisations sent out female missionaries. Historical research on gender and mission has, however, to a large extent been concentrated on Protestant mission.[3] This essay seeks to explore central aspects that characterised women's mission and will look at the ways Protestant mission could act as a liberating force. It has been claimed that missionary women defined themselves in relation to non–Christian women whom they considered subordinate and dependent. Did Western Christian women's success in expanding the scope of gender boundaries build on undisputed notions of racial hierarchies or can mission be seen as a feminist project with implications for women's roles within church and society also in the non–western world?

From the mid–19th century the Christian Protestant mission developed a great momentum. The movement engaged women on a large scale in the USA and in Europe and enjoyed an unparalleled success among married as well as unmarried women. Women played a central role both at home, as fund–raisers and as active agents in 'heathen' countries.[4] Women were a majority in the missionary movements and missionary work attracted women because it combined a gender–specific, Christian way of life with degrees of freedom denied to the Christian woman in the West.[5] It also offered middle class women a wider range of

---

3   On Catholic mission, see Kathleen R Smythe 'The Creation of a Catholic Fiba Society', 129-149, Christopher Comoro and John Sivalon, 'The Marian Faith Healing Ministry', 275-295, and Ronald Kassimiri, 'The Politics of Popular Catholicism in Uganda', 248-274, in Thomas Spear and Isaria N Kimambo (eds.), *East African Expressions of Christianity*, James Currey, Oxford, 1999.

4   Patricia Hill, *The World their Household: the American Woman's mission Movement and cultural Transformation, 1870-1920,* Ann Arbor, 1985; L A Flemming (ed.), *Women's Work for Women Missionaries and Social Change in Asia,* Colorado/London, 1989; L A Flemming, 'A New Humanity: American Missionaries' Ideals for Women in North India, 1870-1930' in Nupur Chanduri and Margaret Strobel (eds.), *Western Women and Imperialism: Complicity and Resistance,* Bloomington and Indianapolis, 1992, 191-206, and Susan Hill Lindley, *You Have Stept Out of Your Place: A History of Women and Religion in America,* Kentucky, 1996.

5   Rosemary Seton, 'Open doors for female labourers: women candidates of the London Missionary Society, 1875-1914', in Robert A Bickers and Rosemary Seton (eds.), *Missionary*

permissible activities than was possible in European and American societies at the time. While spreading the Christian message was initially the main aim, social work, especially health and education, soon became accepted missionary activities, legitimised as the best way of reaching the local population.[6]

The interest among women to be active in philanthropic and missionary activity was a result of developments in 19th century religion: the evangelical movement and the new female role that was implicit in this Protestant revival.[7] This Evangelical revival and its *activism, bibliocentrism, and conversionism* is explained by Steven Maughan as the origin of English Protestant foreign missions.[8] High Church Anglicans as well as Methodist and Baptists were represented among the largest denominational missionary societies. The Evangelical movement was a reform movement within the Anglican Church and in American churches and dominated Anglo-American societies during the 19th century. It had a profound and complex influence on the life and world-view of women.[9] Evangelicalism gendered society and distinguished 'femininity' from 'masculinity' and redefined the relations between a Christian home—identified as a feminine sphere—and the masculine world. A similar development was seen in Protestant Germany and the Scandinavian countries.

The 'paradoxical emancipation'

An important part of the transformative power of the missionary project was its sanctioning of transgressive behaviour as religious exceptions to

---

Encounters: Sources and Issues, London, 1996, 35. See also L A Flemming, 'A New Humanity: American Missionaries' Ideals for Women in North India, 1870-1930', Chanduri and Strobel (eds.); Susan Hill Lindley, *You Have Stept Out of Your Place: A History of Women and Religion in America*, Westminster John Knox Press, Louisville, 1996.

6   See, for example, Hill 1985, and Fiona Bowie, Deborah Kirkwood and Shirley Ardener (eds.), *Women and Missions: Past and Present, Anthropological and Historical Perceptions*, Berg, Oxford, 1993.

7   *Ibid.*

8   Steven Maughan 'Mighty England do good: The major English denominations and organisation for the support of foreign missions in the nineteenth century', Bickers and Seton (eds.), 1996, 14-15. The J and EM was seen as the Anglican Church's tool in the Middle East, and was representative of the 'High Church'.

9   Billie Melman, *Women's Orient: English Women and the Middle East, 1718-1918*, London 1995, 166.

gender rules. It was the pious woman's 'duty' to overcome her 'natural diffidence' in order that she might better serve the mission.[10] While women were often in subordinate positions in terms of missionary hierarchy, the mission movement contributed significantly to the entrance of women into the public domain. It gave women the opportunity to engage in charitable activities outside the home, the chance to learn organisational skills, and the opportunity to enter the labour market as missionaries. Most missions have acted deliberately to change gender structures among the local people they encountered in the mission field, but they have also, intentionally and unintentionally, caused changes in such structures both in their own organisations and in their home countries.[11]

In the United States and Great Britain mission societies by and for women flourished throughout the 19th century. In Germany the first women's mission organisation, 'Morgenländische Frauenmission' was established by ten women in Berlin in 1842. Its aim was to create 'Hilfe für unterdrückte Frauen in Indien'.[12] In the Nordic countries the development of separate women's missions did not take place until fifty years later.[13] An organisation of female Swedish mission workers KMA (Kvinnelige misjonsarbeidere) was organised in 1894, then in Denmark and Finland (1900) and finally in Norway (1902). Even so, women continued to be central in the general mission movement. In Norway which was the leading country in Scandinavia concerning the number of people involved in mission activities, women played a decisive part in the Lutheran Norwegian Missionary Society (NMS), from the time it was established in 1842.[14] NMS, which had close ties to the state church,

---

[10] Susan Thorne 'Missionary-Imperial Feminism' in M Taylor Hubert and N C Lutkehaus (eds.), *Gendered Missions: Women and Men in Missionary Discourse and Practice*, Ann Arbor, 1999, 45.

[11] Line Nyhagen Predelli and Jon Miller, 'Piety and Patriarchy: 'Contested Gender Regimes in Nineteenth-Century Evangelical Missions' in Taylor Huber and N C Lutkehaus (eds.), 1999.

[12] Magdalena Möbius, *Frauenmission als protestantischer Beitrag zur Frauenbewegung in Deutschland? Eine Untersuchung anhand von Materialien aus der Geschichte der Moregnländischen Frauenmission*, Wissenschaftliche Hausarbeit in der I. Theologischen Prüfung, Unpublished paper, 1993.

[13] On gender and religion in the Nordic countries, see Pirjo Markkola (ed.), *Gender and Vocation: Women, Religion and Social Change in the Nordic Countries, 1830-1940*, Helsinki, 2000; Inger Hammar, *Emancipation och religion: Den svenska kvinnorörelsens pionjärer i debatt om kvinnans kallelse ca 1860-1900*, Stockholm, 1999, and Inger Marie Okkenhaug (ed.), *Gender, Race and Religion: Nordic Missions 1860-1940*, Studia Missionalia Svecana, Uppsala 2003.

[14] Hilda Rømer, Christensen, 'Building an Empire at Home and Abroad. Front Figures of the Danish Missionary Work for Women 1890-1940', in Okkenhaug 2003.

became one of the largest popular movements in the country. When NMS in 1904 decided to give women formal rights, this happened nine years before Norwegian women in general received the right to vote. In this way the mission could be an explicit model for women's liberation in society at large.[15]

In general, however, the various mission movements in the Scandinavian countries as in the rest of the Western world tended to defend and conserve ideologically defined gender boarders. One of the strongest hindrances to change was the biblically founded position that women should not have authority over men. Many organisations also held that women could not preach in gatherings with men present. This rule originated from the Lutheran and Evangelical Christian view of womanhood, where male and female belonged to two separate spheres. While a man's ability to support and order his family and household was the sign of masculinity, a woman's femininity was expressed in her dependence.[16] The primary religious explanation for woman's subordination to man lay in the Fall. Eve had introduced transgression to the world and must suffer for it. Christian notions of womanhood assumed a link between the godly woman and her family duties. A woman's salvation lay in her responsibilities as mother, wife, daughter or sister. Established bible teaching said that women were and should be subordinate to men socially. At the same time, however, Protestants believed in the right of all women to salvation and the spiritual equality of men and women. Women's subordination did not mean that they were inferior, but they were operating in different spheres. In fact women were seen as more open to religious influence than men because of their greater separation from the temptations of the world in the domestic sphere and because of their

---

[15] For more information on Nordic women missionary organizations see Kristin Norseth, 'Two of a Kind: The female Teacher's Missionary Association (LMF) and Women Missionary Workers (KMA) in a Norwegian, Nordic and International Perspective', *Norsk Tidsskrift for Misjon (Norwegian Periodical for Mission)*, no. 2 2002, 91-106, Line Nyhagen Predelli, 'Processes of gender democratization in evangelical missions: The case of the Norwegian Missionary Society', *NORA (Nordic Journal of Women's Studies)*, 1, vol. 8, 2000, 33-46, and Nyhagen Predelli, *Contested Patriarchy and Missionary Feminism: The Norwegian Missionary Society in Nineteenth Century Norway and Madagascar*, Unpublished Ph.D. thesis, University of Southern California, 1998, and Karina Hestad Skeie and Kristin Norseth, 'Creating a Voice—Acquiring Rights. Women in the Norwegian Missionary Society and the Process Towards Formal Oganizational Rights in 1904', forthcoming article in *NORA (Nordic Journal of Women's Studies)* 2003.

[16] Leonore Davidoff and Cathrine Hall, *Family Fortunes*, Hutchinson, London, 1987, 114.

'natural characteristics of gentleness and passivity'. As mothers and wives, women were the makers of men. Thus women's moral and religious influence was undisputed. It was held that Christian societies had played a vital part in raising the status of women and that Protestantism, in particular, *manifested a high level of civilisation in terms of its attitudes about them*.[17]

In the Protestant faith femininity was constituted in motherhood. However, motherhood was dependent on marriage, and during the 19th century this was not an avenue open to all because of the period's demographic imbalance, with an excess of women and lack of men. The Protestant emphasis on women's profession as wives and mothers became an obstacle for representatives of the religious discourse who, from the middle of the 19th century, had to address the issue of how an unmarried woman's vocation should be defined. The need to expand women's sphere of action challenged the Protestant teaching's firm assertion of a complementary view of the sexes.[18] Even so, prominent Evangelicals like Hannah More had from the early 19th century argued that once women had looked after her domestic duties in a proper manner, they could consider doing some religious and philanthropic work outside the home.[19]

Thus domesticity was emphasised while at the same time Evangelicalism encouraged women to move away from the home and into the 'world', since it was a practical religion that placed service and manners before doctrine. It stressed self-sacrifice and service to others; characteristics that were seen as 'naturally feminine' and thus encouraged women to leave the home sphere to do charity work in the 'outside' world. Women's moral superiority, her generic spirituality, the very qualifications that had made her the custodian of the 'home', qualified her as a social and religious reformer. The notion of 'un-Christian', that is being in need of missionary attention and concern, was applied to groups outside the middle classes, for example the urban poor. Women in other cultures were also perceived as less fortunate and in need of help. Besides proselytising, female missionaries wanted to extend what they saw as the superior position women had in Protestant Christianity to

---

[17] *Ibid.*, 114–115.

[18] Inger Hammar, 'Protestantism and Women's Liberation in 19th-Century Sweden' in Inger Marie Okkenhaug (ed.), *Gender, Race and Religion; Nordic Missions, 1860-1940*, Studia Missionalia Svecana, Uppsala, 2003.

[19] Davidoff and Hall, 162–172.

non-Christian women.[20] Images of women's intellectual deprivation, domestic oppression and sexual degradation were used to justify missionary work in Africa and Asia. Within the mission movement this is a universalist theme; men and women share a common humanity, and christianization entails a restoration of women's humanity.[21] Western women had a moral duty to uplift the non-Christian women and in many societies, for example in Asia and the Middle East, women could only be reached by women. Thus Western women went out to do Christian work in far away places. While the subordinate female ideal prevailed, this was constantly being contested by the practical every day life of women in the mission.

How have Christian women negotiated change within a patriarchal hierarchy? How have women attempted to challenge the established, male missionary regime? This 'paradoxical emancipation' is characterised by the question: is it possible for women located within a patriarchal structure to transcend traditional boundaries? Is it possible to speak of emancipation and liberation in connection with women who choose to work and act within a traditional hierarchy?[22]

Contrary to the popular image, a substantial number of women in the mission movement were far from passive and submissive. There are numerous examples of women missionaries who were charismatic preachers, writers and leader figures, and who also worked for sexual equality in their own organisation. One prominent Scandinavian woman missionary who became a successful religious authority in her own right was Marie Monsen (1872-1962) in the Norwegian Lutheran Mission. Her Christian calling and personal religious experience legitimised her own roles as a preacher for men as well as for women and children in China, and as spiritual counsellor for male Christian leaders.[23] Another example from a Norwegian mission Society shows, however, that women missionaries could also fail in their attempt at transforming a practical reality into a formalised right. In the 1890s Emma Dahl was preaching to Malagasy men, thus crossing the ideologically justified prohibition.

---

[20] Flemming, 'A New Humanity: American Missionaries' Ideals for Women in North India, 1870-1930', (1992), 192.

[21] Lisbeth Mikaelsson, 'Gender politics in female mission autobiography' in Okkenhaug 2003, 31-53.

[22] Gunilla Gunner and Karin Sarja, 'Den Paradoxala befrielsen', *Svensk Missionstidskrift*, vol. 84, NR. 1, 35-36. See also Susan Thorne, 'Missionary-Imperial Feminism', in Taylor Huber and N C Lutkehaus, eds., 60- 75.

[23] Mikaelsson, 37-49.

However, when she sought formal permission to do so, the mission headquarters in Norway opposed to give her such rights. In the end Dahl had to resign from the organization.[24]

But there were other women missionaries who were able to exceed limits in the mission field, before the mission leadership had officially approved the changes. The geographical distance and the cultural and practical difference between the headquarters and the mission field allowed for a discrepancy between the ideal of gender roles and real life. While work and space in theory were strictly defined according to gender, in practical terms all churches had to be a great deal more flexible in the missionary and frontier situation than it was at home. In the field practical need required pragmatic solutions. Eventually the discrepancy could also influence the gender hierarchies within the mission organisation at home. Ideology had to be reformulated to fit the new reality. In her work on Swedish women missionaries, Karin Sarja defines three levels in the missionary organisation that, to varying degrees, were characterised by patriarchal hierarchy and female subjection.[25] These levels, the central management 'back home', the mission station 'out in the field' and the missionary conference, are to be found in most Protestant missions.[26] Sarja argues that precisely because of these several layers, women missionaries had certain opportunities to gain space and influence. The geographical distance between headquarters in Stockholm or Helsinki and the mission fields in Madagascar or the Natal province, with only slow means of communication, also meant that there was a discrepancy between the ideal of gender roles and real life. While work and space in theory were strictly defined according to gender, in practical terms all churches had to be a great deal more flexible in the missionary and frontier situation than they were at home. Here practical needs created pragmatic solutions. Such flexibility could only redound to the advantage of those who at home were deprived of much opportunity to express or assert themselves.

---

[24] Line Nyhagen Predelli, *Contested Patriarchy and Missionary Feminism: The Norwegian Missionary Society in Nineteenth Century Norway and Madagascar*, Unpublished Ph.d. thesis, University of Southern California, 1998, 272-283.

[25] Karin Sarja *Ännu en syster till Afrika* ('Another sister to Africa'), Studia Missionalia Svecana, Uppsala 2002, 316-329.

[26] Robert Bickers and Rosemary Seton, 'Introduction' in Bickers and Seton (eds.), 5-8.

Class was another factor that was decisive in women missionaries' ability to influence their own position. Social class and financial freedom were important factors that influenced women's latitude. An aristocratic class background and financial independence allowed the Swedish missionary Hedvig Posse to ignore many of the boundaries that existed for other missionaries in the Swedish Church's Mission to South Africa. Moreover, for women from the elite, a calling to mission work could be a way out of a restricted existence. Unmarried women from the upper classes had to care for ageing parents and after their death assist their female relatives with housework in their homes. Hedvig Posse´s decision to become a missionary can be regarded as a resourceful choice at a time in her life when she was economically as well as socially independent.[27]

Caroline Mary Defflis Thackeray is another example of a wealthy, single woman from a' good' family, who made a career out of mission life. She was handpicked by Edward Steere, Bishop of Zanzibar (1874–1882), to head the St Mary's School for Girls at Mbweni, Zanzibar in 1877. The school was established by the Universities Mission to Central Africa (UMCA) in 1873, to cater for children of freed slaves and orphaned girls taken straight from the slave dhows. While being freed from their enslavement, these people still were seen as the lowest of the low. Miss Thackery's school 'restored them back to humanity'.[28] Thackery was a wealthy woman and founded part of the school building by her own means and she run the school herself for twenty-five years. Her family background, close relations to Bishop Steere, and long-time standing at Zanzibar (she lived there for 49 years) made Miss Thackeray a highly respected and influential person in the mission community and among the local population.[29]

The UMCA missionaries at Zanzibar were especially keen to educate the young women 'in hope that they would provide good Christian wives for the (male) seminarists'. The best pupils were trained as teachers to be sent to the African mainland to help run mission stations there. The girls who were not 'academically minded' were taught useful skills: needlework, patchworking and traditional plaited mats of strips of dyed palm leaves which were used as 'seats, curtains and sheets for the

---

[27] Karin Sarja, 'The Missionary Career of Hedvig Posse 1887-1913', in Okkenhaug 2003, 110-142.

[28] Flo Liebst, *Zanzibar: Hisotry of the Ruins at Mbweni* Zanzibar 1992, 31-41.

[29] *Ibid.*, 51.

living and as palls to wrap the uncoffined dead'. They also did field work. These were skills that would be useful for the girls when they left the school and had to cater for themselves in a society in which they had no standing as freed slaves and Christians. The UMCA strategy was thus characteristic of the two key motifs in European as well as American Protestant mission activity: *an emphasis on direct evangelicalism and an emphasis on the civilising activities thought necessary for making evangelicalism more effective.*[30] Both received equal emphasis in late 19th and early 20th century mission thinking. The twin concern for evangelicalism and social change was reflected both in the number of mission personnel engaged in direct preaching and teaching of the Bible and in the considerable proportion of mission resources committed to institutions dedicated to concrete social change. A chief agent for this anticipated social transformation would be the education of women. Education became the most widespread and effective form of women missionary activity and was seen as the primary avenue for social change. Girls' schools were the best way of getting access to the female half of the population for the purpose of evangelisation. Besides teaching local girls and women hygiene and child care among other things, education thus played a central role in the proselytising itself. The education of women would besides provide Christian wives for the native Christian workers also *subvert the very foundations of 'heathen' society and would catalyze the profound social changes needed to accompany broad conversion to Christianity.*[31]

In 19th century Europe education was considered a *means of both social control and individual betterment.*[32] One way of securing that both these aspects were taken care of was the system of boarding schools. This principle was adopted by many missionary societies and transferred to various 'mission fields'. In general, Protestant missionaries were eager to found boarding schools and especially boarding schools for girls, *in hopes that more sustained and pervasive influence of the teachers would result in more effective evangelism and the formation of 'Christian Character'.*[33] Kumari Jayawardena has found the same strategy in her study of Methodist boarding schools for girls in Sri Lanka, where the students were seldom

---

[30] *Ibid.*, 191. Caroline Thackeray was a cousin of the author William M Thackeray.
[31] D L Robert *American Women in Mission: A Social History of Their Thought and Practice*, Macon, Georgia, 1997, 82-3.
[32] J N Burstyn *Victorian Education and the Ideal of Womanhood*, London, 1980, 11.
[33] Hill Lindley, 81.

allowed leave from the school, because they should be kept away from heathen influence until old enough to form a steady *Christian character.*[34] The same argument is found in Palestine where the Anglican Jerusalem and East Mission (J&EM) established a boarding school for girls. This was an opportunity to influence young Arab women, since this was seen as the primary arena in which the new Christian woman would be created; *the gem of all the future hope is the education of girls—education in its broadest, deepest meaning—the building of character far more than mind; the training that gives them a higher aim and a greater scope than the last generation knew.*[35]

Missionary feminism

The position of women in different cultures was commonly used by Western observers as an indicator of the general status of a society. Most female reformers of the 19th century believed that *the guarantor of social progress, the agent of civilisation, was woman herself.*[36] Western missionaries were committed to effecting a substantial change in the social norms affecting women. Among the majority of missionaries in India, for example, this commitment was reflected in a rhetoric that stressed women's low status in Indian society and urged conversion to Christianity as a means of raising women's status.[37] In the mission discourse much emphasis was put on the issue of solidarity between the 'mission sisters' in the home country, 'the serving sisters' in the field and the sisters 'out there', i. e. the local women. This sympathy for the local women's situation is part of what has labelled 'missionary feminism'. Included in the concept

---

[34] Kumary Jayawardena, *The White Woman's Other Burden: Western Women and South Asia During British Rule*, London and New York, 1995, 37.

[35] Jerusalem and East Mission papers, St Antony's College Middle East Archives, Oxford, (StAp) *Bible Lands* III, 1908, 70-73. This report from the headmistress Emmeline Woodhouse, shows the daily schedule of the St Mary's: *By 7 o'clock the girls are dressed and have done a good deal of housework. Prayers at 7.30. The remainder of the housework is finished before 9 o'clock, when they go to Matins at S. George's church. Lessons are over by 4 o'clock. Three days a week girls go for one hour walk; the other three days they play in the garden. Eveningsong: 6.00. They all go into the Oratory to say their Prayers before going to the dormitories.*
Bible Lands IV, 1911, 26. Article by Bishop Blyth, StAp.

[36] A M Burton, 'The White Woman's Burden: British Feminists and the "Indian Woman", 1865-1915', in Chauduri and Strobel (eds.), 139.

[37] Flemming, 'A New Humanity: American Missionaries' Ideals for Women in North India, 1870-1930', (1992) 194.

are such elements as the improvement of women's social conditions, extension of women's social and religious roles, and the underscoring of women's value as human beings on a par with men.[38]

Is it possible for women from one race or ethnic group to promote effectively reforms or institutions designed to modify or improve the conditions of women of another race or ethnic group in a colonial society that embodies such a pervasive dominant-subordinate power structure?[39] Thus Barbara Ramusack formulates one of the essential questions in the debate on Western women as social reformers and missionaries in the non-Western world. Her analytical categories *cultural missionary, maternal imperialist* and *feminist ally* have been adapted by several historians who focus on Western social reformers' and missionaries' efforts to promote social reforms within an imperial relationship.

According to Ramusack's definitions, the 'cultural missionaries' wanted to transfer Western models of social and political improvement for women to the colonies, while the 'maternal imperialists' saw the indigenous women as immature daughters who needed socialisation in order to reach their adult rights and responsibilities.[40] These two categories tend to overlap and Ramusack herself ends up preferring to incorporate the 'cultural missionaries' within the term 'maternal imperialists.' This as a female counterpart to the paternalistic autocracy that characterised British political imperialism in India, which was justified as the long-term preparation of child-like Indians for self-government. The third category, 'feminist allies' were women whose personalities and skills made them able to understand and sympathise with the local women and who created institutional and personal alliances in order to achieve improved conditions. An individual woman might, however, embody two or all three of these categories.[41]

---

[38] Nyhagen Predelli (1998), 298-336, and Mikaelsson, 31-53.

[39] Barbara Ramusack, 'Cultural Missionaries, Maternal Imperialists, Feminist Allies: British Women Activists in India, 1865-1945', in N Chauduri and M Strobel (eds.), *Western Women and Imperialism: Complicity and Resistance*, Bloomington and Indianapolis, 1992, 119-136.

[40] *Ibid.*, 120. Ramusack defines 'cultural missionaries' as *women who preached the gospel of women's uplift based on models evolved in England.*

[41] The white woman as female imperialist is also the theme of Antoinette Burton, who writes about middle class Victorian feminists, who were engaged in social work in India. Burton argues that identification with Britain's empire was implicit in a variety of middle-class feminist programs. The sense of national and racial superiority based on Britain's imperial status was an organizing principle of Victorian culture, and the Victorian women activists identified their cause with British imperialism. A Burton, 'The White Woman's Burden:

World Christianity: politics, theology, dialogues

The usefulness of the term 'maternal imperialist' as an analytical category is questioned by Jayawardena, who argues that the term 'maternal imperialist' tends to homogenise the experience of the Western women.[42] She is concerned with female missionary's motivations, which she identifies as a concept of global duties and obligations towards women in other countries. Unlike Burton, Jayawardena argues that there was a genuine empathy with and wish to elevate the status of indigenous women. In her study of missionaries and social and political reformers in South Asia, Jayawardena shows that, for example, female missionaries´ work for women reflected awareness about women's problems.[43] These women would be 'feminist allies' according to Ramusack's categories. It was the individual woman's *personality and skills* that enabled her to understand the local women's situation. Jayawardena argues that the strong, independent, often single women who became important missionaries were feminists in their own way.[44]

Feminism and mission, or 'religious feminism' is also the theme of Gulnar Eleanor Francis-Dehqani, whose research is based on Protestant women missionaries in Iran in the period 1869-1934. Francis-Dehqani argues that these women missionaries can be seen as 'feminists'. However, this was not because of their achievements in improving the status of local women. On the contrary, the missionary women improved their own situation at the expense of the local women: her conclusion is that

British Feminists and "The Indian Woman", 1865-1915' in Chaudhuri and Strobel, 1992, 137-157.

[42] Jayawarden, 22-29.

[43] *Ibid.*, 25.

[44] *Ibid.* The term 'feminism' has various implications, and has a different meaning today than in the nineteenth and first part of the 20th century. Jayawardena as well as Allison Wilke, who has looked at nationalist Arab women and feminism in the 1930s, are both concerned with the importance of understanding 'feminism' in its historical and geographical contexts. Jayawardena defines feminism as a consciousness of injustices based on gender hierarchy, and a commitment to change, linking women's issues and imperialism. See Ida Blom, 'Feminism and Nationalism in the Early Twentieth Century: A Cross-Cultural Perspective', *Journal of Women's History*, Vol. 7 No. 4, 1995, 81-94, and Karen Offen, 'Defining Feminism: A Comparative Historical Approach', *Signs* 1988 vol. 14, no. 1, 119-157. While the individualist feminist tradition stress individual human rights, relational feminism emphasise women's rights as *women* (defined principally by their childbearing and/or nurturing capacities) and the idea that women are fundamentally different from and even superior to men. This superiority has been linked to the role as mothers and housewives. The *equality in difference* aspect of relational feminism is interesting in regards to for example 19th century Middle Eastern society, where the family in an extended sense is the unit which society is structured around.

these missionaries undoubtedly forwarded the public position of British women and can, therefore, take their place in the historical feminist movement. However, their success was based upon an undermining of the egalitarianism that is the essence of feminism in its search towards equality for all women. For as they expanded their possibilities for western women, they defined themselves in relation to Persian women whom they considered subordinate and dependent in many respects. Therefore, the evolution of the western feminist movement advanced, whilst at the same time its progress relied upon an unequal relationship between the CMS women and the women of Iran ... [45]

The issue of race is, however, very much bound up to time and place. In South Africa in the late 1950s, Hannah Stanton, a white missionary, was jailed for her work against apartheid.[46] My own study of Anglican women missionaries in the inter-war period in Palestine shows that the racial hierarchy of the Church Missionary Society was challenged and rejected. The following example from inter-war Palestine is given in detail, since race is such a crucial issue in the mission encounter. In addition, as Fiona Bowie, co-editor of one of the path-breaking anthologies on women and mission argues: *Although broad patterns do emerge, each context is different. It is in detailed examination of particular missionary encounters that the authentic experience of women is revealed and their presence made visible.*[47]

While Ellen Fleischmann argues that the British attitudes about Muslims and Christians during the Mandate were *oddly racialized—they considered these two groups and the Jews as 'races'*,[48] Billie Melman maintains that Western women (and men) did not simply import notions of race to a directly ruled colonial subject. They negotiated between prejudice and a multifarious social and cultural structure already found in the Middle East.[49] The evangelical writers in Melman's study described their relations

---

[45] G E Francis-Dehqani, *Religious Feminism in an Age of Empire: CMS Women Missionaries in Iran, 1869-1934*, CCSRG Monograph Series 4, University of Bristol, 2000, 7. See also M Kosambi and J Haggis, 'Reconstructing Femininities: Colonial Intersections of Gender, Race, Religion and Class', *Feminist Review* no 65, Summer 2000, 1-4.

[46] Deborah Gaitskell, 'Female Faith and the Politics of the Personal: Five Mission Encounters in Twentieth-Century South Africa', *Feminist Review* no 65, Summer 2000, 68-91.

[47] Fiona Bowie, 'Introduction' in *Women and Missions: Past and Present, Anthropological and Historical Perceptions*, (eds.) F Bowie, D Kirkwood and S Ardener, Oxford, 1993, 18.

[48] Ellen Fleischmann, comment in Bergen 1999. There are really no preconceived conceptions of different 'races' in the Middle East, since intermarriage and conversion among different peoples have long historic roots going back to the early Islamic conquest.

[49] Melman, xxviii.

with Christian and Jewish women in Palestine as a 'mother- and daughter'-relation, which combined the idea of protective care with that of parental authority. In Victorian Britain the metaphor of motherhood was typically applied to relations between middle-class reformers and philanthropists and working-class women. In the Middle Eastern context, the mother–daughter metaphor acquired novel meanings: *The female relationship of protection and deference replaces the patriarchal construct typical of the oriental family and society in general. The evangeliser thus replaces the biological father and the religious mentor.*[50]

This hierarchical relationship was also typical of the pre-World War Anglican missionary's relations to the Palestinian (Christian Arab) teachers. The English women were not only 'mothers', they had also taken on the paternal authority of the employer, denying the Arab teachers their personal names and giving them the meanest duties: *Previously the British staff had always been addressed by their surnames, and collectively referred to as 'The Ladies', and the ladies had done few, if any, playground duties. The Palestinian staff, on the other hand, had been addressed as 'Miss Kareemeh' or Miss Rosie' without a surname, and had been referred to as 'the teachers', and they had done all the playground duties.* [51]

The pioneer Mabel Warburton, headmistress of the British Syrian Mission's Training College from 1901-1914, and founder of the Jerusalem Girls' College in Jerusalem after World War I, had sufficient authority to initiate a lasting change in the relations between European and 'native' teachers. This difference between the pre-World War One missionaries and the new generation is explicitly expressed by a younger teacher, S P Emery[52] who clearly defined herself as different from the old generation: *During that first year Miss Warburton had modernised some customs which the 'pre-war' missionaries had taken for granted. ... Miss Warburton swept all this away, at a memorable staff meeting. From now on, all members of staff would be addressed in the same way, with surnames, not Christian names, and all would take their due part in school duties. It was a real step forward, and was much appreciated by everybody on our staff, though it met with criticism from some country schools, where the old ways died hard.*[53]

---

[50] *Ibid.*, 203.
[51] Emery papers, 2/4, StAP, 21.
[52] S P Emery later became principal at the English High School for Girls in Haifa, also run by the Jerusalem and East Mission.
[53] Emery Papers, 2/4, StAP, 21.

The Church Missionary Society's school headed by a Miss McNeile at Bethlehem was one example of a mission school where the racial stratification was kept; English teachers were *Ladies* while the Palestinians were *teachers*. During Christmas 1919 Emery stayed there and was surprised by this division. The revolutionary aspect of the Girls' College in Jerusalem in regards to keeping a low national profile and introducing the same titles for the all nationalities is seen by Emery's indignation at a missionary committee meeting six years later, when she was still teaching at the Jerusalem Girls' College. The issue was to prepare statements on 'the missionary—his personal life and demeanour, in relation to non-Christians', a topic Emery felt strongly about: *I got thoroughly worked up about the way English people, missionaries and others, treat Palestinians on their staffs. These get treated either as perfect beings, or else much oftener, as rather stupid underlings. In our school we assume all to be equal, that is, the junior English staff and the junior Arabs are equally junior, and when we meet together each of us has a right to her opinion. Ours is the only household in the country where that is so, I am afraid. The reverse does untold harm. In other places only English staff attend staff-meetings, and the Palestinians are simply issued orders. The result is that the local staffs are often discontented and disloyal in their work. However, perhaps we will reform the situation.*[54]

During her time as Principal at the Anglican English High School in Haifa, Emery tried to follow these ideals of equal relations between the non-English and English teachers. A practical and visible start was to revise the practice of playtime duties: *I (...) made a list of staff playground duties, and as I was accustomed to in Jerusalem I gave all the members of staff equal duties. This was an innovation, and the British members of staff complained that they had never done playground duties, and Haifa was very hot. The new plan was accepted, but reluctantly.*[55]

The pre-war missionary generation's prejudices and attitudes to the 'local' population were also found in the British community that came to Palestine after 1918. In dealings with the Arab population, many of the career officials *had a sense of mission and an implicit faith in the psychological ascendancy they derived from knowledge, a knowledge which seemed all the more powerful because it was believed to be unilateral.*[56] One British teacher gives the same description of the British community relations

[54] Emery Papers, 2/4, StAP, 75, 10.5.1925.
[55] Emery papers , 2/4, StAP, 136.
[56] K Tidrick, *Heart-Beguiling Araby*, London, 1981, 207.

with the 'local population' in Jerusalem. Despite being determined to *avoid the harsh segregation, which was rife in Egypt, (...) some of our colleagues believed this doctrine more in theory than in practice.*[57]

During the 1930s a former Jerusalem Girls' College student was teaching at the British Community School, mainly for children of British missionaries and government officials, and run by the Anglican College. She was rejected by some of the parents because she was half Arab, but she kept her job.[58] Thus Warburton's girls' college seemed to be more progressive than the British Mandate community, which has been described as governed by a *coherent imperial ethos that enjoyed attitudes of superiority and prescribed rigid, socially approved behaviours for virtually all contingencies.*[59]

Mission legacy

As education for girls and young women was one of the main areas of activity, it has been used as a central indicator of the legacy of Christian missionaries. While Ellen Fleischmann who has looked at American women missionaries in Ottoman Syria argues that *missionaries were largely responsible for merely 'modernising' the domestic dimension of Middle East women's identity,*[60] Fatma Hassan Al-Sayegh in her study of American women missionaries in early 20th-century Persian Gulf region, argues that the missionary schools were a *landmark in female education* in the tradition-bound societies of the Arabian Gulf.[61] Women missionaries had a far-reaching impact and were among the most effective agents of cultural change. New ideas of female higher education, employment and social liberation and equality touched the lives of many Gulf women, and contributed much to their social and cultural transformation.[62]

---

[57] H and N Bentwich's Archive, A 255/47, Israeli State Archives. H Bentwich Diary, 12 (Unpublished).

[58] E Mead in interview with Okkenhaug, Kingham, 1.2.1996.

[59] A J Sherman, *Mandate Lives: British Lives in Palestine 1918-48*, New York, 1997, 33.

[60] Ellen Fleischmann, 'Our Moslem Sisters: women of Greater Syria in the eyes of American Protestant missionary women' in *Islam and Christian-Muslim Relations*, Vol. 9, No. 3, 1998, 319.

[61] F Hassan al-Sayegh, 'American Women Missionaries in the Gulf: agents for cultural change', *Islam and Christian-Muslim Relations*, Vol. 9, No. 3, 1998, 346.

[62] *Ibid.*, 340.

Jayawardena, whose study is by far the most thorough on the subject, goes even further and maintains that the women missionaries' *lasting contribution was their creation of modern schools for girls, which imparted a good liberal education, including a concern about women's status.*[63] Despite the negative aspects of religious intolerance, racial arrogance, cultural conformist and eurocentrism of the missionary project, missionary education was a key factor in the emancipation of local women.[64]

While mission policy as a medium for cultural change has been acknowledged, Al-Sayegh points to a understudied side of the missionary encounter: the extent to which missionaries were themselves altered by their own experiences. The simple beliefs that were part of the missionary's intellectual equipment gave way to deeper understanding as they got to know the language and the local population as individuals. Al-Sayegh argues that despite racist attitudes and ethnocentrism, women missionaries won the respect of the local people and that there was an inter-cultural experience that altered both sides.[65] This tendency is also found among Anglican women teachers in Palestine, who became life-long friends with some of their Arab colleagues and students.[66]

Another study by Eleanor Doumato of women missionaries in the Middle East i.e. American Protestants in the Persian Gulf area concludes, however, differently and highlights the 'outsider' aspect of the missionary. Despite many years' experience, knowledge of language and local conditions, the missionaries did not have a personal relationship with the people. Doumato does not find any traces of reciprocity implicit in equal relationships.[67]

While Fleischmann maintains that a majority of the American women missionaries in Syria lacked a sense of history, from 1880 till the 1940s, international politics and Arab nationalism were not an issue in their writings,[68] Jayawardena shows that none of the Western women in

---

[63] Jayawardena 1995, 262.

[64] *Ibid.*, 262.

[65] Hassan al-Sayegh, 347.

[66] I-M Okkenhaug *'The quality of heroic living, of high endeavour and adventure': Anglican Mission, Women and Education in Palestine, 1888-1948* Brill, Leiden 2002, 173-197.

[67] Eleanor Abdella Doumato, 'Receiving the Promised Blessing: missionary reflections on Ishmael's (mostly female) descendants', *Islam and Christian-Muslim Relations* Vol. 9, No. 3, 1998, 335.

[68] Fleischmann 1998, 318.

South Asia could ignore the basic issue of national liberation. Many of them supported gradual reforms and visualised a benevolent British Empire where women would be liberated. The rising nationalism in India and Ceylon, especially after the 1920s, led some Christian missions to become more flexible, trying to adjust to demands for self-rule.[69] The same can be seen in Palestine in the inter-war period, when female missionaries actively sided with the Arab nationalist cause against their own British government.[70]

Conclusion

This essay is an attempt to shed light on some aspect of the many-faceted issue of women and mission. Clearly factors like national background, religious and social conditions 'in the mission field' and denominational background influenced the relationship between women missionaries and local women. The individual woman missionary, her personal religiousness and educational and social background, also influences this encounter. The women receiving Western missions and the implicit Protestant ideal of womanhood has only recently began to write their histories. Even so, it is possible to say that women missionaries were role models for the local girls, who saw the opportunities mission offered, but adopted and accommodated the Western, Christian female ideal to suit their own needs and societies. While conversion was common in Africa, especially among women, in the Middle East proselytising was almost impossible. Even so, the various forms of education offered by mission organisations were to a high degree utilised in both areas, and in both Jerusalem and Kampala female missionaries were among the first to work towards university education for local girls.

The British women missionaries taught us 'empowerment' before the word was invented, claims Lydia, a former student of the Gayaza High School in Uganda. After graduation the teachers insisted that she should study art at the University in Kampala, and Lydia followed their advice. Besides raising her family she has worked as a teacher for many years.

---

[69] *Ibid.*, 32.
[70] Okkenhaug 2002, 173-213.

Lydia is also famous for her batik prints and has employed a tailor who makes beautiful clothing after her design.[71] Like the first girls attending Gayaza a hundred years earlier, for Lydia and her co-students Western mission represented new possibilities in their roles as women.

---

[71] Interview with Okkenhaug, Kampala, February 2001.

CHURCHES AS GUARDIANS OF THE PUBLIC SPHERE

Ian Linden

The 20th century has been described as the century of the Self. From the impact of Freud's ideas in psychoanalysis to the use of St Ignatius' spiritual exercises in religious retreats, from the influence of post-modernism to the biochemistry of the brain, there was a sustained focus on 'me, my, and mine'. The idea of being a person came repeatedly under sustained threat. The 'I', the 'acting subject' was threatened by dissolution, whether in the utter helplessness of Hitler's concentration camps or as an intellectual by-product of Freud and French philosophy. At the same time, the communal 'we', socialised belonging to a group or a community, was never more in question. The Holocaust and the threat of nuclear war hung over the latter half of the century, both terrible symbols of the power of the communal in nationality and ideology to bring about mass annihilation.

In defence at this tortured lurch towards nihilism, taken up into the framework of international law in the UN Charter of Human Rights and its protocols, came the assertion of human rights as the contemporary resolution of the clash between the collective—notably Nation, Party, Religion—and the individual. The individual has inalienable rights or entitlements, emerged from the shadow of the Second World War as the manner in which 'modernity' said 'never again' and thereby found a way to talk about ethics through law. It seemed a hopeful escape from the dialectic of despair. Indeed 'modernity'—an artificial construct of modernisation theory that saw human development as the enlargement of human freedoms and choice after totalitarianism—defined itself principally as the attribute of those using this language.

The core list of what human beings may fairly expect to enjoy in their lives, their human rights, describes what growing numbers around the world believe is necessary for their well-being—however variously 'well-being' may be conceived. They lie at the heart of humanist faith and hope in betterment. Or, if we cannot manage to agree with the list in a formal assent of the intellect, denial of these rights to children, transgression of these rights for the young and vulnerable, adds a necessary emotional impetus that facilitates the acceptance of 'rights language'. Denial of the items agreed by states as properly included on this list, or their transgression, defines the nearest secular thought comes to the religious concept of sin.

In short, human rights are the necessary condition for the human happiness, indeed, they are the dominant contemporary account of what you need to be happy. Human rights language has thus become the principal way in which modernity talks about how to be happy, about what is usually meant by ethics. This may arguably not yet be a universal language—there are other ways to talk about how to be happy—but it is clearly promoted as such, and has striven to be so since its codification in United Nations protocols.

It goes without saying that human rights language became an important political weapon in the hands of the First World against the Second during the Cold War. The USA, for example, often used other states' human rights violations as a propaganda weapon in the struggle for what became know as 'the moral high ground', which, like any other high ground was worth occupying in order to attack the enemy more effectively. But to describe this process as the 'politicisation' of human rights might incorrectly give the impression that human rights talk might lack the dimension of a political project. Human rights language, in as much as it is a modern way of talking about ethics, is a discourse about human relatedness, about how we are in the world with each other, about what politics means. Amnesty International, of course, has been the most political example of human rights talk but only in that it has expressed an absolute faith in a check-list of rights as the dominant project of human flourishing and well-being. Not, it should be underlined because it has shown a bias for any existing political group or party.

When I first undertook commissioned work for the Catholic Institute for International Relations in the late 1970s, they had just published a booklet 'The Man in the Middle' with the Rhodesian Justice and Peace Commission. It detailed human rights violations by the Rhodesian Front forces and was in many ways an archetypal document of catholic modernity. The title expressed the neutral innocence of those caught between two contending political projects and Smith's brutal quest to retain white supremacy through the land and take power. How many 'men' were at the time 'in the middle' was a moot point. More important was that human rights language provided a semi-protected way of entering political debate and advocacy. The title in the charged atmosphere of the late 1970s sought to gainsay any specific political project though the publishers, CIIR, were clearly in favour of democracy and black majority rule. 'Semi-protected' in that a British judge ruled against Amnesty International being given charitable status because the overriding nature of its work was the 'promotion' of human rights.

The document was intended to discredit the Smith regime and to be a counter to the Smith propaganda machine. It was only later in 'Rhodesia to Zimbabwe' series that CIIR set out what specific changes in a number of sectors, education and agriculture for example, would in its opinion be required for well-being and flourishing in Zimbabwe, and put them out for dialogue. I remember at the time chafing at the limitations of human rights language. How did you move from a pose of God's eye neutrality which The Man in the Middle sought to achieve to the difficult task of talking to other interlocutors about what might become of Zimbabwe—or Namibia and South Africa come to that? How did you take up a place of neutrality between the torturer and the tortured? There seemed something inherently dishonest about it all. 'The truth never lies', as Christopher Hitchens once said, 'but if it did it would lie somewhere in between'.

My feeling was that two 'levels' existed: a 'human rights level' of commitment, with clean hands, and a 'higher' political level of commitment which meant taking sides, taking risks and proposing futures. The latter was surely where Dietrich Bonhoeffer had ended up in Nazi Germany. But I was not sure how you moved logically from one to the other, or how they related, except by an insight into the necessity of Christian political commitment with all its dangers, betrayals and disappointments.

A deeper look at the core concept of human rights proved more disturbing. Rights turned out to be not something primarily that you 'had' as an individual, like a brain, but something that was socially recognised and realised, and you exercised as a member of a society and product of human relatedness. But they emerged historically as the antithesis of the communal, as an assertion of 'mine against yours', to be precise as an absolute claim on the possibility of private property rather than a practise of shared use. Over four centuries claims of this nature slowly gained ground and proliferated most often as a consequence of social and political struggles or changes of power. The entitlements implied in such imagined inalienable endowments only made sense as a claim on somebody or some corporate legal entity. As formulated in the UN charter, this legal entity was the state.

So the question arose what happened to human rights when states ceased to exist, as in parts of Africa, or when states obviously were unable to realise a particular entitlement single-handedly, as most notably in the right to development? And what of the erosion of rights language that allowed it to be claimed that animals had rights, and that there is a 'right' to abort a Down's syndrome baby in the womb, or, come to that, a right to free health care at the point of delivery with no obligation to pay taxes to make this possible? As part of what became known—with subtle elitism—as the 'human rights community' in a rights language organisation, I found these troubling questions.

Moreover, the individualistic fit between the subject of human rights discourse and the liberal promotion of the market as the sum total of individual wills and choices was disquieting. Max Weber had been clear that political community required 'value systems ordering matters other than the directly economic disposition of goods and services'. But the 'meta-ethics' of the market had as the only value increasing the amount of choice, and the subject of choice was considered to be the autonomous 'consumer'. Where was the concept of Citizenship? Did we then no longer have a political community in a neo-liberal capitalist society?

Today it is hard to find shared value systems. This is the central problem of 'Third Way' social democratic and liberal forms of government. Freedom to choose, tolerance and respect for 'the other' are essentially formal values. They lack content and substance. They do not indicate what kind of society we would like to be living in ten years hence and why. In this sense they do not represent a political project. Indeed language indicates that the role of community as a healing word is to be sprinkled like ketchup to obscure intolerable levels of fragmentation and human isolation. People no longer 'live in community'. They choose 'lifestyles' and these lifestyles segment the market and dictated reinforcing advertising. Conduct is not right or wrong but 'appropriate' or 'inappropriate' as if it were a fashion accessory for fashionable ways of being human. 'The community' exists either as new—or old—forms of exclusive identities i.e. a particular community, or in some universal way is expressed in powerful institutions of the state such as the National Health Service with its specific values. And the former makes rights claims on the latter.

This was the world in which Margaret Thatcher could make the confident statement that society did not exist, only individuals and families. But it was no less the political world in which she tellingly denounced the inertia of welfare state Britain where those with entitlements sought them from the State and were dubbed 'scroungers' for their pains. She meant, I suppose, after due allowance for her poisonous political rhetoric, that they enacted a diminished citizenship as a result of an enforced passivity. But her image of the social security recipient passively engaging with the state from behind protective glass is the microcosm of the wider liberal society in which growing areas of life cause citizens to be defined as consumers of different classes of 'goods'—understood in both the material and abstract sense—some of which are conceived of as 'realised rights'.

And this relationship of state to people has inevitably extended in the 1990s to popular views of legitimate political engagement that go beyond passivity to action. As Rowan Williams writes 'the purpose of political action, on such models, is to persuade the power-holder to honour or realise the rights of the citizen'. The problem with this model is that it transforms the political arena into the terrain of jostling claims and counter-claims made on the state, with state imagined as acting as impartial arbiter between them. The citizen enters the political terrain as bearer of sectional, sectarian, demands, and identity politics is not far behind.

In this area of conflicting claims there is no place for any radical challenge to each entitlement claim, for example, as to whether it is a social good being sought rather than the good of 'mine against yours'. Those, for example, claiming the right to three single, rather than a triple vaccination, against the serious childhood diseases, measles, mumps and diphtheria because of a unwarranted fear of the risk of autism, provide an instructive example. They are unable to heed the social consequences of their claim having been formed in a discourse of 'my good', in this case the emotive 'My baby's good', overriding any intellectual grasp of the simple social good of 'herd immunity'. Such conflicts ought to provide an opportunity for all concerned to debate society's understanding of risk and the social good, but, of course, this is precluded by the very nature of the conflict.

The same structure of political intervention applies to civil society organisations and 'pressure groups'. The problem is, of course, noted by the Right in relations to claims by trades unions but it applies to all 'interest groups' and is characteristic of modern political dialogue. This may be observed most obviously in 'rights' based conflict about abortion where debate seems deliberately to preclude a challenge to the ethical foundations of each position in favour of the emotive assertion of the starting point of each side's argument: the supremacy of the mother's autonomy and choice, or the opposing religiously-based assertions about the beginning of human life, its divine creation, and the corresponding rights of the human embryo as a potential person. This conflict is often described as a product of the clash between traditionalism and modernity, often in particular, between Catholicism and liberalism, but it is far deeper than that.

Now, the normally attributed nature of the 'traditional'—the artificial construct understood as the opposite of modernity—is that the communal, social, and traditional in important respects limit the freedom of the individual and circumscribe choice. Few living in an African village would argue that. And so far, at least, the dominant theme of many 20th-century novels. But, Rowan Williams suggests, the politics of modernity and liberalism constrain no less genuine open ended dialogue about individual and social 'goods'—as an indirect consequence of the unconstrained growth of human rights style claims on the state by contending interest groups. It is simply too risky to ask radical questions in such a mode of bargaining and litigation. As with vaccination, abortion and trades union cases the prosecution of claims for rights on the state invariably precludes a political process that enables contending parties to reach a position different from their starting point.

But an alternative political process is possible. 'Ideally this process is one of defining what is arguably good in some measure for all involved; and thus one of discovering in what ways my good is "invested" in yours,' Williams writes. Or put in another way this political process is a shared quest for how human rights discourse and common good talk might form a single language. Such would be the beginning of a genuinely Christian politics and ethics.

So if the disparate political actors did indeed wish to discover what was good for them in this sense of investment in the good of others there would be a way forward. But in the Dominican Herbert McCabe's words, a certain distortion of the nature of man is built into the capitalist culture which makes it difficult for us to recognise ourselves for what we are, to recognise, in fact, what we want. 'We can see', Herbert McCabe wrote, 'that ethics is the quest for less and less trivial forms of human relatedness. In this quest ethics points towards, without being able to define or comprehend, an ultimate medium of human communication which is beyond humanity and which we call divinity.' In other words ethics, how to be happy, is something we are predisposed to be wrong about.

Our chances of getting ethics right, Rowan Williams suggests, depends on a willingness to take the risk of participating in a political process of genuine dialogue which may take us where we might not want to go, and 'seeing the other as involved in exactly the same history of risk, error and unacknowledged need of the other as oneself'. It involves us recognising ourself in the Other and thus finding the 'I' anew through 'We'. The possibility of doing so, of course leads directly into a theological narrative, a story that involves talking about what God means and does. 'Ethics is entirely concerned with doing what you want', he wrote 'that is to say with being free. Most of the problems arise from the difficulty of recognising what we want.'

It has been necessary to engage in this rather convoluted preamble in order to underline that ethics are not a given, a neat set of rules, or even a helpful manual for assembling an acceptable form of national society or form of globalisation—though it may spin off all of these. Ethical behaviour is to be discovered in reflection and dialogue in the complex interactions of politics and economics. This requires rigorous prior demythologisation and cannot simply be read of human nature. 'It is evident', Marx wrote, 'how political economy establishes an alienated form of social intercourse as the true and original form and that which corresponds to human nature'. In consequence Churches should not be taken in by ideological accounts of what it is to be human or by any facile reading of human nature as they promote political dialogue.

If such a political engagement does begin to define a Christian response to our ethical dilemma, and thus what goes on in the public sphere today, then it follows that Churches have an enormous responsibility to promote the kind of open-ended political dialogue discussed above, and to contribute towards it. For who else will do so? Normally such dialogues only occur after intense armed conflict, as part of national peace processes, when a wounded polity trying to find a compass bearing for the future, stumbles into profound ethical debate. Often this demands first a re-evaluation of the past under the heading of a quest for the truth and reconciliation. But, if crime, drugs, marriage breakdown and single parenthood, suicide and general angst is any measure, we also live in a wounded society that does not know how to be happy, despite generally high levels of prosperity and an end to the Anglo-Irish conflict in the north of Ireland. So, such processes should be normative, not confined to small think-tanks, and they cannot confine themselves to interlocutors drawn only from inside a nation-state. The nature of contemporary identities—indeed the identity of the Churches—is an amalgam of local and global so that 'inside' and 'outside' has greatly reduced significance.

The corollary of this approach is that the Churches only have their tradition of theology to bring to the party and their convenor power. This should dictate the nature of their intervention into the political space and the structures they require to undertake it. Their role in relation to the public sphere is largely to create it. What Gandhi said of Western civilisation applies to democracy as a mode of communication: 'it would be a good idea'. The boast of democracies is to sustain such a space in parliaments and mass media. But it is evident that the space for serious political debate—rather than interest group claims—about, for example, equality, multiculturalism, our relationship with the stranger, globalisation and the way we make our living, and indeed religion, with an intent to change and implement rather than just talk, is in reality small and shrinking. This is an enormous challenge to the Churches who either cling to a modest and diminishing purchase on the legislative process in the House of Lords, the Anglicans, or denounce and propose from the periphery, and sometimes privately from the centre, the Catholic bishops.

Such a form of guardianship of the public sphere poses a similar but greater challenge to a significant part of contemporary Islam. 'As for (those) who consider Islam separate from government and politics' the Ayatollah Khomeini wrote 'it must be said to these ignoramuses that the Holy Qu'ran and the Sunnah of the Prophet contains more rules regarding government and politics than in other matters'. It would be difficult to disagree him on this matter. But this makes it far more difficult for Muslims to consider the human enterprise of building a just and peaceful society in obedience to God as involving dialogue that is fully open to the other and to risk. If the communism of the early Christian community is ignored, Christianity has no outline plan for a just society, and the 'building of the kingdom' is open in hope to the future. Catholic social teaching offers pointers, concepts, denounces aberrations and injustices, but provides no 'rules'. This is not to say that Christians bring to Christian-Muslim dialogue a unique openness. Far from it. They bring a considerable and sometimes unacknowledged baggage from 'Western' political thought together with their particular set of theologies.

As the Iranian revolution illustrated, one form of guardianship of the public sphere that may emerge from a Qu'ran-centred faith is for legislation to be tested against Islamic orthodoxy (and orthopraxis) by religious, legal specialists, *vilayat-i faqih*. The work of the Council of Guardians in Iran presupposed the absolute agency of the Prophet of God in legislative matters, though in reality a superior body, the High Council for the Discernment of Interests, had to be set up to resolve disputes between the Guardians and the Majlis, parliament, by Ayatollah Khomenei. So even in such a theocratic dispensation two 'interest groups' emerged with claims on the state, those with a vision of popular sovereignty based in the people and those who saw sovereignty vested in God alone. The Iranian constitution attempts to harmonise the two. The idea that government could exercise power 'only within the bounds of divine statute' was reversed by the Ayatollah Khomenei himself in favour of the creation of an absolutist state under his direction.

It is ironical that Islamist thought with its clear political alternative to western secular societies and varied approaches to guardianship of the public political space, features most notably as 'the other' for non-Muslims today. There were, of course, many reformist Muslim thinkers before the 1980s who were attempting to engage with the best of 'Western' political thought and practice rather than escape from it. But they do not catch the headlines and they cannot be described as in the ascendancy today.

For to some extent, we can recognise a certain brand of Catholicism in the prescriptive, closed and non-dialogical approach of, for example, the early days of the Iranian revolution. But can we recognise what it was saying to our own society? That we have seriously debilitating moral problems including that our international relations are those of domination and irresponsible power, and that our religious leaders have not got much idea of what to do about it? The answer is not to go back in time and have Councils of Guardians sitting plumb in the middle of our political space and closing it down—there are plenty of politicians doing that right now—but more modest councils on the periphery opening it up. It is time the Churches structured their activity ecumenically in such a way as to make this possible and effective.

MICHEL DE CERTEAU:
A POST-MODERN PERSPECTIVE
ON EARLY MODERN CHRISTIANITY
Peter Gallagher SJ

The Jesuit historian Michel de Certeau (1925-1986) concerned himself with, among other topics, the work of certain spiritual writers from the beginning of the modern period: Favre, Surin and Labadie. His discussion of these authors and their religious itineraries took on, gradually, a post-Modern flavour. Their sincere Christianity notwithstanding, he portrays the three as retreating from their first confidence in the 'grand narrative' of Ignatian spirituality. These Jesuits, in different ways, according to de Certeau, lost their faith in a mechanistic understanding of the *Spiritual Exercises* of St Ignatius Loyola. They stopped believing in the *Exercises* as a mechanism for bringing about the individual's self-giving to God, the conquest of the passions and the conforming of the thoughts, feelings and imagination to the teaching of the Church. The case histories of Favre, Surin and Labadie also reinforced in Michel de Certeau a scepticism about the persistence of the self which might be alleged to experience spirituality. He presents his three authors as coming, implicitly, to share, in different degrees, this sceptical view. The philosophers of their day were busily describing a self which was accessible and powerful. The spirituality in which they were trained, and in which they trained others, also purported to give access to the self and to empower it. De Certeau portrays the three spiritual writers as baffled by the fugitive character of the subject and disappointed by the weakness and fragility of the self.

The early-modern period is sometimes thought to have been characterized by a new confidence in the possibilities of science and technology, but de Certeau shows his three early moderns discovering limitations of the mechanism of the *Exercises*. This device can produce not self-giving but selfishness, not self-control but madness, and not religious conformity but heterodoxy. De Certeau reads back into the experience of his authors a post-Modern diffidence about the power of knowledge. The *Spiritual Exercises* are intended to promote understanding, not least of the self, but they do not always work. Even if they do confer knowledge it is not always as practical or as effective as was hoped. In addition to general doubts about perfectibility and even about the possibility of improvement, de Certeau finds in some early Modern records of spiritual experience particular hesitations about what can be achieved by the Ignatian *Exercises*.

Even if we find ourselves a little resistant to de Certeau's general conclusion that the entirety of religion, theology and spirituality can be detached from the transcendent order, and are merely strategies that shape and control certain patterns of human experience,[1] we might nevertheless be intrigued by his case-studies in which religious discourse is revealed to be less about a tension between spirit and matter, body and soul, and much more a dynamic of power and embodiment. De Certeau's historical research into mystical experience and writing in the early modern period illuminates this dynamic. Despite a biographical fallacy that too naïvely proposes *rapprochements* between the lives studied by the historian and his own life, nevertheless, there is no doubt that de Certeau invested himself to an unusual degree[2] in his research. He returned repeatedly to certain lives, and was haunted[3] by them. They were other selves for him.

A first case study by de Certeau is of Pierre Favre 1506-1546, said to be the most likeable of the founders with Ignatius Loyola of the Society of Jesus. In Favre's spiritual autobiography, the *Memoriale*, begun in 1542, de Certeau discerns a person endeavouring to describe a very particular religious experience. The quiet companion, Favre, was mainly silent about his mystical life,[4] in the absence of a better vehicle for expressing it than the language into which he had been initiated by the Ockhamist theology of the University of Paris, by his devout Savoyard upbringing and by his experience of the *devotio moderna*. Favre was a traveller and pilgrim. His itinerant Jesuit life was spent under the constant shadow of danger 'from animals, wild beasts in forests, denunciation as a spy, hunger, thirst, infested bedding and nights in the open.'[5] De Certeau considers Favre to have been a somewhat rootless person, always the stranger, and ill-at-ease amid the always customs, languages and ideas with which he was confronted by his work and travels.

---

[1] M de Certeau, *La Faiblesse de Croire*, Paris, 1987, 183-266.
[2] L Giard (ed.), *Le voyage mystique Michel de Certeau*, Paris, 1988, introduction.
[3] L Giard, 'La passion de l'altérité', in her *Michel de Certeau*, Paris, 1987, 27.
[4] De Certeau, *Bienheureux Pierre Favre Mémorial*, Paris, 1959, introduction, 39-40.
[5] *Fabri Monumenta*, Rome, 1941, 185.

Just as some philosophers try to establish the point-of-departure for metaphysics, so spiritual travellers, like Favre, are on de Certeau's account, endeavouring, by their numerous departures, to find the Other, in a new way. The pilgrim or missionary, on this view, is transporting the body to many different places partly in the hope of finding the right circumstances or context for a certain sort of departure from the self. De Certeau himself has been described as expressing his own 'desire for the Other' in a 'vast array of journeys, institutional affiliations and writings'[6] on diverse subjects. Favre and de Certeau have in common a tendency to look back and to represent even the most innovative departure as a recovery, investigation or survey of the past Favre's writings are full of expressions of nostalgia and of regret at parting: his ambition is to re-unite and to be re-united.[7] De Certeau's project was not so much nostalgic or refoundational as expressive of the hope that to revisit the mystical works of the past, with all their inhibitions and reticences, might help construct a framework for interpreting today the silence of others and the Other.

Bodily separations entail silence and breaks in communication. Language was constantly failing Favre, as he arrived in a new place where he could not make himself understood. Memory and prayer allowed him to make present to himself those others with whom he could communicate and from whom he was separated. The network of his friends and acquaintances sustained a populous inner life. 'The Spirit who can exile people from their native land can also *fill the whole surface of the earth.*'[8] Favre understood his travelling as part of a strategy of unification, which, ultimately, was preferable to stability and rootedness.[9] Difference came to seem less important to Favre as he travelled widely and noticed the similarities between people. His considerable human sympathy was enlisted especially by the inarticulate frustrations of those who were suffering.[10] The parallel movement in de Certeau himself was the desire to extend his interest in the history of cultures to ones ever more remote and different from his own.

---

[6] F C Bauerschmidt, 'The Abrahamic Voyage: Michel de Certeau and Theology', *Modern Theology* 12, 1, 1996, 4.

[7] E.g., *Fabri Monumenta*, Rome, 1941, 166.

[8] *Ibid.*, 34.

[9] *Ibid.*, 398.

[10] Pierre Favre, *Memoriale*, sections 385-6, pp. 394-5 in De Certeau's edition.

The planned journey to Jerusalem of the first companions of Ignatius can be understood, in de Certeau's analysis of Favre, as an emblem of the belief that the diversity to which, in a certain sense, incessant travelling draws attention, is not as important as the unity between different peoples, revealed by common experiences and parallel faith-commitments. De Certeau, however, in his own case 'deliberately fragments his discourse,'[11] and resists any globalising schematisation that might unify his erudite contributions to a number of intellectual disciplines in different places. By contrast, he schematises Favre's backwards and forwards journeys between Rome, Madrid and Cologne in 1536 and 1546 to illustrate what he perceives as a tension between the desire to be in places where he had friends, ease-of-access and sympathy and an opposing impulse, missionary and counter-reforming in character which took him to destinations, for example, in the Rhineland, where he was much less welcome. His prayer and apostolate were directed towards unifying, or reunifying, a divided Christendom. His personal experience was acute of the suffering which division between persons and communities could inflict. The quiet companion's written reflections on this include as much regret for the past as vision of the future.

As editor of the *Memoriale*, de Certeau similarly, sought an alternative to the violence with which the Other can sometimes be represented to the subject, the 'I', and the sort of fragmentation which turns the subject into the other. The archetypal *soixante-huitard*, Michel de Certeau saw in Favre, even twenty years before the Bastille of post-war austerity came tumbling down, the wandering prophet of harmony.[12] Just as he would one day see himself as a revolutionary plotting *la prise de la parole*,[13] so de Certeau's Favre is an often silent traveller towards an utopian destination in which the European subject could tolerate not only the differences between the self and others, but also between the self and the great Other. De Certeau's own pilgrimage was a search for a place where 'the fragile and necessary boundary between a past object and a current praxis begins to waver',[14] and where the Other can be met

---

[11] F C Baurerschmidt, *op. cit.*, 5.

[12] See J Kristeva, *Strangers to Ourselves*, Paris, 1989, translated by L S Roudiez, New York, 1991, ch. 4, 'the therapeutics of exile and pilgrimage', 87.

[13] M de Certeau, *La prise de parole et autres écrits politiques*, Paris, 1968, 1994, translated by T Conley, as *The Capture of Speech and other political writings*, Minneapolis, 1997.

[14] M de Certeau, *L'Écriture de l'Histoire*, Paris, 1984, translated by T Conley, as *The Writing of History*, New York, 1988, 36.

as truly other and not just as some alter-ego 'forced into a fragmenting passivity.'[15]

'Spaces' 'maps' and 'tours' abound in the collection of de Certeau's work, published in 1980 as *The Practice of Everyday Life*,[16] which might also serve as the general title for his philosophy and spirituality. This language of place and location (and a parallel and darker discourse of dislocation) was anticipated in his exegesis of Favre's memoirs. The early Jesuit's missionary geography was presented as a sort of image of his understanding of the movements of spirits. The quiet companion found his destinations embodied in shrines of the saints, and in other holy places. The self, the *subiectum*,[17] was described as being in easy intimacy with spiritual forces. There were certain echoes of all of this in de Certeau's own life. The Jesuits had directed him towards scholarship in Europe instead of the missionary work in China or Africa which he would have preferred. He understood his vocation as implying a degree of homelessness. The Other would be encountered through a willingness, a desire, even, to be perpetually on the move. Luce Giard says that 'he had had from childhood an intense desire to 'not belong', to free himself, to overcome the limits of family, milieu, of a province and a culture, and to encounter the Other in order to be 'transformed' and 'wounded'.'[18] For de Certeau, interest began to focus less and less on the Other, abstractly conceived, and perhaps known, and more and more on a rich variety of fragmentary instances of particular 'others'. If there is violence in conceptualization, de Certeau began to want to resist it by seeking to speak of the Other only through those 'others' which and whom one might encounter, say, in walking about the city or on a railway journey. He was unsympathetic, however, to an impulse he detected in Favre to 're-locate' attention on the Other to less powerful others. There is in the *Memoriale* much less about God than about intermediaries, saints and angels.

De Certeau responded to his subject's angelogy with a certain condescension: 'Favre is very much of his time, and the range of his

---

[15] M Barnes, *Traces of the Other*, Chennai, 2000, 73.

[16] M de Certeau, *L'Invention du quotidien*, volume 1, *Arts de faire*, 1980, 1990, translated by S Rendall, as *The Practice of Everyday Life*, Berkeley, 1984.

[17] Series of allusions in the *Memoriale* for December 1542, written at Mainz, de Certeau's edition, 262-265.

[18] L Giard, 'Michel de Certeau's Heterology and the New World', *Representations*, Winter, 1991, 216.

experience clearly very limited, but the important thing is to retrieve the interior intuition which guided him in his travels, and both in his spiritual direction and his personal conduct.'[19] Yet there was perhaps something Aristotelian about wanting to explain cosmic reality by reference to superior beings, and de Certeau also suspected a Neoplatonist rationale for constructing an elaborate celestial hierarchy. He perceived these old philosophies as being a dream of reason addressed principally to people's worries, 'their obscure desires, the well-founded anxieties which haunted them, and their extreme sensitivity to invisible forces.'[20] In Favre's world witchcraft, astrology and sorcery abounded, and the pilgrim jousted with evil spirits, helped by good angels and spiritual solidarity. The quiet companion mapped out a plan of campaign, which involved the capture of both speech and silence for those Christian subjects who sought his help. The itineraries which he proposed took people to 'places' of both colloquy and mystical quiet.

The *Spiritual Exercises*, which Ignatius Loyola thought Favre the best of his first companions at giving, were the context for patterns of spiritual experience of different sorts. This experience could be expected to generate a docility, in the self, to the Spirit, which would stimulate the person making the *Exercises* towards a personal faithfulness to God, away from 'immobilization in painful narcissism'.[21] The *Memoriale* is the personal record of a subject seeking, within such patterns, the sort of interior silence which would allow the free discernment of different feelings and thoughts. It is a record of grace. De Certeau draws attention to a constant dialogue, in this work, between an 'I' and a 'You', where most often the I is a self or subject who is on the side of God, and the You is a self or soul called to some transformation such as repentance or conversion.[22] A mechanistic understanding of the *Exercises* imposed such dualistic limitations. Favre is presented by de Certeau as an active mystic with a daily and everyday experience of the living God. If the contemporary crisis of the European subject is anticipated in de Certeau's version of the life of this remarkable wanderer in early modernity it would be in Favre's experience of a long-running interior conversation between a

---

[19] M de Certeau, *Bienheureux Pierre Favre Mémorial*, Paris, 1959, introduction, 72.
[20] *Ibid.*, 50.
[21] J Kristeva, 'Europe Divided: Politics, Ethics, Religion' 1998, in her *Crisis of the European Subject*, translated by S Fairfield, New York, 2000, 160.
[22] M de Certeau, *op. cit.*, introduction, 80-82.

self, understood in relation to a transcendent and generous Other, and another more isolated, 'on-the-move' self, conceiving itself, principally, within, from some modern perspectives, a rather constricting structure of religious practice, and ways of knowing.

A second case-study by de Certeau is that of Jean-Joseph Surin 1600–1665 whose thorough spiritual education under Louis Lallemant did not prevent prolonged physical suffering after his attempts to help the diabolically possessed Ursulines of Loudun in 1634–7. The body and its problems were arguably the chief factors in his spiritual development. De Certeau edited Surin's *Guide Spirituel* [23] and his *Correspondance* and frequently alludes to him in such important works of his own as *The Mystic Fable*[24] and *La faiblesse de croire.*[25] Like Bossuet, who often quotes the *Catéchisme spirituel* 1659 and *Les Fondements de la vie spirituelle* 1667, de Certeau is not one of those readers of Surin who feel that his psychological problems raise serious questions about the reliability of his spiritual doctrine. In the early 17th century, there was a certain reaction among Jesuits and in the Church, more widely, against what were seen as the excesses of undisciplined mysticism, and Lallemant's pupils, and even the texts of their teacher, were the victims of this reappraisal.

The detachment, generosity and simplicity of spirit which are Surin's chief recommendations to any person seeking intimacy with God are perhaps the correlatives of his enthusiasm for visions, and other extraordinary phenomena of the mystical life. He veers between 'aphasia and glossolalia'.[26] Some Jesuit superiors were also concerned that intimacy or union with God should not be presented to students of the spiritual life as an end in itself, considering that service and mission were higher aims, at least in their particular calling. De Certeau again found himself in the subject of his research. Surin's efforts to find a language in which to communicate that loss of self which is the mystic's delight and sorrow, was bound to provoke anxiety in his religious superiors. They were looking to provide recruits to the order with a strong identity rooted in a certain experience of the *Spiritual Exercises* and could not be expected to smile on an educator who lapsed into silence and dwelt, when speaking at all, on the fragility of the self. De Certeau, analogously, saw himself, at least,

---

[23] Left unfinished at Surin's death, and first published in 1801.
[24] Paris, 1982, translated by M B Smith, London and Chicago, 1992.
[25] Edited by L Giard, Paris, 1987.
[26] J Ahearne, *Michel de Certeau Interpretation and its Other*, Cambridge, 1995, 112.

at first, as a believer looking for a way to express belief in a world which feels that God has become absent. Like the melancholic Surin, he thought himself cruelly limited by the narrow expectations about religious experience which were to be found among his contemporaries, both inside and outside the Christian Church.

In 1634, already bodily fragile, Surin was sent to Loudun to be one of the exorcists of Jeanne des Anges and her companions. For three years he visited the Ursulines, but did not consider that he had been able to be of much help to them. His own health never recovered from the strain under which this work placed him. For the rest of his life, nearly thirty years, he needed fairly close supervision. De Certeau traces Surin's fragility to difficulties in Lallemant's tertianship (1629-30) and to his feeling thereafter that he was on his own. 'Surin knew he was not a saintly person, but one exiled from salvation.'[27] Self-destructive impulses and a suspicion that he was hated by God accompanied all sorts of bodily and mental troubles. This was worse than the asceticism, that inscribing of religious ideals on the body, to which his initiation into religious life had inured him. His old instructor might have thought it was simply a matter of generosity. Lallemant, 1587-1635, himself a martyr to headaches and stomach cramps, encouraged heroic generosity in his pupils, who included Jean de Brébeuf, Isaac Jogues and other missionaries to North America.

The itinerant life-style of the Jesuit spiritual, with its numerous contacts, and the varied networks in which, in an earlier generation, Favre, for example, had learned to thrive, does not really seem to have suited Surin, who was not without reclusive tendencies. He felt that his training had been cut short and that he was ill-prepared for the service required. Lallemant had warned: 'We spend entire years, and often our whole lives, haggling over whether we will give ourselves totally to God.'[28] Surin's body, one might say, refused to allow the spiritual transaction to proceed in the way suggested by the teacher. Illness and confusion would thwart Surin's efforts at allowing in himself abandonment and docility to the Spirit. As de Certeau puts it, 'His defeat is already inscribed within himself by that other who nonetheless is himself and who opposes his

---

[27] M de Certeau, *Heterologies Discourse on the Other*, translated by B Massumi, Minneapolis, 1986, ch. 7, 'Surin's melancholy', 102.

[28] F Courel (ed.), *La vie at la doctrine spirituelle de Louis Lallemant*, Paris, 1959, 90.

desire.'[29] Surin experienced an intense frustration at being unable to divide the subject, that is separate radically not only from everyone and everything else but also from his own self. The 'I' could not be abstracted from the body and its ills. The 'possessed', whether in upheaval in Loudun, or in the tranquillity of the Jesuit tertianship, could not even describe the symptoms of their own malady, far less hope for a cure. Surin felt himself in solidarity with the Loudun women, and felt himself lost.

A third case study in de Certeau's anticipation, in early modernity, of the contemporary crisis of the European subject is Jean de Labadie 1610-1674. De Certeau examines the life and work of yet another nomadic Jesuit, this time, one whose spiritual itinerary took him out of the order in 1639 after fourteen years of membership, 1625-39. Labadie had been a brilliant student, and, very young, had a high reputation as preacher, teacher and spiritual guide. In this success, and in his wistfulness and utopianism, de Certeau would find yet another mirror to hold up, with fascinated curiosity, to his own life and personality. In 1637, however, Father General Vitelleschi, cautiously observing the spread of mysticism among some French Jesuits, was alarmed to hear that Labadie, then still a theology student, was living *per modum puri spiritus*. The prayer of silence which he was practicing seemed less-well adapted to the spirituality of service which the Jesuit authorities considered most suitable, even for someone very far from being a recent recruit. De Certeau points out that in just fifty years, 'the Jesuits had increased their membership tenfold, multiplied the number of their foundations, diversified their occupations, extended their influence and increased their wealth.'[30] Vitelleschi's predecessor, Claudio Aquaviva, (Superior General from 1581 until 1615) had, in de Certeau's view, adopted a more flexible view of regional variations in the Ignatian pattern, and had, incidentally, been more relaxed about the secular academic specialities taken up by his subjects.

In 1638 and 1639 at Bordeaux, Surin, with whom he had much in common, tried to help Labadie to find his place in the Jesuits, but their discussions seem to have brought the difficulties to a head and he sought dismissal from the Society. One suffering mystic was not able to rescue another. There was a resistance to ecclesiastical authority in Labadie which was not present in Surin, or, for that matter, in de Certeau, whose

---

[29] M de Certeau, *La fable mystique*, volume 1 XVIe-XVIIe siècle Paris, 1982, 1987, translated by M Smith, as *The Mystic Fable, 1 Sixteenth & Seventeenth Centuries*, Chicago, 1992, 226.
[30] *Ibid.*, 242.

close reading of the French Jesuit mystics did not move to any notable longing for martyrdom, even of the gentler sorts inflicted within the modern Church. The given reason for Labadie's departure from the Jesuits was his poor health, and, in particular, sleeplessness. Labadie worked as secular priest from 1632 until 1650 in various cities, including Bordeaux, Amiens and Toulouse. His ministry was Jansenist in temper, which seems to have been much more than mere theological anti-Jesuitry. Godly intensity of life and eucharistic temperance were the characteristics of a devotional attitude, which, nevertheless, probably owed as much to the *Spiritual Exercises* as to Port-Royal. The spiritual itinerary of Jean de Labadie was far from over, however, since in 1650, at Montauban, he embraced Protestantism and became a pastor. Resisting an attractive summons to a pulpit in London, he preferred to minister for several years in Geneva. In due course, Labadie found he wanted to reform the reformers in the direction of an even more primitive church, and founded his own ecclesial community, the Labadists, in 1669.

For three or four years the sect tried to put down roots in Holland and Denmark, where Labadie died, at Altona, in 1674. The creed of Labadism included the view that contemplation was the key to knowing God, that the scriptures were a hindrance to spiritual progress. The Labadists avoided infant baptism, devotion to the real presence and Sunday observance. De Certeau, however, was less interested in details of the content of Labadie's teaching, mystical or theological, or in the precise beliefs of his followers, as in that 'movement of perpetual departure'[31] which constituted his religious 'style' or practice. Religious practice without belief, which some might consider rather pointless, attracted de Certeau, for a time. He began to see, however, in Labadie the type of a certain kind of perpetually frustrated religious quest, upon which one embarks 'at the behest of an Other, without knowing one's destination, and without even knowing what it could possibly mean to arrive.'[32]

Labadie and his followers were helped by various grandees.[33] The present crisis of the European subject unfolds in a society, and, to some extent, in a Church, less hierarchised. The spiritual nomad has

---

[31] *The Mystic Fable*, 299.
[32] F C Bauerschmidt, 'The Abrahamic Voyage: Michel de Certeau and Theology', *Modern Theology* 12,1, 1996, 16.
[33] Including James I and VI's granddaughter, Princess Elizabeth of the Palatinate, Abbess of Hervord.

fewer fixed points by which to measure progress towards or away from that self which has now become other. De Certeau felt that he himself had been engaged in 'migrations through institutions of meaning'.[34] Following his own spiritual itinerary had left him remote from the beliefs and practices of the church and religious order in which he had begun: he was quietly coping, as best he could, with a life led according to a theology of absence. De Certeau was quite open about the autobiographical, even self-regarding character of his scholarship. His research into Surin, for example, was 'a mirror-like structure'[35] which allowed him to understand himself as an historian of mysticism who 'seeks one who has vanished, who in turn sought one who had vanished, and so on.'[36]

Absent, in the end, from de Certeau was belief in God, about which he could only read in the writings of the mystics, and, absent too was faith in the European subject, an identifiable self, or 'I' who could respond to the invitation of the hidden God to lead a particular life in a particular way. Labadie, for all his 'apostasies', seems the more committed figure. The ceaseless wandering was not a substitute for some more constructive activity but was itself a life of action. Suspicious of even the most sacred texts, Jean de Labadie was not reduced to finding God in books, but remained faithful, after his fashion, to the call which Surin and Favre, in their way, had understood, as not so much a rejection of the self discovered in one's places of origin, but an invitation to discover the subject in other places as well. As Ahearne puts it, 'They aspired to convert their own *I* into the site of the Other.'[37] This is the very opposite of relegating religion to being mere interiority or spirituality. Labadie, disappointed as he was by the various communions, gave up neither on God nor on common life. The content of his youthful mystical experience, looked at askance by the Jesuit General, was such as to impel and inform a very energetic evangelization, from within the different denominations to which he belonged. Although perhaps a marginal figure, Labadie did not move to the edge of mainstream Christianity because of an inability to settle, or out of a wish to sample everything, but in the hope of finding the truth.

---

[34] *The Mystic Fable*, 292.
[35] *Ibid.*, 10.
[36] *Ibid.*, 11.
[37] J Ahearne, *Michel de Certeau: Interpretation and its Other*, Cambridge, 1995, 116.

As an historian, de Certeau was preoccupied by two conditions which he felt informed his research: absence and difference. He is struck by the absence of much that he would wish to know. Historical texts, for example, are, and contain, only traces of the past. He was also very conscious of the difference between ways of thinking which were practised in the past and those which go on now. As he studied the spiritual writings of the 17th century he was acutely aware of their strangeness and that theirs was a Christianity quite different from his own. Many religious and cultural upheavals separate us from them. He had to give up the 'proximity'[38] to his authors which had initially drawn him to them. Luce Giard has described[39] the humiliation which de Certeau experienced in this discovery that the old spiritual writers had something which he could not possess. He shared the 'internal exile' of Surin, by whom he felt so haunted, and the experience of being held suspect by institutions, which Labadie had known.

As a religious person, de Certeau considered himself to be in an awkwardly persistent state of bereavement. The family need not, however, wear mourning. De Certeau's embarrassment in the presence of the religious convictions of others, or of himself when young, did not turn out to be an invitation to reconsider the content of those beliefs. The sense of being cut off from something lost might have prompted projects for securing its retrieval.[40] De Certeau, notwithstanding this possibility, was well and truly exiled from his subject–matter[41] and mourned painfully the loss of that presence of God which is celebrated by his mystic authors in their texts. He felt severed not only from the writers but also from the One about whose felt presence they had so much to say. The mystics, of course, had also felt the absence of God, and loss, and separation. This absence is inscribed in their texts, and many of them felt acutely that inscription in the body also. The present crisis of the European subject is a loss of the known self with which the mystics of the threshold of

---

[38] *L'Absent de l'histoire*, 155-6.

[39] 'La passion de l'altérité' in L Giard (ed.), *Michel de Certeau*, 17-38, and see also M de Certeau, 'La faiblesse de croire' in *La Faiblesse de croire*, 307-14.

[40] 'La rupture instauratrice, ou le christianisme dans la culture contemporaine', *Esprit*, June, 1971, 1177-1214, an article and phrase which encouraged Henri de Lubac to include de Certeau in a survey of contemporary neo-Joachimists in his *La Postérité spirituelle de Joachim de Flore*, volume 2 *de Saut-Simon à nos jours*, Paris, 1981, 447-50.

[41] *The Mystic Fable*, 9.

modernity would have sympathized, and, even, in a certain sense envied. Their somewhat anguished historian, Michel de Certeau, entered into parts of their experience very fully.

THE FUTURE CONFIGURATION OF A
GLOBAL AND LOCAL TRADITION

Alister McGrath

What will the future of the Christian faith look like?[1] A recent highly-acclaimed study by Philip Jenkins paints a picture which many western Christians need to heed. For those who believe that liberal western forms of Christianity are normative, Jenkins' book makes profoundly disturbing reading. Jenkins argues that by the year 2050 the centre of gravity of the Christian world will have shifted firmly to the southern hemisphere. Within a few decades Kinshasa, Buenos Aires, Addis Ababa, and Manila will eclipse Rome, Athens, Paris, London, and New York as the focal points of Christianity. Moreover, the styles of Christianity associated with these centres will not be the culturally-accommodated faiths of the western churches. Jenkins shows that the churches that have grown most rapidly in the global south are far more traditional, morally conservative, evangelical, and apocalyptic than their northern counterparts.[2]

So futures exist for Christianity? We may begin by exploring the question of how global changes are affecting the world's largest religious grouping.

Introducing globalization

Globalization is generally held to represent the emergence of an increasingly global culture, which displaces local cultures. The world has been undergoing a massive change through technological innovation and global restructuring. Social theorists argue that the world is now structured by global forces, which reinforce the dominance of a global capitalist economic system, eroding the primacy of the 'nation state'

---

[1] For a fuller analysis, see Alister McGrath, *The Future of Christianity*, Blackwell, Oxford, 2001.
[2] Philip Jenkins, *The Next Christendom: The Rise of Global Christianity*, Oxford University Press, Oxford, 2002.

through multinational and transnational corporations, and degrading local cultures and traditions through the emergence of a global culture. This agreement amongst academics naturally papers over quite a few significant cracks.[3] For some, globalization is just another way of acknowledging the supremacy of capitalism; others regard the movement as simply the expansion of western influence. Globalization, it is argued, is just Westernization by a more acceptable name.[4]

Whether globalization is a good thing or a bad thing rather depends on your politics. The critics of the trend suggest that it is the outcome of the economics of the Reagan and Thatcher era of the 1980s, which can only bring about the destruction of local identities, traditions and languages, and the continued subordination of poorer nations and regions to rich ones. It will lead to a homogenization of culture and everyday life, which fails to respect individual regional and national identities. Its supporters, however, see the movement in more explicitly Darwinian terms. It is the inevitable outcome of progress. Globalization is possessed of an irresistible and inexorable trajectory, which can be resisted no more than the advent of radio and television. Developments such as the 'information superhighway' make it inevitable that the world will converge towards an increasingly uniform business and social culture. The proliferation of media technology will inevitably bring about Marshall McLuhan's vision of a 'global village', in which a global television audience watches—and is shaped by—the same entertainment spectacles, political events, and economic developments.[5]

Globalization and Christianity

So what might the implications of this process of globalization be for religion in general, and Christianity in particular? Nobody is really sure. Yet this has not prevented a surge of publications speculating on the

---

[3] Barrie Axford, *The Global System: Economics, Politics, and Culture*, St Martin's Press, New York, 1995; Martin Albrow, *The Global Age: State and Society beyond Modernity*, Polity Press, Cambridge, 1999.

[4] Serge Latouche, and Rosemary Morris, *The Westernization of the World: The Significance, Scope and Limits of the Drive towards Global Uniformity*, Polity Press, Cambridge, 1996.

[5] McKenzie Wark, *Virtual Geography: Living with Global Media Events*, Indiana University Press, Bloomington, In, 1994.

matter,[6] ranging from the wacky to the more cautious and reflective. It is clear that a number of possible scenarios may be envisaged.

The first possible scenario rests on the assumption that globalization necessarily leads to secularisation. On this view, the modernization process implicit in globalization inevitably entails ideological progress, leading to the erosion of religion. This approach does not sit easily with the events of recent years, such as the Islamic revolution in Iran, and the resurgence of religion as a marker of national identity in the former territories of the Soviet Union. Additional hypotheses thus have to be introduced to accommodate the theory to the happenings of the real world. Here, religious revival is seen as an attempt to resist the advance of globalization. The Islamic revolution in Iran and the rise of the Hindu National Party in India can both be seen as irrational reactions against the imposition of a global culture upon these regions. However, these reverses are to be seen as transient. In the course of time, modernization must prevail.

Global theorists thus predict the coming of a future uniform global culture with much the same confidence as an earlier generation of Soviet theorists proclaimed the historical inevitability of Marxism-Leninism. 'The most illustrious figures in sociology, anthropology and psychology have unanimously expressed confidence that their children—or surely their grandchildren—would live to see the dawn of a new era in which, to paraphrase Freud, the infantile illusions of religion would be outgrown.'[7]

The difficulty with this view is that it clearly rests on the assumptions of the Enlightenment—a movement which arose within Western culture, affirming the autonomy of reason and logic, which reacted against religion as an improper persistence of irrational ideas. The Enlightenment was not a global phenomenon, and its ideas cannot be regarded as possessing universal validity or as commanding global support. In effect, this approach to religion only works if globalization is explicitly understood as *Westernization*, and if the ethos of the West is defined in terms of the secularism which was typical of the immediate postwar period, especially in western Europe. In the year 2001, many

---

[6] Among the more sane, see Peter Beyer, *Religion and Globalization*, Sage Publications, London, 1994.

[7] William S Bainbridge and Rodney Stark, *The Future of Religion: Secularization, Revival, and Cult Formation*, University of California Press, Berkeley, CA, 1985, 1.

would regard such an analysis of Western culture as seriously skewed. A new interest in spirituality is likely to lead to increasing respect, for example, for the religions of Asia in the West, rather than any kind of pressure for them to conform to the rather dry and sterile secular creed of the now-defunct Enlightenment—a creed which is irreducibly ethnocentric, rather than universal.

The second approach argues that religion will continue to be part of a global culture. In contrast to the previous view, which envisaged the secularist agenda of the West being imposed upon—or accepted by—global culture, this viewpoint sees the emergence of a global religion which is basically a fusion of the religious traditions of the world. The rise of consumerism points to the desire of many to construct their own worldviews, rather than accept pre-packaged non-negotiable ideologies. This can only lead to the idea that the global religion of the future will not be any one of the present-day contenders, but an amalgam, constructed according to taste.

So what is the most likely option? Perhaps the most reliable prediction is the simplest: that today's religions will continue to be of significance in the next century. Futurist Hebert G Gerjouy suggests that the next millennium will see continuing growth within the world's religions, along with the proliferation of new variants within a global culture.[8] A process of adaptation and development will unquestionably take place, especially within Christianity. Some theorists suggest that Christianity might respond to continuing pressure from other religions and anti-religious forces through a process of convergence between its leading elements—Roman Catholicism, Eastern Orthodoxy and revivalist or conservative forms of Protestantism.[9]

Let us explore the prospects for each of these, before returning to consider the future of mainline Protestant denominations.

Roman Catholicism

Roman Catholicism is by far the world's largest Christian grouping, and

---

[8] Herbert G Gerjouy, 'The Most Significant Events of the Next Thousand Years', *Futures Research Quarterly* 8.3 (1992), 5–21.

[9] As in Hans Küng, *Theology for the Third Millennium: An Ecumenical View*, HarperCollins, London, 1991.

is universally expected to be the most successful such grouping in the next century. It represents by far the largest religious group in the United States, with four times the membership of its nearest rival, the Southern Baptists. Recent statistics suggest a modest growth in its membership in the United States over the last few years. It is by far the largest and most widely distributed Christian group in the world, and continues to expand. It can expect to face problems everywhere; nevertheless, its past history suggests that it will be able to face these, and make the necessary adjustments.[10]

A concern for social justice has propelled the Roman Catholic Church into the forefront of the global struggle for human rights, as can be seen from the role in recent decades of the church in the overthrow of President Marcos of the Philippines, the liberation of East Timor from a particularly vicious annexation of the territory by Indonesia, and the libertarian struggle in South America under military dictatorships, which claimed the lives of several notable bishops.

After the Second Vatican Council, the Catholic Church increasingly came to see itself more as a community of believers than as a divinely ordained and hierarchically-ordered society. The laity was given an increasingly important place in the life of the church. The Council also followed the example of Leo XIII in stressing the social aspects of the Christian faith, including its implications for human rights, race relations and social justice. Within the Church, the idea of 'collegiality' became of increasing importance. This expresses the notion that the Church is itself a community of member Churches, with authority dispersed to some extent among its bishops, rather than concentrated in the pope.

The Second Vatican Council is a landmark in the history of Catholicism. It remains to be seen how it will influence the development of Christianity into the next millennium. While many Catholics welcomed the new atmosphere which it introduced, others felt that it had betrayed many central concerns of traditional Catholic teaching and practice. Traces of this tension remain in the modern Catholic Church.

---

[10] Though factually incorrect at several points, there are still insights of importance to be found in Jaroslav Pelikan, *The Riddle of Roman Catholicism: Its History, its Beliefs, its Future*, Hodder and Stoughton, London, 1960. For other aspects of its history, see J Corish Patrick, E Handley James, and Denis Gwynn, *A History of Irish Catholicism*, Gill, Dublin, 1968; Martin E Marty, *A Short History of American Catholicism*, Thomas More, Allen, Tx, 1995.

It is, however, a creative tension, and can be expected to lead to a healthy process of self-examination in the future.

Other tensions have subsequently emerged as significant within Catholicism. Increasingly, Christianity is becoming a religion of the developing world, with its numerical centre of gravity moving away from the Western world towards the emerging nations of Africa and Asia. Much the same pattern is reflected in other Christian Churches. Yet there are some specific issues relating to Roman Catholicism, including a startling decline in the number of men offering themselves for the priesthood. This is especially evident in the Irish Republic, traditionally a Roman Catholic bastion in western Europe. Allegations of child abuse have seriously eroded the status of the priesthood. In 1979, there were just under 8,000 priests in Ireland, of which fewer than 400 were under the age of 29. More than 6,000 are over the age of 40. A serious shortage of priests confronts the Irish church, and it is difficult to see what can be done about it. Similar patterns can be discerned throughout the Western world. In the developing world, however, things are much more encouraging.

This means that the agenda of the developing world is increasingly coming to dominate Catholicism, as the traditional agenda of the west becomes of lesser importance. For many observers, the ultimate confirmation of this trend would be the election of non-western Catholic as pope. This development, which is now widely seen as inevitable, would mark the final stage in the rebirth of Roman Catholicism since the disaster of the 1790s. It would be a powerful demonstration of what everyone knows to be true—that Roman Catholicism has moved decisively from being a western European to a global faith in the last two centuries. There are no compelling reasons to assume anything other than that the Roman Catholic church will continue to be the major player in global Christianity in the next century.

Its leading competitor in most regions of the world will not be Protestantism, but Pentecostalism—to which we now turn.

Pentecostalism

The origins of Pentecostalism are complex, but are usually traced back to the first day of the 20th—1 January 1901. Charles Parham (1873–

1929) had launched the Bethel Bible College in Topeka, Kansas a few months earlier. One of his particular interests was the phenomenon of 'speaking in tongues', which is described in Acts 2:1-4. Most Christians had taken this to be something that happened in the early Church, but was no longer part of the Christian experience. On New Year's Day, 1901, one of Parham's students experienced this phenomenon. A few days later, Parham experienced it for himself.[11]

Parham began to teach about this apparent recovery of the 'gift of tongues'. One of those who heard him speak was the African-American preacher William J Seymour (1870-1922), who opened the 'Apostolic Faith Mission' at 312 Azusa Street, Los Angeles in April 1906. Over the next two years, a major revival broke out, characterized by the phenomenon of 'speaking in tongues.' The term 'Pentecostalism' began to be applied to the movement, taking its name from the 'Day of Pentecost'—the occasion, according to the New Testament, when the phenomenon was first experienced by the early Christian disciples (Acts 2:1-4).

The movement spread rapidly in America, appealing especially to the marginalized.[12] Unusually, it seemed to appeal to and be embraced by both white and African-American Christian groupings. Although Pentecostalism can be thought of as traditionalist in its Christian theology, it differs radically from other Christian groupings in the emphasis which it placed on speaking in tongues, and its forms of worship. These are strongly experiential, and involve prophesying, healings, and exorcisms. The worship style and lack of intellectual sophistication of the movement led to its being ignored by mainline denominations and the academy. Yet after the Second World War, a new phase of its expansion began, which paved the way for its massive growth in the second half of the 20th century.

The incident which brought Pentecostalism to wider public attention took place in Van Nuys, California, in 1960. The rector of the local Episcopalian church, Dennis Bennett, told his astonished congregation that he had been filled with the Holy Spirit and had spoken in tongues. Reaction varied from bewilderment to outrage; the local

---

[11] For a survey, see Walter J Hollenweger, *Pentecostalism: Origins and Developments Worldwide*, Hendrickson Publishers, Peabody, Ma, 1997.

[12] On this aspect of the movement, see R M Anderson, *Vision of the Disinherited: The Making of American Pentecostalism*, Oxford University Press, Oxford, 1980.

Episcopalian bishop promptly banned speaking in tongues from his churches. However, it soon became clear that others in the mainline denominations had shared Bennett's experience. They came out of their closet, and made it clear that they believed that they had experienced an authentic New Testament phenomenon, which would lead to the renewal of the churches.

By the late 1960s, it was evident that some form of renewal based on charismatic gifts (such as 'speaking in tongues') was gaining a hold within Anglican, Lutheran, Methodist, and Presbyterian circles. Perhaps most importantly of all, a growing charismatic movement began to develop within the Roman Catholic Church. Using the term 'Pentecostal' to describe this now became problematic, as this term was used to refer to a family of Churches—such as the Assemblies of God—which placed particular emphasis on 'speaking in tongues'. Accordingly, the term 'charismatic' was used to refer to movements within the mainline churches based upon the ideas and experiences of the Pentecostalist movement.

Charismatic renewal within the mainline churches has led to new and informal worship styles, an explosion in 'worship songs', a new concern for the dynamics of worship, and an increasing dislike of the traditionalism of formal liturgical worship, especially when this involves the cumbersome use of hymn books or service books. It is not just those outside the churches who find this alienating (note how Willow Creek Community Church avoids their use in their 'seeker friendly' services); this trend is now spreading within mainline churches.

The Pentecostalist movement—which we shall here take to include charismatic groups within mainline churches—has changed considerably since World War II. The most obvious change is the massive surge in growth. It is now estimated that there are 500 million Pentecostalists in the world, with a very wide geographical distribution. Although the movement may be argued to have its origins primarily within African-American culture, it has taken root in South America, Asia, Africa and Europe.[13]

Why has this form of Christianity become so popular? Two factors are generally agreed to explain the growing global appeal of

---

[13] W Dempster Murray, D Klaus Byron, and Douglas Petersen, *The Globalization of Pentecostalism: A Religion Made to Travel*, Regnum Books International, Oxford, 1999.

Pentecostalism. First, Pentecostalism stresses a direct, immediate experience of God, and avoids the rather dry and cerebral forms of Christianity which many find unattractive and unintelligible. It is thus significant that Pentecostalism has made huge inroads in working class areas of Latin America, in that it is able to communicate the divine without the need for the alienating impedimenta of a bookish culture.

Second, the movement uses a language and form of communication which enables it to bridge cultural gaps highly effectively. Walter Hollenweger, the most distinguished historian of the movement, pointed to the importance of this in a recent interview:[14]

[Pentecostalism] is an oral religion. It is not defined by the abstract language that characterises, for instance, Presbyterians or Catholics. Pentecostalism is communicated in stories, testimonies and songs. Oral language is a much more global language than that of the universities or church denominations. Oral tradition is flexible and can adapt itself to a variety of circumstances. When you become a Pentecostal, you talk about how you've been healed, or how your very life has been changed. That's something that Pentecostals talk about over and over, partly because people are interested in hearing that sort of thing. Pentecostalism today addresses the whole of life, including the thinking part. More mainline forms of Christianity address the thinking part first, and that often affects the rest of life—but not always.

If 'mainline' is defined numerically, then Pentecostalism is already the most significant Christian alternative to Roman Catholicism. It has displaced to the sidelines those Protestant groupings that once saw themselves as mainline. Pentecostalism is poised to become an increasingly important element in the Christianity of the future. So is its cousin, evangelicalism, to which we now turn.

Evangelicalism

Evangelicalism is a form of Christianity whose origins can be traced back to medieval Europe, but whose modern forms date from the 18th-century evangelical revivals in England. John and Charles Wesley

---

[14] Walter Hollenweger, 'Pentecostalism's Global Language', *Christian History* 17/2 (Spring, 1988), 42.

pioneered a renewal movement within the Church of England, which eventually led to their being thrown out of that Church for excessive 'enthusiasm'. Both Wesleys believed that many of their colleagues within the English national Church were but 'half-Christians', who had no serious emotional or personal commitment to their faith. A renewal of the heart and mind was required.

Evangelicalism became increasingly important in British religious life in the late 18th and early 20th century. Emigration from Britain to the United States led to the movement developing there, virtually achieving the status of a 'folk religion' in many parts of the country, particularly the southern states. However, its recent history owes much to the growing reaction against Fundamentalism in the late 1940s. Many conservative Protestants who were sympathetic to the aims of the fundamentalist movement became alienated by its belligerence, anti-intellectualism and cultural separationism. Surely there was a way in which the basic beliefs of the movement could be articulated in a more sensitive, intelligent and culturally interactive manner? Billy Graham rapidly became a figurehead of a new movement, initially called 'neo-evangelicalism' and then simply 'evangelicalism'. Institutions such as Wheaton College and Fuller Theological Seminary, and journals such as *Christianity Today* became flagships of the new movement, which moved rapidly to gain momentum and influence.[15]

The British scholar David Bebbington argues that evangelicalism is basically a form of orthodox Christianity which possesses four distinctive hallmarks:

1. *Conversionism*—the belief that lives need to be changed through the personal appropriation of faith. A biblical text which is often cited in this context by evangelical preachers, such as Billy Graham, is 'you must be born again' (John 3: 7).
2. *Activism*—the actualization of Christian faith in life, particularly in evangelism (the preaching of the gospel to others) and other forms of Christian activity. One of the reasons that so many evangelical churches

---

[15] Donald Bloesch, *The Evangelical Renaissance*, Eerdmans, Grand Rapids, Mi, 1973; David Bebbington, *Evangelicalism in Modern Britain: A History from the 1730s to the 1980s*, Hyman, London, 1989; George M Marsden, *Reforming Fundamentalism: Fuller Seminary and the New Evangelicalism*, Eerdmans, Grand Rapids, Mi, 1987.

are so succesful is that their memberships tend to be very active in outreach and discipleship programmes.

3. *Biblicism*—a focus on the Bible as the most fundamental resource for Christian life and thought. Bible study is often at the heart of evangelical spiritual life, both individual and corporate. A sure-fire indicator of this trait is the enormous number of devotional and academic works produced by evangelical publishing houses in an attempt to meet this huge demand from their constituency.

4. *Crucicentrism*—a focus on the cross of Christ, and the benefits this brings to humanity. Many evangelical hymns take the form of meditations on the cross—such as George Bennard's 'The Old Rugged Cross', or Isaac Watts' 'When I Survey the Wondrous Cross'.

Evangelicalism is undergoing considerable change at the moment, mainly on account of its substantial expansion in South America, Africa and Asia. It is evident that the developing world has discerned that some of evangelicalism's traditional viewpoints are shaped, to varying extents, by the unacknowledged influence of Western culture. The further expansion of evangelicalism in the non-Western world is likely to involve a further critique of implicit western assumptions within the movement (for example, its individualism), and the emergence of new forms of the movement, responsive to regional issues. By the end of the 21st century, evangelicalism will have changed, reflecting these new patterns of global action and reflection.

Eastern Orthodoxy

The final element of contemporary Christianity which may be expected to flourish in the 21st century is Eastern Orthodoxy. Orthodoxy is no longer a presence restricted to its original territories of central and eastern Europe. It has been dispersed throughout the world through complex patterns of emigration. As might thus be expected, this has been especially significant in the United States, with substantial Orthodox communities resulting from immigration from Russia, Greece, the Balkans and the Lebanon from the 19th century onwards. Large Greek-speaking communities have also grown up in the Australian cities of Sydney and Melbourne, and generally see their Orthodox faith as integral to preserving their traditions and identity. As Will Herberg has suggested, the role of religion in preserving the identity of immigrant communities needs to be appreciated here.[16]

The ability of Eastern Orthodoxy to reach beyond its traditional communities—for example, through conversion from various forms of Protestantism, especially in the United States—suggests that it might undergo significant development in the 21st century. This should not be understood to mean a change in its doctrines or worship patterns, which most Orthodox regard as a fixed aspect of its tradition. Rather, it means a changed perception of its relevance and influence within global Christianity. While there are no compelling reasons to suspect that it will lose its traditional loyalty on the part of Greek and eastern European communities, a major shift may take place. A faith community which was once defined in ethnic terms may well break out of this hitherto restricted role, and become a universal option within the global Christian market.

So what of the mainline Protestant denominations? The future for these bastions of Western Christianity is very doubtful, for various reasons.

The vulnerability of Protestant denominations

In 1929, H Richard Niebuhr published a study of the origin of the modern American religious denomination.[17] They were, he argued, a distinguishing mark of American religious life, and they were here to stay. While Niebuhr did not especially like them, he could not see any way of getting rid of them. They were rooted in historical differences of social class, wealth, national origin, and race.

The next decades seemed to confirm everything Niebuhr argued. Throughout the 1950s, the growth of the traditional Protestant denomination surged in the United States. Congregationalists, Episcopalians, Methodists and Presbyterians reported net annual membership gains. Their membership reflected precisely the issues Niebuhr

---

[16] Will Herberg, *Protestant-Catholic-Jew: An Essay in American Religious Sociology*, University of Chicago Press, Chicago, 1983.
[17] H Richard Niebuhr, *The Social Sources of Denominationalism*, Meridian Books, New York, 1957.

had noted. When Methodists got rich, they became Episcopalians. Each denomination vigorously defended its sovereignty and vested interests. In 1956, a survey showed that 80 per cent of Episcopalians believed that it was wrong to hold worship service with other Christian groups. A year earlier, a Gallup poll shows that 96 per cent of the adult population of the United States belonged to the same denomination as their parents. Their churchgoing habits had not changed over a generation.

Yet by 1990, something had gone wrong for many of these denominations. It was not simply that their growth had stalled. They were in decline. By 1990, the denominations just mentioned had lost between one fifth and one third of their 1965 memberships, at a time when the population growth of the United States had surged. A real numerical decline thus converted into a massive slump in the proportion of America's population associating with these denominations. Why?

The traditional (and rather cosy) answer to this question locates the erosion of church membership in the secularizing impact of industrialization and urbanization, which, it is argued, erode the credibility of religion. This is certainly a neat little idea, which plays well to academic sociological faculties. On the ground, however, it seems rather less satisfactory. Church attendance is far more complex than these figures suggest. The mainline denominations may be in decline, but others are in growth mode—even in industrial and urban centres, traditionally seen as citadels of secularism. In fact, the best predictor of church attendance seems to be whether it affirms traditional Christian beliefs and makes demands of its congregations, or takes a more liberal view concerning both beliefs and demands. To simplify the situation: the former grow, the latter do not. A 1994 study showed that Pentecostal churches have grown by 300 per cent and conservative Protestant churches by 200 per cent since 1950.[18]

The view of mainline church leaders has tended to be that modern America will only take seriously those churches which are progressive and liberal on core beliefs—such as the transcendence of God, the resurrection of Jesus, and so on. This was certainly the perception of the 1960s, when many of the Church leaders of the 1990s were in college. The decisive ethos of those years has remained firmly stamped in their minds. It's just too bad that things have moved on since then, leaving them beached. To their critics—and there are plenty of them—the

---

[18] C S Clark, 'Religion in America', *CQ Researcher* (1994), 1035-52.

mainline denominations have got stuck in a rut, and are being overtaken by new understandings of what it means to be church—like the megachurches, with average Sunday attendances numbered in thousands. Alongside the numerical decline of the traditional American denomination, another trend can be observed, calling into question whether the 'denomination' has any real future. The denomination is increasingly being seen as an historical anomaly which the future does not seem to want. Christian denominations in America are one of the very few institutional expressions of European culture still in existence. But why, many Americans began to wonder, should modern America's religious life be made dependent upon a European model—especially when that model was now seen as having failed back in its homelands?

Both individual churches and Christians in America are showing an increasing reluctance to define themselves denominationally. I have attended churches in California which have described themselves as 'in the Presbyterian tradition'—meaning that they do things like the Presbyterians used to, but do not care to be associated with the institutional politics and policies of this mainline denomination. Is this because it has become slightly outdated to do so? Or because it is seen as associating with an outmoded establishment?[19] Many churches have named themselves after their localities, skilfully dropping any reference to their denomination. The inclusion of denominational identities is no longer viewed as a positive in marketing terms.

So what, then, are the futures of Christianity? There is little doubt as to where that future lies—in the developing world. Jenkins is right: the Christianity of 2050 will be very different from the faith of Europe. The new Christianity will be the faith of poor nonwhites living south of Europe and the United States of America. It will revive Christianity's root emphases on healing and prophecy, not least because its adherents will identify themselves with the poor and oppressed who first embraced the redemption, healing and blessing that Jesus promised.

It remains to be seen how the western church will cope with this shift, and what it can learn from it. Might this be an act of divine judgement against a complacent and lazy church? However we answer this question, we must realize that the future will not be like the past. The

---

[19] See Wade Clark Roof, Jackson W Carroll, and David A Roozen, *The Post-War Generation and Establishment Religion*, Westview Press, Boulder, Co, 1995.

forms of Christian lifestyle, worship and theology favoured by believers in these regions has little interest in traditional western ways of acting and thinking, especially as these have developed in the 20th century. Christianity unquestionably has a future, and a bright one at that—but not in the regions and in the forms that we in the west have come to accept as normative.

THE FUTURE OF LIBERATION
THEOLOGY IN LATIN AMERICA*
David Tombs

Introduction

During the 1970s and 1980s Latin American liberation theology attracted
international attention and was widely acclaimed in progressive theological
circles for its methodological innovations and theological insights.[1]
However, by the 1990s there was a growing consensus that Latin American
liberation theology confronted a crisis.[2] Hostile critics proclaimed the
final end of liberation theology. Proponents and sympathisers were more
likely to speak in terms of 'change' or 'transition' but largely agreed that
an important period was coming to a close. This leaves a question as to

---

* This paper was presented at 'World Christianity: A Contemporary Encounter Between
Religion, Politics and Culture' Postgraduate Conference, St Catharine's College, Cumberland
Lodge, Windsor (15 March 2002). An earlier version of this chapter was published as D
Tombs, 'Liberation Theology Faces the Future', in S E Porter, M A Hayes and D Tombs (eds.),
Faith in the Millennium, Sheffield Academic Press, Sheffield, 2001, 32-58.

[1] There is now an extensive literature on Latin American liberation theology, its significance
beyond Latin America and criticisms raised against it; see esp. A F McGovern, *Liberation
Theology and its Critics: Towards an Assessment*, Orbis Books, Maryknoll, NY, 1989.
[2] On the crisis of the 1990s, see for example, F Betto, 'Did Liberation Theology Collapse
with the Berlin Wall?' *Religion, State and Society* 21.1 (1993), 33-38; P Berryman, *Religion in
the Megacity: Catholic and Protestant Portraits from Latin America*, Orbis Books, Maryknoll, NY,
1996; R Nagle, *Claiming the Virgin: The Broken Promise of Liberation Theology in Brazil*,
Routledge, New York and London, 1995; I Linden, *Liberation Theology: Coming of Age?*,
Catholic Institute for International Relations, London, 1997; J M Vigil, 'Is there a Change
of Paradigm in Liberation Theology?', *SEDOS* 29.12 (1997), 315-21 (315); M Löwy, *The
War of the Gods: Religion and Politics in Latin America*, Verso, London, 1996; G De Schrijver
(ed.), *Liberation Theologies on Shifting Grounds*, Leuven University Press, Leuven, 1998; J
Comblin, *Called for Freedom: The Changing Context of Liberation Theology*, trans. P Berryman,
Orbis Books, Maryknoll, NY, 1998; M A Vásquez, *The Brazilian Popular Church and the Crisis
of Modernity*, Cambridge Studies in Ideology and Religion, University of Cambridge
Press, Cambridge, 1998; J L Kater, 'Whatever Happened to Liberation Theology? New
Directions for Theological Reflection in Latin America', *Anglican Theological Review* 83.4
(Autumn 2001), 735-773.

which aspects of liberation theology are likely to be relevant to Latin America and other theological contexts in the future. In what follows I suggest that even though the terminology of 'liberation' now has many difficulties and liberation theology may have reached the end of an era as a cohesive theological movement, nonetheless many of liberation theology's insights from the 1960s to the 1990s will be valuable guides for any Christian theology that is to offer a prophetic social witness in the future. To understand how so much of liberation theology can remain an important long-term legacy, despite the crisis of the 1990s and the end of the movement itself, it is helpful to give an overview of different phases in the development of liberation theology since the late-1960s and highlight the separate strands that became part of its theological approach.[3]

Liberation theology in the 1960s

Vatican II (1962–65) introduced sweeping reforms into the Church and re-orientated its relationship to the world. This new social emphasis encouraged the church in Latin America to embrace the poor as its special concern in the years immediately after Vatican II. In so doing it drew upon and developed ideas that dated back at least as far as the very first Catholic social encyclical (Leo XIII's *Rerum Novarum* in 1891). *Rerum Novarum* recognised that 'the poor and helpless have a claim to special consideration' by civil authorities.[4] John XXIII had recently restated the same principle of special consideration in *Pacem in Terris*

---

[3] For a more detailed treatment of these ideas, see D Tombs, *Latin American Liberation Theology*, Brill Academic Publishers, Boston and Leiden, 2002. Alfred Hennelly has published many of the most significant source materials on liberation theology in chronological order in A T Hennelly (ed.), *Liberation Theology: A Documentary History*, Orbis Books, Maryknoll, NY, 1990.

[4] *Rerum Novarum*, § 29. The full passage reads: '… it is the duty of the public authority to prevent and punish injury, and to protect each one in the possession of his own. Still when there is a question of protecting the rights of individuals, the poor and helpless have a claim to special consideration. The richer population have many ways of protecting themselves, and stand less in need of help from the State; those who are badly-off have no resources of their own to fall back upon, and must chiefly rely upon the assistance of the State.'

(1963).[5] Prior to the 1960s the church had seen the defence of these rights as the responsibility of the civil authorities. The church's own role had been restricted to charity rather than justice. After Vatican II, social justice for the poor was also to be an issue for the church and integral to its mission. The urgency of this task was reiterated in Paul VI's encyclical *Populorum Progressio* (1967). Where civil authorities failed to heed their responsibility to the poor then the church would need to take up their cause. Catholic social teaching along these lines prepared the way for the church in Latin America to make their distinctive commitment to the poor in the late 1960s.

At the end of Vatican II the Council of Latin American Bishops (CELAM) decided to hold a major meeting in 1968 at Medellín (Colombia) to discuss the implications of Vatican II for their continent.[6] The Medellín Conference was the single most important church event for the development of liberation theology as an effective social movement with a political commitment to justice.[7] Not all the documents from Medellín reflected this commitment with the same strength and consistency but it came out strongly in the *The Message to the Peoples of Latin America* and the *Document on Justice, Document on Peace* and *Document on the Poverty of the Church*. In these four documents, the church made a commitment to the poor that had three key features.[8]

---

[5] In 1931 Pius XI used the fortieth anniversary of *Rerum Novarum* to issue his own social encyclical *Quadragesimo Anno* ('After Forty Years'), in which he quoted Leo's principle and made it his own (*Quadragesimo Anno*, § 25). In 1963 John made the same point in his social encyclical *Pacem in Terris*, 'Considerations of justice and equity, however, can at times demand that those involved in civil government give more attention to the less fortunate members of the community, since they are less able to defend their rights and to assert their legitimate claims' (*Pacem in Terris*, § 56).

[6] CELAM is commonly used to designate both the Council of Latin American bishops as an organisational body and their general conferences. CELAM (the organisation) was set up at a meeting in 1955 in Rio de Janeiro at a conference now referred to as CELAM I. The conference at Medellín is widely known as CELAM II. The other two general conferences are CELAM III (Puebla, Mexico, 1979) and CELAM IV (Santo Domingo, Dominican Republic, 1992). In addition to the major conferences (sometimes called 'extraordinary' meetings) CELAM also meets annually for 'ordinary' meetings. It was the annual meeting in 1965 (held in Rome during Vatican II) that led to second general conference at Medellín.

[7] The origins of liberation theology as a cohesive social movement in the 1960s and its development in the 1970s have been superbly documented by C Smith, *The Emergence of Liberation Theology: Radical Religion and Social Movement Theory*, University of Chicago Press, Chicago and London, 1991.

[8] CELAM, *The Church in the Present-Day Transformation of Latin America in the Light of the Council* (2nd edn), Bishop's Conference, Washington DC, 1973 (ET 1970). The

Firstly, they denounced injustice and defended the poor as an integral part of Christian mission. In the *Document on Justice* the bishops committed the church to assisting the poor and serving as their advocates and promised that: 'The church—the people of God—will lend its support to the downtrodden of every social class so that they might come to know their rights and how to make use of them'.[9]

Second, Medellín called for a clearer witness to the church's teaching in its own institutional life. The *Document on the Poverty of the Church* summarised the challenges that the church needed to address:

> In this context a poor church: denounces the unjust lack of this world's goods and the sin that begets it; preaches and lives in spiritual poverty, as an attitude of spiritual childhood and openness to the Lord; is itself bound to material poverty.[10]

In § 10 the bishops spoke of their 'duty of solidarity with the poor'. They also emphasised that the commitment to the poor in wider society and the commitment to poverty in the church's institutional life were closely linked. The church committed itself to material poverty so that it could strengthen its solidarity with the poor and live more easily in spiritual poverty.[11]

---

documents that were most significant for the development of liberation theology are reprinted in Hennelly (ed.), *Liberation Theology*, 89–119.

[9] *Document on Justice*, § 20. Recognising and naming the suffering of the poor as injustice rather than misfortune (or providential ordering) reflected a new political awareness in CELAM's social teaching; for example, see the declaration in the *Document on Justice* (which echoed *Populorum Progressio*, § 30) that '... misery, as a collective fact, expresses itself as injustice which cries to the heavens' (§ 1). The denunciation of poverty in the *Document on the Poverty of the Church* was equally emphatic: 'The Latin American bishops cannot remain indifferent in the face of the tremendous social injustices existent in Latin America, which keep the majority of our peoples in dismal poverty, which in many cases becomes inhuman wretchedness. A deafening cry pours from the throats of millions of men and women asking their pastors for a liberation that reaches them from nowhere else' (§ 1–2).

[10] *Document on the Poverty of the Church*, § 5. The bishops set out the consequence of this in § 9: 'The Lord's distinct commandment to "evangelize the poor" ought to bring us to a distribution of resources and apostolic personnel that effectively give preference to the poorest and most needy sectors and to those segregated for any cause whatsoever, animating and accelerating the initiatives and studies that are already being made with that goal in mind. We, the bishops, wish to come closer to the poor in sincerity and fellowship, making ourselves accessible to them.'

[11] 'This solidarity means that we make ours their problems and their struggles, that we know

The third feature of Medellín's commitment to the poor was the recognition of poverty as a structural problem in terms of class oppression, and the theological judgement that this was a 'sinful situation'. This was clearest in the *Document on Peace*, where the bishops took-up a line from *Populorum Progressio* (§ 87) that suggested that development might be a new word for peace. The bishops pointed to the injustice of underdevelopment as a sinful feature of Latin America:

> If development is the new name for peace' Latin American underdevelopment, with its own characteristics in the different countries, is an unjust situation which promotes tensions that conspire against peace ... When speaking of injustice, we refer to those realities that constitute a sinful situation ...[12]

The *Document on Peace* addressed both class-tensions in terms of internal colonialism and international tensions in terms of neo-colonialism. It pointed to 'Extreme inequalities between social classes' (§ 3) in Latin America and deplored the way that 'some members of the dominant sectors occasionally resort to the use of force to repress drastically any attempt at opposition' (§ 6). At an international level it repeated *Populorum Progressio*'s condemnation of the 'international imperialism of money' (§ 9).[13] It also noted that the countries that produced raw material remained poor whilst the manufacturing countries enrich themselves (§ 9) and criticised the progressive debt that absorbed the greater part of Latin American gains (§ 9).[14]

The social commitments made at Medellín were drawn together into a cohesive theology under a name provided by Gustavo Gutiérrez, a Peruvian priest. Gutiérrez developed the term 'liberation' in a way that would be crucially important in focussing the new outlook into a

---

how to speak with them. This has to be concretized in criticism of injustice and oppression, in the struggle against the intolerable situation that a poor person often has to tolerate, in the willingness to dialogue with the groups responsible for that situation in order to make them understand their obligations' (*Document on the Poverty of the Church*, § 10).

[12] *Document on Peace*, § 1.

[13] Catholic social teaching that stretched back to the social encyclical *Quadragesimo Anno* (1931).

[14] See also the complaint in the *Document on Justice* that 'Many of our workers ... experience a situation of dependence on inhuman economic systems and institutions: a situation which, for many of them borders on slavery' (§ 11).

challenging theology.[15] Discussions of 'dependency' in other disciplines—most especially economics—emphasised the need for 'liberation' as an alternative to development in the social, political and economic sphere. This inspired Gutiérrez to make the same shift in theology. In July 1968—the month before Medellín—he presented a paper at a meeting of priests and laity in Chimbote, Peru. It was entitled 'Towards a Theology of Liberation'.[16] The political, existential, and theological applications of the term liberation reflected a holistic understanding of salvation that supported the commitments the bishops made at Medellín.[17] The language of liberation was ideally suited to the revolutionary context of the late 1960s and was a rich and inspirational term for theology.

After Medellín Gutiérrez continued to reflect on the issues discussed at Chimbote and presented a revised version of the paper in 1969 at a conference in Cartigny (Switzerland).[18] In the Chimbote and Cartigny papers, Gutiérrez developed the political implications that accompanied an authentic pastoral commitment to the poor in history and argued for a new methodology in Latin American theological work. He stressed that theology had to be responsive to new times and circumstances; it could not just repeat abstract and timeless truths. For Gutiérrez, theology had to interpret people's historical commitment to God (and to their human neighbours) in the light of revelation. In a now

---

[15] The term liberation can be found in many places at Medellín and Gutiérrez noted at Chimbote that there was already talk of the theology of liberation. However, it was his use of the term between 1968 and 1971 that was especially important in making it such a central term for the new movement.

[16] Independently of Gutiérrez, the Brazilian Protestant theologian, Rubem Alves, submitted his doctoral dissertation at Princeton in 1968 under the title 'Towards a Theology of Liberation'. This was published the following year but the publisher requested that the title be changed to *A Theology of Human Hope*, Corpus Books, Washington DC, 1969. In Spanish translation it changed again to *Opio o instrumento de liberación*, Tierra Nueva, Montevideo, 1970. Alves and Gutiérrez realised the similarities of their perspective when they met at the conference in Cartigny, 1969.

[17] Gutiérrez attended Medellín as a theological adviser to the Archbishop of Lima and CELAM's pastoral commitments to the poor at Medellín reflected many of his contributions.

[18] G Gutiérrez, 'Notes on a Theology of Liberation' in SODEPAX, *In Search of a Theology of Development: Papers from a Consultation on Theology and Development held by SODEPAX in Cartigny, Switzerland, November, 1969*, WCC, Geneva, 1970, 116-79. SODEPAX (Committee on Society, Development and Peace) was set up jointly by the WCC (World Council of Churches) and the Pontifical Commission for Justice and Peace early in 1968 and ran for three years.

famous passage he said 'theology is a reflection—that is, it is a second act, a turning back, a re-flecting, that comes after action. Theology is not first; the commitment is first. Theology is the understanding of the commitment, and the commitment is action'.[19]

Viewed in this perspective the Latin American liberation theology that emerged in the 1960s had at least three distinctive features. Firstly, it advocated a pastoral commitment to the poor that had political implications for both church and society. Second, it endorsed a methodological approach that put commitment to social action first and made participation in struggles for justice a precondition for theology. Third, it used a terminology of liberation that expressed the movement's distinctive features in a way that was both relevant and profound. Hopes for liberation and freedom went to the heart of the movement's political ideals, methodological process, and theological emphasis.

'Liberation theology' was a perfect name to represent the new course that the church in Latin America set for itself in the late 1960s.[20] However, since it was the *terminology* of liberation that was the major problem in the 1990s, it is important to be clear that liberation theologians never saw their work as just the terminology of liberation. Liberation theologians stressed that liberation theology involved a whole new approach to theology; it was not just about a new theological term or the addition of a new theme to theology. From the very earliest works it involved a new commitment to the poor and a new methodological approach to the practice of theology. It was because these three innovations—terminology, political commitment and methodology— came together in such a mutually empowering way that liberation theology would be so influential in the 1970s. To understand these three strands in the origins of liberation theology as separate but highly complementary is a first step to understanding a future of liberation theology in which the commitment to the poor and the theological method it encouraged might have longer term relevance than the terminology of liberation. However, to develop a fuller sense of what this

---

[19] G Gutiérrez, 'Toward a Theology of Liberation' in Hennelly, *Liberation Theology*, 62-76 (63).
[20] At the same time, but entirely independently, James Cone was developing an equally prophetic black theology of liberation to address race and racism in the USA; see esp. H Cone, *Black Theology and Black Power*, Seabury, New York, 1969, and *A Black Theology of Liberation*, Lippincott, Philadelphia, 1970

might mean, the subsequent evolution of liberation theology and further strands in its methodology and theological focus must also be considered.

The development of liberation theology in the 1970s

In the 1970s many church leaders and laypeople responded to Medellín's commitment to the poor. The 1970s were difficult years in Latin America. Military coups took place in Bolivia, Chile and Uruguay (1973) and later in Argentina (1976). Repression also increased in countries already under military regimes (especially noticeable in Brazil after 1968, El Salvador after 1969 and Peru after 1975). By 1978 only Colombia, Venezuela and Guyana in South America were free from military dictatorship.[21] In Central America, the Somoza dictatorship held sway in Nicaragua and the military controlled Honduras, El Salvador and Guatemala.

In the face of widespread repression and harassment liberation theology and the popular church made impressive headway and seemed to offer signs of a major church renewal. As liberation theology grew and consolidated as a social movement there were also a number of new developments in its theology and methodology. The Documents of the third General Meeting of the Council of Latin American Bishops at Puebla, Mexico in 1979 (known as CELAM III) reflect three particularly important new emphases that received greater attention as the movement developed during the 1970s: first, the terminology of the 'option for the poor'; second, a new form of popular participation, which incarnated the ideals of liberation theology in the base communities; third, the 'conversion' of the church and the transformation of theology through its contact with the poor, especially in the base communities.

If the language of 'liberation' played a crucial role in initiating the movement in the late 1960s and early 1970s, the idea of an 'option for the poor' was equally important in setting the agenda for the next phase.[22] At the end of the decade, the classic phrase 'preferential option

---

[21] See P Lernoux, *Cry of the People: The Struggle for Human Rights in Latin America—the Catholic Church in Conflict with U.S. Policy*, Penguin Books, New York, rev. edn., 1982 [1980], especially 10.

[22] Some critics of liberation theology objected to the idea of an 'option' for the poor and claimed that it made the church and theology partial and exclusive. However, although the

for the poor' expressed at Puebla (§ 1134) clarified that liberation theology's option for the poor was—and always had been—a 'preferential' concern and never an exclusive one.[23] What made the option so significant was that liberation theology did not shy away from the political conflicts that solidarity with the poor inevitably involved in situations of structural injustice and military dictatorship. Furthermore, talk of an option for the poor also went alongside a major development in liberation theology during the 1970s, which transformed its relationship to the poor and its methodological approach to theology.

For any assessment of the long-term future of liberation theology in Latin America or elsewhere, it is vital to appreciate that the 'option for the poor' had two separate dimensions. Firstly, there was the political option itself, which was initiated in the late 1960s, when liberation theologians committed themselves to the poor. Second, there were the implications of this commitment for theology as a discipline. Working through the methodological implications of the option in the 1970s pointed to a new theological approach based on what might be called an 'epistemological option'. It was the epistemological option—a new way

---

precise phraseology might have been new, the basic idea of an 'option' had clear precedents in the Catholic social tradition identified above. Special concern for the rights of the poor (as a responsibility for civil authorities) had been part of the social tradition since *Rerum Novarum*. The Church's recognition of its own social responsibilities to the poor (beginning in the early 1960s and reinforced by Vatican II) suggested that the principle should be extended from civil authorities to the Church itself. Liberation theologians also pointed out that the bible—and especially the gospels—showed the same preferential interest in the poor; the poor were most in need and the Church had a special responsibility to stand alongside them.

[23] 'We affirm the need for conversion on the part of the whole Church to a preferential option for the poor, an option aimed at their integral liberation' (CELAM, *Puebla: Evangelization at Present and in the Future of Latin America: Conclusions* [Official English Edition of the Third General Conference of Latin American Bishops, Puebla, Mexico, 1979; St. Paul Publications, Slough; Catholic Institute for International Relations, London, 1980], § 1134). It would be mistaken to see the term 'preferential' as a later toning-down of a previously more 'exclusive' option. The option for the poor had always been intended in the preferential rather than the exclusive sense. In November 1971 the Peruvian bishops presented their forceful contribution to the Bishops' Synod on Justice in Rome. In this they pledged themselves to: 'opting for the oppressed and marginal peoples as personal and communal commitment'. This was clarified in the next sentence: 'This option does not exclude any individual from our charity; rather opting for those who today experience the most violent forms of oppression is for us an efficacious way of also loving those who, possibly unconsciously, are oppressed themselves by their very different situation of being oppressors'; see Bishops of Peru, 'Justice in the World', *IDOC* (December 1971), 2-18 (§ 8); reprinted Hennelly (ed.), *Liberation Theology*, 125-36 (128).

of knowing God in and through the lives of the poor and their struggle for justice—which unexpectedly transformed liberation theology in the 1970s and led some to speak of the poor 'converting' the church.

There were a number of factors that encouraged this development. The work of Brazilian educator Paulo Freire on a 'pedagogy of the oppressed' was one critical factor. Freire had emphasised that liberating education needed to treat people as subjects and not just objects. This required a faith in the people as partners in a dialogue and not just recipients of information.[24] Friere's critique of traditional education was easily transferable to traditional approaches to theology. His work set out the challenge to traditional didactic approaches and provided a theoretical framework in which to understand the new alternative. At a more direct and experiential level, however, it was the base communities that proved the most decisive factor.

Medellín gave support to the nascent base community movements and during the 1970s the CEBs (Base Ecclesial Communities) spread rapidly in many Latin American countries.[25] Their strength varied from place to place but they were especially influential in Brazil and Central America.[26] The communities played an important role in the dissemination of liberation theology amongst ordinary people and many base communities members were transformed into social activists through contact with liberation theology. However, a less expected feature of this process was that priests, women religious, pastoral workers and theologians were themselves transformed by their contact with the poor. Many communities showed that they were able to take-over and live out the church's option for them with enthusiasm and dignity. The poor were not just passive objects of an option made by the church; they were active subjects who took the option forward in new ways.

---

[24] See P Freire, *Pedagogy of the Oppressed*, trans. M Bergman Ramos, Continuum, New York, 1970 [Portuguese orig. 1968]. On Freire's remarkable life and contribution to radical thought in Latin America, see D Collins, *Paulo Freire: His Life, Works and Thought*, Paulist Press, New York, 1978. On the extensive similarities in structure between Freire's approach to education and the mature work of liberation theology, see D Schipani, *Religious Education Encounters Liberation Theology*, Religious Education Press, Birmingham, Al, 1988.

[25] See *Document on Justice*, § 20. In English the CEBs are sometimes referred to as BCCs (Base Christian Communities or Base Church Communities).

[26] A classic example is the record of the Solentiname community presented in the work of E Cardenal, *The Gospel in Solentiname*, trans. D D Walsh, 4 vols, Orbis Books, Maryknoll, NY, 1976–82.

In the base communities, this was developed in bible reading circles that valued the contribution of all participants in a mutual search for new understanding. The bible readings in base communities showed how the poor could bring their personal experiences to the bible and offer theological insights that professional exegetes might miss.[27] Contact with the communities encouraged many liberation theologians to develop their awareness not just as 'teachers' but also as 'students' with much to learn from the painful wisdom of the poor.[28]

The new political context of the 1970s made this all the more important. The first phase of liberation theology had been set in the 'atmosphere of liberation' of the late-1960s. The second phase was marked by repression and persecution in the 1970s. The rise of authoritarian regimes throughout the region and escalating conflict between church and state provided a context of persecution and martyrdom. The church committed itself to the poor at a time when their suffering was most acute and it was particularly dangerous to challenge the powers of the militarized state. Thus in 1980 Gutiérrez looked back on the changes liberation theology had undergone in the 1970s and noted the transformative influence of the poor on the church:

After Vatican II and the stimulus of the Medellín Conference, we creatively reappropriated the gospel expression about evangelizing or 'preaching the good news to the poor'. Reinforced by an option for the oppressed and a commitment of solidarity with them, a series of rich and promising initiatives took place all over Latin America... Then came the irruption of the poor. At a terrible price the common people began to become the active protagonists of history. This fact gave us deeper insight into the whole matter of evangelization. Working in the midst of the poor, exploited people, whom we were supposedly going to evangelize, we came to realize that we were being evangelized by them. Here the CCBs [church base

---

[27] See especially C Mesters, *Defenseless Flower: A New Reading of the Bible*, Orbis Books, Maryknoll, NY, 1989 [Portuguese orig. 1983]. On the issues raised in such an approach, see C Rowland and M Corner, *Liberating Exegesis: The Challenge of Liberation Theology to Biblical Studies*, SPCK, London, 1990.

[28] See for example C Boff, *Feet-on-the-Ground Theology: A Brazilian Journey*, trans. P Berryman, Orbis, Maryknoll, NY, 1987 [Portuguese orig. 1984]

communities] played a major role. The Puebla Conference commented on this when it noted that the church discovered the 'evangelizing potential of the poor' through its involvement with the poor and such communities.[29]

Jon Sobrino described how the new contact and appreciation of the poor contributed to the shift within liberation theology in the 1970s:

The important thing about the decade of the 1970s, then, was our rediscovery of the real life of the impoverished majorities, together with our evangelical rediscovery that it is to them that the good news of the gospel is addressed. In this perspective, the poor become the locus, the place, of the Christian life ...[30]

The lives of the poor became not just an ethical priority for social work but also a historical *locus* where God was revealed in a special way. Sobrino expressed this clearly when he said 'This means that the poor are the authentic *theological source* for understanding Christian truth and practice'.[31] The epistemological commitment to the poor meant that Latin American liberation theologians like Gutiérrez and Sobrino judged their priorities and procedures in terms of their relevance to the poor and took the experiences of the poor as the starting point for their theological work.

---

[29] G Gutiérrez, 'The Irruption of the Poor in Latin America and the Christian Communities of the Common People' in S Torres and J Eagleson (eds.), *The Challenge of Basic Christian Communities*, EATWOT International Ecumenical Congress of Theology, São Paulo, Brazil, 20 February–2 March, 1980, Orbis Books, Maryknoll, NY, 1981, 107-23 (120). At the same conference, Sobrino pointed to the impact of persecution: 'Neither *Evangelii Nuntiandi* nor Medellín placed any stress on persecution or martyrdom either. They both re-emphasise the need for subjective witness in the evangelization process. Both, Medellín in particular, stress the need for poverty and the necessity of becoming poor in order to be in solidarity with the poor. But the essential nature of witness is not viewed in terms of persecution and martyrdom' (J Sobrino, 'The Witness of the Church in Latin America' in Torres and Eagleson [eds.], *The Challenge of Basic Christian Communities*, 161-88 [171]).

[30] J Sobrino, *Spirituality of Liberation: Towards a Political Holiness*, trans. Robert R Barr, Orbis Books, Maryknoll, NY, 1988 [Spanish orig. 1985], 3.

[31] J Sobrino, *The True Church and the Poor*, trans. Matthew O'Connell, Orbis Books, Maryknoll, NY, SCM, London, 1984, 93. See also: 'The poor are not simply beneficiaries of liberation. By the mere fact that they exist, for believers they are the historical locus of God, the 'place' where God is found in history' (Sobrino, *Spirituality of Liberation*, 24).

Works in liberation theology in the 1970s built on and deepened the work of the late-1960s to initiate a new phase in liberation theology. The terminology of an 'option for the poor', the spread of the base communities and the distinctively new epistemological orientation were three of the liberation theology's most important developments of the decade. They did not replace the earlier breakthroughs (which remained essential to the movement) but took them in unexpected directions and extended them to new levels.[32] The result was in continuity with the early work but distinctly different from it and opened the way for further changes in the 1980s.[33]

The maturation of liberation theology in the 1980s

In a passage in the 'Conclusions' at CELAM III the bishops had signalled a broader understanding of poverty than the mainly economic focus that had tended to dominate the very early works of liberation theology. The bishops noted that: 'the poor do not lack simply material goods. They also miss, on the level of human dignity, full participation in socio-political life' (§ 1135). In a footnote they added: 'Those found in this category are principally our indigenous peoples, peasants, manual laborers, marginalized urban dwellers and, in particular the women of these social groups. The women are doubly oppressed and marginalized' (§ 1135). This broader sense of poverty and the poor pointed to a shift that would find even greater prominence in the 1980s and was one of the most significant marks of the maturation of liberation theology during the new decade.

The need to extend the analysis of oppression from a class-based economic and political analysis to a more inclusive social framework was both one of the great strengths and the great weaknesses of the liberation

---

[32] For example, just as liberation theology's political option for the poor had developed out of existing strands in the traditions; so the epistemological option came out of what had already gone before. There were hints in this direction at Vatican II and Medellín but it was the progressives in the Latin American church that developed these tentative suggestions and made them central to their practice in the 1970s.

[33] Juan Luis Segundo, who was rather uneasy with the way that liberation theology had changed went as far as to say that it amounted to two different liberation theologies; see J L Segundo, 'Two Theologies of Liberation', *The Month* 17 (October 1984); reprinted Hennelly (ed.), *Liberation Theology*, 353-366.

theology in the 1980s.[34] It was strength in as much as a more comprehensive analysis was urgently required and provided new horizons for theological reflection. Theologians in other contexts (especially feminist and black theologians in North America, and other Third World theologians in Africa and Asia) increasingly criticised the limitations of Latin American liberation theology in its dealing with gender, race and indigenous cultures.[35] Gutiérrez (who was more sensitive to these wider concerns than many other liberation theologians) sketched the new agenda in his contribution to the meeting of the Ecumenical Association of Third World Theologians in São Paulo.[36] The final document from the meeting echoed his concerns:

> The church of the Third World must commit itself to those struggles for liberation that take up specific concerns of ethnic, racial and sex groups, within the overall framework of the struggle of the poor. Indigenous peoples, blacks, and women of the popular classes will always deserve special attention from our church and a growing concern on the part of our theology.[37]

In some cases this made it easier for new voices within the movement, which were often more sensitive to the challenges and better able to deal with them, to take on a greater role. This was especially true

---

[34] George De Schrijver examines the 1980s and 1990s in terms of a shift from economic class analysis to a broader cultural analysis in 'Paradigm Shift in Third-World Theologies of Liberation: From Socio-Economic Analysis to Cultural Analysis?' in De Schrijver, (ed.), *Liberation Theologies on Shifting Grounds*, Leuven University Press, Leuven, 1998. De Schrijver's book offers useful responses (and his own reply) to his thesis.

[35] Engagement with sexuality was equally absent from the work of Latin Americans in the 1960s and 1970s but unlike gender, race and culture there was scarcely even the attempt to address it in the 1980s or 1990s. Despite its importance for understanding the real lives of the poor, and especially the oppressions that women face in a traditional machista culture, liberation theology has been very reluctant to engage with sexuality. I examine this silence in more detail in D Tombs, 'Machismo and Marianismo: Sexuality and Liberation Theology' in M A Hayes, W Porter and D Tombs (eds.), *Religion and Sexuality*, Sheffield Academic Press, Sheffield, 1998, 248–71. For a forceful criticism of liberation theology's weakness with regard to gender and sexuality, see M Althaus-Reid, *Indecent Theology: Theological Perversions in Sex, Gender and Politics*, Routledge, London and New York, 2000.

[36] Gutiérrez, 'The Irruption of the Poor in Latin America', esp. 111.

[37] EATWOT International Ecumenical Congress of Theology, São Paulo, Brazil, 20 February– 2 March 1980: Final Document, in Torres and Eagleson, *The Challenge of Basic Christian Communities*, 231–46 (245).

for women theologians who had been marginalised in the 1970s.[38] In the 1980s women theologians in Latin America took the lead in addressing the sexism and gender issues that their male colleagues either did not acknowledge as a source of oppression or were reluctant to reflect upon theologically. However, Latin American women theologians with academic training were few in number. Unfortunately, despite a general readiness in the 1980s to pay lip service to the importance of women's oppression, few male theologians allowed their theology to be radically changed by it. There were therefore limits to the progress that liberation theology as a movement could make towards a fuller understanding of the different dynamics of oppression. The same was true for the engagement with race and culture. The attempts to broaden the awareness of oppression in the 1980s did not generate the creative and empowering response that was required. Many male liberation theologians made only token attempts to widen their perspective and some dismissed the new agenda as merely secondary issues, which could be addressed after the real priorities (politics and economics) had been resolved. Others made more genuine efforts but provided few new insights.[39]

Liberation theologians had found the transition from the first phase of liberation theology (late 1960s and early 1970s) to the second phase (late 1970s) an empowering experience that strengthened their commitment to the poor. It proved harder to adjust to the challenges of a third phase in the 1980s. Their difficulties reflected many factors, including their areas of academic expertise, their personal backgrounds and their institutional traditions. Few liberation theologians that had been prominent in the 1970s were suitably trained or experienced to take work on gender or race forward with the same force and energy that they had shown in earlier work. Apart from a small number of theologically articulate women, the majority of Latin American liberation theologians found gender and race to be alien issues. In confronting poverty, many liberation theologians had experience in poor neighbourhoods, had undertaken personal vows of poverty as part of their vocation and had found ready support for their stance in the bible.

---

[38] See the various contributors to E Tamez (ed.), *Through Her Eyes: Women's Theology from Latin America*, Orbis Books, Maryknoll, NY, 1989 [Spanish orig. 1986].

[39] See Elsa Tamez's interviews of leading male liberation theologians, *Against Machismo: Rubem Alves, Leonardo Boff, Gustavo Gutiérrez, José Míguez Bonino, Juan Luis Segundo and Others Talk about the Struggle of Women*, Meyer-Stone Books, Oak Park, Il, 1987.

By contrast, their personal experiences usually did not prepare them to recognise or address race, cultural or gender differences as pressing concerns. They also lacked a strong heritage within their institutional identity that would support them with such challenges. The patriarchal culture that the church shared with every other social institution in Latin America was a major barrier to their engagement with sexism. The privileges of the European heritage that many of them shared may also have impeded their recognition of racial issues. The Catholic social traditions that had offered such firm support when dealing with economic poverty and political freedoms offered very little of value on gender issues, indeed it was usually part of the problem rather than part of a possible solution. Likewise the bible is permeated with patriarchal values and feminist theology therefore requires a more complex hermeneutics than generally adopted in Latin American liberation theology. The attempt to explore new dimensions of oppression and deepen the appreciation of poverty therefore met with limited success. Male liberation theologians had been emotionally and intellectually open to transformation by poverty but were both less familiar and less open to the challenges of race and gender.

As a result, instead of re-energising their work, attempts to explore wider issues of oppression often undercut the insight, creativity and impact of their work. There is some justification in talk of the 'failure' of Latin American liberation theology on these grounds. It would, however, be very misleading to see these difficulties as the only—or even the primary causes—of liberation theology's crisis in the 1990s. Other factors in the 1980s also need to be recognised as preparing the way for crisis. Perhaps most importantly, that the political and economic map of Latin America had started to change.

The 1980s saw a shift to formal democracy in many countries, for example, Argentina 1983, Brazil 1985 and Chile 1989, and the worst of the political repression abated with the transition to civilian rule. However, the majority of poor Latin Americans remained excluded from meaningful participation in the political process. At the economic level, during the 1980s 'Silent Revolutions' swept the continent and ushered in new neo-liberal economic policies that widened the gap between rich and poor.[40] In response to the debt crisis many countries looked to boost

---

[40] See D Green, *Silent Revolution: The Rise of Market Economics in Latin America*, Cassell, London, 1995.

growth by giving the free market and free trade a free reign. At the same time, governments imposed harsh 'structural adjustment' plans to slash spending on social services (including food subsidies, welfare benefits, education and health). Working conditions and union rights suffered as private enterprise capitalised on its new freedoms. The result was a partial gain in economic productivity in some sectors, but the destruction of whole industries elsewhere and unemployment or underemployment for many.

Liberation theology in the 1960s and 1970s called for liberation from dependency and dictatorship. In the new democracies of the 1980s the political option for the poor remained a pressing priority, but 'liberation' was as distant as ever and dependency was deepening. Limited political freedoms had been won but they did little to address the economic injustices. Liberation theology's class based analysis had initially developed in the very different atmosphere of the 1960s and was less suited to the new situation. The earlier language of liberation was quickly becoming less relevant to the new economic and political realities. The new poverty did not fit the straightforward class terms and there were no ready alternatives to replace them. Furthermore, the epistemological shift in the 1970s had reoriented liberation theology's focus on poverty in ways that told against prioritising new theoretical analysis. Early works had drawn on the wide-scale structural analysis of dependency theorists; later works had turned to the more immediate daily impact of poverty and oppression at grass-roots level. In addition, even if there had been a wish to return to more structural analysis, any sustained exploration of radical economic and political analysis in the 1980s was severely hampered by the need for liberation theology to defend itself against Vatican criticisms.

Under pressure from the Vatican many liberation theologians became more cautious in their direct comments on economic and political issues in the 1980s.[41] Gustavo Gutiérrez and Leonardo Boff, were under special scrutiny. They had to spend more time responding to criticisms (often very unfair ones) and less time on their own creative theological work. To speak of the poor and God's love for the poor was acceptable; to discuss political and economic analysis provoked complaints of politicising the gospel and Marxist reductionism.

---

[41] See P Lernoux, *People of God: The Struggle for World Catholicism*, Viking, New York, 1989.

There were also more indirect attacks against liberation theology by appointing more conservative bishops to dioceses that had previously been supportive of the base community movement. Training courses, national meetings and other resources that had supported the base communities were withdrawn.[42] In addition, the Vatican moved to absorb some of the key language of liberation theology more explicitly into its own vocabulary and muted the distinctiveness of the Latin American approach. Thus in *Sollicitudo Rei Socialis* ('On Human Concern', 1987) John Paul II endorsed the 'option or love of preference for the poor' (§ 42). Essentially, the Vatican's restoration policy combined firm discipline for 'errant' liberation theologians alongside a take-over and implicit correction of the original liberation theology enterprise.

At the same time, the creative dialogue with liberation theology's grass-roots base came under more strain. The religious situation was far more pluralist than ever before and liberation theology could no longer expect to be the only active and energetic church presence amongst the poor. Protestant churches—most usually fundamentalist or Pentecostal—spread dramatically during the decade, especially in Central America and Brazil where the base communities had previously been strongest.[43] Some critics claimed that although liberation theology opted for the poor, the poor opted for Pentecostalism.[44]

On a more positive front the 1980s witnessed a new attention to spirituality and contemplation in the work of some liberation theologians. Gutiérrez had already indicated in *A Theology of Liberation*

---

[42] The process of political democratization in many countries opened up alternative forums for political discussion and social action and some members of the communities left as a result.

[43] On the challenges raised by the Pentecostal Churches, see especially D Stoll, *Is Latin America Turning Protestant? The Politics of Evangelical Growth*, University of California Press, Berkley, Ca, 1990; D Stoll and V Garrard-Burnett, *Rethinking Protestantism in Latin America*, Temple University Press, Philadelphia, 1993; P Berryman, *Religion in the Megacity*, 9-101; M A Vásquez, *The Brazilian Popular Church*, 74-98; J Burdick, *Looking for God in Brazil: The Progressive Catholic Church in Urban Brazil's Religious Arena*, University of California Press, Berkeley, Ca, 1993, 182-220.

[44] Both the progressive and traditionalists saw the spread of Protestant Churches as detrimental to society but for rather different reasons. The progressives focussed their criticism on the depoliticized gospel of heavenly salvation whilst the traditionalists saw it as a challenge to institutional role of Catholicism in society. The tendency was to stereotype and dismiss the entire movement rather than recognise its diversity and seriously engage with the factors that made the Protestant churches so organisationally effective and so attractive to converts in Latin America's new political and economic context.

that there was a 'great need for a spirituality of liberation'.[45] In the 1980s he developed this in a number of his writings.[46] The rise of Sendero Luminoso or 'Shining Path'—an armed revolutionary movement based loosely on Maoist strategies and committed to the violent overthrow of society—and the response of government security forces unleashed new terror in Peru.[47] Gutiérrez's heart-felt meditations on the 'God of Life' in a culture of death are very different in tone from his work of the early 1970s but conveyed in an equally impressive way his solidarity with the poor and outrage at the injustices that they suffered. Particularly noteworthy in this regard was Gutiérrez's reformulation of his methodological principle to encompass contemplation as well as action as the first step on which critical reflection builds as the second step.[48]

Likewise, the 'suffering in hope' of the Salvadoran people influenced Jon Sobrino's focus on spirituality as the country degenerated into civil war during the 1980s.[49] His work during the period focussed on Christology with increasing attention to the experiences of a Crucified people in the present. In close collaboration with his fellow Jesuit Ignacio Ellacuría—and inspired by the legacy of Archbishop Oscar Romero—Sobrino read the idea of the Suffering Servant and Crucified Christ into the suffering and deaths of the Salvadoran people in ways that brought both ancient history and current reality to life.[50]

---

[45] Gutiérrez, *A Theology of Liberation*, 136.

[46] See especially G Gutiérrez, *The God of Life*, trans. M O'Connell, Orbis Books, Maryknoll, NY, SCM Press, London, 1991 [Spanish origs. 1982, 1989]; *We Drink from Our Own Wells: The Spiritual Journey of a People*, trans. M J O'Connell, Orbis Books, Maryknoll, NY, SCM Press, London, 1984 [Spanish orig. 1983]; *On Job: God-Talk and the Suffering of the Innocent*, trans. M J O'Connell, Orbis Books, Maryknoll, NY, SCM Press, London, 1987 [Spanish orig. 1985].

[47] On Sendero Luminoso, see D Scott Palmer (ed.), *Shining Path of Peru*, Hurst and Co., London, 1992; D Poole and Gerardo Rénique, *Peru: Time of Fear*, Latin America Bureau, London, 1992.

[48] See esp. G Gutiérrez, *On Job*, xi–xiv.

[49] J Sobrino, *Spirituality of Liberation: Towards a Political Holiness*, trans. Robert R Barr, Orbis Books, Maryknoll, NY, 1988 [Spanish orig. 1985].

[50] J Sobrino, *Jesus in Latin America*, trans. Various, Orbis Books, Maryknoll, NY, 1987 [Spanish orig. 1982]. After Ellacuría's assassination along with five other Jesuits, their housekeeper and her daughter by the Salvadoran military on 16 November 1989, Sobrino continued to develop this theme into the 1990s. See especially, J Sobrino, *Jesus the Liberator: A Historical-Theological View*, trans. P Burns and F McDonagh; Orbis Books, Maryknoll, NY, Burns and Oates, Tunbridge Wells, Kent; 1994 [Spanish orig. 1991]; *The Principle of Mercy: Taking the Crucified People from the Cross*, trans. various, Orbis Books, Maryknoll, NY, 1994 [Spanish orig. 1992].

The works by Gutiérrez, Sobrino and others in the 1980s are some of the most thought provoking writings by liberation theologians. They deepen the spiritual commitment to the liberation process and generate provocative insights into God's concern for the poor. However, they were not enough to overcome the growing problems that the movement faced as the 1980s progressed. Whilst the new insights were very valuable, they could not rectify the difficulties that the movement faced in its terminology of liberation. There was increasing recognition that straightforward talk of liberation was misleading, and earlier assumptions about economic dependency over-simplistic, but there was little that was offered as an alternative.

In retrospect, the 1980s was the decade in which liberation theology reached methodological maturity and many of the most profound works of liberation theology were written. Nonetheless by the end of the decade liberation theology was facing serious problems. These included: its terminology of liberation and its political and economic analysis growing steadily less relevant to a new context; the difficulties of engaging with wider dimensions of oppression in a creative and energising way; local pressures from conservative bishops and centralised opposition in the Vatican; a decline in the base communities as some members moved to more secular politics and others joined Pentecostal churches. It was still a powerful theological influence in Latin America and in progressive theological circles around the world but as a social movement its ability to provide leadership in responding to the forces that were transforming Latin America and the entire the global economy had been severely weakened. Its strengths and weaknesses were illustrated in an ambitious project to systematise liberation theology's contribution to theology. The *Theology and Liberation Series* was planned in the mid–1980s as a comprehensive statement on doctrinal areas in a 50-volume work that involved a number of the best-known liberation theologians. However, the project never realised its ambitious hopes and it was eventually suspended in 1993. The difficulties with the *Theology and Liberation Series* were a clear indication that despite the maturity of its theological writing, the liberation theology movement at the turn of the decade was entering a critical new phase.

The crisis in liberation theology in the 1990s

The fall of the Berlin Wall in 1989 showed the power of the market forces at work across the world. It would be far too simplistic to see the fall of the wall as proof of the 'triumph' of capitalism or the 'failure' of liberation theology, because the primary influence on liberation theology had always been the experiences of the poor and not Marxist theory or hopes for a socialist state; nonetheless the fall of the wall was an important symbol of how much economic and political assumptions had changed from liberation theology's origins in the 1960s.[51]

The globalisation of the free-market confirmed the neo-liberal trend apparent in Latin America in the 1980s and exposed the major questions that this raised for the economic analysis and terminology commonly associated with liberation theology. Despite the many flaws of the socialist regimes in the Soviet Union and Eastern Europe, at least they had shown that there was an alternative to free-market capitalism.[52] The possibility of an alternative informed the basic formulation of liberation and dependency in liberation theology's early works. In the 1990s they had to rethink many of these assumptions and hopes and were left with more questions than answers. There were few grounds for optimism that capitalism would bring relief to the poor but no clear alternatives. The financial shocks that hit Mexico and Brazil in the 1990s and Argentina in 2002 suggested that neo-liberalism could not bring economic salvation or promote social equality. However, although the economic problems were obvious the solutions remained elusive. The suffering of the poor was largely the same but the faith and hopes of the 1960s and 1970s had been replaced with uncertainty and doubt.

To make matters worse, the Vatican's continued opposition to the movement compounded the problems that liberation theology faced. John Paul II's consolidation of control over national bishop conferences

---

[51] Whilst a social analysis influenced by Marxism and the discussion of the importance of socialism had featured strongly in some of liberation theology's earliest works, since the mid-1970s they had given little time to these issues.

[52] Liberation theologians had recognised areas where even an imperfect socialism had strengths as well as weaknesses when compared to unchecked capitalism but there was never any significant enthusiasm for the versions of socialism institutionalised in the Soviet Union or Eastern Europe. See especially the discussion in McGovern, *Liberation Theology and its Critics*, 156-94.

(mainly through conservative episcopal appointments) and disciplinary action against individual theologians maintained the pressure on liberation theologians. Pressure on Leonardo Boff led him to resign from the Franciscan order in 1992. In 1995, Ivone Gebara (a Brazilian nun who had been at the forefront of women's contributions to liberation theology) was criticised for remarks she had made to the magazine *Veja* in 1993 about abortion, which the magazine misleadingly published under the title 'Nun Says Abortion Not a Sin'.[53] In 1995 her religious order—the Canonesses of St Augustine—were pressured into sending her to study in Europe for two years.[54]

At the same time the Vatican continued to make the language of liberation its own whilst emphasising the distinction between the 'reductionist' political version and the 'authentic' gospel version of liberation. The overall effect of this was that the overt conflict with liberation theologians receded. In a way, liberation theologians could legitimately claim official support and Vatican sanction for their work. However, it became much harder for liberation theologians to preserve the political edge in their message and distinguish themselves from the de-politicised way that others used their language.

At a theological level, some liberation theologians continued to engage with more diverse perspectives in their writing. Indigenous and ecological issues were added alongside the 1980s interest in race, culture and gender to further extend and expand the original class analysis.[55] As in the 1980s, in principle this wider perspective was an appropriate and necessary development for their message to preserve its integrity. However, in practice the diffusion and greater complexity of the issues made communication of a central message even more difficult and may have contributed to the feeling that the movement had in some sense lost its way. Grappling with new issues tended to fragment their previously clear

---

[53] See *The Tablet* 249 (1 July 1995), 851; I Gebara, 'The Abortion Debate in Brazil: A Report from an Eco-Feminist Philosopher and Theologian Under Siege', *Journal of Feminist Studies in Religion* 11.2 (1995), 129-136.

[54] She was originally meant to go to France but instead ended up in Belgium (where she had previously been a student at Louvain).

[55] On ecology and the environment, see L Boff, *Ecology and Liberation: A New Paradigm*, trans. J Cumming, Orbis Books, Maryknoll, NY, 1995 [Portuguese orig. 1993]; *Cry of the Earth, Cry of the Poor*, trans. Phillip Berryman, Orbis Books, Maryknoll, NY, 1997 [Portuguese orig. 1995]. On inculturation and indigenization, see M M Marzal *et al.*, *The Indian Face of God in Latin America*, trans. P R Hall, Orbis Books, Maryknoll, NY, 1996.

focus on poverty. Any one of these factors would have been a significant challenge for liberation theology, coming together in the way that they did they created a major crisis.

As the impact of the first generation of liberation theologians fades there are few signs of a new generation revitalising and sustaining the liberation theology movement in its original form. Many critics of the movement have been eager to call it a failure and pronounce it dead. However, even if liberation theology does not recover from the crisis as a movement, it would be misleading to think that it has no future as an important legacy. Its extraordinary achievements should never be forgotten. Whilst liberation theology always had important limitations— and these certainly became more apparent in the 1990s—the same is true for any theological attempt to engage with social issues on the historical plane. Liberation theology's terminology may now seem dated in the neo-liberal world economy, its social analysis has often been too limited, and postmodernism raises questions about its underlying philosophical foundations. However, the same criticisms could be made of many other theologies. Liberation theology's difficulties in reading the signs of the current times and presenting a prophetic response do not belong to liberation theology alone.

Looking to the future, the terminology of 'liberation' (which was once a key strength) now makes liberation theology vulnerable to dismissive superficial judgements. If the strong emphasis on liberation is no longer the helpful language that it once was—and others have co-opted it anyway—the 'theology of liberation' may be at an end. As Gustavo Gutiérrez has said, 'I was a Christian long before liberation theology and I will be a Christian long after liberation theology'.[56] New terminology may be needed to do justice to the complexity of the social realities of the present and future. Whether the new language will supplement the language of liberation or largely replace it remains to be seen.[57] However, in an unjust world that remains far from the promise of the kingdom of God, much of liberation theology's legacy will continue to be relevant for a politically engaged Christian faith.

---

[56] R M Brown, *Gustavo Gutiérrez: An Introduction to Liberation Theology*, Orbis Books, Maryknoll, NY, 1990, 22.

[57] In terms of terminology, it should not be forgotten that it is the early works of liberation theology that provide an inspirational example of how a new and relevant theological language can be found, even if they can no longer provide the language itself.

Conclusion

The 1990s was a decade of crisis for liberation theology but many of the announcements proclaiming the failure of liberation theology were superficial and misinformed. To discern the valuable theological legacies that Latin America liberation theology might have in the future it is helpful to understand its past and the separate strands that can be discerned in its chronological development. The brief overview of different phases in liberation theology offered above outlines the 1990s crisis in liberation theology against the successive development of the movement in the 1960s, 1970s and 1980s. Looking back on these earlier decades it is possible to identify the key advances that were made in the late-1960s. First, a pastoral concern for the poor that involved political commitment and solidarity with the struggle of the poor; second, a terminology of 'liberation' that provided a clear focus for the movement; third, a methodology that linked theology to social analysis and rooted reflection in action.

In the 1970s this was developed in at least three related ways. First, the language of an 'option for the poor'; second, the active involvement of the poor in the process of liberative action and reflection in the base communities; third, an epistemology that recognised the struggles of the poor as a special *locus* of God's revelation (developing in second half of the 1970s).

The achievements of liberation theology and the growth of the church of the poor in the 1970s were based on these principles. Military repression provided a clear vision of the economic and political challenges, a firm basis for solidarity and a unified programme for change. Against this background, the 1980s created new challenges for liberation theology. The restoration of limited democracies in the political sphere and the rise of neo-liberalism and globalization in the economic arena posed questions over the analysis that liberation theology had previously depended upon to articulate its option for the poor. In the 1960s and 1970s liberation theology's class-based analysis of political and economic issues had been its greatest strength. The new situation of silent revolutions was harder to interpret. Liberation theology's old social analysis started to lose its critical edge. Unfamiliar with the new economic issues, uncertain over new political forces, and now less committed to this level of theoretical analysis it did not develop a cohesive political–economic alternative. In addition the Vatican's sustained attack on liberation theology diverted its energies and made the movement more cautious in its political and economic stances. Finally, these difficulties coincided with liberation theology's own attempts to diversify the analysis of oppression beyond class based political and economic categories. This was an important and necessary development but not all liberation theologians were fully committed to it or well placed to undertake it.

When neo-liberal capitalism 'triumphed' with the fall of the Berlin Wall it seemed to many observers that liberation theology no longer had a valuable contribution to make on social justice matters. The argument here has been that the crisis in liberation theology in the 1990s had more complex origins, which were rooted in developments in the 1980s and earlier. Furthermore, although the problems in the 1990s were real ones—especially in regard to the terminology of liberation and the outdated socio-economic analysis—they do not invalidate the importance of the principles on which liberation was built or the significance of its legacy. Liberation theology first arose in response to the cries of the poor. Inequality in Latin America and across the world shows clear signs of getting worse rather than better in the future. As the 21st century begun, there were more poor people in Latin America than when liberation theology began in the 1960s and those who were poor were poorer than ever before. The movement called liberation theology may have come to an end, but the issues that it dealt with will remain just as pressing and many of its commitments just as important. Even if the terminology has to change, Christian theology in Latin America and elsewhere will need to keep faith with and build upon the core political, methodological and epistemological principles of liberation theology if it is to adequately engage with these issues in the future.

CHRISTIANITY IN
THE MIDDLE EAST
John H Watson

The world is drawing to a close. Only for one reason can it last longer; just because it happens to exist ... Suppose it should continue materially, would that be an existence worthy of its name, and of the historical dictionary? ... We shall furnish a new example of the inexorability of the spiritual and moral laws, and shall be their new victims: *we shall perish by the very thing through which we fancy that we live.* Technocracy will Americanise us. Progress will starve our spirituality so much that nothing of the bloodthirsty ... or unnatural dreams of the revolutionary will be comparable to these incontestable facts ... Universal ruin will manifest itself; not solely or particularly in political institutions, nor in general progress (or whatever else might be a proper name for it); it will be seen, above all, in the baseness of hearts.[1]

Not from Baghdad or Damascus; not from Brussels or Moscow; not from Islamabad or Kabul—though, within the boundaries of a particular speech, these words might well have come from any of these. The date is not 11 September 2001,[2] 14 May 1948[3] nor 5-10 June 1967[4]—though it might be any of those days. The writer is Baudelaire in the aftermath of the 1848 revolution. The sense of *living within an apocalypse* is common to many times and many places.

---

[1] Charles Pierre Baudeliaire (1821-67), *'Fusées', Oeuvres Complètes*, Gallimard, Paris, 1975, 665-66.
[2] R T Kendall, *The Day the World Changed*, London, 2001. Rowan Williams, *Writing in the Dust*, London, 2002. Eds. Jenny Baxter and Malcolm Downing, *The Day that Shook the World*, London, 2001.
[3] Lucas Grollenberg, *Palestine Comes First*, London, 1980, 44-74.
[4] Martin Gilbert, *Challenge to Civilisation*, London, 1999, 365-368.

Eschatology

The specific language of Eschatology is the primary language of Christian discourse in the Middle East. There is the colourful monk Fr Theophanes who meets William Dalrymple at Mar Saba in November 1994: 'Be careful. These are the Last Days. They are near their goal. They are everywhere now. Always be on your guard … the Arabs will be in Rome and the Whore of Babylon will be in the Vatican.'[5] Then there is the famous desert mystic Abba Justus el-Antoni, who died in 1976. Sacred silence was, for nearly forty years, the overruling ascetic accomplishment of his eremitical life. When he broke the silence, which was extremely rare, he had only one question to ask, 'What time is it now?' His posthumous fame rests upon this question. One commentator suggests that Justus was, with this question, calling attention to the *Parousia*.[6] Another says that Justus asked the time as a warning that all human time passes away as a vapour: 'Man must surely be vigilant for the ultimate salvation of his soul.'[7] A third observer attributes Justus with insight into the distinction between *chronos* and *kairos*. Justus was teaching that when the eternal breaks into the temporal there is a moment of *kairos*.[8] Certainly, pointing to the *Parousia* would be consistent with two millennia of commentary at the Monastery of St Antony the Great in the barren foothills of the Qalalah Mountains. Here the Abba lives in the endtime, embracing a life of physical privation in recompense for the vision he has been granted. Comparable Christian voices are as frequently heard in Syrian Aleppo and Iraqi Baghdad. (In the context of this paper, it must remembered that the Coptic Church in Egypt is the largest Church in the region: what can be said of the Copts can usually be said of the other Churches). Eschatology disturbs those Arab Christians who sense that we shall perish by the very thing through which we fancy that we live. But '*Faith-the-destroyer*' is something that dare not be articulated in any Middle Eastern faith community. Richard Dawkins is not a familiar name in Beirut. There could be danger in questioning regional eschatology in Western academic terms. Popular theology concentrates

---

[5] William Dalrymple, *From the Holy Mountain*, London, 1997, 308.
[6] Rodolph Yanney, 'Modern Coptic Saints', *The Coptic Church Review* Vol. 6 No.3 Fall/ Autumn 1985, Pennsylvania, USA, 1985, 84.
[7] Hegumen Maximus al-Antoni, *The Life of the Anchorite Saint Yustus Al-Antuni*, Cairo, 1989.
[8] John Watson, *Abba Justus: A Modern Desert Father*, Kent, 1993, 23.

upon an American End-Time message. The Coptic Church at Ard El Golf, Heliopolis was comfortable in the 1980s with Hal Lindsey's *Late Great Planet Earth* (which purports to describe the situation since 14 May 1948) and copies of Tim LaHaye can be found everywhere in Egypt at the beginning of this millennium.[9]

The most important aspect of current eschatology in Middle Eastern churches is its concentration upon biblical literalism with reference to specific geographical locations and historical events. Illustrative material is found in 'Research in trying to explain the time equations of the book of Daniel'.[10] The writer of this representative piece is Bishop Dioskoros who is now responsible for communications at the Coptic Patriarchate in Cairo. In the USA he had studied at the California Institute of Technology gaining a doctorate in seismology. He returned to Egypt and joined a monastery, adopting the name of his spiritual father, the parish priest of St George Sporting, Alexandria, Abouna Bishoi Kamel Ishak.[11] The young monk, Bishoi al-Antuni, 'of the monastery of St Anthony the Great', was consecrated Amba Dioskoros on 10 June 1979. In his Biblical study, he set out to solve what he calls 'the three simultaneous equations' that relate to the times referenced in the book of Daniel:

1. Daniel 9: 20-27. The time Jesus was crucified
2. Daniel 8: 13,14. The time of the birth of the false Christ
3. Daniel 12: 12,13. The time of the Second Coming of Christ

Dioskoros concluded that the Second Coming of Christ was to be expected in the autumn of 2001. The location for the *Parousia*, developed from his work as a seismologist, is to be the Haram al-Sharif.[12] This book is cited here because, far from being eccentric, it is an excellent example of the genre.

In eschatology and in regional politics location is everything.

---

[9] LaHaye is co-author of a series of books entitled the 'Left Behind Series' which offer a crude, unorthodox, fictional account of 'the last things'.

[10] Amba Dioskoros; the Arabic title is *Bahth fi Tafsir al-Mu'adalat al-Zamaniyya Allati fi Sifr Daniel*, Abbasiya, 1994.

[11] John H Watson, *The Transfigured Cross: A Study of Father Bishoi Kamel (6 December 1931- 21 March 1979)*, Pennsylvania, USA, 2002.

[12] 'The Noble Sanctuary' is the Temple Mount above the Western (Wailing) Wall and the site of the Dome of the Rock and Al-Aqsa ('the furthermost') mosque.

The sense of place

Metropolitan Abraham[13] of Jerusalem presents an Arab Christian view of the sense of place: 'Holy sites are a physical, tangible proof, and an archaeological, historical witness of the reality of salvation through our Lord ... To come and see the empty tomb' is to 'be sure that he rose from the dead as he said he would' ... 'Pilgrims are able to live through the events of salvation' ... 'We see the holy sites and feel them ... with our eyes and senses.'[14] For Orthodox, this is the normative experience. This sense of place is expressed when we so frequently see the Oriental Orthodox removing their shoes at the entrance to every sanctuary. The practice is very primitive. It has its origin in 'the general Semitic sense that a condition of shoelessness is a sacrament of reverence'.[15] It is natural to reflect upon the record in Exodus; 'Come no closer! Remove the sandals from your feet, for the place on which you are standing is holy ground'.[16] The casting off of footwear is a 'placing-to-the-side' of the more tangible pre-occupations of the pilgrim. Barefoot, the intention is to remain within the Holy.[17] A failure to sense the significance of place, and of sensitivity towards place, is surely at the root of Al-Aqsa *Intifada*. When General Sharon entered the sensitive space of the Haram al-Sharif on 28 September 2000, it was particularly provocative, given his actions in South Lebanon in 1982, where an Israeli enquiry found him indirectly responsible for the massacres in Sabra and Shatila.[18] The desecration of sacred space was deliberate.

The Egyptian sense of a holy site defiled predates Sharon. The Coptic Pope Shenouda III has prohibited pilgrimages to the Holy Land

---

[13] Amba Abraham worked for many years as a research pharmacist at the National Research Centre, Dokki, Cairo before a brief period as a monk, Sidrak El Amba Bishoi, *c.* 1981. He was consecrated 17 November 1991. Named at birth Ibrahim Sedrak, BSc in Agriculture, mid-1960s. PhD in Agriculture, early 1970s, both from Cairo University. He also received a PhD in Theology circa 1975 at the Coptic Institute.

[14] Ed. Naim Ateek *et al.*, *Jerusalem. What makes for Peace!*, Melisende, London, 1997, 107-110.

[15] Kenneth Cragg, *Sandals at the Mosque*, London, 1959, 25.

[16] Exodus 3.5. The scriptural quotations are from the NRSV. © Division of Education NCCC, USA,1995.

[17] Muslim practice at the mosque is based upon the Qur'an's gloss on Exodus 3 in Surah 20.12: 'Take off thy sandals! Behold, thou art in the twice-hallowed valley.' Al-Tabari dates the custom from the time of 'Umar, but other authorities suggest the second year of the Hijrah.

[18] Robert Fisk, *Pity the Nation: Lebanon at War*, London, 1990, 569.

for thirty years. Disobedience meant excommunication. Shenouda even reiterated this prohibition when placed under house arrest by Anwar Sadat in 1981. In the mid-90s sources in Egypt stated that 10,000 Copts had been excommunicated and would be required to make public confession in newspapers before they could be reinstated.[19] The newspaper *Al-Keraza* and the magazine *Al-Mosauwar* published cautions on May 5, 1995. At Easter 1996 further warnings appeared. Many ignored them. Records in the 1960s and 70s have shown that tens of thousands of Copts were usually in Jerusalem for Holy Week and Easter. Pilgrimage to Jerusalem has a vital place in Coptic Folk religion. In Easter 1995 it was calculated that 15, 000 Copts went to Jerusalem despite the Pope's ban.[20]

The prohibition was often mentioned in Egypt. In April 1995 a government publication debated the issue. The Pope stated his view that pilgrimage was 'a matter of Church discipline'. Copts must 'support Arab rights before the Israelis.'[21] He claimed that tour companies, angry at loss of revenue, backed his critics. But a characteristic response from a Copt in the American Diaspora was, 'As for the Pope's ban on visiting Jerusalem, I wish that His Holiness stayed away from politics that put restrictions on him and the majority of the Copts. As the Muslims can go to Mecca and Jerusalem, the Copts can go to the Holy Sepulchre.'[22] Monks from the monastery of St Macarius continued to lead pilgrimages because the physical presence of Copts at the sacred sites was indispensable. For other Christians it might not be the same. Commenting on Western, and specifically Catholic sensibilities Glen Bowman has said: 'It is from the significance, not the places, that one draws inspiration, and the places serve primarily as *loci* where the pilgrims are better able to body forth the subjects of their meditations in their imaginations.'[23] But a Coptic pilgrim writes: 'I visited Jerusalem twice. It was a moving experience every time. I remember being at the holy tomb of Christ for the first time and thinking that all Christianity depends on it—the resurrection

---

[19] Wolfram Reiss, *Erneuerung in der Koptische Orthodoxen Kirche*, Hamburg, 1998.

[20] See *Syndesmos*, Orthodox Press Service No. 59 April 1995, 1-4; cf. *Sourozh* No. 60 London, May 1995, 50.

[21] Lee Keath in *Egypt Today*, April 1995, 87-91.

[22] Private E-mail.

[23] Glenn Bowman. *Christian Ideology and the image of the Holy Land. The place of Jerusalem Pilgrimage in the various Christianities* in Eade and Sallnow eds., London, 1991, 114 and cf. *Contemporary Christian Pilgrimage in the Holy Land*, ed. O'Mahony *et al.*, 1995, and *Palestinian Christians*, ed. O'Mahony, 1999.

of Christ—tears were in my eyes. The second time I visited Jerusalem, I stayed with a family a few minutes walk away from the tomb. So, every night before closing I went there in the Church and sat across the tomb in silence.'[24]

At the Cairo International Bookfair in August 2001, Shenouda said that Jerusalem remains at 'the very core of the Arab–Israeli conflict and each party holds firm to its rights ... Consecutive Israeli governments get even more extreme.' He was happy to receive an invitation from the Iraqi government to visit Baghdad, but continued to hold firm on his refusal to visit Israeli controlled Jerusalem. He would only go at the invitation of Yasser Arafat, with a visa issued by the Palestinian National Authority and hand in hand with the Grand Imam of Al Azhar, Mohamed Sayed Tantawi. 'This position does not require any reconsideration, given the steady deterioration in the political and humanitarian conditions in the occupied lands'. A visit in 2001 would mean 'normalisation'. 'We will not gain anything by it, and only the Israelis will gain economic prosperity. Jews have no rights to Jerusalem; they did not rule it except for a short period before the birth of Christ. Most of the time, the Persians, Romans and Arabs reigned.' Shenouda has always been consistent on this issue. When the Pope met President Carter he told him that God could not regard the Jews as God's specially chosen people, because this would mean that the Christians had not been chosen. The patriarch's rather dubious rider was, 'As for political questions we only talk about general principles, and leave details to the politicians. Jerusalem is both a theological and political question.'[25] Orthodox American comment is guarded: 'Talk of Jerusalem is unwelcome in the USA. In Orthodox churches it is never mentioned. It is recognised that Eastern Orthodox, Syrians, Ethiopians and Copts control many shrines. Catholics seem hardly aware of the Latin sites. Protestants know that 'our Old Testament brethren' have a lobby so strong that any criticism regarding Jerusalem is considered a slight.'[26] Certainly, the painful account of Rosemary Radford Ruether's confrontation with *B'nai Brith*

---

[24] Private e-mail. cf. Iris Habib El Masri, *Magnetic Radiation: the story of Father Pishoi* [sic] *Kamel*, Alexandria, 1989. John H Watson, *The Transfigured Cross*, Philadelphia, 2002.
[25] See *Al-Keraza*, September 1981; cf. Mohammed Heikal, *Autumn of Fury*, London, 1983, 161.
[26] Private e-mail but quoted with permission.

and the Council of Christians and Jews at North Western University has a painful ring of truth.[27]

There is some secularist sympathy for the idea of Jerusalem as an international city. The Palestinian negotiator, Ahmed Qrei a.k.a. *Abu Alaa* told the European Parliament that the Palestinians could be willing to accept 'international sovereignty': 'Jerusalem would then not be the capital of Israel or Palestine but of the world'. Israel and the US are unlikely to embrace that proposal, but if Qrei is talking about the Old City, it might serve as the basis for negotiations with Israeli liberals. But 'internationalisation' would mean a retreat from the Palestinian position of total sovereignty over East Jerusalem.[28] The overwhelming fear is of a lost Christian presence. There is a Christian political consensus concerning the daily tragedy, to which we are armchair witnesses. Bishop Riah Abu El-Assal: 'If we do not find a solution quickly, the land where our faith was born and survived for two thousand years will soon be empty of indigenous Christians. The living faith will be represented only by dead stones and their imported custodians.'[29] The politically assertive Orthodox identify with the radical Palestinian opinions of the Latin Patriarch Michel Sabbah whom they firmly believe to be a cardinal *in pectore*,[30] another victim of Israeli propaganda. The association of Zionist oppression with Nazi oppression is a common theme in private conversation throughout the region. In examining the 'victim of the victimised' it has been carefully argued that European error must not be used as an excuse for silence when Arabs are victims. Palestine was never the arena of the Holocaust, but Palestinians have become victims of the Shoah.[31]

'Replacement Theology'

Geography and History have a central role in the Christian theology of the Middle East, and Eschatology is confused with both in what is described as 'replacement theology'. This term might appear to be the

---

[27] *They Came and they Saw*, ed. Michael Prior, London, 2000, 69-76.
[28] Graham Usher in *Al-Ahram* Weekly, 7-13 September 2000, Issue No. 498
[29] Riah Abu El-Assal, *Caught in Between*, London, 1999, 15; cf. *Demanding Peace; A Church Response to the Al-Aqsa Intifada*, A Report by the Church of England's Board of Social Responsibility, London, October 2001.
[30] Held in Pope John Paul II's heart: one of two *in pectore* from 21 February 1998.
[31] Kenneth Cragg, *Palestine: the prize and price of Zion*, London, 1997, 89-108.

invention of Melanie Phillips in her *Spectator* article of 16 February 2002 were it not for the fact that a search machine on a computer offered over 19,000 occurrences of this term, in pieces about so-called Messianic Judaism. The standard term was 'supercessionism'. In the *Spectator* of 23 February, an Israeli commented, 'a genuine article is 'replaced' with a substitute, while an outdated idea is 'superseded' by a newer one.'[32] This is a territory of confusion rather than anti-Semitism. Pope John Paul II, in his Easter letter of 1986 stated 'the covenant remains with the Jews'. A resolution of the Lambeth Conference in 1988 rejected 'any view of Judaism which sees it as simply superseded by Christianity.' The Vatican Declaration *Nostra Aetate* had a similar agenda.

Western declarations cannot represent the regional Christian understanding of the relationship between Judaism and the Church. Pope Shenouda does not use the term 'replacement theology', but encourages the use of his book 'Christianity, Israel and the issue of Jerusalem' in connection with the Aqsa *Intifada*.[33] His views appeared recently in the Egyptian press under the headline: *No room for the idea of God's chosen people*. He quotes extensively from the Scriptures. 1 Kings 9: 6-9 is illustrative of the rejection of Israel when it disobeys God. 'If you turn aside from following me, you or your children, and do not keep my commandments and my statutes that I have set before you, but go and serve other gods, and worship them, then I will cut Israel off from the land I have given them ...' Israel would be 'a proverb and a taunt among all peoples'. Even the temple would be destroyed.

We have to ask an important question, which is: Did the children of Israel keep the promise of the Lord so that they deserve the Promised Land or did they not keep the covenant of God? Even Solomon did not obey God. His wives turned his heart away. He burnt incense to their gods. His kingdom

---

[32] Melanie Phillips. *Christians who hate Jews*. Spectator 16 February 2002. Israel Shamir Internet: *To the Angel of the Church in Canterbury*. 20 February 2002. Jaffa, Israel; and in Letters to Spectator 23 February 2002.

[33] The source of all the news items in this paper is RNSAW. The author has been a member of the Board of the Religious News Service from the Arab World since its inception over a decade ago. RNSAW offers weekly translations and summaries from the Arabic press on Islam, Christianity and Muslim-Christian relations, with regional religious reportage from the Lebanon to Sudan. The RNSAW offers the widest variety of opinions ranging from government directed publications to left wing, liberal and Islamist periodicals. RNSAW attempts to avoid the often one-sided presentation of these subjects.

was divided. God's promise to David was not fulfilled because David violated the commandments. Writing primarily for Muslims readers, Shenouda says: The children of Israel made the Prophet Musa (Moses) suffer because of their complaining. Did the children of Israel stop their complaints? No. Shenouda cites Scripture at length. (Exodus 16:2. Numbers 11:11. Exodus 17:4.Numbers 14:11.Exodus 32:4.Exodus 32:9).

Now I want to ask: Where was the promise of God when He said that His wrath might wax hot against the children of Israel? There is no room then for the idea of God's chosen people. According to Christianity, God's chosen people are all the people who truly believe in God.[34]

Shenouda's populist 'supercessionism' is given at his weekly teaching sessions in St Mark's Cathedral Abassiya. They were called 'the lesson of Friday' (*dars el-guma'a*) and it is appropriate to note that Mohamed Heikal believes them to be based upon the 'Lesson of Tuesday' conducted by Hassan el–Banna.[35] Shenouda has been banned from Cairo on Fridays since September 1981 and now holds the 'Lesson' midweek. Thousands attend. The communal-political value of the event cannot be doubted.

The clash of civilisations and religious dialogue

A mirror faced a mirror: ire and hate
Opposite ire and hate; the multiplied,
The complex charge rejected, intricate,
From side to sullen side;
One plot, one crime, one treachery, nay, one name,
Assumed, denounced, in echoes of replies.
The doubt, exchanged, lit thousands of one flame
Within those mutual eyes.[36]

---

[34] *Al-Ahali*, Cairo, 6 February 2002.
[35] Hassan el–Banna was the Guide of the Muslim Brotherhood. See Gilles Kepel, *The Prophet and Pharaoh; Muslim Extremism in Egypt*, trans. Jon Rothschild, London, 1985; cf. Heikal, *op. cit.*, 161.
[36] Alice Meynell (1847-1922).

Alice Meynell, the poet of these fine lines, would find a gazeteer of such hatred—usually in its relgious form—stretching from Papua New Guinea to Belfast. There is, to be sure, a dark history of treachery and enmity in all faiths.[37] There is a clash of civilisations.

In the Middle East the enmity runs with the spirituality. There is a need to define by difference. Edward Said's demolition of Samuel Huntington has always been unconvincing.[38] Said has refused to accept that there is a clash though it is evident that there are people who wish to be confronting, clashing and colliding. We are condemned to strife because the choice is made for strife. No culture is pure, monolithic, nor eternally decreed by an act of divine genesis. Of course not. But such things are wished to be. Shenouda wishes to define his difference from Rome, Canterbury and Geneva. Victoria Clark's central thesis is unanswerable.[39] Anyone who has lived and worked with Eastern Christians knows this. For official Islam and Christianity there is a form of mutual display but not dialogue. Reverting to eschatological mode : 'On a worldwide basis Civilisation seems in many respects to be yielding to barbarism, generating the image of an unprecedented phenomenon, a global Dark Ages, possibly descending on humanity.'[40]

The Cairene press has refused to see any connection between terrorism and Islam, believing that *the clash of civilizations* is nothing but a false mask behind which America conceals its real target, which is to consolidate its international control. Western media defames Arabs by relating the actions of terrorists, war mongers and opponents of democracy to Islam. The Cairene journal *Al-Akbar* affirmed its creed that Islam interacted tolerantly with all civilizations. Muslim and Coptic coexistence in Egypt is a unique example of interreligious co-operation. Islam is capable of coexistence with the other, according to *Al-Akbar*. Those who believe that the Western-Islamic clash means that Arab Christians are in one trench with the West, because they are Christians, are wrong. If the issue was really a clash of civilizations—between Islamic civilization and

---

[37] Kenneth Cragg in H B Dehqani-Tafti, *The Unfolding Design of My World*, Norwich, 2000, 258.

[38] Samuel P Huntington, *The Clash of Civilisations and the Remaking of World Order*, London, 1997. Edward Said's review, *The Uses of Culture*, appeared in *Al-Ahram* Weekly, 13 February 1997

[39] Victoria Clark, *Why angels fall: A journey through Orthodox Europe from Byzantium to Kosovo*, London, 2000.

[40] Huntington, *op. cit.*, 321.

Western civilization—which is wrongly called Christian civilization—
why then, Coptic and Arab Christians would always be in one trench
with Egyptian and Arab Muslims. There is not, and there will never be a
religious clash. The clash is a political clash that aims at achieving financial
goals and American interests. In the Arab world, Islamic civilization
encompasses Muslims and Christians, making of them one unity.[41]

Al-Akbar's creative exposition was certainly supported by the
Coptic weekly, *al-Keraza*. Shenouda's editorial stated that 'Jews' have
intensive public relations efforts, including direct communications with
US media and with Congress. Arabs wail about their luck without taking
any positive action to improve the situation. Arabs—Muslim and
Christian—ought to form an Arab lobby to offset the Jewish lobby. Shenouda
asked why all Arab embassies and politicians did not engage in political
communication with congressmen and politicians, media outlets, and
broadcasters. 'The international climate is ready for such a step' because of
tense Israeli—US relationships. For Shenouda, Professor Huntington's clash
is between a spiritually directed Middle East and a misdirected materialist
West. There is no clash between Christian and Islamic civilization.

Perhaps there is no clash because there is no dialogue. Islam and
Christianity in the Middle East have the capacity to make statements to
each other without reciprocity. In a February 2002 interview with the
Grand Imam of the Azhar, Sheikh Muhammad Sayyed Tantawi, it was
reported that the dialogue with the Anglican Communion was established
to clear the confusion and uncertainty that was caused by the terrorists
and focus upon the support of oppressed people, articulating the 'voice
of religion'. Dr Tantawi said that all religions preach peace but Islam
especially does so. The interview conveyed the impression that
pronouncements would have priority over dialogue. 'I explain the
Palestinian issue from the religious point of view. Islam preaches tolerance
and the support of the oppressed. An international force should go to
Palestine and mediate between the two groups. The Islamic *Shari'a* is
based upon tolerance and giving each person his rights. The *Shari'a* also
stresses the necessity of forgiveness.'[42] The Imam believes that the most
important thing is that dialogue should be focused not on 'creeds' but on

---

[41] Gamal Asaad, *Civilizational Islam and the coexistence among religions* in *Al-Akhbar*, February 14
2002.
[42] God's forgiveness is integral here and Surah 100 of the Qur'an (*Nasr*, or Help) should be
explored.

supporting the oppressed and 'sending reports to presidents informing them that a specific country is being attacked and needs their support'.[43]

These glimpses into popular perceptions of dialogue are merely illustrative.

The Qur'an and the Bible

Anyone examining the potential for Muslim-Christian dialogue in the Middle East must address the question of religious texts. Copts and Muslims have comparable dogmas of infallible and inerrant scripture: dogmas proclaimed by ideologues with an accompanying and absolute rejection of any exploration of possible historical sources or textual criticism. Shenouda has constantly and usually angrily rejected the idea that biblical study should involve *asking about a biblical book the same kind of questions that one would ask about any other book, were one trying to discover what message was trying to be conveyed*.[44] Textual criticism is anathema in Orthodox seminaries. *The revelation is secure in the church*, is a popular Coptic phrase.

The most influential Christian text in the region is the Arabic Bible, the work of the American Arabists Eli Smith (1801-57) and Cornelius Van Dyck (1818-95) with their Syrian colleagues Butrus al-Bustani (1819-93) and Nasif al-Yaziji (1800-71). The accessibility and ubiquity of this text has produced a defensive biblical literalism. The final recension of the Qur'an dates from the 7th century. The Qur'an 'by virtue of its brief temporal incidence of twenty-three years in one country, through one prophet',[45] stands in vivid contrast to the library of the Christian Scriptures. The Copts are Biblical fundamentalists, adhering to the doctrine of the verbal infallibility of the Holy Bible. The context is not Coptic history and tradition. Before the Smith-Van Dyck Bible the Copts were not Biblical fundamentalists. The context is Islam, but an Islam related to the Evangelical Christian incursions of the 19th century. Islam speaks of the *Umm al-Kitab*, 'the mother of the Book', heaven's

---

[43] Iqbal Al-Siba'ai, *Dialogue between religions is an order from God.* An interview with the Sheikh al-Azhar on inter-religious dialogue, in *Rose El-Youssef,* February 9-15 2002.
[44] See Raymond E Brown, *Responses to 101 Questions on the Bible,* New York, 1990.
[45] Kenneth Cragg, *Readings in the Qur'an,* London, 1988.

eternal counterpart of the Qur'an here on earth. Islam speaks of *Tanzil*, the sending down of the contents of the Qur'an piecemeal, whereby the heavenly Book, at Allah's side, comes down to the lips of the prophet Muhammad. 'The Bible says' is a Protestant phrase. When the Qur'an is quoted in Islam, 'God says'. It has been one of the most urgent programmes of the Oriental Orthodox in the last century to *qur'anise* the Bible. The enormous passages of narrative, poetry and theology in the Hebrew Bible and Greek New Testament do not easily compare with the chapters (*surahs*) of the Qur'an but since infallibility is claimed for the Islamic text then the Copts must '*quranise*' the Bible.

Middle Eastern Christians are uncomfortable with reflections about 'Jesus the Jew'. When the Second Vatican Council promulgated the declaration *Nostra Aetate* (1965), absolving the Jewish people of deicide, Coptic Pope Kyrillos the Sixth (reigned 1959-1971) condemned the declaration as an imperialist-Zionist plot against the Arab nations and their churches. The Arabic word *Isra'iliyun* refers to both Old Testament Jews and modern Israelis. Recent attempts to expunge the word from liturgical texts are highly problematic, considering the Jewish provenance of the Gospel. Jesus as an authoritative preacher is not unlike a prophet in Islam or a rabbi of Judaism. But for the Coptic exegete the *Logos* of the Fourth Gospel, a book regarded as authoritative narrative, even marginalises Jesus as miracle-worker, healer and exorcist. The Bible is read as confirming the insights of Alexandrian Christology, and the distinction between the Jesus of the New Testament and the equivalent *Isa* of the Qur'an must be expressed as the deepest divergence between a prophet in Islam and the Divine *Logos* of the Christians.

Most Middle Eastern Christians reject the methods of historical criticism. All Muslims are deeply suspicious of any attempt to compare and contrast the *surahs* of Meccan or Medinan provenance. A valuable comment from a moment in the Iranian Revolution should be noted: 'Accents in the Medinan part of the Qur'an might have 'justified' the bitter hostility, where 'killing' is seen as a lesser evil than *Fitnah*, or alleged divergence from Islam. In the longer Meccan period, however, Muslims in the Qur'an were innocent of all power-politics and lived on the receiving end of much adversity themselves.'[46] The passion of *Bilal El-*

---

[46] Kenneth Cragg, in H B Dehqani-Tafti, *op. cit.*, 258.

Habashi[47] and the *Muhajirun*[48] might be contrasted with the effective military policy of the first Islamic society, and this might be consequential. But only modernizers and Christian sympathizers can be heard saying that this would be beneficial.

It is clear that the dialogue about public policy lacks the force and virtue of spiritual intimacy. The Qur'an and the Bible cannot speak to each other. Dialogue is only a word.

Ecumenism

The Ecumenical situation in the Middle East may be glimpsed in the Church of the Holy Sepulchre in Jerusalem where we hear the 'cacophony of warring chants'[49] More: 'One desires holiness, only to encounter a jealous possessiveness.' Beyond the failure of ecumenism 'the frailty of humanity is nowhere more apparent than here (Jerusalem); it epitomises the human condition.'[50]

The legal confrontation between Ethiopians and Copts at Deir As-Sultan is one of the most extraordinary illustrations of the breakdown in ecumenical relations. 'Who holds the monastery's keys?' has been the subject of much litigation. The case has been thoroughly documented. Sufficient to say that the relations between these sister churches are at their lowest in forty years.[51] In David Burrell's memorable phrase, 'the sharpness of the feelings testifies to the depth of the realities at work.'[52]

The names of heretics are lost in the mists of time and most Christians in the first decade of the third millennium do not know what a heretic is. With names like Nestorius and Arius they might just as well be extra terrestrials. For Armenian, Coptic and Syrian laity the debates

---

[47] Mustafa Akkad's 1975 film (Polygram video) *The Message*—with Anthony Quinn as Hamza and Irene Papas as Hind—offers an intensely dramatic presentation of the suffering of Bilal, an Ethiopian and the first muezzin of Islam.

[48] The immigrants who took part in the *Hijrah* from Mecca to Medina.

[49] Jerome Murphy O'Connor, OP, *The Holy Land; An archaeological guide from Earliest Times to 1700*, 49.

[50] *Op. cit.*, 50.

[51] Otto Meinardus, *The Copts in Jerusalem*. AUC Press, Cairo, 1960. Otto Meinardus, *Coptic Church Review*, Pennsylvania, USA, 1995. Aziz Attiya, *The Copts and Christian Civilisation*, Utah, USA, 1979. Cf. (ed.) Anthony O'Mahony, *The Christian Communities in Jerusalem*, University of Wales Press, 2003.

[52] David C Burrell. *Jerusalem after Jesus*, in *The Cambridge Companion to Jesus*. Cambridge, 2001.

of the 5th century are not merely insignificant but petty. For Armenian Catholicos Aram the First, Pope Shenouda the Third and Syrian Orthodox Patriarch Zakka the First such names and debates were sufficiently important to keep them occupied for several days in March 1998, preparing a paper condemning heresy.[53]

The reasons for this Armenian–Coptic–Syriac declaration are bad and sad.

For many years the Assyrian Church of the East has attempted to gain membership of the Middle East Council of Churches. They were founder members of the World Council of Churches in Amsterdam in 1948. This small Church has suffered terribly for centuries. Recent patriarchs were martyred in Iran.[54] Nestorian studies in recent years have shown that theological issues separating the Assyrians from larger churches are related entirely to language and technical terminology.[55] The circumstances are similar to those in which Oriental Orthodox were accused of the Monophysite heresy, but Shenouda, Aram and Zakka are believed to have deliberately excluded the Indian and Ethiopian churches from their gathering. The ecclesiastical politics lying behind their declaration is more significant than the condemnation itself. It is directed against the WCC and the Vatican.

On 11 November 1994 Pope John Paul II and Patriarch Mar Dinkha IV signed a joint Christological declaration. This was reported in Egypt and condemned by the Copts. Rome was wrong and if the WCC had once accepted Nestorians it also needed to be put in its place. Shenouda's incessant condemnation of women priests and homosexuals is widely advertised, but his strongest criticisms are always directed against the Roman Catholic Church. It alone has been a serious threat to Coptic Orthodox autonomy in Egypt. Its theologians have invariably been scholars of great distinction. The statement against the Assyrians was published as a catch-all condemnation. The damage done to every Middle Eastern Christian in the House of Islam is inestimable.

A more encouraging discovery is that the natural ecumenical partners in many parts of the Arab world are the Anglicans and Catholics. Of special importance is the relationship between His Beatitude Stephanos

---

[53] *El Karaza,* 13.14, 10 April 1998.
[54] H B Deqhani-Tafti, *op. cit.,* 165, cf. 218, 232.
[55] Sebastian Brock, *The Christology of the Church of the East,* Athens, 1985. D W Winkler *Koptische Kirche und Reichskirche,* Innsbruck, 1997.

the Second, the Patriarch of the Coptic Catholic Church in Egypt[56] and Dr Mouneer Anis the Anglican Bishop in Egypt. These two immensely impressive bishops provide a model for Christian cooperation, which is, to say the least, encouraging. They are men of honesty and holiness. Stephanos experienced his formation as a Lazarist[57] father in the Congregation of the Mission in Paris. Mouneer was a general practitioner for many years before his ordination. Intellectually, it is fair to say that the influence of Anglicans and Catholics has been out of all proportion to their size in Egypt and the Arab world. Christiaan van Nispen, Henri Boulad, and Samir Khalil with Kenneth Cragg, William Taylor and Naim Ateek are examples of those who have made distinctive and outstanding contributions in Ecumenical-Christian and inter-faith studies.

Tragically, the overwhelming model of church government throughout the region has been autocracy guaranteed by privilege. The problem is common to all churches: an unwelcome Anglican insistence on the reestablishment of the Jerusalem archbishopric, an episcopal *grotesque* who against all tradition requires his flock to kiss his hand, and the Episcopalian demand for denominational separation within a Muslim state: these are modest pretensions compared with a tradition bound system where the patriarch's head is turned by the obsequious adulation of the populace. It should not be thought, however, that all Orthodox are willing victims of a hierarchical system.

Looking to the future of the Church in Egypt

A work of enormous significance was published in Egypt in February 2002, and has been reviewed in the secular press.[58] It is only available in

---

[56] Stephanos Cardinal Ghattas was born at Sheik Zein Eddin near Sohag in Upper Egypt, 16 January 1920. He trained in Rome and was ordained priest on 25 March 1944. He served most of his life in Egypt and was elected Patriarch of Alexandria on 9 June 1986.

[57] The Lazarists—Congregation of the Mission—are a congregation of secular priests with religious vows founded by St Vincent de Paul. The members add the letters CM to their name. As with many other communities, an appellation from the founder, or the place they dwell in, has superseded the original title. Thus in France and in almost all countries they are called Lazarists, because it was in the Priory of St Lazare in Paris that St Vincent de Paul dwelt and there that he established his principal work. In the Irish province, which includes practically all English-speaking countries except the United States, they are called Vincentians, and this name is gradually replacing that of Lazarists in the United States.

[58] Osama Salama, 'What is the relationship between the church and politics? An overview of

Arabic but its English title would be 'The Divine Wisdom behind the Structure of the Church.' A monk who belongs to Abu Maqar monastery in the Wadi Natroun edited the book. The Abbott there is Abouna Matta El Meskeen.[59] All the current issues of Coptic commonalty are revealed in the most revealing document on the Copts that has been produced in the last three decades. Only a bald précis is possible, but each sentence is of immense significance for the future of Middle Eastern Christianity:

Egyptian Christians cannot be passive, but no mixing between religion and politics should take place. Christians should contribute to intellectual, cultural and social concerns. The Copts are not a minority. They should collaborate with other groups in Egypt. Their abilities and their talents—not their numbers—are the true measure of their value.

Copts appealing to the Minority Rights Group at the UN have often been excluded.

Clergymen not laymen represent the church. So, it is important to know what the relationship between church and state should be. What can the church offer society? The duty of the church toward the country is to help politicians to see a practical example of what the world should be like. The church should be an example of the ideal social system. It should be a positive power that pushes the world towards a better future. The church cannot be silent in regard to injustice and violence, but it is a shame when the church confines its efforts to the defence of its members. The church has an interior life, which is based on the sense of cooperation and love among its members, and knows how to settle debates. The church's credibility depends upon defending anyone who is persecuted, without regard to religion or race. This will illustrate the purity of the church.

This is all straightforward, but the proposed reforms are contentious.

The Divine Wisdom behind the Structure of the Church, *Rose El-Youssef*, 23 February-1 March, 2002, RNSAW.

[59] See Matthew the Poor, *The Communion of Love*, New York, 1984.

The author explains that the patriarch and synod should depend upon the *Maglis Al-Milli*—the official and elected Council of the Coptic Community. Its role must be restored to include independent priests and Copts with senior positions in the state. 'To reactivate the role of the *Maglis Al-Milli* is a central concern for the Church.' The *Maglis Al-Milli* will contribute to society when it offers a considered solution to major issues: crime, drugs and international relations.

The present patriarch has conducted a careful tactical campaign against the Community Council, excommunicating members who opposed him. But a greater danger to the Church in Egypt is with those who have left their homeland.

The international Coptic Diaspora must stick to the policy of the church at home. 'It must not replace the mother church.' The focus of the emigrant church must be the kingdom of God. Migrant clergy who concentrate upon political and ideological issues violate the gospel.

The American Coptic Association is a powerful political organisation directed by Professor Shawky Karas, a brilliant mathematician and militant from Sohag in Upper Egypt. There are parallel organisations in Australia, Canada and the United Kingdom.

Priests have no authority to take part in party politics. Priests are for prayer. 'If we pray for the President, we should not participate in any action that offends him'. To offend the President is to offend all Copts. Misrepresenting the President in a foreign country will make things worse. Emigrant churches have a mission, which is taking care of the new generation and revealing the spirit of Eastern Christianity in the West. The problems of Egypt's Christians can only be solved in Egypt by the whole nation.

The real problems of the Church are revealed by the following remarks:

Divorces, trials of the clergy and excommunications must

be judged by the entire Church not by the patriarch alone. Monks should stay in monasteries. There must be restrictions on confessions. Confessors should 'keep secrets and not accept presents'. Confessors should not look women in the eyes or ask for specific details.

Candidates to the monastic life must be 18 years old and able to read and write. They must be unmarried, without children and not required to give parental support. Candidates with sexually transmitted diseases, a criminal record or mental illness cannot be accepted. Candidates must have completed their national service. If the abbot of the monastery is sure that there are no obstacles to a candidate then a one-year novitiate will take place. The new monk 'will be examined to see if he is eager to worship God and is ready to live a humble life in which he will be totally submissive to monastic law.'

Coptic Papal Elections have been controversial for centuries. The author suggests that candidates should not be less than 50 years old. Candidates should have spent at least 15 continuous years in monasticism. 'No consecrated bishop is eligible.'[60] The author adds that the patriarch has to practice his duties in co-operation with all the institutions of the Church: the Holy Synod, the Clerical Council of senior bishops, the *Maglis Al-Milli*, the Supreme Council of Ecclesiastical Judiciary, the Supreme Council of Theological Studies and the High Council of Monasticism.[61]

This book is the most important work of Coptic polity published since 1971.[62] In that year Shenouda's election took place, but not without much criticism. He had only been a monk for eight years before joining

---

[60] See esp. *The Transfigured Cross, op. cit.*, 35-45. *Church Rules*, trans. Dr Nabil Raphael, 2001. *Historical Documents*, trans. by Dr Rodolph Yanney, 2001. *Ecclesiastical Teachings*, trans. by Nirmeen Fawzy and Eng. Sawsan G A Hulsmann-Khalil.

[61] Osama Salama, *op. cit.*

[62] The book should be compulsory reading for the Churches Together in Britain and Ireland team who exhibited a high degree of naiveté concerning Egypt in their report, *Who is my Neighbour? A report of an ecumenical visit to the Middle East in March 2001*, London, July 2001.

the episcopate of the Coptic curia. Being a bishop ought to have disqualified him from election as patriarch. The 2002 publication from Abu Makar may not endear the anonymous author to the Coptic establishment. In the history of the Copts it will be a defining document of immense weight, and its significance will reach far beyond the Middle East. Throughout the entire Christian World insistent prophecy confronts sclerotic Establishment. Power, in all ecclesial practice, is satisfying the human passion for control. There is a chasm between institution and Gospel.

The liturgical mystic

After the inevitable politicking in this kind of presentation we must turn to the real glory of Oriental Orthodoxy. Coptic culture embodies the wonders of pharaonic Egypt, Greco-Roman society in the Nile valley and the Christian adoption of Arabic civilisation: all these marvels can be seen and heard in the liturgy of the Coptic Orthodox Church. The pivotal figure and the emissary of the past-and-future Church is the liturgical mystic. This person is the one who sees in the Divine Liturgy of St Basil the Great the summation of Christian life and thought. The liturgical mystic is the most memorable and least remembered of all the saints. The Middle East provides many examples. The greatest in modern times was *Abouna Mina al-Muttawahad al-Baramusi*, a solitary and ascetic called from his hermitage to be patriarch of the Copts in 1959.[63] Azer Yussef Atta was born on 2 August 1902. From his ordination on 25 February 1928 he attended the Eucharist every day, at first as an assistant and then for over forty years as the daily celebrant. The Eucharist was the central action of his life. He celebrated the Liturgy on the day of his death on 9 March 1971. It is not usual for Coptic monks to attend the Liturgy every day. Orthodoxy has tended to emphasise the necessity of the presence of an earthly congregation, brought before the gate of heaven and the heavenly congregation. The altar is the divine throne set amongst the people of God. But on many occasions Kyrillos was quite alone. If required to celebrate the Eucharist alone, we discover, immediately, that

---

[63] See Iris Habib El Masri, *The Story of the Copts*, Cairo, 1978. John Watson, *Abba Kyrillos. Patriarch and Solitary*, Pennsylvania, 1996. N Van Doorn-Harder and K Vogt, *Between Desert and City: the Coptic Orthodox Church Today*, Oslo, 1997.

we are not alone. A modern English preface in the Eucharist describes our condition: 'In communion with angels and archangels and all who served you on earth and worship you now in heaven, we raise our voices to proclaim your glory' (*Common Worship* 2000). In his hermitage, Abba Kyrillos was always conscious of the heavenly presences. In this perception he was close to the Catholic mystic Charles de Foucauld (1858-1916), who lived in the remote oasis of Tamanrasset in the Sahara.[64] Charles was granted a rare dispensation to celebrate the Eucharist alone in the North African wasteland. Catholic and Copt had similar experiences, but a deacon always attended Kyrillos when patriarch. His comment on the daily Eucharist was invariably the same: 'If the priest is accessible, the flour is handy and the altar is available, and then if we do not pray, what shall we say to God?' Each day was his first and last day of his pilgrimage on earth. He was deeply convinced of the strength gained from the food of the Eucharist. This was his life. (Abba Kyrillos presided over the Liturgy on over fifteen thousand occasions: the total time in the *Heikal*—Coptic 'sanctuary'—amounting to a minimum of at least five years and six months, possibly twice as long). One parallel in the North may be noticed. A Russian priest, glorified in the last decade of the 20th century as St John of Kronstadt, celebrated the liturgy on over nineteen thousand occasions.[65] Ignoring the Church in the daily liturgy has been a central error in Eastern and Western Christian thought.

We have already noted the presence of Abba Justus al-Antuni (1910-1976) who was a monk for thirty-five years. He did not leave the lonely monastery of St Antony the Great, near the Red Sea. He held no position in the hierarchy. Although he was not ordained as a priest, he was always at the liturgy: the first to arrive and the last to leave. He was invariably barefoot and prostrated himself before the altar at each entrance. The Liturgy of St Basil, like all ancient and traditional rites, is sometimes weighed down with hierarchical formalism. Ambitious men become monks solely because it is the only route to the episcopate. Justus would sometimes go into the sanctuary and put on all the vestments— alb, stole, cowl and girdle. Some of the vestments were those reserved for the episcopate. He would take them too. The monks said nothing. Some

---

[64] Carlo Carretto, *Letters from the Desert*, London, 1972. René Voillaume, *Seeds of the Desert*, London, 1955. *Charles De Foucauld*, (ed.) Robert Ellsberg, Modern Spiritual Masters, New York, 1999.

[65] See Sergius Bolshakoff, *Russian Mystics*, London, 1977, 257-259.

felt that he hallowed the vestments. Justus wearing the hierarchical robes was a fool for Christ. The foolishness achieved at the cost of personal dignity is that type of obstinate folly that mocks all ecclesiastical pretentiousness. On several occasions Justus was in chapel at the moment of Holy Communion. He placed his hand in his pocket and raised it to his mouth: 'All we could see was that he was eating something. He would not enter the sanctuary for Holy Communion. He hid before the icons and ate. The fathers of the monastery were convinced that he was already in the realms of the anchorite saints.'[66] It would be absurd to suggest that this was in any sense a denial of the sacrament of the altar. It was rather a mystical sign from Christ's fool; pointing an often forbiddingly sacramental church to the spirituality of holiness. Kyrillos and Justus already lived in the Kingdom of God because they spent their lives in a Liturgy which embraced the entirety of Creation. For them the Church was not an organisation but the new life.

That new life finds universal, daily expression. Every liturgy has its own cultural merits and spiritual virtues. Particular music, gesture, costuming, setting and diction works somewhere for someone. Some churches value simplicity, clean lines of speech, and clarity of expression with educational and instructional values. Other churches cherish long, solemn realisations of the Eucharist, employing the whole complex of senses. In the transcendent mystery of the Oriental Orthodox the angels are perceived as primary actors. Eastern mysticism is inevitably contrasted with the Western demand for direct communication. To share in the liturgy in the Mariout Desert, Vatican City, Taizé, Zagorsk, or in the Sahara are rare and wonderful experiences.

The only tragedy is that not all altars and tables are open to all Christians all the time. In terms of brotherhood the Christians have nothing to teach *al-Ikhwan al-Muslimin*.[67]

A new Apocalypse

Like the Oriental Orthodox Christians described in this essay, Western Christians may need to turn their minds to the panorama of apocalypse.

---

[66] Hegumen Maximus al-Antoni, *op. cit.*, 8.
[67] 'The Muslim Brotherhood'. Hasan Al-Banna founded this powerful and effective movement at Ismailiyya in 1928.

We shall live in some version of apocalypse. Christianity and Islam are especially alike in their multiplicity of versions: 'Versions forever condemned by versions that deny each other.'[68] Politically, some versions are destined to alarm us with their collisions—nuclear, chemical and unimaginable collisions. There has been the vengeful anger of riches and power thrown against Palestine, Iraq, Afghanistan. We have seen the unimagined and unimaginable terror of the ingenious launched against the mighty. The Christians of Pakistan are living with martyrdom and the threat of extinction. But as a means of addressing the reality of the times in which we are now living, and in which we may soon live, we shall all need new images of apocalypse:

> Wild, dark times are rumbling towards us, and the prophet who wishes to write a new apocalypse will have to invent entirely new beasts, and beasts so terrible that the ancient animal symbols of Saint John will seem like cooing doves and cupids in comparison.[69]

---

[68] Kenneth Cragg in DehqanTafti, *op. cit.*, 259.
[69] Heinrich Heine (1797-1856) in *Lutezia* (1855).

MALAYSIAN CHRISTIANS
AND ISLAMISATION
Peter G Riddell

The Islamic context

Malaysia is often cited as one of the best examples of a democratic, pluralist Islam: a country where an Islamic majority can exercise power in a way which is inclusive of non-Muslim minorities. Indeed, a country where Muslims only constitute a small majority (60 percent) of the population provides a crucial laboratory to test whether Islam empowered can reflect the democratic, pluralist values espoused by much of the world in the 21st century.

The founding of the state

Tunku Abdul Rahman, the first Prime Minister of Malaysia and father of the nation, said in Parliament at the time of Malaya's independence in 1957:

> I would like to make it clear that this country is not an Islamic State as it is generally understood; we merely provide that Islam shall be the official religion of the State.[1]

This was clearly the mood at the time of independence and throughout the 1960s. Muhammad Suffian Hashim, the first Malay Chief Justice, expressed the modernist leanings of the early leaders of the new nation in saying:

> Politics and religion cannot be combined together, and the implementation of Islamic law in criminal and civil affairs

---

[1] Mohammad Hashim Kamali, *Islamic Law in Malaysia. Issues and Developments*, Ilmiah Publishers, Kuala Lumpur, 2000, 30.

(not including personal law) to all people in the country is not suitable because Malaysia is a multi-racial state.[2]

Thus Islam was seen as falling outside the realm of national politics, administration and the judiciary. Although Islam was defined as the official religion of Malaya (1957) and Malaysia (1963), its primary functions at the national level in the early years were ceremonial and ethnic: it provided a backdrop for public functions and served to define the identity of the majority ethnic group, the Malays.

Islamic affairs fell within the jurisdiction of the different states of Malaysia. The state Sultans bore responsibility for Islamic matters, and the Malay Reservation Enactments passed by the various state governments of Malaysia maintained Islam as a defining element of Malay identity. Under the Courts Ordinance of 1948 the Shari'a Courts continued to function in matters of personal and family law, but were not integrated into the Federal court system. Islamic law in these specific areas applied only to Muslims.

Insecurity and Islamisation

The Islamic resurgence which took place in Malaysia from the 1970s has been widely studied and documented.[3] It did not merely result from the world-wide resurgence taking place at that time, but also drew on important domestic factors, primarily a sense of insecurity on the part of the Malay majority in the face of a substantial non-Malay minority, leading to an increased ethnic awareness and assertiveness. The 1969 riots in Malaysia were a watershed event,[4] leading to a dramatic rise in Islamic consciousness among Malay Muslims as an instrument for asserting their ethnic identity and to a struggle among Muslim leadership over the best direction for the community. Former Deputy Prime Minister Anwar

---

[2] Mohammad Hashim Kamali, *Islamic Law in Malaysia. Issues and Developments*, Ilmiah Publishers, Kuala Lumpur, 2000, 32.

[3] See for example Chandra Muzaffar, 'Islam in Malaysia: Resurgence and Response', *Islamic Perspective*, 2 (1), 1985, and S Batumalai, *Islamic Resurgence and Islamization in Malaysia*, Charles Grenier, Ipoh, 1996.

[4] Triggered when the governing alliance had its parliamentary majority cut from 89 of 104 seats to 74 in the new 144-seat parliament.

Ibrahim captured the ethnic underpinnings of riot and resurgence in saying:

> It was all a question of the survival of the *umma*, of the Malay race. Previously we had been thinking about these problems outside Islam, when actually we could have solved them through Islam.[5]

Further crises in the late 1990s—the 1997 economic crisis and the 1998 Anwar Ibrahim political crisis—served to fuel the debate in Malaysia over modernisation, Islamisation, and the path for the future. These crises further destabilized the fine balance established by the policies of Tunku Abdul Rahman and the nation's founding fathers. In a climate of political infighting, economic downturn and inter-ethnic friction, political divisions became more clearly delineated. The last 30 years of the 20th century in Malaysia were characterised by a struggle for control of the Malay Muslim community between modernising Muslims (represented by the United Malays National Organisation—UMNO) and more traditionalist-minded Muslim activists (represented by the Islamic Party of Malaysia—PAS). In the midst of this struggle, non-Muslim Malaysians have had to assess their options and take action to shore up their position within society.

One side of the Malay Muslim equation, that of PAS, considers that the solution to Malaysia's political, social and economic challenges lies in a return to sacred scripture and law, the *shari'a*.[6] Hence PAS efforts have been put increasingly into agitating for the introduction of *shari'a* in a holistic way, not merely in the personal and family realm which already was the case, but also in areas of criminal law. The UMNO-led Barisan Nasional Government of Malaysia has vigorously resisted this push, arguing instead that Islamisation should take the form of gradual inculcation of Islamic values rather than enforcement of Islamic legal provisions through Islamic courts.[7] This was based on a notion of Islamic universalism, defining '... the role of Islam as the solution to the nation's racial problems. It was

---

[5] M Nash, 'Islamic Resurgence in Malaysia and Indonesia ', in M E Marty, *Fundamentalism Observed*, Univ. of Chicago, Chicago, 1991, 705.

[6] Olaf Schumann, 'Christians and Muslims in Search of Common Ground in Malaysia', *Islam and Christian-Muslim Relations*, 2/2 (December 1991), 250.

[7] S Batumalai, *Islamic Resurgence and Islamization in Malaysia*, Charles Grenier, Ipoh, 1996, 142.

contended that as a belief-system it is not only in accord with human requirements, but would also allow a high degree of pluralism.'[8]

This intra-Muslim struggle arouses concern from different wings of the Malaysian population, with non-Muslims worried about the degree to which Islamisation of any form has come to dominate public discourse and policy, and devout traditionalist Muslims disappointed in what they regard as a wishy-washy policy on the part of the national government.

Islamic politics at the national level

At the time of writing, more than one third of the members of the Malaysian Parliament and its Federal Cabinet were drawn from non-Malay and non-Muslim communities. This is broadly reflective of population distribution, and represents an important piece in the mosaic of Malaysian pluralism. Nevertheless, the presence of twenty-seven representatives from PAS in the 193 seat Parliament meant that the push for increased Islamisation and a *shari'a* -minded rhetoric made a regular appearance in parliamentary discussion.

In response to such pressure from an enlarged PAS presence in federal parliament after the 1999 national elections, the Barisan Nasional Government under Prime Minister Mahathir Mohamad responded with an increased Islamisation rhetoric of its own. In October 2001 Dr Mahathir declared that the PAS calls for an Islamic state were redundant, as Malaysia was already an Islamic state, and that constitutional change was not necessary. Mahathir's religious advisor Abdul Hamid Othman invited Muslim jurists from Cairo's al-Azhar Mosque to assess whether Malaysia met the criteria to be considered as an Islamic state.[9] In a further development, Mahathir announced in mid-June 2002 that Malaysia was 'an Islamic fundamentalist state' because the government adhered to the fundamental teachings of Islam.[10]

Responses to these declarations by the Malaysian Prime Minister were diverse. Lim Kit Siang, the former leader of the Chinese opposition Democratic Action Party, threatened to take Mahathir to court over his

---

[8] Nakamura Mitsuo, Sharon Siddique and Omar Farouk Bajunid (eds.), *Islam & Civil Society in Southeast Asia*, Institute of Southeast Asian Studies, Singapore, 2001, 64.

[9] 'Malaysia seeks views from Cairo on Islamic state', MSNBC News/Reuters, 24 October, 2001.

[10] 'Mahathir: Malaysia is "fundamentalist state"', CNN.com, 18 June, 2002.

remarks, saying that they went against 'the 1957 independence Constitution, the social contract of the major communities'.[11] In a different vein, PAS scorned Mahathir's declaration that the country is already an 'Islamic state'. The chief minister of the PAS-governed state of Kelantan, Nik Abdul Aziz Nik Mat, said that the declaration made Malaysia an 'instant Islamic state just like instant noodles'.[12]

The push for increased Islamisation had various manifestations in national forums. In another development which caused considerable concern among both moderate Muslims and the non-Muslim communities, the Muslim Scholars Association (MSA) spearheaded a campaign to crack down on media comment deemed derogatory to Islam or the prophet Muhammad. After initially failing to get support from state government authorities through Malaysia, the MSA took the matter to the nine state Sultans, who referred the matter to the National Islamic Affairs Committee[13] chaired by Dr Mahathir. In response, the national government announced in mid-April 2002 that they would begin implementing existing but little used laws which stipulated that anyone found guilty of insulting Islam would be fined and/or jailed.[14]

Islamic politics and law at the state level

In Malaysia, legislative powers relating to Islamic Law fall under the jurisdiction of the various states. *Shari'a* is widely applied throughout Malaysia at the state level in areas of marriage, child custody, divorce and inheritance for Muslim citizens. *Shari'a* law of transactions and commerce is increasingly applied, not only in specifically Islamic banks, but also through Islamic banking windows in conventional banks.[15]

[11] ' "Islamic" remark: DAP may take Mahathir to court', *The Straits Times Interactive*, June 20, 2002.

[12] 'Hardline Islamic opposition presents new challenge to Mahathir', *Yahoo! Asia*, 25 March, 2002.

[13] Established in 1968 by the Conference of Rulers 'to advise ... the Conference of Rulers, State Government and State Religious Council on the administration of Islamic law with a view to encouraging uniformity among the various states of Malaysia.' Mohammad Hashim Kamali, *Islamic Law in Malaysia. Issues and Developments*, Ilmiah Publishers, Kuala Lumpur, 2000, 45.

[14] 'Malaysia to enforce ban on articles insulting Islam', Reuters, 15 April, 2002.

[15] Mohammad Hashim Kamali, *Islamic Law in Malaysia. Issues and Developments*, Ilmiah Publishers, Kuala Lumpur, 2000, 10.

While such a situation may seem to ensure consistency across the states in terms of application of *Shari'a*, in fact the opposite is often the case. In each state there is a Council of Islamic Religion and Malay Custom headed by a *Mufti* who is authorised to issue *fatwa*s, or legal opinions and decisions. The result is often variation from state to state. In the words of Prime Minister Mahathir:

> Despite the fact that all Malays are Sunni Muslim of the Shafei school, the different states have got different and frequently contradictory laws. Such are the differences that it is entirely possible for a Muslim from one state to escape the specific Islamic law by going to another state ...

Dr Mahathir sees this situation as justifying caution in applying Islamic Law, adding the following comment:

> ... if Islamic laws governing the people of the same sect and school in one country cannot be made uniform, how much more difficult it would be to have uniform laws for all the Muslims of the world ...[16]

PAS governments in Kelantan and Terengganu

Leaders of PAS do not share Dr Mahathir's caution about implementing the *shari'a*. On the contrary, a major part of the efforts of PAS since winning government in the states of Kelantan (1959-78, 1990-) and Terengganu (1999-) has been devoted to increasing the areas of application of *shari'a* in the states in question.[17]

Manifestations of PAS Islamic legislation in Kelantan during the 1990s related to the banning of gambling, discotheques, karaoke lounges and unisex hair salons, prohibiting the sale of alcohol to Muslims, and requiring official permission to organise carnivals, theatre

---

[16] Mahathir Mohamad, 'Chapter 3. Islamic Law in the Contemporary World', *Islam and the Muslim Ummah*, Pelanduk Publications, Subang Jaya, 2000, 28-29.

[17] For a discussion of the perspectives of the two PAS figures presently serving as Chief Ministers of Kelantan and Terengganu, Nik Abdul Aziz Nik Mat and Abdul Hadi Awang respectively, cf. Peter Riddell, *Islam and the Malay-Indonesian World: Transmission and Responses*, Horizon Press, Singapore, 2001, 224-230.

performances, dances, beauty pageants and song festivals. In addition, the PAS state government legislated for gender-based checkout counters in supermarkets.[18] In June 2002, a senior UMNO official in Kelantan was convicted of polygamy under the Kelantan shari'a legal code, and was jailed for four days and fined. He had married a second wife without obtaining the required permission from both his first wife and the religious authorities.[19]

The above legislation falls within the state government remit, and PAS was able to move ahead without hindrance (though not without criticism) from the federal government. However, PAS government moves to implement an Islamic criminal code in Kelantan produced a different response from the federal government. In November 1993 the PAS government in Kelantan passed a bill instituting *Hudud*, or Islamic penal codes, in that state. However they could not come into force without approval from the federal government, which withheld such approval.

PAS won government in the State of Trengganu for the second time in late 1999, and moved quickly to increase the Islamic profile of the state. Within days of the victory, the new PAS Chief Minister of Trengganu, Abdul Hadi Awang, announced that his government would ban gambling outlets, sale of alcoholic drinks, and entertainment centres.[20] From 1 January 2000 hotels in Trengganu were prohibited from selling alcohol, and two months later a dress code for women was announced, to start with government office staff and workers in business premises.[21] In mid-2000 the PAS government in Terengganu ruled that women should not take part in Qur'an recitation competitions as the female voice was considered 'aurat' (that part of the body which incites men).[22] Pressure was placed on local supermarkets by Government officials to separate males and females into different queues at cash registers.[23] On 16 April

---

[18] Olaf Schumann, Christians and Muslims in Search of Common Ground in Malaysia', *Islam and Christian-Muslim Relations*, 2/2 (December 1991): 251; Roger Mitton, 'Inside Story Malaysia. Return to Islam', *Asiaweek*, 7 June, 1996.

[19] 'Malaysian ruling party official sentenced to jail for polygamy', *The Star Online*, 13 June, 2002.

[20] *The Star Online*, 2 December 1999.

[21] 'PAS to introduce dress code for Muslim women', *Bernama*, 20 March, 2000. This was not to apply to non-Terengganu women visiting the state.

[22] 'Furor Over Quran Recitals By Women', 10 August, 2000, http://www.asiafeatures.com/current_affairs/0008,1010,02a.html.

[23] Francis Harrison, 'Malaysian state swaps tourism for morality', *The Guardian*, 21 April 2000.

2002 the PAS government in Terengganu announced in the State Assembly a dress code for foreign visitors to the state, banning bikinis, and stipulating that new chalets and resorts should provide segregated swimming pools in premises.[24]

As with Kelantan, the Federal Government expressed displeasure and, at times, ridicule of these measures, but was powerless to act. However, the Terengganu Government followed the lead of its PAS colleagues across the Kelantan border by taking on the Federal Government in the area of criminal law. On 7 July 2002 the Terengganu Syariah Criminal (Hudud) Bill was presented at the State Legislative Assembly. Abdul Hadi Awang, in presenting the Bill, commented as follows:

> The Syariah Criminal Law is intended more at educating society with the greatness of the law to invoke fear on criminals so that they would stop and repent, and to deter would be criminals from becoming criminals.[25]

The inevitable clash between Federal and Terengganu governments over this matter is underway at the time of writing. It is likely that the Federal Government will once again veto implementation of a State Criminal Bill, justifying such a veto by recourse to the Malaysian constitutional stipulation that crime is a federal matter under the Penal Code.

Whether such legislation is implemented or not, the effect of such struggles is to increase the Islamisation ante, as it were. The Federal Government's opposition to widespread consolidation of the hold of shari'a on Malaysia's legal structure is counterbalanced by the Mahatir government's efforts to conduct its own, more nuanced, Islamisation programme through education, the media, and provision of public funds to bodies such as the Institute of Islamic Understanding (IKIM), inaugurated on 3 July 1992 by Dr Mahathir. IKIM defines its own mission statement on its website as

> Striving to uplift the understanding of Islam among Muslims and non-Muslims by highlighting its universal values and

---

[24] 'PAS bikini ban hurting Malaysia's tourism industry', *The Straits Times Interactive*, 29 April, 2002.

[25] 'Hadi Tables Syariah Criminal (Hudud) Bill', *Utusan Online*, 8 July, 2001.

all-encompassing principles which are realistic and relevant to our daily lives.[26]

So although the Mahathir Government strongly opposes the more direct approach of PAS towards Islamisation, through devices such as announcing in March 2000 that it would draft legislation requiring the separation of religion and politics,[27] the Federal Government's own moves towards Islamisation themselves contribute to the upward spiral of Islamising rhetoric which is a cause of considerable concern to Malaysia's non-Muslim minorities. As Robert Hunt observes:

> Malay politicians have not been shy of using religion as a political lever by which to exhibit their Islamic credentials ... These developments have put Christians on the defensive while at the same time confronting them with a bewildering array of supposedly authoritative opinions about the direction of Islam and its relation to the state.[28]

In response, the minorities have moved to organise themselves, seeking safety in numbers, as it were. Mohamad Abu Bakar captures this in saying:

> One aspect of this Islamization drive, which was to have a significant impact on race relations, was the central and state governments' attempts to bring their administrations in line with religious requirements ... [Non-Muslims] entered the fray by activating their own organizations, mobilizing their members, or forming their own societies in order to champion the cause of their co-religionists in the face of the Islamists' challenge.'[29]

We will now turn our attention to the minorities, paying particular

---

[26] http://www.ikim.gov.my/, copied June 2001.

[27] 'Laws To Separate Religion From Politics', *Utusan Express*, 3 March 2000.

[28] Robert Hunt, 'Christian Theological Reflection and Education in the Muslim Societies of Malaysia and Indonesia', *Studies in World Christianity* 3/2 (1997), 211.

[29] Mohamad Abu Bakar, 'Islam, Civil Society, and Ethnic Relations in Malaysia', in Nakamura Mitsuo, Sharon Siddique and Omar Farouk Bajunid (eds.), *Islam & Civil Society in Southeast Asia*, Institute of Southeast Asian Studies, Singapore, 2001, 69-70.

attention to Malaysia's Christian community, listening to voices from its membership which articulate the perspectives and concerns of the Christian masses.

Christian responses to Islamisation in Malaysia
A Profile of the Christian Community

Malaysian society is undergoing great change at the turn of the 21st century. Political, social and economic factors have been discussed in previous paragraphs. Demographic changes have also been in evidence in Malaysia according to the year 2000 census. In that year the Bumiputera—ethnic Malays and indigenous groups in Sarawak and Sabah—constituted 65.1 percent of the population, an increase of 4.5 percent since the 1990 census. In contrast, Chinese represented 26 percent of the population, down from 28.1 percent in 1990 and 37 percent in 1957. In terms of religious allegiance, the Muslim proportion of Malaysia's population increased from 58.6 percent to 60.4 percent in the same period. In 2000 19.2 percent of Malaysians were Buddhist, 9.1 percent Christian and 6.3 percent Hindu.[30]

The 9.1 percent Christian population is diverse in terms of history, ethnicity and denomination. Our study will be helped by focusing on three church groups: the Catholic Church of Malaysia, the Council of Churches of Malaysia, and the National Evangelical Churches Federation.

Catholic Church of Malaysia

The history of the modern Catholic Church in Malaysia dates back to the Portuguese, who conquered the port city of Malacca in 1511. Dominicans and Franciscans arrived with the Portuguese with missionary goals, but in this early period the Christian community remained largely an expatriate community, of various ethnicities. Francis Xavier visited Malacca on five occasions between 1545-1552 and was shocked by the moral decadence which he saw.

---

[30] 'Malaysia census shows minorities dwindling', *The Straits Times Interactive*, 8 November, 2001.

In 1641, when the Dutch conquered Malacca from the Portuguese, the local Catholic community stood at 20,000 with twenty churches present. The Dutch banned the practice of Catholicism and priests were driven out. Nevertheless, Catholicism survived alongside the Protestantism promoted by the Dutch. In 1712 there were six times more Catholics than Protestants in Malacca,[31] and the community was to flourish under successive Dutch and British rule, as well as after independence. In late 1995 the numbers of Catholics in Malaysia stood at 637,000, constituting 3 percent of the population, and one third of the overall Christian minority.[32]

Following the dramatic reforms of the Second Vatican Council, held in Rome from 1963-65, the Catholic Church of Malaysia held substantial meetings every ten years to plan the way ahead as a response to the Vatican II initiatives. The Aggiornamento, held in 1976 in Penang, included 123 Bishops and Clergy. It identified the building of basic ecclesial communities as the Core Need, and also identified four Related Needs: Unity Formation, Ecumenical and Inter-Religious Dialogue, and Integral Human Development.[33] The Peninsular Malaysia Pastoral Convention (PMPC) I, held in 1986 in Kuala Lumpur, was attended by 183 bishops, clergy and laity. The PMPC II, held in Johor in 1996, identified a primary goal for the church in the immediate future of planning for the Jubilee 2000 year.

Council of Churches of Malaysia

British rule in Malaya from the late 18th century brought with it a range of Protestant denominations, which grew especially among expatriate and immigrant communities during the 19th and 20th centuries. The nature of missionary efforts during this period produced ethnic churches with 'distinct Christian identities and polities.'[34] These groups provided the ingredients for the Malayan Christian Council,

---

[31] Anne Ruck, *Sejarah Gereja Asia*,Gunung Mulia, Jakarta, 1997, 216.

[32] *1998 Catholic Almanac: Our Sunday Visitor*, USA (1997), 333-367, cited at http://www.adherents.com/adhloc/Wh_192.html#463.

[33] 'Our Journey as Church in Peninsular Malaysia', http://www.catholic.org.sg/web_links/AVE/pmpc/pmpc1.html, copied 22 May 2002.

[34] Robert Hunt, 'Christian Theological Reflection and Education in the Muslim Societies of Malaysia and Indonesia', *Studies in World Christianity* 3/2 (1997): 212.

which was founded in January 1948, and brought together local Anglicans, Methodists, Presbyterians, the Orthodox Syrian Church, Lutheran Church, Salvation Army, and YMCA.

The Communist Emergency which broke out in the same year led to the creation of over 400 New Villages by the government with British support to cut off communist insurgents from their base of support among local populations. Missionaries from various agencies were very active in working among New Villages. There was also an influx of missionaries from other areas, especially China, with the expulsion of foreign missionaries following the Communist victory in 1949. These events provided a great stimulus to both the growth of the church and to denominational variety, with missionaries coming from wide-ranging denominations. A mass conversion movement among animist tribespeople in the British Borneo territories in the post–war years further stimulated the growth of the Christian community in Malaysia.[35]

With the establishment of Malaysia in 1963, the Malayan Christian Council became the Council of Churches of Malaysia and Singapore in 1967 and then the Council of Churches of Malaysia (CCM—Majlis Gereja-Gereja Malaysia) in 1975. The CCM has suffered from internal disunity, as had the MCC before it. Problems of language worked against ecumenical effectiveness, as many churches were ethnically based. To address this, the CCM has followed a policy of promoting the use of the Malay language at all levels of church life, in order to fulfil the 4th CCM objective of promoting 'discussion and action among churches in Malaysia towards Church union.'[36] There has been some resistance to this, because many Christians 'still feel the impact of Islam on the Malay language and its traditional link and limitation to the Malay race.'[37]

National Evangelical Christian Fellowship (NECF) Malaysia

The third grouping of Christians which demands our attention is the National Evangelical Christian Fellowship. It was formed in May 1983,

---

[35] A S Walters, *Contemporary Presentations of the Trinity in an Islamic Context: A Malaysian Case Study*, Unpublished PhD thesis, University of Birmingham, 1999, 49-51.
[36] http://www.newwomen.net/affiliates/ccm/CCMALAYSIA/ccm/objectives_of_ccm.htm, copied 24 July 2002.
[37] Olaf Schumann, Christians and Muslims in Search of Common Ground in Malaysia', *Islam and Christian-Muslim Relations*, 2/2 (December 1991), 253.

and includes among its members churches from wide-ranging Protestant denominations: Assemblies of God, Baptist, Brethren, Full Gospel Churches, the Evangelical Free Church, Full Gospel Assembly, Independent, Latter Rain, Lutheran, Methodist, Presbyterian, Sidang Injil Borneo Sabah, Sidang Injil Borneo Sarawak, Para Churches, Bible Seminaries, Hope of God Church, and others.

The NECF is an active member of the World Evangelical Association. It has diverse programmes and commissions, including an Evangelism Commission and a Mission Commission. It has developed a specialised Bahasa Malaysia [BM]/Malay Language Ministry in order

> to encourage English speaking churches to start at least 200 BM speaking congregations in Peninsular Malaysia by the year 2000, reaching out to BM speaking Malaysians, particularly the younger generations and also East Malaysians.[38]

The NECF has thus added another piece to the mosaic of Malaysian Christianity, underscoring the diversity of the community and the need for attention to Christian unity.

Safety in numbers

The coming together of evangelical churches to form the NECF in 1983 heralded a wider trend at this time both within the broad Christian community, and indeed within other non-Muslim communities. The Islamic resurgence within Malaysia which had become well established by the early 1980s, the Islamisation measures taken by the federal government, and the rise of PAS caused non-Muslim groups to seek 'safety in numbers', as it were, as a means of addressing what many non-Muslims saw as their increasingly precarious and marginalised position within society.

---

[38] http://www.necf.org.my/html/ministry_f.htm, copied 20 May 2002.

The Malaysian Consultative Council of Buddhism, Christianity, Hinduism and Sikhism

In a dramatic example of interfaith co-operation which underscored non-Muslim concern at Islamisation in Malaysia, Buddhists, Christians, Hindus and Sikhs jointly formed the Malaysian Consultative Council of Buddhism, Christianity, Hinduism and Sikhism (MCCBCHS) in 1983. Since its establishment, the MCCBCHS has lobbied both federal and state governments in Malaysia about matters of concern to non-Muslim minorities. These include religious rights of non-Muslims, increased access to burial grounds, obstacles to construction of places of worship, banning of certain Christian symbols, banning of teaching of non-Muslim faiths in schools, exclusion of non-Muslim programming from public media, restriction over distribution of Bibles in hotels, and other issues.

In support of its lobbying activities, the MCCBCHS has produced printed materials, such as a pamphlet entitled 'Should Islamic Law be Introduced in Malaysia', prompted by the Hudud Bill introduced by PAS in the Kelantan state legislature in 1993, and the periodical *Harmoni.*

Christian Federation of Malaysia

The Islamisation environment in Malaysia has also stimulated intra-Christian ecumenical cooperation of a kind which could serve as a valuable model in other parts of the world. In 1986 the Christian Federation of Malaysia (CFM—Persekutuan Kristian Malaysia) was founded, consisting of almost all Christian denominations, including the Catholic Church, the Protestant CCM, and the NECF. In December 2001 the CFM represented around 5,000 member churches,[39] and spoke for about 90 percent of the Christian population of Malaysia.

In terms of Catholic involvement, the 1976 Aggiornamento, drawn up in Penang, identified Ecumenical and Inter-Religious Dialogue as a key priority. This placed the Catholic Church in an ideal position to join the CFM one decade later.

---

[39] 'Arson Attacks on Churches—CFM Urges Restraint', *Berita NECF* January/February 2002, 1.

The third of the stated aims and objectives of the CFM constitution is as follows:

> To look after the interests of the Christian community as a whole with particular reference to religious freedom and rights enshrined in the Federal Constitution.[40]

This provides a context to the insightful comment by Walters, who succinctly points out:

> The real integration of ecumenism into the life of Malaysian churches had to wait until there were Malaysian issues which proved beyond doubt the value of this sort of co-operation.[41]

The CFM is a member of the MCCBCHS, thus ensuring broad-based Christian support for this cutting-edge interfaith endeavour.

Christians speak out

Church leaders regularly hold meetings with the Malaysian political leadership to seek assurances that the inculcation of Islamic values throughout society will not undermine the position of their community. For example, church leaders, along with leaders of other faiths, met Prime Minister Mahathir Mohammad on 27 November 1998 in Sabah. Bishop Datuk Yong Ping Chung, President of the Christian Federation of Malaysia, the Council of Churches of Malaysia and the Sabah Council of Churches, said of the meeting that '… what was significant was the P.M.'s emphasis that no one group should dominate others and that all should respect and understand each other.'[42]

However, Christian concerns are not completely assuaged by such statements by Dr Mahathir and other government leaders to eminent Church leaders such as Bishop Datuk. We will now turn our attention to specific concerns which are expressed by Malaysian Christians in various forums.

---

[40] http://www.ccmalaysia.org/ie/images/together.htm.
[41] A S Walters, *Contemporary Presentations of the Trinity in an Islamic Context: A Malaysian Case Study*, Unpublished PhD thesis, University of Birmingham, 1999, 50.
[42] http://www.ccmalaysia.org/netscape/events/past1.htm, copied 20 May 2002.

Problems perceived by Malaysian Christians

The dramatic turn in world events following the terrorist attacks on targets in the United States on 11 September 2001, has been a subject of considerable discussion among Christians in Malaysia. Malaysian Christians have taken care to avoid linking their comments about radical Muslim activity with Islam per se. For example, in a press release following the terrorist attacks in New York and Washington, NECF commented that 'the global struggle against terrorism is not a conflict with Islam.' However, it drew links between the events in the USA and specific aspects of the Malaysian scene in the following terms:

> In the Malaysian context, religious extremism has a significant bearing on our multi-cultural, multi-ethnic and multi-religious society. What happened in the United States should give us a new urgency and perspective in evaluating the radical religious movements, which sow seeds of religious militancy in the country.[43]

Concerning domestic marginalisation under Islamisation

Malaysian Christians regularly express concerns about what they see as the marginalisation of the non-Muslim communities resulting from Islamisation in Malaysia. The prominent Anglican writer, Sadayandy Batumalai, encapsulates these concerns:

> Malaysians in general are aware and appreciate that the government is concerned with the spiritual development of the Malay ethnic group. However, neglect of this important concern for the non-Malay part of the population may create two types of communities in Malaysia; one spiritually oriented and the other materially oriented. To be true to their tradition the Malays need to pay attention to spirituality across the board.[44]

---

[43] Press release, http://www.necf.org.my/html/press_release_27sept2001_f.htm, 27 September 2001, copied 20 May 2002.

[44] S Batumalai, *Islamic Resurgence and Islamization in Malaysia*, Ipoh, Charles Grenier, 1996, 134.

Any Government ignoring of Malaysian Christianity may result in part from the faith being seen as a Western implant by Malaysian Muslims.[45] Albert Walters, an academic at the Malaysian Theological Seminary (STM), points out that such a perception runs counter to the fact that 'today the Christian Church in Malaysia is largely local in leadership, membership and finance.'[46] As a result of this feeling of exclusion, Christians have tended to retreat into a ghetto mentality, resulting in a lack of commitment to engaging through their faith with the world around them.

The Government's introduction of an 'Islamic Civilisation' subject as a compulsory component of university programmes for both Muslims and non-Muslims finds little support among non-Muslims. Paul Tan, the former Director of the Catholic Research Centre, takes particular issue with this move by Government, commenting somewhat ironically as follows:

> If the intention of introducing the subject of Islamic Civilization was that the non-Muslims would come to understand Muslims better through it, then for the same noble reason the Government should introduce a subject of other major religious civilizations so as to help the Muslims to understand the non-Muslims.[47]

The more dramatic attempts by PAS to consolidate the position of Islamic Law in the country are a cause of great angst among all sections of the Christian community. The editorial of the NECF periodical *Berita NECF* responded to strident PAS statements in 2001 with alarm: 'PAS' public declaration of its intent to set up an Islamic state should it come into power has once again sent jitters through the non-Muslim community...' This particular editorial gives voice to the feeling of some Christians that PAS plans and the Government's Islamisation programme are two sides of the same coin:

---

[45] Y Hwa, 'Vision 2020 and Theological Education in Malaysia', in S W Hwa (ed.), *Christian Response to Vision 2020*, Persatuan Penulis-Penulis Kristian Malaysia, 1993, 26.

[46] A S Walters, *Contemporary Presentations of the Trinity in an Islamic Context: A Malaysian Case Study*, Unpublished PhD thesis, University of Birmingham, 1999, 50.

[47] Ghazali Basri, *Christian Mission and Islamic Dakwah in Malaysia*, Kuala Lumpur, Nurin Enterprise, 1990, 32.

... resurgence, consolidation and expansion of Islam is expected to continue irrespective of whichever party is in control, an alarming trend to communities of other religious faiths. Generally, the Government is of the view that religious freedom—as enshrined in our federal constitution—is a pre-requisite for national harmony and integration. In reality, however, the practice is not consistent with this view.[48]

NECF organised a forum of 50 leading Christians in July 2001 to discuss current events in Malaysia. Participants were unanimous in calling for the Malaysian Constitution to be upheld and defended 'to ensure the continuance of religious freedom, a right which has been continually threatened by calls for an Islamic state.'[49] University of Malaya law lecturer Dr Khoo Boo Teong said at this forum:

> Unless orthodox *Shariah* can be reformed, the treatment of non-Muslims will always be a major stumbling block in enabling the *Shariah* to be consonant with the definitions of Rule of Law today and into the 21st century.[50]

It thus seems that reassuring statements by politicians to local Christian leaders have not succeeded in wiping away Christian concerns. Some Christians offer as further evidence of their marginalisation the fact that the Government agency IKIM often organises dialogue events, inviting international Christian scholars for discussions, but generally ignores local Malaysian Christians in dialogue activities. Robert Hunt speaks more generally of this problem in the following terms:

> Christians have felt systematically excluded from discussion and debate on Islamisation and its implications. Non-Muslim criticism, or even comment, on government policies promoting Islamisation has been regarded as highly offensive

---

[48] 'Rising Religious Activism. Ready to respond', *Berita NECF* September/October 2001, 1.

[49] 'Defend Constitution to Protect Religious Freedom', *Berita NECF* September/October 2001, 3.

[50] 'Defend Constitution to Protect Religious Freedom', *Berita NECF* September/October 2001, 4.

by Muslims, despite the fact that such policies impact the entire Malaysian society.[51]

Concerning anti-Christian actions and statements

Malaysian Christians also look beyond the somewhat intangible process of marginalisation under Islamisation to more specific actions and statements which they consider to have undermined their position within the country.

NECF came into being in response to three specific developments: the 1981 government legislation forbidding ownership of the Bible by any Malaysians except Christians; the limiting of the number of sites for worship and the outlawing of public gatherings of five or more people without official approval.[52]

The first of these is still in place, and creates obstacles to the importation of non-Islamic religious literature. A US State Department report states that

> For a long time, the Government has discouraged—and in practical terms forbidden—the circulation in peninsular Malaysia of Malay-language translations of the Bible and distribution of Christian tapes and printed materials in Malay.[53]

Regarding the second reason for the establishment of NECF, a Malaysian government quota exists whereby the proportion of Mosques to Muslims is 1:800 but this extends to 1:4000 for non-Muslims.[54] This means that it is far more difficult to obtain official approval for the construction of new churches than it is for the construction of new mosques.

---

[51] Robert Hunt, 'Christian Theological Reflection and Education in the Muslim Societies of Malaysia and Indonesia', *Studies in World Christianity* 3/2 (1997), 215.

[52] 'A Brief History', http://www.necf.org.my/html/history_f.htm, copied 20 May 2002.

[53] 'US Department of State Annual Report on International Religious Freedom for 1999: Malaysia', Bureau for Democracy, Human Rights and Labour, Washington CD, 9 September, 1999, http://www.state.gov/www/global/human_rights/irf/irf_rpt/1999/irf_malaysia99.html.

[54] 'Country Profile: Malaysia', Christian Solidarity Worldwide, http://www.csw.org.uk/malaysia.html.

The third motivation for NECF's emergence finds its most stark expression in the Internal Security Act (ISA).

One of the most contentious pieces of legislation from a Christian perspective was the banning in 1991 of the use of four terms in any non-Islamic literature: *Allah, Kaabah, Baitullah* and *Solat*.[55] Only the first of these raised serious debate, as the latter three all have primary Islamic connotations, whereas *Allah* was hitherto widely used by Malaysian Christians as a standard term of reference for God in their literature. The implementation of this law impacts directly upon the issue of importation of religious literature. For example, in early 1997 some 230 Christian books imported into Malaysia from Singapore and Indonesia were confiscated by the Johor State government authorities, under the law prohibiting the use of the above words in non-Muslim literature.[56]

In contrast with restrictions on the production and distribution of Christian literature, Muslim literature of an orthodox kind enjoys freedom from official interference. This includes writings of a type which causes consternation in Christian circles. As Robert Hunt observes:

> anti-Christian polemical works are commonly found in Muslim bookstores and anti-Christian comment is allowed in the context of larger presentations of Muslim theological concerns.[57]

Anti-Christian activities went far beyond Government legislation. In a sign of worsening communal relations at the grassroots level, arson attacks occurred on churches in Kedah and Selangor in July and October 2001. Five churches were badly damaged or destroyed. While this action was most likely carried out by anti-Government extremist groups, it caused considerable concern among Christians as to the future direction of inter-religious relations.

---

[55] S Batumalai, *Islamic Resurgence and Islamization in Malaysia*, Charles Grenier, Ipoh, 1996, 262, 270.
[56] *The New Christian Herald*, 15 March 1997.
[57] Robert Hunt, 'Christian Theological Reflection and Education in the Muslim Societies of Malaysia and Indonesia', *Studies in World Christianity* 3/2 (1997), 217.

The issue of apostasy

This issue is a festering sore on the Malaysian religious landscape. On the one hand, it is technically possible for a Malay Muslim to convert away from Islam. The High Court of Malaysia upheld this right in a landmark case on October 6, 1988. Yeshua Jamaluddin's writ of *habeas corpus* was upheld after he had been arrested under the ISA, which allowed for arrest for subversion, violence and threats to national security. A High Court judge ruled that the ISA did not extend to the issue of converting away from Islam.[58]

However, other cases suggest that the issue is far more complex than this case suggests. In the celebrated case of NorAishah Bokhari,[59] this 26 year old Malay renounced Islam on 22 October 1997 in the presence of a Commissioner of Oaths to marry Joseph Arnold Lee, 28, a Catholic Chinese. Her family was 'saddened and shocked', and PAS, in a clearly intimidatory move, printed and circulated 100,000 posters bearing her photo. The PAS periodical *Harakah* called on the government to arrest apostates under the ISA. In November 1997 NorAishah's family found her and took her home, saying she had returned to Islam, regretting her earlier action. On December 30 NorAishah disappeared from her home and then reappeared, accusing her father and brother of originally kidnapping her to take her home. She then appealed to the High Court for the right to choose her own religion. However, contrary to her request, a warrant of arrest was issued against her fiance for kidnapping NorAishah, and NorAishah's lawyer was then detained.

This case brought tensions surrounding the apostasy issue to the surface. In 1998 a Bill came before Federal Parliament prescribing the punishment for apostasy as up to three years' imprisonment or a maximum fine equivalent to about £900 or both.[60] This bill was proposed on two occasions by then PAS member for Marang Abdul Hadi Awang, later Chief Minister of Trengganu.[61] The UMNO-led Barisan Nasional Government voted it down both times, stating on 4 August 1998 that

---

[58] Bert Breiner, "Christians and Muslims in Search of Common Ground in Malaysia": A Response', *Islam and Christian-Muslim Relations*, 2/2 (December 1991), 270.
[59] Mohammad Hashim Kamali, *Islamic Law in Malaysia. Issues and Developments*, Kuala Lumpur: Ilmiah Publishers, 2000, 203ff.
[60] *Straits Times*, 17 April 1998.
[61] Suhor Husin, 'Cubaan Kedua PAS Ditolak', *Harakah Internet Edition*, 10 August 1998.

apostates would not face government punishment so long as they did not defame Islam after their conversion.[62]

The issue of apostasy is ongoing. On 24 April 2001 a Muslim convert to Christianity was denied permission to have her identity card changed to reflect her religious conversion. The woman, who has already changed her name from Azlina Jailani to Lina Joy, was told by a judge that she must take up the issue with the Islamic Shari'a Court.[63]

Actions proposed and taken by Malaysian Christians

Malaysian Christians are by no means remaining inactive in the face of what they consider as marginalisation and, at times, threat. Their responses can be considered under several headings.

The need to lobby government

Christians in Malaysia are becoming increasingly adept at lobbying the Federal Government in pursuit of their interests and concerns. We discussed previously the meeting between Prime Minister Mahathir and Bishop Datuk and other church leaders in 1998. In an earlier example, Christian leaders challenged the Government prohibition on Christian use of terms deemed Islamic. The Christian Federation of Malaysia assembled bishops from member churches in 1989 to draw up a letter to Prime Minister Mahathir which stated the following:

> It is inconceivable to us that the Bible in any translation can be regarded as a threat to national security in any country ... Nowhere else in the world, as we know, have people been forbidden to use words which are part of their National Language.[64]

---

[62] 'US Department of State Annual Report on International Religious Freedom for 1999: Malaysia', Bureau for Democracy, Human Rights and Labour, Washington DC, 9 September, 1999, http://www.state.gov/www/global/human_rights/irf/irf_rpt/1999/irf_malaysia99.html; 'Country Profile: Malaysia', Christian Solidarity Worldwide, http://www.csw.org.uk/malaysia.html.

[63] 'Malaysia—Christian Persecution in Malaysia', *International Christian Concern*, May 2001, http://www.persecution.org/humanrights/malaysia.html.

[64] Cited in Olaf Schumann, Christians and Muslims in Search of Common Ground in Malaysia', *Islam and Christian-Muslim Relations*, 2/2 (December 1991), 258.

In response to the attacks on churches in July 2001, the Christian Federation of Malaysia issued a statement urging Christians to exercise discretion in sharing their faith, and calling on the Government to publicly condemn acts of violence and provide greater protection. In the same statement the CFM called on the government to ban inflammatory media presentations. The MCCBCHS also expressed concern to the Government about these attacks.[65]

More generally, Dr S Batumalai drew up a detailed list of recommendations which he said the Malaysian Government needed to consider in addressing the concerns of Malaysian non-Muslim communities.[66] These recommendations are best summed up by his statement that

> The quest for more inclusive greater Malaysian identity must be realised ... a way must be found where by sharing one's faith with others without becoming controversial, one becomes an agent of change. This change can also be understood as conversion not to a particular doctrine but to a common bond to build the nation.[67]

The need to participate in the political process

Malaysian Christians are not merely engaging in lobbying of Government. There are periodic calls by community leaders for Christians to increase their participation in the political process.

The CFM issued a press release prior to 1999 national elections, stressing three priorities:

—the need to carefully examine the integrity and the ability of candidates;
—the need to assess the political parties 'on the basis of their manifestos, their stand on various issues related to citizens' rights, national unity, economic development, protection of the environment and welfare of those who are

---

[65] 'Arson Attacks on Churches—CFM Urges Restraint', *Berita NECF* January/February 2002, 1.
[66] S Batumalai, *Islamic Resurgence and Islamization in Malaysia*, Charles Grenier, Ipoh, 1996, 131-155.
[67] *Ibid.*, 143.

sick, disabled and those who are poor';
—The need to vote: 'Through our vote, we aspire with all
Malaysians to live in a nation, where all citizens may enjoy
freedom, love, justice, peace, stability and economic prosperity.'

The press release further urged Christians in selecting their
preferred candidates to 'see how far views expressed and political
programmes espoused meet with God's standards and Christian values.'
This was a significant statement, in that it was clearly linking Christian
identity, values and beliefs with participation in a political process which
was increasingly marked by an Islamic agenda.

With particular reference to religious issues, the CFM press release
expressed a thinly-veiled concern at PAS campaigning methods, stating:
'The Christian Federation of Malaysia joins all other Malaysians in
expressing the wish that ... there will be no attempt by politicians to
publicly misrepresent or miscast any particular religion, or, subject any
particular religious community to unfair and adverse publicity for the
purpose of political gain.'[68]

While such CFM statements purport to represent the vast
majority of the Christian community, there were similar calls for
involvement in the political area from specific segments of the Christian
community. Writing in *Berita NECF*, former member of parliament
Dato' Lew Sip Hon urged Christians to participate in politics through
the formation of pressure groups, joining political parties, standing for
parliament (especially for a party likely to win government) and forming
a Christian political party.[69]

These calls for greater Christian involvement in the political
process mask the extent to which the Christian community in Malaysia
operates as a ghetto. The NECF Malaysia Survey of Churches (2001)
found that less than 2 percent of Christians surveyed contacted a member
of parliament or took some action on a public issue during the previous
twelve month period.[70]

---

[68] Council of Churches of Malaysia Press Release, http://www.ccmalaysia.org/netscape/press/
press2.htm, copied 20 May 2002. I have corrected linguistic flaws in the English language of
the internet version of the Press Release, without making any change to meaning.
[69] Lew Sip Hon , 'Christians and Political Realities', *Berita NECF* September/October 2001,
4-5 and 14.
[70] Edmund Ng, 'A Post-Survey Analysis: Towards Greater Community Involvement', *Berita
NECF* March/April 2002, 11.

The need to engage with non-Christians

A theme which occurs frequently in Christian comment is the need for Christians to engage with non-Christian Malaysians. The meaning of 'engagement' is, of course, crucial, and the term is used to signify mission in all its forms, as well as simple interaction. Whatever the use of this term, the existence of an inward-looking Christian ghetto seems to be widely recognised.

The NECF Malaysia Survey of Churches (2001) produced some striking details. Around 48 percent of Christians surveyed rarely interacted with Muslims, while 36 percent of churches did not organise any activities that involved interaction with non-Christians in their neighbourhoods. On the average, churches surveyed spent only 8 percent of budgets on social concern and community involvement, compared within 32 percent on salaries and 23 percent on building maintenance.[71]

The same feature seems to characterise the Catholic Church of Malaysia, with Archbishop Anthony Soter Fernandez, in his keynote address to the PMPC II in August 1996, asking the following questions of his fellow Catholics:

> Why is there so much participation in sacrament and worship with so little commitment to living out the Gospel in our lives? … Has our Catholicism been one that observes certain religious practices and ceremonies without adequately understanding them, experiencing their reality, and living them out in daily life? We need to find out if our tepidity and our indifference and a lack of proper understanding of our evangelising mission has promoted an incoherent Christian life.[72]

Archbishop Fernandez challenged the Catholic Church in Malaysia 'to proclaim the Gospel through the simplicity of our lives and caring for others through mercy and justice.' Such an incarnational approach to proclamation of the Gospel would be less likely to run foul

---

[71] *Ibid.*

[72] Anthony Soter Fernandez, 'Our Journey as Church in Peninsular Malaysia toward the Third Millennium', http://www.catholic.org.sg/web_links/AVE/pmpc/key.html, copied 22 May 2002.

of government legislation prohibiting the proselytisation of Muslims than would be street evangelism, for example. Nevertheless, Catholics were clearly very wary of anything that could suggest the kind of mission forbidden by the government. The Catholic Church of Malaysia distributed a questionnaire among parishes, seeking feedback on priorities and concerns. Brother Anthony Rogers collated responses, and commented as follows:

> It is interesting to note that in all the Responses received, there was no mention of the word 'Mission' or 'Evangelisation'. Is this an indication that we are still preoccupied with 'Intra-Church' activities that we have no time to respond with a greater commitment to the people around us? It is obvious that it is our Communion that is genuine that will lead us to 'Mission' that is integral.[73]

In an attempt to demonstrate a more outward-looking face, the NECF made a donation of 50,000 Malaysian dollars for Turkey's earthquake victims on 24 August 1999. This drew praise from Muslim leadership, Malaysian Deputy Prime Minister Abdullah Ahmad Badawi observing that despite being a Christian movement NECF contributed to mainly Muslim victims. 'I hope other quarters will emulate this action,' he said.[74]

However, the most pressing need in terms of engagement with Muslims in the view of Christian commentators was for inter-religious dialogue.

The Catholic Church of Malaysia's Aggiornamento (1976) identified Ecumenical and Inter-Religious Dialogue as a priority. This was reinforced by PMPC I and II in subsequent years. In response, the St Francis Xavier Parish in Kuala Lumpur launched a 'Movement for Interfaith Enhancement' in 1999. This focused on meetings with other faiths devoted to topics such as 'Islam and Buddhism's attitude towards other religions' (April 1999) and 'Islam and Hinduism's attitude towards Justice and Peace' (August 1999). St Francis Xavier Parish is in fact acting as a catalyst to involve other parishes in dialogue, so the impact of

---

[73] Anthony Rogers, 'Synthesis and Reflections on Collated Responses to Questionnaire', http://www.veritas.org.sg/web_links/AVE/rogers.html, copied 22 May 2002.
[74] 'Deputy PM Praises Christians', *Berita NECF* November/December 1999.

this initiative is bound to increase. There thus seems to have been considerable progress since the mid-1990s, when Catholic Archbishop Emeritus in Kuala Lumpur, Tan Sri Vendargon, commented that 'There is very little dialogue with Muslims. The Christian churches are working only among non-Muslims in Malaysia.'[75]

As for the Protestant Council of Churches of Malaysia, its commitment to dialogue with other faiths is expressed on its website in the following terms:

> Being a Christian community in a multi-religious Malaysia demands that the churches keep all channels of communication open and through dialogue with the government and others, to resolve issues and build religious harmony.[76]

Some Christians express concerns about Muslim willingness to dialogue. The prominent evangelical writer Ng Kam Weng articulates the following concern:

> Muslim scholars are only interested in pursuing a dialogue with Western Christians rather than local Christians... because Dialogue with local Christians ... confers legitimacy on local Christian Movements.[77]

However, Sadayandy Batumalai suggests a marginally more optimistic picture, in saying 'Despite lack of much encouragement from the government, dialogue has continued informally.'[78] Clearly, there are instances of Muslims taking the initiative to dialogue with non-Muslims. For example, the International Islamic University of Malaysia requested that a group of its students visit The Assumption Catholic Church in Petaling Jaya, Kuala Lumpur, on 19 May 2002. The Muslim visitors attended a full Mass in the morning, mingled with Assumption Church

---

[75] S Batumalai, *Islamic Resurgence and Islamization in Malaysia*, Charles Grenier, Ipoh, 1996, 144.

[76] http://www.ccmalaysia.org/netscape/events/past1.htm, copied 20 May 2002.

[77] K W Ng, 'Dialogue and Constructive Social Engagement: Problems and Prospects for the Malaysian Church', *Trinity Theological Journal*, vol. 5 (1995), 32.

[78] S Batumalai, *Islamic Resurgence and Islamization in Malaysia*, Charles Grenier, Ipoh, 1996, 145.

worshippers during refreshments, and then joined in a discussion session. Nevertheless, the NECF probably sums up the present situation concerning dialogue accurately in the following comment:

> Though dialogues at local and national levels have been convened, much remains to be done to create a more permanent and stable climate that is conducive to religious harmony.[79]

The need to contextualise the faith

As noted previously, one of the burdens which the Christians of Malaysia bear is that they embrace what is seen to be a foreign faith. Albert Walters addresses the need for contextualisation of Christianity in the following terms:

> The challenge remains for the churches to relate themselves more fully to the soil of [Southeast Asia]—to get down to the rice-roots level of Asian civilisation.[80]

One Malaysian Christian who has attempted to contextualise the Christian message into a Malaysian context is the Jesuit priest, Jojo M Fung. In an article in the *East Asian Pastoral Review*, Fr Fung summarises four everyday Malaysian practices: *tea tarik*, *gotong royong*, *pakai tangan*, *kaki ayam*. He explains the symbolism within the Malaysian culture of each of these terms. He then reinterprets them into a Christian context: having a drink (*tea tarik*) is related to the meal table fellowship of the New Testament; eating with one's hands (*pakai tangan*) is related to the breaking of the bread in the Eucharistic event; mutual help (*gotong royong*) is related to Jesus and the disciples working as a group; and going barefooted (*kaki ayam*) is related to Jesus walking on the water in Matthew 14:25-26. Fung then proceeds to link the symbolism of these Malaysian terms with the symbolism of the Christian faith; e.g. *gotong royong* is

---

[79] 'Rising Religious Activism. Ready to respond', *Berita NECF* September/October 2001, 1.
[80] A S Walters, *Contemporary Presentations of the Trinity in an Islamic Context: A Malaysian Case Study*, Unpublished PhD thesis, University of Birmingham, 1999, 71.

seen as 'a symbol which points to an ever–creative God who continues to collaborate with humankind in the ongoing process of co-creation.'[81]

Other Christian individuals and groups are similarly seeking to articulate the Christian faith in more indigenous terms. Sadayandy Batumalai sets out to interpret the Gospel in a way which reduces it as an expression of particular communities and ethnicities. Furthermore, during the 1990s a group of Christian women took the title 'Women in Theology and Ministry' and set out 'to develop feminist theologies related specifically to the Islamic context, dealing primarily with issues of justice for women.'[82]

Conclusions

It is necessary to stress the multi-racial and multi-geographical nature of the Barisan Nasional governing coalition. At the time of writing it consisted of fourteen political parties, including UMNO; the Malaysian Chinese Association (MCA); the Malaysian Indian Congress (MIC); Parti Progresif Rakyat (PPP); Parti Gerakan Rakyat Malaysia (Gerakan); Sarawak United People's Party (SUPP) and a collection of small parties from Sarawak and Sabah. Each party has three representatives in the BN Supreme Council, regardless of the party size or total members. The President of each BN member party holds the BN Vice-Chairman post on a rotational basis. Decisions of the BN Supreme Council, the highest party forum, are reached through consensus. So it should be noted that BN Islamisation measures are taken by a governing coalition including non-Muslim parties, with some Christian membership and support.

Nevertheless, UMNO is clearly the dominant partner in this coalition. This is signalled by the fact that the position of Chairman of the BN Supreme Council is always filled by the UMNO President. UMNO is the driving force behind the BN Islamisation programme, and has the weight in the coalition to carry this programme through.

---

[81] Jojo M. Fung, SJ, 'Faith: A Malaysian Perspective', *East Asian Pastoral Review* 38/1 (2001): 87–90.

[82] Robert Hunt, 'Christian Theological Reflection and Education in the Muslim Societies of Malaysia and Indonesia', *Studies in World Christianity* 3/2 (1997): 217.

It is not the purpose of this paper to adjudicate in any difference of opinion between some Malaysian Christians and their Government. Rather we have been primarily concerned here to present Christian perspectives, and specifically to show how an increasingly intense intra-Muslim struggle has led to increased efforts by Christians to organise themselves. This has resulted in an exciting brand of ecumenical cooperation, both inter-faith and inter-denominational, which contrasts with the considerable diversity and historical fragmentation of the Malaysian Christian community.

In promoting its approach to Islamisation and combating that of its chief rival among the Muslim Malays, PAS, the Federal Government has stated repeatedly that minority rights and faiths should have a clear voice in such a pluralist context as Malaysia. As Anwar Ibrahim said before his fall from favour, 'There cannot be an Islamic agenda devoid of and oblivious to the realities of a multi-racial society.'[83]

Challenges and complaints by Christians of the type reported in preceding pages can and have received responses from Muslim authorities, groups and individuals. For example, Mohammad Hashim Kamali provides a reasoned Islamic response to MCCBCHS documentation and concerns in his seminal study of Islamic Law in Malaysia.[84] Indeed, Kamali suggests that Malaysian non-Muslims sometimes tend to exaggerate the threat posed by Malaysian Islamisation:

The Islamic leanings of [Malaysia today] tend to be more pronounced when seen through the eyes of the non-Muslims of Malaysia, and yet far too committed to secularity and pragmatism when seen from the perspective of a devout or even moderately religious Muslim Malaysian.[85]

It should be noted that the Malaysian Government is far more

---

[83] Speaking on *Islamic Conversations*, London: Epicflow (for Channel Four), 1993, cited in Peter Riddell, *Islam and the Malay-Indonesian World: Transmission and Responses*, Horizon Press, Singapore, 2001, 243.

[84] Cf. chapter 9 of Mohammad Hashim Kamali, *Islamic Law in Malaysia. Issues and Developments*, Ilmiah Publishers, Kuala Lumpur, 2000.

[85] Mohammad Hashim Kamali, *Islamic Law in Malaysia. Issues and Developments*, Ilmiah Publishers, Kuala Lumpur, 2000, 10.

intrusive in its critique of the theology of 'devationist' Islamic groups than it is of Christian theology. The Department of Islamic Development of Malaysia (JAKIM) of the Prime Minister's Department campaigns actively against Muslim 'deviationist sects'.[86]

Nevertheless, it could be argued that the Government's tolerance of the publishing and distribution of anti-Christian polemical literature by Muslim groups has had a similar effect, though in that instance it does not come directly from Government activity. In response to this literature, Malaysian Christians Ng Kam Weng and Paul Tan have developed a specifically Malaysian apologetic for Christianity to respond to Muslim theological criticisms. [87]

Speaking at the Johor Barisan Nasional Convention in July 2002, Prime Minister Mahathir said that the BN could take great pride in its successful management of racial differences in the almost fifty years since Malaysia's independence.[88] There is much truth in this statement. However, there are signs that at the beginning of the 21st century inter-religious relations are fraying under the impact of political rivalry between the UMNO-led BN Government and PAS. If Malaysia is to live up to its claim of being a model of democratic, pluralist Islam, these tensions will need to be addressed and resolved.

---

[86] Cf. Peter Riddell, *Islam and the Malay-Indonesian World: Transmission and Responses*, Horizon Press, Singapore, 2001, 258-260.

[87] Robert Hunt, 'Christian Theological Reflection and Education in the Muslim Societies of Malaysia and Indonesia', *Studies in World Christianity* 3/2 (1997): 217.

[88] 'BN has managed racial differences successfully—Dr M', Barisan Nasional Official Website, http://www.bn.org.my/cgi-bin/newsdetail.asp?newsID=482, copied 29 July 2002.

CATHOLIC ENGAGEMENT WITH INDIA AND ITS THEOLOGICAL IMPLICATIONS: JULES MONCHANIN, HENRI LE SAUX, AND BEDE GRIFFITHS

Judson B Trapnell +

In the history of Christian encounters with India several key events could be claimed as definitive, beginning with the legendary arrival of the apostle Thomas in Cranganore, South India, in 52 CE and his later martyrdom.[1] Even if St Thomas was not the first disciple of Jesus Christ to reach India, we know that missionaries from Syria arrived by the 4th century and established churches among Hindu communities on the Malabar coast. Here began what has been touted as an exemplary period of interreligious co-existence, explained in part by the Christians' participation in the caste structure and commerce of the area.

The beginning of the 16th century also constitutes a definitive period in the history of Christian engagement with India, shaped by the arrival of Europeans with both commercial and religious motivations. A pattern of co-existence between Christians and Hindus was quickly replaced by one of conflict, grounded not only in cultural myths but religious convictions as well. The decades following Vasco da Gama's arrival on the Malabar coast in 1498 are notorious for the violent persecution of Muslims, the negative stereotyping of Hindus, and the zealous confrontation of the existing Syrian Christianity by the Portuguese—all in the name of the Catholic faith.

The early encounters of India by European Catholics wore a less violent face as well, creating a quite different model for Hindu-Christian relations that would also endure, though with much less influence, into the 20th century. That face was worn most visibly by the Italian Jesuit Roberto de Nobili (1577-1656). Unlike his fellow Jesuit Francis Xavier (1506-1552) whose harsh criticisms of Indians and their religions are perhaps as legendary as his prolific efforts to baptize the 'heathen', de

---

[1] As a general source on the history of Christianity's relationship to Hinduism in India, see Harold Coward, ed., *Hindu-Christian Dialogue: Perspectives and Encounters*, Orbis Books, Maryknoll, NY, 1989.

Nobili immersed himself in the traditions of the priestly caste, the Brahmins, believing that this approach would facilitate the reception of the Gospel from the top down. De Nobili, through his learning of Sanskrit, his adoption of the lifestyle of the *sannyāsin* or renunciate, and his serious effort to understand a non-Christian religion from its own sources, set an example of engagement that would directly inspire the three Europeans discussed in this chapter.[2]

To identify Jules Monchanin's arrival in Bombay in 1939 as a further defining event in the history of Christian encounters with India requires qualification. Like de Nobili, Monchanin did not enter a world in which his own tradition was absent. Christianity had been a part of the Indian religious landscape, however miniscule, for at least sixteen hundred years, increasing in influence after the overthrow of Muslim rule in the mid-18th century by the British. Specifically, a modern Indian Christianity was already in formation through the efforts of Indian Christians such as Brahmabandhab Upadhyay,[3] Narayan Vaman Tilak, and A J Appasamy. Other Indians, like Mohandas Gandhi and Keshub Chunder Sen, while never formally embracing Christianity, clearly influenced its modern Indian form as well.

One may justify a claim for the importance of the work of Monchanin, Le Saux, and Griffiths by taking into account two forces of change that meet in them: first, in distinct ways, each represents questions within the Roman Catholic Church prior to the Second Vatican Council regarding its relation to other religions that each sought to resolve through following a vocation to India. As importantly, each of them maintained

---

[2] See Vincent Cronin, *A Pearl to India: The Life of Roberto de Nobili*, Rupert Hart-Davis, London, 1959.

[3] Brahmabandhab Upadhyay (1861-1907) directly influenced the theological and liturgical explorations of Monchanin, Le Saux, and Griffiths. It was Upadhyay who drew a connection between the Trinity and the Hindu imaging of the divine as *sat-chit-ānanda* (or *saccidananda*), who extolled Vedanta philosophy for its potential role in expressing an Indian Christian theology, who nevertheless upheld Christ as the fulfillment of Vedanta, and who founded a monastery in the model of the Hindu ashram in 1900, though this experiment was short-lived due to ecclesiastical opposition. See B Animananda, *The Blade: The Life and Work of Brahmabandhab Upadhyay*, Roy & Son, Calcutta, 1945; and Julius Lipner, *Brahmabandhab Upadhyay: The Life and Thought of a Revolutionary*, Oxford University Press, Delhi, 1999. For a strongly negative evaluation of de Nobili's and Upadhyay's motives and missionary efforts from a contemporary Hindu, see Sita Ram Goel, *Catholic Ashrams: Sannyāsins or Swindlers?*, 2nd ed., Voice of India, New Delhi, 1994, especially chapters 3 and 4.

connections to theologians in Europe for whom the experiments of these three pioneers provided revealing data about not only the future of missions but also the direction of theology that indirectly informed Vatican II.[4]

Simultaneous with the movements of change within the Catholic Church, a second group of forces were at work in India that impacted any European Christian there. The so-called Hindu Renaissance had begun in the 19th century, a movement that as a whole both drew from and rejected European influence. As a result, the Hinduism that Monchanin, Le Saux, and Griffiths would encounter was one that contained two currents: a liberal, inclusive vision of other religions (e.g., S Radhakrishnan), and a politicised, exclusive criticism of them (e.g., the Arya Samaj and its offshoot, the RSS). In the decades from Independence (1947) to the present, strife between the two has increased, affecting the climate within which all three figures conducted their interreligious explorations.[5]

If one may productively image Monchanin, Le Saux, and Griffiths as Catholics attempting to construct bridges between Christianity and Hinduism, one must somehow represent the fact that the two worlds they were trying to connect were both in the throes of creative change. As we shall see, it was the calling of each figure to seek the contemplative depths of both traditions beneath the turbulent surfaces in order to discern a living connection between them and express it in fresh theological terms. In this chapter we shall examine 1) the approach to this vocation taken by each figure, 2) some of the theological directions prompted by their experiences in India, and 3) the legacies that each left behind for future theologians. If one dares to assert that they together represent a defining moment in the history of Christian encounters with India, one must acknowledge at the outset that their common intention was to pass on their contemplative vocation and theology for Indian Christians to develop more fully.

---

[4] The possible influence of the three on the Council is most apparent in Monchanin. See Donald Nicholl, 'Other Religions (*Nostra Aetate*)', in *Modern Catholicism: Vatican II and After*, (ed.) Adrian Hastings, SPCK, London, 1991, 126.
[5] See Gerald James Larson, *India's Agony over Religion*, State University of New York Press, Albany, NY, 1995. For a highly critical modern Hindu account, see Sita Ram Goel, *History of Hindu-Christian Encounters (AD 304-1996)*, rev. ed., Voice of India, New Delhi, 1996.

Jules Monchanin, SAM (1895–1957):[6]
the challenge of 'rethinking' theology

In the spring of 1939, just prior to his long-awaited departure from France for India, Jules Monchanin, priest of the Church of Lyon, met for a final time with his friend, Henri de Lubac, SJ. Monchanin's record of the visit articulates a principle for theological reform given to him by de Lubac that would guide not only his mission in India but Le Saux's and Griffiths's as well:

> [T]o rethink everything in the light of theology and to rethink theology through mysticism, freeing it from everything incidental and regaining, through spirituality alone, everything essential … He believes that it is in coming into contact with India that I will be able to rework theology much better than by going into theological problems in themselves.[7]

This quotation raises significant questions for our examination of Monchanin's approach to theology: First, what is involved in 'rethinking'? Second, what view of theology is assumed by the advice to 'rethink everything in the light of theology' and by what must be the prior task of rethinking theology 'through mysticism'? Finally, in what ways would transplanting the theologian to a foreign culture that is shaped primarily by a non-Christian religion facilitate this process of rethinking?

Theological method

In French as in English, the verb *repenser* or 'rethink' suggests either the

---

[6] Almost all of the works of and about Jules Monchanin are in French and remain untranslated into English. An important exception is Joseph G. Weber (ed. and trans.), *In Quest of the Absolute: The Life and Work of Jules Monchanin* (Kalamazoo, Michigan: Cistercian Publications, 1977) which includes a substantial biographical essay by Weber with ample quotations from Monchanin, an anthology of Monchanin's writings, and a selected bibliography (though now 25 years old). For further bibliographical information, see Etienne Fouilloux, 'Jules Monchanin in the Intellectual Milieux of Lyon in the Period between the Two World Wars,' in *Jules Monchanin (1895–1957) as Seen from East and West: Acts of the Colloquium Held in Lyon-Fleurie, France and in Shantivanam-Tannirpalli, India (April–July 1995)*, vol. 1, ISPCK, Saccidananda Ashram, Delhi, 2001, 31–45.

[7] Quoted in Weber, p. 25 from a letter by Monchanin to Marguerite Prost, 20 April 1939.

simple act of thinking again in familiar ways about something, or the more challenging tasks of re-viewing and re-formulating, that is, allowing unanticipated structures of conception to emerge from relatively unprocessed experiences and then expressing them in words. Monchanin was intellectually and religiously formed in a time and place in which these more difficult tasks seemed possible and urgent.[8] Nevertheless, throughout his life he would have been mindful of the Oath against Modernism (which he had to take as a priest) and of the later papal encyclical against the so-called 'new theology' (*Humani Generis,* 1950) that was so personally devastating for de Lubac as well as for himself.[9] Rethinking demands that one risk not only the comfort of familiar frameworks of meaning but also the approval of one's faith community. Unlike de Lubac, Monchanin would not live to see the opening to significant reconceptualization represented by the Second Vatican Council.

Creative insight and fresh articulation are not easily achieved without some catalyst to deconstruct one's existing thought structures and languages. De Lubac's advice to Monchanin just before his emigration suggests two such stimuli. The first is mysticism, which was already central to Monchanin's approach to theology.[10] On the one hand, Monchanin exhibited an intellectual gift for Indology and philosophical analysis, including comparative studies, e.g., Eckhart and Shankara. On the other, Monchanin was himself a contemplative whose prayer moved him beyond mere theorizing about theological matters. The relationship between these two urges is effectively described in the following:

> What I wish for is the Absolute (I mean a participation in the Absolute) in truth and Its truth, even if no intellectual construct is linked to it—although I find it difficult to breathe in too pure an atmosphere where ideas cannot be crystallized. The God of mysticism is beyond all feeling, all

---

[8] For six articles about Monchanin's life and work in France, and about the theological situation there between the two world wars, see *Jules Monchanin (1895-1957) as Seen from East and West,* vol. 1, 5-71. No doubt, he was familiar with de Lubac's own efforts at rethinking, especially the latter's seminal *Catholicisme* (1938). This book by de Lubac also influenced Griffiths. See Bede Griffiths, 'Catholicism To-day,' *Pax* 40 (1950), 11-16.

[9] See Francoise Jacquin, 'The Spiritual Journey of Jules Monchanin, or a Passion for the Universal,' in *Jules Monchanin (1895-1957) as Seen from East and West,* vol. 1, 133, 141.

[10] Jacques Gadille, 'Jules Monchanin, a Prophet in the Culture and in the Church of His Day,' in *Jules Monchanin (1895-1957) as Seen from East and West,* vol. 1, 23-27.

hope, in the burning solitude where he reflects himself and unifies himself.[11]

Monchanin's proclivity for thought and ideas thus conditions his passion for the Absolute or for a God beyond all thought and feeling. A method is also suggested here that resonates with de Lubac's 'rethinking': Dare to experience the 'God of mysticism,' yet also allow ideas to crystallize out of that experience.

De Lubac's parting advice to Monchanin suggests a second stimulus in addition to mysticism for the process of rethinking: immersion in a non-Christian culture. Monchanin had felt a call to India from an early age, one to which he eventually committed himself in 1932 in response to a serious illness, joining the *Société des auxiliaires des missions* (SAM).[12] When he did finally leave France and arrive in India in 1939, Monchanin experienced this transplanting as a cross, a mental and spiritual stripping, an opening to God's Spirit.[13] It was this ascesis through immersion in the unfamiliar, and the mystical openness it engendered, that would clear the mental ground for fresh conceptualization during the next eighteen years, a project he would describe as follows: 'India must be rethought in terms of Christianity, and Christianity in terms of India, as was done previously in Greece.'[14]

During his first ten years in India, as had been his experience in France, he was frequently moved by his bishop from one post to the next, serving in small villages where he adapted himself to their Tamil language and customs and to the poorest of conditions shared by Hindu, Muslim, and Christian alike. During this decade of pastoral ministry, private study, and solitary prayer, an idea developed to found a Christian contemplative community in which the mystical depths essential to the project of rethinking theology could be experienced in a way that was both thoroughly Christian and fully Indian.[15] In 1948 Monchanin was

---

[11] Quoted in Weber, 105–106; see also 131. Cf. de Lubac's account of mysticism in Henri de Lubac, SJ, 'Preface,' in *La mystique et les mystiques,* (ed.) A Ravier, SJ, Desclee, Paris, 1965, 7–39; idem, *Theology in History,* trans. Anne Englund Nash, Ignatius Press, San Francisco, 1996, 38, 178–200.

[12] Weber, 15–18. The *Société* had been founded in Belgium in 1926 by Frs Boland and Lebbe for the purpose of assigning priests to autochthonous bishops, first in China and later in India.

[13] *Ibid.,* 31.

[14] *Ibid.,* 95.

[15] *Ibid.,* 72; and Jacquin, 139.

joined by another French priest, Henri Le Saux, OSB, who shared this vision. Together they founded in 1950 a contemplative community at Shantivanam near the sacred Kavery River and the village of Kulithalai where Monchanin had served as pastor.[16] The double name they gave to the new community, Saccidananda Ashram and Hermitage of the Most Holy Trinity, signified the interreligious and Trinitarian commitments they shared.[17] For the next seven years, the solitude and the unfulfilled potential of this community would serve as the crucible out of which Monchanin's mature theologizing would arise.

Theological directions

In what directions did the method of rethinking stimulated by both his mysticism and his immerson in India take Monchanin by 1957? Especially significant for consideration here are his writings on apophatic and Trinitarian mysticism, and on the relation of Christianity to the other religions—two areas that correspond to the two stimuli for rethinking suggested by de Lubac, the first representing an intra-religious and intra-personal process, the second an inter-religious and inter-personal one. The creative interaction of both processes directed the theological explorations of all three figures we are discussing.

In one of his final lectures, 'The Quest of the Absolute' (1956), Monchanin distinguishes two types of Christian mysticism, the analogical and the apophatic. While the former begins with the creature and by discerning traces of its creator rises to a knowledge of God, the latter ascends by means of negating the creature and all that is not God. Nevertheless, Monchanin also concurs with Dionysius that the positive

---

[16] Symbolizing their adaptation of Christian monastic life to the indigenous spirituality, Monchanin and Le Saux assumed traditional Indian names, respectively Parama Arubi Ananda ('Bliss of the Supreme Formless One') and Abhishikteshvarananda ('Bliss of the Anointed One, the Lord'), later shortened to Abhishiktananda—a name by which he is often known.

[17] Saccidananda is a traditional Sanskrit appellation for the Absolute or Brahman: Being (*sat*), Awareness (*cit*), and Bliss (*ananda*). The resonances of this name with the Christian Trinity appealed to both founders. For discussions of the parallels, see Jules Monchanin and Henri Le Saux, *Ermites du Saccidānanda: un essai d'intégration chrétienne de la tradition monastique de l'Inde*, 2nd ed., Casterman, Paris 1957, 176; and Abhishiktananda, *Saccidananda: A Christian Approach to Advaitic Experience*, rev. ed., ISPCK, Delhi, 1984, especially Part Three (161-202), and Appendix 1 (203-214).

or analogical way and the negative or apophatic way are completed by a third mystical approach and theological perspective:

> The third degree, called supereminent, asserts once again what the previous degree [the negative] has denied, but not in the same way ... [T]his supereminent theology is, above all, a deeper immersion into the abyss of nescience; the more the mystic contemplates God and experiences him—*patiens divina*—the more does he measure an unplumbed depth of the 'supra-divine Deity.'[18]

Here is at once an affirmation of the positive contribution of theological discourse and a reminder that such discourse must always be grounded in an ever-deepening experience of not-knowing before the divine mystery—a conclusion with important implications for Le Saux and Griffiths as well.

Monchanin completes his discussion of apophatism in 'The Quest of the Absolute' with a reflection on the Trinity, an effective illustration of how the ascent above images or *via negativa* culminates in a more profound reappropriation of Trinity as constitutive of mystery.[19] The philosophical and theological implications of this connection are profound for Monchanin: To be is to be-in-relationship. Christian mysticism, then, can be defined 'in its essence' as 'the sharing of God's life; that is, the sharing of the trinitarian relationship,'[20] thus fulfilling the apophatic path and correcting an imbalance he identifies in Hindu philosophy:

> Christian mysticism is trinitarian or it is nothing. Hindu thought, so deeply focused on the Oneness of the One, on the *kevalin* in his *kevalatva,* cannot be sublimated into trinitarian thought without a crucifying dark night of the soul. It has to undergo a noetic metamorphosis, a passion of the spirit.[21]

---

[18] Weber, 130.
[19] See also Monchanin's 'Apophaticism and Apavada,' as discussed by Ysabel de Andia, 'Jules Monchanin, Apophatic Mysticism, and India,' in *Jules Monchanin (1895-1957) as Seen from East and West,* vol. 1, 89-93.
[20] Weber, 131.
[21] Weber, 132. The two Sanskrit terms are derivatives of *Kaivalya* which means the final state of the soul once freed from all earthly attachments according to Vedanta and the Yogasutras.

Similarly, in lectures given during his post-war visit to Europe, he criticized Hinduism's tendency to conceive of and experience the goal of oneness with the divine as a unity that abolishes the knower or lover, rather than as a communion between the human and the divine in which some duality remains.[22] Such prognoses of what Indian philosophy needs to receive from Christianity suggest an inclusivist theology of religions, one in which Christianity is understood as fulfilling the aspirations of non-Christian traditions in which the Spirit has nonetheless been present—a position that would have been at the cutting edge of Catholicism in the mid-1950s. Monchanin, however, did not articulate a definitive or systematic theology of religions. His lifelong search for synthesis remained open-ended, intentionally unfulfilled, reinforced by his philosophical assumptions and his experience in India.[23] He concludes 'The Quest of the Absolute' as follows:

> Meanwhile, our task is to keep all doors open, to wait with patience and theological hope for the hour of the advent of India into the Church, in order to realize the fullness of the Church and the fullness of India. In this age-long vigil, let us remember that very often *amor intrat ubi intellectus stat ad ostium* (Love can enter where the intellect must stand at the door).[24]

Theological legacy

In a 1939 letter to his mother written from the ship that carried him to his new home, Monchanin evoked a comparison that others would echo

---

[22] Ysabel de Andia cites three lectures from this period in which such critiques of Hinduism are found: 'L'Inde et la contemplation, Gitagovinda,' and 'L'Hindouisme,' both in *Mystique de l'Inde, mystère chrétien*, (ed.) Suzanne Siauve, Fayard, Paris, 1974; and 'Un itineraire et un dessein missionaire,' in *Theologie et spiritualite missionaires*, (ed.) Edouard Duperray and Jacques Gadille (Beauchesne, Paris, 1984).

[23] Reserve about creating a theoretical synthesis, nevertheless, did not weaken his sense of mission to 'Christianize' India through a clear intellectual strategy that shows how he adapted de Lubac's parting advice: 1) rethink Christianity by returning to its biblical origins prior to any European shaping; 2) isolate the heart of the other civilization by returning to the period of awakening at its origin; and 3) once the purity of both Christianity and the non-Western civilization have been identified, graft the former onto the latter (Weber, pp. 123-25).

[24] Weber, 132.

in describing his legacy: 'I must be buried in this land of India—somewhat like Father de Foucauld in the land of the Sahara—to be sanctified and to make it fertile.'[25] Monchanin longed for as fruitful a death as de Foucauld's, understanding that he would see little growth from the seed he planted and that the transformation of India he foresaw would take generations. In part due to the radicalness of its ideal for its time and in part to the increasing conflicts between Monchanin and Le Saux over the years, the ashram at Shantivanam attracted no lasting vocations. Bede Griffiths, the English Benedictine who received responsibility for the ashram from Le Saux in 1968, did see the seed germinate with the arrival of Indian monks and identified Monchanin as the origin of this growth: 'He gave his life for the ashram without seeing any immediate hope for the future, but it is from his sacrifice that the ashram has continued to live.'[26]

In addition to leaving behind him an ashram as a laboratory for rethinking an Indian Christian theology grounded in contemplation, Monchanin also passed along to Le Saux, Griffiths, and others, specific directions for theological investigation that these others would develop. In particular, Monchanin emphasized the importance of the doctrine of creation as free gift that he believed was needed to correct a serious flaw in Hinduism,[27] as well as the value of a Christian reinterpretation of *advaita* in the light of the Trinity in order to portray God as love more adequately. Monchanin also recognized the vital role that India with its spiritual traditions could play in teaching Europe and the Church the importance of the inner life[28]—a recognition that would be echoed strongly in Le Saux and Griffiths, in the contemporary contemplative renewal in the Catholic Church, and in the general receptivity of the West to Eastern forms of meditation from the 1960s to the present. Finally, with his attempts to 'rethink Christianity in terms of India' by first 'disassociating it by thought from the conceptual modalities in which it was incorporated into Mediterranean civilizations,' Monchanin anticipated the challenges of inculturation with which his successors, especially after Vatican II, would have to grapple.[29]

---

[25] Weber, 27. See also p. 49. 'Unless a grain of wheat falls to the ground and dies ...' (Jn. 12.24).
[26] Quoted without reference on the back cover of *Jules Monchanin (1895-1957) as Seen from East and West*, vol. 1. See also Griffiths's Preface to Weber (p. 3).
[27] See passages quoted in Weber, 126, 148-52.
[28] Jacquin, 138.
[29] Weber, 123.

As the eldest and most conservative theologically of the three figures we are examining in this chapter, Monchanin may appear less of a pioneer in interreligious understanding. One must recall, however, that for his time his very presence in India as a priest with the poor under the guidance of an autochthonous bishop and in particular his vision of a contemplative ashram as a center for dialogue were radical. Prior to Vatican II, more adventurous 'rethinking' was both difficult and dangerous; he illustrates both the obstacles to, and the promise of, serious Western Christian engagement with a non-Christian tradition that will shape the efforts of Le Saux and Griffiths.

Henri Le Saux (Abhishiktananda) (1910-1973):[30] the mystical plunge beyond thought

Not long after his arrival in India, Monchanin wrote of his dream of discovering a Hindu guru, a dream whose fulfillment was 'essential if I am to know India otherwise than through books ... Otherwise I shall never reach the *centre*—the intuition from which everything radiates ...' Over a decade later and only a month after he and Le Saux began their ashram experiment, Monchanin concluded that fulfilling this dream was 'impossible.'[31] When the two priests had visited Sri Ramana Maharshi in 1948, Monchanin had described this Hindu teacher as follows: 'A truly human being, there is not an *atom* of Christianity in that serene and beautiful spirit. Such examples indicate better than anything else the gulf which I perceive ever more clearly between the *summits* of Christianity and of Hinduism.'[32] The visit thus confirmed for Monchanin the difficulty in building a bridge, even a contemplative one, between the two traditions.

Le Saux's response to Ramana Maharshi was significantly different. He had read the writings of this teacher before leaving France and, although he was initially unimpressed, the presence of the Maharshi, and with him 'the very soul of India,' eventually penetrated Le Saux

---

[30] Le Saux's writings are primarily published in Delhi, India (under Abhishiktananda) by the International Society for the Promotion of Christian Knowledge (ISPCK). A complete bibliography of these as well as studies of Le Saux (articles and book-length) are found in James Stuart, *Swāmī Abhishiktananda: His Life Told through His Letters*, ISPCK, Delhi, 1989.

[31] Quoted in Stuart, 98.

[32] Quoted in Stuart, 32-33; see also 98.

deeply: 'It was a call which pierced through everything, rent it in pieces and opened a mighty abyss.' In the following days, he dreamed frequently of the Maharshi and became aware of a mental conflict that would continue for most of the rest of his life:

> My dreams included attempts—always in vain—to incorporate in my previous mental structures without shattering them, these powerful new experiences which my contact with the Maharshi had brought to birth; new as they were, their hold on me was already too strong for it ever to be possible for me to disown them.[33]

Le Saux's self-analysis here reveals his experience of du Lubac's project of 'rethinking': Existing 'mental structures' are shaken by 'powerful new experiences'—experiences that cannot be 'disowned', presumably through either reasoned explanation or appeal to orthodoxy. At work here as well are the two stimuli of mystical awakening and interreligious encounter implied by de Lubac. In contrast, however, to Monchanin's interpretation of his friend's advice, Le Saux's 'rethinking' springs from an unusual willingness to open through non-Christian sources to a level of experience 'which pierced through everything,' i.e., all thought and image, revealing 'a mighty abyss.'[34]

In this detail of difference between the two French *sannyasins* regarding their openness to learning to plunge beyond thought from Hindu gurus one may discern a contrast in their engagement with India that would have important consequences for their respective theological methods and explorations.

Theological method

For weeks at a time during the early 1950s Le Saux immersed himself in the silence of non-discursive meditation in the caves of Arunachala near

[33] Abhishiktananda, *The Secret of Arunachala: A Christian Hermit on Shiva's Holy Mountain*, ISPCK, Delhi, 1979, 8-9.

[34] Monchanin strongly disapproved of Le Saux's spending three weeks in retreat with another Hindu guru, Sri Gnanananda, in 1956. See Stuart, 98-100. For Le Saux's account of this retreat, see his *Guru and Disciple: An Encounter with Śrī Gnānānanda, a Contemporary Spiritual Master*, trans. by Heather Sandeman, ISPCK, Delhi, 1990.

Ramana Maharshi's ashram, consciously following the models of the early Christian desert fathers and of the Hindu *sannyāsins*. Inspired by these retreats, Le Saux composed a series of essays that he gathered into a volume entitled *Guhāntara: au sein du fond*.[35] These writings, he would say later, 'had poured forth even before I had become aware of them' and are 'the direct expression of the first overwhelming experiences.'[36] Their message was inherently apophatic, arising from the discovery that the God that Christians and Hindus alike worship under various traditional forms is One beyond those forms. Yet that message was also inherently Upanishadic, conveying his realization that this One is also one's Self. To uncover a similar depth within Christianity the Church must respond to the 'grace of interiority' offered to it through India.[37] While this message and the experience from which it sprang would remain central to Le Saux's theological writings for the rest of his life, he would refine its expression in relation to Christian doctrine, especially the Trinity. Important here, however, is what we learn of his theological method which received significant reshaping in these experiences in the caves of Arunachala. From this point on, Le Saux was unremittingly mindful of the principle that the thought processes of theology must be founded upon experience of nonduality beyond thought, an experience that relativizes all formulations yet also empowers all formulations with the power to draw the hearer of them to his or her source.[38] In contrast to Monchanin, Le Saux also concluded that through such a plunge beyond thought into silence, beyond the inherited structures of theology into an unstructured state, one could bridge the gulf between Hinduism and Christianity.[39]

---

[35] *Guhāntara* (Sanskrit) means 'the dweller in the cave,' and is a pseudonym for the author, while the French subtitle may be translated, 'at the heart of the depth' (Stuart, 76, 78, 364). Only portions of this text have been published so far, primarily in Abhishiktananda, *Initiation a la spiritualité des Upanishads: 'Vers l'autre rive'*, ed. M–M. Davy, Presence, Sisteron, 1979, and *idem, Intériorité et Révélation: Essais théologiques*, ed. M–M. Davy, Presence, Sisteron, 1982. See bibliographic details in Stuart.

[36] Stuart, 76, 223.

[37] Abhishiktananda, 'La Grace de L'Inde,' in *Initiation à la Spiritualité des Upanishads*, 41.

[38] See excerpt from his spiritual diary (May 21, 1954), quoted in M-M Davy, *Henri Le Saux— Swāmī Abhishiktānanda: le passeur entre deux rives*, Le Cerf, Paris, 1981, 118-19.

[39] For Monchanin's skeptical assessment, see Weber, 132. For Le Saux's different conclusion, see his *Intériorité et révélation*, 119. On the 'gulf' between the traditions, see also Stuart, 56, 58. The limits of Monchanin's approach to dialogue, in contrast to Le Saux's, are analyzed by Michael Amaladoss, SJ, in his 'The Theological and Missionary Project of Monchanin in Today's Indian Theological Context,' in *Jules Monchanin (1895-1957) as Seen from East and West*, vol. 2, 122.

It was precisely here that Monchanin felt increasingly uncomfortable with Le Saux's method and conclusions: 'I feel a growing horror for all those muddled modes of thinking in which this *beyond thought* proves to be *short of thought,* in which everything is drowned.'[40] As though in response, Le Saux diagnosed his colleague's inability to grasp the true significance of these essays as symptomatic of an attachment to Western conditioning: 'I think he is too 'Greek' to go to the depths.'[41]

Not surprisingly, Le Saux's skeptical attitude toward the method and content of traditional theology was encouraged by the Church censors' rejection of *Guhāntara* and by his increasing conflicts with Monchanin who came to represent a rigidity of thinking that he was trying to purge in himself.[42] This strong ambivalence toward theology and theologians would continue, even as he later in life attempted to integrate the explosive message of *Guhāntara* into the minds of the Indian and Western churches through a more patient concern for his audience.

Theological directions

Monchanin's death in 1957 left responsibility for Saccidananda Ashram fully in Le Saux's somewhat reluctant hands. It would not be until 1968, however, that Le Saux would relinquish this responsibility to fellow Benedictine, Bede Griffiths, and move permanently to a hermitage in the north near Uttarkashi. During this middle period of Le Saux's sojourn in India, he became increasingly involved in the tasks of articulating an Indian theology and of composing an Indian liturgy. While maintaining his contemplative focus, he organized and participated in several meetings, primarily among Christians, in which the potential dialogue between Christian and Hindu spiritualities was explored.[43] In 1968, in preparation

---

[40] Quoted in Jacquin, 143. For Monchanin's Preface to *Guhāntara,* see Monchanin, *Mystique de l'Inde, Mystère chrétien,* 271-73; quoted in full in de Andia, 82-84. See also Weber, 119.
[41] Quoted in Stuart, 81.
[42] For the censors' comments and Le Saux's reactions to them, see Stuart, 82-84, 104. On Le Saux's own abiding caution in plunging into the advaitic experience, note diary entry (23 March 1953) in Abhishiktananda, *Ascent to the Depth of the Heart: The Spiritual Diary (1948-1973) of Swāmi Abhishiktānanda (Dom H. Le Saux),* (ed.) Raimon Panikkar, trans. by David Fleming and James Stuart, ISPCK, Delhi, 67. For a particularly revealing criticism of theologians, see *Ascent to the Depth of the Heart,* 142.
[43] See Abhishiktananda, *Hindu-Christian Meeting Point: Within the Cave of the Heart,* rev. ed., trans. by Sara Grant, ISPCK, Delhi, 1976.

for the All-India Seminar of the Catholic Church in Bangalore, he composed a book-length memorandum in which he reflected upon the renewal of the church through liturgical reform, openness to Hindu sources, and contemplation.[44] His most notable theological work dates from this period as well, published in 1965 as *Sagesse hindoue mystique chretienne: du Védanta à la Trinité*.[45] This work was an ambitious attempt to synthesize his early experiences of nonduality into a coherent Trinitarian spirituality and thus represents a more accessible kind of bridge-making between Hinduism and Christianity than *Guhāntara*.[46]

Le Saux's apophatic emphasis in the early chapters of *Sagesse*, heightened by his appeal to the Hindu experience of nonduality, forces the question more powerfully than one finds in Monchanin of how to reconcile apophatic theology and the efficacy of Christian symbols. Is the doctrine of the Trinity, for example, an aid to contemplation that is functionally equivalent to the Vedantic image of *saccidānanda* and that one must finally transcend in opening directly to the divine mystery? The exigencies of analysis and the assumptions of Christian theology guide Le Saux to articulate the relationship between the Vedantic and Trinitarian experiences within a hierarchical and sequential framework. He thus presents the Vedantic experience of Self-realization in which one's sense of self is lost in an awakening to Brahman as an essential stage in one's union with the divine mystery. This experience constitutes a thorough purification of concepts, images, and all that reinforces duality between oneself and God, and represents the culmination of and justification for the apophatic way.

However, Le Saux affirms, relying upon similar theological sources as Monchanin, that the apophatic stage is completed by the important recovery of the Trinity as a mystery that underlies the theological doctrine but cannot be reduced to it, a mystery revealed in Jesus' relation to the Father. That relation does not constitute a simple monism but rather a

---

[44] Abhishiktananda, *Towards the Renewal of the Indian Church* (Bangalore: Dharmaram College, 1970).

[45] Centurion, Paris.

[46] For a comparison of these two works, see Stuart, 192. For Le Saux's anticipation of this task of integrating Hindu and Christian understandings of the divine mystery into a 'Christian *advaita*' as early as 1954, see Stuart, 79. For a detailed and insightful analysis of *Sagesse* in the context of Le Saux's developing thought, see Edward Theodore Ulrich, 'Swāmī Abhishiktānanda's Interreligious Hermeneutics of the Upanishads' (Ph.D. diss., Catholic University of America, 2001), chap. 6.

communion in which the partners are paradoxically conceived as one-in-relation.

Vedanta obliges us to recognize in man a level of consciousness deeper than that of reflective thought, more basic than man's awakening to himself through sense-perception or mental activity. Christ's experience compels us to admit the existence in man of something even deeper still ... Only he who proceeds from the Father at the fount of Being itself could tell us that Being is not a monad, but communion.[47]

Le Saux's strategy for reconciling Vedantic and Trinitarian experiences discloses a theological framework similar to Monchanin's: the 'theology of fulfillment' which assumes 'the convergence upon the historical Christ and the Church, of all the religious and spiritual experiences of mankind.'[48] Like Monchanin, however, Le Saux balances the fulfillment framework with an affirmation of the fact that Christianity will learn much from the encounter with India.[49] Nevertheless, one must take seriously Le Saux's reminder about the provisional nature of this and any theological work as an exercise in 'rethinking.' He was, even at his most explicitly theological, consciously using words to point toward silence.

Theological legacy

If *Sagesse* represents a resolution of the creative tension between Vedantic and Trinitarian experiences that characterizes *Guhāntara*, Le Saux would soon move beyond that resolution into fresh and pregnant disequilibrium, even as he was revising *Sagesse* in an English translation. Symptomatic of this internal change was a growing dissatisfaction with the 'fulfillment theology' as a framework for relating Hinduism and Christianity.[50] The solution, he was coming to realize, was not a new theological framework

---

[47] Abhishiktananda, *Saccidānanda*, 82-83, 84.
[48] *Ibid.*, xv.
[49] *Ibid.*, 223-24.
[50] Stuart, 261.

but a stance at a different level, an openness outside all frameworks. Already in 1970 he had written in a letter that *Sagesse* failed to solve the problem of how to bring together the depths of Christian and Hindu mysticisms:

> The best course is still, I think, to hold on even under extreme tension to these two forms of a unique 'faith' until the dawn appears. For advaita and theology are on two different levels. The lofty assurance of the advaitin philosophers is as empty as that of the theologians.[51]

As his enthusiasm about the project of revising *Sagesse* steadily lessened, his skepticism about theology as a response to the divine mystery heightened. He judged his book flawed by the same limitations of thought that he had criticized in Monchanin.[52] These conclusions reflect a fuller mental kenosis, a more thoroughly apophatic realization than seemed to inform *Sagesse,* an emptying that the events of his final years can in part explain, especially his permanent move to his hermitage in the north in 1968, his deepening meditation upon the Upanishads with disciple Marc Chaduc, and his heart attack in 1973.

In the year before his death, Le Saux wrote:

> No wish to be a theologian. The only thing I try to do is turn souls inward, where every question is moot—to the primordial silence of the Father, or to the consuming silence of the Spirit, where the Verbum dawns, and whither it leads.[53]

In spite of such caveats, Le Saux has strongly influenced theologians and other Christian authors who knew him or who have been drawn to his writings, including *Sagesse.*[54] Yet few of these authors would point to specific theological conclusions as his primary legacy. Instead they are inclined to identify his importance for Christian theology

---

[51] *Ibid.*, 268.

[52] Stuart, 312, 317, 318.

[53] Letter quoted in Jacques Dupuis, *Jesus Christ at the Encounter of World Religions,* trans. by Robert R Barr, Orbis Books, Maryknoll, NY, 1991, 75.

[54] Such a list would include Jacques Dupuis, SJ, Raimon Panikkar, Michael Amaladoss, SJ, Murray Rogers, Sr Sara Grant, RCSJ, Sr. Vandana, RCSJ, George Gispert-Sauch, SJ, Klaus Klostermaier, Bettina Baeumer, James Stuart, and, as we shall see, Bede Griffiths.

in his ability to live the tensions created by a life in dialogue and to speak from experience with unusual integrity.[55] In contrast to Monchanin, Le Saux remained convinced to the end of his life that the key to de Lubac's project of rethinking as well as to building any kind of bridge between the mystical depths of Hinduism and Christianity was the mystical plunge beyond thought. In a letter written several weeks before his death, he asserts, 'So long as we have not accepted the *loss* of all concepts, all myths—of Christ, of the Church—nothing can be done! Everything has to spring up anew from the depths ...'[56]

Bede Griffiths, OSB Cam. (1906-1993):[57] toward the integration of mysticism and theology

In a 1976 article, Bede Griffiths praised Le Saux's recently published English translation of *Sagesse* as 'without doubt the deepest study which has yet been made of the basic problem, the relation between advaita and the Trinity.'[58] Yet, Griffiths, like some of Le Saux's other colleagues, appears to have been surprised when the French *sannyasin's* spiritual diary (first published in French in 1986) and his letters (the basis for James Stuart's 1989 biography) revealed how disillusioned he was with this book by the end of his life. At issue for Griffiths was not Le Saux's abandonment of the 'fulfillment theology' as a framework for comparing Hindu and Christian spiritualities, for Griffiths had himself let go of this theology of religions by the early 1970s.[59] Instead, Griffiths objected to

---

[55] On the unique quality of Le Saux's theological method, see Antony Kalliath, CMI, *The Word in the Cave: The Experiential Journey of Swāmī Abhishiktananda to the Point of Hindu-Christian Meeting*, Intercultural Publications, Delhi, 1996, 135. See also Jacques Dupuis, Introduction to Abhishiktananda, *Intériorité et révélation*, 11-34.

[56] Stuart, 358.

[57] A complete list of Griffiths's numerous books and articles are listed in Beatrice Bruteau (ed.), *The Other Half of My Soul: Bede Griffiths and the Hindu-Christian Dialogue* (Quest Books, Wheaton, Illinois, 1996. A number of studies of Griffiths are also listed there, to which one may add Shirley du Boulay, *Beyond the Darkness: A Biography of Bede Griffiths*, Doubleday, New York, 1998; and Bruno Barnhart (ed.), *The One Light: Bede Griffiths' Principal Writings*, Templegate, Springfield, Illinois, 2001.

[58] Bede Griffiths, 'Dialogue with Hinduism,' *Impact* (May 1976), 155.

[59] See interview with Griffiths in Jesu Rajan, *Bede Griffiths and Sannyasa*, Asian Trading Corporation, Bangalore, 1989, 226.

Le Saux's renewed attraction to a dichotomized view of absolute reality and relative creation, and thus of *advaita* and theology—a view reflected in the heightened skepticism toward language expressed in the letters and diary entries of Le Saux's final years.

In his 1991 lectures at the John Main Seminar, Griffiths expressed his critical evaluation of Le Saux in this way:

> Toward the end of his life, I get the impression the world had become too much an illusion for him. He was just leaving it behind and centering on the one reality alone. And I think that's not the fullness. I think in each tradition you have to go beyond the dualities and open up to the one beyond, and *then* you have to reintegrate the whole of humanity and the human experience into that unitive vision.[60]

One may dispute whether Griffiths is portraying Le Saux accurately here, but these statements are significant in capturing the key principles of Griffiths's own approach to theology and nonduality.[61] In particular, Griffiths consistently affirmed throughout his life the need to integrate a radical openness to the divine mystery 'beyond' with a consistent valuing of the creation and the individual self. He articulated this need for integration in terms of a various polarities: East and West, immanence and transcendence, feminine and masculine, intuitive and rational. It was this instinct for reconciling opposing values that also guided his approach to the relationship between mysticism and theology that we have been examining in Monchanin's and Le Saux's responses to the charge given them by de Lubac.

---

[60] Bede Griffiths, 'Plenary Discussions,' side 3, tape recordings of *Christian Meditation: The Evolving Tradition*, John Main Institute, Chevy Chase, Maryland, 1991. (These lectures and discussions have been edited and published as *The New Creation in Christ: Christian Meditation and Community*, ed. by Robert Kiely and Laurence Freeman, OSB, Darton Longman and Todd, London, 1992; Templegate, Springfield, Illinois, 1992.)

[61] For a more thorough comparison of Le Saux and Griffiths, see the author's 'Two Models of Christian Dialogue with Hinduism: Bede Griffiths and Abhishiktananda,' *Vidyajyoti* 60/ 2-4 (February-April 1996), 101-110, 183-91, 243-54; and *idem*, 'The Comparative Study of Religious Experience: Implications for Dialogue,' *Dialogue & Alliance* 11/2 (Fall/Winter 1997), 59-87.

Theological method

Griffiths moved to India from England in his mature years (age 48) when he was already to a large degree formed intellectually, theologically, and spiritually. Like Le Saux, he had spent two decades as a Benedictine monk and priest; like Monchanin, Griffiths was a public figure, although he had published considerably more, including numerous articles and an autobiography, *The Golden String* (1954). One of the central themes of these early writings, contemplation, connects the three figures, in large part explaining their mutual attraction to India.[62] Griffiths agreed with his two predecessors that both Christianity and the West will benefit from an encounter with Hinduism and the East where contemplation and nonrational means of knowing in general have been more consistently valued. The 'marriage of East and West' that Griffiths first articulated in 1953 and that became the title of his 1982 sequel to *The Golden String* would also aid the East by encouraging its rational capacities.[63] Thus in his dialogue with Hinduism, Griffiths instinctively preserved a careful balance of rational and non-rational means, ever vigilant to integrate theology and mysticism, words and silence.

In his article, 'The Mystical Dimension of Theology' (1977), Griffiths argues that the vital interrelation between Christian theological discourse and mystical realization has been neglected by the modern church.

[T]he most urgent need in the Church to-day is to recover her mystical tradition, not merely in the sense of encouraging contemplative prayer and contemplative life, but rather in the sense of learning to see religion itself as a way of mystical experience. We have to show that Christianity is not merely a way to know about God but a

---

[62] See in particular a series of articles Griffiths wrote for *Life of the Spirit* in the fifties: 'The Priesthood and Contemplation,' vol. 5 (April 1951), 439-46; 'The Divine Office as a Method of Prayer,' vol. 6 (August-September 1951), 77-85; 'Liturgical Formation in the Spiritual Life,' vol. 6 (March 1952), 361-68; 'The Mystery of the Scriptures,' vol. 7 (August-September 1952), 67-75; and 'The Cloud on the Tabernacle,' vol. 7 (May 1953), 478-86.

[63] Bede Griffiths, 'The Incarnation and the East,' *The Commonweal* 59/12 (25 December 1953), 300. This essay was later reprinted in Bede Griffiths, *Christ in India: Essays Towards a Hindu-Christian Dialogue*, Templegate, Springfield, Illinois, 1966, 1984, 69-76.

way to know God, that is to experience the reality of God in one's life.[64]

An important effect of the modern divorce of the scriptural, liturgical, and doctrinal aspects of Christianity from the mystical has been to sap theology of its transforming power and to reduce it to formulae intractably identified with one cultural context:

> Christian mystical experience is...the experience of God in the Spirit through Christ, but the terms in which Christ is understood are subject to continuous change. The function of theology is to reflect on the terms in which the mystery of faith is expressed in the Scriptures and in the history of the Church and the world and so to renew the experience of the mystery of faith. Thus theology derives from a mystical experience and seeks continually to renew it by means of the words and images and thoughts through which that experience is expressed.[65]

As in Monchanin's project of 'rethinking Christianity in terms of India,' Griffiths advocated a reconnection to Jesus' experience of God, which for him is inherently mystical, and the rebuilding of theology from that experience expressed in terms meaningful to an Indian context. The Church's recovery of its mystical tradition and subsequent renewal of theology is, for Griffiths, one important fruit of its encounter with India where the mystical element of religion remains more prominent.

It is appropriate, then, that Griffiths concludes his 1977 article on the integration of mysticism and theology by reflecting upon de Lubac's advice to Monchanin 'to rethink everything in terms of theology and to rethink theology in terms of mysticism.'[66] By opening himself more fully to Indian mystical sources than Monchanin, Griffiths could

---

[64] Bede Griffiths, 'The Mystical Dimension in Theology,' *Indian Theological Studies* 14 (1977), 230.

[65] *Ibid.*, 244. See also Bede Griffiths, 'The Advaitic Experience and the Personal God in the Upanishads and the Bhagavad Gita', *Indian Theological Studies* 15 (1978), 71-72.

[66] Griffiths, 'The Mystical Dimension in Theology,' 246. Griffiths also cites de Lubac's advice in his *The Cosmic Revelation: The Hindu Way to God*, Templegate, Springfield, Illinois, 1983), 85, and in another important article for Griffiths's understanding of theology: 'The Mystical Tradition in Indian Theology', *Monastic Studies* 13 (Autumn 1982), 159-73. On

discern the common contemplative source beyond thought and image from which Hinduism and Christianity then diverge in scripture, ritual, and doctrine. By clinging to a principle of integration more tenaciously in his intra– as well as interreligious exploration than Le Saux, Griffiths could articulate a theological bridge not only between Hinduism and Christianity but between the worldviews of East and West. If rethinking theology in an Indian context in the 20th century depended upon de Lubac's two stimuli of mysticism and interreligious encounter, Griffiths's method clearly built upon the breaking up of the existing ground of theological structures by his predecessors using these same two means.

Theological directions

The guiding principle of Griffiths's integration of apophatic and Trinitarian theologies was his theory of religious symbol. Drawing upon Aquinas, Jacques Maritain, and Karl Rahner, Griffiths defined the religious symbol as the expression of the divine mystery in human consciousness, a communication further explicated in ritual and doctrine.[67] Far from being a simple artifact or sign, the religious symbol mediates communion between the divine Spirit and the human spirit, between mystical realization of the nondual reality and theological reflection within the world of language, or between what Le Saux described as the separate levels of *advaita* and theology. Thus, for facilitating theological renewal, Griffiths believed the role of India is providential due to its fuller sense of the power of symbols as representations of the the divine mystery.[68]

---

this general topic, see also his 'The Two Theologies', *Tablet* 234/7299 (31 May 1980), 520–1 (with his responses to critics in 234/7305 [12 July 1980], 677); and 'A Symbolic Theology', *New Blackfriars* 69/817 (June 1988), 289–94, in which he allies himself with the positions of Karl Rahner and Avery Dulles. For a fuller analysis of Griffiths's theological methodology, see Wayne Robert Teasdale, *Toward a Christian Vedanta: The Encounter of Hinduism and Christianity according to Bede Griffiths*, Asian Trading Corp., Bangalore, 1987, 61-68.

[67] For discussion of Griffiths's theory of religious symbol, see the author's *Bede Griffiths: A Life in Dialogue*, State University of New York Press, Albany, New York, 2001, and *idem*, 'The Mutual Transformation of Self and Symbol: Bede Griffiths and the Jesus Prayer', *Horizons* 23/2 (Fall 1996), 215-41. Other important modern interpreters of symbols for Griffiths included Carl Jung, Seyyed Hossein Nasr, Suzanne Langer, and Lama Anagarika Govinda.

[68] On the more vital sense of symbolism that Griffiths found in India and that he wishes to revive in the Church, see Bede Griffiths, *Christ in India: Essays toward a Hindu-Christian Dialogue* [first published in England as *Christian Ashram*], Templegate, Springfield, Illinois,

As an important qualification to his theory of symbols, Griffiths upholds the apophatic principle of Dionysius's 'radical criticism of language':

Dionysius says about the language we use to speak of God, that all words we use about God are symbols in which divine reality is present but is beyond the grasp of the mind ... Here we are at the heart of mystical theology. God cannot be known directly. He is only known through signs and symbols by which the divine mystery makes itself known.[69]

In this apophatic principle Griffiths finds a powerful link to those Hindu philosophers like Shankara who have emphasized the Upanishadic teaching that ultimately what we can most truly say about the Absolute (Brahman) is *neti neti*, 'not this, not this.' But the above quote makes an additional point, one that received less emphasis by Le Saux, especially in the later correspondence and diary entries of which Griffiths was critical: The symbols through which one may come to know God are also themselves means through which the divine mystery expresses and communicates itself. For Griffiths, the most important such symbol in the Christian revelation is the Trinity. Building on the stages of spiritual ascent espoused by Dionysius, Griffiths states that the apophatic way beyond symbols is not final but is completed by 'the way of transcendence' in which symbols such as Father, Son, and Word regain their power but in a sense that is 'beyond human comprehension.'[70]

Griffiths finds a similar spiritual dynamic in Ruysbroeck's Trinitarian mysticism. Through contemplation, one leaves the created world of multiplicity in order to return to the one divine source, only to discover that within that unity all multiplicity is present in interrelationship, modelled upon the unity in relationship of love that is the Trinity. 'This is

---

1966, 1984, 101-102, 175-76; and *idem, The Marriage of East and West: A Sequel to The Golden String*, Templegate, Springfield, Illinois, 1982, 47. On the ambiguous character of symbols to both facilitate and block experience of the divine mystery, see *The Marriage of East and West*, 43.

[69] Bede Griffiths, *A New Vision of Reality: Western Science, Eastern Mysticism and Christian Faith*, ed. by Felicity Edwards, Collins, London, 1989, 243, 245. Cf. Karl Rahner, 'The Theology of the Symbol,' in *Theological Investigations*, vol. 4, tr. by Kevin Smyth, Helicon Press, Baltimore, Maryland, 1966, 221-52.

[70] Griffiths, *A New Vision of Reality*, 247.

the climax of Christian mysticism, as of all mysticism, where there is a return to the original unity of being beyond all distinctions and yet embracing all distinctions.'[71] The model of a differentiated unity, symbolized in the fullest sense by the Trinity, is the key to Griffiths's 'Christian *advaita*,' a model that he could not find as clearly presented in Hindu teachings on nonduality.

As for Monchanin and Le Saux, Griffiths's way of resolving the tensions between *advaita* and Trinity is reflected in his theology of religions. Just as the Trinity symbolizes the inner dynamics of the divine mystery, so it reveals a principle of differentiated unity that characterizes all relationships in creation, including potentially those between the religions whose revelations may thus be understood as complementary. In place of the 'fulfillment theory' that he, like Le Saux, had earlier advocated, he articulated the following theology of religions in 1973:

> The divine Mystery, the eternal Truth, has been revealing itself to all men from the beginning of history. Every people has received some insight into this divine mystery—which is the mystery of human existence—and every religion, from the most primitive to the most advanced, has its own unique insight into the one Truth. These insights, insofar as they reflect the one Reality, are in principle complementary. Each has its own defects both of faith and practice, and each has to learn from others, so they may grow together to that unity in Truth which is the goal of human existence.[72]

Nevertheless, Griffiths also discovered that in putting such a vision into language, he could not avoid setting it within a Christ-centered theological framework—both because this is the limitation of language and because this is the limitation of the human heart devoted to a particular symbol.

---

[71] *Ibid.*, 251. See also Bede Griffiths, 'A Meditation on the Mystery of the Trinity,' *Monastic Studies* 17 (Christmas 1986), 69-79.

[72] Bede Griffiths, *Vedanta and Christian Faith*, Dawn Horse Press, Clearlake, California, 1973, vii-viii (from author's preface, not included in 1991 edition). See also *A New Vision of Reality*, 286.

Theological legacy

At his ashram in January 1990 Griffiths suffered a stroke that, like Le Saux's heart attack in July 1973, was accompanied by a profound spiritual awakening. In describing 'the greatest grace I've ever had I my life' he focuses on a shift in mental function, similar to his account of what happens during meditation:

> I had died to the ego, I think. The ego-mind and also maybe the discriminative mind that separates and divides, all seemed to have gone. Everything was flowing into everything else, and I had a sense of unity behind it all.

Several days later, Griffiths felt a call to 'surrender to the Mother'. His prayerful response evoked 'a psychological breakthrough to the feminine': 'An overwhelming experience of love came over me. It was like waves of love.' Both events, he believed, awakened the feminine, intuitive side that had been repressed so long both within himself and his culture of origin, bringing a new balance with his dominant rational side.[73] Gradually, as his normal consciousness returned, rational activity resumed but without overshadowing the simultaneous intuitive awareness of nonduality.

In his transformed mental state Griffiths experienced the basis for a more profound rethinking. Yet one does not discern significant developments in his theology as a result of the stroke. What one can see is a heightening of prophetic charism due to a more total transparency to the Spirit and a more vital grounding of theory in experience. Griffiths continued to pursue his project of the preceding decade of identifying a principle of nonduality as differentiated unity within not only Christianity and the other major religions but Western science as well.[74] By broadening

---

[73] Griffiths, 'Plenary Discussions,' side 2, *Christian Meditation*. See also John Swindells, ed., *A Human Search: Bede Griffiths Reflects on His Life, An Oral History*, Triumph Books, Liguori, Missouri, 1997, chap. 7.

[74] For a particularly effective treatment of the topic of nonduality, see Bede Griffiths, 'Transcending Dualism: An Eastern Approach to the Semitic Religions,' (ed.) Wayne Teasdale, *Cistercian Studies* 20/2 (1985), 73-87. In the area of Western science, Griffiths relies in particular upon the 'new scientists' in the fields of psychology (especially Ken Wilber), biology (especially Rupert Sheldrake), and physics (especially Fritjof Capra and David Bohm)—all with inspiration from Pierre Teilhard de Chardin.

the scope of his synthesis in this way, Griffiths's clearly aspired to fulfill de Lubac's intuition 'to rethink everything in the light of theology' to a degree not possible for his two predecessors. To address this same project of exploring the principle of nonduality in a crosscultural context, Griffiths's final work was an anthology of scriptures from the major religions.[75]

One may certainly take issue with such synthetic projects; Griffiths himself did not claim to have based them on exhaustive research. Instead, he would have argued that they represent theology rethought 'in terms of mysticism,' for it is at the mystical level, he claimed, that the various religions converge, a convergence that his own experience, both contemplative and interreligious, confirmed. It is in the breadth and depth of such conclusions that his unique legacy lies, a legacy, however, that bears continuity with and dependence upon the contributions of Monchanin and Le Saux.

Conclusion

To examine Monchanin, Le Saux, and Griffiths together in one essay invites diachronic analysis as well as theological comparison in terms of method, substance, and legacy.[76]

In his response to de Lubac's charge to 'rethink' theology on the basis of mystical and interreligious experience, Griffiths employed a method that was more daring than Monchanin's, yet more cautious than Le Saux's. In contrast to Monchanin and like Le Saux, Griffiths allowed his dialogue with Hinduism to be more than intellectual by incorporating symbols from Hindu ritual more centrally in the liturgy, terms from Hindu scriptures more constitutively in his theology, and practices from Hindu spirituality more thoroughly in his daily meditation. Like Monchanin and in contrast to Le Saux, however, Griffiths did not immerse himself in the experience of nonduality without concern for losing his religious and intellectual bearings. In the same 1991 seminar cited above,

---

[75] Bede Griffiths, *Universal Wisdom: A Journey through the Sacred Wisdom of the World*, (ed.) Roland Ropers, HarperCollins, San Francisco, California, 1994.

[76] For another comparison of the three figures, see Sten Rodhe, 'Christianity and Hinduism: A Comparison of the Views Held by Jules Monchanin and Bede Griffiths,' in *Jules Monchanin (1895-1957) as Seen from East and West*, vol. I, 169-81; reprinted in *Vidyajyoti* 59/10 (October 1995), 663-77.

Griffiths concludes that Le Saux may have plunged too carelessly into the *advaitic* experience.[77] As is apparent from their methodological criticisms of one another, the three represent a range of options for balancing the radical and conservative exigencies that are both required for any project of theological reform to remain intelligible to the community of faith. Nevertheless, their friend and colleague in Hindu–Christian dialogue, Raimon Panikkar, has praised all three as 'trespassers' who were 'prosecuted' both by Christians who doubted their orthodoxy and Hindus who questioned their sincerity.[78]

Monchanin, Le Saux, and Griffiths also shared a deep interest in the relationship between the apophatic (*advaitic*) and Trinitarian approaches to theology. This similarity is partially explained by their common focus on the nondualist philosophy of Shankara and his interpreters who were their primary partners in dialogue, rather than the more numerous devotees of various Hindu gods. As contemplatives, they felt affinity with those in India who affirmed that God is a mystery beyond all thoughts, images, and forms (*nirguna Brahman*) more than with those who worshipped God in or through a particular form (*saguna Brahman*). Their *inter*religious dialogue, then, with Hindu *advaita* and its presentation of the formless God stimulated their *intra*religious dialogue on the relation of the formless God of contemplation and the Trinitarian God of doctrine. Generally, they came to a common conclusion: The dialogue with Hinduism disclosed by similarity the significance of the apophatic way in both traditions and by contrast the essentially Trinitarian nature of Christianity. Reflecting the tension between their theological commitments and their intra- and interreligious experience, there lingers in each not a small measure of mystical humility in comparing *advaita* and the Trinity.

Nevertheless, as a result both of their differing methods and of the different stages of the Church's development in which they lived, they arrived at different conclusions regarding a theology of religions. Monchanin concluded that no bridge, even a contemplative one, could be constructed over the abyss between the summits of Christianity and Hinduism. To reconcile this antinomy in a pre-Vatican II worldview, he

---

[77] Bede Griffiths, 'Plenary Discussions', side 3. Cf. Le Saux's own sense of his 'plunge' in Abhishiktananda, *Intériorité et révélation,* 135-36.
[78] Raimon Panikkar, 'Remarks at a Memorial Service for Bede Griffiths', tape recording, September 1993, Chicago, Illinois.

assumed an inclusive theology of religions in which all human religious aspirations, including the Hindu, would find fulfillment in Christ and the Church—though not without significant contributions from India to that fullness. Le Saux experienced a bridge between the summits in his awakening to nonduality, then attempted to express that connection within a theological framework similar to that of Vatican II, but finally despaired of all such attempts due to the limitations inherent in language. In the end he let go of all comparative frameworks for resolving the tension between *advaita* and Trinity as well as for understanding the relationship between the religions. Griffiths was aided by an explicit theory of religious symbol that salvages the power of images like the Trinity to make present the divine mystery to which they point, and by a post-Vatican II openness to the spiritual riches of other traditions of symbols. As a result, he was able both to envision and to articulate a convergence between the various religions at their mystical summits (or depths) in a way that was true to his instinct for integration but was perhaps not possible for Monchanin or Le Saux for historical as much as theological reasons.

Their legacies are most constructively conceived as sequential and cumulative, suggesting that their own efforts were inherently incomplete. Each recognized that their contemplative vocation and theology would only bear fruit if thoroughly transplanted to Indian soil, a process that would change that vocation and theology in ways they could neither anticipate nor control. Each, therefore, measured their success by the degree to which they could pass on their legacy to Indian monks. Only Griffiths would live to see this fulfillment, but the achievement belongs to the Spirit that moved through each of them.

Their common legacy extends beyond the Indian Church to the broader Christian community's understanding of the theological task. The challenge of rethinking theology in the light of mystical experience and interreligious dialogue is not something to be feared, as difficult as it may be. Nor is the additional task of rethinking everything in the light of theology to be avoided in the face of an increasingly secularized world. Monchanin, Le Saux, and Griffiths each demonstrate that through the inevitable sacrifices involved in such rethinking a transforming grace is present.

FAITH IN JESUS CHRIST AS EXPRESSED IN AFRICAN CONCEPTS?

Stanislaw Grodz SVD

African theologians search for their place in contemporary contextual christology. For the time being it looks as if they are in the shadow of the Latin American and Asian Christian theologians whose christologies seem to attract much more attention. When their work becomes noticed, it is its Africanness that comes to the fore. The contemporary world tries to overcome its prejudice against African cultures. Although tolerance is officially stressed old suspicions pervade. In theology that bias meant that African concepts were considered as inappropriate for expressing the faith in Jesus Christ. Starting from the 1960s many theologians in Africa (African and non-African) began exploring African concepts showing their deep meaning and religious significance. The African cultural context became a useful theological source for expressing the Christian faith in an African way. In order to present the message of Christ to the Africans in comprehensible terms one must begin by building on their current religious understanding. That means using the old familiar concepts. Since the new transcends the old, the current religious concepts often require modification. My aim is to explore the Africanness of African christology and discover the extent of transformation of meaning that African concepts undergo within the scope of African christology. For that purpose I will examine three paradigms—Christ the ancestor, Christ the healer and Christ the ruler (chief)—used for presenting Jesus Christ in Africa. These three ways or trends have become the most prominent ones in the last two decades of the 20th century. I want to point out that the modifications are quite significant, though they do not jeopardize the overall Africanness of the theological reflection. An analysis that shows which elements of the concepts are emphasised and which tend to be overlooked may give an idea as to how firmly grounded the African christology is in the African cultural background. The future direction of African christology seems to be one of the critical issues. Should African christology stay on the level of 'adaptations in African tools and languages of traditional declarations' or, should it take a new step and express the formulations of Nicea and Chalcedon in a new language meaningful for the Africans?[1]

Reasons for the new perspectives on Jesus

The new perspectives on Jesus gained prominence with the intensification of trends that tried to reinstate the value of African identity. That was done in the turmoil of striving for political independence and the reaction against European cultural domination. After a long insistence on using only European ideas for expressing the faith in Jesus Christ, Christians became more aware of the fact that every proclamation of the Gospel was culturally conditioned. That strengthened the conviction that European ways of presenting Jesus to the Africans were often ineffective.[2] This did not mean that they were wrong but it certainly meant that they did not answer the questions the Africans were asking. This led to the realization that theology developed in one cultural situation could not be transplanted into a new context and simply adapted to it. This even led to the expression of extreme views that the question of who Jesus was for the Africans could not be answered by non-Africans. A more moderate opinion prevailed that this was possible as long as the answer was free of cultural imperialism. Any authentic theology must develop in a given context starting from the most important question about the crucial event—the death and resurrection of Jesus of Nazareth. The emergence of contextual theologies fostered the new trends in proclaiming Jesus Christ using local culture. Is Jesus Christ only a guest in a local culture and will He remain a mere stranger? Or should He be perceived and expressed in the local African terms? If the latter were the case, He should be freed from the European cultural expression and integrated into the local context. This implies that there must be ways in that local culture for expressing His existence and role. The conciliar rediscovery

---

[1] Y C Elenga, 'African Descriptive Christologies on Naming Jesus', *Sedos bulletin* 34.5 (2002), 158.

[2] See e.g. J Kirby, 'Cultural Change and Religious Conversion in West Africa', in T Blakely, W E A van Beek, D L Thomson (ed.), *Religion in Africa*, J Currey, London, 1994, 60-62; E Messi Métogo, 'La personne du Christ dans l'oeuvre de Mongo Beti', in F Kabasélé, J Doré, R Luneau (eds.), *Chemins de la christologie africaine*, Desclée, Paris, 1986, 58-63; J Baur, *2000 Years of Christianity in Africa. An African History 62-1992*, Paulines Publications, Nairobi, 1994, 2.

of the *logoi spermatikoi* theology served the quest for Christ present in the world cultures well.[3] All this means that the acceptance of Jesus and of His message does not necessarily lead to the denial of the former African cultural values. Jesus was born as a Jew but He transcended his own particular cultural context. In a similar way the attempts at expressing Him in African terms were not meant to bind Him within the confines of African cultures.[4] The African Christians have taken up the challenge of presenting Christ as someone very close to the people of Africa and described in terms of their culture. That was not totally new. Inculturation of the Christian faith has been going on with more or less success within many African Independent (Instituted) Churches (AIC) for dozens of years. That 'oral' theology has only recently been considered as a valuable source of African Christian theology. All this shows a growing awareness that African christology can be developed only on the basis of the experience of Jesus' presence in the vital problems of African communities.

Another reason for the new approach to the presentation of Jesus can be seen in the fact of the persistence of the indigenous African perception of the world or in other words of the primal worldview. In spite of all the expectations on the part of missionaries Africans still cherish the memory of their ancestors, seek the help of diviners and healers when things go wrong and look up with esteem, despite all their shortcomings and drawbacks, to their traditional rulers. It means that these concepts are still current and meaningful.

Pope Paul VI's famous sentence in which he stated during his visit to Uganda in 1969 that the Africans not only can but they must have an African Christianity was further enhanced by John Paul II in Nairobi in 1980 when he said that 'Christ in His members is Himself an

---

[3] J M Bahemuka, 'The Hidden Christ in African Traditional Religion', in J N K Mugambi, L Magesa (eds.), *Jesus in African Christianity. Experimentation and Diversity in African Christology*, Initiatives Ltd., Nairobi, 1989, 11; K Bediako, 'Biblical Christologies in the Context of African Traditional Religions', in V Samuel, C Sugden (eds.), *Sharing Jesus in the Two Thirds World*, Partnership in Mission—Asia, Bangalore, 1983, 143; J S Mbiti, 'Is Jesus Christ in African Religion?' in J S Pobee (ed.), *Exploring Afro-Christology*, Peter Lang, Frankfurt am Main, 1992, 21, 28; J S Ukpong, 'Christology and Inculturation: A New Testament Perspective', in R Gibellini (ed.), *Paths of African Theology*, Orbis Books, Maryknoll, NY, 1994, 42.

[4] *The Paschal Mystery of Christ and of All Humankind*. Volume 4 of an Experimental Source-book for Religious Education. Spearhead 59 (1979), 51.

African'.[5] The post-synodal document *Ecclesia in Africa* (EA) issued in 1995 encouraged African Christians to assimilate the Gospel message while remaining faithful to all authentic African values (EA 78). It also stressed the need for further research concerning such matters as: 'marriage, veneration of ancestors, and the spirit world, in order to examine in depth all the cultural aspects of problem from the theological, sacramental, liturgical and canonical points of view' (EA 64).

African christological paradigms

Although the current African christological paradigms had taken their shape before the synodal recommendations were made, they definitely need more in-depth examination. The number of publications on particular African christological paradigms dropped significantly after the mid-1990s. Whether this is because the reflection had reached the limits set by the paradigms or because the recommendations were really being taken seriously and efforts were being diverted for the time being to those issues remains to be seen.

Three African christological paradigms have drawn my attention: Christ the ancestor, Christ the healer and Christ the ruler (chief). The ancestor paradigm gained its prominence in the ecclesiastical milieu due to the academic work of such African theologians as Charles Nyamiti, Bénézet Bujo, Efoé Julien Pénoukou, or François Kabasélé. The healer paradigm is widely spread at the grass-roots level and only recently has been incorporated into the academic theology by such scholars and missionaries as J Matthew Schoffeleers, Michael Kirwen, Aylward Shorter, Cécé Kolié, Kofi Appiah-Kubi, Joseph Healey and Donald Sybertz. The ruler (chief) paradigm got a boost from a Nigerian theologian Ukachukwu Christopher Manus, who supported earlier efforts made by Kabasélé, and John Samuel Pobee.

Some theologians use the phrase 'christological models' to describe these ways of presenting Jesus. In my view a more general term such as 'paradigm' seems to be more appropriate since the efforts of theologians have neither been coordinated, nor focused on creating a homogenous 'model'. The African concepts employed in christology for

---

5   B Hearne, 'Christology and Inculturation', *AFER* 22.6 (1980), 336. Papal addresses were published in: *AFER* 11.4 (1969), 404 and *AFER* 22.4 (1980), 198. See also A Shorter, *African Christian Theology*, Orbis Books, Maryknoll, NY, 1977, 20-22.

that purpose form rather umbrella notions that cover a variety of theological presentations.

Christ the ancestor

Damian Lwasa sees in Jesus Christ a new Adam, i.e. the 'universal ancestor'. Christ attained this status by the blood covenant He made with the people. He is also the divine ancestor who governs His mystical body. In a similar way the spirit of the common ancestor continues to govern the clan.[6] For John S Pobee Christ could be perceived as Nana—the Great and the Greatest Ancestor who has authority over all beings. However, Pobee has been more inclined to presenting Christ as the spokesman (*okyeame*; the king's *alter ego*) in the Akan (Ghanaian) royal court. This image has its solid foundation in the Akan concept of the sacred status of power.[7] Another Ghanaian, Kwame Bediako searches for the presence of Christ in the Akan cultural heritage and sees Christ as someone who assumes authority over all the powers of the invisible world, including the ancestors. Only after establishing this fact does Bediako call Christ the great ancestor of all mankind [sic].[8] François Kabasélé tries to relate the image of the ancestor to the image of the eldest brother. It seems that their mediatory role is the linking element between the two images. Jesus fulfils a similar role to that of African ancestors in the transmission and safeguarding of life. Like the ancestors He accompanies those living on earth. The mediatory role of the ancestors can serve as a help in understanding the fullness of the mediatorship exercised by Jesus Christ.[9] For Efoé Julien Pénoukou the ancestor, the life-giver (*joto*—*l'ancetre co-fécondateur*) offers an indigenous parallel to Christ. As the *joto* conquers death and gives new life, so Christ offers re-birth to people through the resurrection. In spite of the differences between the notions of *joto* and Christ people understand that the latter fulfils a cosmotheandric relation in the universe.[10] The gift and flow of the life-force becomes the

---

[6] D Lwasa, 'African Traditional Community As a Preparation for Christian Community Life', in A Shorter (ed.), *African Christian Spirituality*, Geoffery Chapman, London, 1978, 141-150.

[7] J S Pobee, *Towards an African Theology*, Abingdon Press, Nashville, 1979, 94-97.

[8] Bediako, 'Biblical Christologies', 146-156.

[9] F Kabasélé, 'Christ as Ancestor and Elder Brother', in R Schreiter (ed.), *Faces of Jesus in Africa*, Orbis Books, Maryknoll, NY, 1991, 116-127.

[10] J E Pénoukou, 'Réalité africaine et salut en Jésus Christ', *Spiritus* 23.89 (1982), 383-390.

most important issue for Bénézet Bujo. God is its source but gives it through the ancestors. The undisturbed flow of the life-force forms a basis for the harmony in the community created by those living in the visible and those in the invisible world. Human beings were created to live in such harmony, and the ancestors mark the way to it (the restoration of such a state of harmony has a salvific dimension). Through His incarnation Jesus remains in solidarity with the living on earth and with their ancestors. His actions fulfil the best aspirations of the ancestors. Although the category of ancestor can be attributed to Christ only analogically (there are no biological ties between Him and the people) one can say that Christ is the Proto-Ancestor, the ancestor par excellence. He has acquired that status by His death and resurrection. The African ancestors find in Him the basis for their existence and vitality and through Him they can be better understood. They become the forerunners, images of the Proto-Ancestor. Jesus' divine sonship becomes the source and foundation of human re-birth in God. The ancestors' striving after righteousness becomes in Jesus a meeting-place with the God of salvation. From now on the narratives about His deeds and the remembrance of his passion, death and resurrection mark the way to salvation.[11]

Nyamiti noticed that Jesus' ancestorship finds its basis in His divinity (because of His ancestral relationship within the Trinity) and in His humanity (due to His incarnation). Christ's ancestorship in relation to the people is linked to His mediatory role. Nyamiti saw the fact of their being God's children as the link between Christ and the people. However, unlike Bujo, he adopted a concept of brother-ancestorship, because he sees it as 'grounded on the social constitution of man'. The African concept of brother-ancestorship applies analogically to Christ's relationship with the people. The differences which exist between the notions of bother-ancestor and Christ emphasize that the latter is the ancestor par excellence. Christ's ancestorship is the best fulfilment of the African concept of ancestorship. Jesus Christ became the ancestor of the people because of His divine and human natures. He was the brother-ancestor of the people from the very beginning but He perfected it through His death and resurrection. Jesus' death on the cross and His resurrection are the perfect example of fidelity in the mutual relationship

---

[11] B Bujo. *African Theology in Its Social Context*, Orbis Books, Maryknoll, NY, 1992, 17-24, 75-87.

between a descendant and his ancestor. The resurrection perfected the five constitutive features of the ancestor selected by Nyamiti (natural relationship, supernatural status, mediation, title to regular sacred communication, exemplarity). Christ redeemed people by uniting them with God and filling the gap that separated them. In order to have Christ as one's brother-ancestor one has to maintain one's status of the child of God. The Eucharist fulfils the cult of ancestors in the best way.[12]

Christ the healer

The term 'healer' has been adopted here although some writers prefer other words. Using the image of the indigenous healer as a figure of Christ in the academic field theologians point to the fact that Jesus fulfils both African and Christian values. R Buana Kibongi, the pioneer of this trend in academic theology, focused on the function of mediator-priest. He emphasized that Jesus perfected and fulfilled the human need for salvation, felt and addressed by the indigenous healers in an imperfect way.[13] The healing function, left aside by Kibongi, was taken up by Pobee. He stressed its importance while reflecting on the authority and power which Jesus wielded as proofs of His divinity. Both the African healer and Jesus healed because they were 'ensouled' with God. But as the former only experienced that on certain occasions, Jesus was permanently 'ensouled' with God. Again the conviction that Jesus fulfilled and perfected the indigenous values becomes prominent.[14] The discovery that the Africans had been using for a very long time the image of Jesus as the one true healer (*nganga*) both in catechesis and liturgy became the point of departure for Matthew Schoffeleers. The figures of Christ and the African healer come together in their ability to know hidden things (divination) and in their mediation between the human world and the invisible world (prophetism). A more detailed analysis of perception of Jesus by some African people led Schoffeleers to focus on the apparently contradictory images of the slain and slaying *nganga*, whose salvific death initiates a

---

[12] C Nyamiti, *Christ as Our Ancestor. Christology from an African Perspective*, Mambo Press, Gweru, 1984, 15-17, 25-93; *idem*, 'The Mass as Divine and Ancestral Encounter Between the Living and the Dead', *African Christian Studies* 1.1 (1985), 35-36.
[13] R Buana Kibongi, 'Priesthood', in K Dickson, P Ellingworth (eds.), *Biblical Revelation and African Beliefs*, Lutterworth, London, 1969, 47-56.
[14] Pobee, *Towards an African Theology*, 92-93.

new social order freed from evil. The slain and slaying *nganga* uproots witchcraft, eliminating its proximate and distant causes.[15]

According to Shorter the image of the indigenous healer (he uses sometimes a very misleading term 'witchdoctor') helps the Africans to understand Jesus better. Jesus assumed the role of a Palestinian exorcist of his time. He healed and revealed the coming of God's Kingdom. He did not use any divinatory practices but had a mysterious knowledge about the situation of His patients. He demonstrated that sickness was not a necessary punishment for sin but emphasized that repentance for sins could have a bearing on physical healing. He explained neither the origin, nor the reasons for the existence of evil and suffering, but showed His ability to conquer them. Similarly to the indigenous healer Jesus approached healing in a holistic way. Healing and revealing, He fulfilled the work of the indigenous healer in every respect.[16] Cécé Kolié pays attention to the fact that Jesus always took the whole social context of the healed into account. Healing also means the reintegration of the person into his/her community. The indigenous healer acted in a similar way. As a healer Jesus fought evil and allowed Himself to be wounded. By his death He gave a meaning to his healings, and consequently to suffering and evil. Suffering together with the Crucified becomes a cure for sickness, and one experiences healing in the name of Jesus. Kolié states that the Africans find it difficult to establish the true reason for Jesus' death using their traditional methods. They can only turn to God and trust that He will eventually provide the answer. All difficulties are linked to the acceptance or the rejection of the event of Jesus' death and resurrection.[17] Joseph Healey and Donald Sybertz notice that the Africans see Jesus as the chief diviner-healer and that they creatively transform indigenous names in order to apply them to Jesus. The African diviner reveals the causes of misfortune. Using a secret power he heals and prevents the reoccurrence of a misfortune. In order to explain Jesus' role better the theologians search for figures of saviours in folk tales and point out that Jesus exceeds and fulfils all that the indigenous healers could do.[18]

---

[15] M Schoffeleers, 'Folk Christology in Africa: The Dialectics of the Nganga Paradigm', *Journal of Religion in Africa* 19.2 (1989), 157-183.

[16] A Shorter, *Jesus and the Witchdoctor. An Approach to Healing and Wholeness*, Geoffrey Chapman, London, 1985, 7-17.

[17] C Kolié, 'Jesus as Healer?', in R Schreiter (ed.), *Faces of Jesus in Africa*, Orbis Books, Maryknoll, NY, 1991, 128-150.

[18] J Healey, D Sybertz, *Towards an African Narrative Theology*, Paulines Publications, Nairobi, 1996, 62-103, 291-336.

The motif of fulfilment of the actions of the indigenous healer is present in almost every theological reflection.

Christ the ruler

In the first attempt at using the concept of the African ruler in the Christian academic theology, the centrality of the position of the ruler was emphasized. The ruler is the focal point of the world and covers everything in his shade like a tree (in the tropics shade is a blessing), encompasses the whole life of his subjects and ensures their security. Pobee based his model on the centrality of the ruler's position. In order to express the differentiated unity of God the Father and of Jesus Christ he employed the concept of the spokesman (*okyeame*), the *alter ego* of the king. Pobee pointed to the sacred status of the ruler and to the fact that he could not be approached by ordinary people. At the same time he emphasized the human nature of the king. He also indicated the priestly mediatory and judicial functions exercised by the king and the fact that the ruler was the symbol of the identity, unity, and continuity of the people. The transcendence of ethnic boundaries was the new quality brought by Christ because He was the ruler of all the people. Employing some of the royal titles Pobee pointed to king's fidelity, and also to the belief that the king was the giver of new life and the deliverer from oppressors, and someone who removes pain and misfortune. Pobee also emphasized a feature of the king which was rather neglected in the Akan milieu—his concern for peace.[19]

In a similar way, i.e. by using titles, Kabasélé approached Christ. The titles reserved for indigenous rulers—*ntita, luaba*—were applied to Him, indicating that He had the power to enthrone other rulers. For Kabasélé the application of these and other titles to Christ is a sign, that Christians acknowledge that Christ fulfils the tasks of the indigenous ruler in a perfect way. The theologian pointed to some features of the indigenous ruler: his generosity, might, concern for the benefit of his people, wisdom, and also the fact of his being the mighty victorious hero who unities the people and defends them against evil. Kabasélé paid attention to the ambivalence that surrounds the ruler as the one who stands on the border line between the visible and invisible worlds. The ruler belongs to the group of 'mighty people', who are able to see

---

[19] Pobee, *Towards an African Theology*, 94–97.

and perform things not possible for the uninitiated. The indigenous ruler transmits and does the will of the ancestors.[20] The Ashanti Catholics of Ghana have a similar practice of applying local royal titles to Christ. The metaphor of the leopard underscores such royal prerogatives as the real and highest command in the community at all levels, passing judgements on the members of the community, prestige and power used for defence of the subjects against all threats. There are, however, new elements that are introduced into the metaphor: accessibility of the king as opposed to the isolation of the indigenous king from ordinary people, and his being the leader of a community that exceeds ethnic borders.[21]

Manus developed his own servant-king christology inspired by what he had discovered among the Nigerian Aladura Churches. He stated that the African royal categories (taken from four African nations: the Yoruba, the Shilluk, the Ganda and the Zulu) are related in an analogous way to the New Testament ideas of the Messiah-King. There are no exact parallels but there is certain continuity and discontinuity. He emphasized four interconnected elements of the structure of African kingship: sacrality, rulership and authority, protection, benevolence. Manus stressed the sacred status of the indigenous ruler. The ruler has a divine genealogy and in consequence he exercises a mediatory function: he belongs to the earthly community and at the same time overcomes its boundaries. The ruler reigns and rules, he generously endows his people with gifts and honours. He is the ritual head of the community, the judge and the law-giver who embodies order. The election of the rulers depended on the will of the divinities and cultic heroes. The enthronement of the ruler was a community event, during which the council of elders confirmed that choice. The ruler had to protect, heal and guard the integrity of individual persons and of the community. Manus stated that Jesus fulfilled all the royal functions of the indigenous ruler in the best way.[22]

Transformation of meaning of African concepts

The impact of African religious culture on African christologies is

---

[20] F Kabasélé, 'Christ as Chief', in R Schreiter (ed), *Faces of Jesus in Africa*, 103–115.
[21] P Obeng, *Asante Catholicism. Religious and Cultural Reproduction Among the Akan of Ghana*, E J Brill, Leiden, 1996, 201–215.
[22] U C Manus, *Christ, the African King. New Testament Christology*, Peter Lang, Frankfurt Main, 1993.

obvious.[23] However, the question of how firmly the latter remains rooted in the former requires attention. There are at least two reasons. Firstly, the incarnation transcends all cultural frames and Jesus cannot be confined to an African cultural milieu. Secondly, religions, as parts of culture, interact with each other. This interaction can create completely new and surprising situations and is not totally controllable. Efforts made by many early missionaries to translate and express the Biblical message and Christian teaching using African notions led to a demonization of the African spirit world.[24] In the new approach the indigenous African religious concepts and ideas used for expressing the Christian teaching again undergo certain modifications.

When African theologians employ the term 'ancestor' they focus mainly on the intermediary role of the African ancestors (e.g. Kabasélé, Nyamiti). They also underline the fact of the ancestors' humanity. Ancestors used to be human beings and still stay in close contact with the human world, though they themselves live in the invisible world and have been endowed with features unattainable to those living in the visible world. The theologians also stress the conviction that the ancestors (to a greater or lesser extent in cooperation with the Supreme Being) are sources of life and are responsible for sustaining it (e.g. Pénoukou, Bujo).

However, many features of African ancestors have been overlooked or omitted. Theologians tend to forget that along with respect, people approach the ancestors with a feeling of ambivalence. There is a strong conviction in many African societies that ancestors punish their descendants for transgressing tribal tradition and other misconduct. In some African societies ancestors seem to be really feared.[25] Theologians also overlook specific forms of contact between ancestors and those living in the visible world such as reincarnation or possession and forms of prophecy and dreams that are linked with them. This is a very significant matter. Nyamiti acknowledges the right to sacred communication between the people and their ancestors but seems to narrow it down only to Christian sacramental rituals.[26] By doing so he gives a new meaning to the African concept of sacred communication between the inhabitants of the visible and invisible worlds.

---

[23] Elenga, 'African Descriptive Christologies', 155.

[24] See e.g. B Meyer, *Translating the Devil. Religion and Modernity Among the Ewe of Ghana*, Africa World Press Inc., Trenton, NJ, 1999, 83-111.

[25] See e.g. Bujo, *African Theology*, 79.

[26] Nyamiti, 'The Mass as Divine and Ancestral Encounter', 34, 42-46.

Theologians also skip over the problem of the unclear form of ancestors' existence. Many African societies believe that ancestors lead a life resembling their earthly existence but find themselves somehow closer to the Supreme Being. However, no one living in the visible world seems to be eager to join the ancestors. Though death in African societies is not considered to be such a dramatic event as for example in Europe, Africans clearly prefer their earthly existence to anything else.

When the African theologians state that Christ attained the status of the ancestor through his death and resurrection, they say nothing about the African ancestral installation rituals, and little about the condition of a 'good death'. The latter, in the light of research carried out by John C McCall and conclusions drawn by Louis-Vincent Thomas and René Lunaeu, may not be so significant.[27] The omission or transposition of the former seems to pose a more serious problem. It is the human community of those living in the visible world that establishes a dead member of that community as an ancestor in the indigenous African religions. In African Christian theology attempts are made to stress that it is God, the Father, and not the Christian community, who establishes Jesus as the ancestor.

The theologians still have to tackle another problem. The idea of ancestorhood in African indigenous religions is based on the condition of blood-relationship. But Jesus and the Africans are not blood-relatives. Kabasélé focuses on the transmission of life in general. Nyamiti uses the concept of 'brother ancestorship' and supports it by emphasizing God's fatherhood towards Jesus and all the people. Bujo, acknowledging the lack of biological ties between Jesus and the Africans, emphasizes the primordial character of Christ's ancestorship and calls Him the Proto-Ancestor.

Some theologians have a tendency to create their own concept of ancestors to meet the needs of Christian theology. Nyamiti, who is the most explicit example in this respect, enhanced his concept of ancestor. While in the 1980s he named only five features characteristic of an ancestor, in the 1990s his texts include a recourse to the idea of the vital force, as the central element in the African world view.[28] One can also

---

[27] J C McCall, 'Rethinking Ancestors in Africa', *Africa* 65 (1995), 258–266; L.-V. Thomas, R Luneau, *La terre africaine et ses religions. Traditions et changements*, Librairie Larousse, Paris, 1975, 100–102.

[28] C Nyamiti, 'African Ancestral Veneration and Its Relevance to the African Church', *African Christian Studies* 9.3 (1993), 14–17; *idem*, 'The Trinity from an African Ancestral Perspective', *African Christian Studies* 12.4 (1996), 38–41.

find attempts at telescoping abundance of anthropological data with synthesizing statements like: 'Without violence being done to the essence of the concept of ancestorship, one could gather its different meanings into one formula: "Ancestor is essentially a mediator of life, goodness and wisdom."'[29] All theologians agree that Christ took over the prerogatives of African ancestors due to the power He had received from God and completely fulfilled ancestors' aspirations.

Christian theologians in Africa stress the healer's mediatory role between the visible and invisible worlds. They also emphasize his priestly function and the fact that African Christians themselves see a parallel between healer and Christ (Kibongi, Kirwen). Some theologians indicate that healing power comes from God and the healer cures only because he is 'ensouled with God' (Pobee). The healer's holistic approach to the human person is often stressed. This approach encompasses all aspects of life: physical, psychological and social (Shorter, Kolié, Appiah-Kubi). It has also been underlined that the healer fights evil in every-day life, leaving aside the speculative search for its ultimate causes (Shorter). Finally theologians explicitly state that the healer is not 'a miracle worker' but a person, who having his own faults and weaknesses, becomes vulnerable to the forces he fights against in the process of healing (Kolié, Schoffeleers). The theologians point out that healer can obtain access to hidden knowledge and can serve as a prophet in his community (Schoffeleers, Healey and Sybertz). All those who foster the paradigm of Christ, the healer, agree that Jesus fulfils all the aspirations of the African healer.

However, some important elements are left out. Difficulties arising from the fact that the same person may diagnose the imminent causes of evil, perform a healing ritual and take preventive action against evil and its agents tend to be overlooked. The healer is seen as a very ambivalent person by some people. Many Africans are convinced that the healer has constant access to supernatural forces, that are neither explicitly good, nor explicitly evil. When they ask a healer to prevent a future evil, they believe (and sometimes clearly expect) that he may go as far as to launch a mystical attack on the perpetrator.

So far not much has been done by African Christian theologians in terms of conducting a deeper analysis of the beliefs concerning the supernatural forces with which healer is dealing. Though some emphasize

---

[29] B Mpasi Loude, 'Kultura afrykańska wobec Ewangelii', *Communio* 4 (1990), 81.

that the Supreme Being is the source of all spiritual power in the universe (Pobee), the indigenous healers themselves talk mainly about their contact with spirits, divinities, heroes and ancestors, and they mention the Supreme Being as the ultimate source of their power only when urged to do so by their Christian interlocutors.[30] Many healers consider contact with supernatural forces as dangerous. On the part of the healers this contact requires effective preparation and each healer has to work out his own ways of dealing with the supernatural. The Christian theologians seem to forget about the whole issue of spirit possession and the fact that for many healers spirit possession becomes a prerequisite for performing effective healing rituals or diagnosing the causes of evil. A stern reaction of senior Vatican officials that stopped the experimental activity of archbishop Milingo in Zambia in the early 1980s might be seen as an unwillingness or inability for a deeper analysis of this phenomenon within the framework of Christian academic theology. Milingo's case was further complicated by the fact that distancing himself from spirit possessions practiced in African indigenous religions, he tended to use similar means for creating an openness on the part of Zambian Christians to the activity of the Holy Spirit.[31] Healers working in the African Indigenous (Instituted) Churches distance themselves from indigenous healers but retain many African elements and forms of ministry.

Turning to the concept of the African ruler (king, chief), we find theologians underlining the centrality of the position of the ruler not only in society, but also in the whole universe. The African ruler is an intermediary between the visible and invisible worlds, and is one of the 'powerful people'. The theologians expose the sacred status of the ruler (Pobee, Manus) while pointing to his divine genealogy (Manus). The inaccessibility of the African ruler for ordinary people is noted, but at the same time his human nature is also stressed. The theologians notice the fact that the ruler is chosen by the will of supernatural forces and this is approved by the council of elders. It is accepted that as a mediator the ruler fulfils a priestly function. He has to provide harmony and well-being for those who are in his care. The ruler is the judge, conciliator

---

[30] M Kirwen, *The Missionary and the Diviner. Contending Theologies of Christian and African Religions*, Orbis Books, Maryknoll NY, 1987, 84, 97, 101.
[31] G Ter Haar, *Spirit of Africa: The Healing Ministry of Archbishop Milingo of Zambia*, Hurst, London, 1992, 127-130.

and giver of life. As a mediator he does not his own will but that of the ancestors.

However, it seems that focusing on the sacredness of the status of the ruler theologians overlook the fact discovered by anthropologists that it is not so much the ruler as a person who is sacred but the power. Rulers, though often considered as incarnations of the divine ancestors, are seen as sacred and not as saints. The theologians also tend not to notice that the ruler (a human being) elevated to the sacred status does not become an autocrat. The sacred status was not conferred on him for ever. Even if it was believed that other ritual specialists could fulfil their functions only because the ruler maintained the contact with the supernatural, he was not thought of as the sole channel by which these forces could communicate with those living in the visible world.

The central position of the ruler in the universe also brings about an aura of ambivalence, an ambivalence that again somehow escapes the attention of the theologians. His being the central figure in the universe means that opposing forces (not only morally neutral ones) affect the person of the ruler. He becomes their focal point. In many African societies the ruler, considered as the embodiment of order, commits unforgivable crimes during his installation rituals.[32] The fact that Christianity exercised a highly destructive role on the African concept of kingship is another important omission in the Christian theological discourse on Christ, the African ruler. Only Bediako gives a lot of attention to this problem.[33]

In applying the notion of African kingship to Christ certain elements were obviously modified. Firstly there is an emphasis on the universal kingship of Christ that goes beyond ethnic borders and secondly the abolition of the separation of the ruler from ordinary people. In his reflection on whether African tradition can say anything about Jesus a French theologian René Luneau states that the African concepts (ancestor, healer, ruler), each of which exposes the idea of mediation, provide images, imperfect though they be which are useful, for explaining who is Jesus Christ for Africans.[34]

---

[32] See e.g. W MacGaffey, 'Kingship: Kingship in Sub-Saharan Africa', in M Eliade (ed.), *Encyclopedia of Religion Vol. 8*, Macmillan Publishing Co., New York, 1987, 322-325; Thomas, Luneau, *La terre africaine et ses religions*, 190-191.

[33] Bediako, 'Biblical Christologies', 149-157.

[34] R Luneau, 'Jésus-Christ est-il aujourd'hui africain?', *Studia missionalia* 50 (2001), 412-413.

'Pan-African' christology?

Christological reflection in Africa conducted within the ancestor, healer and ruler paradigms is diverse. These are not homogenous models. Rather they use a common concept but the specifics vary according to main interests of those who do the theological reflection. It seems that attempts at homogenizing the perceptions of Jesus within the three above mentioned paradigms at the present stage of development of African theology are premature. They tend to lead towards the creation of a 'pan-African' christology, i.e. christology easily applicable and relevant all over Africa. That would be to repeat mistakes made in the past by missionaries. The appearance of 'pan-African' christologies could be the next step in the development of African christology. However, there are still not enough local ways of interpreting the Christ event that would serve as data for a synthesis. The approaches of Pénoukou, Kolié, Pobee or Bediako should be followed by many others.

Nyamiti argued that the development of 'ethnic' theologies in contemporary Africa which is plagued by separatist tendencies, carries with it the danger of exclusivism.[35] Recognizing this danger one may ask about the point of creating christologies that, though based on anthropological data, tend to overlook the actual experience of people. Bujo, who also seems to be tempted to create a 'pan-African' christology, pays more attention to the everyday experience of the Africans. The systematization and reflection on the christology of the Aladura Churches, from which Manus began his reflection on Christ, the African ruler, seems to be more meaningful and convincing than his own formulation of a 'pan-African' King-Christology.[36] This does not mean that models developed within the 'pan-African' perspective are unsuitable. They mark a certain direction in which the African christology will most probably develop. However, it seems that jumping over the stage of creating local christologies is to try to go too fast.

---

[35] C Nyamiti, 'Contemporary African Christologies: Assessment and Practical Suggestions', in R Gibellini (ed.), *Paths of African Theology*, 68.
[36] U C Manus, 'Jesu Kristi Oba: A Christology of "Christ, the King" Among the Indigenous Christian Churches in Yorubaland, Nigeria', *Asia Journal of Theology* 5.2 (1991), 311-330.

Complementarity

Diversity in African christology makes theologians aware of the need for complementarity. Bediako oscillates between the ancestor paradigm and that of the eldest brother. Abraham A Berinyuu points out that acceptance of Christ as ancestor implies the African perception of Him also as healer, because the ancestor takes care of the health of those living in the visible world.[37] Emmanuel Milingo who worked within the healer paradigm acknowledges the accuracy of applying the ancestor concept to Jesus.[38] Those working within the ruler paradigm point out that the African ruler belongs to the people 'endowed with power'. The healer belongs to this group. Kabasélé moves between the models of ancestor, ruler and eldest brother. He is fully conscious that none of the models, and not even all of them together, can express the richness of the self-revelation of God in Jesus Christ.[39] The necessity of complementarity and of an inclusive approach is seen and practiced by all the African theologians.

Differences in the academic quality of the paradigms

All three paradigms differ from each other in terms of the depth of academic reflection. The ancestor paradigm has been extensively developed by academic theologians. This paradigm clearly bears the marks of professional theological reflection. Efforts have been made to incorporate the popular models of Christ, the healer and the ruler into academic reflection. These popular models have developed within the African Independent (Instituted) Churches and on the margins of the mainline Churches in Africa. The existing academic reflection concerning the healer paradigm is mostly characterized by 'postulative' language (what could or should be done). It describes and analyses what has already been done in the field and it lacks new and original approaches. In the ruler paradigm one can notice a different process. Starting from the situation

---

[37] A A Berinyuu, *Pastoral Care to the Sick in Africa. An Approach to Transcultural Pastoral Theology*, Peter Lang, Frankfurt a. Main, 1988, 101-103.

[38] E Milingo, *The World in Between: Christian Healing and the Struggle for Spiritual Survival*, Orbis Books, Maryknoll, NY, 1984, 78.

[39] F Kabasélé, 'L'au-delà des modèles', in F Kabasélé, J Doré, R Luneau (eds.), *Chemins de la christologie africaine*, Desclée, Paris, 1986, 204-228, esp. 226-228.

as found in the Independent Churches, the theologians are trying to formulate an academic christological model based on that situation.

Theological reflection conducted within the paradigm of Christ the healer requires special attention. Non-African theologians and anthropologists feature prominently among those who foster it. Perhaps that is how it should be in the present initial phase. Since expatriates enforced a negative point of view on the whole domain of contact with invisible forces, they should also attempt to restore an unbiased approach to all that has been demonised. African Christians employ the healer paradigm in their every day life regardless of the official ecclesiastical approach. They do so, however, within the frame of 'oral theology'. Practice, that is the perception of Christ the healer and its application in the Christian healing ministry, is far more developed than theoretical reflection. The pace of the latter has been slowed down due to a lack of a clear position of the mainline Churches on the issue of indigenous ways of contact with the supernatural world and maintenance of a sharp European distinction between medicine and religion. The Africans see a disparity between the practice of Jesus and the mission Churches as far as healing is concerned and emphasize the fact of the Apostles carrying on Jesus' ministry in the way He himself understood it. Several African theologians express their conviction that the Christian message about salvation will reach the Africans only when the Church takes seriously the African understanding of health and sickness, and when it reasserts the fact that medicine and religion have the same roots. They also appeal for a new reflection from the Christian perspective on the gift of healing as given to their ancestors.[40] A change of attitude of the mainline Churches towards African beliefs would facilitate the discovery of Christ for the Africans.

This poses a major problem for the mainline Churches because it would require a return to a 'pre-Enlightenment' mentality with its acceptance of spiritual beings such as demons and their active role in causing sickness and disasters in the visible world. Schoffeleers and Gifford indicated these difficulties.[41] Though the 'pre-Enlightenment' vision of the universe is considered as archaic in Europe, one has to remember that Jesus lived and acted among people who subscribed to such a world view.

---

[40] Kolié, Christ the Healer?, 144.
[41] P Gifford, *African Christianity. Its Public Role*, Hurst, London, 1998, 328-330; M Schoffeleers, 'Christ in African Folk Theology: The 'Nganga' Paradigm', in T Blakely *et al.* (eds.), *Religion in Africa*, 86. This version of his earlier article contains a more explicitly articulated concern.

A German biblical scholar Joachim Gnilka states that 'the synoptic Gospels share a belief in demons with the majority of the ancient world'. People in Jesus' time believed that suffering (possessions, sicknesses) was caused 'by demons who were considered as despotic and malicious beings that have effective power over people'.[42] Gnilka underlines that several times the Gospels stress Jesus' power over demons who cause sickness (e.g. Mt 8: 9; Lc 4: 39). The Gospels also emphasize that demons' activity was not directly linked with sin. Demons were considered as beings that act in order to harm people physically and spiritually.[43] Such statements correspond with opinions expressed by African theologians about Jesus the healer.

Limitations of African christologies

John Parratt states that African theologians have not yet developed new categories suitable for expressing African theology. In his opinion up to the early 1990s even the most innovative African theologians were reluctant to leave the theological language stemming from the Council of Chalcedon. It may be added that it is still the case. Parratt points out that e.g. Pobee accepted the statement about the divine and human nature of Christ without making efforts to explain what both descriptions mean in the African context. Attempts at comparing the African meaning with the meaning they had in the Greek context could help to come to a deeper understanding who Jesus is.[44]

The whole field of soteriology has been neglected so far, though Parratt indicated there has been some development. According to Kwesi Dickson, given the African understanding of death as fulfilment (and not as failure), the African perception of redemption should emphasize the cross as the basis of Christian hope.[45] Acceptance of the African perspective

---

[42] J Gnilka, *Jezus z Nazaretu. Orędzie i dzieje*, Kraków, 1997, 153–154. (German original: *Jesus von Nazaret. Botschaft und Geschichte*, Herder, Freiburg im Breisgau, 1993).

[43] *Ibid.*, 154–155.

[44] J Parratt, *Reinventing Christianity. African Theology Today*, Eerdmans Publishing Co., Grand Rapids, Mich., 1995, 197. He acknowledged that initially he had been convinced about impossibility of avoiding old images in new theologies. In the early 1990s he was no longer sure whether that was the right way for non-Western theologies. Perhaps the African theologians have not gone far enough yet in their search for new images and concepts?

[45] K Dickson, *Theology in Africa*, Darton, Longman, Todd, London, 1984, 185–187; Parratt, *Reinventing Christianity*, 89–90.

on life will lead to a perception of death not as its antithesis but as a different form of existence in the universe. According to Kolié, African tanatological symbolism focuses more on rebirth than on failure or disaster. Such a perception is not distant form the authentically Christian attitude towards death in the perspective of Christ's resurrection. The Ghanaian theologian Abraham A Akrong points out that a new approach to the soteriological aspect of incarnation is appearing along with the new perception of Christ. Seeing Christ as the ancestor, salvation becomes a return to God's family, because only there a human being can lead a healthy life. Jesus, the ancestor takes parental care of all members of God's family and protects them.[46] In Parratt's opinion soteriology has been neglected because African theologians have concentrated their efforts on finding bases for Christian dogma in the indigenous culture. Such concentration does not help in discovering relevant expressions of Christ's redemptive role. Over and above that African religions are ahistorical. Christological models are also to certain extent beyond time. Such a situation leads Parratt to emphasize the fact that the central event of the Christian faith has neither equivalent nor points of contact in African religions. No one has presented any comprehensive explanation of the Christ event from the African perspective so far.[47] A hermeneutical problem has not yet been resolved—should African experience be interpreted in the light of the Christian sources, or vice versa.[48]

Two opposite tendencies can be detected in African christology. On the one hand, in the functional approach, that Parratt considers as the most promising, Africans emphasize Jesus' deeds in relation to individual human being. Though they acknowledge the divine and human nature of Jesus, they present His divinity in functional categories and show it through His humanity. Much more attention has been devoted to this latter aspect.[49] Such seems to be the attitude within the systematic theological reflection. On the other hand, in the Independent Churches

---

[46] A A Akrong, '*Christology from an African Perspective*', in J Pobee (ed.), *Exploring Afro-Christology*, 127.

[47] Parratt, *Reinventing Christianity*, 198-199.

[48] *Ibid.*, 201.

[49] Pobee, *Towards an African Theology*, 85; H Sawyerr, *Creative Evangelism: Towards a New Christian Encounter with Africa*, Lutterworth, London, 1968, 72; Parratt, *Reinventing Christianity*, 81-82.

and in the individual responses the Africans seem to pay more attention to Jesus' divinity.[50]

Some African theologians (Nyamiti, Manus) employ the comparative method in order to show the similarities and differences between the elements of indigenous religions and the Christian message.[51] However, the concentration on finding parallels in both traditions creates a danger of motivating the theologians more eagerly to search for similarities and to overlook differences. In this context Parratt's reminder about the lack of parallels in indigenous religions with the most important event of the Christian message becomes more significant.[52]

In the 1990s Nyamiti argued for his own general approach indicating the changing situation in Africa. There are homogenizing processes taking place also in the sphere of religious beliefs as a result of migration and easier communication. The appropriate tendency towards unity has been promoted by various socio-political and ecclesiastical groups. Nyamiti stated that though his method is open to the possibility of generalization, this in itself does not discredit the method. Critical voices said that his ancestor concept did not reflect the real situation of any ethnic group. Nyamiti defended his general ancestor concept saying that it was being used within Christian theology and not in social anthropology.[53] He pointed out that one should not expect a theologian to use cultural data in the way an anthropologist would do so. The selection, and particularly the application of certain cultural elements are directed towards theological goals and may require their modification in the sense of submitting them to a process of 'purification' from all that is contrary to the Christian spirit.[54] In Nyamiti's opinion since the Africans accept 'euroatlantic' cultural values, why could they not accept the cultural values from other parts of Africa? Besides that the understanding of certain African values such as the contact with the ancestors is expanding as a result of an increasing interchange of insights.[55]

---

[50] K Ross, 'Current Christological Trends in Northern Malawi', *Journal of Religion in Africa* 27 (1997), 167–168; J S Mbiti, 'Some African Concepts of Christology', in G F Vicedom (ed.), *Christ and the Younger Churches*, SPCK, London, 1972, 54.

[51] Nyamiti, 'Contemporary African Christologies', 70.

[52] Parratt, *Reinventing Christianity*, 83; Luneau, 'Jésus-Christ', 416–417.

[53] Nyamiti, 'African Ancestral Veneration', 18–19; *idem*, 'The Trinity', 42–43.

[54] This reflection appears in Nyamiti's works for the first time in: 'The Trinity', 45.

[55] Nyamiti, 'African Ancestral Veneration', 20; *idem*. 'The Trinity', 44.

Within the current christological trends

We have to notice with astonishment that the African christological thought often remains beyond the scope or merely on the margin of interest of those who systematize the world theology. It is even more surprising that they do notice the christological trends from other parts of the world.[56] The 50th issue of the Roman *Studia missionalia* which is dedicated to christology in the third millennium may serve as an example of this. The editors focus almost entirely on Asian christology to the complete neglect of any Latin American input and with minimal reference to Africa. Among 18 articles only one deals with African christology and it was written by a non-African, although undoubtedly his is the voice of a specialist.[57]

Meanwhile African theologians working on a christology 'from below' do not forget about the necessity of supporting it by the perspective 'from above'. Developing their own attempts at grasping who Jesus Christ is through the titles, they see their insufficiency and the need for a complementary approach. The efforts of African theologians can be placed in the category that Dupuis calls the 'critico–dogmatic' approach.[58] They are also familiar with the 'fundamental challenge to Christology [...] of holding fast to both continuity and discontinuity in the profession of christological faith: continuity in the sameness of meaning; discontinuity in the mediation of concepts'.[59] The other contemporary approaches to christology named by Dupuis: the salvation history approach, the anthropological approach, the approach of liberation Christology, the feminist liberation approach and christology in an interreligious perspective find their reflection in the work of African theologians.[60]

R S Sugirtharajah indicated that the third quest for the historical Jesus had its own impact on Third World theologians. However, he stated that the non-Western Christians are not searching who Jesus was, because there are many answers and it is certain that no one will be able to

---

[56] J Dupuis, *Jesus Christ at the Encounter of World Religions*, Orbis Books, Maryknoll, NY, 1991; idem., *Who do you say I am? Introduction to Christology*, Orbis Books, Maryknoll, NY, 1994.

[57] The issue bears the title: ' "Who do you say that I am?" Christology in the Third Millenium'. The article on African christology was written by René Luneau, 'Jésus-Christ est-il aujourd'hui african?', 407–420.

[58] Dupuis, *Who do you say I am?*, 21.

[59] *Ibid.*, 22

[60] *Ibid.*, 22–31.

confine Christ to dogmatic formulations. The non-Western Christians have been more interested in where they can find Jesus. The Magi's quest for Jesus (Mt 2:2) presents a more suitable model for non-Western search for Christ than that of trying to imitate Peter in his answer given to Jesus (Mt 16: 16).[61]

Africans' practical attitude is echoed in the statements made by theologians that authentic and coherent Christology can be developed only when the liturgies of the Churches reflect the real problems and joys of everyday life of the African Christians.

Conclusion

The Africanness of this theological reflection comes from the fact, that the Christ-event is being addressed, studied and analysed by Africans who are searching for Jesus' presence in the vital problems and issues of their communities. They are reflecting on their current situation from the perspective of the primal world view which still exists in African societies and they use concepts that operate within it or at least they employ a vocabulary which is rooted in this world view. Having this in mind the Africanness of African christology will not be jeopardized even when the theologians modify some of the indigenous concepts. Most of the African Christian theologians engaged in christological reflection focus on the mediatory role of Christ and assume that He perfectly fulfils all the aspirations of ancestors, healers and rulers. This assumption could be placed within the framework of the suggestions made by the Vatican II that emphasize the need for 'purification' of cultures from elements that do not go along with the spirit of Christ. It is not that obvious, however, that all the African cultural elements left out by the theologians are really contrary to the spirit of Christ. Then, the 'purification' understood either as the absorption and modification (sometimes considerable) of African cultural elements, or understood as the search for the deeper meaning of these elements which would be applicable to the Christian context, still requires further explanation of its role in the attempts made by the Africans to express the faith in Jesus Christ in a new theological language.

---

[61] R S Sugirtharajah ' "What Do Men Say Remains of Me?" Current Jesus Research and Third World Christologies', *Asia Journal of Theology* 5.2 (1991), 337.

RUSSIAN ORTHODOXY: CONTEMPORARY CHALLENGES IN SOCIETY, INTERRELIGIOUS ENCOUNTERS AND MISSION

Basil Cousins

Today, the Russian Orthodox Church (ROC) is riven by the struggle to re-establish itself and its identity. What is its mission in post-communist Russia? Where does it stand in relation to Putin's Russian Federation? Where indeed does it stand in the modern world beyond? Indeed, it is not alone in this. Islam has a similar dilemma, albeit against a different scenario. Closer to home, where does Islam within Russia—Domestic Islam—stand *vis-à-vis* Russian Orthodoxy and *vice versa*?. Finally, what Mission does the ROC see in relation to Domestic Islam?

This essay seeks to summarise the current missionary challenges facing both the Russian Orthodox Church (ROC) and Islam in Russia (Domestic Islam) in the light of history since the accession of Tsar Nicholas II and to outline tentatively possible future directions for both. The thread running throughout is the struggle to re-establish both ROC and Domestic Islam within the highly secularised and fractured society—the legacy of the Communist era. The essay will focus on:

—The broad socio-political context
—The re-establishment of a national identity—the role
    of ROC and Domestic Islam
—The relationship between religion and the state
—Concepts of freedom of conscience
—The role of Mission in a multi-cultural world
—Church and Society
—Inter-Christian and Interfaith relationships
—Conclusions

The letters RF signify the Russian Federation; ROC = the Moscow Patriarchate of the Russian Orthodox Church and the phrase 'Domestic Islam' = the Muslim communities encompassed within the Russian Federation. The Russian word *Sobor* describes the local Council of Bishops of the Russian Orthodox Church. Where possible, I will contrast the attitudes of the ROC and Domestic Islam. The term 'Russian Orthodoxy' covers the full spectrum of those who claim to adhere to the Russian Orthodox sense of Christianity whether they be united with the Moscow Patriarchate or not.

Caveats

It is almost humanly impossible to describe the profound depth of the trauma inflicted on the people of the former Russian Empire during the 70-year Soviet Communist period by the 'Red Terror'. The effects of this extreme trauma are vividly reflected in the psychological mirror provided by the Russian Orthodox Church. The type of extreme social engineering devised by Lenin and executed (often literally) by his henchman Stalin aimed to remodel the Russian Soul—a soul whose very existence atheistic communism vehemently denied. The effects of the profound social damage caused by the attempt at the forcible replacement of traditional values, both Christian and Muslim, with a 'revolutionary conscience' will continue to blight for decades the social fabric throughout the former USSR and countries that fell under its hegemony.

We observe through the lens of semi-complacent Western eyes the contemporary political, economic and social developments within the Russian Federation—coupling this with the Russian Orthodox Church under the tutelage of the Moscow Patriarchate. It is difficult to discern the underlying motivations and causes as well as to comprehend the real meaning of the slavophile-eurasiatic movement with its rooted objections to 'Western Influences' observable throughout the history of both the Russian State and Russian Orthodoxy. This difficulty arises in no small part due to the profoundly different perceptions of Christianity generally held by Eastern Orthodoxy influenced by more mystical Greek traditions and the more legalistic Western traditions, both Catholic and Protestant, which emanate from the Roman background. For example, important terms such as 'Catholicity' have different nuances of meaning between East and West—differences which affect the concept of Mission.

We should remember that in the '*Rus*' we are seeking to understand a particularly strong psychology with enormous endurance —an endurance which has enabled the Russian people to withstand centuries of onslaught from both the Muslim East and challenges from the Catholic West as well as its own internal struggles and civil wars of which Communism was but a episode—truly awful but now mercifully a closed chapter in a cruel history.

With this strong defensive psychology in mind, we should consider whether Russia in general and the ROC in particular has yet developed a 'World Vision'. The Russian Communists certainly had such a view inherited from international socialism—a western import, if ever there was. With certain exceptions like Peter I, neither the Russian state nor ROC developed a westward view, let alone a 'World Vision' but remained in essence eurasiatic-slavophile in spirit—looking eastwards. Incursions were made into North America—just because it was East. This underlying outlook affected the ROC Mission as much as anything else.

The key lies in the search for a national identity universally applicable throughout the Russian Federation. To achieve real success, this national identity needs to incorporate and bring into focus a comprehensive political and social unity amid all the myriad nationalities, belief systems, cultures, languages along with their tortured individual histories and accumulated experiences latent in the Federation today. The process of establishing a strong pervasive consciousness of such a generic national identity at the ground level may be well be modelled, albeit unconsciously, on the strong national identity successfully established in the USA. An important difference between the USA and the Russian Federation lies in how the multi-ethnic mix arose in the first place: with the USA it was by voluntary migration—in Russia it was achieved by conquest.

The Russian Orthodox Church and Russian Domestic Islam could have an important, not to say, a critical role to play in enabling this strong self identification—a pervasive self-image which will be a vital element in the peaceful development of the whole region.

No one should underestimate the complexity of the situation facing the Russian Orthodox Church nor that of its tortuous relationship with domestic Islam. Orthodoxy has evolved from being one of the independent founding forces behind the Russian state itself, to an almost complete dependency on the Russian State, particularly from the time of Peter I—the Great. It felt that it had been effectively cast adrift in 1905; almost annihilated by the Communism Regime only to be almost completely re-cast adrift again from the state in the multi-cultural, multi-ethnic, multi-belief modern society that may be being engineered in contemporary Russian Federation. The 1997 Law 'Freedom of Conscience and Religious Associations' sought to re-establish a special relationship between the ROC and the Russian State but at the price which includes an identification with the Russian state and ethnicity as well as the explicit acknowledgement of the presence of other significant non-Christian religious bodies—particularly Domestic Islam. On the surface, Islam would appear to be perceived as less of a threat to Russianness and the ROC than Western Christian and other influences. However, there is increasing evidence that Domestic Islam is claiming equal rights energetically within the Russian Federation and is very likely to present a significant challenge to the ROC in its heartlands. There is evidence of considerable nervousness about this. President Putin justified the renewed attack on Chechnya: 'if the Chechen extremists' were not stopped 'we will have the Islamisation of Russia'[1]—a fear met within the writings of Il'Minsky—a leading 19th century Russian Educationalist—and in the proceedings of the Russian Orthodox Missionary Society.

A final caveat, and an important one, lies in the different nuances of understanding the nature of Christianity between Eastern Orthodox and Western Christianity both Catholic and mainstream Protestant. David Fairbairn, an American Reformed Protestant, sets these out well in his book *Eastern Orthodoxy though Western Eyes*.[2] By and large Western Christianity, both Catholic and Protestant, reflects the Latin mind and Roman culture whilst Eastern Orthodoxy mirrors Greek mind and culture. The differences may be summarized as:

—Western Christianity, especially Protestantism, emphasizes the individual; Eastern Orthodoxy focuses on the whole— the group—hence the concept of *sobornost*—the collective— individual rights contrasted with corporate responsibility.
—Western Christianity sees Scripture through a legal lens in contrast with the more personal and mystical Eastern orientation, focused on participation in divine life—*theosis*.

[1] *The Times*, 21 March 2000, 8, quoted by Vera Tolz, in '*Inventing the Nation—Russia*', Arnold, London, 2001, 259.
[2] Donald Fairbairn, *Eastern Christianity through Western Eyes*, Westminster John Knox Press, Louisville, 2002.

I would add the greater Eastern emphasis on the Holy Spirit. An Orthodox criticism of Vatican II is that it was not sufficiently oriented to the action of the Holy Spirit. —The approaches to 'meaning' are quite different—Western tends to be textual, Eastern tends to be pictorial. To a Western Christian the 'Word of God' is likely to mean Scripture; to an Orthodox it will mean 'Christ'.[3]

These differences affect the attitude both to Mission and religious revival. Whilst the Western Christian approach will focus on the conversion and salvation of each individual soul, the Orthodox focus on an institutional conception of revival—the individual is subordinate to the community and is safe under her umbrella.[4]

Finally, it is important to view the actual place occupied by the ROC and Domestic Islam within the full context of contemporary Russia. I therefore begin with a brief overview of the state of the RF, the ROC and Domestic Islam contrasted as far as possible, with the situation before 1917. I will refer to the events during the Communist Period where necessary in the context of the current situation.

The broad socio-political picture

To begin to understand the role being played out by the ROC and Domestic Islam, it is necessary to acknowledge the innate historical Russian attitude to leadership—an attitude which runs from Tsars via general secretaries to presidents. Andrew Kutchins notes in *Russia after the Fall* President Putin's reflection: 'From the very beginning, Russia was created as a supercentralized state. That's practically laid down in its genetic code, its traditions and the mentality of the people'[5]

A second key factor to consider is the nature of the processes through which today's society in the Russian Federation have been and

---

[3] Fairbairn, *ibid.*, 5-7.
[4] Sharon Linzey and Iakov Krotov, 'The Future of Religion and Religious Freedom in Russian', *Religion in Eastern Europe*, ed Walter Sawatsky, Vol. XXI, No. 5 Oct 2001, 31.
[5] Andrew C Kuchins, *Russia after the Fall*, Carnegie Endowment for International Peace, Washington 2002, 5, citing N Gevorkan, A Kolesnikov and N Timakova, *Ot pervogo litsa: Razgovory s Vladimirom Putinym* ('From the First Person: Conversation with Vladimir Puton'), Vargius, Moscow, 2000, 167-8.

are passing. It can be argued reasonably cogently that the ROC generally mirrors the political ambiance of Russia and therefore the same processes. Boris Kagarlitsky in *Russia under Yeltsin and Putin* argues that between 1990 and 1999 'what occurred ... was not 'reform', still less 'revolution'. It was Restoration ... a natural continuation of the political cycle that began by the Russian Revolution in 1917'[6]

There are other critical socio-economic factors—of which the most telling is the loss of status as a global superpower, both economically and militarily. The World Bank Development Indicators 2001 compares the 1999 GDPs as:

USA	9152.1
Russia	401.4—below Australia.[7]

In 1980, the World Bank had assessed that the Soviet GDP was a little less than 50 percent of the USA. Even bearing in mind the Soviet apparatchiks' false accounting proclivities, the current imbalance is monumental.

Hidden among other appalling effects of Communism lie other key concerns such as demography. The overall population of the Russian Federation has been in long-term decline, particularly in urban, industrial centres. In 1914, the Russian Empire had an estimated population of 140.4m,[8] by 1939 the USSR had 194.1m inhabitants. This fell to 178.5m by 1950 despite the forcible annexation of new territories. By 1997, the population of the Russian Federation stood at 147.5m of which about 120m were ethnic Russians. The fall is partly explained by the independence of the Ukraine and other former republics of the Soviet Union—there are some 25.0m ethnic Russians living in the newly independent states.[9] Nevertheless, it has been estimated that the overall 1991 population of the former Soviet Republics would have been 150.0m

[6] Boris Kagarlitsky, *Russia under Yeltsin and Putin Neo-liberal Democracy*, Pluto Press, London, 2002, 3. He builds this concept around Kondratyev, the outstanding Russian economist and statistician who discovered long waves in the development of capitalism. It would be intriguing to build a parallel theory of 'long waves' in the evolution of religion!

[7] Kutchins, *ibid.*, 297.

[8] Geoffrey Hosking, *A History of the Soviet Union 1917-1991*, Fontana Press, Final Edition, 1992, Table A, 518.

[9] Andrew Evans, 'Forced Miracles: The Russian Orthodox Church and Postsoviet International Relations', *Religion, State and Society*, Vol. 30, No 1, 2002, 36.

greater without the huge population losses of the Soviet period. Apart from the horrific effect of the Soviet social re-engineering and the Great Patriotic War, the demographic decline is due to long-term falling birth rates among the Russian population coupled with increased social malaise leading to rising death rates, especially among men of working and parenting age.[10] Uniquely in modern Europe, male life expectancy fell from 64 to 57 between 1989 and 1994. Among the contributing factors is the significant growth in male 'anomic' suicide which now exceeds female by 5:3.1; the overall rate having risen from .334 per 1000 in 1990 to .53 in 1996[11]. As a result of these and other factors, the overall population is declining by over half a million each year.[12] These trends are partly counterbalanced by higher birth rates and better social cohesion among rural populations—predominantly non-Russian, generally Muslim and more conservative, concentrated along the southern rim and east from the Urals. This imbalance between Russian and non-Russian populations is likely to reach significant proportions since the overall fertility rate has dropped from 2.51 children per women in 1950-1955 to 1.35 in 1995-2000. Allowing for 7.4 million net inward migrants from 2000- 2050, the total population will decline to 121.3million.[13] It is an open question as to what the proportion of ethnic Russians would be in such as scenario. Finally, Russia suffers from an exceptional health crisis, due to the catastrophic decline in medical and social services since the fall of Communism.[14] The only realistic level of detailed support is available at the 'kitchen table'— putting emphasis back on the family unit.

In 1997, some 27m+ were non-Russian although only half of them lived in the autonomous republics. This means that nearly 20 percent of the population of the principal Russian states which make up the Federation are non-Russian. There are good reasons to question such a

---

[10] Harley Balzer, 'Human Capital and Russian Security in Twenty First Century', Andrew C Kutchins (ed), *Russia after the Fall*, Carnegie Endowment for International Peace, 2002, 164.

[11] Sharon Linzey and Iakov Krotov, 'The Future of Religion and Religious Freedom in Russian', *Religion in Eastern Europe*, ed Walter Sawatsky, Vol XXI, No.5 Oct 2001, 37.

[12] Anders Aslund, 'Ten myths about the Russian Economy', *Russia after the Fall*, 119.

[13] United Nations, *Replacement Migration: Is it A Solution to declining and aging Populations?*, ESA/P/WP.160, 21 March 2000, 61.

[14] Dennis J B Shaw, *Russia in the Modern World—A New Geography*, Blackwell, 2001, 153 citing C Haub (1994), 'Population change in the former Soviet republics', *Population Bulletin* 49(4), 4.

low figure as it fails to take account of 'unofficial' immigration into the wealthier urban, industrial centres. The proportion of ethnic Russians in the Federation was temporarily boosted by the reverse migration—*in-migration*—during the early 1990s of such Russians back from the newly independent states of the former USSR and indeed from the autonomous ethnic republics within the current Federation—places in which the ethnic Russians are no longer the 'ruling class' and no longer feel comfortable. These figures are provided to give context to the religious statistics from various sources:

	1914[15] Russian Empire	1917[16] Revolution	1989[17] USSR	2003[18] Russian Federation
Total Population	140.4m		286.7m	142.0m[19]
Orthodox	117m	90m	51.6m	80m[20]
Churches/chapels	70,000	69,000	6,893	19,000
Dioceses	67		67	128[21]
Bishops	130	163		150
Priests and deacons		51,105		19,800
Seminaries	58	58	3	26
Academies/university		4		3
Monasteries		1257	18	480
Monks/nuns		73, 463		
Parish schools	35.000[22]	40,000		
Sunday School				

---

[15] Dimitry Pospielovsky, *The Orthodox Church in the History of Russia*, St Vladimir's Seminary Press, NY, 1998, 198.

[16] Wacheslav Maiyer, 'Research in the Archives of the ROC; in the field of translations and publishing in native languages', *Religion, State and Society*, Vol. 25, No 4 1997, 369

[17] Library of Congress Country Studies, via www.adherents.com.

[18] www.russian -orthodox-church.org.ru/today

[19] G Yemelianova, 'Russia's *Umma* and its Muftis', *Religion, State and Society*, 2003/1

[20] www.oca.org, Fr John Matusiak as at 05/05/03. Estimates vary widely ranging from 23m to 100m. They are difficult to compare, say, with the statistics of Orthodox Church in America which are more likely to be based on church attendance. It is estimated that actual church attendance in the RF is 2-3m.

[21] www.russian-orthodox-church.org.ru/dioceses/index.htm lists 37 dioceses in the Russian Federation with 13 outside including 8 in the Ukraine.

[22] Richard Pipes, *The Russian Revolution 1899-1919*, 88, notes that half of the grade schools in the Russian empire with one third of the pupils were under Church supervision at the behest of the government. Cf. John S Curtiss, *Church and State in Russia*, New York, 1972.

In addition, there was a considerable ROC presence in America, China, Japan, Western Europe and elsewhere.

	America[23] 1985[24] 2003[25]		ROW outside RF 2003
Autocephaly		1970	
Orthodox	1m	2-3m	100m[26]
Parishes		2000	
Churches/chapels	558		
Dioceses			
Bishops	10		
Priests and Monks	681		
Seminaries	3		
Seminarians	123		
Academies	1		
Monasteries	7		
Nuns	19		
Parish schools			

Domestic Islam statistics

Various estimates are made of the Muslim population in the Russian Federation—mostly based on ethnicity. These vary from 14 m—the official figure—to 20m possibly reflecting the higher birth-rate. Predictions were made in the 1980s that the Muslim population would now be 30m. Henry Balzer in *Russia after the Fall* notes that 'immigration to Russian ... 'will most likely involve populations that are neither Slavic nor Orthodox'.[27]

---

[23] Dimitry Pospielovsky, *The Orthodox Church in the History of Russia,* St Vladimir's Seminary Press, NY, 1998.

[24] Michael A Meerson, 'The Orthodox Church in America', *Eastern Christianity and Politics in the Twentieth Century,* (ed.) Pedro Ramet, Duke University Press, 1988, 134-135.

[25] www.oca.org, Fr John Matusiak as at 05/05/03

[26] *Ibid.* Fr Matusiak notes that The Russian Orthodox Greek Catholic Church of America (ROBCCA) was finally granted 'autocephaly' from the Patriarchate of Moscow in 1970. Romanian, Bulgarian and Albanian Orthodox Churches then merged with the Russian to form the pan-Orthodox church in America with English liturgy in some 600 parishes. In addition, there are also some 50 parishes directly within the canonical jurisdiction of Moscow and a larger number of parishes belonging to the Russian Orthodox Church Outside Russia (ROCOR) which is not in communion with Moscow. Fr Matusiak's figures relate to estimated overall Orthodox numbers.

[27] Harley Balzer, 'Human Capital and Russian Security', *Russia after the Fall,* 170-1.

	1913		*1999*
	Russian Empire	*USSR*	*Russian Federation*
Total Population	140.4		142
Muslims	31m		15m
Mufti Boards	3		40[28]
Mosques and prayer			
houses	26,279[29]		
Clerics	5,339		

In 1917, the Muslim presence was largely concentrated well to the east of Moscow from the Upper Volga beyond the Ural Mountains through Siberia and along the southern rim of the Russian Empire. Today, such presence is more pervasive—fuelled by 'unofficial' migration of non-Russian, generally Muslim peoples from the Autonomous Republics and elsewhere. The recent opening of an important Mosque in Moscow in the teeth of local opposition evidences this. There is a large and growing illegal Chinese presence in many parts of the Federation. A short visit to one of the main railway stations in Moscow will confirm the huge influx of non-Russians—legal and illegal.[30]

Religious practice

However, the survival of both Orthodoxy and Islam during the Communist experiment and their comparative renaissance since the 1980s lead one to feel that physical measures are insufficient. We need some means of measuring underlying spirituality.

The level of Muslim religious practice pre-1917 is not known but was thought to have been reasonably high as the majority were living in tightly knit rural communities where it was socially important to be seen to conform. However, opinions about Orthodox religious practice pre-1917 vary considerably. Geoffrey Hosking in *Russia—People and Empire 1552-1917* describes the presence of Orthodox belief and practice in the peasant communities—uniquely in Europe peasants were know as *krestianin*—Christians. In general they were illiterate supported

---

[28] Yemelianova, 'Russia's *Umma* and its Muftis', *Religion, State and Society*, Vol. 31, 2003/2, 140 (quoting Asadullin 1998).
[29] Yemelianova, *ibid.*, 1; Maiyer cites 25,000 mosques, 369.
[30] Interview with Patrick Doyle, 18/04/03.

by a poorly paid, generally ill educated clergy. They would wear Christian symbols and take part in Orthodox liturgies usually conducted in archaic Church Slavonic. They generally saw life in religious terms but tacitly supported a range of pagan practices—they were *dvoeverie* (supported two faiths). It is believed that Russian Muslim communities had much the same characteristics. The landowners in Russia were generally lukewarm about Orthodoxy and many of the intelligentsia turned strongly against the Church.[31] Pospielovsky notes one delegate to the 1917-18 Sobor saying 'We say we have 110 million Orthodox Christians but what if [in reality] we have as few as 10 million!'[32] Only 10 percent of Russian soldiers took communion in 1917 compared with 100 percent in 1916 when it was obligatory.

There is reckoned to be an upsurge in religious practice within the former Communist Empire. Clearly the emergence of the Church—and Islam—from the catacombs after 60 years of the most intense persecution—is remarkable. However, the depth of this new religiosity needs to be very carefully assessed and put into context. In July-August 1995 the All Russian Centre for Opinion Research questioned 3000 Russian immigrant inhabitants. Little is known about their religious affiliation, if any.

The following replies were received to questions about religious orientation:

Do you believe and if so to which religion do you adhere?

Orthodox	53 percent
Other Christian	2 percent
Islam	3 percent
Jewish	0.1 percent
Other faiths	1 percent
Unbelievers	28 percent
Don't knows	13 percent

How important a role does religion play in your life?

Fundamental	4 percent
Important	19 percent

---

[31] Geoffrey Hosking, *Russia—People and Empire 1552-1917*, Fontana Press, 1998, 210ff.
[32] Pospielovsky, *ibid.*, 199.

Of little importance   30 percent
Practically nothing   19 percent
Atheist   14 percent
Don't knows   14 percent

Summary
| *Declared adherents* | *59 percent* |
| *Unbelievers and Don't knows* | *41 percent* |

Summary
Religion Fundamental/Important	*23 percent*
Of little or no importance/Don't know	*63 percent*
Atheist	*14 percent*

Segodnya 2/9/95

One of the difficulties with these figures is that they do not make clear the balance between the practice of adherents to Christianity and Islam which could be significant.

Other later surveys of considerable interest are cited by Sharon Linzey and Iakov Krotov. These focused on the life values held by the population, particularly the younger element. Linzey and Krotov write: 'It is commonly thought that since the collapse of Communism, there has been a resurgence of interest in religion—a veritable revival of sorts. This is largely a myth'[33] They cite the case of Moscow which has over 300 churches serving a population of 8m. On Easter Sunday 170,000—2.1 percent—attended Church; the Ministry of Internal Affairs militia recorded 4m—50 percent of Muscovites visiting the cemeteries to commemorate the dead. Various sources consistently agree that the 2-3 percent regularly attend ROC services. This is far high than in Communist times but lower than in non-Communist countries, however secularized they may be.[34] Irena Borowik reinforces the view that there may be indications of the gradual growth of a 'traditional believing group'. She cites Lev Mitrokhin and others who have suggested that the new religiosity is only a surface social awareness and an indicator of anti-communist orientation.[35]

---

[33] Sharon Linzey and Iakov Krotov, 'The Future of religion and Religious Freedom in Russian', *Religion in Eastern Europe*, (ed.) Walter Sawatsky, Vol. XXI, No. 5 Oct 2001.

[34] Linzey etc, *ibid.*, 34.

[35] Irena Borowik, 'Between Orthodoxy and Eclecticism: On Religious Transformations of Russia, Belarus and Ukraine', *Social Compass: International Review of Sociology of Religion*, Vol. 49 (4), 2002.

Measures of Muslim religiosity are less available but studies of Friday prayers seem to indicate a low level of practice.

Is religion considered to be an important issue in modern Russia? The indicators are not encouraging. In most of the studies reviewed, the subject is only mentioned, if at all, in relation to ethnic conflict, particularly Chechnya. The ROC hardly merits a mention.

National identity and the re-establishment of ROC identity
National Identity

The historical unity of the ROC and the Russian State was succinctly expressed by S S Uvarov, Minister of Public Education (1838-1849), in the formula: '*Orthodoxy, Autocracy, Nationality*; national-religious and state integrism.[36] This was firmly based on the sacralization of the state. The type of state organization thought to be compatible with Orthodoxy is still one of considerable importance to the ROC today. Emperor Justinian's 6th *Novella* in the 6th century described a model for church-state, idealized as a *symphonia*. In contrast, the Western Church frequently confronted the state in its various forms. This confrontation led to a political culture of balance and compromise. This whole process is eloquently described in *Saints and Sinners* by Professor Eamon Duffy of Cambridge University. In contrast, Eastern Orthodox churches frequently merged with the state, leading to Caesaro-Papism—a church state symbiosis with a simple formula 'One Tsar on earth corresponds with One God in heaven'. Whilst the 1994 Sobor opted for 'non-preference of any state system for the Church'[37], the monarchical form of government is felt by the ROC to be 'more religiously rooted'. It is noteworthy that the 1917-18 Sobor cancelled the 11th anathema against those who denied the role of God in the appointment of the Tsar and the descent of the gifts of the Holy Spirit during the anointing—in effect taking a step towards desacralising the Tsardom and hence the state. However, this act is little known and has not penetrated the Orthodox monarchical consciousness, even today.

---

[36] Fr Benjamin Novik, 'Analysis of 'The Fundamentals of Social Conception of the Russian Orthodox Church', *Religion in Eastern Europe*, Vol. XXII, No 5, October 2002, 5.
[37] 'Principles of Social Conception of the Russian Orthodox Church', 2000, para 3.7.

The national identity of the USSR was partly built on the status it achieved as a global superpower and partly on the comprehensive social infrastructure it built. Judyth Twigg argues that 'a significant portion of the Soviet Union's national identity and political legitimacy derived from its provisions of social benefits'[38]

She argues that the rate of explosion of inequality has caused the loss of all sense of a common national identity. 'In the midst of socio-economic chaos, no common set of unifying principles has emerged to replace the ideal, flawed as it was, of Soviet socialism'[39] Twigg is one of the few authors who draws attention to the potential role of the ROC. Well over 50 percent of Russians classify themselves as Orthodox even if they appear to have little grasp of the essence and practice of Orthodoxy and are tending towards 'supermarket' religion, picking up the bits that attract them from various belief systems. She notes the 'jealous reaction' of the ROC: 'Officially sanctioned discrimination against religious minorities, ... may undermine spirituality and religion as a sustainable source of family stability and social cohesion'[40] The ROC may be able to capitalize on the positive Russian nationalism of the emerging middle class.

Twigg writes that the ROC has deliberately sought to place itself at the centre of post-Soviet Russian National Identity, 'referring repeatedly to a uniquely Orthodox 'Russian Idea' or 'Russian Soul'.[41]

However, the role of the growing Muslim populations within the Russian Federation could be crucial in the re-establishment of an agreed set of unifying principles from which would flow a common national identity. Kutchins states that the overall population of the Federation in 2022 will be 135m, 10m less than today,[42] back down to the 125.7m counted in the 1897 first Russian census.[43] Given the higher birth-rate of the non-Russian population, Muslims may well number 30-40m with a heavy emphasis on youth as opposed to the Russian population skewed to the more elderly.

---

[38] Judyth L Twigg, 'What has happened to Russian Society?' *Russia after the Fall*, Carnegie Endowment for International Peace, Washington, 2002, 148.

[39] Twigg, *ibid.*, 155.

[40] Twigg, *ibid.*, 159

[41] Twigg, *ibid.*, 158.

[42] Kutchins, 'Russia Rising?', *Russia after the Fall*, Carnegie Endowment for International Peace, Washington, 2002, 302.

[43] Pipes, 'The Russian Revolution 1899-1919', 55.

The nature of Russian Orthodoxy—the re-establishment of identity in the modern world

Is Russian Orthodoxy a national religion principally focused on the Russians in Russia—and outside? It has traditionally seen itself in this role—the religious protector of the *Rus*. But the 1st Russian Diaspora, unwittingly engineered by Lenin and Stalin, has resulted in a rebalancing of its putative membership. Today's role call of Russian Orthodox bishops reflects this. In 1917, there were few Russian Orthodox bishops outside the confines of the Tsarist Empire; today there are a significant number—many of whom acknowledge the jurisdiction of Constantinople rather than Moscow. including the leaders of the important autocephalous Russian Orthodox Churches and independent exarchates. Looked at on a global basis, the Russian Orthodox Church is highly fissured. The particular historic tension between Moscow amd Constantinople was significantly exacerbated during the Communist Period. In 2003, there are few signs of it being resolved. The Russian Orthodox Exarchate of Western Europe acknowledges Constantinople whilst in the UK and Ireland it was agreed after the Second World War to return to the jurisdiction of Moscow. However, various versions of Russian Orthodoxy operate in the same geographical area including the Church in Exile which broke from Moscow in the 1920s on the grounds that the ROC leadership in Moscow had compromised with the atheistic communist Regime. This Church in Exile has opened a number of parishes in Moscow and other parts of the Russian Federation.

In Spring 2003, the Moscow Patriachate has begun a significant charm campaign aimed at reuniting all the various parts of Russian Orthodoxy under its jurisdication. This campaign is in no small part motivated by the Second Russian Diaspora that began with the fall of Communism. A large number of Russians, particularly the young, are leaving the Federation and settling in the West. The Moscow Patriachate in putting pressure on Russian Orthodox communities in the West to accommodate them. Estimates of the size of this diaspora vary widely. Further, the low level of religious practice within the RF itself is reflected in the Russian Communities overseas. Relatively few Russian expatriates are appearing at Russian Orthodox services in the West. As noted below, this desire by Moscow can run counter to the development of flourishing Russian Orthodox communities outside the RF which are successful in attracting non-Russian converts.

Broadly, the question needs to be asked: 'is the ROC seeking to establish where its future lies as:

—An ethnic, national religion for the Russians both at home and overseas; or
—A religion specially privileged by the state for Russians and others—within the Russian Federation; or
—An authentic orthodox version of Christianity—an integral part of the 'broad' catholic church embracing both Russian and non-Russians within the Russian Federation and elsewhere with no special state privileges?

A strong impulse can be seen in Russian Orthodoxy in Russia to define and defend its 'canonical territory', whether this be physical landmass or ethnic Russians. Mirroring the implementation of the so-called 1997 *Law on Freedom of Conscience and Religious Associations* in modern Russia, strange moves can be observed seeking to try to limit membership of Russian Orthodoxy overseas to native Russians resident or travelling outside the Federation. Such a mindset would appear to want to discourage indigenous converts.

This strong nationalistic orientation constrains the outlook of Orthodox clergy. They do not generally see their faith as a universal faith in the same sense as the Western Churches do. The separation of Church and State that has come to be accepted, however unwillingly, in the West, has no real emotional equivalent in the East. The constant resistance to the right of the Catholic and Protestant Churches to proselytise on the soil of the former Russian Empire, not just the Russian Federation, remains a constant feature.

In support of this attitude is the belief nursed throughout Russian Orthodoxy history at least since the 14th century that it is the only 'true church'—the Third Rome with a mission to bring the rest of Christianity into line. Russian Orthodoxy refused to support Byzantium when it accepted the proposals of the Council of Florence on the issue in the 15th century.

As a direct result of this pretension, Russian Orthodoxy still expends much effort in fighting off Catholicism when it should be tackling the steady advance of Islam in modern day Russia. The Orthodox protests against papal visits to Azerbaijan and Bulgaria clearly evidence this as does the 'black-listing' of Bishop Jerzy Mazur at Moscow Airport on 19 April 2002 for unstated reasons. *Keston News* and other media have cited many examples of similar application of administrative measures to defend the ROC's canonical territory.

Russian Orthodoxy today is wrapped in a ferment of discussion about its mission, organization and indeed about its 'Soul'. Della Cava[44] in his overview of the ROC describes the main factions ranging from the 'ultra-nationalists' and the 'ecumenists' on opposite wings of the Church to the largest, most powerful faction whom he typifies as the 'institutionalists' all under the leadership of the Patriarch Alexi II. Russian Orthodoxy's supreme governing body is the Local Council *(Pomestnii Sobor)* made up of Russian Orthodox archbishops and bishops (no lay participation) from outside as well as inside the Russian Federation, 'has set Russian Orthodoxy's present course. Between these meetings, decisions are constitutionally taken ... by the Holy Synod (Sviashchenii Synod), the single most powerful interim policy making committee of the Church.'

Much energy of these bodies has been 'dedicated to keeping the moral hegemony and ecclesiastical jurisdiction of the Moscow Patriarchate intact'. The main threats are seen to be Intra-Orthodox division and the advance of foreign missionaries—not Islam! Significantly, the advance of Islam and Buddhism within the 'the canonical territory' defined in ecclesiastical law is not even mentioned in Della Cava's study.

Russian Orthodoxy is trying to reclaim its 'home ground' among the Russian peoples scattered throughout the Federation and outside it in the Ukraine, Byelorussia, Estonia and elsewhere. Symbolically, the religious buildings stolen by the Communists are being progressively restored and brought back into full operation with the new generation of Orthodox clergy and believers. Orthodoxy is 'sacralising' a whole range of civic celebrations once dedicated to demonstrating the 'prowess of Communism'; famous battlefield victories such as Kursk are being developed as centres of Orthodox pilgrimage.

It is important, at this juncture, to consider the significance of religious nationalism. Fairbairn states that it is not a product of official Orthodox Church doctrine. Indeed, the more Western oriented Russian Orthodox theologians oppose it strongly. Vladimir Lossky (1903-1958) asserts that the very notion of a national church is erroneous in the face

[44] Ralph Della Cava, 'Reviving Orthodoxy in Russia—an overview of the factions in the Russian Orthodox Church', *Cahiers du Monde Russe et Sovietique*, Vol. 38, 1997, 137.

of the 'wholeness'—the catholicity of the Church. John Meyendorf (1926–
1992) describes it as 'that bane of modern Orthodoxy'.[45] Another
theologian Alexandre Schmemann defines it as a heresy, that prevents
catholicity—the *sobornost* is centred around the Eucharist. O'Callaghan
writes 'The Church cannot be limited to a function of one's ethnic
heritage'.[46] There is not the space to examine the reasons for ethnicity
within Orthodoxy in general except to propose that the various ethnic
Orthodox Churches evolved under the pressure of Islamic conquest. The
result is that it is commonplace in the West to find separate Russian,
Greek, Serbian etc Orthodox Churches in the same city. This fragmentation
has been partially resolved within North America by the amalgamation
of various ethnic Orthodox churches into the Orthodox Church in
America with an American English liturgy. This church does not include
the patriarchal parishes directly controlled by Moscow nor the Russian
Orthodox Church outside Russia which broke away in the 1920s and
still does not recognize the Moscow Patriachate.[47]

Religious nationalism is the fruit of an outburst of quite
widespread aggressive Russian nationalism. The spectrum of such
nationalism ranges from extremist groups not unlike the pre-Revolutionary
Black Hundreds *(Chernaya sotnya)* to mainstream organisations like
Russian National Unity *(Russkoye natsional'noye yedinstvo)*. Alexandr
Verkhovsky describes the significant linkages and active cooperation
between ROC bishops and clergy with many of these movements[48]. Within
the ROC itself, there are a large number of Orthodox brotherhoods
espousing extreme nationalist ideological positions. Anti-semitism is
noticeable—The Protocols of the Elders of Zion is to be found on sale in
ROC churches.[49] Unsurprisingly such attitudes are coupled with various
anti-western manifestations and anti-globalisation tendencies. Verkhovsky
typifies many of these movements as Orthodox Fundamentalist. One of
the more bizarre examples has been the so called *'INN Jihad'* which

---

[45] Donald Fairbairn, *Eastern Christianity through Western Eyes*, Westminster John Knox Press,
Louisville, 2002, 146, quoting Schmemann in 'Church, World and Mission', 98.
[46] Fairbairn, 147. 'An Eastern Orthodox Response to Orthodox Claims', 34.
[47] www. oca.org.
[48] Alexandr Verkhovsky, 'The Role of the Russian Orthodox Church in Nationalist
Xenophobic and Antiwestern Tendencies in Russia to day: Not Nationalism but
Fundamentalism', *Religion, State and Society*, Vol. 30, No. 4, 2002, 333.
[49] Verkhovsky, *ibid.*, 333.

campaigned vigorously against the introduction of barcodes in which the fundamentalists discovered the 'Seal of Antichrist' or the Number of the Beast' such as 666. The issue was finally resolved in a sensible manner at a Broadened Plenum of the ROC Theological Commission in Feb 2001.[50]

Finally, spiritual nationalism manifests itself in opposition to the 'West'—a multilayered concept most frequently interpreted as Catholicism itself—thus *Russian 'spirituality', statehood and culture were all seen in antithesis to 'papism'*[51] There is not space to analyse the interplay of Catholic and Anti-Catholic traditions in Russia except to note that in the background there is a strong upswell of pro-Catholic sympathy, particularly among the younger, more Western looking sections of the ROC.

Against the background described above, the Moscow Patriarchate is remaking the institutional church and its links with the broader social order.

Four new Patriarchal departments have been created focusing on:

—Religious Education and Catechetics
—Charitable Activities
—Communication with the armed forces and law
  enforcement agencies
—Mission to the Orthodox

The apparent complete omission of any mention of Mission outside the Orthodox is noteworthy.

Della Cava underlines that the Mission to the Orthodox is 'specifically charged not with preaching to the potential believer in distant lands, but to the Orthodox and nominal Orthodox ... targeted by foreign missionaries on the Church's own turf ....—its canonical territory.' The term 'canonical territory' flies in the face of the right of free choice and religious liberty, constitutionally guaranteed Russian citizens by the 1990 Law of Religion.

Della Cava suggests a possible fourth faction within Russian Orthodoxy—the Pastoralists—'those clergy, laymen and women who ...

---

[50] Verkhovsky, *ibid.*, 340.
[51] Sergei Filatov and Lyudmila Vorontsova, 'Catholic and Anti-Catholic Traditions in Russia', *Religion, State and Society*, Vol. 28, No 1. 2000, 69.

are engaged at the grass roots, who in some significant way break from the past' and 'who are not slow in talking of the future.'

Russian Orthodoxy has found it difficult to handle these often powerful intellectual and other movements. Jane Ellis[52] and others have described the suppression of new movements within the ROC even during times of persecution and difficulty, for example Fr Men and many others. These movements are generally motivated by a very strong sense of Christian Mission and are less likely to 'compromise' with current 'religo-political correctnesses'.

The movement started by Fr Alexander Men is prominent in this respect. Since his unexplained assassination in 1990, his philosophy and work have been actively developed. They take the form, among other initiatives, of two institutes, St Andrew's Biblical Theological College and its sister Institute which focuses on Pastoral Issues. Both institutes have a broad world view of Christian Mission in its most profound sense and its relationship with other faith structures. St Andrews has very recently published a number of important, far-seeing studies including: *Christianity and Islam—Problems of Dialogue, Theological Dialogue between the Orthodox Church and Eastern Orthodox Churches, Christian-Hindu Dialogue and Orthodoxy and Catholicism—from confrontation to dialogue.*[53]

At the roots of any significant reform must lie the education of future clergy in the seminaries. Della Cava highlights Dimitri Pospielovsky, a Canadian Orthodox university historian who has drawn attention to today's outstanding reformers of seminary life. They have come to the fore at a point when Pospielovsky considers the standards of contemporary clergy have reached their nadir.

At a time when 'the most interesting and promising seminarians are adult converts with secular degrees' , the general standard of seminary formation is marked by the anti-intellectualism of their narrow minded monastic mentors and by their 'desire to isolate themselves from the sinful world around them'. Pospielovsky places his hope for the Faith and the Church squarely on seminary reforms.

---

[52] Jane Ellis, *The Russian Orthodox Church—A Contemporary History*, Routledge, London, 1986(1988). Her chapters on the growth, flowering and suppression of Orthodox Dissent portray the fundamental difficulties that the ROC has in this respect.

[53] *Christianity and Islam—Problems of Dialogue* contains a wide range of important documents from Orthodox, Roman Catholic and Muslim sources including translations of key Second Vatican Council declarations such as *Nostra Aetate*.

One other factor that needs to be mentioned at this point is the widespread anti-Semitism that pervades much of Russian Orthodoxy.

The ROC relationship with domestic Islam

The relationship between the ROC and Domestic Islam within the Federation remains an enigma. The interpretations of 1997 Law with their restrictive definitions of 'Traditional Religions' incorporate a very strong sense of 'canonical territory'. This sense favours a status quo between the ROC and Domestic Islam coupled with a strong resistance to outside influences—particularly from the West. It is built on a presumption that ethnic Russians 'belong' to the ROC while the Tatars and other indigenous peoples generally 'belong' to Islam. Both the ROC and Domestic Islam share this strong sense of 'canonical territory' or *umma*, which give them exclusive religious rights over their 'own' people. Proselytisation is unwelcome, particularly by the various forms of Western Christianity. However, it is far from clear how much Domestic Islam is influenced by external forces in the Muslim world emanating from Egypt, Saudi Arabia, Turkey and Iran. It is very hard to believe that, in a period of Islamic resurgence, the Muslims in the Federation are not continuing to 'proselytise' and consolidate their position within Russia on an extensive scale. There is certainly evidence of very significant Islamic investment in the reconstruction of mosques, madrasahs and other components of the Islamic faith.[54] Yet, not for the first time in the history of this relationship, Russian Orthodoxy would appear to turn a blind eye to Domestic Islam in its midst.

Domestic Islam generally appears to be regarded somewhat more benignly by the Russian Orthodox than Western Christianity, apart from *wahhabism* in the Caucasus. Orthodox priests have been heard to remark that they would prefer someone to become a Muslim rather than a Roman Catholic.[55] Sharon Linzey and Iakov Krotov explore the complex issues

---

[54] Yemelianova, *ibid.*, Yemelianova gives an impressive list sources of the important financial underpinning from ' foreign Islamic assistance ... triggered by Gorbachev's religious liberalisation in the late 1980s which reached its peak in 1991-92.' A study needs to be done comparing the financial assistance that has flowed from Christian sources such as aid to the Church in need with Muslim financial support over the past 20 years.

[55] Orthodox source.

involved in their article 'The Future of Religion and Religious Freedom in Russia'.[56]

The relationship between religion and the state—its affect on Mission
Russian Orthodoxy

The start of this chapter reflected on the nature of the political process in modern Russia, concluding that there are powerful currents supporting the concept of '*Restoration*'—a form of turning the clock back to the imagined world pre-1917. However, this is not all bad. The period from the accession of Tsar Nicolas II to 1917 was one of enormous change and soul searching both within Russia and the ROC. The Communist Revolution forcibly interrupted a process which could have enabled the Russian People to develop into its own version of an industrial based democracy recognizable as such in the West. *Restoration* could entail stepping back into the unfulfilled pre-revolutionary thought processes both for the Russian State and the ROC. However, it could also take a more sinister form seeking to recreate a Tsarist style state with full autocracy and all the benefits of an imaginary glorious past.

That said, Putin's judgement about the centrifugal tendencies of Russian society may well be applied to the ROC. It goes some way to explaining its ambivalent attitude to the Church-State relationship. This ambivalence should not be that surprising since it can be argued that the Russian State would not have come into existence and survived without the support of Russian Orthodoxy. Tsarist Russia was a symbiosis of Church and State.

President Putin is paying careful attention to the Russian Orthodox Church. On the political front, he faithfully pursues the aims of his predecessors, both Tsarist and Communist, by defending the frontiers of the current Russian Empire and seeking to influence strongly the surrounding countries, particularly those like Kazakstan—formally members of the Russian/Soviet empires. The current war against terrorism has enabled him to acquire a new and powerful ally in the USA who has tacitly supported quite extreme measures to eradicate

---

[56] Sharon Linzey and Iakov Krotov, 'The Future of Religion and Religious Freedom in Russia', *Religion in Eastern Europe*, Vol. XXII, Number 5, October 2001, 26-47.

Islamicist insurgency. The future of this relationship is now in the balance again—post the Iraq episode. Further, quite how such anti-terrorist activity will help or hinder inter-religious relationships remains to be seen.

In May 2002, the Russian Orthodox Patriarch Alexi II stated: 'The Russian Orthodox Church does not aim to achieve state status.' [57] He was responding to concerns voiced at of the European Council that the Russian Orthodox Church was seeking ways of making Orthodoxy the state religion. He insisted that 'before the 1917 Revolution, Russia had already been through every possible negative consequence of Orthodoxy being the state religion when the Church was just another governmental institution'. Interestingly, he 'stressed that the Church should be separated from the State so that it can ethically assess an event occurring in the country and society.' Recent ROC decisions point towards their desire to be independent of the Russian State and yet enjoy a unique special status within it. There is significant risk of being re-swallowed by the state in this.

Does Alexi's statement reflect the underlying reality of his church today? In an era with a nostalgia for the 'Restoration' of imagined pre-revolutionary models in both Russian society and the church, this could be doubted. Quite why the ROC should want to nestle up so closely to the Russian state is paradoxical when it becomes clear from Russian history that, despite, or perhaps even because of, the symbiosis of Church and State, the Tsarist governments generally saw the Orthodox Church as a political rival. (Lenin, Stalin and their successors certainly did so). The Tsarists consistently sought to bring the Moscow Patriarchate and Orthodoxy in general under their direct political control—to make the Church an instrument of the State—the same type of motivation that lay behind the nationalization of the Catholic Church by Henry VIII and with broadly the same effects. The French monarchy tried to achieve political dominance over the Catholic Church on numerous occasions, possibly the most famous of which was the Avignon episode when the Papacy was forcibly relocated to Avignon under the tutelage of the French monarchy.

---

[57] *Pravda*, 5 June 2002, Moscow.

This political domination made the Russian Church subservient to the state, ensuring that the clergy frequently acted as state officials working in close collaboration with the police and civil administrations. It significantly undermined and discoloured the development of the Christian mission of Russian Orthodoxy, which itself frequently became yet another instrument for the colonization of conquered peoples.

The Russian Orthodox Church became deeply frozen by its subservience to the Russian State. Fr Eugene Smirnoff, a Russian Orthodox priest, wrote from London in 1903 in his book *Russian Missions* that 'the parish clergy came to ... (Asia) in response to the religious requirements of the Russian Government officials, and of the troops and colonists.'[58] Fr Eugene sets out to refute the view that 'The Orthodox Church is not ... often thought of as a missionary church. Indeed one sometimes hears it said that the Church is not an 'evangelistic church.'[59] He adds that 'In the history of the Russian Missions a period of stagnation set in ... from 1756-1824.'[60] In the Western Churches there was an immense surge of missionary activity, closely associated, it has to be said, with the development of trading empires.

Although there were examples of Russian Orthodox who sought to resist the impact of state control, the general state of subservience profoundly affected the mission of the Church. In effect, it became a political mission, not a spiritual one. Missionaries followed the Russian settlers into the furthest reaches of Asia as they were conquered by the Tsarist armies, not primarily to convert the indigenous peoples to Christianity but to service the needs of the Russian settlers along with those of the army and government administrators. In many ways, the only real spiritual successes of the Russian Orthodox mission occurred in places like Alaska, China and North America, well beyond the political reach of Moscow.

During the 19th and early 20th centuries, the dependency on the state was beginning to diminish somewhat. Possibly, this was due to a sense developing within the ruling circles that religion was no longer so important to the political process. The key reform sought by the ROC at the start of 20th century was the autonomy of ecclesiastical

---

[58] Fr Eugene Smirnoff, *Russian Missions*, Rivingtons, 1903, (republished by Stylite Press in 1986) 14.
[59] Smirnoff, v.
[60] Smirnoff, 15.

administration, the removal of the *réglement* imposed by Peter I in 1721 which both abolished the Patriarchate and subordinated church affairs to the Government—profoundly damaging the ROC's sense of its spiritual mission.[61]

Whatever the cause, a new sense of genuine spiritual Mission awoke from about the 1820s, encouraged by a number of broader minded Patriarchs. They, and others, began the process of weaning away the Church from its psychological dependency on the State, more particularly away from attempts to convert and Russify Turkic and other indigenous nationalities by force and/or administrative means as part of a state sponsored Russification process. This development of a degree of independence from political control took place at a time when the Russian society was slowly beginning to absorb the liberalization concepts and initiatives flowing from Western Enlightenment. Perhaps the greatest example of this process was the abolition of Serfdom by Tsar Alexander II in 1861. This can be compared with the anti-slavery movement in the West.

However, it is essential for the ROC to acknowledge the realities of the modern world, most particularly resurgent Islam as well as endemic secularity within its midst.

Andrew Evans in his article 'Forced Miracles: The Russian Orthodox Church and Postsoviet International Relations' builds on Huntington's view that since the end of the Cold War, the East-West axis has shifted to a clash of civilisations. Different cultures are 'the main source of division among human beings today'.[62] He specifies Slavic Orthodox Christianity as one of the world civilisations. The German theologian Dietrich Bonhoeffer, describing the relationship between Russian Orthodoxy and the State as theologically unique, wrote 'the Church in Orthodoxy is the spiritual organ of the state and special protector of the ethos.'[63] He forecast that in the post-communist era the state would have a propensity to approach the ROC as a national standard for ethics and values—a political culture of fused church and state.

---

[61] James Cunningham, 'Reform Projects of Russian Orthodox Church at the beginning of XXth Century', *The Legacy of St Vladimir*, St Vladimir's Seminary Press, Crestwood, 1990, 107.

[62] Evans, *ibid.*, 33.

[63] See Vigen Guroian, *Ethics after Christendom: Toward an Ecclesial Christian Ethic*, William B Eerdmans, Grand Rapids, Mi, 1994, 5.

Bonhoeffer's prediction, written at the end of the Stalinist era, has turned out to be prescient. Evans argues that the ROC has never been effectively free from the state throughout Russian history. The ROC has featured, especially in the later Communist Period, as a state sponsored actor in international relations. The ambiguous state of democracy makes it difficult to define what is state and what is not. He writes 'Soviet infiltration of the ROC, the post-Soviet tradition of joint church-state leadership and the attitudes inherited from both eras make the ROC much more a state actor than a non-state actor.'[64]

Since 1917, the ROC has inadvertently become a trans-national player to a very much larger extent than it ever was in Tsarist times. This arose initially because of the diaspora of Russians, principally to Western Europe and America. It was reinforced by the appeals for help that the persecuted church in Russia made in the 1920s and 1930s to the West and even to the Vatican. In the post-Great Patriotic War period, the State sponsored and encouraged ROC's activity in the Communist inspired international peace movements. Unlike the rest of their Orthodox brethren, the ROC sent delegates to the Second Vatican Council, motivated, it is said, by a Communist desire to drive political wedges between Europe and USA.

The ROC is caught in a dilemma between defending its hegemony over the native Russian population in the Federation and living with the now extensive Russian global diaspora—one that is particularly concentrated in North America, Japan and Europe.

It is evident that Russian Orthodoxy fears marginalisation in a world in which there is full freedom of conscience. Uzzell writes: ' While the greater Orthodox Community acknowledges the pluralist nature of the new millennium, the ROC has taken a step away from pluralism.' But it has done this at a price! Domestic Islam is, at least in theory, acknowledged as of equal status within the Russian Federation. The Russian Muslims have not been slow in claiming full equality of treatment within the Russian Federation.

---

[64] Evans, *ibid.*, 34.

The relationship between religion and the state—
domestic Islam

Yemelianova in her study of domestic Islam records that: 'The Bolsheviks ... demonstrated a surprising continuity with the ancien régime in their approach towards Russia's *umma*. Against a background of institutionalized atheism, the Bolsheviks pursued a policy of control and accommodation of Islam rather than its complete eradication.' They preserved, under various guises, the Ufa Muftiate but 'at the climax of the Second World War, the Stalin leadership created three more Muftiates', known as Spiritual Boards in Tashkent, Uzbekistan; Baku, in Azerbaijan and Dagestan '... designed to tighten state control over Soviet Muslims who were regarded by the German Commanders as a potential fifth column.'[65]

Yemelianova concludes that 'throughout the Tsarist and Soviet periods muftiates proved to be effective tools of control and regulation of the Muslim community by the state.'[66]

Paradoxically, the end of Soviet rule was followed by the creation of dozens of new Islamic Spiritual Boards or Muftiates, headed by 'young imams' often covering particular nationalities in various states which either remained within the new Russian Federation or in the newly independent states such as Azerbaijan. The flow of foreign Islamic assistance was an important factor in this 'mufti boom' under the banner of *da'wa* (summons to Islam). These funds have been used for the construction and staffing of Mosques, madrassah, Islamic universities and other Islam-related institutions as well as heavy investment 'in the work of Islamic missionaries and the organization of various Islamic training camps and courses'[67] It is noted that not all the funds were used for the purposes intended and there have been accusations of misappropriation. There are intense political struggles between the various principal Muftiates, particularly the 'Court Muftiates' seeking influence in Moscow.

Paul Roth in the review *Glaube in der 2 Welt* describes the background to the Peoples Council held in Moscow during December 2001 attended by President Putin and Patriarch Alexi II as well as many senior Muslims, along with Gennadi Sjuganow, head of the Communist

---

[65] Yemelianova, 'Russia and its Muftis', *Religion, State and Society*, Vol. 31, No. 2, 2003,-139
[66] Yemelianova, *ibid.*, 140.
[67] Yemelianova, *ibid.*, 2, citing Osmanov, 1999, 140.

Party and Vladimir Shirinovski of the extreme right. The main topic was the relationship between Orthodoxy and Islam in the light of 9/11. The sub-theme was to develop joint approaches to combat the spread of secular humanism. The apparent aim of the Council was religious but the Muslims used it to promote political points of importance to them, particularly equality of treatment and opportunity as well as a solution to the conflict in Chechnya.

With the collapse of Marx-Leninism, Yeltsin sought a new 'Russian Idea'. This may be typified as the theory of 'Eurasianism'. The religious aspects of this political theory are tinged by the redevelopment of an understanding between Church and State with an Orthodox colouring, balanced by the view that the Asiatic and Islamic elements of Russian Federation society should be given more respect in Russian history and within the present political framework; in particular the Muslim population must be given due consideration in elections. [68]

The friendly government attitude to Islam does not reflect popular feeling which is influenced by factors such as the report in *Isvestia* that 10,000 Soviet citizens (presumably mainly Muslims) fought with the Iraqis in the Gulf War. A Moscow poll in 1991/92 showed that 60 percent of those polled regarded Islam as a threat but not Western expansionism.

It is difficult to separate out the relationship of Domestic Islam to the Russian State from its relationship with the ROC. The Peoples Council described above contains many statements by the Muslims which are religious at one level and deeply political at another, reflecting the Muslim concept of the indissolubility of Church and state.

The Muslim speakers denied that Islam is linked to terrorism, pointing out that Islam has been in Russia as long as Christianity and that Muslims fought alongside Russians in the 'Great Patriotic War'. They criticised the special position of Orthodoxy in the Russian State, focusing on complaints that no Muslim chaplains were allowed in Russian prisons and that Muslim press should be given a wider distribution among non-Muslims. They proposed a Ministry of Muslim Interests.

The Muslim Russia Movement was formed in 1996 which, apart from demanding an apology form the Russian Government for their behaviour towards the Chechens, made four main demands:

---

[68] Paul Roth, 'Orthodoxe-Islamische Zusammenarbeit' ('Orthodox Muslim Collaboration'), *Glaube in der 2 Welt* 01/2003, 18-21.

—Proportional representation for Muslims at all levels in the administration and Media;
—National territory units should remain intact;
—Russia must not exercise majority power in favour of the Orthodox in districts with a large Muslim population
—Muslim feasts should be recognized alongside Orthodox.

Accusations of favour shown towards the Orthodox by the Russian government are frequently levelled by the Muslims—and others. F Asadullin, a journalist, wrote in *Moscovski Novosti* [No 13/1996]: 'The authorities place Christianity under special state protection; freedom of religion before the law is the basis of democracy—a fundamental democratic right.'

All in all, there is increasing evidence of a powerful Muslim lobby within the RF.

This will continue to challenge the special privileges claimed by the ROC, particularly in the autonomous republics like Tatarstan.

Concepts of freedom of conscience—and religion

Geraldine Fagin of Keston College reports that the two great patriarchates of Moscow and Constantinople place markedly different emphases on religious freedom. 'While Moscow is unenthusiastic about (it) and does not regard it as integral to Orthodox teaching, the Ecumenical Patriachate embraces it as the supreme manifestation of the divine gift to humanity: free will.'[69] Laurence Uzzell, writing in his article 'The Problem of Religious Freedom in Modern Russia' states categorically that the most evident and dramatic about-turn in post-Soviet Russia occurred in September 1997 with the adoption of the Law on Freedom of Conscience and Religious Associations, signed by President Yeltsin in October 1997, which formally re-established state control of religious life. This law was the result of a long period of intensive ROC lobbying. This replaced a more democratic Act of 1990. The new act seeks to re-establish the hegemony of the Moscow Patriarchate in the Russian Federation which the Church regards as its *Canonical Territory*—its exclusive home ground—

---

[69] Fagin, *op. cit.*, 11.

that is exclusive to other versions of Christianity both Catholic and Protestant but particularly the Roman Catholic.

Uzzell asserts that the process began at least three years earlier when government and federal organs began to ignore increasingly the 1990 Law on Religious Freedom and the 1993 Constitution. He draws the conclusion that there is considerably less religious freedom in 2000 than there was in the early 1990s.[70] The new law restricts the rights of foreign missionaries and all newly established religious groups. Linsey and Krotov record that 'the passage of this bill has had disastrous effects on Orthodox-Protestant relations. ... Many Protestants feel that the Moscow Patriarchate is waging war against them.'[71] It is very sad to observe the Russian Orthodox Church retreating behind old fashioned 'Administrative Measures' such as the physical exclusion of western clergy to defend itself.

Linsey and Krotov go on to describe the fierce debate that surrounded the Religious Freedom Act which the Russian Orthodox Church defended on the grounds that 'the simple Russian people are defenceless to the onslaught of totalitarian cults.' In November 1998 'the Presidential Committee for Collaboration with Religious Organisations met to discuss the numerous anti-missionary laws that have been adopted in thirty regions of Russia. The general Prosecutor of Russia declared that all these laws to be unconstitutional for violating the constitutional right of freedom of religion. Metropolitan Poyarkov defended these unconstitutional and discriminatory laws as a 'natural and necessary reaction of self-defence ... One could not put Russian Orthodoxy on an equal basis with foreign missionaries ...' (Ivan Arakelyn, *Russkaya Mys,* 28 November 1998, 21).[72] This was reinforced by Metropolitan Kiril of Smolensk, Head of the Foreign Relations Department of the Moscow Patriarchate who affirmed at the Peoples Council held December 2001 in the light of 9/11 that faith and religion were the basis of the nation— every Russian was Orthodox by birth—adherence to any other religion was the result of 'criminal proselytism'.[73] Strong language!

[70] Lawrence Uzell, 'The problem of religious freedom in modern Russia', *Religion and Society—Characteristics of Religious Life in Modern Russia,* Lietnii Sad (*Summer Garden*), Moscow, 2002, 22ff.

[71] Sharon Linsey and Iakov Krotov, 'The Future of Religious Freedom in Russia', *Religion in Eastern Europe, ibid.,* 42.

[72] Linsey and Krotov, 43.

[73] Paul Roth, 'Orthodoxe-Islamische Zusammenarbeit' ('Orthodox Muslim Collaboration'), *Glaube in der 2 Welt,* 01/2003, 18.

At that Council, Patriarch Alexi II claimed that Muslims were not responsible for 9/11—the root cause of which was injustice in the World. The Metropolitan reinforced this line of thinking by stating that the Russian Orthodox Church opposes terrorism but can understand the underlying reasons. Western civilization is no longer Christian but secular humanist. It is in conflict with Islam and the 'Traditional Religious World to which the Russian Orthodox Church belongs'. His thesis was that non-traditional religious communities were to be criticized. 'Non traditional religious communities' is a ragbag phrase used to incorporate every form of Western Christianity as well as the totalitarian sects which the Russians typify by the Moonies. The term *Wahhabism* is used to describe any fundamentalist movement whether Islamist or Christian.

After the lifting of religious persecution during *Perestroika* the Moscow Patriarch was not unreceptive to ecumenical approaches from Rome but since 1995/96 a widespread campaign against the West has developed under the slogan 'Resistance to [Western] Proselytism in the Canonical Territory of the Russian Orthodox Church'

A more thoughtful approach may be found in 'The basis of the social concept of the Russian Orthodox Church' approved by the Russian Council of Bishops (Sobor) held to celebrate the Christian Year of Jubilee— 2000. This document represents something completely new in Russian Orthodoxy. Wil van der Bercken writing in *Exchange* October 2002 writes: 'For the first time in her existence the Russian Church formulated fundamental principles in relation to Church and Society ... the end of blind obedience of the Church to the state ... in Eastern Orthodoxy in general. No other Autocephelous Orthodox Church had ever expressed her social view in an official document'[74]

This document is ambivalent about freedom of conscience. Its recognition as a generally accepted human right has proved that 'in the modern world religion has turned from a 'social' into a private 'affair', that 'the spiritual value of system (in society) has disintegrated' and that the modern state has lost its 'religious commitments'. Freedom of conscience in laws ... evidence the fact that society has become massively apostate but this principle enables the Church's existence in a nonreligious world'[75]

---

[74] Wil Van den Bercken, 'A Social Doctrine for the Russian Orthodox Church', *Exchange* Vol. 31 4, October 2002, 373.
[75] Van den Bercken, 378.

The role of Mission in a multi-cultural world

Redefining the Mission of Russian Orthodoxy has to be an integral component in the re-establishment of its identity in the global multi-cultural society apparently developing today. It is an area in which there are more questions than answers. Is the ROC mission simply focused on 'winning back' its ethnic Russian flock from a state of agnostic secularisation? Presumably, such a mission would extend to win back its non-ethnic Russian flock such as the Tatars and other non-Russian converts to Russian Orthodoxy. Does it seek to encourage non-ethnic Russian 'converts' within the Federation, or elsewhere? Is this area—the Mission to Domestic Islam—one area in which the concept of 'Restoration' is not being pursued? Finally, what is the ROC relationship with autocephalous and other overseas forms of Russian Orthodoxy? It might well be seeking to act as the 'Vatican' of Orthodoxy—a restoration of the concept of the Third Rome.

Aleksi II, in his report to the 1994 Sobor focused on *Mission in the Contemporary World* stressed broader issues, in particular making Orthodoxy accessible to the contemporary World. He put particular stress on making the Orthodox Liturgy more accessible to all, particularly the urban populations and the young. He advocated the creation of a special synodical commission to pick up the work begun at the 1917 Sobor designed to re-order liturgical practice and modernise translations. At the same time, Aleksi proposed ROC involvement in social issues. This eventually gave rise to the document of social policy published in 2000. He called for the creation of missionary structures within the ROC, particularly the training of Orthodox missionaries who can operate within a post-Soviet society whose 'state of mind' is 'stamped by secularisation and agnosticism'[76]

There is no doubt that Domestic Islam faces a similar set of challenges. How do the various Muslim communities within the Federation interpret their *da'wa* mission—call to Islam? Clearly this will vary from more extreme Islamist interpretations in the Caucasus and Chechnya to the more 'moderate' in central Russia. Is the aim to win back former Muslim peoples from secularism or indeed from Russian

---

[76] Giuseppe Alberigo, 'Towards a Common Future', *The Holy Russian Church and Western Christianity*, Concilium 1996/6, 153-157.

Orthodoxy? Does Islam continue seeking to proselytise other 'heathen' tribes and even ethnic Russians as it has consistently in the past? Finally, is the currently muted but long term aim still to convert the whole of Russia to Islam?

There would appear to be a 'tacit' compromise between the two faiths in the form of a 'non-proselytisation agreement'—a clear reversal of history for both parties. We will need to look hard for real, as opposed to superficial, evidence of mutual collaboration and understanding between Orthodoxy and Islam. How would such collaboration affect their respective missions? What is really happening at ground level? Are ethnic Russians converting to Islam in the same manner as we can observe in the UK with some ethnic English?

It is, of course, all too easy to seek to view the whole picture at the 'corporate' level i.e. in the ROC case at the level of the hierarchy. This is more difficult in the case of Domestic Islam as, at least in theory, Islam does not have a clerical hierarchy. In practice, the institution of a Muftiate in Ufa, Urals by Catherine the Great has given Domestic Islam the semblance of a religo-political structure.[77]

Islam, by its nature, is strongly focused on The Book—the Qur'an and other canonical writings. In its current form, it is non-hierarchical and has no 'official' central leadership similar to the ROC, the Roman Catholic Church and some Protestant churches, although it appears to be heavily dominated and influenced by clerics. It does have its own very strong forms of 'religo-political correctnesses' and is motivated by an overall call—*da'wa* to bring the whole of humanity to Islam. Despite the lack of a hierarchy, there is evidence of a degree of hidden central direction and Islamic coordination, mainly emanating from the oil rich Middle East, particularly the puritanical Saudi Wahhabist sect.

Da'wa is interpreted in different ways down the ages and in different territories. The historical missionary flow and counterflow of Russian Orthodoxy and Islam appears to show a consistently more successful Muslim Mission to non-Russians. All the efforts of various Tsarist governments at least since Ivan II—The Terrible—to use the Orthodox Mission as a crude political tool to integrate all the conquered peoples within the Tsarist Empire into a common Russian Orthodox culture met with little success. The 19th century is dominated by mass

---

[77] Galina Yemelianova, 'Russian and its Muftis', *Religion, State and Society*, Vol. 31 No. 2, 2003, 139.

apostasies of so called 'New Christians' among the Tatar and other groups reverting to Islam. Each time a Tsar ushered in a period of comparative 'toleration', Domestic Islam was able to re-assert itself. Il'Minski and others, particularly in the Russian Missionary Society, frequently gave dire warnings about the advance of Islam in the late 19th and early 20th centuries. The 1905 Decree on Religious Tolerance re-opened the floodgates to the open declaration of Islamicity by native populations across Russia no longer fettered by police and administrative pressures to appear to be Orthodox.

Church and society

As mentioned above in the discussion about Freedom of Conscience, the *Sobor* of 146 bishops adopted '*The Principles of Social Conception of the Russian Orthodox Church*' (PSC ROC*)* in August 2000. The PSC was the result six years work by a group of 26 bishops, clergy, theological professors and officials of Synodal departments—all clerical without lay participation.

Fr Benjamin Novik has critically reviewed first the five chapters of the total of sixteen.[78] He writes that 'religiously apprehended acknowledgement of earthly well-being offers a considerable difficulty for Russian Orthodoxy where sanctity was traditionally associated with evangelic poverty.'[79] Orthodox Christianity is of a deeply spiritual nature—transcendental—'reaching beyond' towards God and eternal life. This conception of Christian spirituality is expressed in the Russian Orthodox attitude to the liturgy and in the tendency to regard monastic ascetism as the ideal way. It has difficulty in correlating the earthly and the heavenly. 'What is earthly life?' a test, a waiting room or 'a garden that needs to be endlessly tilled?'[80]

The very separation of Church from the state forces out questions as to the nature of Christian life and the nature of mission which need to be answered, not just in relation to the secular state but particularly in relation to Islam. Christianity is not just a religion for inner use but a principle for one's whole life social, cultural, political, economic, ecological,

---

[78] Fr Benjamin Novik, 'Analysis of 'The fundamentals of social conception of the Russian Orthodox Church', *Religion in Eastern Europe*, Vol. XXII, No. 5 December 2002.
[79] *Ibid.*, 1.
[80] *Ibid.*

bio-ethical. Christ's message is all-embracing. Islam, from its inception, has always been 'all-embracing' enfolding the whole spectrum of life on earth within a unitative concept of Church, morality and state. Orthodoxy, to some extent, matched this, with the concept of *symphonia* between church and state mentioned in the PSC 3rd chapter but it has relied on a friendly state to provide the social context.

Novik argues that, in an era of secularisation and differentiation of society, the church has not only been separated from the state but also from society. 'Its prophetic function proved to be weakened, if not totally lost.'[81] Perhaps it could be adduced that Russian Orthodoxy had generally looked to its close relationship with political power to provide the 'social conception' for a Christian state, leaving politics to handle the 'dirty bits'. This Manichean dualism distinguishing the 'spiritual' from the 'profane', although condemned in the PSC, pervades Orthodoxy. It is expressed with great beauty in its liturgical-ascetic monastic disciplines.

Under Communism, the church was cut out of any public presence whatsoever and could not form a social teaching even if it had wanted to do so. 'There was only one 'social conception' namely Communist, for all people.'[82]

Novik is critical of the PSC in many respects, particularly its clear preference for a mono-confessional Orthodox Community e.g. a civil or ethnic nation. The PSC has not faced up fully to the modern realities of Christian life in a multinational, multi-confessional state. The document does not use expressions such as 'common values of all mankind' or the 'common good' as found in Roman Catholic documents. It does discuss 'Christian patriotism' whatever that may mean. It does not mention 'Christian humanism. A notion that was elaborated in Russian religious philosophy.'[83] 'A theologically motivated conception of Christian responsibility for society is absolutely absent from this document.'[84] It makes no mention of important Russian philosophers such as V S Solovyov (1853-1900) although it does use some of their concepts such as the law as a minimum of ethical norms.[85] He also wrote: 'One cannot deny the fact that social progress happened in the spirit of love and justice, that is

---

[81] *Ibid.*, 2.
[82] *Ibid.*
[83] *Ibid.*, 9.
[84] *Ibid.*, 4.
[85] *Ibid.*, 4.

in the spirit of Christ. Elimination of tortures and cruel executions, cessation of persecutions of heretics and adherents of a different faith at least in the West, abolition of feudal slavery and serfdom—if all these Christian reorganisations had been made by non-believers, then so much the worse for believers.'[86]

There is no section devoted to 'Church and Society' in the PSC which contains itself no statement about a Christian understanding of society. Novik finds this strange as an officially sponsored scientific theological conference 'Church Mission—Freedom of Conscience—Civil Society' (July, 2000) affirmed that ' a task of the Church and its mission is to promote the formation of civil society by finding its historically proper place'[87]

There is not space here to discuss the influence on the ROC Mission of many other important aspects of the SPC and other ROC initiatives but we may ask how does the development of 'Some Principles of a Social Conception of ROC' affect its mission in the modern world, particularly its mission to domestic Islam? Almost for the first time, it enables the ROC to begin presenting itself, not just a means of gaining eternal life, but as a credible correlation of the spiritual and the earthly. How one 'tills one's garden in the love of Christ' determines one's posthumous destiny. This is a significant move away from politically motivated 'superficial' conversions based on baptism and the undoubted *beauty* of the liturgy to a deeper personal conversion based on the fuller understanding of Christianity advocated by Il'Minski in 19th century. What the SPC does signal is the start of a process of modernising ROC thought and practice. Novik clearly believes it has a long way to go before it has completely faced up to the realities of the modern secular world.

Inter-Christian and interfaith relationships

The Jubilee *Sobor* accepted a declaration on ecumenism , 'Basic principles of the attitude of the Russian Orthodox Church toward other Christian Confessions'. Van der Bercken states that this is no more than a

---

[86] Vladimir S Solovyov, 'About the Decay of a Medieval World Outlook' in *Works*, Vol. 2, Moscow, 1988, 349 (Russian), cited by Novik, 11.

[87] Novik, *op. cit.*, 7.

confirmation of the actual reserve of the ROC towards the World Council of Churches and its troubled relations with the Roman Catholic Church.[88]

Conclusions

I am concerned in this article to describe the broad background to the contemporary Mission of the Russian Orthodox—Moscow Patriarchate, particularly its traditional mission to Domestic Islam—predominantly Muslim peoples such as the Tatars within the Russian Federation. I have sought to balance this with some feel for Muslim concepts of its *da 'wa*—call to Islam—within the same context. Both religions need to tackle the widespread agnosticism and syncretism within the highly secularised population. Prior to the 1917 Revolution, the fundamental strength of both religions lay in traditional, rural, agricultural communities.[89] At that time over 70 percent of the population was rural, today some 70 percent+ are urban.

Perhaps, in summary, one should start by answering the question posed above: does Russian Orthodoxy see itself a national religion focused on Ethnic Russians in Russia? Every indication would seem to point to a strongly affirmative answer. The steady strengthening in practice of the provisions of the 1997 Law on Freedom of Conscience and religious Associations strongly indicates this. What are the consequences?

—Russian Orthodoxy in diaspora would seem to be of secondary importance; The continued arguments for 'the principle of the local church—responsible to its people before God' put forward by Metropolitan Kirill of Smolensk and others appears to take no account of Russian Orthodoxy overseas; nor, as Philip Walters notes, of the share of such responsibility with other Christian denominations.[90]

—Unsurprisingly, ecumenical relationships with other

---

[88] Van den Bercken, *Exchange* Vol. 31:4 October 2002, 373.

[89] Geoffrey Hosking, *A History of the Soviet Union 1917-1991*: Official Soviet classifications show that in 1913 some 67 percent were individual peasants with 16 percent bourgeoisie/landowners; 15 percent workers: by 1937, 12 percent had become 'collective peasants' leaving 62 percent 'workers and 26 percent 'white collar'.

[90] Philip Walters, 'Pluralism versus community: religious challenges in Russia today', *Sobornost*, Vol. 24: 2, 2002, 55.

Christian bodies like the World Council of Churches and the Roman Catholics have distinctly worsened;
—Islam and other non-Christian 'Traditional Religions' are, at least implicitly, given equal standing. The ROC may live to regret this bitterly, particularly as the demographic impact of higher Muslim birth rates begins to make itself felt.
—The Law firmly opens the door to discrimination not just against the Sects but directly against the ROC itself. At the start of this essay, Putin indicated his view of Russia as a 'supercentralised state' by its very nature. Linzey and Krotov wrote ' ... where all the resources are in the hands of state officials, persecution may arise not only in the form of direct aggression but in the form of passive unfriendliness ... Some Russian politologists and scholars feel that the ideological basis for a future persecution may well be in place'[91]

What of the ROC Mission to Domestic Islam? So far, I have detected no activity in this important area—rather a blind spot. What, if anything, is being done to support and develop the Christian faith of Tatar and other non-Russian Christians in the semi-autonomous states? We know from the studies of Yemelianova that significant financial support has been given by Muslim sources to the Islamic infrastructure and educational resources in the key Muslim enclaves in Russia—principally semi-autonomous states such as Tatarstan. The local ethnic Christian communities may well feel at a considerable disadvantage to their Muslim neighbours, particularly as the Russian population diminishes as a result of immigration back to Russia.

It is to be suspected that, unless a significant missionary effort is put in by the ROC into these territories, the local Christian communities will wither away—as they have so often in the past. Consolidation of the hold of Islam in these states is to be expected.

It is also to be suspected that, as so often in the past, the 'supercentralised' Russian state will take the 'line of least resistance' and tend to let the Muslim communities run their own affairs as have both their Tsarist and Communist predecessor administrations. Such Muslim communities will remain less prone to the effects of central

---

[91] Linsey and Krotov, *ibid.*, 46-47.

interference and persecution in its various forms than the ROC and other Christian groups.

Overall, the persistent impulse still evident within much of the Moscow Patriarchate of the Russian Orthodox Church to claim special status within the Russian Federation will, as it has in the past, cripple its spiritual Christian mission to its own people as well as to non-Russians. In the long run, it will significantly impede the evolution of an effective modern national identity that will unite the vast medley of different cultures contained within in the borders of the Russian Federation.

JEWISH ISRAELI ATTITUDES TOWARDS CHRISTIANITY AND CHRISTIANS IN CONTEMPORARY ISRAEL

David M Neuhaus SJ

Introduction

My focus here will be on Jewish Israeli attitudes towards Christians and Christianity in Israel today as observed by one reasonably attentive Christian Israeli, myself. My aim here is not historical or socio-political. I will seek rather to sketch impressionistically the contemporary scene. Jews in Israel are very heterogeneous. There are believing, practising Jews and non-believing, non-practising Jews and many varieties in between. Well-known is the division among ultra-Orthodox, modern Orthodox, traditional, Conservative, Reform and Reconstructionist Jews. As important for understanding Jewish life in Israel are the diverse cultural backgrounds of the Jewish communities that originate in Western and Eastern Europe, North America, Latin America, the Middle East etc. A helpful distinction with regard to our subject is the distinction between Jews that come from the countries of Christendom and those that come from the Islamic world. However, each community has its own history that moulds attitudes towards Christians and Christianity.

Jewish Israeli society is still in formation and this does not always facilitate relations with those defined as outsiders. It is also important to be aware at the outset that the historical context of European anti-Semitism and its culmination in the Holocaust is formative for and remains at the forefront of the attitudes of many Jewish Israelis towards non-Jews in general and Christians in particular. In fact, Zionism, the motivating ideology behind the establishment of the State of Israel, is, in many ways, a reaction against what is perceived as the inability of Christendom to accept Jews, Judaism and Jewish life in its midst.

Christians in Israel are a tiny statistical minority, officially less then 2 percent of the general population.[1] They are also far from

---

[1] Official population statistics for 2003 give the figure 2.1 percent of the population of Israel is Christian. It should be noted, however, that this figure includes Christians from East Jerusalem, annexed in 1967, most of whom are not Israeli citizens.

homogeneous, including Orthodox (Greek, Russian, Romanian, etc), Catholic (Eastern and Latin Catholics), Eastern non-Chalcedonians (Armenians, Coptic, Ethiopian and Syrian Orthodox) and Protestants (Anglican, Lutheran, Evangelicals etc.). Here, though, it might be more helpful to distinguish among four groups of Christians in Israel defined by social, political and cultural factors rather than focus on the denominational breakdown of Christians in Israel.

A first group consists of the Christian Arabs, who, according to the official statistics, make up more than 90 percent of the Christians in Israel. The Christian Arabs who reside within the borders defined in 1948/9 are citizens of Israel.

A second group of Christians consists of the large number of expatriates (many being priests and religious), mostly of European and North American origin, attached to the numerous Christian religious institutions. Most are not citizens of Israel although some are long-term residents.

A third group, less clearly identifiable and of yet unknown proportions, consists of the myriad of Christians who have immigrated to Israel in recent years, particularly from Russia, the countries of the former Communist bloc (and also from Ethiopia) within the waves of Jewish immigration. They receive citizenship on arrival.

A fourth group consists of the tens of thousands of foreign workers (many from the Philippines, Latin America, Eastern Europe and Africa), most of them Christian, who have found employment in Israel. Although the vast majority may be considered a temporary population, among the foreign workers there are those who have established families, speak Hebrew and seem to be establishing a more permanent presence in Israel.

Jewish Israelis often seem to give priority in their perception of Christians and Christianity to the Catholic Church. In fact, it often seems that the Pope is perceived as leader of all Christians and that the diversity of Christian Churches and groups goes unnoticed. This was particularly evident in the March 2000 pilgrimage of Pope John Paul II to the Holy Land. Secular Israelis, in particular, were fascinated by the Holy Father and many attitudes and issues about Christians and Christianity surfaced during this visit. It must be stressed though that there is a wide diversity on all issues in Jewish Israeli society and a presentation of attitudes towards any subject certainly risks being stereotypical. What will be outlined here is necessarily an over-simplified picture of Jewish Israeli attitudes towards Christians and Christianity.

General attitudes to Christianity

The pilgrimage of John Paul II should not be underestimated in its profound impact on Jewish Israeli attitudes towards Christians and Christianity. A prominent Israeli journalist described the visit in these terms:

> He has left behind a series of pictures that will not be quickly forgotten: Catholic Christianity standing at attention to the strains of Hativka (the national anthem), Catholic Christianity standing up before the Palestinian refugees and announcing that it is on their side, Catholic Christianity descending from the Popemobile into Heikhal Shlomo, the seat of the Chief Rabbinate and shaking the hands of the rabbis, Catholic Christianity entering the gates of Jewish sovereignty, the President's House, Catholic Christianity at Yad Vashem and at the Western Wall.[2]

The Pope's moving addresses and, even more importantly, his symbolic acts—his visits to the Western Wall, to the chief rabbis, to the president and to Yad VaShem—were followed with close attention. These acts drove home for many Jewish Israelis, as never before, that the Catholic Church and many other branches of the Christian Church have evolved in their attitude to Jews and Judaism, having worked hard to eradicate certain Christian traditional teachings of contempt for Jews and Judaism.[3] One Jewish Israeli activist in Jewish–Christian dialogue commented: 'Following the Pope's recent pilgrimage it will be easier for Jewish Israelis to understand that Christianity is not only a negative phenomenon in history but that it is a positive redemptive force.'[4]

---

[2] *HaAretz* (Ari Shavit, 'The road to reconciliation'), 27.3.2000.

[3] The Anti-Defamation League published a full page statement in all the important Israeli newspapers acclaiming the 'historic visit to the Jewish state' and informing the public of the 'Pope's views on Israel, Judaism and the Shoah', underlining the profound changes in Catholic Church teaching.

[4] Y Landau quoted in 'Envisioning the Future of Jewish Christian Relations in Israel', *Service international de documentation judéo-chrétienne* XXXIII, 3 (2000), 10.

I will mention here some of the dominant general attitudes, which are still widespread, but at the end I will present some perspectives for change that were heralded during and after the Pope's visit.

First and foremost, there is a problem of *general ignorance.* Jewish Israelis tend to have little knowledge of Christianity in general and also little knowledge of the Christian minority that lives in their midst. The Hebrew press pointed to this ignorance about Christianity in the time leading up to the Pope's visit.[5] In a survey of attitudes carried out just before the papal visit, it was shown that many Israelis were unaware of any common ground between Christianity and Judaism.[6] In a study of the education system, it was shown that Jesus is hardly mentioned at all during the twelve years of elementary schooling.[7] Many Jewish Israelis have never consciously met a Christian Israeli or a Christian Palestinian. Some would not even know that there is such a thing as a Christian Israeli or a Christian Arab.

Secondly, there is the problem of *a monochromatic reading of the historic relations* between Jewish and Christian Europeans. The little Jewish Israelis do know about Christianity and Christians relates directly to the negative side of the history of Jewish-Christian relations in Europe. Two national museums, Yad VaShem (the Holocaust Museum) and Beth HaTefutsot (the Diaspora Museum) tend to focus predominantly on the dark side of Christian intolerance of Jews and point directly to the link between Christianity and Nazism. Visits to these museums are integrated into the Israeli educational curriculum. Little distinction is made between Christian and European national identities or between manifestations of modern anti-Semitism and Christianity at large. Debates within the Catholic Church like those concerning the canonisation of Pius XII and Edith Stein or the establishment of the Carmel at Auschwitz perpetuate the perceived link between Christianity, especially Catholicism, and the Holocaust. In addition, Christians are suspected of being missionary, desirous of converting Jews whenever possible. Interestingly, even today many Jewish Israelis have a more positive attitude towards Islam than towards Christianity, Islam still being widely perceived as a religion that

---

[5]   See in particular the article of Orna Coussin, 'It is time for Israelis to learn that Jesus was Jewish', *HaAretz*, 23.12.1999.
[6]   Survey conducted by Hanoch and Rafi Smith for the Elijah School, 15.3.2000.
[7]   See Coussin in *HaAretz*, 23.12.1999.

offered a relative tolerance to Jews in history when compared with Christianity.

Thirdly, there is a problem of *traditional Jewish hostility towards Christianity*. The general ignorance about the basic elements and history of Christianity builds upon a relatively widespread religious anti-Christian polemic. When Jesus is mentioned he is most often called Yeshu (a rabbinic acronym for 'May his name and memory be erased') instead of Yeshu'a or Yehoshua (Jesus-Joshua). Mythic fabrications about his birth and career as contained in polemical tracts like *Toldot Yeshu* (an early rabbinical anti-Christian tract) are known. These polemical inventions are often repeated even by well-meaning, educated Jewish Israelis. They have inherited them from tradition without questioning them (or being questioned about them). Traditionally, Islam is considered closer to Judaism than Christianity. Islam is seen as monotheist, respectful of Law and having a history of tolerance for Jews whereas Christianity is perceived as polytheist, idolatrous, antinomian and profoundly anti-Jewish.

Fourthly, this all goes hand in hand with a *fascination about Christianity* in its more traditional and exotic forms among secular Jewish Israelis. On Saturdays (the secular Israeli day-off) the traditional monasteries are swamped by visitors who seek out the atmosphere of 'overseas' right at home. This is part of a general secular Jewish Israeli fascination with non-Jewish and esoteric spirituality whether Buddhism, Hare Krishna, New Age sects or Christianity. This fascination is usually for a Christianity as 'other-worldly' as possible, celibate monks and nuns often swathed in monastic garb, chanting angelically, in unknown languages, in incense filled and dimly lit churches.

Fifthly, there is the inescapable issue of the *denominational ('ethno'-centric) nature* of Israeli society and state. The majority of Israelis are Jews[8] and many perceive society and state as being of an intrinsically Jewish character. The Jewish character of the state is propagated by official Zionist ideology and through the use of national symbols (the flag, the anthem, etc.) which are drawn exclusively from the Jewish tradition. This is true for Israelis who regard Jewish identity as primarily religious as well as many of those who are secular Jews. Christians and Muslims are in the same boat when it comes to this fact, that the defining

---

[8] According to the 2003 official Israeli statistics, 81 percent (5.4 million) of Israelis are Jews, 19 percent (1.3 million) are non–Jews of whom 82 percent are Muslim, 9 percent are Christians and 9 percent are Druze.

characteristic of belonging in the country is predominantly Jewish rather than Israeli. Discrimination based upon denominational identity (Jewish or 'non-Jewish') is widespread and moulds attitudes as well as motivates official policy in many cases. Discrimination affects funding of all services, holding public office, buying land, rights of residence, education, development, etc.

Finally, the creation of a Jewish majority state in Israel has begun to influence Jewish attitudes towards non-Jews in a more positive way too. The *self-confidence of a majority* liberates some Jews to interact with non-Jews in general and Christians in particular in less self-defensive and more interactive and dialogic ways. Some Jewish Israelis are becoming more aware that ignorance and prejudice are not helpful in understanding the Jewish relationship with Christians and the Christian world. It is becoming more acceptable to challenge both the monochromatic reading of history and traditional anti-Christian attitudes in a search for a new approach towards Christianity in general and the Christians in Israel in particular. I will develop some of these aspects later.

One might conclude in general terms though by saying that Christianity and Christians are generally perceived as foreign and extraneous to the Israeli reality.

Attitudes to specific issues concerning Christianity in Israel

Israel attributes great importance to denominational identity (Jewish, Christian, Muslim, etc). The state itself is defined as Jewish and despite extensive guarantees of democracy and equality for all citizens within a series of basic laws,[9] in practice those who are not Jews are considered at best marginal in the society and at worst as outsiders. Very few Christians, Arab or expatriate, have managed to achieve positions of prominence in Jewish Israeli society.[10] In general, the Christian presence is restricted to

---

[9] The State of Israel has no constitution. Basic freedoms are rooted in the Declaration of Independence. Orthodox Jews have resisted the formulation of a constitution, arguing that Jewish Law is that constitution.

[10] One of the rare examples is the Christian Arab author Anton Shammas who writes in Hebrew and is considered one of the most innovative writers of Hebrew today. Shammas now lives in the US. There have been some noted expatriate figures who are Hebrew-speakers and have held positions within academic and scientific institutions; the best known case is that of Marcel Dubois, OP. who served for many years as head of the

closed-off communities, which are formed according to culture, language and rite. Here I will deal with Jewish Israeli attitudes concerning a number of issues which are of direct concern to Christians in Israel: a) religious freedom, b) the 'new' Christian Israelis, c) Christian positions on the Israeli-Arab conflict and d) Jewish-Christian dialogue.

Freedom of religion

Israel does guarantee extensive religious freedom and there is no religious persecution in the State of Israel.[11] At the same time, there are a number of issues that are cause for concern in the general Jewish Israeli attitude to religious freedom.

Jewish Israelis are generally proud that the State of Israel is a Western-style democracy and that it guarantees religious freedom to all its citizens. The claim is often made that Israel is the only Western-style democracy in the Middle East. At the same time, religion plays a central role within the formal apparatus of state. This is because of an agreement, known as the *status quo*, reached by the Zionists and the Jewish orthodox community in 1948, and according to which religious authorities play a central role in the personal status of every citizen. Many Jewish Israelis are painfully aware of the limitations of the *status quo*. The system was created within the context of a struggle between Jewish 'secularists' and Orthodox Jews regarding the exact character of the 'Jewish' state. The civil and political system in Israel today remains under constant pressure as a result of this continuing conflict. In the resulting denominational system, denominational communities (Jewish, Muslim, Christian, Druze, etc.) are granted extensive autonomy, but every individual, like it or not, belongs to a community defined along religious lines, and the clerics of that community control his or her personal status. The system, partly inherited from the Ottomans and partly based upon the idea that Israel is a 'Jewish' state, limits the freedom of individuals especially on issues of personal status, marriage, registration of children, divorce, burial etc. In

---

Philosophy Department at Hebrew University. Another Dominican, himself a Jew by origin, Bruno Hussar, OP, was the founder of the Israeli Jewish-Arab peace village of Neve Shalom.

[11] For an Israeli perspective on religious freedom see R Lapidoth, 'Freedom of Religion and Conscience in Israel' in R Lapidoth and O Ahimeir (eds.), *Freedom of Religion in Jerusalem*, Jerusalem Institute for Israel Studies, 1999, 3-46.

fact, the Israeli political system in its present form does not allow for the separation of religion and state, so fundamental to most Western-style democracies.

It is interesting to note, in this context, that Christians enjoy more freedom in the selection of their leadership than any other religious community. Jewish, Muslim and Druze religious leaders and functionaries are selected by state officials whereas Christian religious functionaries are selected by and from within their own Church organs. Whereas Jewish, Muslim and Druze religious functionaries are bureaucrats of the state and receive state stipends, Christian clergy remain outside the structures of state bureaucracy. Within the realm of education and healthcare, Christians have retained their network of private schools and hospitals, receiving certain subsidies from the state whereas no such parallel private education or healthcare facilities have been developed for Muslims or Druze.

It should be noted that Jewish Israeli attitudes toward the entirety of the 'non-Jewish' population in Israel are affected by the definition of the state as 'Jewish'. There is discrimination, both legal and social, against non-Jews, particular against the Arab citizens of the state and the Christian Arab citizens among them.[12] I am not referring here to the population in the Palestinian territories who are struggling for political independence but rather to that population that is, by definition, Israeli, living within the borders of Israel since 1948, having full citizenship. The tension between a state which is 'Jewish' and/or 'democratic' is debated continuously among Jewish Israelis but the reality of second-class citizenship is lived by the population defined as 'non-Jews', predominantly Arab in its composition. Many Jewish Israelis are generally unaware that the lack of separation between religion and state is also a major impediment to the full guarantee of civil and political rights for Israel's non-Jewish citizens, Christians included.[13]

Although attitudes and even official policies towards Christians sometimes seem to be based upon specifically anti-Christian prejudices, many Jewish Israelis are very sensitive to the issue of maintaining good relations with the West and most particularly with the US and cautious

---

[12] For a detailed analysis see I Lustick, *Arabs in the Jewish State: Israel's Control of a National Minority*, University of Texas Press, Austin, 1980. See also (in Hebrew) *Erets Aheret*, no. 16 (May-June 2003) on the Arab citizens of Israel.

[13] One important study is R Gavison, *Israel as a Jewish and Democratic State: Tensions and Opportunities*, HaKibbutz HaMeuchad, 2000 (Hebrew).

about harming Christian interests. In general, Western countries are often perceived as Christian and good relations with them are seen as connected to Israeli treatment of local Christians. Specifically anti-Christian policies and laws have been rare, yet certain steps have been taken to restrict religious freedom. In 1970, the Israeli Law of Return, which grants automatic citizenship to Jews from the Diaspora who immigrate to Israel, was amended in order to prevent converted Jews from receiving automatic citizenship.[14] The debate about who is eligible for automatic Israeli citizenship under this Law has not ended and, since the 1970 amendment, further debates have been conducted about Jews who define themselves as Messianic believers in Jesus. In 1977, an anti-missionary law was passed, limiting traditional Christian missionary activity. A more recent proposal to enact restrictions on the distribution and even possession of the New Testament was scuttled due to extensive outside pressure, particularly from pro-Israeli evangelical groups in the US. Israel has known sporadic violent attacks against Christians and Christian places of worship by extremist Jewish groups. Groups that are suspected of being missionary have been particularly targeted. This anti-Christian (and anti-'non Jew') sentiment seems to be increasing in some circles because of the general context of fear and suspicion generated by the present violence and political crisis. However, violent acts that target Christians are generally presented as acts of marginal individuals.

The claim of guaranteed religious freedom goes hand in hand with the claim that Israel guarantees freedom of access to the Holy Places. This is often taken as a basis for Israeli demands to administer the Holy Places of not only Judaism but also of Christianity and even Islam within the territories occupied by Israel after the 1967 War.[15] The pervasive idea is that only Israel has guaranteed freedom of access to the Holy Places. This is often based upon the additional claim that access to the Holy Places was restricted under Jordanian rule in Jerusalem. Although Jewish Israelis insist that freedom of access to the Holy Places is guaranteed

---

[14] The law was ammended following the court case involving Carmelite Father Daniel Rufheisen, a converted Polish Jew, who asked for Israeli citizenship under the Law of Return. His request was refused by the Supreme Court in 1962. The 1970 amendment added to the definition of a Jew as someone 'born of a Jewish mother', the new distinction of not belonging to another religion.

[15] For coverage of a document circulated by an official of the Israeli Ministry of Foreign Affairs to the Israeli participants in the Camp David negotiations concerning the Holy Places, see *Kol HaIr* (Hebrew), 14.7.2000.

and this is generally scrupulously upheld for foreign Christians, freedom of access has been severely restricted for both Christian and Muslim Palestinians on what has been defined as security grounds. It is not uncommon to meet young Christians from Bethlehem who have never visited the Church of the Holy Sepulchre in Jerusalem, 20 minutes away, because freedom of movement for Palestinian Arabs from the Palestinian territories has been drastically limited for long periods of time. Limiting access of Muslims to the Aqsa Mosque has been at the centre of much of the violence in these past years. A further problem is the refusal of Israeli bureaucrats to grant entry visas to some diocesan seminarians, clergy and religious who come to study in the Holy Land or serve the institutions there. This is particularly the case for those from the surrounding Arab countries.[16]

The sensitivity to Israel's reputation as a guarantor of religious freedom only marginally influences attitudes to Christian Arabs. Towns at the centre of Christian consciousness like Nazareth and Bethlehem were indeed treated with special care by the Israelis when they were occupied in 1948 and 1967 respectively. However, the rural Christian Palestinian Arab population, far from the important Christian sites, met with the same fate as their Muslim compatriots. Christian Arabs were an integral part of the exodus of refugees particularly from Galilee and from the major Palestinian towns like Jaffa, Haifa, Acre, West Jerusalem, Ramleh, Lydda, Bisan etc. Yet it would be true to say that Israeli Jews are often more 'embarrassed' by acts of hostility committed against Arabs when they happen to be Christian. In the recent events in the Palestinian territories this was clear in the way that the Israeli press presented the repeated bombardment of Beit Jala, a town with a large Christian population. Many Israeli commentators insisted that the town was suffering because of the Muslims who came from out of town and used the town to force the Israelis to bombard Christian homes and churches.[17]

Israeli policy and attitudes towards the Christian Arabs in Israel are marked by attempts to fragment them according to denominations (Orthodox, Catholic, Protestant etc.) and to separate Christians in general

---

[16] This state of affairs endangers the continuity of Christian institutional life particularly for the Roman Catholic Church as Jerusalem is the center of a diocese that includes Jordan. The diocesan and Franciscan seminaries have numerous vocations from Jordan and these young seminarians are often refused visas.

[17] See, for example, Hila Altschuler in *HaAretz* magazine, 22.12.2000 or *Kol HaIr* (Hebrew), 4.5.2001.

according to their extraction, non-Arab expatriates or Arabs. Christian Arabs are also encouraged to separate themselves from their Muslim and Druze neighbours by underlining denominational (Christian) rather than civic-national (Arab or Palestinian) identity. Many Jewish Israelis seem to feel more comfortable talking about Muslim, Christian and Druze minorities rather than about an Arab (or Palestinian) minority in Israel. One of the most effective means of fragmenting the Arab minority by the state has been the imposition of military service on certain denominational groups. For example, since the early 1950s the Druze have been enlisted in the army and later certain Bedouin tribes were also subject to compulsory military service. Israeli officials have repeatedly formulated the idea of enlisting Christian Arabs into the army and although compulsory military service has never been imposed there are increasing numbers of Christian Arab youths who have been enlisted. The two main incentives for these youths are the high unemployment in the Arab sector and a strong sense of denominational identity when there are tensions with Druze or Muslim neighbours. The attempts by Arab civic leaders and intellectuals to combat denominational fragmentation and to forge national unity on the basis of Arab (or Palestinian) identity is repeatedly undermined by active state involvement in the fanning of denominational fragmentation. Most recently this has been seen in the official state positions on the construction of a mosque by a group of Muslim activists alongside the basilica in Nazareth.[18]

Jewish Israeli officials have often courted the expatriate Christian presence in Israel in order to promote Israeli interests. There are special areas of interest that motivate Israeli courtship of Christian religious leadership. Firstly, there is the issue of foreign pilgrim groups that visit the Holy Land. The desire to be perceived as trustworthy custodians of Christians and Christian Holy Places means that Israel is particularly interested in influencing as much as possible the Christian pilgrim groups that visit the Holy Land. There has been a long and unresolved struggle regarding who has the rights to lead these pilgrim groups during their sojourn in the Land. Needless to say Israeli-trained Jewish guides and Christian Arab guides do not tend to present the history of the Land, the

---

[18] For the details of this controversy see D Christiansen, 'Nazareth journal' in *America*, 4/182 (12.2.2000), 8-13. Finally, after extensive US pressure, the construction of the mosque was forbidden and its foundations were destroyed in 2003.

Christian presence in the Land and the present conflict in the same light. Secondly, the Israelis have continually co-opted expatriate Christians living in Israel for official 'information' campaigns overseas. The use of expatriate clergy as semi-official Israeli spokespeople has drawn mostly on the Protestant and Evangelical Churches but a number of Catholics have been mobilised too. Thirdly, the various traditional Churches (particularly the Greek Orthodox, the Armenians and the Franciscan Custody of the Holy Land) own extensive property all over Israel. Israel, which gained control over the extensive Muslim religious endowment land in 1948, has continuously tried to gain control strategic parts of this Church land too. The factor of land has been particularly evident in the Israeli attitude towards the Greek Orthodox Church, a major landowner in Israel, which is still led by almost totally Greek expatriate bishops despite the fact that the faithful are overwhelmingly Arab.

The context of the continued hostilities between Israel and her neighbours certainly explains to some degree the attitudes to and limitations on religious freedom described above. At the same time, the fact that Israel is by definition a denominational state, defined as 'Jewish' in both popular opinion and by law, means that Israel is not yet the state of all its citizens and this constitutes a certain obstacle to the full realisation of religious freedom.

The 'New' Christian Israelis

There is a new and little-known Christian reality in Israel today, the myriad of new Christian immigrants, mostly from the former Soviet Union (and some from Ethiopia). As most of these immigrants have identified themselves in some way as Jews on entering the country, it is extremely difficult to know how many Christians there are among them and what is the nature of their religious identity. A figure published for 1999 illustrates the reality of this phenomenon: out of about 86,000 new immigrants that year, 53 percent were not Jewish according to Jewish Law (i.e. did not have a Jewish mother) and 38 percent did not even have a Jewish father.[19] The official statistic of 2001 did include this population by stating that a total of 225,000 new Israelis were not

---

[19] See *HaAretz*, 31.1.2000.

registered as Jews because they were not Jewish according to Jewish religious law. Of these, though, only 25,000 were registered officially as Christian.[20] These trends have led many Orthodox Jews to propose amending once again the Law of Return in order to guarantee the Jewishness of those who are receiving citizenship in the country. Others are proposing new processes by which this large population of non-Jews might be formally incorporated into the Jewish people by individual or mass conversion or some other process of civil incorporation.[21] Israeli identity cards, carried by all citizens, registered 'nationality' (Jewish, Arab, Druze, etc.) rather than 'civic identity' (Israeli) until 2002. In that year, the Ministry of the Interior, controlled at that time by an Jewish Orthodox political party, after a conflict with the judiciary, refused to recognise the legitimacy of certain conversions to Judaism and annulled the registration of nationality on the identity card.[22]

Population statistics that traditionally broke down the population into Jews, Muslims, Christians, Druze etc., now have an additional breakdown of the ostensibly Jewish population into Jews and non-Jews. This has created a new category in the public mind 'the non-Jewish Jewish new Israeli'. These 'new' Israelis sometimes wear crucifixes under their shirts, hide icons in their bedrooms, put up Christmas trees at Christmas time and one of their major representatives, the former government minister Yuri Edelstein, a newly observant Jew, is the son of a Russian Orthodox priest of Jewish origin. The reality of a non-Jewish or even explicitly Christian immigrant community in Israel living among the Jewish Israeli population is not new. Since 1948, Christians, particularly from Eastern Europe, have found their way to Israel within the waves of predominantly Jewish immigration. In the past, the vast majority of these Christians have had close family links to Jews and either assimilated into the (secular) Jewish population or left Israel for other countries. It

---

[20] See *HaAretz*, 17.9.2001. Those not registered as Jewish or Christian are registered as Russian, Ukranian, etc. Some, it was revealed, have no registration at all on their identity cards (see *HaAretz*, 17.1.2000). The 2002 statistics counted 27,000 official Christians among the new immigrants. According to Dr Z Khanin of Bar Ilan University the number of self identified Christians is slighter higher than the official statistic (see *HaAretz* [Hebrew], 11.6.2002 and *The Jerusalem Report*, 26.8.2002, 22).

[21] See the fascinating discussion (in Hebrew) in the issue of conversion to Judaism in *Eretz Aheret*, no. 17 (July-August 2003).

[22] Identity cards issued after this date still have a place for nationality (*le'om*) but it is left blank by the issuing authorities.

does seem though that those who have arrived within the very large waves of immigration, about one million immigrants in the past ten years, and who are Christians are in Israel to stay and many are not losing their Christian identity.

Clandestine communities have been formed (evangelical Protestant, Orthodox and Messianic) and many Israeli Jews realise that it is becoming increasingly important to deal with the issue. Many of these Christians live in towns and neighbourhoods that are defined as Jewish. Many hide their Christian identity and even tend to adopt external Jewish identity markers in order to fit in. The children of these immigrants often hide their Christian identity at school and some of these children, who have explicitly Christian names, have been renamed by their parents or by school authorities. It is not uncommon for these Christians to pass through the Jewish rites of passage in order to pass as Jews, their children are circumcised, they are often married in Jewish ceremonies and many are buried in Jewish cemeteries. As non-Jews cannot be officially buried in Jewish cemeteries, there are now 'civil' cemeteries in which those who are explicitly non-Jewish can be buried with no religious rites.

Clearly, the state has promoted the mass immigration to Israel in order to increase the Jewish (by definition non-Arab) population of the state as part of the 'demographic struggle' with the Arabs. The emissaries who were sent to promote immigration did not have strict scruples about the 'Jewishness' of candidates for immigration but on arriving in Israel those who are overtly Christian have met obstacles to the preservation of their religious identity.[23] In one illustrative case, for example, two Ethiopians who frequented Christian prayer services were threatened with expulsion from the country on the basis of having claimed to be Jewish and yet prayed as Christians.

Clearly, Jewish Israelis hope that the majority of these Christians (particularly those who have family ties with Jews and who are not overtly believing or practising Christians) will assimilate themselves into the Jewish majority. Even in the time of Ben Gurion, the first prime minister of the state, he considered the possibility of mass conversions of different populations to Judaism. Yitzhaq Ben Zvi, the second state president, was well known as an ethnographer who sought out different ethnic groups

---

[23] For a description of the work of these emissaries see the article of Yossi BarMuha, 'The Sixteenth Tribe of Israel has been discovered,' *HaAretz*, 8.8.1997.

who might be descended from the Ten Lost Tribes of Israel and even proposed that the Druze in Israel were one of these peoples.[24] There has been a limited academic debate on the exact religious identity of the Ethiopian Falashas. Most Israelis have accepted without questioning that this group should be considered fully Jewish, even if the Orthodox rabbis were very reluctant to do so and have tried to forbid inter-marriage between Jews and Falashas without the Falashas undergoing a ceremony that affirms rabbinic Judaism.[25] In 1999, the State established a Joint Institute for Jewish Studies which promotes formal conversion for new Israelis who are not Jewish. The institute is an official government body and is staffed by representatives from different streams of Judaism.[26] 250,000 immigrants to Israel who are not considered Jewish according to Jewish Law are envisioned as the target population of this institute. In 2000, about 4,600 immigrants were converted to Judaism.[27]

Small groups of Christian immigrants have tried to establish permanent institutional frameworks in order to guarantee Christian survival and one of the best known of these groups is the *Œuvre de Saint Jacques* ('Work of St James'), founded in the 1950s. The *Œuvre* has Hebrew speaking Catholic communities in the main cities of Israel. In August 2003, the presiding prelate of the *Œuvre*, Dom Jean-Baptiste Gourion, the Benedictine abbot of the monastery in Abu Ghosh, near Jerusalem, was named an auxiliary bishop to the Latin Patriarch of Jerusalem. This step gave unprecedented exposure to the community of Hebrew-speaking Catholics. In an interview in an Israeli daily, the new bishop explained that part of his new task was 'to build relationships with those of the Christian immigrants who seek such a relationship with the Church.' According to the paper, the new bishop called on the Israeli establishment to stop trying to convert the non-Jewish immigrants.[28] Alongside the Catholic expression, the Orthodox Church has also named a pastor for

---

[24] See *HaAretz*, 3.1.1999.
[25] Public debate in Israel still rages over the fate of the Falasha Mura, Ethiopian Falasha who adopted official Christianity. Some of the Falasha Mura have relatives in Israel and many seek to immigrate to Israel. For details on the Falasha and Falasha Mura see the articles of Yair Sheleg in *HaAretz*, 4.3 and 6.3.2003
[26] For background to this institute see 'The Birth of Israel's New Jews', *The Jerusalem Report* 29.1.2001.
[27] See *HaAretz*, 24.12.2000.
[28] *HaAretz* (Hebrew), 14.10.2003

the mainly Russian Orthodox Christian immigrants.[29] Evangelically linked groups of 'Messianic Jews' have sprung up too, recently reinforced by their outreach to the tens of thousands of Russian and other Eastern European Christians who have found their way to Israel as immigrants or as foreign workers.[30]

In all of this, the questions for the state are numerous. Among them, one might ask:

—Who is a Jew? There is a general confusion regarding the identity of this new group of Christian Israelis. Some do have Jewish ancestry. Are they 'Jewish Christians'? Many Jews find this term offensive.

—Who is an Israeli? Is Israel a Jewish state? What does this mean in terms of integrating these Christians? Can the children of these Christians be educated as Christians? What would this type of education entail within the context of a Jewish majority? Can Hebrew be used as a medium of Christian instruction?

It should be mentioned in this context that Jewish Israelis who convert to Christianity (or any other religion) are free to do so according to a basic law which deals with religious freedom. There is only a very small number of such cases and whereas conversion to Christianity is odious to all traditional Jewish sources, these Christians of Jewish origin remain Jews for the purposes of the state unless they explicitly seek to change this identity. Most conceal their religious identity to some extent although some have entered religious orders and communities.

In addition to the 'new' Christians who are Israeli citizens, there is an important presence of Christian foreign workers from Eastern Europe (Poland, Romania, Ukraine, etc.), South America, Africa and Asia (particularly Philippines and Sri Lanka). Although most of these workers are in Israel on limited work contracts, there are some who clearly hope to stay on in a country considered substantially more affluent than their countries of origin. These foreign workers are served by the

---

[29] For the Russian Orthodox community and the work of Father Alexander Winogradsky see 'The New Israelis' by Lauren Gelfond in *The Jerusalem Post* magazine, 1.11.2002.

[30] See *The Jerusalem Report* 11.8.2003, 17-19. For an excellent survey of the Messianic Jewish communities, see K Kjaer-Hansen and B Skjott, *Facts and Myths: About the Messianic Congregations in Israel*, Caspari Center, Jerusalem, 1999.

traditional churches (Orthodox, Catholic, Protestant) to some degree but have also established a new and as yet fragile presence in Israeli cities where previously there was no visible Christian presence. In Israel it is extremely difficult to attain citizenship as a non-Jewish expatriate,[31] however some of these foreign workers stay on illegally, marry in Israel and have children here. In fact, the presence of a large foreign worker population is one factor that Israel has in common with many other countries in the Middle East and throughout the world.

The Israeli-Palestinian conflict

Within the context of the conflict between Israelis and Palestinians and the broader Israeli-Arab conflict, there is a consistent Jewish Israeli attempt to seek foreign Christian support based upon the historic and often troubled relations between Jews and Christians. In addressing Christians about the present conflict, Jewish Israelis often insist on the following:

> —True repentance for the history of Christian anti-Semitism necessitates support for Jewish aspirations today, including Jewish political aspirations.
> —The Biblical heritage, shared by Jews and Christians, unequivocally supports the Jewish God-given right to the Land, a Land which is at the centre of the Jewish religion, like Rome for Catholics and Mecca for Muslims.
> —The Jews are a bastion of Western democratic and liberal political and cultural presence in the Middle East, the only guarantee of religious freedom and access to the Holy Places.

However, Jewish Israelis often think that Christians are by definition foreigners. There is a general ignorance among Jews in Israel about local Arab (and Jewish) Christians. Many Jewish Israelis think that Arabs are by definition Muslims. According to this perception, Christians are perceived as foreign also to Arab culture and have been consistently persecuted by Muslims. The popular version of the events in Lebanon is

---

[31] Whereas Jews are granted citizenship automatically under the provisions of the Law of Return and can retain their previous citizenship, non-Jews who make application have to wait many years and eventually have to give up their original citizenship.

often used to predict direly what the fate of Christians in the Muslim Arab world will be. This often leads to a position, sometimes formulated by Israeli government officials, that the Christians need Israeli protection from supposed Arab or Muslim aggression.[32] This motivated a certain Israeli policy towards the Christians in Lebanon during the Israeli invasion there and is used in order to justify Israeli claims to sovereignty over parts of the Old City of Jerusalem—the claim is that the Christians will not be safe in a Palestinian state.

Some Jewish Israelis tend to think that the whole world is against the State of Israel and that includes the local Christians. Despite this rather monolithic attitude, a distinction is often made among pro-Palestinian, neutral and pro-Israeli Christian positions. The traditional Churches, Orthodox, Catholic and Protestant, are considered pro-Palestinian. The reasons given by some Israeli officials for this supposed pro-Palestinian position are:

—Muslim pressure on local Christians in particular on Arab Christians.
—The Christian Arab desire to prove that they are as loyal as Muslim Arabs to the national cause.
—The indigenisation of the Christian leadership that has led to the mixing of religion and politics as Christian Arab nationalists have gained key leadership positions in the traditional Churches.

The Israeli government has consistently opposed the indigenization of the local Church leadership. The Israeli state has an understandable preference for expatriate Christians as representatives of Christian interests. The degree to which the Christian community is headed by expatriate Europeans or Americans is also often considered the extent to which it might be friendly towards Israeli political interests or at least be indifferent to the Arab-Israeli conflict. Until recently, foreign

---

[32] See the important article of Danny Rubinstein 'Who will defend the Christians' in *HaAretz*, 13.9.2000 and the strident response of Father Raed Abusahlieh in *Al-Quds*, 24.9.2000. Also, Danny Rubinstein, *HaAretz*, 6.11.2001 and Nitzan Horowitz, *HaAretz*, 30.12.2001. A video cassette, entitled 'Holy Land: Christians in Danger', has recently been circulated in France. It argues that Christians are being persecuted by Muslims in the Palestinian territories and that the Israeli Army defends Christians.

Christians controlled all Church institutions and even now constitute an important part of Church personnel within many of these institutions. The Greek Orthodox Church is still exclusively controlled by expatriate Greek bishops.[33] This creates great tension between the hierarchy and the faithful. Most other traditional Church hierarchies (Roman Catholic, Anglican, Lutheran etc.) have undergone extensive indigenisation. Local Christian Church leaders who have adopted a more political discourse and taken stands on peace and justice are consistently condemned by state officials. A few Christian leaders have been accused of terrorist activity and have been imprisoned, exiled or placed under various restrictions.[34]

Among the various evangelical Protestant Churches and even in some still limited Catholic circles there is a trend known as Christian Zionism. Evangelical fundamentalist groups, which are attracted to Israel because of its Biblical significance, are increasingly present in Israel. Their strong support for even rather extremist Zionist positions goes hand in hand with a barely concealed missionary drive towards the Jews. Whereas some Jewish Israelis welcome the political support, these groups are kept at arm's length by many because of their missionary agenda. They are primarily encouraged to influence the foreign policy of their own countries (particularly the USA) through their lobbying. The subject of Christian Zionism has been of some concern to the local Christian Churches as the Christian Zionists have often spoken out in support of Israeli political claims in the name of all Christians. In addition, many of these Christian Zionist groups seem to encourage local indigenous Christians not only to throw in their lot with Israel, but to deny their own Arab identity, express hostility towards Islam and often to emigrate.[35]

---

[33] See the extensive coverage of the election of the new Greek Orthodox Patriarch, Ireneos I, in 2001 in the Israeli press (eg. *Jerusalem Post* 16.9.2001, *HaAretz*, 1.9.2002.

[34] The Anglican Revd Elia Khoury was accused of terrorist activity and expelled in 1969, The Greek Catholic Patriarchal Vicar of Jerusalem, Hilarion Cappucci, was convicted of gun running for the PLO and condemned to prison in 1974 (and released after extensive Vatican intervention in 1977), Greek Catholic Revd Fawzi Khoury was accused of belonging to a terrorist organization and briefly imprisoned in 1983 and both he and Anglican Revd (now Bishop of Jerusalem) Riah Abu al-Assal were subject to severe limitations on their freedom of movement in the 1980s. More recently the Greek Orthodox Father Atallah Hanna (an Israeli citizen from Galilee was questioned by the police and had his travel documents confiscated (see *HaAretz*, 23.8.2002).

[35] For Christian Zionism see the illimunating series of five articles by Donald E Wagner in the Lebanese *Daily Star*, 7.10, 8.10, 9.10, 10.10 and 14.10. 2003.

Jewish-Christian dialogue

Jewish-Christian dialogue has been increasingly important in Europe and the US in the past decades. In Israel, the dialogue is hardly at the centre of Jewish Israeli consciousness due to the fact that most Jewish Israelis rarely meet identifiable Christians in their day-to-day lives. Yet, some Israelis do recognise the importance of dialogue with Christians.[36] Israel's insistence that it is at the centre of the Jewish world today has meant that there has been an increasing attempt by Israeli Jews to take leadership roles in the official and institutional Jewish-Christian dialogue internationally. Some themes of this dialogue include:

—How is the Bible read? How can Christians become more aware of their 'Jewish' roots?
—What is anti-Semitism? What is its link with anti-Judaism?
—How did the Holocaust come about? Is the attitude to the Jews in certain New Testament passages anti-Jewish?
—What is the significance of the State of Israel for the dialogue? What are Christian attitudes to Zionism?
—How can Christians reformulate their theological discussion about Judaism and Jews in order to promote respect for Jews and appreciate God's 'ongoing covenant with Israel'?

Within the dialogue, Jews are often expected to teach Christians and help them change. For the moment, this is rarely mutual. Within these frameworks the Jewish side is perceived as the embattled minority whereas the Christian side is perceived as the dominant majority.

In Israel there are numerous organisations that promote inter-religious dialogue and recently they have been searching out more and more indigenous (i.e. Muslim and Christian Arab) partners in dialogue.[37] In almost all these organisations, Western (often foreign born) Jews or

---

[36] In the former Israeli government, a minister in the government, Rabbi Melchior, was made responsible for contacts with the Christian world as well as being responsible for Jewish Diaspora affairs.

[37] The *Guide to Interreligious and Intercultural Activities in Israel* (published by the Interreligious Coordinating Council in Israel, 2000) lists about 67 organisations working in dialogue.

expatriate Christians are the dominant figures. This often means that the agenda for dialogue is the same as that used in Western countries where Jews are the minority. However, within the State of Israel the Jews are the dominant majority and this is a major change in the meeting between Jews and Christians in the Israeli context. Unfortunately, this fact has not yet been assumed within the Jewish-Christian dialogue in Israel. In Israel, with Jews no longer an embattled minority but a dominant majority, the dialogue must now include an evaluation of the experience of the Israeli reality from a Christian point of view. Jews often insist on this, pointing out that Christians must deal theologically with the return of Jews to their Land and their empowerment there. According to this view, such a Christian reflection on Israel will overturn deeply rooted Christian ideas about the perpetual wretchedness of the Jews because of their rejection of the Christ.[38] This is not a one way reflection, though as a Christian reflection on the reality of Israel as a state brings to the forefront the voices of those Christians who live in Israel.

Unfortunately, there is almost no dialogue between the indigenous Jews and indigenous Christians in Israel. Within the Pastoral Plan of the Catholic Churches in the Holy Land, the result of a five-year synod which ended in 2000, a ground-breaking document calls for the nurturing of exactly this kind of dialogue.[39] In fact, an agenda that could be imagined for just such a Christian Arab-Jewish Israeli dialogue is substantially different from that which is proposed for Europe or the US:

—What has been the experience of the 'non-Jewish' minority within the Jewish state? How has the Israeli state dealt with issues of pluralism? democracy? religious freedom? What are the patterns of co-existence, co-operation, domination, discrimination, prejudice?
—How does one read the history of the Holocaust, Zionism and the establishment of the State of Israel within the context of this dialogue? What is the future of the Palestinian people?
—How can Judaism and Christianity (and Islam too) contribute to the values of democracy, pluralism, justice and peace in Israel?

---

[38] See David Hartman in *HaAretz*, 25.4.2000.
[39] See 'Assembly of Catholic Ordinaries in the Holy Land', *The General Pastoral Plan*, n. 13 'Relations with believers of other religions', see 'Our relationship with Jews,' 153-157.

—What role does the Bible play within the political context of the State of Israel?[40]

—This particular type of Jewish-Christian dialogue also gives rise to its own theological issues. What is the Christian understanding of the election of Israel, the connection between Israel and the Land of Israel? What does the Christian commitment to peace and justice imply within the Israeli-Palestinian context?

There are other elements of the Jewish-Christian dialogue which are particular to the Israeli context and cannot be overlooked. First and foremost, Jewish-Christian dialogue in Israel is faced with the reality of Islam and the Muslim world. The State of Israel exists at the centre of the Islamic Arab world. Whereas Christians involved in dialogue often argue for the privileged place of the Jews in dialogue, Jewish Israelis often see Muslims as equal, if not preferred, partners in the dialogue. Not only is Islam seen as religiously and theologically closer to Judaism, but the long centuries of Jewish co-existence with Muslims were often less traumatic than the centuries spent with Christians. In addition, almost half the Jewish Israeli population (those with their cultural roots in Morocco, Iraq, Yemen, Egypt, Tunisia, Algeria, Syria, Lebanon, Iran, Turkey etc.) share a cultural world with Muslim and Christian Arabs. This shared heritage is still evident among these Jews in Israel (particularly in liturgical, folk, musical and culinary culture). Arabic was a very significant language of Jewish life for hundreds of years during which dialogue with Muslims and Christians was conducted with greater or lesser ease depending on the period.

A second element particular to the Israeli context is that religion, in and of itself, is often perceived as contributing more to the tensions between communities than to understanding and co-existence by many Jewish Israelis. Among both Jewish Israelis and Christian Arabs, many participants in the inter-religious or inter-cultural dialogue are either marginal in their own communities or non-practising. Many practising (Orthodox) Jews are not interested in dialogue and the various streams of Liberal Judaism are still small and marginal on the Jewish Israeli scene.

---

[40] See the Pastoral Letter of HB Mgr Michel Sabbah, Latin Patriarch of Jerusalem, *Reading the Bible Today in the Land of the Bible*, November 1993.

Within Jewish-Christian dialogue, Jews have been particularly helpful to Christians in an evaluation of the price paid for the Christian embrace of political empowerment at the time of Constantine and thereafter. At present, the dialogue in general, and Israeli-Christian Palestinian dialogue in particular, can and should help Jews in evaluating the current embrace of power by contemporary mainstream Judaism in the context of Zionism and the State of Israel.

Conclusion: perspectives and new trends

In conclusion, it must be repeated that Jewish Israeli attitudes are far from static and many factors might transform these attitudes in the period ahead. I would like to briefly mention, in conclusion, a few of the perspectives and new trends in Jewish Israeli life that might alter attitudes towards Christians and Christianity which have been presented above.

The need for education

Ron Kronish, a leading Israeli activist in Jewish-Christian dialogue, commented on the Pope's visit, saying that the visit was a watershed. 'What particularly impressed me was what we call "the great educational opportunity". During the month before the Pope's visit and during the visit itself there was more about the Pope and Christianity on television and in the newspapers than during the last 30 years.'[41] Some Jewish Israelis are becoming aware that ignorance about Christianity is an impediment, on the one hand, to general culture and, on the other hand, to respect for the local Christian community. Slowly small steps are being taken to rectify this. The Hebrew University of Jerusalem inaugurated a Centre for the Study of Christianity in 2000 although no departments for the study of Christianity or the New Testament exist in any of the Israeli universities. There is still much work to be done, particularly the work of collaborating with local Christians, especially Christian Arabs, in the task of educating the general public.

---

[41] R Kronish, quoted in 'Envisioning the Future of Jewish Christian Relations in Israel,' *SIDIC* XXXIII, 3 (2000), 10.

Israeli secularism

The increasingly strident formulation of an Israeli secularism which has begun to challenge the Jewish identity of the state will undoubtedly affect attitudes to non-Jews. The question, already clearly formulated, is whether the state will recognise 'Israeli' identity as the only defining civil identity, thus privatising denominational identities, particularly 'Jewish' identity. The de-denominationalisation of the State is not only presented by some Israelis as a condition for the democratic character of the state but also a condition for putting an end to discrimination against Christians and all non-Jews.[42] However, it should be pointed out that important work on developing a religious Jewish *modus vivendi* with democracy, pluralism and modernity is also being carried out in Israel.[43]

Re-reading Islamic-Arab Culture

It is difficult to imagine how peace with the Arab world might influence the Israeli scene. Undoubtedly, peace will necessitate a re-reading of Islamic-Arab civilisation from the Israeli point of view. The reclaiming of Jewish rootedness in the Islamic-Arab world is already current in certain circles and is expressed in the rebirth of interest in Arabic-speaking Judaism, a dominant form of Judaism of the early medieval period. Jews and Christians have both played an important role in the formation of Islamic Arab civilisation and their continued existence within the larger context of the Middle East depends on a re-evaluation of their respective relationships with the diversity of Islamic Arab culture. Within the context of Middle Eastern Arab Islamic civilisation, Jews and Christians have found a common language on many issues in the past and this might indeed be a fruitful context for a dialogue today as well.

---

[42] See the cover story 'Who gets to be an Israeli,' *The Jerusalem Report*, 30.6.2003, 12–15.

[43] One of the most important Jewish think-tanks in Israel is the Shalom Hartman Institute, founded by Orthodox rabbi and philosopher, David Hartman. This institute confronts the problems of the encounter between Judaism and modernity in all its forms including the encounter with other faith traditions.

Hebrew speaking Christians

Since the inception of Zionism, some have asked whether a Hebrew speaking Christianity will emerge. This has begun and the seeds have been sown. Byzantine Orthodox, Roman Catholic, Protestant and Messianic congregations where Hebrew is the language of prayer and communication already exist. The coming years will certainly be decisive in the emergence of a Hebrew-speaking, Israeli Christian community that is not only inculturated in Israel but also integrated within the Jewish milieu in the country. This community might then act as a bridge with Christianity in general and with the Christians of the Arab world in particular.

Re-reading the history of Jews and Christians

Jews as a dominant majority in Israel are faced with the challenge of re-writing and teaching their own history.[44] Embattled minority Jewish communities have focused almost exclusively on the negative and dark sides of the relationship between Christians and Jews, particularly Christian failings in this relationship. Part of the challenge is now to uncover more positive modes of relationship that did and do exist. In addition, the prickly subject of anti-Christian trends in Judaism must be dealt with in order to facilitate a change in Jewish attitudes towards non-Jews in general and Christians in particular.[45]

Finally, it is important for Christians in Israel to engage themselves fully in the whole range of social, educational, political and cultural domains in order to transform the attitudes of the majority society. It is my experience that many Jewish Israelis are ready to be challenged in their attitudes and perceptions. A Christian witness to the values of peace and justice on the one hand and unity, democracy and human rights on the other hand has a significant role to play in Israeli society today.

---

[44] A pioneering series of books on this subject has already been published by the Open University. The head of the editorial board is Dr Ora Limor. The first volume was published in 1993.

[45] A recent contribution to this kind of study is the book by the Hebrew University historian, Israel J Yuval, *Two Nations in Your Womb: Perceptions of Jews and Christians*, 2000, (Hebrew).

RESPONSES OF THE CATHOLIC CHURCH TO ISLAM IN THE PHILIPPINES FROM THE SECOND VATICAN COUNCIL TO THE PRESENT-DAY

Rocco Viviano SX

Introduction

2 April 2003: a bomb in Davao City, Mindanao, Philippines, kills thirteen people and injures thirty-five. President Arroyo-Macapagal declares the city under a state of 'lawless violence' and orders police and military intervention.[1] It is just another incident in the violent confrontation between the Government and the *Abu Sayyaf* rebel forces.

Siocon, Zamboanga del Norte, Mindanao, 4 May 2003: twenty-eight people are killed in a clash between the rebel forces of the MILF and the Government military.[2] The President calls off GRP–MILF peace talks scheduled for the 9-11 May Malaysia.[3]

18 July 2003: a ceasefire agreement between the Government and the MILF seems promising for peace in Mindanao.[4] Hardly, however, can it be saluted as the solution to the problem, which will require much harder and painstaking work.

In the 21st century, reflection on interreligious dialogue cannot be purely academic. Globalisation has changed the nature of the interaction between cultures and religions: communities and individuals struggle to negotiate between local and global identities. One effect is an increase in local conflicts worldwide.[5]

---

[1] Cf. F B Zamora, 'State of 'lawless violence' declared in Davao', in *The Philippine Daily Inquirer*, 2 April 2003, in Internet: http://www.inq7.net, accessed 21 July 2003.

[2] Cf. 'Twenty-two dead in attack on Zamboanga del Norte town', in *The Philippine Daily Inquirer*, 4 May 2003, Internet: http://www.inq7.net, accessed 21 July 2003; 'Government troops in massive hunt for MILF rebels', in *The Philippine Daily Inquirer*, 5 May 2003, Internet: http://www.inq7.net, accessed 21 July 2003.

[3] Cf. 'Malaysia hopes RP Government, MILF resume peace talks', in *The Philippine Daily Inquirer*, 6 May 2003, Internet: http://www.inq7.net, accessed 21 July 2003.

[4] 'Church Mediates a Cease-fire in Southern Philippines', in *Zenit*, 21 July 2003, Internet: http://www.zenit.org, accessed 21 July 2003; 'MILF chief to head peace talks with Government', in *The Philippine Daily Inquirer*, 19 July 2003, Internet: http://www.inq7.net, accessed 21 July 2003.

[5] Robert Schreiter, *Reconciliation. Looking towards Mission in the 21st Century*, Lecture delivered at the Missionary Institute of London, 21 March 2002.

The Philippine conflict, which is generally perceived as a religious clash, is one example, calling the Church to reflect on interfaith relations amid an urgent need for reconciliation and peace.

It is insufficient for the Church to take a position vis-à-vis those who are directly responsible for the violence—the MILF and *Abu Sayyaf* are only symptoms of a deeper problem, whose roots need to be identified and addressed to reach an adequate and constructive response.

This study considers how, during the past four decades, the Catholic Church in the Philippines has become increasingly aware of the complexity of the problem, and how it has approached interreligious engagement with the Muslim community both to respond to the local conflict and to fulfil its missionary mandate.

Firstly, the historical roots of the Philippine conflict are examined to allow better appreciation of the progress that the Catholic community has made regarding its encounter with the Filipino Muslim community after Vatican II, from the point of view of the teaching and of the praxis. The final part identifies some elements emerging from the ongoing dialogue, which reveal the direction in which it is desirable that the Church in the Philippines continue its engagement with Islam. The aim is not just peace in the country, but also a relationship of greater trust and friendship, within which it is possible to learn from one another's faith experience and commitment.

The roots of the conflict: the background to Christian-Muslim relations in the Philippines

The relationship between Christians and Muslims in contemporary Philippines is complex: the result of historical, geographical, social and economic factors.

This section briefly presents the encounter between the Catholic Church and the Islamic community in the Philippines in past and recent history. This will provide an important basis to understand the present situation better.

Christianity and the Catholic Church in the Philippines

The Philippines is often described as 'the only Christian Country in Asia' because of its majority Christian population.[6] This is the result of the past four centuries of the country's history, particularly marked by its belonging to the Spanish Empire.

The Catholic Church arrived in the Philippines with the Spaniards and was formally established when the diocese of Manila was created, as suffragan to Mexico (6 February 1579). Its first bishop was the Spanish Franciscan Domingo Salazar. After 16 years, the diocese of Manila was raised to an archdiocese, and three new dioceses were created as suffragan to it (Nueva Caceres, Nueva Segovia and Cebú). In 1910 the diocese of Lingayen was created by separating twenty-six parishes from Manila. Other dioceses began similarly: San Fernando (1948), Imus and Malolos (1961) and Antipolo (1983).[7]

The southern part of the Archipelago, where the Muslim presence is mainly concentrated, remained under the jurisdiction of the bishop of Cebú until the diocese of Jaro was created in 1985. The Church started developing in Mindanao-Sulu with the institution of the diocese of Zamboanga in 1910, comprising the Island of Mindanao and the Sulu archipelago. The dioceses of Cagayan de Oro and Surigao were formed before World War II, whilst before the end of Vatican II a number of prelatures were constituted and Jolo was made an Apostolic Prefecture first (1953) and then Vicariate (1958). More jurisdictions were instituted after the Council, including the Marawi Prefecture (1974), created as an element of reconciliation in the troubled area of the south.[8]

This rapid overview demonstrates that, although Christianity reached the southern Philippines around 1565, the Catholic Church in the Mindanao-Sulu area is relatively young.[9]

In 1968, in line with Vatican II developments, the Catholic Bishops' Conference of the Philippine (CBCP) became the official organisation of the local hierarchy. Its origins may be traced back to the Catholic Welfare Organisation, which started in 1945 to provide spiritual aid to the Filipino Catholics and to coordinate their activities. The CBCP

---

[6] Peter G Gowing, 'The Muslim Filipino Minority', in *Crescent in the East*, Humanities Press, Atlantic Highlands, NJ, 1982, 211.

[7] 'Archdiocese of Manila', in Internet: http://cbcponline.org/jurisdictionn/manila.html, accessed 12 June 2003.

[8] See note 98.

[9] William LaRousse, *A Local Church Living for Dialogue*. Muslim-Christian Relations in Mindanao-Sulu (Philippines), 1965-2000, Pontifical Gregorian University, Rome, 2001, 19.

was restructured in 1972 and its new constitution received Holy See approval in 1988.[10]

The CBCP participates in the Federation of Asian Bishops' Conferences (FABC), which brings together the bishops of the Churches of Asia in fellowship and mutual cooperation. The FABC began in November 1970, when 180 Asian bishops gathered in Manila for Pope Paul VI's visit. It is a sign of the spiritual affinity, common moral and religious values, patterns of socio-political conditions and similar challenges and concerns among the various Asian Catholic Churches.[11]

In recent years, a key event in the life of the Catholic Church in the Philippines was the celebration of its Second Plenary Council, held in Manila from the 20 January to 17 February 1991. It represents an important development in the Church's process of self-understanding, particularly with regard to interreligious relations.[12]

Islam in the Philippines: Muslims in the contemporary Philippines

According to the Catholic missionary Sebastiano D'Ambra, the Philippines constitutes an exceptional case in the history of Islamic expansion, whereby a large majority has become a small minority in a particular country.[13] In fact, at present, Muslims make up only 4–5 percent of the entire population of the Philippine Republic (65 million), alongside 90 percent Christians (83 percent Catholics and 7 percent Protestants) and 5 percent followers of other religions. The majority of Muslims (94 percent) are concentrated in the western and southern area of Mindanao,

---

[10] Cf. Lope C Robredillo, 'The Challenge of the Times and the CBCP's Responses: A Historical Essay on the Catholic Bishops' Conference of the Philippines', in Catholic Bishops' Conference of the Philippines, *Pastoral Letters 1945-1995*, compiled and edited by Pedro C Quitorio III, Peimon Press, Manila, 1996, xix-xlviii. Cf. also Internet: http://www.rc.net/philippines/cbcp/cbcphist.htm, accessed on 21 June 2003.

[11] The documents of the FABC are available in Gaudencio B Rosales and C G Arevalo (eds.), *For all the Peoples of Asia*, Claretian Publications, Quezon City, Manila, 1992. Cf. also Internet: http://www.fabc.org.

[12] Cf. Secretariat of the Second Plenary Council of the Philippines & Catholic Bishops' Conference of the Philippines, *Acts and Decrees of the Second Plenary Council of the Philippines. 20 January-17 February 1991*, Catholic Bishops' Conference of the Philippines, Manila, 1992.

[13] Sebastiano D'Ambra, 'Christian-Muslim Relations in the Philippines', in *Islamochristiana*, Vol. 20, 1994, 180.

in the Sulu archipelago (Basilan, Sulu and Tawi-Tawi), and in the southern part of Palawan.[14]

Thirteen ethnic groups generally associate themselves with the Muslim religion.[15] Among these groups, the Maranao, Maguindanao and Tausug make up 76 percent of the Muslim population; the Sama, Yakan, Sanguil and Badjao constitute 21 percent, while the residue six groupings constitute the remnant 3 percent.[16]

Muslims constitute the majority population in the five southern provinces of Tawi-Tawi, Sulu, Basilan, Mindanao and Lanao del Sur.[17]

Protestant missionary and scholar Peter Gowing observed that, '2.2 million Filipinos who embrace Islam are not a minority' if considered as part of the Southeast Asian Region, which is the most densely Muslim-populated area of the world. Muslim Filipinos are aware of being part of this majority, having more in common with the Muslim Malays of Indonesia and Malaysia (in terms of religion, culture and of historical, political and economic relationships) than with the Christian Malay majority of the Philippines.[18]

Arrival of Islam in Southeast Asia and in the Philippines

Therefore the process of Islamisation of the Philippine Archipelago cannot be studied in isolation, but needs to be considered against the background of the spread of Islam across Southeast Asia.[19] Oscar Evangelista defines trade as the 'dynamic force' in 'the courtly centres and coastal principalities' of Southeast Asia at the time of the arrival of Islam. According to him it is possible to trace the presence of Arab traders in that region back to the 5th century AD. In the 13th century, however, the southern area of the Philippines (along with Central and East Java, Bali

---

[14] William LaRousse, *A Local Church Living for Dialogue*, 12-13.

[15] Cf. *Ibid.*, 15; Sebastiano D'Ambra, 'Christian-Muslim Relations in the Philippines', 180.

[16] William LaRousse, *A Local Church Living for Dialogue*, 15-16.

[17] Peter G Gowing, 'The Muslim Filipino Minority', 211.

[18] *Ibid.* Cf. also Peter Riddell, *Islam and the Malay-Indonesian World*, London, C. Hurst and Co., 2000.

[19] Carmen Abubakar, 'Islam in the Philippines—The Moro Problem', in Asghar Ali Engineer, *Islam in Asia*, Vanguard Books, Lahore, 1986, 41; Oscar Evangelista, 'Some Aspects of the History of Islam in Southeast Asia', in Peter Gordon Gowing (ed.), *Understanding Islam and Muslims in the Philippines*, New Day, Quezon City, 1988, 16; Paolo Nicelli, *The First Islamisation of the Philippines*, Silsilah Publications, Zamboanga City, 2003, 15-16.

and the Moluccas) became an important centre for Arab Muslim trade.[20]

Islam came to Southeast Asia from the sub-Indian continent gradually, especially in areas strongly influenced by Hindu and Buddhist traditions. Evangelista identifies diverse factors to explain Islam's success in rooting itself in the region: firstly, it seems that Sufism favoured Islam's acceptance by local populations, on account of its capacity of integrating elements of other religious traditions, as well as with a more direct and emotional approach to spirituality. The second factor was political, as loyalty to the Islamic world constituted a possible political alternative to Hindu Majapahit and Buddhist Siam. Finally, at the time of European colonial expansion, acceptance of Islam was possibly a reaction against attempts to introduce Christianity into the region.[21]

Generally, the expansion of Islam in the Philippines paralleled its development in the Malay Peninsula and Sumatra.

A Muslim settlement in the Sulu Archipelago was probably started at the end of the 13th century by foreign traders who intermarried with members of the local ruling families, and possibly assumed some political importance. The *tarsilas*[22] mention Tuhan Masha'ika and Tuhan Maqbalu as the important figures of this period. The possible arrival of Sufi missionaries (*makhdumin*) in the late 14th century also encouraged the local population's receptivity to Islam. A second Muslim wave came from Sumatra in the early 15th century). By the mid 15th century the sultanate of *Sharif ul-Hashim* was established and Islam spread inland. By the early 16th century, thanks to increased contacts with Malaysia, Sulu became part of the wider *dar-al-Islam* in South East Asia. From Sulu, Islam moved to Mindanao (mid-15th century), which became the springboard for further expansion in the Philippine Archipelago. Towards the end of the 16th century, connection with Sulu and the Moluccas, especially through marriage alliances, contributed to deepen the process of Islamisation, also favoured by the reaction to Spanish attempts to extend their sovereignty and Christianity to Mindanao. Towards the end of the 16th

---

[20] Oscar Evangelista, 'Some Aspects of the History of Islam in Southeast Asia', 17.

[21] *Ibid.*, 18-21.

[22] The word *tarsila* is the Philippine adaptation of the Arabic *silsilah*, and among other meanings, designates a genealogical account to trace the chain (*silsilah*) of succession back to a mythical or religious leader. Cf. Nagasura T Madale, 'The Hejra Towards Muslim-Christian Dialogue: Problems and Options, in Nagasura T Madale, *Essays on Peace and Development in Southern Philippines*, Capitol Institute for Research and Extension, Cagayan de Oro City, 1999.

century, Islam was beginning to impose its rule in the Manila area, but the arrival of the Spaniards interrupted the process.

The expansion of Islam in the Southern Philippines was relatively slow. Its adoption, however, by part of the local population influenced their sense of identity and cohesion.[23]

Historical relations between Muslims and Christians in the Philippines
First Encounter: the Spanish Period (1565-1898)

Centuries of interaction between Christians and Muslims have shaped the attitudes which characterise present–day engagement.[24]

The first historical encounter between Muslims and Christians in the Philippines occurred with the arrival of the Spanish in the early 16th century. Although Ferdinand Magellan reached the Archipelago in 1521, Spanish hegemony in the newly discovered territories started with Miguel Lopez Legazpi in 1565.[25] The aims of the Spanish expedition were threefold: to find a channel of communication with the Orient, then controlled by the Portuguese;[26] to establish a platform for new commercial and missionary activities with China and Japan; and the Christianisation of local populations.[27]

According to Abubakar, the fact that the encounter between Filipino Islam and Christianity was mediated by Spanish Catholicism determined the 'tone and style' of the meeting. Burning in the minds of the Spanish *conquistadores* was the memory of the Moorish occupation of Spain ending with the Fall of Granada in 1492. When they realised

---

[23] Cesar Adib Majul, *Muslims in the Philippines*, University of the Philippines Press, Quezon City, 1999, 84; Carmen Abubakar, 'Islam in the Philippines—The Moro Problem', 44.

[24] Cesar Adib Majul, 'Muslims and Christians in the Philippines', in Kail C Ellis, *The Vatican, Islam and the Middle East*, Syracuse University Press Syracuse, NY, 1987, 310.

[25] Sebastiano D'Ambra, 'Christian-Muslim Relations in the Philippines', 182.

[26] Gowing writes that, 'The European discovery and conquest of the Philippines occurred in the context of this rivalry between Portugal and Spain for trade routes to the Orient. The conversion of the Philippines to the Christian faith must be seen against the background of Spain's sixteenth century role as the premier Catholic nation of Europe. Possessing the lion's share of the Iberian Peninsula, Spain was to inherit the Kingdom of Portugal at the end of the century.' (Peter Gowing, *Islands under the Cross*, 16-17).

[27] Peter Gowing, *Islands under the Cross*, 16-17.

that the newly discovered territories were inhabited by people who shared the same religion of their old Moorish enemy, they approached them feeling that they were involved in a new stage of 'the struggle fought between Christianity and Islam several hundred years before during the Crusades (11th to the 13th centuries) and during the *Reconquista* in Spain itself (12th to the 15th centuries).'[28]

The confrontation between the *Moros*, as the Filipino Muslims were called by the *conquistadores* on account of their religious connection to the Moors, and the Spaniards, who were identified with Christianity, fostered distrust, which was soon extended to the Christianised Filipinos of the northern islands, as they were involved in fighting the Muslim Filipinos on behalf of the Spanish colonisers during the three-century long Moro Wars. This constituted the beginning of 'the alienation that came to characterise Muslim-Christian relations' in the Philippines.[29]

Vis-à-vis the Spanish invasion, resistance was fierce: in fact while the Spaniards succeeded in driving the Muslims away from Luzon and Visayas, they never succeeded in controlling the Muslims of Mindanao and Sulu.[30]

The scars left by the Moro Wars are still visible today. To subjugate the Moros, forcing them into Catholicism, the Spanish pursued the destruction and depopulation of Muslim villages, destroyed their commercial maritime activities by capturing and burning their sea craft, and rendered their islands uninhabitable, by cutting and burning their coconut and fruit trees. Moreover, many Moros were deported to Luzon and forced to convert to Catholicism. The response of the Moros was equally fearful: warriors would attack and destroy the villages of locals who had become Christians, and sell hundreds of them on the slave market of the East Indies.

The Spanish Catholics viewed Islam as a false religion from which the Moros had to be delivered,[31] while the Muslims fought to preserve their religion, way of life, land, their freedom and independence.[32]

---

[28] Carmen Abubakar, 'Islam in the Philippines—The Moro Problem', 45

[29] *Ibid.*, 48-49.

[30] Cf. Michael J Diamond and Peter G Gowing, *Islam and Muslims. Some Basic Information*, New Day, Quezon City, 1981, 77. Also cf. William L Yam, 'Islam in the Philippines', in, Cyriac K Pullapilly (ed.), *Islam in the Contemporary World*, Cross Roads Books, Notre Dame, Indiana, 1980, 361.

[31] Cesar Adib Majul, 'Muslims and Christians in the Philippines', 312-313.

[32] William L Yam, 'Islam in the Philippines', 360-361.

American rule and commonwealth (1898-1946)

With the Treaty of Paris (1898), Spain ceded the Philippines to the USA. The Americans initially adopted a policy of non-imposition, and seemed to be aware of the differences and deep-rooted hostility between the Christianised Filipinos of the north and the Muslims of the South.[33] After succeeding in breaking Muslim resistance through military intervention, they adopted a 'politics of attraction', 'designed to uplift the Muslims politically and economically' and integrate them into the Philippine nation.[34] A period of calm followed the treaty signed by General Bates and the Sultan of Sulu on 20 August 1899.

However, whilst Government's efforts were aimed at bringing both communities to cooperate for their mutual benefit, American officials saw Mindanao as the 'land of promise'. Settlers from other islands, mainly Christians from Luzon and the Visayas, were introduced in what the Moros considered their ancestral land. They soon felt that this policy of migration was aimed at taking control of their area, and perceived 'integration' as the imposition of a Christian government and the destruction of their cultural and religious identity.

When the Commonwealth period was inaugurated in 1935, as a transition period towards Philippine independence, the Muslim Filipinos were 'handed over to Christian Filipinos to be governed'.[35] The transfer of settlers in Mindanao was accelerated, and towns with Christian majorities appeared in traditionally Muslim areas. Following the old Spanish and American pattern, Christian Filipino officials regarded the Moros as inferior and as 'wards to be educated in a superior culture'.[36] Similarly, the Church looked at Mindanao-Sulu as an area for proselytising. In response, the Muslims harboured the same feelings of distrust and hostility of the past.

Independence: the first stage (1946-1968)

Independence was granted on 4 July 1946 and the Republic of the Philippines was born. Despite previous requests on the part of the Muslim

---

[33] Cesar Adib Majul, 'Muslims and Christians in the Philippines', 315.
[34] Michael J Diamond and Peter G Gowing, *Islam and Muslims. Some Basic Information*, 78.
[35] Cesar Adib Majul, 'Muslims and Christians in the Philippines', 312.
[36] *Ibid.*, 317.

Filipinos for their territories either to remain under American rule or to be granted independence as a separate state, the southern islands were incorporated into the new Filipino jurisdiction.[37]

Muslim Filipinos had long feared this as sanctioning the destruction of their own identity and culture. The sense of alienation already experienced under American rule deepened.[38] They resisted the Filipino Government as they had rejected previous foreign rulers.

During the first period of the Republic, the crucial issues were the question of the land (as part and parcel of the Government's policy of integration) and the gradual development of the idea of Moro secession from the Republic (as a Muslim Filipino response to that policy).

In 1954, responding to Muslim insurgencies over the issue of the land, the Government resolved to investigate the problem. The outcome was that Muslims did not identify themselves as Filipinos, nor feel part of the nation.[39] Unfortunately, the Commission for National Integration, created in 1957, failed because of the Government's lack of support,[40] and also because of Moro fear that integration would bring about the dissolution of their identity and way of life.[41] They still wished to be part of the Muslim Malay-Indonesian world.

In 1955 about two hundred Muslim Filipinos were granted scholarships for education at Al-Azhar University in Cairo, as part of the programme sponsored by Egyptian President Nasser.[42] This generated a movement of intellectual Muslim Filipinos which favoured the crystallisation of the 'Moro identity', and enhanced the long nourished quest for self determination and independence of the *bangsa*[43] *Moro*. Although it was perceived as an isolated episode, it was significant that in 1961, Ombra Amilbangsa from Sulu, presented a bill in Congress asking for the creation of an independent Republic of Sulu. This was followed by the short-lived Hajal Ouh revolutionary movement for the independence of Sulu, Basilan and Zamboanga, ending with the death of its founder at the beginning of the insurrection.[44]

---

[37] *Ibid.*, 318.
[38] Carmen Abubakar, 'Islam in the Philippines—The Moro Problem', 56.
[39] William LaRousse, *A Local Church Living for Dialogue*, 123.
[40] *Ibid.*, 123-124.
[41] Carmen Abubakar, 'Islam in the Philippines—The Moro Problem', 61.
[42] William LaRousse, *A Local Church Living for Dialogue*, 125.
[43] In Filipino, the term *bangsa* denotes the concept of nation and community.
[44] William LaRousse, *A Local Church Living for Dialogue*, 127.

Developments and status of Christian–Muslim relations from 1968

After the March 1968 massacre, when several Muslim recruits were killed within the military base of Jabidah, *datu*[45] Matalam of Cotabato announced the birth of the Muslim Independence Movement (MIM), for the creation of the independent Republic of Mindanao and Sulu.[46] Conflict was now open; violent clashes followed, from mid 1970 through 1971, between the Christian armed group of the *Ilagas* and their Muslim counterparts, the *Blackshirts* and the *Barracudas*.

The climate of violence offered President Marcos the opportunity to declare Martial Law, in September 1972. Consequent action aimed at disarming Muslims provoked clashes with the army. Against this background the Moro National Liberation Front (MNLF), led by Nur Misuari, came into prominence. The MNLF considered the Government insensitive to the Muslims and threatening their religion, culture and institutions, and saw political separation as the only solution.[47]

Soon the MNLF earned the support of the Conference of Islamic Ministers, which favoured their negotiations with the Filipino Government. The process led to the Tripoli Agreement, in 1976, in which the two factions reached a compromise: the MNLF shifting its objective from secession to autonomy, and the Government granting autonomy to the Muslim areas of the Republic.

The shift in the MNLF objectives caused the less moderate fringes of the movement to form the Moro Islamic Liberation Front, officially announced in 1984 by Salamat Hashim, former collaborator of Misuari. The MILF put emphasis on Islam and regarded itself as a religious movement, while considering the MNLF as secular.[48] An Islamic matrix is noticeable, whereby only Muslims can rule Muslims in *dar-al-Islam*.[49]

---

[45] *Datu* denotes the Filipino traditional community leaders.

[46] On the issue of Islamic separatism in the Southern Philippines, cf. Eric U Gutierrez, *Rebels, Warlords and Ulama, A Reader on Muslim Separatism and the War in Southern Philippines*, Institute for Popular Democracy, Quezon City, 2000.

[47] Cesar Adib Majul, 'Muslims and Christians in the Philippines', 321.

[48] William LaRousse, *A Local Church Living for Dialogue*, 160–161.

[49] *Dar al-Islam* (House of Islam) is 'the whole territory in which the law of Islam prevails. Its unity resides in the community of the faith, the unity of the law and the guarantees assured to members of the *umma*.' (Cf. A Abel, 'Dar al-Islam', in H A R Gibb et al. (eds.), *The Encyclopaedia of Islam*, Brill; Leiden, Luzac, London, 1960, Vol. II, 127). By contrast, everything outside *dar al-Islam* which is not part of *dar al-'ahd* (House of the Covenant, i.e. allied nations), is *dar al-harb*, the 'House of War'.

Unfortunately the Tripoli Agreement was only partially implemented: whilst the cease-fire was observed immediately, it soon became evident that the Government had no intention of honouring the other commitments.[50] Marcos unilaterally announced the formation of the Autonomous Regions IX and XII, and called for a referendum regarding their structure.

To prove the sincerity of its intentions, the Government implemented projects to benefit Muslim Filipinos.[51] Many Muslims, and particularly the MNLF, regarded the Government's steps as palliatives seeking international publicity rather than the welfare of Muslim Filipinos.

In 1986, Marcos' removal from power created a 'breathing space' amid Christian–Muslim tensions. New President Aquino met Misuari, seeking a solution to the problems and the Jeddah Accord was signed in January 1987. Unfortunately this too yielded no meaningful result.[52]

Following other attempts, the Congress held a plebiscite over the issue of Autonomy: on 19 November 1989 only four provinces out of thirteen voted to be part of the Autonomous Region in Muslim Mindanao (ARMM).

The National Unification Commission[53] (NUC), formed by President Ramos in June 1992, resumed negotiations with the MNLF, and in September 1996 the final accord on the implementation of the Tripoli Agreement was signed.[54]

The NUC also attempted negotiations with the MILF. Talks were held in August and September 1996. An initial accord was signed on 7 January 1997 to cease hostilities and carry out further negotiations.

---

[50] Sebastiano D'Ambra, 'Christian–Muslim Relations in the Philippines', 188.

[51] In October 1976 the Agency for the Development and Assistance of Muslims in the Philippines was created; in February 1977, a Code was presented reflecting the *Shari'ah*, and the *Shari'ah* Court was established; in April 1977, the Manila Mosque was completed; in February 1978, the Philippine Pilgrimage Authority was launched; in July 1978, the Commission for Islamic Affairs was set up; in June 1980 an International Conference was held in Manila on the 600th anniversary of Islam in the Philippines and the 14th century of Hijra. (Cf. Peter G Gowing, 'Christian–Muslim Dialogue in the Philippines, 1976-1981', in *South East Asia Journal of Theology*, Vol. 23 No 1 (1982), 38-40).

[52] Sebastiano D'Ambra, 'Christian–Muslim Relations in the Philippines', 191.

[53] The NUC was set up as an advisory body to the peace process, on the basis of consultations with various sectors of society. (Cf. 'Profiles', in Mindanao State University's Research and Development Centre, *A First Step to Peace: Mindanao in Transition, Accord* Series, April 1999, also available on the Internet: http://www.c-r.org/accord, accessed 27 June 2003).

[54] William LaRousse, *A Local Church Living for Dialogue*, 171-178.

Despite the continuing hostilities between the MILF and the Government Military, peace talks continued and formal negotiations began on 25 October 1999. Hostilities persisted and violence escalated. On 17 March 2000 the Military attacked MILF's main camp at Abubakar, as well as others. In response, Salamat Hashim called for a *jihad* against the Government.

Another protagonist on the scene of Christian-Muslim engagement in the Philippine is the *Abu Sayyaf Group*. Reportedly, it started in 1991 and came into prominence in 1995 with a raid on the predominantly Christian town of Ipil, in Zamboanga del Sur. The group was founded by an Islamist, Abdurajak Janjalani, who had trained with radical groups in Egypt and studied in Libya, returning to the Philippines with an agenda for establishing an independent Muslim State.

Abu Sayyaf, which means 'bearer of the sword', believe that the only way to save Islam from succumbing to materialism is to eliminate any Western influence; they also assert that co-existence with unbelievers is not an option for Muslims. The group, which allegedly is connected with the wider radical movement within Islam and with other terrorist groups, is involved in notorious kidnapping for ransom, and uses violence to achieve its goals.

Abu Sayyaf opposes both MNLF and MILF. The fact that it functions in small autonomous units rather than a whole, makes negotiations more difficult. Although Janjalani was killed in a confrontation with the police on 18 December 1998, the activities of the group have continued.[55]

Given the complexity of the situation, talk about Christian-Muslim relations in present-day Philippines cannot be confined to the religious level, but necessarily involves the socio-political dimension. It is the inevitable consequence of how the relationship began and historically developed.

---

[55] For a detailed profile of the MNLF, MILF and Abu Sayyaf, and their activities, cf. Peter Chalk, 'Militant Islamic Extremism in the Southern Philippines', in Jason F Isaacson and Colin Lewis Rubenstein (eds.), *Islam in Asia. Changing Political Realities*, Transaction Publishers, New Brunswick, NJ, 2002, 187-222. Chalk argues that by 'implementing a sustained program for socio-economic growth and development' the Government of the Philippines could remove the civilian support-base to the MILF and Abu Sayyaf, thus removing their very *raison d'être* (*ibid.*, 211-212).

Catholic teaching on Islam and Christian Muslim relations in the Philippines

Since the Second Vatican Council, the Catholic Church in the Philippines has developed a deeper awareness of the presence of Islam and the importance of Christian-Muslim dialogue for better understanding of its own identity and mission.

This section considers how the Church in the Philippines has gradually responded to the interreligious challenge at the level of teaching. John Paul II's teaching on Islam in the Philippines is presented first, and then some of the documents of the local Church are explored, which best illustrate the above mentioned development.

John Paul II on Catholics and Muslims in the Philippines

Pope John Paul II has devoted much of his teaching to interfaith relations, with particular attention to Islam.[56] His attitude towards Islam is grounded on the vision inaugurated by the Second Vatican Council.[57]

From this perspective, despite the insurmountable difference regarding the identity and the role of Jesus Christ according to the two traditions, there exists a core of faith which is shared by Christianity and Islam which constitutes the foundation for joint endeavour to make the world more just and harmonious, where the dignity of every human being is respected and enhanced.

Usually, and especially in his pronouncements of the early years, John Paul II has shown remarkable openness to Islam and Muslims, alongside sincere desire for mutual understanding, deeper trust and esteem.

Within his general teaching on Christian-Muslim relations, John Paul II has also specifically addressed the context of the Philippines.

---

[56] Cf. Thomas Michel, 'Islamo-Christian Dialogue: Reflections on the recent teachings of the Church', in *Bulletin Secretariatus Pro Non-Christianis*, 59 (1985—XX/2), 177.

[57] Second Vatican Council, *Nostra Aetate* no. 3; *Lumen Gentium* no. 16.

The message to the Muslim Filipinos

In 1981 the Philippines welcomed John Paul II on his first pastoral visit. The memory of the violence of the 1970s was vivid, and the country was still ruled by President Marcos, who would be dismissed five years later.

On 20 February, the Pope met three Muslim leaders representing the Muslim Filipinos in Davao, Mindanao, and responded to their addresses with a message to all Muslim Filipinos.[58]

John Paul II's address presents some of the themes that recur in his general teaching on Christian-Muslim relations.

He mentions the 'brotherhood' between Christians and Muslims which is founded on the shared membership in the human family, created by God, and united in the effort to 'reach *Him* in our own ways, through faith, prayer and worship, through the keeping of his law and through submission to his designs.'[59] In the light of this, John Paul II stresses the particular bond between Filipino Christians and Filipino Muslims. Bonds of nationality, history, geography, culture unite them, as well as 'hope for a better future', which they are building together.[60]

Secondly, the Pope speaks of the importance of relationships based on mutual trust and esteem, which are necessary for the wellbeing of both Muslims and Christians. He indirectly refers to the historical conflict that has affected the Philippines since the first encounter between Christianity and Islam, observing that in the past their relationship 'has too often deteriorated, to the detriment of all concerned.'[61] This past, however, need not continue to be an obstacle to the betterment of present-day relationships.

---

[58] John Paul II *et al.*, '20 February: Davao Airport: Meeting with the Representatives of the Muslim Community', in *Bulletin Secretariatus Pro Non-Christianis*, 46 (1981), 6-11. The Muslim leaders, Mohammad Ali Dimapcro (for the Maranao), Simeon A Datumarong (for the Magindanao) and Albert-Ulama Tugung (for the Tausug), expressed their gratitude for the Pope's visit and highlighted its importance for the Muslim Filipinos.

[59] 'I deliberately address you as brothers'. Cf. John Paul II, 'To the Representatives of Muslims in the Philippines', in Francesco Gioia, *Interreligious Dialogue. The Official Teaching of the Catholic Church (1963-1995)*, Pauline Books and Media, Boston, 1997, (hereafter referred to as Gioia), no. 363.

[60] *Ibid.*

[61] *Ibid.*, no. 365.

Thirdly he mentions freedom founded on respect for human dignity, which demands not only justice but also love and mercy,[62] while the fourth element is co-operation for a more peaceful and just Philippine society. Both by recognising and encouraging the initiatives of dialogue that are already taking place, and by explaining the need for co-operation between Christians and Muslims as a necessary consequence of their shared 'religious framework', John Paul II focuses on the 'common willingness to build a more fraternal society.'[63]

Addresses to the bishops of the Philippines

On 12 October 1985, four years after his visit and one year before the overthrowing of Marcos, the Pope's message to the Philippine bishops centred on Christian-Muslim collaboration in educational and social activities. Alongside the fact that in many dioceses of the Philippines Catholics and Muslims live side by side, he acknowledged that 'here and there certain tensions have arisen in the area of political matters,' however he preferred to stress the ongoing joint work between Catholic and Muslim institutions, and the need for mutual respect.[64]

In 1990, in a very different political context the Pope called the Philippine bishops' attention to the necessity to work for Catholic-Muslim agreement on religious freedom in the Philippines. He acknowledged that 'interreligious relations between the two communities are generally marked by friendship and cooperation,' and that 'opportunities for dialogue on matters of common interest and on religious themes are not lacking.' Mutual respect must be fostered, based on 'the right of every individual to freedom of conscience', if Christians and Muslims are to be 'partners in building a society shaped by the values taught by God: tolerance, peace, and concern for the poorest and the weakest.'[65]

In 1996, the Pope's message centred on the 'special vocation' of the Church in the Philippines: 'to bear witness to the Gospel in the heart

---

[62] *Ibid.*, no. 366.
[63] John Paul II, 'To the Representatives of Muslims in the Philippines', in Gioia, nos. 365-367.
[64] John Paul II, 'To the Bishops of the Philippines on their Ad Limina Visit', Rome 12 October 1985, Gioia, no. 478.
[65] John Paul II, 'To the Bishops of the Philippines on their Ad Limina Visit', Rome 30 November 1990, Gioia, no. 696.

of Asia.' He called on all Catholics in the Philippines to be builders of peace and, to emphasise that dialogue is essential for peace building, he recalled his words to the Muslims in 1981: 'Dialogue is built upon trust, and trust presupposes not only justice but mercy.'[66]

Observations

While acknowledging the value of John Paul II's pronouncements on Islam and Christian-Muslim relations in the Philippines, it is also important to notice that the subject has not always been his main concern.

For example, on the occasion of his visit in 1981, except the message to the Filipino Muslims, all his other speeches never mention Islam or Muslims, or the conflicts in the South.

On his arrival, in fact, he saluted 'those who belong to non-Christian religions' in general.[67] In a different context, the Pope referred to the Philippines as a nation 'whose people has remained faithful to the Christian faith'; spoke of a 'clear national identity which is unequivocally Filipino and truly Christian,' and stated that the 'special qualities of the Filipino people originate from a solid Christian tradition of faith and love for their neighbour', paying no attention to the Muslim component.[68]Moreover, speaking of the bishops' concern for the poor of the country, he did not mention that, in proportion, the Muslim Filipino population is particularly poverty-stricken.[69]

Despite all, John Paul II's has clearly affirmed the need for better Christian-Muslim relationships in the Philippines. His stance signifies the Universal Church's acknowledgement of the presence of Muslims in the Philippines, as the enriching religious *other* whom the Catholic Church needs, in order to be itself.[70]

---

[66] Cf. John Paul II, 'To the Bishops of the Philippines on their Ad Limina Visit', 27 September 1996 in *Bulletin Pro Dialogo*, Vol 95 (1997), 175-177.

[67] 'Discorso del Santo Padre Giovanni Paolo II durante la cerimonia di benvenuto all'aereoporto internazionale di Manila', Manila 17 February 1981, Internet: http://www.vatican.va, accessed 15 July 2003. (My translation.)

[68] 'Messagio del Santo Padre Giovanni Paolo II al Presidente della nazione filippina', Manila 17 February 1981, Internet: http://www.vatican.va, accessed 15 July 2003. (My translation).

[69] 'Discorso del Santo Padre Giovanni Paolo II all'episcopato filippino e ai vescovi asiatici riuniti a villa San Miguel a Manila', Manila 17 February 1981, in http://www.vatican.va, accessed 15 July 2003. (My translation.)

[70] John Paul II, 'To the Representatives of Muslims in the Philippines', in *Gioia*, no. 367.

Especially significant is the fact that dialogue actually took place between John Paul II and the representatives of the Muslim community, showing the willingness on both sides to build a pluralistic and harmonious community of people of faith.

The Catholic Church in the Philippines and Christian-Muslim Relations
The Catholic Bishops' Conference of the Philippines

The teachings of the Catholic Bishops' Conference of the Philippines show a twofold gradual shift with regard to interreligious dialogue, Islam, the Muslim Filipino minority and their demands for self-determination. The first shift is from equating 'Filipino' and 'Christian' to realising that the Filipino nation is a culturally and religiously pluralistic society. The second regards the notion of dialogue: from the idea of 'negotiations aimed at ending conflicts' to the idea of 'engagement for building a culture of peace'.

Up until the early 1980s, the bishops' pronouncements reveal a certain lack of sensitivity towards the Muslim Filipinos, as they employ expressions like 'our people' and 'our nation' often referring to Christians, rather than to all Filipinos, and as they tend to identify the Philippines as a 'Christian country'.

In a letter of 1973, for example, despite explicitly addressing 'God's People and Fellow-Citizens', the bishops' still call the Philippines a 'Christian nation'.[71] This motif returns in 'Evangelisation and Development' issued the same year.[72] In the letter for the Marian year (1975), the bishops also state that, 'we consider ourselves the Christian country of Asia'.[73] A letter published in 1982, after the Pope's visit, referred once again to the country as 'a Christian nation' and, surprisingly,

---

[71] CBCP, 'On Plebiscite', January 1973, in Catholic Bishops' Conference of the Philippines, *Pastoral Letters 1945-1995*, compiled and edited by Pedro C Quitorio III, 360-361, (hereafter referred to as PL 1945-95). Cf. William LaRousse, *A Local Church Living for Dialogue*, 418.

[72] CBCP, 'On Evangelisation and Development', 4 July 1973, in *PL* 1945-95, 380.

[73] CBCP, 'Mary in Philippine Life Today', 2 February 1975, in *PL* 1945-95, 411.

overlooked the important meeting of John Paul II and the Muslim representatives.[74]

Despite all, during the 1980s the pronouncements begin to display a greater awareness of the Muslim presence and of the violent Christian–Muslim conflict in Mindanao. The letter, 'A Dialogue for Peace', published in 1983, acknowledged the urgency of dialogue and spoke of the Philippines as a pluralistic society, although, according to LaRousse, some of the language ('our people' and 'their faith') still seems to contradict the content. At this stage 'dialogue' is understood as between the Church and the Government and not with Muslims.[75]

The same year, however, in their letter on reconciliation the bishops specifically acknowledged people of other religions as fellow citizens and part of *the Philippine* nation.[76]

In 1984 a survey on the concerns of the Church in the Philippines, showed that interreligious engagement was not high in the scale of priorities. The same year bishop George Dion, of the Apostolic Vicariate of Jolo, published some of his Pastoral letters in a book entitled *Attitudes of Christians towards Muslims,* and circulated it among the bishops. He denounced Christian Filipinos' attitudes towards Muslims as distant from the teachings of Vatican II, and urged the episcopate to help Christians change those attitudes. He also pointed out the common error of identifying 'Filipino' with 'Christian', as revelatory of a need to broaden national consciousness.

During the 1990s the bishops took a more attentive posture. Documents display greater sensitivity to Muslims, greater awareness of the conflict in the South and stress the necessity to engage in serious dialogue to end bloodshed and suffering, and build a culture of dialogue.

In 2000, the CBCP addressed a letter of appeal for peace in Mindanao to the MILF, the Government, and 'all people of good will'. The document explicitly recognises Christians, Muslims and *Lumads*[77] as Filipinos, and calls for trust, respect and understanding between Muslims and Christians as the foundations for durable peace in the country.[78]

---

[74] CBCP, 'A Church Sent', 17 February 1982, in *PL* 1945–95, 559.
[75] CBCP, A Dialogue for Peace, 20 February 1983, in *PL* 1945–95, 568.
[76] CBCP, 'Reconciliation Today', 27 November 1983, in *PL* 1945–95, 574.
[77] Followers of traditional religion.
[78] Cf. William LaRousse, *A Local Church Living for Dialogue*, 432–433. CBCP, 'An Urgent Appeal for Peace in Mindanao', 6 July 2000, Internet: http://cbcponline.org, accessed 12 June 2003.

The Second Plenary Council of the Philippines

The Second Plenary Council (1991) provided a unique point of reference for the Philippine Catholic community seeking a renewed definition of its identity. Thirty-eight years after the First Plenary Council (1953), the 1991 event saw members of the hierarchy and laity embark on a joint endeavour to apply the conclusions of Vatican II to the particular context of the Philippines.

Besides a Conciliar Document, the Plenary Council also produced 132 Decrees, which formed the core of the National Pastoral Plan of renewal that followed. Although they are not mentioned in the Decrees, interreligious dialogue and Christian-Muslim relations are addressed several times in the Conciliar Document.

It explicitly considers the Philippine nation as pluralistic and Muslim Filipinos as an integral part of it.[79] 'Filipino' is no longer identified with 'Christian',[80] and there exist a 'Filipino matrix' that underpins Filipino identity regardless of religious adherence.[81]

Being viewed as a necessary component of the Church's task of evangelisation, interreligious dialogue is described as 'an imperative of mission.'[82]

The document openly acknowledges the existence of conflicts between Christians and Muslims, with which the Church has to deal and that can only be understood in the light of past history and within the broader context of Southeast Asia.[83] Past animosities still affect present relationships, therefore the Church has to 'be the first to start in undoing past effects of our mutual grievances.'[84]

Four tasks for the Church are identified: 'a deeper knowledge and appreciation' of their faith on the part of Catholics;[85] a movement 'towards openness in understanding the religious convictions of others;[86]

---

[79] Secretariat of the Second Plenary Council of the Philippines & Catholic Bishops' Conference of the Philippines, *Acts and Decrees of the Second Plenary Council of the Philippines. 20 January-17 February 1991*, Manila: Catholic Bishops' Conference of the Philippines, 1992, (hereafter indicated as PCP II), no. 111.

[80] PCP II, nos. 19; 114; 250–255.

[81] PCP II, no. 72.

[82] PCP II, no. 111.

[83] *Ibid.*

[84] PCP II, no. 115.

[85] PCP II, no. 113.

[86] *Ibid.*

having acknowledged the existence of an ongoing 'dialogue of life' between Muslims and Christians,[87] the Church has the duty to encourage such initiatives;[88] and finally, the Church should 'make a common cause with Filipino Muslims... on the fundamental issues of justice and development', paying particular attention to the fact that many Muslim Filipinos suffer from poverty and inequality.[89]

The document could have been more precise on certain issues,[90] nevertheless it affirms that interreligious engagement is essential for the definition of the identity and mission of the Church in the Philippines.

The Catechism of the Catholic Church in the Philippines

Approved and published in 1997, the Catechism was aimed at 'presenting the faith specifically for Filipino Catholics, taking into account the actual concrete situation, Filipino values, belief systems and culture.'[91]

Although it retains the linguistic ambiguity of 'the Philippines as the only Christian nation in Asia', the Catechism has the merit of bringing interreligious dialogue back to the attention of the Church, after it had been ignored in the National Pastoral Plan.[92]

Another important aspect, according to LaRousse, is that the Catechism makes a direct connection between the Sunday profession of faith (Creed) and interreligious engagement, bringing interreligious concern into every Filipino Catholic's everyday life.[93]

---

[87] PCP II, no. 114.

[88] PCP II, no. 115.

[89] *Ibid.*

[90] For example: 1) In section 10 it is stated that it was the implanting of the Christian faith that created the Philippine nation. The cognate idea of the Philippines as a Christian nation appears in section 18-19; 2) In section 251 the preferential option for the poor is affirmed, but there is no reference to the fact that the Muslim provinces are among the poorest provinces of the country; 3) Interreligious dialogue is not included among the 'special concerns' for a renewed evangelization, addressed in sections 216-237, while ecumenism is; 4) Interreligious dialogue and the study of other religions do not appear in connection with formation programs; 5) There is no mention of the role of schools in educating to mutual respect and esteem between people of different religions. (Cf. William LaRousse, *A Local Church Living for Dialogue*, 434-438).

[91] William LaRousse, *A Local Church Living for Dialogue*, 439.

[92] *Ibid.*, 441-442.

[93] *Ibid.*

Conclusion

After Vatican II the Church in the Philippines seriously reflected on Christian-Muslim relations. On the one hand, this development has been stimulated by the teaching of the Universal Church, and in a special way by John Paul II's attention to Christian-Muslim engagement in general and in the Filipino context in particular.

On the other hand, the reflection has involved both the hierarchy and the laity (e.g. the Second Plenary Council). As a result, the entire community has become more aware of its responsibility vis-à-vis the local Christian-Muslim conflict, as well as of the need to adjust the understanding of its own mission accordingly.

Responses to the conflict: Christian-Muslim encounters
Multiple responses

Since the 1970s, the violent conflict in the Southern Philippines has claimed about 125.000 lives.[94] There have been attempts on the part of the Government to address the conflict through political negotiations. The Church has promoted numerous initiatives at various levels.[95]

Religious congregations have played a very important role in promoting a spirit of mutual understanding between Christians and Muslims in Mindanao. Particularly significant has been the contribution of the Oblates of Mary Immaculate (in the dioceses of Cotabato and Jolo), especially through education in peace and dialogue. Their Notre Dame Schools have provided quality education to Christians and Muslims alike in full respect of each person's faith, fostering mutual esteem and trust.[96] The Claretians have had similar role in the diocese of Isabela (Basilan).[97]

---

[94] William LaRousse, 'Is Dialogue Possible?', in *Landas*, Vol. 16 no. 2 (2002), 274.
[95] For a detailed account of all initiatives, sponsored by both the government and other agencies, both at a national and local level, cf. Michael Fitzgerald, 'Christian-Muslim Dialogue in South-East Asia', in *Islamochristiana*, Vol. 2, 1976, 171-185 (with regard to the period 1962-1976), and Peter G Gowing, 'Christian-Muslim Dialogue in the Philippines, 1976-1981', in *South East Asia Journal of Theology*, Vol. 23 No 1 (1982), 37-48, (covering the years 1976-1981).
[96] William LaRousse, *A Local Church Living for Dialogue*, 446-450.
[97] *Ibid.*, 450-452.

At the ecumenical level, the role of Peter Gowing, of the Dansalan Research Centre in Marawi, has been outstanding. Among Catholics the work of Bishop Bienvenido Tudtud must be mentioned. He was the first leader of the Prelature of St Mary in Marawi, which was created when Pope Paul VI expressed his desire that the Church in Mindanao should engage in a specific 'ministry of reconciliation' between Christian and Muslims.[98]

Important was the creation of a Commission for Interreligious Dialogue within the CCBP in 1990, to promote interreligious engagement in the light of Vatican II and more recent documents of the Church, to support and connect existing initiatives, and to keep contact with the Pontifical Council for Interreligious Dialogue.

Among many initiatives and institutions for dialogue and peace, the *Silsilah Dialogue Movement* and the *Bishops-Ulama Forum* have made a highly significant contribution to Christian–Muslim dialogue and to the peace building process. Both started at a local level and have rapidly become important points of reference at the national level.

The Silsilah Movement: beginning and aims

Rooted in the missionary experience of Sebastiano D'Ambra PIME,[99] the Silsilah Dialogue Movement started on 9 May 1984, in Zamboanga City, to foster deeper understanding between Christians and Muslims. It seeks to bring people from both communities together to share the richness of their respective faiths and co-operate in the building of durable peace in Mindanao.

When Fr D'Ambra arrived in the Philippines in 1977, the Moro struggle in Mindanao had already begun.[100] The way Muslims and Christians approached one another because of deeply prejudiced mutual images,

---

[98] Cf. *ibid.*, 467–471. One expression of the ecumenical cooperation in Marawi is the Joint Catholic-Protestant Consultation on Christian Presence among Muslims that took place on 24-27 July 1978. The participants addressed a 'Communication' to both Christians and Muslims (Dansalan College and Prelature of Marawi, 'Joint Catholic-Protestant Consultation on Christian Presence among Muslim Filipinos: Communication', in *Occasional Bulletin of Missionary Research*, no. 3 January 1979, 31-32).

[99] The *Pontificio Istituto per le Missioni Estere* (Pontifical Institute for Foreign Missions) is a Society of Apostolic Life for the Mission, founded in Italy in 1850.

[100] Sebastiano D'Ambra, 'Silsilah Growth. From a Personal Experience to the Movement's Experience', in Internet: www.silsilahdialogue.org, accessed 24 June 2003.

profoundly touched Fr D'Ambra, who resolved to commit his life to the cause of reconciliation through dialogue between the two communities.

After immersing himself in the local language, culture and problems, he shared the simple life of a small community of Muslims. The *Silsilah Movement* sprang from a 'spiritual experience' that D'Ambra describes in these words:

> God was talking through my new Muslim friends, saying to me in the deeper part of my spirit that: 'He, the Lord, is the fountain and source of dialogue ... That ... changed my life and gave me the courage to take a lot of risks, and later, to start the Silsilah Dialogue Movement.[101]

The 'Silsilah Vision Statement' describes the spirit of the Movement:

> In the name of God, the source and fountain of dialogue, Silsilah envisions a life-in-dialogue for all Muslims, Christians and peoples of other living faiths in respect, trust and love for one another and moving together towards a common experience of harmony, solidarity and peace.[102]

The term *silsilah*[103] is used by the Sufis to describe their link of unity with Allah. The *Silsilah Movement* is founded on the conviction that it is possible for every person to rediscover the 'silsilah' that links them to God, whatever one's religious beliefs. This is possible because God initiates and sustains a dialogue with the entire humanity.

God 'reveals' his love for humanity in different ways (i.e. faiths). His style of dialogue, however, is always the same, and *Silsilah* intends to be a response to God's dialogue.[104]

Silsilah is meant to be the 'common house and family' for people of all faiths,[105] where, in the spirit of *silsilah*, all are encouraged to deepen their understanding of God's dialogue with them: Muslims are encouraged

---

[101] Sebastiano D'Ambra, 'Silsilah Growth'.
[102] Silsilah Dialogue Movement, 'Silsilah Vision. The Spirituality of Life-in-Dialogue', in Internet: www.silsilahdialogue.org, accessed 24 June 2003.
[103] Cf. present study, 10, footnote no. 17.
[104] Silsilah Dialogue Movement, 'Silsilah Vision. Spirituality of Life-in-Dialogue'.
[105] Sebastiano D'Ambra, 'Silsilah Growth'.

to re-appropriate the significance of the 'great jihad', the struggle for the purification of the heart, and Christians are encouraged to deepen their understanding of the Beatitudes.[106]

'Culture of dialogue' and 'life-in-dialogue'

The purpose of *Silsilah* is 'to promote a culture of dialogue', which implies 'life-in-dialogue with God, with oneself, with others and with creation', rooted in one's experience of faith.[107]

A 'spirituality of dialogue' is required: on the one hand, to sustain a process of personal transformation according to the values of one's own faith; on the other hand, to encourage individuals to join hands in a process of social transformation, according to common ethics founded on shared religious values.[108]

Thus the 'culture of dialogue' contributes to transforming conflicts into peaceful situations 'where all persons are respected in their human and spiritual aspirations as creatures of God and part of the same human family'.[109] The Silsilah 'vision' strongly emphasises the connection between dialogue and peace.

The promotion of the 'culture of dialogue' is an answer to God's call for unity in diversity in the midst of today's pluralistic world. Its aim is to encourage people of different cultures and faiths to 'learn from the beauty and uniqueness of other cultures and religions, and see in them the signs of God's dialogue with humanity and ... creation'.[110] In this sense the 'culture of dialogue' constitutes the wider framework for interreligious engagement.

'Life-in-dialogue' is not only the visible expression of the 'culture of dialogue', but also the concrete means for promoting it.

According to the *Silsilah Vision*, the first requirement for 'dialogue of life', with the 'religious other' in particular, is 'sincerity of heart' rooted in an act of faith. In fact, in the context of the Southern Philippines,

---

[106] Silsilah Dialogue Movement, 'Silsilah Vision. The Spirituality of Life–in–Dialogue'.
[107] Silsilah Dialogue Movement, 'Culture of Dialogue', in Internet: www.silsilahdialogue.org, accessed 24 June 2003.
[108] *Ibid.*
[109] *Ibid.*
[110] Silsilah Dialogue Movement, 'Culture of Dialogue'.

where the 'religious other' is often perceived as the enemy and a threat, it takes a leap of faith to believe that 'in the heart of each person there is always a "corner" of openness and kindness ready to start a sincere dialogue.'[111]

Secondly, 'life-in-dialogue' signifies a serious commitment to solidarity, paying attention to the less privileged of society and giving voice to their aspirations for the respect of their dignity and rights. Those who commit themselves to this lifestyle of dialogue, become themselves 'living dialogues' providing mediations between sectors of society.[112]

Thirdly, life-in-dialogue means commitment to promoting the 'culture of dialogue' through education and formation. The process of education starts in the family, trying to reach all the structures of society, to 'change the trend of egoism in the world, forming people who understand the importance to relate with brothers and sisters, members of the same family created by God'.[113]

Development and activities

The *Silsilah Movement* started as a 'small group of Muslim and Christian friends praying and reflecting together on their mission of dialogue'[114] and has developed through a wide range of activities and initiatives.

The *Silsilah Centre* was opened in Zamboanga City in 1986. It hosted permanent exhibits on the culture of dialogue and peace, provided a venue for conferences, lectures and meetings, as well as a place for prayer and meditation for people of all faiths, Christians and Muslims in particular.

The *Centre* also issues the *Silsilah Bulletin* and other publications,[115] and has developed programs aimed at forming people of dialogue. The most important education program is the *Silsilah Summer Course on Muslim-Christian Dialogue*, offering intensive courses on Islam, Christianity and Interreligious relations. It includes the opportunity for Christians to

---

[111] *Ibid.*
[112] *Ibid.*
[113] *Ibid.*
[114] Sebastiano D'Ambra, 'Christian-Muslim Relations in the Philippines', 203.
[115] William LaRousse, *A Local Church Living for Dialogue*, 501.

experience life with Muslims families and for Muslims to live with Christian families, as part of their experience of interreligious engagement.[116] *Silsilah* courses are also included in the programmes for the formation of candidates to the priesthood in the Seminaries of Mindanao.[117]

Harmony Village, inaugurated outside Zamboanga City in 1990, includes the 'Oasis of Dialogue', which is a training and formation centre, and the *Silsilah Institute* (since 1999).[118]

An 'Oasis of Prayer/Interfaith-Ashram' was opened in Silang, Cavite, in 1997, providing a place for silence, meditation and prayer according to the 'spirituality of Silsilah'.[119]

Silsilah also contributed to the constitution of the *Movement of Muslim Christian Dialogue,* begun in 1992 in the Diliman Campus of the University of the Philippines, Manila, as a forum on Muslim–Christian dialogue.

A primary school was opened in a predominantly Muslim village, on the idea that the culture of dialogue in the community can be effectively promoted beginning with the youngest generations.[120]

The *Silsilah Prayer* takes place every Saturday at 3 pm, when Christians and Muslims gather to pray and share their faith experiences. Prayer starts with the recitation of the *Al-Fatiah* by a Muslim, Quranic and Biblical readings follow, and then the *Our Father* is recited by a Christian. Then the participants share their personal experiences of interreligious engagement in the light of their faiths.[121]

Silsilah spirituality also inspired the constitution of the Emmaus Community, in 1987, composed of Catholic women who devote themselves to Muslim–Christian dialogue. They are committed to shared life of prayer and work among the destitute Christians and Muslims of a very poor area of Zamboanga City, focussing on the Eucharist as the source of dialogue.[122]

---

[116] *Ibid.*
[117] *Ibid.*, 503–504.
[118] *Ibid.*
[119] *Ibid.*, 502.
[120] *Ibid.*
[121] William LaRousse, *A Local Church Living for Dialogue*, 502.
[122] Sebastiano D'Ambra, 'Christian-Muslim Relations in the Philippines', 203.

The Silsilah Movement has had its share of difficulties. From the beginning, Fr D'Ambra encountered opposition and mistrust of both Christians and Muslims, as well as from Government authority.[123] The greatest test, however, was the killing of Fr Salvatore Carzedda, close friend and co-operator of Fr D'Ambra, on 20 May 1992. It is thought that he was murdered because of his commitment to Christian-Muslim dialogue.[124]

The Bishops–Ulama Forum
Origins

Over the past seven years the *Bishops-Ulama Forum* (BUF) has played an important role in cementing Muslim-Christian relations in the Philippines.[125]

It is composed of the Catholic Bishops of Mindanao, the Muslim religious leaders of the Ulama League of the Philippines, and the bishops of the National Council of Churches of the Philippines (NCCP).

The formula: 'In the service of peace and development in Mindanao',[126] which opens every BUF statement, illustrates that in the spirit of interreligious dialogue BUF members are constantly committed to peace and better Christian-Muslim understanding in the Southern Philippines.[127]

In 1992-93 the National Unification Commission[128] brought different religious leaders together to reflect on the ongoing conflict in Mindanao and identify its causes.[129] After the *Abu Sayyaf* attack on the town of Ipil in April 1995, the Government of the Philippines sponsored

---

[123] Sebastiano D'Ambra, 'Silsilah Growth'.

[124] Sebastiano D'Ambra, 'Christian-Muslim Relations in the Philippines', 203-204. Silsilah Dialogue Movement, 'Padayon', Internet: www.silsilahdialogue.org, accessed 24 June 2003.

[125] For a detailed description and analysis of the BUF, see Sebastiano D'Ambra, *Building a Culture of Dialogue: Bishops-Ulama Forum Experience*, doctoral dissertation, Notre Dame University, Cotabato City, October 2000; in particular 90-141.

[126] Cf. Bishops-Ulama Forum, 'Statements', in *Ibid.*, 177-204. Cf. also Internet: http://www.mindanao.com/kalinaw/buf/dialogues.htm, accessed 12 July 2003.

[127] Kalinaw Mindanaw, 'Primer on the Bishop Ulama Forum', in Internet: http://www.mindanao.com/kalinaw/buf/primer.htm, accessed 12 July 2003.

[128] Cf. present study, 16.

[129] Kalinaw Mindanaw, 'Primer on the Bishops-Ulama Forum'.

a series of meetings in different cities of Mindanao resulting in a 'Mindanao Agenda for Peace and Development.[130]

In this context five Catholic bishops and ten Muslim Ulama met in July 1996 at the Ateneo de Manila University to consider the prospects of peace. This paved the way for the First Bishops-Ulama Forum Dialogue, which took place in Cebú City on 26 November of that year.[131]

The BUF has then developed into a more structured organisation: in May 1997 (Third Dialogue) the Bishops of the NCCP were invited to become part of the Forum; a Tripartite Commission was created to monitor areas of concern and implement the decisions of the Forum; a joint Secretariat was also created to assist the Commission.

Ethos and objectives

The Bishops-Ulama Forum represents the response of religious leaders to the conflict in the Southern Philippines. It started as a 'corrective' to the peace process, as both the Catholic bishops and Muslim leaders felt that an essential element was missing in the attempts at establishing peace. They realised that the socio-economic and political effort for durable and constructive peace has to be grounded on the Philippine cultural and religious traditions. The BUF intends to provide this missing component, without which many peace efforts have proved ineffective.[132]

The starting point of dialogue is 'the spiritual bases for peace in their respective traditions, grounded in the belief in one God, a common origin, and a common destiny for all.'[133] Dialogue within the BUF takes place mainly at the level of common action, and aims at bringing commitment to interfaith relations, peace and development to the grassroots.

Activities and fruits

The BUF works primarily through its 'dialogues'. Since the 1996, the

---

[130] Kalinaw Mindanaw, 'Primer on the Bishops-Ulama Forum'.
[131] William LaRousse, *A Local Church Living for Dialogue*, 480 and 482.
[132] Kalinaw Mindanaw, 'Primer on the Bishops-Ulama Forum'.
[133] *Ibid.*

Bishops and Ulama have been meeting regularly to work for interreligious dialogue and peace.[134]

The BUF has gradually taken up a more definite identity and role in the Mindanao peace process, through continuous attention to the events and receptivity to the most urgent challenges. The agenda is always identified in relation to specific needs.

The BUF has promoted dialogue forums at a regional level, to address local issues.[135] A seminar-workshop was held in April 1998 to advance dialogue locally. It has also encouraged the creation of a network to coordinate the activities of such centres and of other organisations working for the same purpose.[136]

Together with its peace partners (which include Catholic Relief Services and UNICEF), the *Bishops-Ulama Forum* conducts community-based workshops to promote a culture of peace, and co-operates with schools encouraging the introduction of peace education into their syllabuses. All of these activities aim at promoting mutual understanding among Christians, Muslims and *Lumads*.[137]

Prompted by the BUF, the First Mindanao Imam-Priests Conference took place in Davao City on 1-4 December 1998. Various imam-priests meetings have followed since throughout Mindanao, enabling local religious ministers to know one another and practice Christian-Muslim dialogue locally.[138]

In February 1999, the BUF launched its newsletter, *Bitiara*, and in May of the same year the *Mindanao Week of Peace* celebration was approved, to promote the convergence of all peace initiatives in Mindanao. It was held from 25 November to 1 December of that year under the title, 'Healing the Past and Building the Future'.

Since August 1999, the BUF has supported the 'Zones of Peace', an initiative taken by the people with the support of the Church, NGOs, local officials and the Government Peace Commission, to create spaces where weapons are banned in order to protect peace.[139]

---

[134] Cf. William LaRousse, *A Local Church Living for* Dialogue, 482-487. The 21st General Assembly of the Bishops-Ulama Conference has just taken place on 18-20 August, under the title 'Seeking Peace and Development through an Authentic Christian and Muslim Dialogue of Life in Asia'.

[135] Kalinaw Mindanaw, 'Primer on the Bishops-Ulama Forum'.

[136] William LaRousse, *A Local Church Living for Dialogue*, 487.

[137] *Ibid.*, 487-488.

[138] *Ibid.*, 489-490.

[139] *Ibid.*, 508-509.

The BUF has significantly contributed to the peace process in Mindanao, especially as the Forum has gradually gained a position of mediation between the Government and the MILF. It is of great significance for Christian-Muslim dialogue and reconciliation, as it offers the image of Christian and Muslim religious leaders working together in friendship.

As a result, the BUF has authority to denounce any actions contrary to the respect of human rights and dignity. One example is the statement released on 18 May 2000, in which Bishops and Ulama denounced the Government Army-MILF clashes.[140] They urged both the Philippines Government and the MILF to cease the hostilities and to resume peace negotiations. A similar statement was made on 27 November 2000 for the Mindanao Week of Peace. As recently as 12 May 2003, the BUF responded to recent bloodshed in Mindanao.[141]

The members of the BUF have also offered themselves as third party mediators in any negotiations between Government and MILF. This has contributed to the important agreement of 18 July 2003 between the Government and the MILF.[142]

The Catholic Church and the Muslim community in the Philippines: an assessment of the encounter

Why is Christian-Muslim encounter necessary at all in the Philippines? What are the major hindrances to constructive engagement? How is the Catholic Church responding to the challenge? And what are the elements, emerging from the experience of interreligious dialogue, which seem promising for future developments? This section deals with these questions to assess the status of the engagement.

---

[140] Bishops-Ulama Forum, 'Statement', Cagayan de Oro City, 18 May 2000, in Internet: http://www.mindanao.com/kalinaw/peaceproc/statement-buf.htm, accessed 12 July 2003.
[141] 'Philippine Christians and Muslims Call for Return to Dialogue in Mindanao', in *Zenit*, 13 May 2003, in Internet: http://www.zenit.org/, accessed 21 July 2003.
[142] Cf. 'Church Mediates a Cease-fire in Southern Philippines', in *Zenit*, 21 July 2003, accessed 21 July 2003.

Reasons for Christian-Muslim engagement in the Philippines

While since Vatican II the Catholic Church has increasingly acknowledged interreligious dialogue as integral to its identity and mission, there are also specific reasons why such acknowledgement is particularly urgent in the Philippines.

In the first place the Catholic Church in the Philippines must be considered within the framework of Asian Christianity and Catholicity. This has immediate ecclesiological and missiological implications. In fact the FABC has emphasised Asia multicultural and multireligious heritage as essential to the self-understanding of the Church in Asia and its specific mission.[143]

Secondly, in the specific context of the Philippines what makes interfaith encounter and Christian–Muslims relations in particular, immediately urgent, is the need for reconciliation and peace in response to ongoing violent conflict.

This second motive, however, needs clarification. On the one hand there is the danger of reducing, at least *de facto*, interreligious dialogue merely to 'negotiations towards peaceful agreement' and to confine it to the sphere of social justice. This would not do justice to Catholic theological understanding of and teaching on interreligious dialogue as an integral dimension of the life of the Church. The risk is that one aspect, namely the 'dialogue of common action', becomes exclusive of other dimensions, particularly *theological engagement* and *religious experience*.[144]

On the other hand, to reach 'higher' levels of interfaith engagement certain preconditions are necessary. In the Philippine context a necessary precondition is a peaceful environment freed from fear of the *other*. This requires investing in a slow and painstaking process of

---

[143] FABC, 'Evangelisation in Modern Asia', Statement and Recommendations of the First Plenary Assembly, nos. 9-18. Cf. also FABC, 'Prayer, the Life of the Church of Asia', Statement and Recommendations of the Second Plenary Assembly, nos. 30-36. John Paul II spoke of the special missionary vocation of the Church in the Philippine as 'to bear witness to the Gospel in the heart of Asia' (John Paul II, 'Discourse to the Bishops of the Philippines on *Ad Limina* Visit', in *Bulletin Pro Dialogo*, 95(1997), 175-176.

[144] Pontifical Council for Interreligious Dialogue and Congregation for Evangelization of Peoples, *Dialogue and Proclamation*, Rome, 19 May 1991, no. 42.

reconciliation beginning from the grassroots. Work for peace and reconciliation is aimed at phasing out fear and mistrust to make space for respect, mutual esteem and reciprocal enrichment. In this sense commitment to reconciliation is an integral part of work for dialogue. This is what the Philippines need and what the Church in the Philippines needs to address now.

Obstacles to the encounter: contrasting standpoints

It is often argued that the conflict in the Southern Philippines is not a religious conflict.[145] While it is true, however, that it is not possible to reduce the causes of the conflict to the religious differences between Christians and Muslims,[146] an adequate approach to the problem cannot dismiss the religious element altogether. An objective reading requires the complexity of the issue to be acknowledged and dealt with from a broader perspective that takes into account diverse factors.

The contemporary conflict in Mindanao is profoundly rooted in the history of Christian–Muslim encounter in the Philippine Archipelago during the past four and a half centuries. In his speech to the Muslim Filipinos in Davao, John Paul II also spoke about the influence of the past on the present status of the Philippine society.[147] But in what sense does history condition the present?

The events of history have certainly nurtured mutual feelings of fear and mistrust, widening the gap between the two major faith communities of the Philippines.

Far from underestimating the impact of history, however, it must be stressed that the gap between Christianity and Islam pre-existed their historical encounter in the Philippines. Therefore it is important to be aware that the roots of the 'clash' are to be ultimately situated in that original 'irreconcilable' difference.

When analysing the reasons for Christian–Muslim misunderstanding in the Philippines, Peter Gowing has used the expression

---

[145] Cf. Sebastiano D'Ambra, 'Christian–Muslim Relations in the Philippines', 195.
[146] See note 55.
[147] John Paul II, 'To the Representatives of Muslims in the Philippines', in Gioia no. 365.

'of different minds', to illustrate the deeply contrasting 'visions' that underpin the attitudes of the two faith communities.[148]

According to Gowing it is possible to discern the contrast at five different levels. In the first place, although recognising the inadequacy of short-hand, he characterises the Muslim-Christian contrast as the 'Age of Faith versus the Age of Politics',[149] highlighting the difference between the Christian and the Muslim visions of politics and faith and, in particular, of the way these interact.

Secondly, Gowing suggests that the contrast regards 'Filipino' identity, as Christians tend to emphasise a common 'Filipino' character, whilst Muslims tend to emphasise difference.

The third contrast consists in 'special privileges' versus 'human rights'. Where the Muslims maintain that it is a 'question of human rights' to have their own code of personal laws modelled on their belief, Christians regard it as a special privilege whereby certain Filipino citizens are exempted from the obligations of national law.

The fourth divergence concerns the notion of development. The divergence between Christian and Muslim perceptions of development in the Philippines has been a source of misunderstanding. Often, Christians have wondered why Muslims seemed to reject their offer of a better standard of life, whilst Muslims have seen it as a trap aimed at annihilating their identity through absorption into Christian mainstream.[150]

This relates to the fifth point of misunderstanding, which involves the concept of integration. While from the Filipino Christian standpoint, integration does not exclude the right and freedom to practice one's own religion,[151] Muslims often perceive it as a fatal threat to their Islamic

---

[148] Peter Gowing, 'Of Different Minds. Christian and Muslim ways of looking at their relations in the Philippines', *International Review of Mission*, Vol. 67 (Jan. 1978), 74–85.

[149] Cf. *Ibid.*, 75–77. Gowing argues that, because of mounting secularisation, 'Philippine Christian society … tends to see the world in secular-political terms', while in recent times Filipino Muslims 'have become even more self-consciously committed to ordering their lives around the teachings and practices of Islam'. This is not to say that the Christian way of life is detached from Christian faith and that only the Muslim way of life is profoundly religious; rather it is to say that there seems to be more self-consciousness about that link on the part of Filipino Muslims.

[150] Peter Gowing, 'Of Different Minds', 83.

[151] 'No law shall be made respecting an establishment of religion, or prohibiting the free exercise thereof. The free exercise and enjoyment of religious profession and worship, without discrimination or preference, shall forever be allowed. No religious test shall be

identity. Gowing suggests that the use of different terminology (e.g. 'orchestration') might provide a way of conveying the notion of unity-in-diversity.[152]

Gowing's account gives an idea of how easily misunderstanding can occur if the two profoundly divergent standpoints come into contact without the corrective of mutual clarification. In particular, if left 'unattended', contrasting standpoints may favour the perpetuation of images of the *other* based on prejudice and fears rather than on mutual knowledge and trust. Often the 'Moro image' still conditions Christian views of Muslims, while some Muslims still see Christians as invaders, land-grabbers and a threat to their Islamic identity.[153]

Internal 'struggles'

Muslim-Christian encounter in the Philippines is also hindered by differing agendas: in general, the Christian community seeks integration, while the Muslims pursue self-determination. The respective aims determine different 'struggles' within each community.

Since the 1970s the Catholic Church in the Philippines has struggled to appropriate the new outlook inaugurated by Vatican II. During the past thirteen years efforts have been especially significant in the 'struggle' to acknowledge the necessity of dialogue.

There is an ongoing 'struggle' within the Catholic community to make space for the Muslim community.[154] There are opposing forces within the Church which deserve serious attention as they manifest yet another 'struggle': the struggle to come to terms with the memory of past wounds received from elements of the Muslim community, the pain of which makes it difficult to forgive and forget.[155]

---

required for the exercise of civil or political rights' (*Constitution of the Republic of the Philippines*, 1987, art. III, sec. 5).

[152] Peter Gowing, 'Of Different Minds', 84.

[153] Jose' Ante, 'Christian-Muslim Relations in the Philippines', in *Encounter*, 214 (April 1995), 3; Peter Gowing, *Mosque and Moro*, 30.

[154] Cf. William LaRousse, *A Church living for Dialogue*, 526; Sebastiano D'Ambra, 'Silsilah Growth'; also cf. Sebastiano D'Ambra, *Life in Dialogue*, Zamboanga City, Silsilah Publications, 1991, 76-77.

[155] William LaRousse, *A Church living for Dialogue*, 527.

Muslims are struggling too. They share the same 'struggle' to overcome the memory of past clashes and sufferings at the hands of Christians. Some Muslims also share in the 'struggle' for integration into the Philippine nations (Cf. the compromise between the MNLF and the Government in 1976 and, more recently, the agreement with the MILF).

But another struggle is ongoing too, as some elements of the Muslim community are 'struggling' against being integrated into the *bangsa* Filipino. At various levels, Filipino Muslims see the Islamic community of South East Asia as their pivot and pole of orientation. In some cases the sense of belonging to *dar al-Islam* is much stronger than Philippine identity, and this constitutes a significant obstacle to the encounter, particularly when it takes the shape of violent confrontation, as in the case of the Abu Sayyaf.

Ongoing dialogue
Culture of peace and dialogue

Following Vatican II, the Catholic Church in the Philippines has made remarkable efforts towards Christian-Muslim encounter. There has been a large number of initiatives at various levels, of which the Silsilah Movement and the Bishops-Ulama Forum are two significant examples.

In response to the conflict, efforts towards dialogue have taken a specific direction, whereby for the Church in the Philippines to work for Christian-Muslim dialogue is closely related to commitment to peace. On the whole, dialogue is promoted by encouraging a 'culture of peace and dialogue' and by giving priority to *dialogue of life* (e.g. the Silsilah Movement) and *common action* (e.g. the BUF).

The culture of peace is being promoted through education and cooperation on issues of social justice.[156] It seems, however, that two aspects are becoming increasingly important for the encounter: history, and the basic ecclesial communities.

---

[156] Sebastiano D'Ambra, 'Towards a Culture of Dialogue in the Philippines. Muslim-Christian Intercultural Communication in Mindanao', in *Journal of Dharma*, Vol. 24, no. 3 (Jl-S 1999), 290-298. Also cf. De Castro, 'Is Dialogue Possible? A Response', in *Landas,* Vol. 16 no. 2 (2000), 306-307.

History revisited

Given the importance of the past for contemporary Christian-Muslim relations in the Philippines, interreligious engagement demands that the history of the encounter between the two faith communities (and the different worlds they represent) be approached from a new perspective.

On the one hand, for the sake of objectivity and completeness, it is necessary that history be re-written taking into account not just the mainstream perspective of Christian Filipinos, but also the Moro point of view, as well as that of the *Lumads*.[157]

On the other hand, it is also necessary to question interpretations of history which perpetuate commonplaces. For LaRousse, for example, the idea that 'the Spanish held a blind animosity for all Muslims', should be considered alongside cases of Spanish-Muslim cooperation. Similarly, the idea that before 1521 the Muslim community was unanimous against any external 'attempt at colonisation' and that all problems came with the Spanish needs to be reconsidered in the light of existing conflicts among different ethnic groups.[158]

An effort to liberate history from the burden of ideological interpretations, can favour the recognition of the role of each ethnic group and community in the formation of the nation, and allow for better mutual appreciation.

To some extent, such effort could also throw light on the history preceding the arrival of both Islam and Christianity, and thus help the Filipinos to retrieve common roots and identify elements of a common narrative in support of a Filipino national identity.[159]

A more objective reading of history, however, could at least partially favour the 'embracing of memories',[160] forgiveness of past

---

[157] William LaRousse, 'Is Dialogue Possible?', 287-288.

[158] William LaRousse, *A Church Living for Dialogue*, 523-424.

[159] Eric Casiño argues that an anthropological approach to difference could provide an important basis for unity between Christian and Muslim Filipinos. (Eric Casiño, 'The Anthropology of Christianity and Islam in the Philippines: a Bipolar Approach to Diversity', in Peter G Gowing, *Understanding Islam and Muslims in the Philippines*, 36-45). On the same line, Paolo Nicelli argues that despite differences due to religious affiliations, there exist a 'Filipino identity', and 'it is possible to identify some common traits which are part of the character of the different people of the Philippines and this can help us to understand who really are the Filipinos'. (Paolo Nicelli, *The First Islamisation of the Philippines*, Silsilah Publications, Zamboanga City, 2003, 26-34.)

[160] Lilian Curaming, 'Is Dialogue Possible? A Response', in *Landas*, Vol. 16 no. 2 (2002), 299-300.

mutually inflicted wounds and more trustful relationships. In this regard accounts of positive relations and experiences of dialogue and cooperation between Christians and Muslims should become part of Philippine history.[161] In this sense Bishop Tudtud insisted that the Church should contribute to bringing about 'a series of happy events that will be remembered during the years to come in contradistinction to the … unhappy events' of the past.[162]

Basic ecclesial communities and basic dialogue communities

The Church in the Philippines insists that interreligious dialogue is a task of each local Church. In particular, 'basic ecclesial communities' (BEC) provide one effective way of promoting interreligious dialogue at the grassroots.

The encyclical *Redemptoris Missio* describes 'ecclesial basic communities' as

> Groups of Christians who, at the level of the family or in a similarly restricted setting, come together for prayer, Scripture reading, catechesis, and discussion on human and ecclesial problems with a view to a common commitment. [They] are a sign of vitality within the Church, an instrument of formation and evangelization, and a solid starting point for a new society based on a 'civilization of love'.[163]

BECs represent a place for shared responsibility and commitment, and a 'source of new ministries'.[164] Their model is the early Christian communities, gathered to listen to God's Word, to celebrate the Eucharist, and to share according to the needs of each member (Cf. Acts 2:42-47). The Second Plenary Council of the Philippines saw the BECs as a 'great

---

[161] William LaRousse, *A Church Living for Dialogue*, 523.
[162] Bienvenido Tudtud, *Dialogue of Life*, quoted in LaRousse, *A Church Living for Dialogue*, 469.
[163] John Paul II, *Redemptoris Missio, Encyclical Letter on the permanent validity of the Church's missionary mandate*, Rome, 7 December 1990, no. 51.
[164] *Ibid.*

hope for the Church in the Philippines', on account of their 'potential for evangelisation.'[165]

These communities constitute a space where interreligious dialogue can take place at the most basic level and make a difference to the life of the people.[166] In 1999 the Archdiocese of Cotabato, Mindanao, launched a programme for interreligious dialogue, centred on BECs,[167] where particular emphasis is put on the sharing of experiences of life with Muslim neighbours. The Cotabato experience seems to demonstrate that through BECs the 'culture of peace and dialogue' can be effectively promoted among Catholics and thus contribute to the process of reconciliation between Filipino Christians and Muslims.

According to LaRousse, BECs can potentially stimulate the formation of 'Basic Human Communities of Christians and Muslims', taking Christian-Muslim dialogue a step further. In the early 1990s the Silsilah Movement was studying the possibility of creating such 'Basic Dialogue Communities',[168] which could become the context for Christians and Muslims to rethink their relations, history and identities in the light of the encounter with the *other*.[169]

Epilogue

The complexity of the situation does not allow for easy answers and solutions to the ongoing conflict in the Philippines. The local Catholic Church is aware that the response to the situation is ultimately a question of response to Islam and indeed its 'struggle' to 'make space' for the Muslim community shows that the challenge is being taken quite seriously.

It is important, however, that two irreducible 'tensions' be accepted as part and parcel of the Church's specific mission in the Philippines. One is between dialogue and proclamation, and the other between Christianity and Islam.

---

[165] PCP II, nos. 137-140.
[166] *Ibid*.
[167] William LaRousse, 'Is Dialogue Possible?', 286.
[168] Sebastiano D'Ambra, *Life in Dialogue*, 109-111.
[169] William LaRousse, 'Is Dialogue Possible?', 286-287.

How is the Church in the Philippines seeking to integrate interreligious dialogue with its particular mission? This precedes the question of Christian-Muslim relations.

On the one hand the Church's mission is universal in its very nature: firstly, it has the responsibility to be, amongst humanity, the 'sign and sacrament'[170] of the salvation offered by God through Christ (through witness and proclamation); secondly, to represent humanity's aspirations to God (through intercession).

On the other hand, God's offer of salvation through the Paschal Mystery, reaches all human beings through their consciences, cultures and religions, 'in ways known only to God'.[171]

The problem is how to maintain the cosmic dimension of the Church's mission while allowing that religions may have a purpose in God's plan; how to integrate faithfulness to the missionary mandate ('go, proclaim, baptise'), while learning from other religions (i.e. How can 'Tradition' be enriched by 'traditions'?).

These theological questions take up a concrete character in any particular context like the Philippines, where the encounter between Christianity and Islam occurs in the encounter of people. How is this particular Church trying to acknowledge the importance of the Muslim community for its life and mission, without diluting its missionary thrust?

Regarding the second tension, it is not enough for the Church to do its best. Effective and constructive interreligious engagement requires a two-sided commitment: dialogue will function only with the clear will on both sides to make it work.

The situation in the Philippines demands that not only the Christian but also the Muslim community take responsibility and take up the 'challenge' that the very existence of the *other* poses. Both parties are expected to declare their commitment to a constructive relationship, whereby each community may be enriched by the other without losing its own identity. This requires the will to come together and 'negotiate the common space',[172] to grow together as integral parts of a single nation.

Perhaps it cannot yet be taken for granted that the national unity of the Philippine Republic is as important a concern from either

---

[170] Second Vatican Council, *Lumen Gentium*, no. 1.
[171] Second Vatican Council, *Gaudium et Spes*, no. 22.
[172] Cf. Michael Barnes, *Theology and the Dialogue of Religions*, Cambridge University Press, Cambridge, 2002, 230-254.

side. Perhaps it is necessary to invite the Muslim community to say openly how high a priority this is for them.

Fortunately, the BUF and Silsilah—among other initiatives—show that such bilateral commitment is possible, both at the level of leadership and at the grassroots.

Persevering in 'the twofold struggle' (dialogue-mission; Christianity-Islam), and trying to work more 'with' rather than 'for' Muslims, the Catholic Church in the Philippines can function as leaven: it can be a stimulus for all Filipinos to seek authentic and constructive dialogue, aimed not just at reconciliation and peace, but also at mutual help to grow in their respective cultural and religious identities.

Abbreviations

ARMM	Autonomous Region in Muslim Mindanao
BEC	Basic Ecclesial Communities
BUF	Bishops-Ulama Forum
CBCP	Catholic Bishops' Conference of the Philippines
FABC	Federation of Asian Bishops' Conferences
GRP	Government of the Republic of the Philippines
MILF	Movement of Islamic Liberation Front
MIM	Muslim Independence Movement
MNLF	Movement of National Liberation Front
NCCP	National Council of Churches of the Philippines
NUC	National Unification Commission
PCP II	Second Plenary Council of the Philippines

Bibliography

Abel, A., 'Dar al-Islam', in Gibb, H A R et al. (eds.), *The Encyclopaedia of Islam,* Brill; Leiden, Luzac, London, 1960, Vol. II, 127.

Abubakar, Carmen, 'Islam in the Philippines–The Moro Problem', in Asghar Ali Engineer, *Islam in Asia,* Vanguard Books, Lahore, 1986, 39-74.

Ante, José, 'Christian-Muslim Relations in the Philippines', in *Encounter,* no. 214 (April 1995).

'Archdiocese of Manila', in Internet: http://cbcponline.org/jurisdictionn/manila.html, accessed 12 June 2003.

Barnes, Michael, *Theology and the Dialogue of Religions,* Cambridge University Press, Cambridge, 2002.

Bishops-Ulama Forum   'Statements', in Sebastiano D'Ambra, *Building a Culture of Dialogue: Bishops-Ulama Forum Experience,* Doctoral dissertation, Notre Dame University, Cotabato

City, October 2000, 177-204.

Bishops-Ulama Forum, 'Statement', Cagayan de Oro City, 18 May 2000, in Internet: http://www.mindanao.com/kalinaw/peaceproc/statement-buf.htm, accessed 12 July 2003.

Casiño, Eric, 'The Anthropology of Christianity and Islam in the Philippines: a Bipolar Approach to Diversity', in Peter G Gowing, *Understanding Islam and Muslims in the Philippines*, New Day, Quezon City, 1988, 36-45.

Catholic Bishops' Conference of the Philippines, *Pastoral Letters 1945-1995*, compiled and edited by Pedro C. Quitorio III, Peimon Press, Manila, 1996.

Chalk, Peter, 'Militant Islamic Extremism in the Southern Philippines', in Jason F Isaacson, and Colin Lewis Rubenstein, (eds.), *Islam in Asia. Changing Political Realities*, Transaction Publishers, New Brunswick, NJ, 2002, 187-222.

'Church Mediates a Cease-fire in Southern Philippines', in *Zenit*, 21 July 2003, Internet: http://www.zenit.org, accessed 21 July 2003.

Curaming, Lilian M, 'Is Dialogue Possible? A Response', in *Landas*, Vol. 16 no. 2 (2002), 297-304.

D'Ambra, Sebastiano, *Building a Culture of Dialogue: Bishops-Ulama Forum Experience*, Doctoral dissertation, Notre Dame University, Cotabato City, October 2000.

D'Ambra, Sebastiano, 'Silsilah Growth. From a Personal Experience to the Movement's Experience', in Internet: http://www.silsilahdialogue.org, accessed 24 June 2003.

D'Ambra, Sebastiano, *Life in Dialogue*, Silsilah Publications, Zamboanga City, 1991.

D'Ambra, Sebastiano, 'Christian-Muslim Relations in the Philippines', in *Islamochristiana*, Vol. 20, 1994, 179-206.

D'Ambra, Sebastiano, 'Towards a culture of dialogue in the Philippines. Muslim-Christian intercultural communication in Mindanao', in *Journal of Dharma*, Vol. 24, no. 3 (Jl-S 1999), 284-300.

Dansalan College and Prelature of Marawi, 'Joint Catholic-Protestant Consultation on Christian Presence among Muslim Filipinos: Communication', in *Occasional Bulletin of Missionary Research*, no. 3, January 1979, 31-32.

De Castro, Antonio F B, 'Is Dialogue Possible? A Response', in *Landas*, Vol. 16 no. 2 (2002), 305-311.

Diamond, Michael J. & Gowing, Peter Gordon, *Islam and Muslims. Some Basic Information*, New Day, Quezon City, 1981.

Ellis, Kail C, *The Vatican, Islam and the Middle East*, Syracuse University Press, Syracuse, NY, 1987.

Engineer, Asghar Ali (ed.), *Islam in Asia*, Vanguard Books, Lahore, 1986.

Evangelista, Oscar, 'Some Aspects of the History of Islam in Southeast Asia', in Peter Gordon Gowing (ed.), *Understanding Islam and Muslims in the Philippines*, New Day, Quezon City, 1988, 16-25.

Federation of Asian Bishops Conference, 'Evangelisation in Modern Day Asia', Statement and Recommendations of the First Plenary Assembly, Taipei Taiwan, 27 April 1974, in Gaudencio B Rosales and C G Arevalo (eds.), *For all the Peoples of Asia*, Claretian Publications, Quezon City, Manila, 1992, 11-25.

Federation of Asian Bishops Conference, 'Prayer, the Life of the Church of Asia', Statement and Recommendations of the Second Plenary Assembly, Barrakpore, Calcutta, 25 November 1978, in Gaudencio B Rosales and C G Arevalo (eds.), *For all the Peoples of Asia*, Claretian Publications, Quezon City, Manila, 1992, 27-48.

Fitzgerald, Michael, 'Christian-Muslim Dialogue in South-East Asia', in *Islamochristiana*, Vol. 2, 1976, 171-185.

Gioia, Francesco, *Interreligious Dialogue. The Official Teaching of the Catholic Church (1963-1995)*, Boston, Pauline Books and Media, 1997.

'Government Troops in Massive Hunt for MILF rebels', in *The Philippine Daily Inquirer*, 5 May 05, 2003, Internet: http://www.inq7.net, accessed 21 July 2003.

Gowing, Peter Gordon (ed.), *Understanding Islam and Muslims in the Philippines*, New Day, Quezon City, 1988.

Gowing, Peter Gordon, 'Christian-Muslim dialogue in the Philippines, 1976-1981', *South East Asia Journal of Theology*, Vol. 23 no. 1 (1982), 37-48.

Gowing, Peter Gordon, 'Of different minds. Christian and Muslim ways of looking at their relations in the Philippines', *International Review of Mission*, Vol. 67 (Jan 1978), 74-85.

Gowing, Peter Gordon, 'The Muslim Filipino Minority', in *Crescent in the East*, Humanities Press, Atlantic Highlands, NJ, 1982, 211-226.

Gowing, Peter Gordon, *Islands under the Cross. The Story of the Church in the Philippines*, Manila, National Council of Churches in the Philippines, 1967.

Gowing, Peter Gordon, *Mosque and Moro, A study of Muslims in the Philippines*, 1964.

Gutierrez, Eric U, *Rebels, Warlords, and Ulama, A Reader on Muslim Separatism and the War in Southern Philippines*, Institute for Popular Democracy, Quezon City, 2000.

John Paul II et al., '20 February, Davao Airport: Meeting with the Representatives of the Muslim Community', in *Bulletin Secretariatus Pro Non-Christianis*, no. 46 (1981), 6-11.

John Paul II, 'To the Bishops of the Philippines on Ad Limina Visit', Rome, 27 September 1996, in *Bulletin Pro Dialogo*, Vol. 95 (1997), 175-176.

John Paul II, 'To the Bishops of the Philippines on Ad Limina Visit', Rome, 12 October 1985, in Francesco Gioia, *Interreligious Dialogue. The Official Teaching of the Catholic Church (1963-1995)*, Boston, Pauline Books and Media, 1997, no. 478.

John Paul II, 'To the Bishops of the Philippines on their Ad Limina Visit', Rome, 30 November 1985, in Francesco Gioia, *Interreligious Dialogue. The Official Teaching of the Catholic Church (1963-1995)*, Boston, Pauline Books and Media, 1997, no. 696.

John Paul II, 'Discorso del Santo Padre Giovanni Paolo II all'episcopato filippino e ai vescovi asiatici riuniti a villa San Miguel a Manila', Manila 17 February 1981, in http://www.vatican.va, accessed 15 July 2003.

John Paul II, 'Discorso del Santo Padre Giovanni Paolo II durante la cerimonia di benvenuto all'aereoporto internazionale di Manila', Manila 17 February 1981, in Internet: http://www.vatican.va, accessed 15 July 2003.

John Paul II, 'Messagio del Santo Padre Giovanni Paolo II al Presidente della nazione filippina', Manila 17 February 1981, in Internet: http://www.vatican.va, accessed 15 July 2003.

John Paul II, *Redemptoris Missio, Letter Encyclical on the permanent validity of the Church's missionary mandate*, Rome, 7 December 1990.

Kalinaw Mindanaw, 'Primer on the Bishops-Ulama Forum', in Internet: http://www.mindanao.com/kalinaw/buf/primer.htm, accessed 12 July 2003.

LaRousse, William, 'Is Dialogue Possible?', in *Landas*, Vol. 16 no. 2 (2002), 273-296.

LaRousse, William, *A Local Church Living for Dialogue. Muslim-Christian Relations in Mindanao-Sulu (Philippines) 1965-2000*, Pontifical Gregorian University, Rome, 2001.

Madale, Nagasura T, 'The Hejra Towards Muslim-Christian Dialogue: Problems and Options, in Madale, Nagasura T, *Essays on Peace and Development in Southern Philippines*, Capitol Institute for Research and Development, Cagayan de Oro City, 1999.

Majul, Cesar Adib, 'Muslims and Christians in the Philippines', in Kail C Ellis, *The Vatican, Islam and the Middle East*, Syracuse, NY, Syracuse University Press, 1987,. 309-333.

Majul, Cesar Adib, *Muslims in the Philippines*, Quezon City, University of the Philippines Press, 1999.

'Malaysia Hopes RP Government MILF Resume Peace Talks', in *The Philippine Daily Inquirer*, 6 May 2003, Internet: http://www.inq7 net, accessed 21 July 2003.

Michel, Thomas, 'Islamo-Christian Dialogue: Reflections on the recent teachings of the Church', in *Bulletin Secretariatus Pro Non-Christianis*, no. 59 (1985–XX/2), 172-193.

'MILF Chief to Head Peace Talks With Government', in *The Philippine Daily Inquirer*, 19 July 2003, Internet: http://www.inq7.net, accessed 21 July 2003.

Nicelli, Paolo, *The First Islamisation of the Philippines*, Silsilah Publications, Zamboanga City, 2003.

'Philippine Christians and Muslims Call for Return to Dialogue in Mindanao', in *Zenit*, 13 May 2003, accessed 21 July 2003.

'Profiles', in Mindanao State University's Research and Development Centre, *A First Step to Peace: Mindanao in Transition, Accord Series no. 6*, April 1999, Internet: http://www.c-r.org/accord/min/accord6/profiles.shtml, accessed 27 June 2003.

Republic of the Philippines, *Constitution of the Republic of the Philippines*, 1987.

Riddell, Peter, *Islam and the Malay-Indonesian World*, London, C Hurst and Co., 2000.

Robredillo, Lope C, 'The Challenge of the Times and the CBCP's Responses: A Historical Essay on the Catholic Bishops' Conference of the Philippines', in Catholic Bishops' Conference of the Philippines, *Pastoral Letters 1945-1995*, compiled and edited by Pedro C Quitorio III, Peimon Press, Manila, 1996, xix-xlviii.

Schreiter, Robert, *Reconciliation: Looking towards Mission in the 21st Century*, Lecture delivered at the Missionary Institute of London, 21 March 2002.

Second Vatican Council, *Lumen Gentium, Dogmatic Constitution on the Church*, in Tanner, Norman P. (ed.), *Decrees of the Ecumenical Councils*, London, Sheed and Ward, 1990, 849-900.

Second Vatican Council, *Nostra Aetate, Declaration on the Church's Relation to non-Christian Religions*, in Tanner, Norman P. (ed.), *Decrees of the Ecumenical Councils*, London, Sheed and Ward, 1990, 968-971.

Secretariat of the Second Plenary Council of the Philippines & Catholic Bishops' Conference of the Philippines, *Acts and Decrees of the Second Plenary Council of the Philippines. 20 January-17 February 1991*, Manila, Catholic Bishops' Conference of the Philippines, 1992.

Silsilah Dialogue Movement, 'Culture of Dialogue', Internet http://www.silsilahdialogue.org, accessed 24 June 2003.

Silsilah Dialogue Movement, '*Padayon* Spirit of Silsilah', Internet: http://www.silsilahdialogue.org, accessed 24 June 2003.

Silsilah Dialogue Movement, 'Silsilah Vision. The Spirituality of Life-in-Dialogue', Internet: http://www.silsilahdialogue.org, accessed 24 June 2003.

Tolibas-Nuñez, Rosalita, *Roots of Conflict. Muslims, Christians, and the Mindanao Struggle*, Asian Institute of Management, Makati City, 1997.

'Twenty-two Dead in Attack on Zamboanga del Norte Town', in *The Philippine Daily Inquirer*, 4 May 2003, Internet: http://www.inq7.net, accessed 21 July 2003.

Yam, William L, 'Islam in the Philippines', in Pullapilly, Cyriac K (ed.) *Islam in the Contemporary World*, Cross Roads Books, Notre Dame, Indiana, 1980, 358-369.

Zamora, F B, 'State of 'lawless violence' declared in Davao', in *The Philippine Daily Inquirer*, 2 April 2003, Internet: http://www.inq7.net, accessed 21 July 2003.

THE VATICAN, JERUSALEM AND THE PALESTINIAN CHRISTIANS: FAITH, DIPLOMACY AND POLITICS IN THE HOLY LAND

Anthony O'Mahony

Arguably as a sacred city, Jerusalem is the single most important place in the Middle East: for Muslims, the Haram al-Sharif is a symbol of victory; for Jews the Wailing Wall a symbol of loss; and for Christians, the Holy Sepulchre a symbol of victory through loss. Religion and politics have interacted in every sacred story. Political theologies remain at least implicit in the histories of all major faith communities and at the centre of every sacred story is at least one sacred place, which in turn carves out of the cosmos a space held to be inviolable and safe for believers, a sanctuary, the place where everything of ultimate significance has occurred. For the Christian community and in particular for the Christians of Jerusalem, the principal holy spaces are the Church of the Nativity in Bethlehem, the Churches and Holy Places in Nazareth, and especially, Church of the Holy Sepulchre in Jerusalem, which remains an important symbol of Christian presence and custodianship in Jerusalem. Christians have not always enjoyed the right of freedom to make pilgrimage to and worship in the Holy Sepulchre, however, access to the sanctuary has always remained a symbolic anchor for Christians in Jerusalem. Perhaps no single place speaks more eloquently of the diversity of Christianity in Jerusalem than the Holy Sepulchre, with multiple side chapels, belonging to Greeks, Armenians, Latins, Syrians, Copts, Ethiopians, competing liturgical rites and celebrations and the aroma of many shades of incense upon the air.[1] A modern expression of this long historical continuity of the complex makeup of Christianity in the Holy Land is that in Jerusalem today there are three Patriarchs: Greek Orthodox, Armenian and Latin; five Catholic patriarchal vicars: Maronite, Greek Catholic, Armenian Catholic, Syrian Catholic and Chaldean Catholic; four archbishops: Assyrian, Syrian Orthodox, Coptic Orthodox and Ethiopian Orthodox; and two Protestant bishops: Anglican and Lutheran. These Christian

---

[1] These opening thoughts I owe much to John Renard's 'Theological Perspectives on the Middle East', *American-Arab Affairs*, No 34 (1990), 56–63.

communities have come under the rule of numerous political entities: Islamic, the Ottoman empire, the British Mandatory Administration, and the modern states of Jordan and Israel.

From the end of the Crusader period onwards the Christian communities and churches of Jerusalem and Palestine have experienced a succession of political systems and states with no partiality to Christianity. At the same time, these churches were representatives of ecclesiastical traditions older than those states, indeed in many ways older than the ethnic identities that are now prevalent in the region.[2] This has meant that the involvement of Christians in politics has been a natural endeavour and a constant theme in the religious culture of Jerusalem. An expression of this relationship between religion and politics in its Palestinian monastic setting has been described by John Binns in *Ascetics and Ambassadors of Christ: The Monasteries of Palestine 314-631*:

> The Monks were people who withdrew from the secular world of the city but also were conscious of belonging to it. This double vocation is shown most clearly in the contrast between the two best-known monks, Euthymius, who consistently sought the seclusion and silence of the desert, and Sabas, who, although a renowned ascetic, was involved in the life of the Church of Jerusalem to the extent of travelling.

The relationship between Christianity and the politics of the Holy Land has a historical significance, which is often hidden under the weight of the modern conflict which continues to disturb the 'peace of Jerusalem'. It is against this background that we will undertake an historical, religious, political and diplomatic survey of relations between the Vatican, the Catholic Church and the Palestinian Christian communities in the Holy Land.

---

[2] Samuel Rubenson, 'Church and State, Communion and Community: Some issues in the recent ecclesiastical history of Jerusalem', (eds) Heikki Palva and Knut S Vikor, *The Middle East Unity and Diversity*, NIAS, Copenhagen, 1993, 84-102.

Rome and Jerusalem

The years 1945-1949 were a time of profound political and social transformation for Palestine. Few other periods in its history match these changes, which left no community unaffected. The Palestinian-Arab Christian and Muslim community were reduced from a majority to a minority in the west and north sections of Mandate Palestine, subject to the rule of a staunchly nationalistic Jewish and Zionist state.[3] The events of 1948-1949 were particularly devastating: a large number of Palestinians became refugees including approximately 50-70 per cent of the Palestinian Christian population.[4] Nearly half of the Christian community of Jerusalem had lived and had their businesses in the more modern and developed Western sector of the city now under Israeli occupation; their property was sequestered after they fled or were compelled to leave. Most of them were forced to seek refuge in the Old City, in monasteries and other Church buildings. Many others were forced to flee elsewhere, some leaving the former Mandate territory all together. Hence the division of Jerusalem into Jordanian and Israeli sectors was of considerable importance to the Christian communities in Jerusalem. The Arab quarters of West Jerusalem which had been taken by the Israelis were almost entirely Christian Arab quarters and much of the centre of West Jerusalem was Christian Church property on which the Holy Places and other shrines,

---

[3] For a general survey see Ian Lustick, *Arabs in the Jewish State. Israel's Control of a National Minority*, University of Texas Press, Austin, 1980. For the position of the Christian communities within the State of Israel, see Ammon Kapeliouk, *Les arabes chrétiens en Israël (1948-1957)*, Thèse de doctorat, Sorbonne, 1968; and *idem*, L'État social, èconomique, culturel et jurdique des Arabes chrétiennes en Israël, *Asian and African Studies*, Vol. 5 (1969), 51-95.

[4] The number of Christian refugees is a difficult and controversial question, Robert Brenton Betts, *Christians in the Arab East. A Political Study*, John Knox Press, Atlanta, 1978, 212, estimated the figure at 55,000 refugees, or 50 percent of the Christians living in what was to become the State of Israel after the 1949 Armistice. However, according to Edward Duff, 'Honor in Israel' in the American Jesuit review, *America*, 26 March 1949, 677 there were 150,000 Christian refugees, of whom 55,000 were Catholic. Bernard Sabella, 'Palestinian Christian emigration from the Holy Land', *Proche-Orient Chrétien*, Vol. 41 (1991), 74, suggests that the war of 1948 witnessed the forced migration of 714,000 Palestinians of whom 50,000 were Christians, or 7 percent of all refugees and 35 percent of all Christian who lived in Palestine prior to 15 May 1948. However, their travails did not end here. For an attempt to remove Arab Christians from Galilee after 1948, see Nur Masalha, 'An Israeli plan to transfer Galilee's Christians to South America: Yosef Weitz and "Operation Yohanan", 1949-1953', (ed.) Anthony O'Mahony, *Palestinian Christians: Religion, Politics and Society in the Holy Land*, Melisende, London, 1999, 190-222.

monasteries and religious institutions of Eastern Jerusalem depended for their maintenance. In addition the heads of various communities lived and worked, almost without exception, in places, which fell under Jordanian control. The lot of the Christian communities could not escape notice in the Vatican, which had always paid tremendous attention to Jerusalem as the birthplace of Christianity and a place of sacramental significance.[5]

The Holy See during this period tried to steer a neutral course, but in the latter half of 1948 the situation of the Palestinian Arab refugees and the question of Jerusalem's future status made for a modification in the Vatican's position. The Holy See was immediately galvanised into massive relief effort on behalf of all Palestinian Arab refugees without distinction between Christian and Muslim. It also set about the search for a viable long-term political solution to the problem of the refugees and sought in particular the return of Palestinian Christians to Jerusalem.[6] From this date the Vatican maintained several distinct policies: a permanent interest in the fate of all Palestinian Arab refugees;[7] a commitment to help finding a long term solution to the Middle East and to the Israeli-

---

[5] Anthony O'Mahony, 'The Vatican, Palestinian Christians, Israel and Jerusalem: Religion, Politics, Diplomacy, and Holy Places, 1945-1950', *Studies in Church History: The Holy Land, Holy Lands, and Christian History*, Vol. 36 (2000), 358-374.

[6] Catholic institutions and agencies were swift to respond to the crisis, providing humanitarian support for the Palestinian Arab refugees in advance of parallel Protestant and the UN and far exceeding all other Christian and other institutions in their efforts. From summer 1948 to February 1950, the American National Catholic Welfare Conference sent $1.3 million, much more than the American Protestant Church World Service, which contributed $331,000. Catholics outside North America gave some $5 million, while various Red Cross organizations contributed just $2 million. This multinational and well-organized Catholic relief effort was provided for all Palestinian refugees, Muslim and Christian, and was formulated by the foundation of 'The Pontifical Mission to Palestine' on 4 June 1949. The Vatican, moreover, did not intend to limit itself to emergency aid, as its avowed goal was to create a viable and long-term political solution to the Christian refugee problem at least, in order to preserve a stable social base for the Church and to prevent future upheavals in the region. See Andrej Kreutz, *Vatican Policy on the Palestinian-Israeli Conflict: The Struggle for the Holy Land*, Greenwood Press, Westport, Connecticut, 1990, 87-111.

[7] M-A Boisard, 'Le Saint-Siège et la Palestine', *Relations Internationales*, Vol. 28 (1981), 443-455 and the studies by A Kreutz, 'The Vatican and the Palestinians: a historical overview', *Islamochristiana*, Vol. 18 (1992), 109-125; 'The Vatican and the Palestinian question', *Social Compass*, Vol. 37 (1990), 239-254; and 'The Vatican and the Palestinians', (eds.) Peter C Kent and John F Pollard, *Papal Diplomacy in the Modern Age*, Greenwood Press, Westport, Connecticut, 1994, 167-179.

Arab conflict in particular;[8] and a concern with the question of Jerusalem and the Holy Places. [9]

Thus papal policy towards Jerusalem can be divided into three periods.

1.   From 1897 to 1947, when the Popes spoke of the Holy Land in general and of Jerusalem, insisting primarily on the need to project the physical integrity of the Holy Places and on the needs of the local Catholic community and its institutions.

2.   From 1947 to 1964 (Pope Paul VI's pilgrimage to the Holy Land); here the stress is on safeguarding the Holy Places, on freedom of access for all faithful of the three monotheistic faiths and the right of each of the three religions to have control of its own holy places.

3.   From 1964 to the present day, a period during which the emphasis moves to Jerusalem in a global context and to the preservation of its identity and vocation: the Holy Places; the areas surrounding them; guarantees for everybody of their own cultural and religious identity; freedom of religion and conscience for the inhabitants and the pilgrims; the cultural dimension.

The development of Vatican policy towards Jerusalem

The fate of Jerusalem and the other Holy Places in Palestine, so strongly linked with the origins of Christianity, has always commanded the Holy

---

[8]   For a general appreciation of Vatican policy to the Middle East, see Gerald Arboit, *Le Saint-Siège et le nouvel order au moyen orient, de la guerre du Golfe à la reconnaissance diplomatique d' Israël*, L'Harmattan, Paris, 1996 and George E Irani, *The Papacy and the Middle East: The Role of the Holy See in the Arab-Israeli conflict, 1962-1984*, University of Notre Dame Press, Notre Dame, Indiana, 1986.

[9]   Jean-Dominique Montoisy, *Le Vatican et le problème des Lieux-Saints*, Franciscan Press, Jerusalem, 1984 and Edmond Farhat (ed.), *Gerusalemme neidocumenti pontifici*, Libreria Editrice Vaticana, Rome, 1987.

See's interest and has led it on a number of occasions to undertake political initiatives designed to guarantee a Catholic presence in the Holy Land.[10] As early as 1922, Cardinal Gasparri, the Vatican Secretary of State, had publicly expressed the fear that the terms of the British mandate for Palestine, which at the time was being approved by the League of Nations, might give the Jewish population a privileged position, which might compromise the rights of the Catholic Church regarding the protection of the Holy Places. These fears gradually faded away in the following years; but the problem of the fate of Palestine was reawaken by the Second World War. Persecution throughout Europe, increasingly urgent and determined requests to allow Jews to emigrate *en masse* to Palestine and the British government's decision to relinquish its mandate created a new political and religious climate within which Papal Policy had to operate. In the aftermath of the Second World War, the Holy See avoided taking a stance either in favour of or against the creation of a Jewish State in Palestine, although it continued to follow attentively the evolution of the political situation in the Middle East.[11] In an uncertain and changeable political climate, the Holy See decided after some hesitation that the best solution to protect the Catholic Church's rights and the Christian communities in the Holy Land in Palestine would be the internationalisation of Jerusalem.[12] The Holy See set about concentrating its own forces in an attempt to obtain international legal status for Jerusalem, as it was foreseen in the plan for the division of Palestine

---

[10] For a general view of these endeavours, see S I Minerbi, *The Vatican and Zionism. Conflict in the Holy Land, 1895-1925*, Oxford University Press, 1990, 15-95; H F Kock, *Der Vatikan und Palastina*, Herold Verlag, Vienna-Munich, 1973; G Pierazzi, 'Der Vatikan and die Heilgen Statten in Palastina, 1919-1922 und 1947-1950', *Jahrbuch der Diplomatischen Akademie Wien* (1973), 99-110; Daniella Fabrizio, *La questione dei Luoghi Santi e l'assetto della Palestina, 1914-1922*, Franco Angeli, Milan, 2000. For an attempt by Belgium Catholics to get the mandate for Palestine and hence to protect the Holy Places of Christianity, see Roger Aubert, 'Les démarches du Cardinal Mercier en view de l'octroi à la Belique d'un mandate sur la Palestine', *Academie Royale de Belgique. Bulletin de la Classe des lettres et des sciences, morales et politique*, Vol.65 (1979), 145-228.

[11] On the background to the Vatican opposition to the Zionist plan for Palestine, see Meir Mendes, *Le Vatican et Israel*, Editions Cerf, Paris, 1990, 69-96; Andre Chouraqui, *La Reconnaissance, Le Saint-Sèige, les Juifs et Israël*, Robert Laffort, Paris, 1992, 101-168 and for a history of Vatican-Zionist relations, Michael Perko, 'Toward a "Sound and Lasting Basis": Relations between the Holy See, the Zionist Movement and Israel, 1896-1996', *Israel Studies*, Vol. 2, no.1 (1998), 1-26.

[12] Pietro Pastorelli, 'La santa Sede e il problema di Gerusalemme', *Storia e Politica*, Vol. 21 (1982), 57-98.

approved 29 November 1947, by the General Assembly of the United
Nations. To this end the Vatican encouraged several political and diplomatic
alternatives and sought to mobilise the Catholic hierarchy and faithful
throughout the world in support of such a move.[13] The attitude taken by
the Vatican on the Palestine issue at the end of the Second World War was
unequivocally and succinctly stated in the summer of 1949 by the British
plenipotentiary minister at the Holy See:

> The Vatican would have preferred, from the point of view
> of the fate of the Holy Places and of Catholic interests in
> Palestine generally, that neither Jews nor Arabs, but a Third
> Power, should have control in the Holy Land. Such a solution
> it well knew, however, was unattainable, and in the actual
> circumstances it preferred the Arabs to the Jews.[14]

There is considerable evidence proving this diagnosis to be true.
Once the Holy See had overcome its suspicion of the Balfour Declaration,
it was generally satisfied with the British management of the Palestine
mandate, and particularly with the rigorous respect of the *status quo* that
Britain assured, which had prevented the Orthodox Church from gaining
new positions in the possession and administration of the Holy Places
and which had permitted the Vatican to distance itself from France, whose
traditional function as the protector of Catholic interests in the Holy
Land had by now lost most of its meaning.[15] Thus, in respect of the

---

[13] See the fundamental work by Silvio Ferrari on Vatican Policy toward the Jerusalem
question, 'The Vatican, Israel and the Question of Jerusalem (1943-1984)', *Middle East
Journal*, Vol. 39 (1985), 316-331; 'The Struggle for Jerusalem', *European Journal of International
Affairs*, Vol. 1 (1991), 22-39; 'Il Vaticano e la questione di Gerusalemme nel Carteggio
Spellman-Truman', *Storia Contemporanea* Vol. 13, no. 2 (1982), 285-320; 'La Santa Sede e il
problema della Palestina nel secondo Dopoguerra', *Communitá*, (1985), 400-446; 'Per
Gerusalemme una e indivibile', *Limes*, Vol. 2 (1994), 149-162.

[14] London, Public Record Office [PRO], Fo. 371/WV 1011, Perowne to Attlee, 9 August,
1949; see also FO 371/E6425, Perowne to Bevin, 4 May 1948.

[15] On the Vatican and the ending of the French Protectorate in Palestine, see Sergio I
Minerbi, *L'Italie et la Palestine, 1914-1920*, PUF, Paris, 1970; *idem*, 'L'Italie contre le
Protectorat religieux Français en Palestine (1914-1920)', *Asian and African Studies*, Vol. 4
(1968), 23-56; Daniela Fabrizio, 'Il Protettorato Religioso sui Cattolici in Oriente: La
questione delle relazioni diplomatiche dirette tra Santa Sede e Impero Ottomano, 1901-
1918', *Nuova Rivista Storica,* Vol. 82 (1998), 583-626 and Catherine Nicault, 'La fin du
protectorat religieux de la France à Jérusalem (1918-1924)', *Bulletin du Centre de recherche
française de Jérusalem*, No. 4 (1999), 7-24.

arrangements made for Palestine following World War One, the Vatican and the Catholic powers acquiesced in a situation not consonant with their desires but at least not unsatisfactory to them. Control of Jerusalem and the Holy Places went with control of Palestine, and British control in their view was better than Turkish control.[16] If they had been unable to improve the position of the Latins in the Holy Places, they had at least prevented it from deteriorating further. The Orthodox were satisfied with British control of Jerusalem and Bethlehem as long as the status quo of 1852 was adhered to. Since Jerusalem was in the hands of a Protestant power, Protestants found little of a religious nature to complain about. Against this background it was understandable that the British decision to relinquish the Palestine mandate, announced in spring 1947, was greeted with dismay by the Holy See, which could see no satisfactory alternative way of protecting Catholic interests in the Holy Land.[17] As there was now no chance of Britain's mandate in the Holy Land being extended and because doubts were growing regarding the wisdom of entrusting Palestine to UN administration for fear of allowing Soviet penetration in the Middle East, the Vatican was faced with an alternative: a divided Holy Land as the result of the creation of a Jewish State and an Arab State or the creation of a single state in Palestine representing both sides but with an Arab majority, considered to be the lesser evil as compared with the creation of a Jewish State.[18]

The creation of a single Arab-controlled state in Palestine was openly supported by the Middle Eastern Catholic community and by influential Catholic elements in Jerusalem and Palestine. In Rome these positions were greeted favourably in some ecclesiastical circles close to the Sacred Oriental Congregation, highly aware of the implications of the Palestine question for the future of Catholic activities throughout the Middle East. However, the Vatican did not pronounce itself in favour of an Arab State in Palestine although it knew perfectly well that, generally, Catholic communities and most ecclesiastical authorities preferred this solution to the division of the Holy Land. This reticence is explained by

---

[16] Maria Grazia Enardu, *Palestine in Anglo-Vatican Relations, 1936-1939*, Università degli studi di Firenze, Facoltà di Scienze Politiche 'Cesare Alfari', 1980.

[17] Paolo Pieraccini, *Gerusalemme, Luoghi Santi e communità religiose nella politica internazionale*, Edizioni Dehoniane, Bologne, 1997, 47-78.

[18] S Ferrai, *Vaticano e Israele dal secondo conflitto mondiale all guerra del Golfo*, Sansoni Editore, Florence, 1991, 29-54.

the Vatican's hopes for the internationalisation of Jerusalem, which was an important feature of the plan to divide Palestine approved in the summer of 1947 by the majority of the United Nations Special Committee on Palestine (UNSCOP). The creation of a Jewish state in Palestine was viewed even less favourably. The fears and worries of leading exponents of the Curia in Rome and the Holy See's concern over growing Jewish immigration into the Holy Land are well known. There is nothing to suggest that this attitude changed after the end of the Second World War. As well as coming up against the incomprehension and suspicion of those sections of Catholicism inclined to interpret the dispersion of the Jewish people in theological terms,[19] the return of the Jews to Palestine was something of an unknown quantity in relation to the protection of the Holy Places and the safeguarding of Christian interests. The Holy See preferred not to choose between these unsatisfactory alternatives. Despite pressures from Arab countries and particularly intense pressure from the Christian Arab community in the Middle East, the Vatican managed to avoid making any statement about the territorial aspects of the Palestine issue.

Meanwhile, the Vatican continued to oppose any plan for making permanent the division of Jerusalem between Jordan and Israel, since under such an arrangement there would be little prospect for concentrating a Christian population in Jerusalem in sufficient numbers to have much say in the conduct of the affairs of the city or to provide a base for promotion of Vatican interests in the Near East. Proposals for functional

---

[19] See the following studies on the positions taken by some leading Catholic thinkers regarding the theological and political status of the State of Israel. For the leading French philosopher Jacques Maritain, see Esther Starobinski-Safran, 'Judaïme, peuple juif et État d'Israël', *Jacques Maritain face á la modernité. Enjeux d'une approche philosophique. Colloque de Cerisy*, textes réunis par Michael Bressolette et René Mougel, Presses universitaires du Mirail, 1995, 219-243, and Sylvain Guéna, 'La passion d'Israël. Réflexions de Jacques Maritain sur la Shoah', *Istina*, Vol. 45 (2000), 16-36. The Swiss Cardinal Journet and founder of the influence periodical *Nova et Vetera*, Esther Starobinski-Safran, 'Les destinées d'Israël, son mystère et la foi mosaïque selon Charles Journet', *Charles Journet (1891-1975). Un théologien en son sièle*, Actes du colloque de Genève, 1991, sous la direction de Philippe Chenaux, Editions Universitaires Fribourg Suisse, 1992, 72-88. And Louis Massignon the French Islamicist and mythical-political activist, Anthony O'Mahony, '*Le pèlerin de Jérusalem*: Louis Massignon, Palestinian Christians, Islam and the State of Israel', *Palestinian Christians: Religion, Politics and Society in the Holy Land*, (ed.) A O'Mahony, Melisende, London, 1999, 166-189, and Dominique Bourel, 'Massignon face à face Israël', *Louis Massignon: mystique en dialogue*, Collection 'Question de' no. 90, Albin Michel, Paris, 1992, 67-75.

internationalisation of the shrines were also not very appealing. The introduction of the authority of the UN into the already complicated picture of the Holy Places might only serve to erode Latin rights, especially since it would be difficult to control the composition of the proposed UN commission for the Holy Places. Consequently, Pope Pius XII issued an encyclical on Palestine, *Redemptoris Nostri*, on April 15, restating his support for full territorial internationalisation. He urged all the faithful to exert every effort to see that their governments supported this course of action.[20]

The idea of establishing Jerusalem as a separate entity, directly controlled by the United Nations, was developed during the summer of 1947 in a subcommittee of UNSCOP, which was responsible for studying the problem of the Holy Places in Palestine. It was then included among the proposals put forward by the majority of this body and became an essential aspect of the plan to divide Palestine. For this reason, it obtained the support (albeit reluctant) of the Jewish Agency and of the countries which supported the creation of a Jewish state in the Holy Land. Thus it was reproposed in the report made by the first subcommittee set up in October 1947 by the ad hoc committee of the United Nations, approved by the United Nations on 25 November 1947 (as part, however, of a much wider plan for the division of Palestine) and finally accepted by the General Assembly under Resolution 181 (II) on 29 November 1947. During this period of time the Holy See made no request, either publicly or confidentially, for the internationalization of Jerusalem.[21]

It would seem, then, that initially the Holy See came to favour a system of guarantees which did not necessarily imply the creation of Jerusalem as a *corpus separatum*. But it is equally obvious that the Vatican was extremely pleased when this solution received the support of the majority of UNSCOP. The Vatican felt it gave the best protection possible to the Holy Places and the Catholic community in Palestine and, in addition, satisfied a number of spiritual ideals (a legal and institutional framework embodying the universal meaning of the Holy Places) and

---

[20] H Eugene Bovis, *Jerusalem Question, 1917-1968*, Hoover Institution Press, Stanford 1971, 71. The original text is in *Oriente Moderno*, Vol. 29 (1949), 52-53; translated text in *The New York Times*, 16 April 1949.

[21] S Ferrari, 'The Holy See and the Postwar Palestine issue. The Internationalization of Jerusalem and the protection of the Holy Places', *International Affairs*, Vol. 60, no. 2 (1984), 261-283.

political ideals (preventing Jerusalem from becoming part of a Jewish or Arab State) that were deeply rooted in the Catholic world. The origin of the internationalisation plan cannot therefore be directly attributed to requests put forward by Christian religious confessions, even though the desire to remove the Holy Places from Jewish and Arab control undoubtedly contributed to encouraging this solution. Rather, the plan must be attributed to the international policies of those countries, especially France,[22] which were interested in obtaining a sphere of influence throughout the Middle East by virtue of the UN presence in the Holy City.

The question of Jerusalem now moved to the UN. The debate on this occasion centered on three different proposals. The first was the Palestine Conciliation Commission's proposal suggesting Israel and Jordan should each govern the two zones into which Jerusalem was divided as a result of the fighting in 1948 and that a UN Commissioner should be appointed with the task, among other things, of protecting the Holy Places. The second was put forward by Sweden and Holland and proposed to limit UN activity to the protection of the Holy Places, not far removed from the 'functional' internationalisation of Jerusalem that the Israel government had stated it was willing to implement on several occasions. The third proposal was supported by Australia, which proposed a return to the principle of Jerusalem's territorial internationalisation favoured in Resolution 181 (II) of November 29, 1947. The Australian draft resolution, fiercely contested by Israel and opposed by the US and the UK, was supported by the Arab bloc (save Jordan), the Communist bloc (which saw the internationalisation of Jerusalem as a chance to enter Middle East politics) and the majority of Catholic countries, no doubt heavily influenced by the Vatican. In Australia, the Labour Government facing national elections in 1949 was particularly mindful that some 30 percent of the Australain electorate was Catholic. At the end of a heated debate this heterogeneous coalition managed to obtain sufficient votes for the Australian resolution to be approved, and with it the reaffirmation of the principle of territorial internationalisation for Jerusalem.

There can be no doubt, that the Vatican did everything in its

---

[22] On French catholic opinion, see D Lazar, *L'Opinion Française et la naissance de l'État d'Israël, 1945-1949*, Paris, 1972, 177-219, and for the development of that thought, Y Rash, *Deminer un champ fertile: les catholiques français et l'État d'Israël*, Editions du Cerf, Paris, 1982, and *idem, Catholiques de France, un Israëlien vous parle*, Cana, Paris, 1981.

power to support Jerusalem's territorial internationalisation. Had the Australian resolution been rejected, the General Assembly would probably have approved the project for the 'functional' internationalisation proposed by Sweden and Holland. It would have been a very serious blow to the Vatican, which would have been forced, by the will of the UN, to accept a solution that it had refused on every occasion it was proposed by the Israelis in the course of direct negotiations.

The vote taken on December 9 1949, reaffirming the General Assembly's will to internationalise Jerusalem territorially further stiffened the position of Israel and Jordan. They intensified their negotiations to find an agreement based on Jerusalem's division and accelerated the process of integrating the sections of Jerusalem they controlled into their respective States. The Israeli Parliament proclaimed Jerusalem its capital and transferred its headquarters and main government offices there. The King of Jordan, worried by the rise of dangerous rivalry with Amman, merely appointed a Supreme Custodian of the Holy Places in Jerusalem.

Pope Paul VI and John Paul II on the Jerusalem question

The Holy See was firm in its request for the territorial internationalisation of Jerusalem up until 1967. After the 1967 war, however, the new situation that had been created with the unification of the city in Israeli hands pushed the Vatican to reconsider its very strategy.[23]

In the first place it must be kept in mind that after the Second Vatican Council, many theological reserves had been removed with regard to the reconstitution of a Jewish state: the declaration *Nostra Aetate*, in affirming that the death of Christ 'cannot be either indirectly attributed to those Jews living at the time, or to the Jews living in our day', dismissed the traditional theological justification of the Jewish Diaspora, relegating the existence of the State of Israel to an exclusively political dimension.

From this perspective the reconstitution of a Jewish nation, while still continuing to be the object of debate from a theological stand-point, ceased to be a problem on the political landscape, as demonstrated by the

---

[23] S Ferrari, 'Le Saint-Siège, L'État d'Israël et les Lieux-Saints de Jèrusalem', (ed.) J-B D'Onorio, *Le Saint-Siège dans les relations internationals*, Editions du Cerf/Cujas, Paris, 1989, 301-321.

frequent references of John Paul II to the State of Israel and the right of the Jewish people to live in security and tranquillity.[24] The Vatican withheld diplomatic recognition of Israel can be explained by political motives, among which figure the unresolved problem of Jerusalem,[25] the enduring tensions among the states of the Middle Eastern region, the absence of internationally recognised borders and the lack of justice for the Palestinian people, for which the Holy See continues to vindicate the right to the homeland.

Pope Paul VI[26] totally redefined the position of the Holy See with the speech made on December 22, 1967, in which were indicated the elements that the Holy See judged 'essential and indispensable' in any solution to the problem of Jerusalem and the holy places: the first, according to the Pope, regarded the holy places justly so called and considered by the three great monotheistic religions concerned with them—the Jewish, the Christian and the Muslim—and intended to protect the freedom of worship, the respect for, conservation of and access to these very holy places, guarded by special immunities by the means of its very own status, and whose observance was to be guaranteed by an

---

[24] Phillippe Levillain, 'Israël et le Saint-Siège. L'accord fondamentale entre le Saint-Siège et Israël', *Dictionnaire historique de la papauté*, (ed.) P Levillain, Fayard, Paris, 1994, 915-917; F Yerly, 'Le Saint-Siège, l' État d' Israël et la paix au Moyen-Orient', *Vingtième siècle*, no. 51 (1996), 3-14, and for an Israeli perspective, see Sergio I Minerbi, 'The Vatican and Israel', *Papal Diplomacy in the Modern Age, op. cit.*, 189-201; *idem*, 'The Catholic Church, Judaism and the State of Israel', *Christian-Jewish Relations*, Vol. 21, no. 2 (1988), 26-35; and for an alternative Catholic perspective, Georeg E Irani, 'The Holy See and the Israeli-Palestinian Conflict', (ed.) Kail C Ellis, *The Vatican, Islam and the Middle East*, Syracuse University Press, 1987, 125-142. The entire religious and diplomatic environment was subsequently changed by the visit to the Holy Land in March 2000 by Pope John Paul II, see 'Jean-Paul II en Terre Sainte', *Istina* Vol. 41 (2000), 113-195.

[25] The Vatican establishment of diplomatic relations between the Holy See and Jordan on 3 March 1994, for the background to the relationship see Joseph L Ryan, 'The Holy See and Jordan', *The Vatican, Islam and the Middle East*, 163-188. And between the Holy See and Israel on June 14 1994, 'Accord fondamental entre le Saint-Siège et l'État d'Israël', *Istina*, Vol. 41 (1996), 401-428.

[26] For the background and the impact upon Paul VI of his pilgrimage to Jerusalem and the Holy Land, see Claude Soetens, 'Entre Concile et initiative pontificale: Paul VI en Terre Sainte', *Cristianesimo nella storia*, Vol. 19 (1998), 333-365. On the Second Vatican Council and the Jews and Paul VI's relations with the Jewish people and Israel, see the studies by Jean-Marie Delmaire, 'Une ouverte prudente: Paul VI, le judaïsme et Israël', *Paul Vi et la modernité dans l'Église*, École française de Rome, Palais Farnèse, 1984, 821-835; 'Vatican II et les juifs', *Le deuxième concile du Vatican (1959-1965)*, École française de Rome, Palais Farnèse 1989, 577-606.

institution of international character, with particular attention paid to the historic and religious physiognomy of Jerusalem. The second aspect of the question referred to the free enjoyment of religious and civil rights, legitimately due to all persons and activities of all the communities present in the territory of Palestine.

With this speech, the Pope did not revive—nor did he explicitly exclude—the request for the territorial internationalisation of Jerusalem, and indicated the specifics which the Holy See's judgement would have to qualify any alternative formula. These were three: first, the safeguarding of the holy places and of the historic and religious character of the city; second, the international nature of the status as applicable to any and all parties; and third, the protection of the civil and religious rights of the Palestinian communities.

In order to understand the position of the Holy See, particular attention should be directed at the reference to the necessity of protecting (in addition to the holy places) the 'historic and religious physiognomy' of Jerusalem, inserted into Paul VI's speech and constantly repeated afterwards: implicit in this, in fact, was the refusal of a solution founded solely on the extra-territoriality of the holy places, which while it would have adequately protected the latter, would not have been able to provide any guarantee whatsoever against transformations,—demographic, urban, architectural,—that would alter irreparably the sacred character of the entire city.

Of equal importance appeared the reference to the 'religious and civil rights' due to 'all the communities present in the territory of Palestine'. Understood in this appeal was the obvious intention of Paul VI to guarantee the indispensable conditions for the survival of the Christian community in Palestine, with the aim of stopping a flow of emigration that threatened to transform the Holy places into 'museums void of life'.[27] From this preoccupation came an acute sensitivity to the demands of the Arab community (to which the greater majority of Christians in the Holy Land belong) and to the lot of the Palestinian people, whose destiny appeared in a certain way connected with that of

---

[27] On the whole question of Christian immigration from the Holy Land, see Bernard Sabella, 'Socio-economic Characteristics and Challenges to Palestinian Christians in the Holy Land', *Palestinian Christians. Religion, Politics and Society in the Holy Land, op. cit.*, 82-95 and 'Palestinian Christians: Realities and Hopes', *The Holy Land, Holy Lands, and Christian History: Studies in Church History*, 373-397.

Christianity itself in the Holy Land. Here is the source of the close relationship inter-woven in papal documents between the question of the holy places and the Palestinian question. It is certainly no coincidence that it was Paul VI himself—the Pope who most appreciated the opportunity to enlarge the focus from the Holy Places to include the Christian community in the Holy Land—who recognised in 1972 that the Palestinians were something more than simple refugees, but indeed a 'people' which had the right to 'equal recognition of its aspirations' and, as John Paul II would add later, a homeland.

Confronted by these worrying developments, the Holy See—guided by John Paul II—clarified its position in three documents, among which the most important was the apostolic letter *Redemptions Anno* of the 20 April, 1984.

John Paul II described the importance of Jerusalem '... Jews ardently love [Jerusalem] and in every age venerate her memory, abundant as she is in many remains and monuments from the time of David who chose her as the capital, and Solomon who built the Temple there. Therefore they turn their minds to her daily, one may say, and point to her as the sign of their nation. Christians honour her with a religious and intent concern because there the words of Christ so often resounded, there the great events of Redemption were accomplished: the Passion, Death and Resurrection of the Lord. In the city of Jerusalem the first Christian community sprang up and remained throughout the centuries a continual ecclesial presence despite difficulties. Muslims also call Jerusalem "Holy", with a profound attachment that goes back to the origins of Islam and springs from the fact that there have been many special places of pilgrimage and for more than a thousand years have dwelt there, almost without interruption.'

Further he says: 'I am convinced that the failure to find an adequate solution to the question of Jerusalem, and the resigned postponement of the problem, only compromise further the longed-for peaceful and just settlement of the crisis of the whole Middle East'.

In this letter the Pope took care to identify two principles which he judged unacceptable: first of all, methodologically, the unilateral search for a solution to the question of Jerusalem (as Israel had done in proclaiming the city capital of the State), or even by way of 'bilateral understandings between one and other states' (as was the case at Camp David); and secondly, substantially, the reduction of the problem to the simple 'free access for all to the holy places' (which was the text sustained by the government of Israel).

Thus, clearing the field of all possible ambiguities, the Holy See was able to outline the framework its own project for Jerusalem. This plan departs from the establishment of the predominant religious significance of the Holy City, 'crossroads between earth and heaven', a significance that today translates into the vocation of Jerusalem to become the place of encounter and recognition among the believers of the three great monotheistic religions, existing on 'a level of equality, without any one having to feel subordinate, and with respect to the others.'[28]

The political problem of Jerusalem could find its resolution, therefore, in the recognition of a legal status that allowed the city to realise its historical function. From this comes the necessity of legal guarantees that protect on one hand 'the existence of the religious communities, their conditions, their future', and on the other, the *habitat* in which they find themselves, and thus the historic, urban and architectural configuration that the city has assumed.

These legal guarantees in addition must have—in the Holy See's judgement—an international nature, first of all, in order to provide them with a stable character, and secondly, because the involvement of the entire international community in the protection of the city would express the universal significance of Jerusalem. Yet it does not seem necessary that these guarantees cover the entire city, nor that they be incompatible with the sovereignty exercised over them by one or more states.[29]

Considered in the entirety of the thought of Pope John Paul II regarding the Jerusalem question we can delineate an 'organic' development of themes already affirmed by Paul VI, although reformulated in light of the theological and political currents that inspire the current Pope. The accent put on the religious meaning of the Holy

[28] S Ferrari, 'Coabitazioni tra religioni a Gerusalemme', (ed.) A Riccardi, *Il Mediterraneo nel Novecento*, Cinisello Balsamo, San Paolo, 1994, 316-336.

[29] For the development of Vatican and Catholic thinking on the Jerusalem question, see the ensemble of works by the French Franciscan scholar, Bernardin Collin, *Les Lieux-Saints*, Les Éditions internationales, Paris, 1948; *Le problème juridique des Lieux-Saints*, Sircy, Paris, 1956; *Les Lieux-Saints*, PUF, Paris, 1968; *Pour une solution au problème des Lieux-Saints*, Maisonneuvre et Larose, Paris, 1974; *Rome, Jérusalem et les Lieux-Saints*, Éditions Franciscaines, Paris, 1981, and *Recuil de documents concernant Jérusalem et les Lieux-Saints*, Franciscan Press, Jerusalem, 1982.

City—already present in the statements of Paul VI—is coherent with all of the thoughts and actions of John Paul II,[30] and above all the idea (a newer one) that the resolution of the question of Jerusalem is a preliminary condition for a consequent Middle Eastern peace settlement.

It would be simplistic to read this affirmation as merely a report on the attempts to relegate the problem of Jerusalem to the margins of international diplomatic negotiations: in reality, it explains the Pope's conviction that the reconstruction of peace in the Middle East can only be based on the rediscovery of a common faith in God on the part of Christians, Jews and Moslems,[31] just as—indicating another field of application for this very same principle of the priority of the 'religious' over the 'political'—the reconstruction of the unity of the European peoples can be based only on the rediscovery of the Christian soul of Europe according to the Pontiff.[32]

The re-establishment of the Latin Patriarchate of Jerusalem

Whether they are Catholic or non-Catholic, the eleven Christian Churches in the Arab world have in common the fact that they belong to the world of the Christian Orient. Unique in its kind, the twelfth Church is Latin in rite and Roman in discipline: 95 percent of its faithful are Arabs, and its current Patriarch is a Palestinian.[33]

The reasons for this particularity are historical. After seeking for a long time to re-establish the unity of the Church by negotiations between Ecclesiastical hierarchies, from the 16th century onwards the Papacy attempted to reconstitute Catholic unity at grass-roots level,[34]

---

[30] On John Paul II's relations with the Jewish people, see D Cerbelaud, 'Jean-Paul II et le judaïsme: une ténacité exemplaire', *Lumière et vie*, no. 257, 2003, 21-35.

[31] S Ferrari, 'The Religious significance of Jerusalem in the Middle East Peace Process: some legal implications', *Catholic University Law Review*, Vol. 45, no. 3 (1996), 733-743.

[32] Michael Sutton, 'John Paul II's Idea of Europe', *Religion, State and Society*, Vol. 25, no. 1 (1997), 17-30.

[33] Frans Bouwen, 'The Churches in the Middle East and The Churches in Jerusalem', (ed.) Lawrence S Cunningham, *Ecumenism. Present Realities and Future Prospects*, University of Notre Dame Press, 1998, 25-36 and 37-49.

[34] Bernard Heyberger, *Les Chrétiens du Proche-Orient au temps de la Réforme catholique*, Ecole Française de Rome, Rome, 1994.

benefiting from the development of the European influence within the Ottoman empire.[35]

In the whole of the Middle East it has not more than 75,000 faithful, the majority of whom come under the jurisdiction of the Latin Patriarchate of Jerusalem, which largely corresponds to the territories of Jordan, Palestine and Israel. Other small Latin communities exist also in Syria (3,000 people), Lebanon (5,000), Turkey (5,000), Iraq (3,500) and Cyprus (1,000). The influence of this Church is, however, not limited to the meagre number of its flock. It is strongly supported by the Roman institutions and partakes more than any other part of the Catholic Church of the Orient of the power and authority of the Vatican, which might express itself through the Patriarchate on issues relating to the acute important regional and geo-political problems. Moreover, the presence of foreign mission in the Middle East, complemented by a still quite dense network of schools and medical and social establishments gives Latin Catholicism an influence which goes far beyond the modest appearance of its structures at diocese and parish level.[36]

The idea to establish a Latin-rite Church in the Middle East took shape during the Crusades. When the Franks entered Jerusalem in 1099 the Patriarchal see was vacant because the titular had fled.[37] In addition, the victors had, of their own authority decided to replace him with a Latin Patriarch, of Catholic faith, Latin in rite and Roman in discipline. Its jurisdiction was subsequently to extend to the bishoprics of Lebanon (excluding Tripoli and Jbeil). In 1100, a second Latin Patriarchate was created in Antioch. For almost a century the new Church was closely dependent on the Crusader principalities, and the devolution of patriarchal and episcopal charges was decided locally depending on the political balance of power. However, with the fall of Jerusalem and the withdrawal of the Patriarchate to Saint-Jean-d'Acre at the end of the 12th century, the weakening of the Latin States enabled the Papacy to take matters back in hand by imposing its right to nominate the Patriarch. In 1291, the last Latin Patriarch died drowned in the ditches of Saint-Jean-d'Acre when the last Crusader citadel was taken. The

[35] Joseph Hajjar, 'La question religieuse en Orient au déclin de l'Empire Ottoman (1683-1814)', *Istina*, Vol. 13 (1968), 153-260.

[36] Anton Issa, 'Il Patriarcato Latino di Gerusalemme', Giovanni Bissoli (ed.), *Gerusalemme. Realtà sogni e speranze*, Franciscan Press, Jerusalem, 1996, 142-160.

[37] Bernard Hamilton, 'The Latin Church in the Crusader States', (eds.) K Ciggaar, A Davids and H Teule, *East and West in the Crusaders States*, Editions Peeters, Louvain, 1996, 1-20.

Patriarchal title, which was deprived of real jurisdiction, was, however, to survive until 1847 in favour of the Latin titular prelates established in Europe.

The disappearance of the resident Patriarch in Jerusalem, however, did not put an end to all Latin presence. It was maintained thanks to the Franciscan Order which from 1219 onwards established a province and then a 'custody' of the Holy Land; despite the hostility of the Greek Church (which had been re-established in Palestine after the departure of the Crusaders). They pursued the Mamelukes to accept its presence in Jerusalem as well as the existence of 'Catholic rights' over the Holy Places (Church of the Holy Sepulchre in Jerusalem and Church of the Nativity in Bethlehem), which were exercised by the Franciscans. The legal basis of these rights were constituted by an agreement concluded in 1333 between the King of Naples, Robert d'Anjou, and the Mameluke sultan of Egypt, and was ratified by the Pope in 1342.[38] This recognition was, however, not enough to efficiently protect the friars, as they were very isolated in a hostile environment and experienced several difficult moments. In the mid-16th century they were even expelled from their custodial see (on Mount Zion) by the Ottomans and obliged to withdraw to the convent of the Holy Saviour where they are still based today.

In 1847, the Latin Patriarchate was re-established in Jerusalem, up until that point the Greek Catholic Patriarch of Antioch considered itself to be the representative of the Oriental Catholics in Palestine. The choice of Palestine is paradoxical, as the largest Latin parishes were rather to be found in Lebanon. It is explained by the fact that the Holy See was determined to ensure the safeguarding of the Catholic rights over the Holy Places which were threatened by the aggressive machinations of the Greek Orthodox clergy which had only accepted the presence of the Latins in Jerusalem unwillingly. The protection offered by French diplomacy had for a long time been sufficient to preserve the position of the Franciscans.[39] In the mid-18th century the situation changed however with the appearance of Russia, which after the treaty of Kutchuk-

---

[38] M Roncaglia, 'The Sons of St Francis in the Holy Land. Official entrance of the Franciscans as custodians of the Basilica of the Nativity in Bethlehem', *Franciscan Studies*, Vol. 10 (1950), 257-285.

[39] On the modern history of the Franciscan Custody, see A Giovannelli, *La Santa Sede e la Palestina. La Custodia di Terra Santa tra la fine dell'impero ottomano e la guerra dei sei giorni*, Ed. Studium, Rome, 2000.

Kainardji (1774) presented itself as protector of the Orthodox in the Ottoman Empire. This change in the balance of power led to a first retreat by the Latins after 1757 from its position in the Holy Places. The Latins had exclusive rights over the Holy Sepulchre from 1690 with the support of French diplomacy but were partly turned out following an attack by the Greeks, which the Ottoman government ratified.[40]

In the mid-19th century this balance of power evolved even more unfavourably for the Catholics. Jerusalem was the object of a rivalry between the European powers, which was exercised through the Churches.[41] Whereas Britain and Prussia acted in unison to reinforce their political and religious influence by establishing an (Anglican) Anglo-Prussian bishopric in Jerusalem, Russia dispatched an Ecclesiastical high dignitary to the Levant in the following year, in order to mark its interest and concern for the local Orthodox Churches. As far as France was concerned, its retreat during the Syrian-Egyptian crisis in 1840 did not allow it to make any reply. In this unfavourable context for the Catholics, the Greek Church of Jerusalem multiplied its pressure in order to undermine the Latin rights over the Holy Places. In 1847, the Silver Star of the Church of the Nativity, symbol of these rights, was taken down. This incident convinced the Papacy (which was strongly supported by the Catholic powers) that the time had come to put a stop to the process of trying to eliminate Catholics rights. Rejecting the concerns of the Franciscans who wanted to maintain the monopoly over the protection of the Catholic rights as well as of the other Oriental Catholic Churches, Piux IX in his bull *Nulla celebrior* decided to re-establish a Latin Patriarchate residing in Jerusalem five and a half centuries after the disappearance of that which had existed during the Crusades. Guiseppe Valerga was appointed the first Latin Patriarch of Jerusalem.[42]

---

[40] M Roncaglia, 'La questione dei Luoghi Santi .nuovi documenti (1757)', *Studia Orientalia Christiana Collectanea*, Vol. 1 (1956), 135-138 and Vol. 2 (1957), 65-69.

[41] Thomas Stransky, 'Origins of Western Christian Missions in Jerusalem and the Holy Land', *Jerusalem in the Mind of the Western World, 1800-1948*), (eds.) Y Ben-Arieh and M Davis, Praeger, Westport, Conn., 1997, 1-19; Catherine Mayeur-Jaouen, 'Les Chrétiens d'Orient au XIXe siècle: un renouveau lourd de menaces', *Histoire du christianisme des origines à nos jours: XI Libéralisme, Industralisation, Expansion Européenne (1830-1914)*, Desclée, Paris, 1996, 793-849.

[42] S Manna, *Chiesa Latina e Chiese Orientali all epoca del Patriarca Giuseppe Valerga (1813-1872)*, Pontificio Istituto degli Studi Orientali, Naples–Rome, 1972; Pierre Duvignau, *Une vie au service de l'Église. S.B. Mgr Joseph Valerga, Patriarche Latin de Jérusalem, 1813-1872*, Imprimerie du Patriarcat Latin, Jerusalem, 1972.

The creation of a new see which had to be ratified by the Ottoman government was the opportunity to open negotiations with a view to determine its prerogatives; these were in fact to extend to the protection of the Catholic rights in the Holy City. This task was performed by the French diplomacy. The Patriarchate was not formally recognised but was able to exercise jurisdiction and authority in fact and was, on a diplomatic level, treated like the other Patriarchates in the city. The division of rights over the Christian Holy Places between Greeks, Armenians and Latins was the subject of a *firman* in 1852 which settled the dispute concerning the church in Bethlehem and perpetuated the situation which existed in 1757, following the first trespassing by the Greeks. This is the famous *status quo* which is given international recognition by the treaty of Berlin (1878) and which is still *in situ* today.[43]

The Latin Patriarchate of Jerusalem was established without the necessity or the ambition to create a Latin Catholic community in the Holy Land. However, in fact a community did come into being as the result of the creation of the Patriarchate. In only a few decades, the 4,000 Latin Catholics in the Holy Land multiplied by 10 (not counting those who were settled outside of the Patriarchal scope i.e. in Lebanon, Syria, Mesopotamia and Constantinople). Many Christians in the Holy Land rallied to the new Patriarchate, particularly those who felt culturally close to Europe, or those taken by the modernity of the institution and or those just wishing for a more demanding spirituality and discipline. Others were simply aware that by being part of Latin Catholicism they would enjoy better protection in Ottoman Palestine and would be able to benefit from the services of efficient social and educational establishments.

However the creation of the Latin Patriarchate of Jerusalem was questioned by all of the existing Oriental Catholic hierarchies, who understandably felt nervous about the creation of this new and challenging Ecclesia. It became particularly clear during the First Vatican Council when the work of the preparatory commission on the Oriental Churches, which was undertaken in the absence of the Oriental prelates, led to a 'Latinist' programme, but which was not adopted due to the Council being suspended prematurely. The dispute lessened during the Pontificate of Leo XIII who put an end to most of the Latinising tendencies amongst

---

[43] Selim Sayegh, *Le status quo des Lieux-Saints. Nature juridique et portée internationale*, Pontificia Universitá Lateranense, Rome, 1971.

the growing Catholic communities in the Christian Orient, and the Congrès Eucharistique International in Jerusalem called by the Pope in 1893 confirmed this policy. The new Pope was at pains to renew dialogue between Eastern and Western Christendom and was aware of the key role, which the Oriental Catholic Churches might play in disarming the distrust generated between these two parts of the Christian Church.[44] Moreover, among other initiatives he published the Encyclical *Orientalium dignitas*, which recognised the value of the Oriental rites and prohibited Oriental Christians converting to the Latin rite, under threat of punishment. The document provoked the discontent of the Latin authorities in Jerusalem. Under Benedict XV, the founder of the Congregation for the Oriental Church and the Oriental Pontifical Institute, 'Latinism' was again prohibited. The need for Catholicism to be diffused using the Oriental rites was soon realised with such great clarity that Pius XI at one point considered abolishing the Latin Patriarchate of Jerusalem and leave the field for the Franciscan Custody of the Holy Places and the Greek Catholic Melchite Church. Odo Russell of the British Mission to the Vatican wrote:

> The whole question of the Oriental Church is being closely studies by the Holy See, and the tendency is rather to 'delatinise' than to Latinise the Catholics of the East. It may therefore come about that the Patriarchate at Jerusalem will be handed over to the Greek Uniates.[45]

He eventually refrained from doing so, for reasons more to do with diplomacy than with religion. Forceful political intervention and the determined resistance from the Latin Patriarchate Barlassina[46] who had support in the *curia* and among influential members of the French hierarchy, the Pope eventually abandoned the idea. [47]

---

[44] Claude Soetens, *Le congrès eucharistique international de Jérusalem (1893) dans le cadre de la politique orientale du Pape Léon XIII*, Éditions Nauwelaerts, Louvain, 1977, 245-289.

[45] FO.141-667. File no. 6023 Russell to Curzon (November 13, 1923).

[46] P Pierracini, 'Il Patriarcato Latino di Gerusalemme (1918-1938): ritratto di un Patriarca scomodo. Luigi Barlassina', (eds.) G Meynier and M Russo, *L'Europe et la méditerranée*, Harmattan Paris, 1999, 243-258.

[47] S Ferrari, 'Pio XI, La Palestina e I Luoghi Santi', *Achille Ratti Pape Pie XI*, École française de Rome, Rome, 1996,909-924.

After the First World War, it appeared that the departure of the Ottomans and the establishment of the British Mandate would open great opportunities for Christianity in Jerusalem and Palestine. However the competing project the 'Jewish national home' to which Britain had in Balfour Declaration of 1917 agreed to. In the 1920s, fears of the Catholic rights over the Holy Places being questioned led the Latin Patriarch of Jerusalem, Mgr Barlassina[48] to adopt an openly anti-Zionist stance which he also tried to convey to Europe (without great success). It also provided the belated partisans of Latinisation with ammunition, presenting the Latin Patriarchate as bulwark for the protection of the Catholics in the Middle East. Although the future remained heavily threatened, the British mandate period was nevertheless favourable to the Christian communities in the Holy Land including the Latins who were able to develop their institutions and gained in number through converts.

Following the Second World War the dreaded upheavals occurred. Whereas the UN division plan of 1947 provided for the establishment of Jerusalem as *corpus separatum* the Holy City became the subject of fights between Jews and Arabs which led to it being split into two in 1949 (with the Latin Patriarchate and the Holy Places on the Arab side). More seriously, however, the clashes led to a massive exodus of the Palestinian population. For the Latin Church in the Holy Land, whose flock was already small, the result was catastrophic: large parishes were emptied; others, like those in Haifa and Jaffa, were almost ruined. The new State of Israel was not very welcoming towards the Christian Arabs and the economic situation in Jordan was hardly flourishing.

This time the exodus was not restricted to the neighbouring countries: many faithful were aware of how easily they would be able to integrate elsewhere due to their belonging to a global Catholic Church and therefore left to settle in Europe and America. Of the 10,000 Latins, which were found in Jerusalem and the neighbouring towns after the 1948 war, only 3,000 remained in the early 1970s. Yet although the Patriarchate was faced with declining numbers and a weakening of its institutions it became more firmly rooted in the Palestinian Arab experience. It had found its vocation to represent Palestinian Christianity in Jerusalem which neither the Greek nor the Armenian Patriarchate would be able to incarnate. The fact that an Italian Patriarch was at its

---

[48] Pierracini, *loc. cit.*, 250–58.

head (which had been the case since the beginning) constituted an anachronism. The last Italian Patriarch Beltritti[49] has been replaced by Michel Sabbah,[50] a Palestinian Arab (1987), from which moment the Latin Patriarchate in Jerusalem has been able present itself as representative of the Church of the Palestinians in the Holy Land.

The Latin Patriarchate in the contemporary Holy Land

Unlike the other Oriental Catholic Patriarchs the Latin Patriarchate of Jerusalem is not responsible for all Latin Arabs in the Middle East but exercises its jurisdiction in a limited area (Israel, Jordan, and the Occupied Territories including Jerusalem and Cyprus).[51] Apart from this area (two-thirds of the Latins in the region are to be found) there are other Latin communities which fall under the authority of either apostolic vicars (Lebanon, Syria, Turkey, Egypt, Kuwait, United Arab Emirates), or bishops (two in Sudan, one in Iraq), or of apostolic administrators (Djibouti, Somalia). The apostolic vicariate of Lebanon (which was created in 1938 and has been exercised by an archbishop resident in Beirut) is the most

---

[49] The list of Patriarchs since the re-establishment of the Latin Patriarch in 1847: Giuseppe Valerga, 1847-1872; Vincenzo Bracco, 1873-1889; Luigi Piavi, 1889-1905; Filippo Camassei, 1907-1919; Luigi Barlassina, 1920-1947; Alberto Gori, 1949-1970; Giacomo Beltritti, 1970-1987.

[50] Michel Sabbah, who was born in Nazareth in 1933, ordained a priest in 1955. Most of his ecclesiastical career has been in Palestine where he was parochial vicar in Mdaba, Arabic teacher at the Patriarchal seminary, student chaplain, general chaplain of the youth movement and then director general of the schools of the Patriarchate. From 1968 to 1970 he served in Djibouti after which he was curate in the parish of Christ the King in Amman. He holds a doctorate in Arab philology from the Sorbonne, became president of the Pontifical University of Bethlehem in 1981. Elected Latin Patriarch of Jerusalem in 1887, and consecrated in Rome in January 1988.

[51] The term 'Holy Land,' as regards the hierarchy of the Catholic Church, embraces Cyprus, the West Bank, Jordan and Israel. Until 1929, the Holy Land was under the jurisdiction of the apostolic delegate in Syria who resided in Beirut, Lebanon. In March of that year, Pius XI decided that Palestine (which was then under British mandate) should become the responsibility of the pontifical representative in Cairo, Egypt, who had a residence in Jerusalem. On 11 February 1948 Pius XII established the Apostolic Delegation in Jerusalem and Palestine, which covered Israel, Jordan and Cyprus. Following the establishment of diplomatic relations between the Holy See and Jordan on 3 March 1994, and between the Holy See and Israel on 14 June 1994, the apostolic delegation covers only Jerusalem and the Palestinian Autonomous Territories. At the present time there is an apostolic nunciature in Amman, Jordan, and another in Tel Aviv, Israel.

notable Latin structure apart from the Patriarchate of Jerusalem, given the importance of this country for Oriental Christianity (despite the small number of Latin faithful—hardly 5,000). The apostolic vicariate of Turkey has direct authority over the Latins in Istanbul and indirect authority over those in Izmir who fall under the authority of an archbishop. The Latin archbishopric of Baghdad which was established in 1638 only had 3,500 indigenous faithful although until the outbreak of the Gulf wars it provided ecclesiastical services to the 25,000 foreign Catholics resident there.

Within area of jurisdiction of the Latin Patriarchate there are approximately 72,000 faithful[52] which means that the Latins are the second largest Christian community in this area after the Greek Orthodox (slightly less than 100,000) but before the Greek Catholics (40,000). Of these, approx. 25,000 live in Jordan, 17,000 in Israel (mainly in the Nazareth area where the Arabs are in the majority) and 8,000 in the West Bank (of which 4,000 in Jerusalem and the remainder around Bethlehem and Ramallah). Although the Latin community grew until 1973 due to its high birth rate, it has since declined in number due to the high level of emigration; this tendency has gained momentum during the Palestinian uprisings *(Intifada).*[53]

The guardianship of these Latin communities was for a long time ensured by the Sacred Congregation for the Propagation of the Faith; since the Papacy of Pius XI it has been exercised by the Sacred Congregation for the Oriental Churches which is a more flexible structure.[54] From 1984 it has been represented locally by an 'Apostolic Delegation' based in Jerusalem which co-ordinates all Catholic institutions and activities in Israel, Jordan, the Occupied Territories and in Cyprus. Since the Second Vatican Council (1967) there is also a 'Conference of

---

[52] This figure is given by the *Annuaire de l'Eglise catholique en Terre Sanite*, Jerusalem, 1999, 29, although other sources suggest a lower figure 50,000 according to Jean-Pierre Valognes, *Vie et mort des chrétiens d'Orient. Des origines à nos jours*, Fayard, Paris, 1996, 507.

[53] B Sabella, 'Palestinian Christian emigration from the Holy Land', *Proche Orient Chrétien*, Vol. 41 (1991), 74-85. The general question of Christian migration from the region: B Sabella, 'L'émigration des arabes chrétiens: dimensions et causes de l'exode', *Proche Orient Chrétien*, Vol. 47 (1997), 141-169 and Elie Austin, 'L'immigration massive des chrétiens d'Orient', *Études*, Vol. 373 (1990), 101-106.

[54] J Hajjar, 'Les Église du Proche-Orient au Concile Vatican II. Aperçu historique (1958-1978)', *Istina*, Vol. 41 (1996), 253-308 and Emmanuel Lanne, 'Un christianisme contesté. L'Orient catholique entre myth et réalité', *The Christian East. Its institutions and its thought: a critical reflection*, Pontifical Oriental Institute, Rome, 1996, 85-106.

the Latin Bishops in the Arab Regions—Conférence des Evêques Latins dans les Régions Arabes' (CELRA) which meets every year under the presidency of the Patriarch of Jerusalem and the vice-presidency of the apostolic vicar of Lebanon; all Patriarchal vicars, apostolic vicars and Latin bishops in the Middle East are members (archbishopric of Baghdad; apostolic vicariates of Beirut, Alexandria, Aleppo, Kuwait and Arabia; Patriarchal auxiliaries of Israel, Jordan and Cyprus; apostolic administrators of Djibuti and Somalia).

The Latin Church in the Holy Land only has a Patriarchal structure in appearance: it does not have true autonomy, and the legal status of its head is very restricted compared to what the appointment as Patriarch means in the Arab world. Unlike other Oriental Catholic Patriarchs (whose appointment is the task of the local synod although the Holy See plays a role in the process), the Pope directly appoints the Latin Patriarch. Falling under the authority of the Sacred Congregation for the Oriental Churches through the apostolic delegate, to whom he is subordinated, he therefore only ranks number two in the Catholic hierarchy in the Holy Land. However, he presides over CELRA and the Order of Knighthood of the Holy Sepulchre, an institution that dates back to the Middle Ages and is today dedicated to supporting the development of the Patriarchate's education and social activities. Auxiliary bishops called Patriarchal vicars represent the Patriarch in the three districts of his area of jurisdiction (Israel, Jordan and Cyprus), plus an Episcopal vicar for the Hebrew-speaking community. Under his authority, patriarchal tribunals (inherited from the Ottoman system) rule on matters of personal status affecting Latin Christians (three courts of first instance in Israel, Jordan, the Occupied Territories and Cyprus, two appeal courts in Jerusalem and Amman).

Although legally speaking he is hardly more than a bishop, the Latin Patriarchate enjoys a prestige and exerts an influence far beyond his legal powers. In fact since 1987 the see of Jerusalem has been occupied by a Palestinian who, taking into account the particularities of the Greek and Armenian Churches, is the only Arab Patriarch of the Holy City. Sabbah is aware of his responsibilities as figurehead of Palestinian Christianity and of the effects, which his nomination has had in the Christian Arab milieu he plays a very active role both at local level and abroad, in the context of CELRA, as well as among the Oriental Catholic Patriarchs.

The organisational structure of the Patriarchate is Roman. The Patriarch has a *curia* with ten members; a presbytery council consisting of elected and appointed members and which represents the three districts within the Patriarchal area of jurisdiction; and a chapter consisting of three canons. Eleven diocesan commissions consisting of priests and religious deal with questions regarding doctrine, pastoral theology, liturgy, catechism, ecumenism and relations with Islam and Judaism. A patriarchal seminary exists in Beit Jala: it currently has about 60 seminarians. The number of parishes totals more than 60 of which half are in Jordan, a quarter in Israel, a quarter in the West Bank and Cyprus. A secular clergy of approx. 80 priests serves them, although some are held by religious orders (mainly Franciscans). These priests are almost exclusively Arabs and have generally gone through the Patriarchal seminary of Beit Jala where they are trained in Latin discipline; this gives them a homogeneity and superior training in many respects compared to the other Churches in the Holy Land.

Despite its limited human resources and its modest financial means the Latin Patriarchate in the Holy Land shows a dynamism which is unmatched by the other Christian Churches. Its greatest success is in education: about 20 Patriarchal secondary schools, 35 primary schools and approximately 30 nurseries, a total number of 15,000 children and pupils of which 11,000 are in Jordan and 4,000 in the West bank. Those of the religious congregations, which go even further (28,000 pupils in the same area), complement the efforts of the Patriarchate. Thus the majority of pupils from the Christian community in Jordan—a country where the educational public sector is strongly influenced by Islam—can receive a Catholic education.[55] The Patriarchal schools recruit pupils far beyond the Latin community (one-third of their pupils are Greek Orthodox or Greek Catholics, and one-quarter is Muslim) which explains largely why the influence of the Latin Church stretches far beyond its manpower resources into Palestinian Arab society.

This generous contribution to keeping the Palestinian population in Palestine and to promote it would not be complete without higher

---

[55] Jean-Pierre Valognes, 'Les chrétiens de Jordanie', *Vie et mort des chrétiens d'Orient*, 614–635; G Chatelard, 'Jordaine: entre appartenance communautaire et identité nationale', *Les Cahiers de l'Orient: Edition Chrétiens de l'Orient*, no. 48 (1997), 117–122, and M Haddad, ' "Detribalizing" and "Retribalizing": The double role of the Church among the Christian Arabs in Jordan: a study in the anthropology of religion', *The Muslim World*, Vol. 82 (1992).

educational structures; it is when the young people think of going to university that the temptation to leave is greatest. During his visit to the Holy Land, Pope Paul VI had convinced himself of the need for the Catholic university within the Patriarchal area of jurisdiction: it was finally set up in Bethlehem in 1973.

Hebrew-Catholicism in the Holy Land

Within the jurisdiction of the Latin Patriarchate there also exists a body which attempts to express and take care of the Hebrew Catholic community: *Oeuvre de Saint Jacques l'Apôtre*. Its creation was approved by the former Patriarch, Alberto Gori, in 1955, after several years of discussion and preparation, and it received warm encouragement from Cardinal Tisserant, then prefect of the Sacred Congregation for the Oriental Churches. The decision to found the *Oeuvre* was prompted principally by the patriarchates' pastoral solicitude for the Catholics, apparently some several thousand of them, who arrived in Israel as refugees or immigrants in the years following the Second World War and the creation of the State of Israel (1948), and who continued to arrive throughout the 1950s. They came almost invariably from the countries of Eastern Europe and were either converted Jews or descendants of such converts, or Catholic spouses in mixed marriages and their (often) baptised children—though in a few cases they had no connection at all with Jews and Judaism, and were simply anxious to emigrate from their countries, now Communist or in the process of becoming so. The patriarchate, especially in the person of the then vicar in Israel, Mgr Vergani, was conscious of its duty to those immigrants and, fearing that because of differences of mentality and language, as well as of the complexity of the socio-political situation, the immigrants might not easily find their place within the normal parochial organisation, favoured the creation of a distinct framework within its jurisdiction specially designed to meet their needs. It was accepted that the pastoral centres envisaged would adopt Hebrew, as being the *Lingua franca* for immigrants originating from a number of different countries.[56] The

---

[56] In fact the *Oeuvre* was granted permission by the Patriarchate and the Vatican to have the liturgy in Hebrew as early as 1957. For the pioneering work of the French Jewish convert priest, Jean-Roger Henné in creating a Hebrew Catholic culture, see Dominique Trimbur,

statutes of the *Oeuvre* approved on 11 February 1956, exhorts its members to:

> Acquire an understanding of the mystery of Israel. We insist upon a Biblical formation; we try to promote a Jewish Christian culture and a spirituality in conformity with that culture…(We aim) to combat all forms of anti-semitism, attempting to develop mutual understanding, sympathy and friendly relations between the Catholic world and Israel.

The majority of those who supported the creation of the Oeuvre seemed to have felt that, even though an open missionary drive among Israeli Jews would in the circumstances be unthinkable, their task was to make the Christian faith accessible to those Hebrew-speaking Israelis whom God might prompt to seek membership of the church. A smaller number of the 'founding fathers' were (and still are) motivated by a much larger vision, which could be summed up as a desire to implant the Church within the Jewish people in such a way that Jews who become Christians should be able to preserve their national character, in much the same way that members of any other people or nation are able or invited to so do. [57]

Extensive autonomy was granted to the *Oeuvre*, which is officially supervised, on behalf of the Patriarch, by his Episcopal vicar, with four *foyers* (or communities) in Tel Aviv, Haifa, Jerusalem and Beersheva which together constitute between several hundred or a couple of thousand. However in August 2003 due to continuing tension over the question of jurisdiction for the Hebrew Catholic community, John Paul II named Abbot Jean-Baptisté Gourion an auxiliary bishop of the Latin Patriarchate of Jerusalem and charged him with the pastoral care of Hebrew-speaking Catholics in the Holy Land. The appointment of 68 year old Abbot Gourion came amid continuing debate over the advisability of establishing a separate church jurisdiction in the Holy Land for Catholics

---

'Les Assomptionistes de Jérusalem, les Juifs et le sionisme', *Tsafon: Revue d'études juives du Nord*, no. 48 (1999-2000), 71-111.

[57] David-Maria Hunter (D-M A Jaeger), 'Holy Land Christians: Hebrew-speaking communities', *The Tablet*, 7 January, 1978,5-7. S Ferrari, 'La Liberté religieuse en Israël', (ed.) Joël-Benoît d'Onorio, *La liberté religieuse dans le monde*, Editions Universitaires, Paris, 1991, 243-254.

who speak Hebrew and are not of Arab or Palestinian origin.[58] Bishop Gourion is one of the founders of Eglise de la Résurrection at Abou-Gosh, near Jerusalem and was elected its first abbot in 1999.[59] Since 1990 he has been president of the *Oeuvre de Saint Jacques l'Apôtre,* and simultaneously served as the Latin patriarch's vicar for Hebrew-speaking Catholics. Interestingly Bishop Gourion was born to French parents in Oran, Algeria. He attended school in Algeria and study science and medicine at the University of Paris. He was baptised at a French Benedictine monastery in 1958 and entered the order three years later. Ordained a priest in 1967, he and two other Benedictines were sent to Israel in 1976 to the found the monastery at Abou Gosh.[60]

The future identity of the Latin Catholic Church of Jerusalem

The Latin Church has long experienced an identity problem, and it took a long time for its vocation to gain a clear outline. At any rate, its vocation was never clearly outlined by Rome. The defence of the Catholic rights over the Holy Places had been invoked to explain the re-establishment of a Patriarchate residing in Palestine but it could not by itself justify the creation of specific structures at the level of the Middle East as a whole; yet apostolic and diocesan vicariates exist beyond the Patriarchal area of jurisdiction of Jerusalem. Thinking logically, the end of proselytism and the recognition of the Oriental rites by the Holy See should therefore have resulted in the disappearance of the Latin Church in the Orient. However, it had become by then an established reality. What vocation should it be assigned given the conditions? There were

---

[58] Drew Christiansen, SJ, 'A Campaign to Divide the Church in the Holy Land', *America,* 19 May 2003.

[59] For the background to the Benedictine presence in the Holy land see the studies by Dominique Trimbur, 'Vie et mort d'un séminaire syrien-catholique l'établissement bénétctin de Jérusalem', *Proche-Orient Chrétien* (Jerusalem), Vol. 52, 2002, 303-352; 'Religion et politique en Palestine: la cas de la France à Abou Gosh', *De Bonaparte à Balfour—La France, L'Europe occidentale et la Palestine,* (eds) D Trimbur and R Aaronsohn, Paris, CNRS-Éditions, 2001, 265-293; and 'The Encounter between Eastern and Western Christendom in Jerusalem: Syrian Catholics, the Benedictines and France', *Eastern Christianity: Studies in Modern history, Religion and Politics,* (ed.) Anthony O'Mahony, Melisende, London, 2004.

[60] 'Benedictine abbot named as Jerusalem auxiliary', *The Tablet,* 23 August 2003, 27.

considerable obstacles. However, this Church behind which the shadow of the Vatican and the powerful institutions of the Catholic Church are clearly aligned, is attractive: the solidity of its structures, its discipline, the quality of its clergy, the dynamism of its social, educational and pastoral action are all the more seductive as the other Oriental Churches are deprived of external support and far from showing the same degree of vitality. Moreover, the Latin Church in the Orient has to try to steer a medium course. Whereas all religious references link it with the West, it has to legitimise its presence by giving itself an indisputably Arab image.[61]

In order to be accepted, the Latin Church in the Orient has had to remove many prejudices existing even within the other Catholic Churches established in the region. The most reticent one was the Greek Catholic Church which also was strongly established in Palestine and therefore was in competition with the Latins. Although the establishment of a Latin Patriarchate in Jerusalem was beneficial to all Catholic Churches (to which it brought greater protection and a wave of conversions) the Melkite Church has repeatedly claimed that due to the fact that it was itself a synthesis of local religious tradition and in union with Rome, it was the Melkite Church which should represent Catholicism in the Orient and defend the Catholic rights over the Holy Places. The quarrel lasted until the Second Vatican Council when the Melkite Patriarch Maximos IV reiterated his claim for the Latin Patriarchate to be abolished (nearly 120 years after its re-establishment). [62]

The local political circumstances have since emptied this controversy of much of its substance: since for many decades East Jerusalem and the West Bank had been occupied by Israel it would in any case be impossible for the Melkite Patriarch (whose residence is at

---

[61] Apart from the important pastoral letters of the Patriarch, Michel Sabbah in particular 'Reading the Bible Today in the Land of the Bible' (November, 1993). There is a growing body of theological-political reflection from within the Latin Palestinian Catholic community: Rafiq Khoury, *La catéchése dans l'eglise locale de Jérusalem: histoire, situation actuelle et perspectives d'avenir*, Pontifica Universitá Lateranense, Rome, 1978; 'Chréteins arabés de la Terre Sante', *Études*, Vol. 369 (1988), 395-408 and Anton Odeh Issa, *Les minorités chrétiennes de Palestine à travers les siècles. Etude historico-juridique et dévélopment moderne internationale*, Franciscan Press, Jerusalem, 1976.

[62] On the sometimes difficult relations between the Melkites and Latins over who should represent Catholic rights and interests in Jerusalem and the Holy Land, see *Catholicisme ou Latinisme? À propos du Patriarcat Latin de Jérusalem*, Harissa, 1961, and *The Custody of the Holy Land: Status Quo and the Oriental Rites*, Jerusalem, 1961.

Damascus) to efficiently ensure the protection of the Catholics in the Holy Land, or even to make pastoral visits. The Melkites and Latins are moreover aware of the fact that any change in the current situation might upset the fragile balance of the *status quo* in the Holy Places. The Greek Orthodox Church, which already finds it difficult to respect the Catholic rights represented by the Latin Patriarch, could not in any case accept their transfer to the Melkites which it still sees as dissidents who wrongly claim Byzantine religious 'legitimacy'. In Jerusalem where the Orthodox hierarchy has remained Hellenistic in culture whereas the Melkites insist on being rooted in 'Arabness', the divide between the two Greek Churches is even wider than in the rest of the Middle East.

By contrast, the presence of the Israel occupier, the rise of Islamic radicalism and the threat of a complete disappearance of Christianity in the Holy Land have permitted a certain rapprochement between Latins and Greek Catholics, which has been facilitated by both sides renouncing proselytism as well as by the increased Arabisation of the Latin Church. Moreover, the two communities tend to become 'bi-ritual'—they use the services of one or the other church, depending on the circumstances, and practice the two liturgies—whereas there are outlines of pastoral co-operation, the first result of which is the St Cyril Centre in Jerusalem created by the Latin Patriarchate, the Greek Catholic Patriarchal Vicariate and the Franciscan Custody in 1981 for the religious training of adults and the pedagogical preparation of catechists. Still it is not true that all mistrust has been overcome and yet moreover, the relationship between the two religious hierarchies is not yet as close as required by the situation.

The hierarchy is in fact constrained in more than one way: its Church is spread between the West Bank, Jordan and Israel and cannot ignore the feelings of its Palestinian faithful although it cannot either get involved in an open conflict with the authorities of the occupier which would not be without consequences for the situation of the Latin Catholics in Israel and the foreign religious communities. Moreover, it cannot freely take a position as it is placed under the supervision of the Apostolic Delegation which represents the Vatican in the Holy Land, and takes an approach to the Arab-Israeli problem which does not only take the interests of Palestinian Christianity into account.

The appointment of a Palestinian priest as Latin Patriarch in Jerusalem in 1987 was highly symbolic. This event did not fail to have an effect on the political attitude of the Patriarchate: soon after his nomination

Mgr Sabbah adopted a very firm line on the Palestinian question: he limited his formal contacts with the Israel authorities to a minimum, abolished all ceremonies associated with religious feast days (other than the offices of the liturgy) because of the *Intifada*, associated himself to the joint reply of the Churches of Jerusalem when their rights were infringed upon (this reply went as far as the closure of Christian Holy Places).[63] At the head of the Conference of the Latin Bishops of the Arab Regions, Mgr Sabbah has inspired more vigorous viewpoints on the Arab-Israeli conflict; he considered the PLO to be the only representative of the Palestinian people.[64]

This evolution in the political stance of the Latin Church is the logical complement of its Arabisation and should finally provide it with the specific vocation which it has sought since the project of Latinising the Oriental Churches was abandoned. Whereas the Greek Orthodox and Armenian Patriarchate of Jerusalem continue to represent religious milieus and traditions which are not Arab, that the Greek Catholic Church is handicapped by a lack of resident see in the Holy Land (as by his links with Syria where its Patriarch is to be found), the Latin Church finally seem to be in the best position to incarnate Palestinian Christianity. History has made the Latin Church in the Orient a reality. It is probably in the interest of global Catholicism to finally provide it with the necessities for it to express to the full the potentialities of its existence—the process of 'inculturation' as advocated by the John Paul II. An *Ecclesia* for and within Jerusalem which would give the pilgrim and the stranger a home.

---

[63] Andrea Pacini, 'Socio-Political and Community Dynamics of Arab Christians in Jordan, Israel, and the Autonomous Palestinian Territories', (ed.) A Pacini, *Christian communities in the Arab Middle East: The Challenge of the Future*, Clarendon Press, Oxford, 1998, 259-285, and Thomas Stransky, *A Catholic Views Political Zionism and the State of Israel*, The Institute of Judaeo-Christian Studies, Seton Hall University, 2000, 21-54.

[64] For the accord between the Vatican and the Palestinian Authorities, see Paolo Ferrari da Passano, 'L'Accordo tra la Santa Sede e l'Organizzazione per la Liberazione della Palestina', *La Civiltà Cattolica*, no. 1 (2000), 364-371.